Henry George Bohn

The Bibliographer`s Manual of English Literature

Containing an Account of Rare, Curious and Useful Books

Henry George Bohn

The Bibliographer's Manual of English Literature
Containing an Account of Rare, Curious and Useful Books

ISBN/EAN: 9783741179792

Manufactured in Europe, USA, Canada, Australia, Japa

Cover: Foto ©Andreas Hilbeck / pixelio.de

Manufactured and distributed by brebook publishing software (www.brebook.com)

Henry George Bohn

The Bibliographer`s Manual of English Literature

THE
BIBLIOGRAPHER'S MANUAL

OF

ENGLISH LITERATURE

CONTAINING

AN ACCOUNT OF RARE, CURIOUS, AND USEFUL BOOKS, PUBLISHED IN OR RELATING TO GREAT BRITAIN AND IRELAND, FROM THE INVENTION OF PRINTING; WITH BIBLIOGRAPHICAL AND CRITICAL NOTICES, COLLATIONS, OF THE RARER ARTICLES, AND THE PRICES AT WHICH THEY HAVE BEEN SOLD IN THE PRESENT CENTURY

BY

WILLIAM THOMAS LOWNDES.

NEW EDITION, REVISED, CORRECTED AND ENLARGED
BY HENRY G. BOHN.

PART VI.

LONDON:
HENRY G. BOHN, YORK STREET, COVENT GARDEN.
1861.

NOTICE TO THE SIXTH PART.

In several former preliminary notices I have called attention to some of the more important of my additions, and think it as well to continue the practice. I have therefore to state that the present part is increased full one-fourth on the original work, and every page materially enlarged, as reference to the following names, some of which are entirely new, will testify:—
M'Culloch, J. B. Macgregor, John. Mackintosh, Sir James. Malcolm, Sir John. Mantell, Dr. Manuale ad usum Sarum. Markham, Gervase. Marryat, Capt. Martin, R. M. Mary Stuart. Massachusetts. Mather, Cotton and Increase. Mendham, Jos. Milman, Rev. H. Milton John. Missale. Mitford, Miss. Montgomery, James and Robert. Moore, Thos. More, Hannah. Morgan, Lady. Mormon, Book of. Murray, Lindley. Napoleon. Newman, J. H. Newton, Sir Isaac. Nichols, John. Nicholson, Peter. Nicolas, Sir Harris. Norton, Hon. Mrs. Nowell, Alexander. Oliver, Rev. George. Ordnance Survey. Ormerod, George. Ossian. Ottley, W. G. Ovid. Owen, Rich.

It was not my original intention, as stated in a Notice to the Second Part, to introduce any names which had not already been given by Lowndes, taking it for granted that he would be complete to the date of publication, 1834, and that I should

NOTICE TO THE SIXTH PART.

merely have to continue his lists; and to this rule I at first adhered, but afterwards found so many important omissions in the department of contemporary Literature, that it became necessary to abandon the prescribed limit. Accordingly, the present part will be found to contain many such additional names as Capt. Marryat, Dean Milman, John Henry Newman, Sir Harris Nicolas, and Professor Owen; all of whom had acquired literary reputation before the period in question, and were better entitled to mention than some who have been included.

The next part is in progress, and will, I hope, be published in the ensuing spring.

HENRY G. BOHN.

YORK STREET, COVENT GARDEN,
December 26th, 1860.

M.

M. A.—A true and admirable Historie of a Mayden at Confolens, in the Prouince of Poictiers, that for the space of three Yeares and more, hath liued, and yet doth, without receiuing either Meat or Drinke. Lond. 1604, 12mo.
Contains verses by Thomas Dekker. Dedicated to the barbers-surgeons, by A. M. Bindley, pt. III. 1298, 1l. Gordonstoun, 1192, 1l. 6s.

M. A.—Falsehood in Friendship; or, Union's Vizard; or Wolves in Lambskins. Printed for Nat. Fosbrooke, 1605, 4to.
Seventy-three leaves. This discourse is otherwise called 'The Masque of the League and the Spaniard discovered.'

M. A.—The Reformed Gentleman. Lond. 1693, 8vo.
Bliss, 3s. 6d.

M. A.—See MUDIE, Alexander. MUNDAY, Anthony. MURDERS.

M. B.—See MANDEVILLE, Bernard.

M. C.—The second part of the historie, called the Nature of Woman, contayning the end of the strife betwixt Perseus and Theseus. Lond. by the widow Orwin, 1596, 4to.
In the Malone collection.

M. C.—See MARLOWE, Christopher.

M. E.—See MARBURY, Ed.

M. E.—Saint Cicily, or the converted Twins, a Christian Tragedy. Lond. 1666, 4to. 3s.
This play was published by M. Medbourna.—1667, 4to. 3s.

M. E.—See MANNING, Edward.

M. F. F.—See MATTHEWS, Francis.

M. G.—See MARKHAM, Gervase. MARSHALL, George. MERITON, George. MYNSHUL, Geffray.

M. G.—The seconde and last part of the first Booke of the English Arcadia, making a complete end of the first history. Lond. 1623, 4to.
Bright, 1l. 18s.

M. G.—Hobson's Horse-load of Letters; or, a President for Epistles. Lond. 1617, 4to. Two parts.
Black letter. Caldecott, 1l. 1s.

M. G. L.—See MEASON, G. L.

M. H.—See MORE, Henry.

M. H. A. T. H. P. See MACMATION, Hugo.

M. I.—The Funeral Sermon preached at the Burial of the Lady Jane Maitland, by Mr. I. M. Edinb. 1633, 4to. See MAITLAND, Lady Jane.

M. I.—Bachelour of Divinity. A Patterne for Women; setting forth the Life and Death of Mrs. Lucy Thornton, of Little Wratting in Suffolk. Lond. 1619, 12mo.
Bliss, morocco, 10s. 6d.

M. I.—The younger Brother his Apologie. Oxford, 1634, 4to.
Inglis, 949, 9s.

M. L.—A breefe Directory, and playne way howe to say the Rosary of our blessed Ladye with Meditations, &c. whereunto are adjoyned the Prayers of St. Bryget. Brugen Flandorum excud. H. Holost, 1676, a diminutive volume, size four inches by three.
Bliss, fine, in morocco, 3l. 5s.

4 F

M. J.—A Healthe to the Gentlemanly profession of Serving men, or the Serving-Man's comfort, with other things not impertinent to the premises, as well pleasant as profitable to the reader. Lond. by W. W. 1598, 4to.
Black letter. Bright, the margin stained, 1l. 16s. In the Malone Collection.

M. J.—News from Hell, Rome, and the Innes of Court : wherein is set forth the Coppy of a Letter written from the Devill to the Pope, &c. &c. published for the future Peace and Tranquillity of the Inhabitants of Great Britane, by J. M. 1642, 4to. woodcut on title.
This tract has been attributed to John Milton. White Knights, 5153, 13s. King and Lochée's in March, 1810, 11s. 6d. Skegg, 5s. Heber, pt vii. 6s. It is reprinted in the seventh volume of the Harleian Miscellany.

A Reply to the Answer (printed by his Majesties Command at Oxford) to a printed Booke intituled 'Observations upon some of his Majesties late Answers and Expresses.' By J. M. Lond. 1642, 4to. Milton might be supposed to have been the author of this tract, were it not for the following passage at p. 20:— 'What have we to do with Aristocracy or Democracy? God be blessed, we nor know, nor desire, any other government than that of Monarchy!'

Salve for ye Blind, a Def. of ye Parliament by J. M. 1643, 4to. This tract has been erroneously attributed to Milton.

Jus Populi, 1644, 4to. This tract, containing many energetic sentiments and expressions, has been erroneously attributed to Milton.

Neutrality is Malignancy. By J. M. 1648, 4to.

M. J.—Agreeable variety, containing Discourses, Characters, Poems, Letters, &c. Lond. 1717, 8vo.
Bliss, pt. ii. 2568, mor. 7s. 6d. Lond. 1724, 8vo. Bliss, pt. ii. 2582, 2s. 6d.

M. Jo.—Phillippes Venus, wherin is pleasantly discoursed sundrye fine and wittie arguments, in a senode of Gods and Goddesses, assembled for the expelling of wanton Venus from among their sacred societie. Lond. for John Perrin, 1591, 4to.
In the Malone Collection.

M. I. or J.—*See* MAIDMENT, James. MARKHAM, Gervis, or Jervase. MARSTON, John. MAXWELL, James. MELTON, John. MERVINE. MILTON, John.

M. Sir J.—*See* MENNIS, Sir John.

M. L.—*See* MASCAL, Leonard.

M. M.—*See* CULROS, Elizabeth Melvill, Lady. PARIS and VIENNA.

M. M. T.—*See* MORE, Thomas.

M. P.—Sundrie pleasant Flowres of Poesie, newlie plucked from the Hill Parnasse, by the Hand of P. M. and very goodlie to smelle. Lond. 1576. 4to.
Said to be unique.—reprinted, 1825, 4to. for the Rev. Peter Hall. Two copies only.
(Perhaps only a *jeu d'esprit* by the Rev. P. Hall. He presented one of the copies, said to be *reprinted*, to Mr. Grenville, in whose collection it has since passed to the British Museum.)

M. P.—The powerfull Favorite, or the Life of Ælius Sejanus. Paris, 1628, 4to.
Pp. 124. This tract, supposed to be a satire against the Duke of Buckingham, is the subject of a paper in the Craftsman. It has been ascribed to Pierre Marbleu, the French historian, and to Philip Massinger, our English dramatist. Gordonstoun, 1827. 7s. Inglis' Old Plays, 7, 8s. 6d.—First Edition. Paris, 1628, 4to. pp. 62. Gordonstoun, 1896, 2s. *See* MATHIEU, P.

M. P.—King Charles his Birthwright. Edinb. 1633, 4to.
Four leaves. Bindley, pt. iv. 1072, 1l. 16s. Reprinted in 'Various Pieces of fugitive Scotish Poetry,' edited by Laing.

M. P. D.—*See* MOULIN, P. du.

M. R.—A newe Ballade, (beginning O dere Lady Elysabeth). Without Place or Date.
Reprinted from a copy, supposed unique, in the library of the Society of Antiquaries of London, in the tenth volume of the Harleian Miscellany.

M. R.—Scarronides, or Virgil Travestie, a Mock Poem. Lond. 1665, 8vo. by R. Monsey.
Bliss, leaf wanting, 2s.

M. R.—Micrologia. Characters or Essayes: of Persones, Trades, and Places, offered to the City and Country. By R. M. Lond. 1629, 8vo.
Pp. 56, not numbered. Nassau, pt. L 2248, russia, 1l. 11s. Heber, pt. vi. 10s. 6d. Bliss, 19s.

M. R.—Voyage to Buenos Ayres, 1716. *See* BUENOS AYRES, p. 306.

M. R. *See* MAVERICK, Rs.; MANLEY, Roger; MOSSOM, R. D.D.; MURRAY, Sir R.

M. S.—*See* MARMION, Shakerley.

M. T.—Micro-cynicon: Sixe snarling Satyres. Insatiat. Prodigall. Insolent. Cheating. Iugling. Wise. Lond. by Thomas Creede, 1599, 18mo.
Bindley, pt. ll. 1800, 2£. resold Perry, pt. ll. 695, 19£. Again, Heber, pt. iv, 7l. 2s. 6d. No other known.
Formerly attributed to Marston (*see* Bibliotheca Heberiana), but now inserted in the Works (vol. v.) of Thomas Middleton by Mr. Dyce.

M. T.—The Silkwormes and their Flies: lively described in Verse, by T. M. a Countrie Farmer, and an Apprentice in Physicke, for the great Benefit and Enriching of England. Lond. by V(alentine) S(imms) for Nicholas Ling, 1599, 4to. woodcut on Title.
Pp. 76. A didactic Poem, addressed to 'Marie, Countesse of Pembroke,' followed by a table of contents. In some catalogues the author is stated to be Thomas Mouffal. Inglis, 1390, 9£. 8s. Nassau, pt. i. 2575, 2l. 14s. Boswell, 2591, 4l. 7s. Perry, pt. ll. 1177, 4l. 14s. 6d. Bibl. Anglo-Poet. 667, 15l. 15s. resold, Saunders in 1818, 3l. 10s. Skegg, 17s. Heber, pt. iv. 1599, 2l. 2s. Gardner in 1854, mor. 2l. 6s. *See* MUFFET, Thomas.

M. T.—The Copie of a Letter written from Master T. M. neere Salisbury, to Master H. A. at London, concerning the Proceeding at Winchester. Lond. 1603. 4to.
Reprinted in the first number of Morgan's Phœnix Britannicus.

M. T.—The Ant and the Nightingale, or Father Hubbard's [i. e. Oliver Hubbard] Tales. Lond. 1604, 8vo.
A satirical work, a mixture of prose and rhyme, some of which, says Mr. Todd, is extremely beautiful. A copy is in the Duke of Sutherland's collection, another was sold among the Bridgewater duplicates for 5l. Included by Mr. Dyce in his edition of Middleton (vol. v.) *See* HUBBARD, Oliver, p. 1132.

M. T.—The Blacke Booke. Lond. 1604, 4to.
Black letter. Pp. 44. Stevens, 770, 11. 8s. Roxburghe, 6671, 3l. 13s. 6d. Read, 1779, 4l. 14s. 6d. Bindley, pt. ii 697, 6l. 8s. 6d. resold Bright, 6l. 2s. 6d. Bibl. Anglo-Poet. 85, 25l. Saunders in 1818, 7l. 17s. 6d. Inserted by Mr. Dyce as a Work of Thomas Middleton's in Vol. V. of his edition.

M. T.—A Discourse of Trade from England to the East Indies. Lond. 1621, 4to. 4s. (? by Tho. Mun.)

M. T.—A Cloud of Witnesses or the Sufferers Mirror, made up of the Swan-like Songs and other choice passages of several Martyrs and Confessors. Alphabetically disposed, with Appendix, 1665, 12mo. 4 vols. in 3.
Bliss, 6s. Constable, 155, 1l. 2s.

M. T.—*See* MANLEY, Thomas. MAY, Thomas. MERITON, Thomas. MIDDLETON, Thomas.

M. Sir T. *See* MAINWARING, Sir Thomas.

M. W.—A Remembrance of the Worthie Show and Shooting by the Duke of Shoreditch and his associates, the worshipful citizens of London, upon Tuesday, 17 Sep. 1583. Lond. 1583.
Reprinted in Roberts' English Bowman. Lond. 1801, 8vo

M. W.—The Huntingdon Divertisement, an Enterlude, for an entertainment at Merchant Taylors' Hall, June 20, 1678. Lond. 1678, 4to.
Roxburghe, 4176, 19s.

M. W.—The Man in the Moone, telling strange Fortunes, or the English Fortune-Teller. Lond. 1609, 4to.

Twenty-seven leaves. In this trifle, the dedication of which is subscribed W. M., three orators and thirteen characters are introduced. Bright, last leaf inlaid, 2l. 2s. Inserted in Mr. Halliwell's privately printed volume 'Old Books of Characters,' 4to. 1857; and reprinted for the Percy Society. See No. 84, list in Appendix.

See DRAYTON, M. MOORE.

M. W.—The Female Wits; or, the Triumvirate of Poets at Rehearsal; a Comedy. Lond. 1697, 4to.

Roxburghe, 5353, date 1704, 4s.

MABLY, Gab. Bonnot, Abbé de. Observations on the Romans. Lond. 1751, 8vo. 3s.—Lond. 1776, 12mo.

A fit companion to Montesquieu's treatise on the Grandeur and Declension of the Romans.

Observations on the History of Greece; or, the Causes of the Prosperity and Misfortunes of the Greeks. Geneva, 1766, 12mo.

Observations on the Manners, Government, and Policy of the Greeks; translated, with notes and illustrations, by Mr. Chamberland. Oxf. 1784, 8vo.

The Principles of Negociation; or, an Introduction to the Public Law of Europe founded on Treaties, &c. Lond. 1757, 8vo.

Observations on the Government and Laws of the United States of America; translated from the French, with a preface by the Translator. Lond. 1784, 8vo.—Dublin, 1785, 8vo.

Phocion's Conversations; or, the Relation between Morality and Politics, originally translated by Abbé Mably, from a Greek manuscript of Nicocles. With Notes by William Macbean, A.M. Lond. 1769, 1770, 8vo. 5s.

M'ADAM, John Loudon. A practical Essay on Road Making. Lond. 1822, 8vo. 7s.

Remarks on Road Making. Lond. 1822, 8vo. 7s. 6d.

Observations on Turnpike Road Trusts. Lond. 1825, 8vo. 6s.

MAC ALLESTER, Oliver. A Series of Letters, discovering the Scheme projected by France, in 1759, for an intended Invasion upon England with flat-bottomed Boats; and various Conferences and original Papers touching that formidable Design. Lond. 1767, 4to. 2 vols.

This work contains some curious particulars relative to the young Pretender, and the banishment of the Jesuits from the French dominions. Bindley, pt. iii. 300, 5s.

MACARIA.—A Description of the famous Kingdom of Macaria. Lond. 1641, 4to.

Pp. 14. This little treatise, composed in the form of a novel, was designed to intimate a new model of government as the properest means to reconcile the breach which was then beginning between King Charles and his Parliament. It is reprinted in the first volume of the Harleian Miscellany.

MACARIUS, St. Institutes of Christian Perfection, translated by Granville Penn. Lond. 1816, 12mo. 5s.

A good translation.

Primitive Morality; or, the spiritual Homilies of St. Macarius the Egyptian, done out of Greek into English, with several considerable Emendations and some Enlargements from a Bodleian MS. never before printed. Lond. 1721, 8vo. 6s.—Bristol, 1749, in vol. i. of Mr. Wesley's Christian Library.

— The Travels of Macarius, Patriarch of Antioch; written by his attendant Archdeacon, Paul of Aleppo, in Arabic. Translated by F. C. Belfour. See Oriental Translation Fund Publications, in Appendix.

MACARONIC Poetry. Specimens of (edited by W. Sandys). Lond. Beckley, 1831, post 8vo. 6s.

Epistola Macaronica ad Fratrem. A Macaronic Epistle, &c. with an English version for the use of Country Gentlemen. Lond. Johnson, 1790, 4to.

Carminum Rariorum Macaronicorum delectus, in usum indorum Apollinarium. Edinb. 1801, 8vo.

Editio altera, emendata et aucta. Edinb. 1813, 8vo. James Boswell, 493, 1l.

MACARONEANA, ou Mélanges de Littérature Macaroniques des différents peuples de l'Europe, par M. Octave Delepierre. Brighton, 1852, 8vo.

Contains a valuable Bibliography of the subject.

MACALPINE, James. Certain curious Poems written at the close of the XVIIth and beginning of the XVIIIth centuries, &c., edited by W. Motherwell. Paisley, 1828, 8vo.
Only thirty printed.—Eyton, 7s.

M'ARTHUR, John, LL.D. The Principles and Practice of Naval and Military Courts Martial. Fourth Edition. Lond. 1813, 8vo. 2 vols. 12s.
An esteemed work. The first edition appeared in 1792, 8vo. 1 vol. See OSSIAN.

MACARTNEY, George, Earl of. Embassy to China. *See* ANDERSON, Eneas. BARROW, John. HOLMES, Samuel. IRELAND, in 1778, p. 1167. STAUNTON, Sir G. L. Bart.

MACASSAR. — An historical Description of the Kingdom of Macassar, in the East Indies. Lond. 1701, 8vo.
Fonthill, 2912, 5s.

MACAULAY, Catherine. The History of England from James I. to the Revolution. Lond. 1763-83. 8 vols. History of England, from the Revolution to the present time, in a Series of Letters. Bath, 1778, vol. i. (all printed). Together, 9 vols. 4to.
Willett, 1474, 5l. 18s. Hibbert, 8151, russia, 4l. 16s. The other writings of Mrs. Catherine Macaulay are now in little estimation. A list of them will be found in Watt's Bibliotheca Britannica.

— Rev. Aulay, M.A., F.R.S. The History and Antiquities of Claybrook, in the County of Leicester: including the Hamlets of Biticeby, Ullesthorpe, Wibtoft, and Little Wigston. Lond. 1791, 8vo.
Pp. viii. and 186, with additions and list of books, 4 pages, and a view of Claybrook church as a tailpiece to p. 186.

— Rev. Kenneth. The History of St. Kilda; containing a Description of this remarkable Island; the Manners and Customs of the Inhabitants; the religious and pagan Antiquities found there; with many other curious and interesting Particulars. Lond. 1764, 8vo.
Of this work Dr. Johnson observed, that 'it was very well written, except some foppery about liberty and slavery.' Reed, 5039, 7s. 6d. Drury, 2511, 7s. 6d. Sir P. Thompson, 467, 9s. 6d. Dent, pt. i. 1367, 13s. Willett, 1661, 14s. Fonthill, 1276, 19s. Heath, 4731, 11. 4s.

M'BANE, Donald. Expert Swordman's Companion; or, the true Art of Self-defence, with an Account of the Author's Life, and his Transactions during the Wars in France: to which is added, the Art of Gunnery. Glasgow, 1728, 12mo. 10s. 6d.
A curious treatise, with cuts.

MACBEAN, Alexander, M.A. A Dictionary of the Bible, historical and geographical; theological, moral, and ritual; philosophical and philological. Lond. 1779, 8vo. 9s.
A useful book, but now somewhat superseded by the work of the Rev. Dr. John Robinson.

A Dictionary of ancient Geography. Lond. 1773, 8vo. 4s. The preface to this work was written by Dr. Sam. Johnson. Roxburghe, 7107, 8s. 6d.

MACBETH, King of Scotland. The Secret History of Mack-beth King of Scotland, taken from a very ancient manuscript. Lond. 1708, 8vo.
A romance translated from the French.

MACCABEES.—The Third Book of the Maccabees. Lond. by John Tysdale, 1563, 16mo.
A copy is in the Bodleian.

A brief and compendious Table, in a Maner of a Concordaunce, opening the Wayes to the principall Histories of the whole Bible, &c. (to which is added) The Third Boke of Machabees, a Booke of the Bible also prynted unto this Boke which was never before translated or prynted in any Englyshe Bible. Lond. for Gwalter Lynne, dwellynge on Somers Kaye, by Byllinges Gate, 1550, 16mo. FIRST EDITION of the third Book of Maccabees. A copy is in the British Museum, where also is a copy of an edition printed separately by J. Daye in 12mo, dated 1550, which impression was passing through the press about the same period as Lynne's edition. It was again printed by Daye in Becker' edition of the Bible, 1551, folio, (see pp. 179, 180). It is to be

found in Whiston's Authentic Records of the Old and New Testament, 8vo. 1727, and in the edition of the Bible published by Bishop Wilson at Bath, 1785.
The five Books of Maccabees in English, with Notes and Illustrations. By the Rev. H. Cotton. Oxford, 1832, 8vo.

MacCarthy, (Captain). Recollections of the Storming of Badajoz and the Battle of Corunna. Lond. n. d. 8vo.

M'Cleland, T. Reports of Cases in Exchequer, at Law and in Equity, from Hilary to Michaelmas Term, 1624. Lond. 1825, royal 8vo. published at 1l. 12s.
Reports of Cases in Exchequer in Hilary, Easter, and Trinity Terms, 1825. By T. M'Cleland and E. Younge. Lond. 1827, royal 8vo. pub. 1l. 8s. 6d.

M'Cormick, Charles, LL.B. Memoirs of the Right Hon. Edmund Burke. Lond. 1797, 4to. portrait.
Pp. 383, with an advertisement. A disgraceful piece of party virulence. Bindley, pt. iii. 819, 5s. 6d. Fonthill, 1875, 1l. 5s.

M'Creery, John, Printer. The Press; a Poem, in two parts. Part i. Liverpool, 1803. Part ii. Lond. 1827, royal 4to.
An elegant volume, with wood engravings, published as a specimen of Typography. Second edition, both parts. Lond. 1830, crown 8vo. without cuts, 7s.

M'Crie, Thomas, D.D. Works. Edited by his son. Edinb. 1855-7, 4 vols. small 8vo. 1l. 4s.
The historical works of this divine are much valued.
The Life of John Knox, containing Illustrations of the History of the Reformation in Scotland, with biographical Notices of the principal Reformers, and Sketches of the Progress of Literature in Scotland during the 16th Century. To which is subjoined, an Appendix, consisting of Letters and other Papers, never before published. Edinb. 1812, 8vo. 2 vols. An important addition to the Ecclesiastical History of Scotland. Larpe paper. Heber, pt. v. 1l. 1s.—1814, 8vo. 2 vols.—1818, 8vo. 2 vols.—Edinb. 1831, 8vo. 2 vols.—Edinb. 1840, 8vo. in 1 vol.—New edition, with notes and a Memoir by Andrew Crichton. Lond. Bohn, 1854, fcap. 8vo. 2s. 6d.
The Life of Andrew Melville, containing Illustrations of the ecclesiastical and literary History of Scotland, during the latter part of the 16th and beginning of the 17th Centuries. Edinb. 1819, 8vo. 2 vols.—Second edition, Edinb. 1847, 8vo. 2 vols. in 1.
Memoirs of Mr. William Veitch and George Bryson, written by themselves, with other Narratives illustrative of the History of Scotland from the Restoration to the Revolution. Edinb. 1825, 8vo. 12s.
History of the Progress and Suppression of the Reformation in Italy, in the sixteenth Century; including a Sketch of the History of the Reformation in the Grisons. Edinb. 1827, 8vo.
Second edition, enlarged, 1833, 8vo. 10s. 6d. 'A learned and able work.'
History of the Progress and Suppression of the Reformation in Spain in the 16th Century. Edinb. 1829, 8vo. Pp. viii and 424, 12s.
Miscellaneous Writings, edited by his son. Edinb. 1841, 8vo. 10s. 6d.
Sermons. Edinb. 1836, 8vo.
Life. By his son. Edinb. 1840, 8vo. 9s.

Macculloch, John, M.D. A Description of the Western Islands of Scotland, including the Isle of Man. Lond. 1819, 8vo. 2 vols. with plates chiefly geological in 4to. 3l. 3s.
A Mineralogical and Geological work of great merit, valuable and instructive also in the subjects of the agriculture, scenery, antiquities, and economy of these islands.
The Highlands and Western Isles of Scotland, containing Descriptions of the Scenery and Antiquities, &c. &c. &c. Lond. 1824, 8vo. 4 vols. 3l. 12s. 6d.
A Geological classification of Rocks, with descriptive Synopses of the Species and Varieties, comprising the Elements of practical Geology. Lond. 1831, 8vo.
System of Geology and Theory of the Earth. Edinb. 1831, 8vo. 2 vols. 10s. 6d.
Remarks on the Art of making Wine; with Suggestions for the Application of its Principles to the Improvement of domestic Wines. Lond. 1817, 12mo. 8s. The best treatise on the subject.
Proofs and Illustrations of the Attributes of God from the Facts and Laws of the Physical Universe. Lond. 1837, 8vo. 3 vols. 2l. 2s.
A Critical Examination of Dr. Macculloch's Work on the Highlands and Western Isles of Scotland, (by James Brown, LL.D, Author of the 'Highlands, &c.' Glasg. 1827). Edinb. 1829, 8vo.
A violent attack.

M'Culloch, J. R. A Discourse on the Rise and Progress and peculiar Objects of Political Economy;

containing an Outline of a Course of Lectures on that Science. Edinb. 1824. 8vo. Second edition. 1825. 5s.

An esteemed work.

Treatise on the Principles, Practice, and History of Commerce. Lond. (Library of Useful Knowledge), 1831, 8vo. 3s. 6d.

Dictionary of Commerce and Commercial Navigation. Lond. 1832, thick 8vo.—Second edition, 1844.—Third edition, with Supplement. Lond. 1844, 2l. 10s.—New editions, with Supplements, 1854, 1856, 1859, 2l. 10s.

Geographical and Statistical Dictionary of the World. Lond. 1842, 2 vols. 8vo. 4l.—Second edition, Lond. 1846, 5l. 5s. 1849-50, 3l. 3s. Supplement to the same, 1850, 2s. 6d —Third edition, with Supplement. Lond. 1854, 3l. 3s.

Principles of Political Economy, with some enquiries respecting their application, and a sketch of the rise and progress of the science. Edinb. 1825.—Third edition, enlarged, Lond. 1843.—Fourth edition, Lond. 1849, 15s.

Literature of Political Economy, a Classified Catalogue of Books on the science. Lond. 1845, 8vo. 14s.

A Treatise on the Succession to Property vacant by death; including inquiries into the influence of primogeniture, entails, &c., over the public interest. Lond. 1848, 8vo. 6s. 6d.

A Statistical Account of the British Empire, exhibiting its extent, physical capacities, population, industry, and civil and religious institutions. Lond. 1837, 8vo. 2 vols.—Second edition, Lond. 1839, 8vo. 2 vols.—Third edition, stereotyped, Lond. 1846, 8vo. 2 vols.—Fourth edition, with Appendix. Lond. 1854, 8vo. 2 vols. 2l. 8s. Reduced, 1l. 1s.

Treatises and Essays on Subjects connected with Political Policy. with Biographical Notices of Quesnay, A. Smith, and Ricardo. Edinb. 1853, 8vo.

On the Rate of Wages, second edition, 1854, 8vo.

Considerations on Partnerships with Limited Liability. Lond. 1856, 8vo.

On Metallic and Paper Currency. Edinb. 1858, 4to. (from the Ency. Brit.)

Treatises on Economical Policy. Edinb. 1853, 8vo. 14s.

Treatise on the principles and practical influence of Taxation and the Funding System. Lond. 1845, 16s.—Second edition, Lond. 1852, 8vo. 10s.

Some Illustrations of Mr. M'Culloch's Principles of Political Economy. By Mordecai Mullion, private Secretary to Christopher North. Edinb. 1826, 8vo. 3s.

See RICARDO, David, SMITH, Adam.

MACCULLOCH, Robert, D.D. Lectures on the Prophecies of Isaiah. Lond. 1791-1805, 8vo. 4 vols.

In the composition of these lectures the author, who was a minister of the church of Scotland, has made great use of Vitringa's elaborate commentary on Isaiah.

Sermons on Interesting Subjects, 1803, 12mo. 2 vols.

M'CURTIN, H. English-Irish Dictionary, with an Irish Grammar. Paris, 1732, 4to. 2l. 12s. 6d.

Dent, with O'Brien's Irish-English, 2 vols. pt. ii. 707, 1l. 16s.

For the Irish-English Dictionary which forms the usual companion to the above, see O'BRIAN.

A brief Discourse in Vindication of the Antiquity of Ireland: collected out of many authentick Irish Histories and Chronicles, and out of Foreign learned Authors. In two Parts. I. Containing a brief Account of the Travels and Adventures of the Gadelians from Fenius-farsa's Time to the Coming of the Milesians into Ireland, and continued to the Year of Salvation 432. II. Some memorable Actions and Accidents to the Year 1171. Dublin, 1717, 4to. 12s. Pp. 314, besides title, dedication to the Right Hon. William O'Brien, Earl of Inchiquin, preface and catalogue of subscribers, 9 leaves.

The Elements of the Irish Language grammatically explained in English in four Chapters. Lovain, 1728, 8vo. Dent, pt. i. 1809, russia, 1l. 5s.

M'DERMOT, (M.) An Impartial History of Ireland, from the earliest accounts to the present time. Lond. n. d. (circa 1810) 8vo. 4 vols. with portraits.

MACDIARMID, John. Lives of British Statesmen. Lond. 1807, 4to. portraits.

An extremely valuable work, comprehending the lives of Sir Thomas More, Cecil, Burleigh, Strafford, and Clarendon, four portraits. Hibbert, 5l. 5s., 1l. 9s.— 1820, 8vo. 2 vols. with four portraits. Duke of York, 3230, 16s.—Lond. 1838, 8vo. portrait, in one vol. 7s. 6d.

An Enquiry into the System of National Defence in Great Britain. Lond. 1805, 8vo. 2 vols. 7s.

An Enquiry into the Principles of civil and military Subordination. Lond. 1806, 8vo. 2s. 6d.

Scrap Book. Lond. 1823-4, post 8vo. 2 vols. 13s.

MACDONALD, Alex. Schoolmaster. A Gaelick and English Vocabulary. Edinb. 1741, 8vo.
Dent, pt. l. 1371, 4s.

— Alexander. A complete Dictionary of English Gardening. Lond. 1806, 4to. 2 vols. 24 coloured plates, from original drawings by Sydenham Edwards.
White Knights, 2524, 3l.

— Andrew. Miscellaneous Works. Lond. 1791, 8vo.
Roxburghe, 3971, 4s. Many of the productions of this writer appeared under the signature of Matthew Bramble, Esq. He was writer of "Probationary Odes, No. 7," which possesses excellent humour and poignant satire.

— Archibald. Memoirs of Archibald MacDonald, of Barisdale, 1754, 8vo.
With portrait. Dowdeswell, 591, 6s. 6d.

— John. Travels in various Parts of Europe, Asia, and Africa, during a Series of thirty Years and upwards. Lond. 1790, 8vo.
A recital of the adventures, amours, &c. of a servant. Roxburghe, 2316, 5s. 6d. Heber, pt. ii. 1s.

MACDONALD FAMILY.—An historical and genealogical Account of the Clan or Family of Macdonald, of Clanranald, from Somerlett, King of the Isles, Lord of Argyll and Kintyre, to the present Period. Edinb. 1819, 8vo. 10s.
Privately printed. Genealogical and Historical Account of the Clan or Family of Macdonald of Sanda, 1825, royal 8vo. Privately printed. 18s.

MACDONNEL, D. E. Dictionary of Quotations in general use. Lond. 1779. First edition, post 8vo.— Lond. 1797, third edition, post 8vo.—Lond. 1837, ninth edition, 12mo.— New edition, (under the title of 'A Manual of Quotations'), by E. H. Michelsen. Lond. 1856, 12mo. 6s.
(The whole of this book is incorporated and extensively corrected in Bohn's Handbook of Quotations.)

M'DOUALL, Andrew, Lord Banckton. Institutes of the Laws of Scotland in civil Rights; with Observations upon the Agreement or Diversity between them and the Laws of England, in four Books. Edinb. 1751-3, folio, 3 vols.
Roxburghe, 1074, 8l. 13s. 6d. An esteemed work. LARGE PAPER.

MACE, Thomas. Musick's Monument: or, a Remembrancer of the best practical Music, both divine and civil, that has ever been known to have been in the world. Lond. 1676, folio. port. by Faithorne after Cooke, æt. 63.
'A most delectable book.'—Burney. Heber, pt. v. 10s. Skegg, 1l. 1s. Townley, pt. ii. 1020, 1l. 6s. Bindley, pt. ii. 1037, 1l. 12s. LARGE PAPER copies, 2l. 2s.

MACER, Æmilius. Macer's Herbal practysed by Doctor Lynacro, translated out of Laten in to Englysshe. Impr. by me Robert Wyer (1542), 16mo.
Contains W in form. A jejune performance, says Dr. Pulteney, 'written on Galenical principles.' Heber, pt. vii. 6d.

MAC EWEN, William. Grace and Truth: or, the Glory and Fulness of the Redeemer displayed, in an Attempt to explain the most remarkable of the Types, Figures and Allegories of the old Testament. Edinb. 1763, 12mo.
An esteemed work, frequently reprinted. Select Essays upon Subjects doctrinal and practical. To which is prefixed, an Account of the Author, with a brief Description of the Secession. Edinb. 1767, 12mo. 2 vols. 6s.

MAC FARLAN, Robert. Gaelic and English Vocabulary. Edinb. 1795, 8vo.

MACFARLANE (P.). Gaelic and English Vocabulary; and English and Gaelic. Edinb. 1815, 8vo. 2 vols.

MACFARLANE, Robert. The History of the Reign of George the Third, King of Great Britain, 1760-96. Lond. 1770, 82, 94, 96, 8vo. 4 vols.

Horne Tooke, 337, 8 vols. 11s. 6d. A second edition of vol. 1. appeared in 1763, with alterations by another hand.

M'FINGAL: a modern Epic Poem, in four Cantos. Fifth Edition, with explanatory Notes. Lond. 1792, 8vo. 2s. 6d.

A successful imitation of Hudibras, by John Trumbull, first published in Connecticut, in 1782.

MACGEOGHEGAN, M. l'Abbé. Histoire de l'Irlande, ancienne et moderne, tirée des Monuments les plus authentiques. Paris, 1758-63, 4to. 3 vols. 2l. 2s.

Willett, 1002, 3l. 12s. History of Ireland, translated by P. O'Kelly. Dub. 1831, 8vo. 8 vols.—Dub. 1844. royal 8vo. in one vol. 10s. 6d.

MACGILL, Thomas. An Account of Tunis, of its Government, Manners, Customs, and Antiquities, especially of its Productions, Manufactures and Commerce. Glasg. 1811, 8vo. 5s.

A compilation of little value or authority.

Travels in Turkey, Italy, and Russia, in 1803-6. Lond. 1808, 12mo. 2 vols. 6s.

MACGOWAN, Rev. John. Discourses on the Book of Ruth and other important Subjects. Lond. 1781, 8vo. 5s.

MACGREGOR, John. Historical and descriptive Sketches of the Maritime Colonies of British America. Lond. 1828, 8vo. 7s.

Observations on Emigration to British America. Lond. 1829, 8vo.
Account of British America. Edinb. Blackwood, 1832. 8vo. 2 vols. 1l. 10s.
My Note-Book. Lond. 1835, post 8vo. 8 vols. Chiefly a personal narrative of his tours on the continent.
The Commercial and Financial Legislation of Europe and America; with a pro-forma Revision of the Taxation, and the Customs' Tariff of the United Kingdom. Lond. 1841, 8vo. 10s. 6d.
Commercial Statistics: a Digest of the productive Resources, commercial Legislation, custom Tariffs, Navigation, Port and Quarantine Laws and Charges, Shipping, Imports and Exports, and the Monies, Weights and Measures of all Nations; including all British commercial Treaties with Foreign States. Collected from authentic Records, and consolidated with special reference to British and Foreign Products, Trade, and Navigation. Lond. 1844-50, super-royal 8vo. 5 vols. pub. 7l. 10s., reduced (Bohn) 2l. 12s. 6d.

Originally published in Paris. Some of the volumes are sold with independent titles, e.g. 'Germany and her Resources,' 'Holland and the Dutch Colonies.'

The Progress of America from the Discovery by Columbus to the Year 1846. Lond. 1847, roy. 8vo. 2 vols. (The Supplements, 84 pages, are sometimes placed at the end of vol 1.) Pub. at 4l. 14s. 6d., reduced (Bohn) 1l. 11s. 6d.

Financial Reform: a Letter to the Citizens of Glasgow. With an Introduction and supplementary Notes. Lond. 1849, 8vo.

The History of the British Empire, from the Accession of James I.: to which is prefixed, a Review of the Progress of England, from the Saxon Period to 1603. Lond. 1852, 8vo. 2 vols. 1l. 16s.

A synthetical View of the Results of recent commercial and financial Legislation. Second edition. Lond. 1855, 8vo.

Mr. Macgregor was Secretary of the Board of Trade, and in that position inaugurated important reforms in the tariff. Besides the works enumerated above, he was the author of 'Reports on Foreign Tariffs and Trade,' presented to Parliament by royal command, and of some less extensive treatises on kindred subjects.

He also produced the best edition of De Lolme on the Constitution. See DE LOLME.

M'GREGOR, John James. New Picture of Dublin. Dublin, 1821, 12mo.

With plates and a plan of Dublin. Duke of York, 8208, morocco, 14s.
True Stories from the History of Ireland, third series, second edition, engraved titles and front. Dublin, 1829-33, 18mo. 8 vols. 10s. 6d.
Memoir of Lond. 1840, 12mo.

MAC-GREGOR, Robert. See MACLEAY, K. ROB ROY.

M'GRINGER, Joel, D.D. A compendious Treatise of modern Education, in which the following interesting Subjects are liberally discussed: The Nursery, Private Schools, Public Schools, Universities, Gallantry, Duelling, Gaming, and Suicide; to which are added, coloured Designs, both characteristic and illustrative. Lond. 1804, folio, 1l. 1s.

MACGUIRE, Connor, Lord. Trial, with perfect copies of the Indictment. Also the copies of Sir Philome O'Neale's commission, with many remarkable passages in Ireland. Lond. 1645, 4to.

MACHIAVELLI, Nicholas. Tutte le Opere, con una Prefazione di Giuseppe Baretti. Lond. 1762, 4to. 3 vols.

A good edition. Drury, 2789, 1l. 15s.—Lond. 1747, 4to. 3 vols. 12s. Willett, 1597, 2l. 15s. Bright, old mor. 2l. 1s.

— Works. Newly translated from the Originals; illustrated with Notes, Anecdotes, Dissertations, and the Life of Machiavel never before published; and several new Plans on the Art of War. By Ellis Farneworth, M.A. Lond. 1762, 4to. 2 vols.

Nassau, pt. ii. 1564, 1l. 9s. Dent, pt. ii. 708, russia, 2l. 5s. Marquis of Townshend, 2168, 3l. 13s. 6d.—1775, 8vo. 4 vols. Reed, 2512, 3l. 8s. Heath, 3285, 2l. 10s.

The Works of Nicholas Machiavel. Lond. 1675, folio, Brockett, 1849, 1l. 2s.—1694, folio.—1698, folio. Roxburghe, 6916, 12s. 6d.—1720, folio, 10s. 6d.

On good Government. Lond. 1802, folio.

The Art of Warre, set forthe in Englishe by Peter Whitehorne, with an addicion of other like marcialle Feates and Experimenta. Anno MDLX. 4to. 2l. 2s. The title-page to this edition is elegantly cut on wood by W. S.; at the bottom, in type, is 'Niclas Inglande,' subsequently omitted. The volume contains 4} h l in fours, besides the dedication to Queen Elizabeth.—1562, 4to. White Knights, 2525, morocco, 1l. 7s. Heber, pt. i. 4314, 1l.—1573, 4to. Horne Tooke, 448, 1l. 15s. Heber, pt. v. 1l.—1588, 4to. with cuts. Heber, pt. v. 7s.

The Florentine Historie, translated into English by T(homas) B(edingfield). Lond. 1594, folio, 6s.—1595, folio.—By M. K. Lond. 1674, 8vo. Roxburghe, 8263, 2s.

History of Florence, and of the Affairs of Italy; the Prince, and other Works. Farnworth's translation carefully revised. Lond. (Bohn's Standard Library) 1847, post 8vo. 3s. 6d. with portrait.

Discourses upon the first decade of Livy, translated by Edward Dacres. Lond. 1636, 18mo. 3s. 6d.—1674, 18mo. Roxburghe, 7579, 5s.

The Prince, with an Introduction. By J. S. Byerley. Lond. 1802, 8vo. 6s. In this translation the writer compares Machiavel with Buonaparte.

The Meaning of Machivels Instructions to his Sonne: With the Answers to the same. Lond. 1613, 4to. In verse. Bindley, pt. iv. 1081, 8s. Inglis, 951, 8s. Halliwell, 1859, 2l. 12s. Collection.—A—G, 25 leaves.

Machiavel, as he lately appeared to his deare sons, the Moderne Projectors, with characters; divulged for the pretended good of the Kingdoms of England, Scotland, and Ireland. Lond. I. O. for Francis Constable, 1641, 4to. Title and 14 leaves unpaged, in Prose and Verse, probably written by John Taylor, the Water Poet.

Marriage of Belphegor, 1772, 12mo.

Life of Castruccio Castracani, 1722, 12mo.

Belfagor, a tale, translated in verse. Lond. 1840. 8vo.

Machivell's Dogge, a Poem, 1617, 4to. with curious woodcut of a dog. Bindley, pt. iv. 720, 9l. 12s. Heber, pt. iv. 2l. 8s.

MACHIN, Lewis. The Dumbe Knight, a Comedy. Lond. 1608, 4to.

Rhodes, 1811, 1l. 10s. Heber, pt. ii. 16s.—1633, 4to. Roxburghe, 5356, 11s. Bhoden, 1612, 13s. Heber, pt. ii. 5s. 6d. It is reprinted in Dodsley's Collection of old Plays.

Three Eglogs, n. d. 8vo.

M'INTOSH, Brigadier, of Borlam. Essay on Ways and Means for inclosing, and of planting Scotland, and that in sixteen Years at farthest. Edinb. 1729, 8vo.

MACINTOSH, Ch. Flora and Pomona, or the British Fruit and Flower Garden. Lond. 1829, 4to. 71 coloured plates, pub. 4l. 4s.

Practical Gardener and Modern Horticulturist. Lond. Kelly, 1828-9, 8vo. 2 vols. coloured plates, 2l, 2s.

Flower Garden. Lond. Orr, 1840, fcap. 8vo. with coloured plates.—Second edition, 1844.—Third edition, 1847, 10s. 6d.

Greenhouse, Hothouse, and Stove. Lond. Orr, 1839, fcap. 8vo. coloured plates, 10s. 6d.

Orchard and Fruit Garden. Lond. Orr, 1839, fcap. 8vo. coloured plates, 10s. 6d.

The Book of the Garden, in 2 vols. Vol. I. 'Structural,' with 1073 illustrations. Vol. II. 'Cultural,' with 279 illustrations. Edinb. Blackwood, 1853-5, royal 8vo. 2 vols. (published in parts), 4l. 7s. 6d.

MACINTOSH, Donald. A Collection of Gaelic Proverbs and familiar Phrases. Edinb. 1785, 12mo.

Roxburghe, 1440, 10s. 6d. Nassau, pt. i. 2096, 11s. Constable, 615, 11s.—A new

Edition, edited by Alexander Campbell, 1819, 12mo.
See also MACKINTOSH.

MACKAILE, Matb. Account of the Moffet-Well in Scotland. Of the Oily Well. Culpeper's Character. Edinb. 1664, 12mo.
Nassau, pt. I. 2087, 4s. Bliss, 6s.
A translation of the following article.
Fons Moffetensis, seu Descriptio topographico-spagyrica Fontium mineralium Moffetensium in Annandalia Scotiæ. Edinb. 1659, 12mo. White Knights. 2500, 1l. 2s.
A Treatise on Mace. Aberdeen, 1677, 12mo.
The Diversitie of Salts and Spirits maintained, together with a new System of the Order and Gradation in the World's Creation, as also Scurvie and Alchymie discovered. Aberdeen, 1683, 12mo.—Gordonstoun, 1552, 3s. Inglis, 694, 4s.

MACKAY, Andrew, A.M. The complete Navigator. Lond. 1804, 8vo.
A most correct and practical system.—Second Edition improved. Lond. 1810, 8vo.
The Theory and Practice of finding the Longitude and Latitude at Sea or Land: to which are added various Methods of determining the Latitude of a Place and Variation of the Compass, with new Tables. Lond. 1793, 8vo. 2 vols. In 1.—Aberdeen, 1801, 8vo. 2 vols.
A Collection of Mathematical Tables, for the Use of Students in Universities and Academies; for the practical Navigator, Geographer, and Surveyor; for Men of Business, &c. Lond. 1804, 8vo. 7s.

MACKAY, Angus. A Collection of Ancient Piobaireachd or Highland-pipe Music. Edinb. 1833, folio, 1l. 15s.
Dedicated to the Highland Society.

— Maj. Gen. Hugh, of Scoury. Memoirs of the War in Scotland and Ireland. 1689-91. *See* BANNATYNE and MAITLAND CLUBS. Appendix.

— John, of Rockfield. Life of General Hugh Mackay. *See* BANNATYNE and MAITLAND CLUBS. Appendix.

— J. T. Flora Hibernica. Dub. 1836, 8vo.

— History of the House and Clan of. Edinb. 1829, 4to. 1l. 1s.

— *See* MACKY.

MACKENNA, Theobald. Political Essays relative to the affairs of Ireland, in 1791-82-93. Lond. Debrett, 1794, 8vo.

MACKENZIE, Alexander. Voyages from Montreal, on the river St. Laurence, through the Continent of N. America, to the Frozen and Pacific Oceans, 1789-93; with a preliminary Account of the Fur Trade. Lond. 1801, 4to.
Illustrated with maps, and a portrait of the author. Strettell, 1249, 15s. 6d. Fonthill, 859, 1l. 4s. Roxburghe, 7346, 1l. 6s. Willett, 1583, 1l. 7s. Besides the interesting details in this voyage respecting the countries travelled over, and the manners of the inhabitants, it is important, as having affected the discovery of the Polar Sea, by land.—Paris, 1802, 8vo. 2 vols.

— F., and A. Pugin. Specimens of Gothic Architecture, on sixty-one Plates. Lond. Taylor, 1816, 4to. 1l. 10s. LARGE PAPER, 2l. 2s.
Drury, 2793, russia, 1l. 11s. 6d.
Architectural Antiquities of St. Stephen's Chapel, Westminster. Lond. Weale, 1844, imp. folio. 4l. 4s.
Description of the Roof of King's College Chapel, Cambridge. Lond. Weale, 1840, 4to. 7s. 6d.

— George, M.D. The Lives and Characters of the most eminent Writers of the Scots nation. Edinb. 1708, 11, 22, folio. 3 vols.
'A most shapeless mass of inert matter.' Townsley, pt. II. 1011, 2l. 5s. Reed, 8347, 2l. 10s. North, pt. II. 1246, 5l. 10s. Roxburghe, Suppl. 725, 4l. 4s. Dindley, pt. II. 1047, 5l. 5s. Bright, 1l. 1s.

— Sir George, of Rosehaugh. Works. Edinb. 1716-22, folio. 2 vols.
With portrait. Reed, 3345, 1l. 13s. This edition does not contain the author's romance of Aretina, nor a tract on the Discovery of the Fanatic Plot. Mackenzie's writings relative to Scottish antiquities are of little value, but his juridical works are still held in estimation.
Aretina, or the serious Romance. Lond. 1661, 12mo. Mackenzie's earliest publication, omitted in his collected works. This and the next four articles were published anonymously.
Religio Stoici, or the Religious State. Edinb. 1663, 12mo.—1665. Hehar, pt. I.

MACKENZIE, Sir G.—*continued.*
4to, 6d. In the volume of Essays dated
1713.

A moral Essay preferring Solitude to
public Employment and all Appanages.
Edinb. 1665, 12mo.—Lond. 1685, 12mo.—
Lond. 1693, 12mo. (In the vol. dated 1713).
Replied to by John Evelyn.

Moral Gallantry; a Discourse proving
that Point of Honour obliges Man to be
virtuous. Edinb. 1667, 12mo. (In the vol.
dated 1713.)

A moral Paradox, maintaining that it is
much easier to be virtuous than vicious,
and a Consolation against Calumnies.
Edinb. 1667—1669, 8vo.—Lond. 1685, 8vo.

Pleadings on some remarkable Cases
before the supreme Courts of Scotland,
since the Year 1661. To which the Decisions are subjoined. Edinb. 1672, 4to.—
1673, 4to.

A Discourse upon the Laws and Customs of Scotland in Matters criminal.
Edinb. 1678, 4to.—Second edition, Edinb.
1699, folio.

Observations upon the XXVIII Act 23rd
Parl. King James VI. against Bankrupts,
&c. Edinb. 1675, 12mo.

Observations upon the Laws and Customs of Nations as to Precedency. Edinb.
1680, folio. pp. 99, dedicated to the King,
with a portrait of the author by Vander-
banc. Hindley, pt. ii. 1256, 1l. 11s. 6d.
Gough, 2066, 12s. Nassau, pt. — 2299, 12s.
Heber, pt. i. old mor. 2l. 5s. The whole of
this valuable tract is reprinted in the last
edition of Guillim's Display of Heraldry.

The Science of Herauldry, treated as a
Part of the civil Law and Law of Nations:
wherein Reasons are given for its Principles and Etymologies for its harder Terms.
Edinb. 1680, folio. pp. 98, and a table of
sirnames, 6 pages. This learned work
was published along with the preceding.
It was dedicated by the author to his countrymen, and is divided into thirty-four
chapters, each illustrated by a variety of
historical observations. It has been highly
praised by Nicolson, Nisbet, and other
writers. Roxburghe, 8900, 17s.

Idea Eloquentiæ forensis hodiernæ, una
cum Actione forensi ex unaquaque Juris
Parte. Edinb. 1681, 8vo. — In English,
translated by R. Hepburn. Edinb. 1711,
8vo.

Jus Regium, or Monarchy vindicated
against Buchanan, Naphtali, Dolman, Milton, &c. Lond. 1684, 8vo.—1685, 12mo.

On the Discovery of the Fanatick Plot.
(Anon.) Edinb. 1684, folio. This political
tract is omitted in Mackenzie's works.

Institutions of the Law of Scotland.
Edinb. 1684, 12mo.—Edinb. 1688, 12mo.
—Lond. 1694, 8vo. — Edinb. 1706, 12mo.
With Notes by J. Spottiswood. Edinb.

1723. 8vo. by Alexander Bayne, 1730,
12mo.—1758, 12mo. *See* ERSKINE, John.

A Supplement to Sir George Mackenzie's
Institutions. By Alex. Bayne. Edinb.
1731. 12mo.—Edinb. 1749, 12mo.

A Defence of the Antiquity of the royal
Line of Scotland, with a true Account
when the Scots were governed by Kings
in the Isle of Britain. Edinb. 1685, 8vo.—
Lond. 1685, 8vo. 3s. 6d. pp. 190; with Dedication to the King, pp. 6; a Letter to the
Earl of Perth, pp. 14, and advertisement,
pp. 2. This tract was written in answer
to Bishop Lloyd's historical Account of
Church Government.

The Antiquity of the Royal Line of
Scotland farther cleared and defended
against the Exceptions lately offered by
Dr. Stillingfleet, in his Vindication of the
Bishop of St. Asaph. Lond. 1686, 8vo.
4s. pp. 213, with a dedication to K. James
II. pp. 8, and an address to the reader,
pp. 4.

Defensio Antiquitatis Regalis Scotorum
Prosapiæ, Latine versa à F. Sinclare. Traj.
ad Rhen. 1689, 8vo. 7s.

Observations on the Acts of Parliament
made by K. James and his Successors to
the End of the Reign of Charles II. Edinb.
1686, folio. Sotheby's in 1824, mor. 2l. 14s.

Oratio inauguralis habita Edinburgi, Id.
Mar. 1689, de Structura Bibliothecæ pure
juridicæ. Lond. 1689, 12mo. This elegant oration was pronounced at the opening of the Advocates' library, Edinburgh,
of which Sir George was the founder.

Reason, an Essay. Lond. 1690, 12mo.—
1695, 12mo. In the vol. dated 1713.

De Humanæ Rationis Imbecillitate Liber singularis, editus a J. G. Græcio. Traj.
ad Rhen. 1690, 12mo.

The moral History of Frugality, with
its opposite Vices. Lond. 1691, 8vo. In
the vol. dated 1713.

A Vindication of the Government in
Scotland during the Reign of K. Charles
II., with several other Treatises relating
to the Affairs of Scotland. Lond. 1691,
4to. An answer appeared in 1692, 4to.

Essays upon several moral Subjects.
To which is prefixed an Account of his
Life and Writings. Lond. 1713, 8vo.

Memoirs of the Affairs of Scotland from
the Restoration of King Charles II. to
1677. Edited by Thos. Thomson, Esq.
Edinb. 1821, 4to. Drury, 2791, 1l. 2s.
Bright, 19s. Duke of York, 3150, 6s. A
masterly criticism on this valuable work
appeared in the Edinburgh Review, No.
LXXI.

MACKENZIE, Sir George, of Tarbat. *See* CROMERTY, Earl of.

— Sir George Steuart, Bart.
Travels in the Island of Iceland,

during the Summer of 1810. Edinb. 1811, 4to. 2 maps and 15 coloured plates.

A valuable and interesting work, treating on almost every topic. Duke of York, 8l. 4s. Hollis, 70s, 3l.—1812, 4to. Drury, 8799, russia, 1l. 6s. New edition, (in double columns). Edinb. Chambers, 1842, royal 8vo. 1s. 4d.

An Essay on some Subjects connected with Taste. Edinb. 1817, 8vo. 8s.

MACKENZIE, Henry. Works. Edinb. 1808, crown 8vo. 8 vols. Portrait.

Hollis, 803, 1l. 13s. Duke of York, 3240, 1l. 18s.—*Contents*. Man of Feeling; Man of the World; Julia de Roubigné; Papers from the Mirror and the Lounger; Miscellanies; also Poems and Dramas (now first published).

Of Mackenzie's principal work, the Man of Feeling, there have been published many and various editions. The first was anonymous, in 1771. Its sequel, the Man of the World, appeared soon after.

Mackenzie was one of the first to cultivate German Literature, and in 1791 published translations of Lessing's Set of Horses.

— J. Memoirs of John Calvin, 1809, 8vo. 6s. portrait.

1818, 12mo. with portrait, 4s.

— John. A Narrative of the Siege of London-Derry, faithfully represented to rectifie the Mistakes, and supply the Omissions of Mr. Walker's Account. Lond. 1690, 4to.

Pp. 84, besides title, preface, and contents, 4 leaves.

Dr. Walker's Invisible Champion foyled. Lond. 1690, 4to. See WALKER, Rev. George.

— Murdoch, F.R.S. Orcades; or, geographic and hydrographic Survey of the Orkney and Lewis Islands, in eight Maps. Also, an Account of the Orkney Islands. Lond. 1750, folio.

Willett, 1501, 1l. 7s.

A Treatise of Maritime Surveying, in two Parts; with a prefatory Essay on Draughts and Surveys. Lond. 1774, 4to. 5s.

Maritime Survey and Nautical Descriptions of the Coasts of Ireland and of the West Coasts of Great Britain. Lond. 1776, elephant folio, 2 vols. Geo. Chalmers, 1l. 2s.

— Roderick. A Sketch of the War with Tippoo Sultaun, 1789-92. Calcutta, 1793-4, 4to. 2 vols. 10s. 6d. —Calcutta, 1799, 4to. 2 vols. 12s.

An impartial work, full of valuable information.

MACKENZIE FAMILY. The Genealogie of the Mackenzies preceding the year 1661, written in 1669 (by Mackenzie of Applecross). Edinb. 1829, 4to.

NOT PUBLISHED. Only 50 printed, Eyton, mor. 18s.

Another edition, with continuation, 1843, sm. folio.

MACKERELL, Benjamin. The History and Antiquities of the flourishing Corporation of Kings Lynn, in the County of Norfolk. Lond. 1738, 8vo.

Drury, 2517, 5s. 6d. Dent, pt. 1. 1372, 5s. 6d. Sir P. Thompson, 491, 8s. Roxborghe, 8849, 9s. 6d. Towneley, pt. II. 737, 10s. Bindley, pt. II. 1576, 11s. 6d. Willett, 1562, 16s. Heath, 4673, 14s. Fonthill, 2114, 1l. Nassau, pt. I. 2083, with additional plates, 1l. 7s. *Collation*.—Pp. 290, besides title and dedication, 2 leaves; preface, 6 pages; also 11 plates at pp. 1, 8, 76, 156, 160, 161, 182, 184, 213, 220, and 272. There are other plates on the letter-press.

MACKGILL, James. Discours particulier d'Ecosse, escrit par Commandement et Ordonnance de la Royne Douarière et Regente, par Messires Jacques Mackgill, Clerk du Registre, et Jean Bellenden, Clerc de la Justice. xi. Janvier, M.D.LIX. Edinb. 1824, 4to.

Presented to the members of the Bannatyne Club by Thomas Thomson, Esq. Fifty-two copies printed on Club paper. A like number was printed on ordinary paper of a larger size.

MACK GREGORY, John. An Account of the Sepulchres of the Ancients, and a Description of their Monuments. Lond. 1712, 8vo.

Roxburghe, 9016, 9s.

MACKINTOSH. See also M'INTOSH

MACKINTOSH, James. Travels in Europe, Asia, and Africa; begun in the Year 1777, and finished in

1781. Lond. 1782, 8vo. 2 vols. 12s.

Published anonymously. Fonthill, 2763, 1l. 6s.

Some Observations and Remarks on a late Publication entitled Travels in Europe, Asia, and Africa; in which the real Author of this new and curious Asiatic Atalantis, his Character and Abilities, are fully made known to the Public, (by Joseph Price.) Lond. 1782, 8vo. 2s. 6d. Fonthill, 2764, 13s.

MACKINTOSH, Sir James, Knt., M.D.

Vindiciæ Gallicæ. Defence of the French Revolution and its English Admirers against the Accusations of the Right Hon. Edmund Burke; including some Strictures on the late Production of Mons. de Calonne. Lond. 1791, 8vo. Hibbert, 4977, 11s. Horne Tooke, 449, 11 2s.

Second edition, Lond. 1791, 8vo.—Third edition, with additions, Lond. 1791, 8vo.—Fourth edition, with additions, Lond. 1792, 8vo.—New edition, Lond. 1837, 12mo. &c.

This is esteemed the most able of the answers to Burke. The first edition is the most prized, as containing many passages afterwards suppressed.

Pamphlet on the Regency Question. Lond. 1788, 8vo.

A Discourse on the Study of the Law of Nature and Nations; Introductory to a Course of Lectures on that Science in Lincoln's Inn Hall, on Wednesday, Feb. 20, 1799, in pursuance of an Order of the honourable Society of Lincoln's Inn. Lond. 1799, 8vo. 2s. 6d.—Second edition, Lond. 1799, 8vo.—Third edition, corrected and enlarged. Lond. 1800, 8vo.—Reprinted 1828, 12mo. 8s.—Again, Lond. Lumley, 1835, 12mo. 5s.

Translated into French by Paul Royer-Collard; with 'Le droit des gens par Emer de Vattel.' Paris, 1830.

Discourses on the Laws of England. Lond. (1799). 8vo. A pamphlet.

The Trial of John Peltier, Esq. for a Libel against Napoleon Buonaparte, taken in short-hand by Mr. Adams, and the Defence revised by Mr. Mackintosh. Lond. 1803, 8vo. 10s. 6d. Reprinted in "Celebrated Speeches." Philad. 1845, 8vo. 10s.

This splendid specimen of forensic eloquence was translated into French by Madame de Stael.

Substance of his Speech in the House of Commons on presenting a Petition for the Recognition of the Independent States established in the Countries of America formerly subject to Spain. Lond. 1824, 8vo.

Dissertation on Ethical Philosophy, chiefly during the XVIIth and XVIIIth Centuries. Edinb. 1830, 4to. 9s. Prefixed originally to the Encyclopedia Britannica. Reprinted, Philadelphia, 1871, 8vo.—New edition with a Preface by Dr. Whewell. Edinb. and Lond. 1836. 8vo.—Second edition, 1837.—Third edition, Lond. 1839, 8vo. 9s. Prefixed to 8th edition of Ency. Brit. Edinb. 1853, 4to.

A Fragment on Mackintosh, being Strictures on some passages in the Dissertation prefixed to the Ency. Brit. Lond. 1835, 8vo.

History of England, B.C. 55 to A.D. 1572. Lond. (Lardner's Cabinet Cyclopædia) 1830–32, 12mo. 18s.—New edition, revised by his son. Lond. Longman, 1853, 8vo. 2 vols. 1l. 1s.

—— With Continuation to 1760, by Wallace and Bell. Lond. 1830–38, 12mo. 10 vols. 1l. 15s.

Speech on the Second Reading of the Bill to amend the Representation of the People in England and Wales, July 4, 1831. Lond. 1831, 8vo.

History of the Revolution in England in 1688, comprising a View of the Reign of James II. from his Accession, to the enterprise of the Prince of Orange. By the late Sir James Mackintosh, and completed to the settlement of the Crown, by the Editor. To which is prefixed a Notice of his Life, Writings, and Selection of his Speeches. Lond. 1834, 4to. published at 3l. 3s.

The first portion of this volume, consisting of the fragment by Sir James Mackintosh, was published separately under the following title.

View of the Reign of James II. Lond. 1835, 4to. 1l. 11s. 6d.

The Life of Sir Thomas More. Lond. fcap. 8vo. 1844. Printed separately from the Lives of British Statesmen by Mackintosh and others in Lardner's Cabinet Cyclopædia.

Addresses as Lord Rector of the University of Glasgow (in "Inaugural Addresses of Lords Rectors of the University of Glasgow, by John Barras May," Glasg. 1839, 8vo.)

Tracts and Speeches, 1787-1831. Lond. 1840, 8vo. 25 copies privately printed. Eyton, mor. 19s.

Miscellaneous Works. Lond. 1846, 8vo. 3 vols. 2l. 2s.—Another edition, 3 vols. post 8vo.—Compact edition, in 1 vol. Lond. 1850, 8vo. 1l. 1s.—Again, 1851.

Memoirs of the Life of, edited by his son. Lond. 1835, 8vo. 2 vols. portrait, 1l. 1s.

MACKLIN, John, Minister of God's Word at Lesbury, co. Northumberland. A wonderful Account

of, who, being 116 Years of Age, was miraculously restored to a youthful Vigour and Complexion, new Hairs growing upon his Head, new Teeths in his Mouth, and his Eyes restored to a most perfect Sight. Lond. T. Vere, 1657, 12mo.
Black letter. Braod, 3l. 3s. A copy is in the British Museum.

MACLEAN, James, a complete History of, the Gentleman Highwayman. Lond. n. d. 8vo. port.
See in Johnson's (Ch.) Lives of Highwaymen.

MACLEAN, an Historical and Genealogical Account of the Clan of, by a Seneachie. Lond. 1838, 8vo. with Genealogical Tree.

MACKLIN, Charles. The Man of the World, a Comedy; and Love à la Mode, a Farce. Lond. 1793, royal 4to. portrait of Macklin by Condé, after Opie.
Published by subscription, for the benefit of the author and family, at 1l. 1s. The amount received was 1632l. 11s. which was disbursed in purchasing two annuities, one of 200l. for Mr. Macklin, and another of 75l. for his wife, &c. Roxburghe, 3946, 15s.

Memoirs of the Life of Chas. Macklin, Esq. By James Thos. Kirkman. Lond. 1799, 8vo. 2 vols. with portrait of Macklin by Ridley. Reed, 8267, 7s. Roxburghe, 5317, 1l. 1s.

Memoirs of Charles Macklin. Lond. 1804, 8vo. with portrait. Reed, 8266, 5s.

Mackliniana, a series of Papers, detached from the European Magazine. Reed, 8259, 1l. 16s.

MACKNIGHT, James, D.D. A Harmony of the four Gospels; in which the natural Order of each is preserved. Lond. 1756, 4to.
Dr. Macknight closely adheres to the principle of Osiander; but his paraphrase and commentary contain so much useful information, that his Harmony has long been regarded as a standard book among divines. The preliminary dissertations are highly valuable. Bishop Marsh says, that whoever makes use of this Harmony should compare with it Dr. N. Lardner's observations, which were first published in 1764, (reprinted in Dr. Kippis's edition of his works, vol. 11).—Second edition, corrected and greatly enlarged, Lond. 1763, 4to. front. Williams, 1015, 3l. 15s.—Edinb. 1804, 8vo. 2 vols.—Edinb. 1809, 8vo. 2 vols. Earl of Kerry, 336, 1l. 4s.—Fifth edition, Lond. 1819, 8vo. 2 vols. Nassau, pt. 1, 2080, 15s. Dr. Macknight's Harmony was translated into Latin, and published at Bremen and Deventer, 1772, 8vo. 3 vols.

The Truth of the Gospel History shewed, in three Books. Lond. 1763, 4to. 15s. A work of great merit. Hollis, 704, with Macknight's Harmony. 1l 9s. Heath, 513, with the Harmony, 1761, 2l. 12s. 6d. Williams, 1017, 5l. Two portions of the work are printed in Bishop Watson's Collection of Theological Tracts.

A New literal Translation of all the Apostolical Epistles (accompanied by the Greek text, and the old translation, in parallel columns), with a Commentary and Notes, philological, critical, explanatory, and practical. To which is added, a History of the Life of the Apostle Paul. Edinb. 1795, 4to. 4 vols. 3l. 13s. 6d.—The same without the Greek Text. Edinb. 1795, 4to. 3 vols. 2l. 12s. 6d. This work 'was the unremitting labour of nearly thirty years, during which period seldom less than eleven hours a day were employed on it.'—Second edition, with the Greek text and Life of the Author. Lond. 1806, 8vo. 6 vols. 2l. 8s.—Without the Greek Text, Lond. 1806, 8vo. 4 vols. 1l. 11s. 6d.—Lond. 1816, 8vo. 4 vols. 1l. 16s.—Lond. Tegg, 1843, in one vol. roy. 8vo. 1l. 1s.

As a specimen of this work, he published in 1787 a translation of the Apostle Paul's 1st and 2nd Epistles to the Thessalonians.

MACKWORTH, Sir Humphrey. Free Parliaments, or a Vindication of the House of Commons in the Case of Ashby against White. Lond. 1704, 8vo.

Peace at Home, or a Vindication of the House of Commons on the Bill for Preventing the Danger of Occasional Conformity. Lond. 1704, 8vo. (Answered by Defoe.)

The Case of Sir Humphrey Mackworth, and of the Mine Adventurers, &c. &c. Lond. 1705, 4to. (There are two other works on this Case, with titles nearly similar. One is 4to. 1707, the other folio, 1720.)

His Proposal; being a new scheme offer'd for the payment of the publick debts, for relief of the South-Sea Company, and for easing the nation of the land and malt tax. Lond. n. d. 4to.

Observations on the Scheme of Mr. Law in France, and Sir H. M. in Great Britain; and concerning the establishing paper-money and forcing credit. Lond. n. d. fol.

For a full list of Sir Humphrey Mackworth's works, see the Bodleian Catalogue and Watt's Bibliotheca.

MACKY, or MACKAY John. Memoirs of his secret Services, temp. William III., Queen Anne, and George I., with Characters of the Courtiers of Great Britain. Lond. 1733, 8vo.

Roxburghe, 8526, 6s. Hibbert, 4923, 6s. Townley, pt. II. 745, 7s. Nassau, pt. I. 2091, 18s. Bindley, pt. II. 2735, with MS. notes transcribed from original notes by Swift, 1l. 8s. In the British Museum is the copy with MS. notes by Dean Swift.

— Jo. Journey through England, in familiar letters from a gentleman here to his friend abroad, (without name on title page, but dedication signed Jo. Macky), 2 vols. fourth edition with additions. Lond. 1722, 8vo. 2 vols.—Fifth edition, Lond. 1732, 8vo. 2 vols.

Journey through Scotland, being the third volume, which completes Great Britain. Lond. 1723, 8vo.

MACLAINE, Archibald, D.D. Discourses on various Subjects, delivered in the English Church at the Hague. Lond. 1799, 8vo. 7s.

In considerable estimation.—1801, 8vo. Williams, 1150, 11s.

A Series of Letters, addressed to S. Jenyns, Esq., on Occasion of his View of the Internal Evidence of Christianity. Lond. 1777, 8vo.

See MOSHEIM.

MACLAREN, Charles. A Dissertation on the Topography of the Plain of Troy. Edinb. 1822, 8vo. With a Map. Combe, 1147, 6s.

MACLAURIN, Colin. A complete System of Fluxions; with their Application to the most considerable Problems in Geometry and natural Philosophy. Edinb. 1742, 4to. 2 vols.

A masterly performance. FINE PAPER. Constable, 650, 1l. 17s. Willett, 1594, 2l. 9s. Also Lond. 1801, 8vo. 2 vols.—Translated into French, Paris, 1749, 4to. 2 vols.

Geometria organica, sive Descriptio Linearum curvarum universalis. Lond. 1720, 4to.

A Treatise on Algebra. Lond. 1748.

8vo. 5s. Best edition. Also Lond. 1738, 1760, 1796, 8vo. Translated into French, Paris, 1753, 4to.

An Account of Sir Isaac Newton's philosophical Discoveries. With Life and Writings of the author by Patrick Murdoch. Lond. 1748, 4to. LARGE PAPER. Williams, 1010, 15s. — Second edition, Lond. 1750, 8vo.—Again, 1775, 8vo. Hibbert, 5830, 6s. Translated into French, Paris, 1749, 4to.

It is other works consist principally of Papers in the Philosophical Transactions.

— John, Lord Dreghorn, one of the Senators of the College of Justice, and F.R.S., Ed. Works. Edinb. 1798, 8vo. 2 vols. 9s.

This selection is in little estimation; many of the pieces in vol. 1 had been printed before, with some 'levities,' (ex. gr. 'The Keekiad,') at a private press which Lord Dreghorn kept for his amusement. Prefixed is an account of the author's life and writings.

Poems. 1769, sm. 8vo. Privately printed. Geo. Chalmers, pt. iii. 6s.

The Keekiad, a Poem. Privately printed, 1760, 4to. Eyton, mor. 7s. 6d. Other editions in 8vo.

Arguments and Decisions in remarkable Cases before the High Court of Justiciary, and other supreme Courts in Scotland. Edinb. 1774, 4to. 10s.

— John. An Essay on the Prophecies relating to the Messiah. Edinb. 1773, 8vo. 8s.

This work, of a most powerful and accomplished mind, affords much assistance, says Mr. Orme, for understanding the numerous predictions of the Old Testament relative to the Messiah and his times.

The Works of John Maclaurin, containing his Essays and Sermons. Lond. 1819, 12mo. 2 vols. 6s. Glasgow, 1824, 12mo.

MACLEAN, Archibald. A Paraphrase and Commentary on the Epistle to the Hebrews. Edinb. 1811-17. 12mo. 2 vols.

'We are acquainted with no expository work in our language, which, within so small a compass, contains so much valuable matter, and truly scriptural illustration.'—Orme. Lond. 1819, 8vo. 1 vol.

Sermons on the Doctrines and Duties of the Christian Life, 8vo. portrait, 10s. 6d.

The Works of Archibald M'Lean, with a Memoir of his Life and Writings by Jones. Lond. 1823, 8vo. 7 vols. 2l. 10s.

Miscellaneous Works, Lon. 1822, 12mo. 7 vols. 1l. 4s.

MACLEAY, K., M.D. Historical Memoirs of Rob Roy and the Clan Macgregor; including original Notices of Lady Grange; with an introductory Sketch, illustrative of the Condition of the Highlands prior to the Year 1745. Glasgow, 1818, 12mo. 7s.

Description of the Spar Cave in the Isle of Skye. Edinb. 1811, 8vo.

MAC LEAY, W. S. Horæ Entomologicæ. Lond. 1819, 8vo. vol. i. in 2 pts. (all published) 3 plates, 1l. 4s.

Sotheby's in 1825, 3l. 5s.

MACLEOD, Hugh, D.D. Casus Principis; or, an Essay towards a History of the Principality of Scotland; with some Account of the Appanage and Honours annexed to the second Prince of Scotland. Lond. 1791, 4to.

Chalmers, 15s.

M'LEOD, John. Narrative of a Voyage in his Majesty's late Ship Alceste along the Coast of Corea to the Island of Loo-Choo, with an Account of her subsequent Shipwreck. Lond. 1817, 8vo. 12s.

A highly interesting volume. Dent, pt. 1. 1369, 6s.—1818, 8vo. Drury, 2687, 13s. 6d.

MACLURE, William. Observations on the Geology of the United States of America. Philadelphia, 1817, 8vo.

A valuable work, ably noticed in the Edinb. Review, xxx. 574—88.

MACMAHON, Thos. O'Brien. Depravity and Corruption of Human Nature, wherein the Opinions of Rochefoucault, Hobbes, Mandeville, Helvetius, &c. &c. on that Subject are supported, against Hume, Lord Shaftesbury, Sterne, Brown, and other Apologists for Mankind. Lond. 1774, 12mo. 5s.

— Hugo. Jus Primatiale Armacanum, in omnes Archiep. Epis. &c. —assertum per H(ugonem) A(rmachanum) M(acmahon) T(otius) H(ibernia) P(rimatem) Anno Dom. 1728, 4to.

The first piece includes 272 pages, besides an Index; the second, Prosecutio ejusdem Argumenti, 125 pages; then eleven pages, with a prefix 'In Nomine Domini,' and three leaves of Memoranda et Corrigenda. Heber. pt. i. 4319. 5l. 7s. 6d.

MACMICHAEL, William, M.D. A Journey from Moscow to Constantinople, in the Years 1817 and 1818, Lond. 1819, 4to. plates.

Drury, 9794, 2l. 14s.

The Gold-Headed Cane, containing Anecdotes of its many possessors. Lond. 1827, post 8vo.—Second edition, enlarged 1828, post 8vo. 6s.

MACNAB, D. An accurate Description of the Island and Kingdom of Sicily. Falkirk, 1784, 8vo. Fonthill, 2531, 10s.—Lond. 1798, 8vo.

M'NAYR, James, LL.D. A System of English Conveyancing, adapted to Scotland. A new Edition, considerably enlarged and improved. Glasgow, 1800, 4to.

Best edition.—Glasgow, 1780, 4to.

A Guide from Glasgow to some of the most remarkable Scenes in the Highlands of Scotland, and to the Falls of the Clyde. Glasgow, 1797, 8vo. 5s.

MACNEIL, Hector. Poetical Works. Lond. 1801, 12mo. 2 vols.

Roxburghe, 3510, 7s. 6d. Fonthill, 5495, 1l. 6s.—Edinb. 1806, 12mo. 2 vols.—Edinb. 1812. Third edition corrected, 12mo. 2 vols. plates. The productions of this author are 'deservedly popular.'—Byron. It is said that ten thousand copies of his 'Scotland's Skaith' were sold in one month.

MAC NEVEN, William James. Pieces of Irish History, illustrative of the Condition of the Catholics of Ireland, of the Origin and Progress of the political System of the United Irishmen, and of their Transactions with the Anglo-Irish Government. New York, 1807, 8vo.

Pp. xxiii and 305, with title, errata, contents, 3 leaves.

M'NICOL, Donald. Remarks on Dr. S. Johnson's Journey to the Hebrides; in which are contained, Observations on the Antiquities, Language, Genius, and Manners of

4 z

the Highlanders of Scotland. Lond. 1779, 8vo.
In considerable estimation. Roxburghe, 7l. 16s. 6d. Fonthill, 2584, 10s. Dowdeswell, 408, 11s. Bindley, pt. ii. 1569, 13s.— New edition, Lond. 1817, 8vo.

MACPHERSON, Æneas. Edina delineata; or, picturesque perspective Views of the Churches, Castles, &c. &c. in and near Edinburgh. Edinb. 1798, 4to.

— Charles. Memoirs of his Life and Travels in Asia, Africa, and America, chiefly between the Years 1773 and 1790. Edin. 1800, 12mo.
Roxburghe, 8318. 5s.

— David. Annals of Commerce, Manufactures, Fisheries, and Navigation, with Brief Notices of the Arts and Sciences connected with them. Lond. 1805, 4to. 4 vols. 2l. 2s.
Gardner, 1854, 14s. A highly valuable work.
Geographical Illustrations of Scottish History, with explanation of the difficult and disputed points. Lond. 1796, 4to. 10s. 6d. With a map.
The History of the European Commerce with India. Lond. 1812, 4to. with a map. An elaborate work. Hibbert, 6161, 10s.

— James. An Introduction to the History of Great Britain and Ireland. Third Edition, revised and greatly enlarged. Lond. 1773, 4to. 10s.
Pp. 404, with index, also preface and contents.—1771, 4to.
An Examination of the Arguments contained in a late Introduction to the History of the ancient Irish and Scots (by Thomas Leland, D.D.) Lond. 1772, 4to.
Remarks on an Introduction to the History of Great Britain and Ireland. Lond. 1772, 8vo. 3s. 6d. See WHITAKER, Rev. John.
The Highlander, a Poem, 1758, 12mo. Reed, 7114, 1l. 7s.
Fragments of Ancient Poetry, collected in the Highlands of Scotland, and translated from the Gaelic or Erse Language. 1760, 8vo.
The History of Great Britain, from the Restoration in 1660 to the Accession of the House of Hanover. Lond. 1776, 4to. 2 vols. 1l. 1s.—Lond. 1775, 8vo. 2 vols. 10s. 6d.
Original Papers, containing the Secret History of Great Britain, 1690—1714; with Extracts from the Life of James II. as written by himself. Lond. 1775, 4to. 2 vols. 1l. 11s. 6d. Willett, 1595, 2l. 2s. Marquis of Townshend, 2171, russia, 2l. 4s.—Lond. 1775, 8vo. 2 vols. 10s. 6d.
Both works bound uniformly, 4 vols. 8vo. Towneley, pt. ii. 1119, 1l. 11s. 6d.—4 vols. 4to. Roxburghe, 8380, 4l. 5s. Dent, pt. ii. 710, 4l. Drury, 2796, 4l. 16s.
A Letter to James Macpherson, Esq. With an Address to the Public, on his History of Great Britain, and his Original Papers. Lond. 1775, 4to. 6s.
See OSSIAN.

MACPHERSON, John, D.D. Critical Dissertations on the Origin, Antiquities, &c. of the ancient Caledonians, their Posterity the Picts, and the British and Irish Scots. Lond. 1768, 4to.
Pp. xxvi and 382. Garrick, 1557, 9s. Roxburghe, 8725, 1l. 5s. Heber, pt. v. with Notes by David Macpherson, 1l. 12s.

MACQUEEN, Daniel, D.D. Observations on Daniel's Prophecy of the Seventy Weeks. Edinb. 1748, 8vo. 6s.
An able anonymous tract by a man of learning and talents, intended as a reply to a pamphlet on the same subject, in which the prophecy of Daniel was applied wholly to the Jews.

— John, A.M. British valour triumphing over French courage, under the conduct of the Duke of Marlborough, with a Modest Character of his Grace. Lond. 1715, 8vo.
Bliss, pt. ii. 2586, old mor. 12s.

M'QUEEN, James. A geographical and commercial View of Northern Central Africa. Edinb. 1821, 8vo. 7s.
A critique on this work, likewise remarks on the present state of the slave trade, will be found in the Quarterly Review, xxvi. 51—82.
General Statistics of the British Empire. Lond. 1836, 8vo.

MACQUER, Joseph. Elements of the Theory and Practice of Chemistry. Lond. 1758, 8vo. 2 vols. 6s.
A treatise formerly in considerable estimation.
Dictionary of Chemistry, with Plates,

Notes, and Additions by the Translator. Lond. 1711, 4to. 2 vols.—1777, 8vo. 3 vols.

MACQUER, Philip. A Chronological Abridgment of the Roman History, from the Foundation of the City, to the Extinction of the Republic. Translated and improved with Notes, by Thomas Nugent. Lond. 1759, 8vo. 6s.

MACROBIUS, Amb. Aur. Theod. Opera, accedunt integræ Is. Pontani et Variorum Notæ et Animadversiones. Lond. 1694, 8vo. 5s.

Drury, 2524, morocco, 9s. A reprint of the variorum edition. Lug. Bat. 1670.

MACROPEDIUS, George. Methodus de conscribendis Epistolis, etc. Accessit Chr. Hegendorphini Epistolas conscribendi methodus. Lond. 1595, 16mo.

MACSWINEY, Owen. Tombeaux des Princes, des Grands Capitaines, &c. d'Angleterre. See TOMBEAUX.

M'URE, alias CAMPBELL, John. A View of the City of Glasgow. Glasgow, 1736, small 8vo.

With a portrait and Prospect of Glasgow, by Taylor. A work of little value to the historian, abounding in ridiculous descriptions of the city of Glasgow. 5s. Dowdeswell, 401, ll. 7s. — New edition, Glasgow, 1830, 8vo.

MADAN, Martin, D.D. Thelyphthora; or, a Treatise on Female Ruin. Second Edition, improved. Lond. 1781, 8vo. 3 vols. 15s.

The controversy which this singular work occasioned lasted long, and was carried on with great keenness. In it the author maintains the lawfulness of polygamy as being authorised by the Mosaic law, and therefore obligatory on Christians. Lond. 1780-1, 8vo. 3 vols. Fonthill, 40, 1l. 1s.

Thoughts on executive Justice with Respect to our criminal Laws. With an Appendix. Lond. 1785, 12mo. 6s. Horne Tooke, 254, 6s.

Poemata, partim reddita partim scripta. Lond. 1784, 12mo. Not printed for sale.

— Pat. M.D. A philosophical and medicinal Essay of the Waters of Tunbridge. Lond. 1687, 4to.

Pp. 22. Reprinted in the first volume of the Harleian Miscellany.

MADDEN, Samuel, D.D. Memoirs of the Twentieth Century, being original Letters of State under George the Sixth. Lond. 1733, 8vo.

This severely satirical work was intended to be comprised in six volumes. Only one, however, was printed, which was suppressed on the day of publication. Bindley, pt. iii. 31, 3l. 15s. Hibbert, 5023, 5l. 5s. Saunders' in 1818, 3l. 15s. Heber, the Dedication copy, part ii. red mor. 5l. 5s. Collation.—Pp. 527, with dedication to 'His Royal Highness Frederick Lewis Prince of Wales,' x pages, and 'A modest Preface, containing many Words to the Wise,' 31 pages. See Nichols' Literary Anecdotes, vol. 2, page 52.

Reflections and Resolutions proper for the Gentlemen of Ireland, as to their Conduct for the Service of their Country. Dublin, 1738, 8vo. Original edition (pp. 224), with a preface (24 pages), which is not in the privately printed edition of 1816, its existence being therein positively denied by the editor. Hibbert, 5022, 10s. —Reprinted Dublin, 1816, 8vo. 6s.

MADDISON, Sir Ralph. Great Britains Remembrancer, tending to the Increase of the Monies of the Commonwealth. Lond. 1655, 4to.

MADDOCK, Henry. An Account of the Life and Writings of Lord Chancellor Somers. Lond. 1812, 4to.

Hibbert, 5162, 6s. Reports of Cases in the Vice-Chancellor's Court, before Sir T. Plumer and Sir J. Leach, from 55 to 60 George III. Lond. 1815—22, royal 8vo. 5 vols.—1829, royal 8vo. 6 vols.

Treatise on the Principles and Practice of the high Court of Chancery. Lond. 1815, 2 vols.—1820, royal 8vo. 2 vols. —Third edition, 1837, royal 8vo. 2 vols. 3l. 13s. 6d.

— James. The Florist's Directory, by J. Curtis. Lond. 1810, 8vo.

An excellent work.—Lond. 1792, 8vo. Hibbert, 5024, 5s. 6d.

MADEIRA.—A History of Madeira. 1821, imp. 8vo.

With 27 coloured engravings. An historical Relation of the first Discovery of the Isle of Madeira. Lond. 1675. Fonthill, 2690, 1l.

An historical Account of the Discovery of the Island of Madeira, abridg'd from the Portuguese original. To which is added an Account of the present State of the Island, in a Letter to a Friend. Lond. 1755, 8vo. 2s. 6d.

A Description of the Island of Madeira; with an Account of the Manners and Customs of its Inhabitants. Lond. 1783, 12mo. 2s. 6d.

MADNESS, the Mirror of. See MIRROR.

MADOX, Isaac, Bishop of Worcester. A Vindication of the Government, Doctrine, and Worship of the Church of England, established in the Reign of Q. Elizabeth. Lond. 1733, 8vo. 5s.

An excellent treatise 'against the injurious Reflections of Mr. Neale in his late History of the Puritans; together with a Detection of many false Quotations and Mistakes in that Performance.' This celebrated English divine published several sermons. See NEAL, DAN.

— Thomas. The History and Antiquities of the Exchequer of the Kings of England, from the Norman Conquest to the End of the Reign of Edward II. Lond. 1769, 4to. 2 vols.

Best edition of a 'most valuable and accurate work.'—*Nicolson*. Dent, pt. ii. 712, russia, 2l. Reed, 1866, 2l. 2s., Brockett, 2037, 2l. 5s. Marquis of Townshend, 2172, 8l. LARGE PAPER. Heath, 4398, 4l. 4s.—Lond. 1711, folio. Sir P. Thompson, 597, 16s. Bindley, pt. ii. 841, russia, 2l. 6s. Willett, 1543, with the index, 1741, morocco, 3l. 8s. LARGE PAPER. Sir M. M. Sykes, pt. ii. 283, russia, 1l. 9s. Roxburghe, 8609, 2l. 4s. Duke of Grafton, 130, with the index, (taken from the Baronia Anglica), 1l. 19s.

Formulare Anglicanum; or, a Collection of ancient Charters and Instruments, from the Norman Conquest to the end of the reign of Henry VIII. Lond. 1702, folio. A 'useful work, of unspeakable service to our students in law and antiquities.'—*Nicolson*. Gough, 2257, 1l. 9s. Willett, 1505, russia, 2l. 6s. LARGE PAPER. Duke of Grafton, 129, 14s. Sir P. Thompson, 585, 15s. Roxburghe, 975, 19s. Heath, 4397, 1l. 18s. Brockett, 1853, russia, 2l. 5s.

Firma Burgi; or an historical Essay concerning the Cities, Towns, and Boroughs of England. Lond. 1726, folio, 18s. Brockett, 1852, 1l. 2s. Duke of York, 1379, 1l. 5s. Willett, 1504, russia, 1l. 11s. 6d. LARGE PAPER. Hibbert, 5012, 1l. 5s.

Baronia Anglica; or, History of Land Honors and Baronies, and of Tenures in Capite. With an Index to the History of the Exchequer. Lond. 1736, folio. Gough, 2258, 11s. LARGE PAPER. Sir M. M. Sykes, pt. ii. 284, russia, 1l. 1s.—Lond. 1741, folio, pp. 292, with an Index, 97 pages. Reed, 3347, russia, 17s. 6d. Brockett, 1851, 19s. Hibbert, 5011, 1l. 2s. Willett, 1502, russia, 1l. 15s. LARGE PAPER. Heath, 4396, 1l. 9s.

The Ancient Dialogue concerning the Exchequer, published from two manuscript Volumes, called the Black Book and Red Book, remaining of Record in his Majesty's Exchequer. Likewise a Dissertation concerning the Author of this Dialogue, and a Discourse concerning the most ancient Great Roll of the Exchequer, commonly styled The Roll of Quinti Regis Stephani. Published originally in Latin, by Tho. Madox, Esq. Historiographer. Now carefully translated into English by a Gentleman of the Inner Temple. Lond. 1758, 4to. Dent, pt. ii. 711, russia, 14s.

MADRAS.—Transactions of the Literary Society of Madras. Lond. 1827, etc. 4to. 3 vols.

MEONIE, or Certaine excellent Poems and Spiritual Hymnes. Lond. V. Sims, for John Busbie, 1595, 4to.

A copy in the Capell Collection, Camb. See SOUTHWELL, Robert.

MAFFÆUS, John Peter, Soc. of Jesus. Fuga Sæculi, or the Holy Hatred of the World. Conteyning the Lives of 17 Holy Confessours of Christ, selected out of sundry Authors, &c. Translated by H. H. [Henry Hawkins, an English Jesuit at Rome in 1616, and living as Missionary in London in 1641]. Engraved title. Printed at Paris, 1632, sm. 4to.

The Preface (7 pages) and the Arguments by Hawkins are in verse. Amongst the Lives will be found those of St. Malachy, Bp. of Connorthen in Ireland; St. Edward the Confessor; St. Anselm, Archbishop of Canterbury; and St. Hugh, Bishop of Lincoln. Bindley, pt. iii. 273, 1l. 1s. Heber, pt. x. 138.

MAFFEI, Francis Scipio, Marquis de. A complete History of Amphitheatres, more particularly regarding the Architecture of those Buildings, and in particular that of Verona. Translated by Alexander Gordon. Lond. 1730, 8vo.

An esteemed work with cuts.

MAGAILLAN, Gabriel. History of China, translated by John Ogilvy. Lond. 1688, 8vo.

Heber, pt. I. 12s.

MAGEE, William, Archbishop of Dublin. Discourses and Dissertations on the Scriptural Doctrine of Atonement and Sacrifice. Fourth edition, with large Additions. Lond. 1816, 8vo. 3 vols.

One of the ablest Critical and Polemical works of modern times.—1901, 8vo. 2 vols, Vol. iii. (Sermons and Visitation Charges), to complete former editions, was published in 1816, 8vo. 10s. 6d.

Discourses and Dissertations on the Atonement and Sacrifice (complete, but without his Sermons and Charges), in one vol. royal 8vo. double columns. Lond. Bohn, 1842.—Again, 1856, 6s.

Works, comprising his Discourses on the Atonement, Sermons, and Visitation Charges, with Memoir by Dr. Kenney. Lond. 1842, 8vo. 2 vols. 1l. 6s.

MAGENS, Nicholas. An Essay on Insurances. Lond. 1755, 4to. 2 vols.

Willett, 1590, 1l. 13s. This work was originally published at Hamburgh in the German language, but is much augmented in this edition.

MA-GEOGHAGAN, M. l'Abbé. See MACGEOGHEGAN.

MAGGI, Carlo Maria. The Beauties of, paraphrased, to which are added Sonnets. By Mariana Starke. 1811, 8vo.

MAGIC.—A System of Magick. 1727. See DEFOE, Daniel.

A complete History of Magick, Sorcery and Witchcraft (by Rd. Boulton). Lond. 1715-16, 12mo. 2 vols. Roxburghe, 1866, 6s. 6d. Nassau, pt. i. 1804, 17s.

A Vindication of a complete History of Magick, Sorcery and Witchcraft. By Rd. Boulton, author of the previous work. A reply to Hutchinson.

See WITCHCRAFT.

SALVERTE, Eusebe. The Philosophy of Magic, Prodigies, and apparent Miracles. With Notes by Anthony Todd Thomson, M.D. Lond. Bentley, 1846, 8vo. 2 vols.

COLQUHOUN, J. C. A History of Magic, Witchcraft, and Animal Magnetism. Lond. Longman, 1851, post 8vo. 2 vols.

WRIGHT, Thomas. Narratives of Sorcery and Magic, from the most authentic Sources. Second edition. Lond. Bentley, 1851, post 8vo. 2 vols.

Ennemoser's History of Magic, translated from the German by Wm. Howitt. With an Appendix of the most remarkable and best authenticated Stories of Apparitions, Dreams, Table-Turning, Spirit-Rapping, &c. Lond. Bohn, 1854, 2 vols. post 8vo. 10s.

See BREWSTER, David. DEE, John. HUTCHINSON, Francis. SCOTT, Sir W.

MAGNA BRITANNIA. See Cox, Thos. LYSONS, D. and S.

MAGNA CHARTA. Anno Incarnationis Dominicæ Millesimo quingentissimo xiiij decimosexto edibus Marcus (1514). Explicit Lond. cum solerti curis ac diligencia impresse in civitate. Lond. per Bd. Pynson, 1514, 12mo.

FIRST EDITION. Pynson printed it again in 1519, 12mo.; 1625, 8vo.; 1527, 12mo. It was also printed by Redman in 1525, 12mo.; by Berthelet in 1531, cum aliis Statutis, 8vo.; and again in 1532, 12mo.

In 1534 it appeared for the first time in 18mo., with an English translation, 'out of Latyn and Freunshe into Englysshe, by George Ferrers,' printed by Robert Redman. This translation was reprinted by Redman's widow, without date, under the title of 'THE GREAT CHARTER, CALLED IN LATYN MAGNA CARTA,' with divers old Statutes, &c. newly corrected. Again by Berthelet in 1540 and 1541; by T. Petyt in 1542; by Tottel, 1556, 1557, 1556, 1565, 1574, 1576, and 1587. (A LARGE PAPER of this edition, with MS. notes, sold at Bright's sale for 2l. 2s.) The first and the last two named editions are in Latin, the others in English, edited by Wm. Rastell, serjeant-at-law. T. Marshe printed it in 1566, Wight in 1602, and the Stationers' Company in 1608 and 1618. It is also attached to the various collections of Statutes printed by Berthelet in 1543, H. Wykes, 1564, and by C. Barker, from 1579 to 1687; as well as in all modern collections. See STATUTES. The best annotated translations are by BLACKSTONE, Sir W.; and THOMSON, Thomas, which are under their names in the alphabet.

MAGNA CARTA, on a large folio sheet,

1450 MAG — MAI

MAGNA CHARTA—*continued*, surrounded with the Arms of the Barons, engraved and published by JOHN PINE, London Yard, Little Britain, in Aldersgate Street, 1733, price at the time of publication 10s. 6d. Of this edition, copies with the arms coloured have been sold as high as 6l. 6s. Two other editions were taken from the same copperplate: I. Published by J. Pine in Old Bond Street, near Piccadilly, &c. II. Sold by R(obert) E(dge) Pine, Albemarle Street, Piccadilly; and there was a later one made by Mr. Basire for the Record Commission, and a lithograph facsimile in 1819.

But the most magnificent of all editions of MAGNA CARTA WAS PRINTED IN LETTERS OF GOLD by JOHN WHITAKER in 1816, and dedicated to the Prince Regent, afterwards George IV. The ordinary copies were on thick glazed card-board, some white, others tinted of various hues, and these were published at 10l. 10s. Others had decorated borders and emblazoned arms, with portraits in colours, and these were much more expensive. Others, again, were printed on white or purple SATIN OR VELLUM, in super-royal folio, highly decorated with heraldic emblems and armorial bearings, chiefly under the direction of Mr. Thos. Willement. Some copies have in addition finely-painted portraits of King John, Roger Bigod, and the Prince Regent: these were published at from fifty to one hundred guineas. Some few copies were even more expensive than this, and by means of paintings, jewelry, and gorgeous binding, reached a cost of two hundred and fifty guineas.

MAGNANIMITIE, The Mansion of. *See* COMPTON, Richard.

MAGNIFICAT. — An Exposicion vpon the Songe of the blessed Virgins Mary called Magnificat; whereunto are added, the Songes of Salue Regina, Benedictus et Nunc dimittis, translated out of Latine into Englysh by John Hollybush (*query* Bp. Coverdale?) Southwark by Jas. Nicolson, 1538, 16mo.

Copies are in the Bodleian and in the Christ Church College Libraries at Oxford. There is another edition in 1538, without printer's name.

MAGNUS, Olaus. A compendious History of the Goths, Swedes and Vandals and other Northern Powers. Translated by J. S. Lond. 1658, folio.

Bright, 10s.

MAHOMET.—Four treatises concerning the Doctrine, Discipline and Worship of the Mahometans. To which is prefixed the Life of Mahomet. Lond. 1712, 8vo.

Garrick, 1448, 6s. 6d.

A lytell Treatyse agaiust Mahumet and his cursed Secte. Imprinted by Peter Treverys, 16mo.

Life of Mahomet. By Washington Irving. Lond. (Murray) 1850, 8vo. 10s. 6d. Bohn, post 8vo. 1s. 6d.

Mahomet and his Successors. By Washington Irving. Lond. (Murray) 1850, 8vo. 10s. 6d. Bohn, post 8vo. 1s. 6d.

See ABULFEDA, ISD. BEDWELL, William. Koran. OCKLEY. PRIDEAUX, Humphrey. RABADAN, Mahomet.

— (Deen, of Brighton). The Travels of. In a Series of Letters. Cork, 1794, 12mo. 2 vols. 7s.

MAHONY, or MALONY, Father Connor, or Constantine. Disputatio Apologetica, de Jure Regni Hiberniæ pro Catholicis Hibernis adversus Hæreticos Anglos. Francof. 1645, 4to.

Lyte, 1849, 9l. 15s. Horner, mor. 6l. 15s. An attempt 'to excite his countrymen to persevere in their endeavours to extirpate the name, manners, and religion of Englishmen from amongst them.'— *Nicolson.* The book was printed at Lisbon. *See* Bibl. West. no. 4622. Held to be a damnable and seditious work by the Mayor and Council of Galway, and burnt. —Reprinted, 100 copies, Dublin, Mullins, 1829, 4to. Lieber, pt. i. 4606, 14s. At the end of the original edition is a leaf of 'errata,' which are corrected in the modern reprint.

MAICHELIUS, Daniel. Introductio ad Historiam Literariam de præcipius Bibliothecis Parisiensibus. Cantab. 1721, 8vo. 5s.

MAJERUS, Count M. Themis Aurea. The Laws of the Fraternity of the Rosie Crosse. (Rosicrusians.) Translated from the Latin. Lond. 1656, 12mo.

MAID, The Old; folio. A Periodical Publication.
Bright, nos. 1 to 37, 1755-6, 4s.

MAIDS.—The History of the two Maides of More-clacke. With the Life of simple John i' the Hospitall. Lond. 1609, 4to.
Copies are in the British Museum and the Malone Collection. *See* ARMIN, Robert, page 70.

The Not Browne Maid. A Ballad. Reprinted by Pickering, in Black Letter, sq. 18mo. *See* ARNOLD (R.). Chronicle of London, p. 72. Also PERCY Society, No. 27, *Appendix*.

A notable and prodigious Historie of a Mayden, who sundry Yeares neither eateth, drinketh, nor sleepeth, neyther avoydeth any Excrements, and yet liveth. Printed and published in High Dutch, and after in French, and now lastlie translated into English, 1589, 4to. Six leaves. Nassau, pt. ii. 570, 15s.

A true and admirable Historie of a Mayden at Confolens. Lond. 1604, 4to. Contains verses by T. Decker, or Dekker. *See* M. A.

A Letter sent by the Maydens of London, to the Matrons and Mistresses of the same. Lond. H. Hynneman, for Thomas Hacket, 1567, 12mo.

The faire Maide of Bristow; as it was plaide at Hampton before the King and Queenes most excellent Majesties. Lond. 1605, 4to. Roxburghe, 4124, 7l. 1s. A copy is in the British Museum.

The Maidens bloody Garland; or, High-Street Tragedy. (Oxford, 17--). A characteristic imitation of the Newgate ditties, ascribed to Mr. Thomas Warton, reprinted in Brydges' Censura Literaria, vol. iii. p. 374.

MAIDMENT, James. Nugæ derelictæ quas colligerunt Jac. M(aidment) et R(obert) P(itcairn). Edin. 1822, roy. 8vo.
A collection of eighteen small tracts relative to the history and antiquities of Scotland, privately printed. It is said there are only six complete copies extant.

A north Countrie Garland. Edinb. 1824, 12mo. Of this curious selection only thirty copies were printed.

A book of Scottish Pasquils, &c. Edinb. 1827-8, 12mo. (60 small, 15 large paper, printed.) *See* PASQUILS.

A Banquet of Dainties for strong Stomachs. Edinb. (Stevenson) 1829, 18mo. A collection of Scottish satirical and lewd poems of about the middle of the 18th century, from Myius' MSS. The joint publication of Mr. C. K. Sharpe and J. Maidment. Only a few copies printed.

Nugæ Scoticæ; Miscellaneous Papers illustrative of Scottish Affairs, MCCCV—MDCCCXXXI. Edin. (Stevenson) 1829, 8vo. A collection of 22 tracts. Sixty copies of each were printed, but it is believed that not more than 30 complete sets are extant. Edited by James Maidment, G. R. Kinloch, and Charles Baxter.

Analecta Scotica: Collections illustrative of the Civil, Ecclesiastical, and Literary History of Scotland, chiefly from original MSS. Edinb. (Stevenson) 1834-8, 8vo. 2 vols. A valuable work. 106 small, and 6 large paper printed.

Mr. Maidment has edited or compiled many other volumes in Scottish literature, of which he has printed a list, including his volumes printed for the Abbotsford, BANNATYNE, MAITLAND, and SPOTTISWOODE Clubs.

MAILLET, Benedict de. Telliamed, being a Translation from the French. Lond. 1749 or 1750, 8vo. 4s.
A cryptonymous book—Telliamed being the anagram of M. de Maillet. It consists of 'Discourses between an Indian philosopher and a French missionary on the diminution of the sea, the formation of the earth, the origin of men and animals, and other curious subjects relating to natural history and philosophy.'

MAIMBOURG, Lewis. History of the League, translated by John Dryden. Lond. 1684, 8vo.
Roxburghe, 8013, 3s. This translation was made, not, as Dr. Johnson says, 'with the hopes of promoting popery,' but to strengthen the hands of government, and to discredit the party who had acted with Lord Shaftesbury.

An historical Treatise of the Foundation and Prerogatives of the Church of Rome, and of her Bishops. Translated from the French by A. Lovel, M.A. Lond. 1685, 8vo. 4s.

The History of the Crusades, or the Expeditions of the Christian Princes for the Conquest of the Holy Land. Translated by John Nalson, LL.D. Lond. 1685, folio, 15s.

The History of Arianism, translated by W. Webster. With an Appendix containing an Account of the English Writers in the Socinian and Arian Controversies. 1728, 4to. 2 vols.

MAIMONIDES, R. Moses. Porta Mosis, sive Dissertationes aliquot

in varias Mishnajoth sive Textus
Talmudici Partes, etc. Arab. et Lat.
editæ, cum Appendice Edv. Po-
cockii. Oxon. 1654 or 5, 4to. 12s.
A learned and able work.
Canones Poenitentiæ, Latine per G. N.
Cantab. 1631, 4to.
De Jure Pauperis et Peregrini apud
Judæos, Heb. et Lat. Notis illustravit H.
Prideaux. Oxon. 1679, 4to. 8s. 6d. Wil-
liams, 1033, morocco, 1l. 4s.
Laws of the Hebrews relating to the
Poor. Translated. Lond. 8vo. 5s. 6d.
Maimonides de Sacrificiis, de Consecra-
tione Calendarum, et de Ratione Interca-
landi, cum Notis Lud. de Compiegne de
Vlel. Londini, 1683. 4to. A Latin version
of a work by the celebrated Rabbi Mai-
monides, of some importance as a rabbinical performance.
Doctor Dubitantium. 'This famous
book contains the method of the wisest
and most learned Jew that ever was of interpreting Scripture; the last part of
which work is the ground-work of Spencer's De Legibus Hebræorum.'—*Bishop
Warburton.*
De Doctrina Legis, et de Natura et Ratione Pœnitentiæ apud Hebræos, Heb. et
Lat. cum Notis Rob. Clavering. Oxon.
1705, 4to.
The main Principles of the Creed and
Ethics of the Jews, exhibited in selections
from the Yad Hachazakah, with a literal
Translation, Notes, and Glossary. By H.
H. Bernard. Camb. 1832, 8vo. 10s. 6d.
LARGE PAPER, 8vo. 1l. 1s.
The Reasons of the Laws of Moses, from
the More Nevochim of Maimonides, with
Notes, Dissertations, and a Life of the
Author. By James Townley, D.D. Lond.
1827, 8vo. An excellent translation, with
upwards of 100 pages of valuable notes,
together with also dissertations on the
Talmudical writings, and on various other
topics tending to elucidate the 'Reasons
of the Laws of Moses.' The 'More Neve-
chim,' or 'Instructor of the Perplexed,' is
considered one of the most valuable productions of the learned Jewish Rabbi
Moses ben Maimon, better known by the
name of Maimonides.
Book of Precepts. Heb. and Eng., with
Life. Lond. 12mo. 2s. 6d.

MAINE. See MAYNE.

MAINTENON, Mme. de. The Letters of Madame de Maintenon, and
other eminent Persons of the Age
of Lewis XIV. To which are added,
some Characters. Translated from
the French. Lond. 1753, 12mo. 5s.

The letters of this celebrated lady are
still in estimation.
The Life of Madame de Maintenon, translated from the French. Lond. 1752-54,
12mo. 3 vols.
Memoirs for the History of Madame de
Maintenon, and of the last Age. Trans
lated from the French, by the Author of
the Female Quixote (Mrs. Lennox.) Lond.
1757, 12mo. 5 vols. 15s.
Secret Correspondence with the Princess
des Ursins. Lond. 1827, 8vo. 3 vols. port.
Contains several curious and important
historical Notices.

MAINWARING, Edward. *See*
MANWARING, Ed., and MAYN-
WARING.

—— John, B.D. Sermons on several occasions, preached before the
University of Cambridge: to which
is prefixed a Dissertation on that
Species of Composition. Camb.
1780, 8vo. 5s.
The studious reader will receive much
advantage from the justness of the criticism displayed in the dissertation and
notes.—*Bishop Watson.* Williams, 1152,
8s. 6d.—1163, 13s.

—— Roger. Two Sermons, entitled
Religion and Allegiance. Lond.
R. Badger, 1627, 4to.
Called in by Proclamation, 24th June,
1628, and ordered to be burnt. Reprinted,
Lond. 1709, 8vo.

—— Sir Thomas, Bart. The Le-
gitimacy of Amicia. *See* LEYCES-
TER, Sir Peter.

—— Captain F. L. Narrative of
the Surrender of Buonaparte, and
of his Residence on Board H.M.S.
Bellerophon, with a Detail of the
principal Events that occurred in
that Ship, between the 24th of May
and 8th of August, 1815. Lond.
1826, 8vo.

—— Lady Jane. A funerall Ser-
mon preached at the Buriall of the
Lady Jane Maitland, with diverse
Epitaphs written by sundry Au-
thors. By M. J(ames) M(aitland).
Edinb. 1633, 4to.
Bindley, pt. II. 1031, 5l. 3s. *See* M. I.

—— Sir Richard, of Lethington.
Poems, with Appendix, containing

the Poems of Sir John and Sir Thomas Maitland, edited by J. Bain. Glasgow, 1830, 4to.

Seventy-one printed. Eyton, 16s. LARGE PAPER (only 5 copies). Eyton, 1l. 9s.

History of the House of Seytoun. See MAITLAND CLUB, *Appendix.*

MAITLAND, Sir Rd. Life and Character of. *See* in Miscellanea Scotica, 1710, 8vo.

— William. The History of London from its Foundation to the present Times, continued to the Year 1772, by the Rev. John Entick, M.A. Lond. 1772 or 1775, folio, 2 vols.

A work of some authority, but of late superseded. Hibbert, 5209, 1l. 16s. Dent, pt. II. 628, 4l. 8s. Nassau, pt. I. 2344, russia, 3l. 7s. 6d. Reed, 3348. 5l. 12s. 6d. Heath, 4637, russia, 7l. *Collation.*—Vol. I. Title, one leaf; dedication to the Right Hon. Ellingsby Bethell, Esq. 2 pages; list of subscribers, 6 pages; contents, pp. iii–viii; the history, pp. 5–712. This volume contains seven plates, not including a head piece on page 5, and a sepulchral stone, on p. 17. Vol. II. Title, one leaf; contents, 2 pages; the history continued and index, pp. 713–1410; an appendix, pp. 1367–91; continuation, pp. 1–148; directions to the binder for placing the plates. This volume contains 124 plates, of which the following are not mentioned in the list:—117. Black Friars Bridge. Contin. p. 3. 118. New Excise Office, p.148. 119. The Bank of England and New Nowgate, p.148. 120. New River Office, and Front of New Newgate, p. 148. 121. Sessions House in the Old Bailey, p. 148. 122. Magdalen Hospital and Westminster Lying-in Hospital, p. 148. 123. The Circus and Obelisk in St. George. Fields, p. 148. 124. The Adelphi, p. 148. *Other Editions.*—1789, folio. Roxburghe, 8653, 6s. Duke of York, 8181, 16s. Willett, 1511, 16s. LARGE PAPER, 1l. 11s. 6d.—1756, 2 vols. Goldsmid, 577, 1l. 16s. Townsley, pt. II. 1019, 2l. 3s. —1760, folio. 2 vols. This edition contains the same letter-press, dedication, list of subscribers, number of engravings, and even errors of paging, as that of 1772; except that in the second volume of the latter 'The Continuation of the History of London,' in 145 pages, was substituted for the description of the plates of the public buildings, under the title of 'English Architecture,' inserted in the edition of 1760.—A Continuation of the History and Survey of the Cities of London and Westminster, and Borough of Southwark, with the Places adjacent. (Lond. 1772), folio, 16s.

(Printed off separately from the edition of 1772, as a Supplement to preceding editions.)

The History of Edinburgh, from its Foundation to the present Time. Also the ancient and present State of Leith, and a Perambulation of divers Miles round the City. In nine Books. Edinb. 1753, folio. Bindley, pt. II. 637. 1l. 4s. Nassau, pt. I. 2263, 1l. 9s. Hibbert, 5308, 1l. 10s. Heath, 4754, 1l. 19s. Willett, 1513, 1l. 7s. There are copies on LARGE PAPER.

The History and Antiquities of Scotland, from the earliest Account of Time to the Death of James the First, Anno 1437. And from that Period to the Accession of James the Sixth to the Crown of England, Anno 1603, by another Hand. The whole compiled from the most authentic Vouchers. Lond. 1757, folio, 2 vols. Townsley, pt. II. 1012, 1l. 1s. Roxburghe, 8705, 2l. Willett, 1512, 2l. 4s. Heath, 4713, russia, 4l. 6s.

MAITTAIRE, Michael. Annales Typographici, ab Artis inventæ Origine ad Annum 1557 (cum Appendice ad Annum 1664). Hagæ Com. &c. 1719, &c. 4to. — vols.

These Annals will ever be considered a lasting monument of this sound scholar's diligence and zeal, and are indispensable in every bibliographical library. Edwards, 15, 5 vols. without the index (which is often wanting), 3l. 5s. Willett, with Denis' Supplement, 1669, bound in 9 vols. 9l. 9s. Roxburghe, 6597, 9 vols. 13l. 11s. LARGE PAPER. Hibbert, 5166, 9 vols. 1719-41, mor. 32l. MacCarthy, 683 *bi. Contents.* —Vol. I. Ab Artis Origine ad Annum 1500, Hag. Com. 1719. Vol. II. 1500-36, Hag. Com. 1722. In two Parts. Vol. III. 1536-57, Hag. Com. 1725. In two Parts. Some copies bear date Amst. 1725. Vol. IV. *Not so marked on title-page but called* " Tomus primus, editio nova. Amst. 1733, 4to. In two Parts. A reprint of the first volume, with numerous additions and some omissions. This completes Maittaire's own publication, but the following volumes form a desirable supplement:— Vol. V. *but called on title-page,* Tomus quartus, Indicem complectens. Lond. 174L In two Parts (of which the second is sometimes wanting). Supplementa Annalium Typographicorum a M. Denis. Viennæ, 1789, 4to. 2 vols. A set of the 9 vols. on LARGE PAPER is in the Grenville Collection.

Græcæ Linguæ Dialecti. Lond. 1706, 8vo. Duke of Grafton, 124, 3s. 6d. Drury, 2450, Maittaire's own copy, with numerous corrections and additions, 1l. 15s. LARGE PAPER. Heath, 5091, Maittaire's own copy,

MAITTAIRE, M.—*continued*.
with an original MS. letter from J. F.
Reitzius, 1*l*. 16*s*. Williams, 1154, mor.
2*l*. 5*s*.—Præfationem et Appendicem ex
Apollonii Dyscoli Fragmento inedito addidit J. F. Reitzius. Hag. Com. 1738, 8vo.
9*s*.—Lond. 1742, 8vo. 9*s*. LARGE PAPER.—
Post J. F. Reitzium, totum Opus recensuit, emendavit, auxit F. G. Sturzius.
Lips. 1807, 8vo. 12*s*. Best edition. FINE
PAPER, 18*s*. VELLUM PAPER, 1*l*. 4*s*.

Stephanorum Historia, Vitas ipsorum ac
Libros complectens, port. by Sturt. Lond.
1709, 8vo. cum Appendice (often wanting.)
Brockett, 1847, 17*s*. Willett, 1569, russ.
2*l*. 12*s*. 6*d*. LARGE PAPER, Heath. 5083,
2*l*. 10*s*. Roxburghe, 6525, 3*l*. 6*s*. Dibdin,
501, morocco, 4*l*. 14*s*. 6*d*. The Life of Robert Stephens, in Latin, revised and corrected by the author, with a new and complete list of his works, is prefixed to the
improved edition of R. Stephens' Thesaurus Ling. Lat. Lond. 1784. fol. 4 vols.

Historia Typographorum aliquot Pari-
siensium Vitas et Libros complectens.
Appendice. Lond. 1717, 8vo. Constable,
636, 17*s*. Hibbert, 5037, russia, 1*l*. 8*s*.
Sir M. M. Sykes, pt. II. 322, 1*l*. 5*s*. Strett-
ell, 953, 1*l*. 11*s*. 6*d*. Willett, 1568, 1*l*. 13*s*.
Bindley, pt. II. 1606, 1*l*. 15*s*. LARGE PA-
PER. Duke of Grafton, 857, 6*l*. 12*s*. 6*d*.
Fonthill, 2240, 3*l*. 1*s*. Dibdin, 502, mor.
3*l*. 13*s*. Roxburghs, 6526, 4*l*. 10*s*.

The English Grammar. Lond. 1721,
8vo. 3*s*. LARGE PAPER. Williams, 1155,
9*s*.

Senilia, sive Poetica aliquot in Argu-
mentis varii Generis Tentamina. Lond.
1742, 4to. 5*s*.

Miscellanea Græcorum aliquot Scrip-
torum Carmina cum Versione Latina et
Notis. Lond. 1722, 4to. 5*s*.

Epistola de antiquis Quintilliani Editi-
onibus, 4to.

Librorum manuscriptorum Ecclesiæ
Westmonasteriensis Catalogus. Intended
as a supplement to the 'Catalogus Librorum MSS. Angliæ et Hiberniæ. Oxon.
1697,' folio. All the impressions, save one,
were destroyed by fire.

This eminent scholar likewise published
an edition of Homer's Batrachomyoma-
chia, and several of the Latin classics,
with elaborate indexes.
See Oxford. Poetæ Latini.

MAJOR, John. De Historia Gentis Scotorum Libri sex, seu Historia Maioris Britanniæ, tam Angliæ quam Scotiæ, e veterum Mo-
numentis concinnata. Parisiis, apud
Jodocum Badium, 1521, 4to.
Contains fol. cxlvi, with title (at the
back of which are verses to James V, by
Badius Ascensius), a preface and table.
'Written in a Sorbonic and barbarous
style, yet very truly and with great liberty of spirit, not sparing the usurpation
of Rome, and taxing in divers places the
laziness and superfluity of the clergy.'—
Ant. à H'ood. According to Bishop Nicolson, 'This writer mixes the chronicles of
England and Scotland all along; and
seems to have taken the greatest part of
what concerns the affairs of his own nation upon the credit of our writers.' Gordonstoun, 1688, 7*s*. Dent, pt. II. 714, 1*l*. 9*s*.
—Gardner, in 1854, mor. 9*s*. 6*d*.—Edinb.
1740, 4to. Best edition. Heath, 4722, 9*s*.
This edition contains a life of Major, and
a list of his works, mostly printed at Paris
about 1515-29, in folio, which are valued
at about 1*l*. 10*s*. per volume.

— John Henniker. Two Letters
on the Origin, Antiquity, and History of Norman Tiles, stained with
Armorial Bearings. Lond. 1794,
8vo.
Pp. 114, with engravings of 16 painted
tiles from the pavement of the palace of
the Dukes of Normandy, at Caen. Dedicated to Sir John Henniker, Bart., the
author's father. Brockett, 1849, 5*s*. 6*d*.
Roxburghe, 8578, 6*s*. These letters, addressed to George Earl of Leicester, P.S.A.,
were previously printed for private distribution.

— Thomas. The Ruins of Pæs-
tum, otherwise Posidonia in Magna
Græcia. Lond. 1768, imperial
folio.
This work consists of 24 large and 6
small plates. No. 19 is repeated. Drury,
2843, 1*l*. 9*s*. Gough, 7764, 1*l*. 10*s*. Nassau,
pt. I. 2583, 1*l*. 17*s*. North, pt. II. 969, 3*l*. 7*s*.
Bindley, pt. II. 1062, 2*l*. 10*s*. Fonthill,
1803, 5*l*. 5*s*. 6*d*. Willett, 1510, with Cham-
ler's Ionian Antiquities, 1769, 5*l*. 7*s*. 6*d*.
—Lond. 1767, folio. This edition consists
of twenty-four plates, and ten leaves of
text.

Recueil d'Estampes gravées d'après les
meilleurs Tableaux des grands Maitres,
dont on a fait choix dans les Cabinets les
plus célèbres d'Angleterre et de France.
Lond. 1754, folio. Twenty-nine plates on
26 leaves.—Second edition, Lond. 1768, fol.
This edition consists of 67 plates.

MAKGILL. *See* MACKGILL.

MAKINS, Mrs. B. An Essay to
revive the ancient Education of
Gentlewomen in Religion, Manners, Arts, and Tongues, with an

Answer to the Objections against this Way of Education, 1678, 4to.

Mrs. Makins was tutoress to the Princess Elizabeth, daughter of K. Charles I. For an interesting account of this learned lady, see GRANGER.

MAKLUIRE, John. The Buckler of bodilie Health. Edinb. 1630, 12mo.

The General Practice of Medicine, by J. M. (Mr. Makluire.) Edinb. 1634, 18mo.

MALABAR. — Accounts of the Success of two Danish Missionaries sent to the East Indies for the Conversion of the Heathens in Malabar. Lond. 1714-18, 12mo. 4 pts. in 1 vol. 6s.

An Account of the Religion, Manners, and Learning of the People of Malabar, in the East Indies; in several Letters, written by some of the most learned Men of that Country to the Danish Missionaries. Translated from the German of Bartholom. Ziegenbalg by J. T. Phillips. Lond. 1717, 8vo.

The Propagation of the Gospel in the East; being an Account of the Success of two Danish Missionaries lately sent to the East Indies for the Conversion of the Heathens in Malabar. Translated from the German of Bartholomeus Ziegenbalg, &c. by Anth. Will. Bohm. Lond. 1718, 8vo.

A Malabar and English Dictionary, wherein the Words and Phrases of the Tamulian Language, commonly called by Europeans the Malabar Language, are explained in English. By the English Missionaries of Madras (John Philip Fabricius and John Chr. Breithaupt). Vepery, near Madras, 1779, 4to.

An English and Malabar Dictionary, by the English Missionaries of Madras. Vepery, near Madras, 1786, 4to.

A Grammar for learning the Principles of the Malabar Language, properly called Tamul or the Tamulian Language. Second Edition. Vepery, near Madras, 1789, 8vo.

MALACHI.—Paraphrasis Prophetiæ Malacci poëtica. Edinb. 1611, 4to.

Seven leaves, the work of Alexander Julius, published without his name. A copy is in the British Museum.

The Prophets Malachy and Isaiah prophesying to the Saints and Professors of this Generation. Lond. 1656, 4to.

MALALA, Joh. Joannis Antiocheni, cognomento Malalæ Historia Chronica, Gr. cum Interpretatione et Notis Edmundi Chilmeadi, Dissertatione de Autore Humfredi Hodii, et Epistola Richardi Bentleii. Oxon. 1691, 8vo.

Bindley, pt. II. 1812, 7s. Heath. 2190 10s. Williams, 960, morocco, 19s. Gardner in 1834, Gibbon's copy, 11s. See MEXANDER.

MALCHAIR, John. xii Views of the Environs of Oxford, 1763, oblong 4to. consisting of Title and xii etchings, rare.

Bindley, pt. III. 870, 7s. 6d. Hibs, pt. II. 870, 2l. 3s.

MALCOLM, Alexander. A Treatise of Music, speculative, practical and historical. Edinb. 1721, 8vo. 10s. 6d.

An esteemed work.

— David. Genealogical Memoir of the most noble and ancient House of Drummond, and of the several Branches that have sprung from it, from its first Founder Maurice to the present Family of Perth. Edinb. 1808, 12mo.

Privately printed. G. Chalmers, 10s. 6d.

— James. A Compendium of modern Husbandry. Lond. 1805, 8vo. 3 vols.

Principally written during a survey of Surrey, made at the desire of the Board of Agriculture. Collation.—Vol. I. Pp. xx and 456, with a coloured map by John Cary, five plates of Lime Kilns, and a Merino ram. Vol. II. pp. 544. Vol. III. pp. 500. LARGE PAPER.

— James Peller. Londinum Redivivum; or, an ancient History and modern Description of London. Lond. 1803-7, 4to. 4 vols.

Edwards, 652, 4l. 16s. Sturtevill, 1248, with Anecdotes, 2 vols. (forming together 6 vols.) 7l. 10s. Fonthill, 253, with Anecdotes, 2 vols. bl. 15s. Collation.—Vol. I. Pp. 5—452, with two title pages, one engraved (1803), the other printed (1802); advertisement, two pages; authentic particulars, &c. and list of (10) plates, 2 pages, and contents, 2 pages. Vol. II. 1803. Pp. x. and 5—511. Page 611 contains

MALCOLM, J. Peller—*continued.*
the list of the 8 plates contained in this
volume. Vol. III. 1808. Pp. ix and 5–
587. Pages 457–8 are repeated with asterisks, and p. 587 contains the list of 17
plates contained in the volume. Vol.
IV. 1807. Pp. vi and 554. On page 554
is given a list of the 11 plates contained in
the volume.

Anecdotes of the Manners and Customs
of London from the Roman Invasion to
the Year 1700; including the Origin of
British Society, Customs, and Manners;
with a general Sketch of the State of Religion, Superstition, Dresses, and Amusements of the Citizens of London during
that Period. To which are added Illustrations of Changes in our Language,
Literature, Customs, and gradual Improvement in style and Versification; and
various Particulars concerning public and
private Libraries. Lond. 1811, 4to. 1l. 10s.
Collation.— Pp. 576, besides title-page; introduction, contents, and list of (18) plates,
drawn and engraved by the author.—
Second edition. Lond. 1811, 8vo. 2 vols.

Anecdotes of the Manners and Customs
of London during the 18th Century; including the Charities, Depravities, Dresses
and Amusements of the Citizens of London during that Period; with a Review of
the State of Society in 1807. To which is
added a Sketch of the domestic and ecclesiastical Architecture, and of the various
Improvements in the Metropolis. Lond.
1808, 4to. *Collation.*—Title, contents, and
(an imperfect) list of plates, 2 leaves;
introduction, anecdotes, &c., 430 pages;
indexes, 8 pages. The volume contains
50 plates, drawn and etched by the author,
some coloured; Nos. 31–50 are to be
placed between pages 478–9.—Second
edition, Lond. 1810, 8vo. 2 vols. This edition contains 45 plates only (not distinctly
mentioned in the printed list of plates).

Miscellaneous Anecdotes illustrative of
the Manners and History of Europe during
the Reign of Charles II. James II. William III. and Anne. Lond. 1811, 8vo. with
5 plates.

Seventy-three Views within twelve
Miles round London. Drawn and engraved
by James Peller Malcolm. Lond. 1811,
4to. 73 plates, with title and index to
Malcolm's Plates for Lysons' Environs, 4
pp. Lond. 1800, 4to. 15s.

An historical Sketch of the Art of
Caricaturing. Lond. 1813, 4to. with 31
engravings, 15s.

Lives of Topographers and Antiquaries
who have written concerning the Antiquities of England, with (twenty-six) Portraits of the Authors, and a complete List
of their Works, so far as they relate to
the Topography of the Kingdom; together
with a List of Portraits, Monuments, Views,
and other Prints contained in each Work:
with Remarks that may enable the Collector to know when the Works are complete. Lond. 1815, 4to. with 26 portraits,
1l. 1s. LARGE PAPER, 1l. 11s. 6d.

Excursions in the Counties of Kent,
Gloucester, Hereford, Monmouth, and Somerset, in the Years 1802, 1803, and 1805.
Lond. 1807, 8vo. 20 fine plates.—The second edition. Lond. 1814, roy. 8vo. pub. at
1l. 7s. Pp. 246, besides title, advertisement, contents, and list of plates, which
are 29 in number, drawn and etched by
the author.

First Impressions; or, Sketches from
Art and Nature, animate and inanimate.
Lond. 1807, 8vo. NASSAU, pt. i. 2098, 9s.
See GRANGER, James, p. 927.

— Sir John. The History of
Persia, from the most early Period
to the present Time, with an Account of the present State of that
Kingdom, and Remarks on the Religion, Government, Sciences, Manners, and Usages, of its ancient and
modern Inhabitants. Lond. 1815,
royal 4to. 2 vols. map and plates.
A most valuable work. Duke of York
3154, 4l. 16s. Dowdeswell, 577, boards,
4l. 17s. Drury, 2802, russia, 5l. LARGE
THICK PAPER, imperial quarto, with proof
plates. Hibbert, 5171, morocco, 9l. 9s.—
Second edition. Lond. 1829, 8vo. 2 vols.
2l. 2s.

Sketch of the Political History of India,
from the Introduction of Mr. Pitt's Bill in
1784. Lond. 1811, royal 8vo. This valuable manual of modern Indian diplomacy
was afterwards embodied in the first five
chapters of 'The Political History of
India.'

The Political History of India from 1784
to 1823. Lond. Murray, 1826, 8vo. 2 vols.
1l. 4s. A valuable work.

Report on Malwa and the adjoining
Countries. Calcutta, 1821, 4to. pp. 679,
besides Appendix, xxiv. 1l. 1s. A portion
of this volume was afterwards embodied
in the 'Memoir of Central India.'

A Memoir of Central India, including
Malwa and adjoining Provinces. Lond.
Parbury, 1823, 8vo. 2 vols. 'A work of
very considerable importance.'— Third
edition. Lond. 1832, 8vo. 2 vols. 1l. 1s.

On the Government of India. Lond.
1833, 8vo. 15s.

Sketch of the Sikhs, a singular Nation
in the Provinces of the Punjab, in India,
situated between the Rivers Jumna and
Indus. Lond. 1812, royal 8vo. This interesting sketch originally appeared in

the eleventh volume of the Asiatic Researches, and was printed separately at Calcutta, royal 8vo.
Sketches of Persia. Lond. 1828, sm. 8vo. 2 vols. 10s.—Again in 1 vol. 6s.—Third edition, 5s.
Life of Robert, Lord Clive, collected from the Family Papers. Lond. 1836, 8vo. 3 vols. portrait, 7l. 2s. A small number printed on LARGE PAPER, for presents only, 3l. 3s.
The Life of Lord Clive has been re-written from these materials by the Rev. G. R. Gleig, in 1 vol. 12mo. See Murray's Colonial Library, APPENDIX.
Life and Correspondence from unpublished Letters and Journals. By J. W. Kaye. Lond. 8vo. 1856, 2 vols. portrait.

MALCOLME, David, D.D. Essay on the Antiquities of Great Britain and Ireland, containing Letters, Essays, and other Tracts, illustrating the Antiquities of Great Britain and Ireland; together with many curious Discoveries of the Affinity betwixt the Language of the Americans and the ancient Britons to the Greek and Latin, &c.; also Specimens of the Celtic, Welsh, Irish, Saxon, and American Languages. Edinb. 1738, 8vo.
Some copies have new title, dated Lond. 1744, 8vo. Dent, pt. 1. 1375, 12s. 6d. Heath, 4732, 14s.

MALDEN, Henry. An Account of King's College-Chapel, in Cambridge. Camb. 1769, 12mo.
Pp. iv. and 92, with a portrait of Malden, and a plate of the chapel. 'Sam. Ireland. From Rev. Dr. James of Rugby, the Author, Sep. 21, 1793.' MS. Note. Dent, pt. 1. 1377, 3s. 6d. Fonthill, 2146, 9s.

MALEBRANCHE, Nicolas. A Treatise concerning the Search after Truth, translated by Thomas Taylor. Lond. 1694, folio, 10s. 6d.
Translated by Richard Sault. Lond. 1692-4, 8vo. 2 vols.—Second edition (translated by T. Taylor). Lond. 1700, folio.—Third edition. Lond. 1720, folio.
An excellent work. Malebranche, according to Locke, was an acute and ingenious author.
Treatise of Nature and Grace. To which is added, the Author's Idea of Providence, and his Answers to several Objections against the foregoing Discourse. Translated from the last edition, enlarged by many explications. Lond. 1695, 8vo.

MALHAM, Rev. John. The Naval Gazetteer, or Seaman's complete Guide. Lond. 1795, 8vo. 2 vols.
Illustrated with charts.—1801, 8vo. 2 vols.

MALKIN, Benjamin Heath, LL.D. The Scenery, Antiquities, and Biography of South Wales, from Materials collected during two Excursions in the Year 1803. Lond. 1804, 4to.
Embellished with views by Laporte, and a map of the country. From this work may be gleaned interesting notices on the history and antiquities of this part of Wales, as well as manners, &c. Dent, pt. II. 716, 13s. 6d. Duke of York, 8153, 17s. Drury, 2303, 2l. 8s.—Second edition, Lond. 1807, 8vo. 2 vols. Hibbert, 5040, 6s. 6d. Fonthill, 3159, 2l. 10s.
Classical Disquisitions and Curiosities, Critical and Historical. Camb. 8vo. 1830.
A Father's Memoirs of his Child. (Thomas Well Malkin.) Lond. 1806, roy. 8vo. with a frontispiece designed by Wm. Blake, of whom an account is given, pages xviii-xl.
Essays on Subjects connected with Civilization. Lond. 1795, 8vo.
Almahide and Hamet, a Tragedy. To which is prefixed, a Letter on Dramatic Composition. 1804, 8vo.
Dr. Malkin also translated Gil Blas. See LESAGE.

MALIM, Wm. The True Report of all the Successes of Famogosta, a City of Cyprus. Translated from the Italian by Wm. Malim. Lond. 1572, 4to.
The head title of this work is 'The true Report of all the Successes of Famagusta, made by the noble Earle Nestor Martinengo, vnto the renowned Prince the Duke of Venice.' Heber, II. 14. 6s. A copy is in the British Museum.

MALLET, David. The Works of David Mallet, Esq. A new Edition, corrected. Lond. 1759, 12mo. 3 vols.
Reed, 7115, 8s. Hibbert, 5041, 11s. Combe, 1157, 12s. Willett, 1570, 1l. 1s. Edwin and Emma. Birmingham, Baskerville, 1760, 4to.—Reissued, illustrated by Local Subjects, drawn and etched by G. Arnold. Lond. 1810, 4to.—With Notes by Dr. F. T. Dinsdale. Lond. (Bell) 1849, 12mo. 5s.

Ballads and Songs, edited by Dr. F. T. Dinsdale. Lond, Bell, 1857, post 8vo.

The Life of the Lord Chancellor Bacon. Lond. 1740, 8vo. 5s. LARGE PAPER. Williams, 1156, 8s. 6d.—With an Appendix, containing several pieces not printed in the last editions of Bacon's Works. Lond. 1760, folio. Of this work, Bishop Warburton remarked, 'that Mallet, in his Life of Bacon, had forgotten that he was a philosopher; and if he should write the life of the Duke of Marlborough, which he had undertaken to do, he would probably forget that he was a general.'

MALLET, F. Descriptive Account of the Island of Trinidad. Lond. 1802, folio, large map.

— Paul Henry. Northern Antiquities, with a Translation of the Edda, and other Pieces, from the ancient Islandic Tongue. Translated from M. Mallet's Introduction to l'Histoire de Dannemarc, &c. With additional Notes by the English Translator (Thomas Percy, Bishop of Dromore), and Goranson's Latin Version of the Edda. Lond. 1770, 8vo. 2 vols.

A highly valuable work. Dent, pt. I. 1878, 13s. Roxburghe, 7251, 1l. 6s. Fontbill. 1196, 1l. 19s. New edition, entirely revised and considerably enlarged by J. A. Blackwell. Lond. 1847, post 8vo. 5s. (Bohn's Antiquarian Library.)

MALLING, Ove. Great and Good Deeds of Danes, Norwegians, and Holsteinians; collected by Ove Malling, and translated into English. Lond. 1807, 4to. 8s.

MALMSBURY, William of. See CHRONICLES.

MALO, Charles. Panorama d'Angleterre, ou Ephémérides Anglaises politiques et littéraires. Paris, 1817, tom. 1.

A severe critique on this catchpenny publication appeared in the Quarterly Review, xviii. 328—9.

MALONE, Edmund. Historical Account of the Rise and Progress of the English Stage, and of the Economy and Usages of the ancient Theatres in England. Basil, 1800, 8vo.

Pp. 420, with 4 plates on folding leaves. Bright, ls.—1790, 8vo. Privately printed. Bindley, pt. II. 1560, 1l. 17s. Hibbert, 5044, 13s. Enlarged in the edition of Shakspeare, by Boswell. Lond. 1821, 8vo. 21 vols. Same copies taken off separately.

Cursory Observations on the Poems attributed to Thomas Rowley. Lond. 1782, 8vo.

A Letter to the Reverend Richard Farmer, D.D., relative to the edition of Shakspeare published in 1790, and some late Criticisms on that Work (by Joseph Ritson). Lond. 1792, 8vo. 3s.

An Inquiry into the conduct of Edm. Malone, Esq. concerning the Manuscript Papers of John Aubrey, Esq. in the Ashmolean Museum, Oxford (by Joseph Caulfield). Lond. 1797, 8vo. See BOOLEAN LIBRARY.

Enquiry into the Authenticity of certain miscellaneous Papers and legal Instruments attributed to Shakspeare, Queen Elizabeth, and Henry, Earl of Southampton. Illustrated by Fac-similes of the genuine Handwriting of Shakspeare, never before exhibited, and other authentic Documents. Lond. 1796, 8vo. Bindley, pt. III. 1117, 8s. FINE PAPER, Twenty-five copies printed for presents. Reed, 6344, 12s. 6d. Steevens, 1393, 1l. 1s. Baker, 403, 1l 7s. Sir M. M. Sykes, pt. III. 835, morocco, 1l. 17s. Bindley, pt. III. 1118, 2l. 4s.

Account of the Incidents from which the Title and Part of the Story of Shakspeare's Tempest were derived, and its true date ascertained. Lond. 1808-9, 8vo. Eighty copies privately printed. Boswell, 1784, 11s. Bindley, pt. III. 1118. Nassau, pt. II. 450, 17s. Field, 577, 1l.5s. Williams, 1167, morocco, 2l. 12s. 6d. In most of the copies Malone wrote the following note: 'It is requested that this pamphlet may not inadvertently be put into the hands of any person who might be likely to publish any part of it.' An APPENDIX was afterwards issued, but only twenty copies were printed of it.

A biographical Memoir of the Life of Rt. Hon. William Wyndham. Lond. 1810, 8vo. Geo. Chalmers, 8s. 6d. This memorial, the last literary production of this author, originally appeared in the Gentleman's Magazine, and was afterwards, in an enlarged and corrected state, printed in a small pamphlet, and privately distributed.

The Life of William Shakspeare, with an Essay on the Phraseology and Metre of the Poet and his Contemporaries, by James Boswell. 1821, royal 8vo. portraits. Twenty-one copies. Taken off separately from the edition of Shakspeare in demy 8vo. Not printed for sale. Ord 785, 1l. 12s. 6d.

The Essence of Malone; or, the 'Remarks' of 'Some Account of the Life and Writings of John Dryden' 11 Lond. 1800, 8vo. Second Edition, enlarged. Lond. 1800, 8vo. 3s. 6d. Bindley, pt. ii. 442, 15s. Heber, pt. ii. both editions, 9s.
Another Essence of Malone, or the Beauties of Shakspeare's Editor. Lond. 1801, 8vo. 5s.
The above two virulent attacks were written by George Hardinge.

MALONY, Con. O. *See* MAHONY, Father.

MALORY, Sir Thomas. *See* MORT D'ARTHUR.
See ARTHUR. CAXTON.

MALPIGHIUS, Marcellus. Opera omnia. Lond. 1686 or 1687, folio, 2 vols. 39 plates, 10s.
Now in little estimation.
Anatome Plantarum; cui subjungitur Appendix de Ovo Incubato. Lond. 1675, folio, 7s. 6d.
Opera posthuma, quibus præfixa est ejusdam Vita a se ipso scripta. Lond. 1697, folio, portrait by Kip.

MALTA.—Certayn and True good Newes from the Siege of the Isle of Malta, 8vo. No place or date.

MALTBY, Edward, D.D. Illustrations of the Truth of the Christian Religion. Lond. 1802, 8vo. 6s.
A work recommended by Bishop Tomline.
Sermons. Lond. 1819-22, 8vo. 2 vols.
Charges, Visitations, and Tracts (various). Lond. 1807-53, 8vo.
Greek Gradus, or Poetical Lexicon of the Greek Language, with a Latin Translation, an English, Greek Vocabulary, and a Treatise on the most popular Greek Metres. Lond. 1830, 8vo.—Second edition. Lond. 1840, 8vo.—Third edition, 1851, 1l. 1s. Based on the improved edition of Morell's Thesaurus. *See* MORELL.

MALTE-BRUN, Con. Universal Geography, or a Description of all the Parts of the World, on a new Plan, with a general Index. Edinb. 1822-33, 8vo. 9 vols. maps.
The Index is sometimes bound separately, making vol. 10.
System of Universal Geography, founded on the Works of Malte Brun and Balbi; embracing the History of geographical Discovery, the Principles of mathematical and physical Geography, and a complete Description, from the most recent Sources, of all the Countries in the World. With an alphabetical Index of 12,500 Names. Lond. and Edinb. 1844, 2l. 2s.—New edition. Lond. Bohn, 1850, (1078 pages) 8vo. 15s.

MALTHUS, Thomas. A Treatise of artificial Fire-works, both for Warres and Recreation, &c. Lond. 1629, 12mo.
A curious treatise, with plates. Bright, 7s.

— Rev. T. R. An Essay on the Principle of Population. Lond. 1817, 8vo. 3 vols.
This valuable work has been the subject of much controversy and animadversion. Hibbert 6049, 10s. 6d. Drury, 2540, 19s. Duke of York. 3343, 15s.—First edition. Lond. 1798, 8vo. 5s.—Lond. 1803, 4to.—Lond. Fourth Edition, 1807. 8vo. 2 vols. Additions to this and former editions were published separately. Latest edition. Lond. 1826, 2 vols. 8vo. For replies, *see* GODWIN, Wm. HAZLITT, Wm. PLACE, Fr.
Principles of Political Economy considered with a View to their practical Application. Lond. 1820, 8vo. Hibbert, 5050, 7s.—Second edition. Lond. 1836, 8vo. (in part rewritten) with Memoir of the Author, [by Dr. Ed. Maltby, Bp. of Chichester.]
Definitions in Political Economy. Lond. 1827, post 8vo. 7s. 6d. New edition by Cazenove, 12mo. Lond. 1853, 3s. 6d.
A summary View of the Principles of Population. Lond. 1830, 8vo.
Observations on the Effects of the Corn Laws, &c. Lond. 1814, 8vo.—Third edit. 1815, 8vo.
The Grounds of an Opinion on the Policy of restricting the Importation of foreign Corn. Lond. 1815, 8vo.
Inquiry into the Nature of Rent. Lond. 1815, 8vo.
Statements respecting the East India College. Lond. 1817, 8vo.—Second edition in PAMPHLETEER.
The Measure of Value stated and illustrated. Lond. 1823, 8vo.
Letter to Samuel Whitbread on the Poor Laws. Lond. 1807, 8vo.
Letter to Lord Grenville on the East India Company's Establishment, &c. 1813, 8vo.

MALTON, James. Picturesque and descriptive Views of the City of Dublin. Lond. 1792, oblong folio.
Nassau, pt. i. 2598, 1l. 17s.—1793, folio. Hibbert, 5212, 18s.—1794, folio. Dent, pt. ii. 629, morocco, 3l.

1460 MAL · MAN

MALTON, J. An Essay on British Cottage Architecture. Lond. 1798, 4to.
With 21 plates in aquatinta. Fonthill, 1823, 1l. 9s. An essay, containing an attempt to refute Malton, was published by Rich. Elsam, 1803, 4to.
The young Painter's Maulstick, being a practical Treatise on Perspective. Lond. 1800, 4to. 15s. An esteemed work.

— **Thomas.** A complete Treatise on Perspective, in Theory and Practice. In four Books. Lond. 1770, folio.
A work on the principles of Dr. Brook Taylor, with a frontispiece and forty-six plates. Garrick, 1806, 18s. — With Appendix. Lond. 1776–83, fol. 2 vols. 2l. 10s.
The royal Road to Geometry; or, familiar Introduction to the Mathematics. Lond. 1793, 8vo. 10s. An excellent work. — Lond. 1774, 8vo. 5s. Roxburghe, 1520, 8s. 6d.

— **Thomas.** A Picturesque Tour through the Cities of London and Westminster, illustrated with Views in Aquatinta. Lond. 1792, folio, 2 vols.
Hibbert, 5971, russia, 1l. 18s. Roxburghe, 8518, 4l. 4s. Duke of York, 3152, 6l. 12s. Fonthill, 2506, 7l. 7s. *Collation.* — Vol. I. Pp. 60, with list of subscribers and introduction, 2 leaves; the volume contains plates 1–48, not including an engraved title-page and dedication to the Prince of Wales. Vol. II. Pp. 61–112, with plates 48–100, not including the engraved title-page.
Views (30) of Oxford. Lond. 1810, folio.
Views (24) in London and Bath, oblong folio. Beckford in 1817, no. 74, 1l. 13s.

MALVERNE PRIORY. *See* THOMAS, William.

MALVEZZI, Marq. Virg. Discourses upon Tacitus, translated by Sir Richard Baker, Knt. Lond. 1642, folio. 4s.
Romulus and Tarquin, from the Italian by H. C. L. Lond. 1637, 18mo. First edition. Bliss, 8s.
Il Davide perseguitato, David persecuted. Translated by Robert Ashley. Lond. 1647, 8vo. with frontispiece by Marshall. Drury, 2541, morocco, 9s. — 1650, with a print of K. Charles playing on a harp. Bliss, 13s.
Several other works of this Italian author have been translated into English.

MALYNES, Gerard de. Consuetudo, vel Lex mercatoria: or, the ancient Law Merchant, in Three Parts. Lond. 1622, fol. 5s.
The writings of this ingenious author were formerly much esteemed. Geo. Chalmers, Dedication copy to King James, 1l. 11s. — Lond. 1629, folio. — 1636. — 1656, Geo. Chalmers, 6s. — 1686, folio. Best edition, with numerous additions. Geo. Chalmers, 1l.
A Treatise of the Canker of England's Commonwealth, 1601, 4to. Reed, 2584, 18s. 5058, 3s. 6d.
St. George for England, 1601, 4to. Bindley, pt. I. 1964, 8s.
England's View in the Unmasking of two Paradoxes: with a Replication unto the Answer of Maister John Bodine. Lond. 1603, 4to. pp. 197, without introduction. Geo. Chalmers, with the Canker, 1801, 1l. 9s.
The Maintenance of free Trade. Lond. 1622, 8vo. *See* Oldys' British Librarian, 96–105.
An Answer to a Treatise of free Trade lately published. Lond. 1622, 12mo. Gordonstoun, 1521, 2s. 6d.
The Center of the Circle of Commerce, in Answer to the Balance of Trade by E(dward) M(isselden). Lond. 1623, 4to.

MAN, James. Censure and Examination of Mr. Thomas Ruddiman's philological Notes on the Works of the great Buchanan, more particularly on the History of Scotland. Aberdeen, 1753, 12mo. 5s.

— **John.** The History and Antiquities, ancient and modern, of the Borough of Reading, in the County of Berks. Reading, 1816, roy. 4to. 10s. 6d.
Published at 3l. 3s. LARGE PAPER, imp. 4to. 5l. 5s. *Collation.* — Half title and title, 2 leaves; dedication, one leaf; preface, 3 pages; the history, with additions, 430 pages; appendix and index, pp. I–xxxvi; list of (27) plates, one page, and errata, a separate slip.

MAN. — Every Man, a moral Playe. Lond. R. Pynson, 4to.
A copy is in the British Museum. — Lond. by John Skot, 4to. 16 leaves, A 4, B 8, and C 4. Reprinted in Hawkins's Origin of the English Drama.
The dead Man's Song, whose Dwelling was neer Basing-hall in London. Printed for E. Coles, &c. This ballad, described

MAN—continued.
by Warton as worthy of Percy's collection, is reprinted (with the omission of the woodcuts) in Brydges' British Bibliographer, II. 136—40.

The dead Man's Fortune. The plot of this early dramatic performance will be found in Reed's edition of Shakespeare, 1803, vol. III.

Man in the Moone telling Fortunes, 1609. See PERCY SOCIETY, in Appendix.

Man in the Moon discovering a World of Knavery, 1657. See MOON.

The wise old Man, 1671, 4to, with a woodcut title. Nassau, pt. II. 1521, 11. 6d.

A strange Metamorphoses of Man, transformed into a Wilderness. Deciphered in Characters. Lond. 1634, 12mo. Containing sig. I. An entertaining and humorous work. Hibbert, 5334, 8s. 6d. Nassau, pt. II. 648, 9s. Heber, pt. v. 12s.

The Pilgrimage of Man wandering in a Wildernesse of Woe, &c. Lond. 1635, 4to. Gordonstoun, 1787, 4s. 6d.

The Beginning, Progress and End of Man represented in Emblematic folding plates. Lond. E. Alsop for T. Dunster, 1654, 12mo. Heber, pt. iv. (described as unique) 1l. 6s.

Philosophical Essay on Man. [By T. P. Maret] Lond. 1773, 8vo. 2 vols.

Moral and Philosophical Estimate of the State and Faculties of Man. Lond. 1769, 8vo. 4 vols.

The married Man's Feast to all who master their Wives, 1671, 4to. Bindley, pt. III. 583, 1l. 2s.

The History of the Man after God's own Heart. Lond. 1761, 12mo. In this production, which was ably and most satisfactorily answered by Dr. S. Chandler, King David is represented as an example of perfidy, lust and cruelty, fit only to be ranked with such monsters as Nero and Caligula—1764. Hollis, 582, morocco, 13s. See CHANDLER, S., p. 402.

A Letter to the Rev. Dr. Samuel Chandler, from the Writer of the History of the Man after God's own Heart (Peter Annett), 8vo. 1s. 6d.

Man and Woman. Here begynneth an Interlocution with an argument between Man and Woman, and which of them could prove to be the most excellent. 4to.

Unknown to Herbert—the piece has Wynkyn de Worde's device at the end—but not the usual colophon. Heber, pt. iv. 4l. 4s.

MAN, Isle of.—History and Description of the Isle of Man. Lond. 1744, 8vo.

By G. Waldron. [See also under his Works, folio, 1731.] Willett, 1391, 8s. Nassau, pt. I. 1510, 4s.

History of the Isle of Man, by H. A. Bullock. Lond. 1816, 8vo. plates, 10s. 6d.

History and Description of the Isle of Man. Lond. 1744, 12mo. Skegg, 2s.

A Book of Rates, of the Customs of all Goods and Commodities, that are imported into and transported from the Isle of Man. Dublin, 1731, 12mo. 8 leaves.

Chronicon Mannie, or a Chronicle of the Kings of Man. Perth, 12mo. 1784. See JOHNSTON.

A short View of the present State of the Isle of Man. By an Impartial Hand. Lond. 1787.

The Statutes and Ordinances of the Isle of Man now in force, alphabetically arranged. By Thomas Stowell, Advocate. Douglas, 1792, 8vo. pp. 170.

The Statute Laws of the Isle of Man, from the original Records. By C. Briscoe. 1797, 8vo. Another edition by Mills, printed in 1821.

The Lex scripta of the Isle of Man, comprehending the ancient Ordinances and statute Laws from the earliest period to 1818, edited by Mr. Jefferson. Douglas, 1819, 8vo.

View of the Jurisprudence of the Isle of Man, with the History of its Constitution, Government and Practice of the Courts. Lond. 1811, 8vo.

General View of the Agriculture of the Isle of Man, by Quayle. Lond. 1812, 8vo. port. printed 1794. See AGRIC. SURVEYS, p. 19.

Sketches of the Isle of Man, by Bennett. Lond. 1829, 8vo.

Report on the Charities in the Isle of Man. Lond. 1831, folio.

A Six Days' Tour in the Isle of Man. 12mo. 1836.

Descriptive Account of the Isle of Man, by Jeffries, 1838, 12mo.

An Historical and Statistical Account of the Isle of Man from the earliest Times to the present, with a view of its Ancient Laws, Peculiar Customs and Popular Superstitions by Joseph Train, F.S.A, Scot. Douglas, 1845, 8vo. 2 vols. map and plates.

Beyond comparison the most complete History of the Island ever given to the public. It contains a Memoir of the Author, who was a most valued correspondent of Sir Walter Scott.

A Dictionary of the Manks Language, by A. Cregeen. Douglas, 1835, cr. 8vo.

Grammar of the Manks Language. See KELLY, Rev. J.

Bible and Testament, in the Manks Language. Whitehaven. 1772, 8vo. 2 vols. —Another edition. Lond. 1819, 8vo.

New Testament in the Manks Language, translated by Wilson, Bp. of Man. Lond. Oliver, 1768, 8vo.

For other Works on the Island, see FELTHAM, John. JOHNSTONE James. KING,

5 A

History of Vale Royal. ROBERTSON, David. ROLT, Richard. SACHEVERELL, W. TRIONMOUTH. Lord. TOWNLEY, Rich. WALPOLE, G. WOOD, S. G.; and MANKS LITERARY SOCIETY, in Appendix.

MANBY, George William. The History and Antiquities of the Parish of St. David, South Wales; collected from the most ancient Documents in the Bodleian Library. To which is annexed, a correct List of the Archbishops, Bishops, &c. who have filled that See. Lond. 1801, 8vo. plates in aquatinta, 10s. 6d.

Fugitive Sketches of the History and natural Beauties of Clifton, the Hotwells and Vicinity. Lond. 1802, 8vo.

An historic and picturesque Guide from Clifton, through the Counties of Monmouth, Glamorgan and Brecknock; with Representations of Ruins, interesting Antiquities, &c. Bristol, 1802, 8vo. plates.

A Journal of a Voyage to Greenland in 1821. Lond. 1822, 4to. with plates and woodcuts, published at 1l. 11s. 6d. Second edition. Lond. 1823, 8vo. with graphic illustrations.

On the Preservation of Shipwrecked Persons. Lond. 1812, 8vo.

MANCHESTER, Henry Ley Montague, Earl of. Manchester al Mondo: a Contemplation of Death and Immortality. 12mo.

First edition. Lond. 1633—1635. 12mo. with portrait of the earl.—1636. 12mo. with portrait and frontispiece. Hibbert, 5052, 4s. Bindley, pt. II. 1560, 11s.—1635, 12mo.—Lond. 1636, 12mo.—Fourth edition, 12mo.—1638, front. and portrait. In the Granville Collection.—1639, Fourth edition. Hebor, pt. vi. 4s. 6d.—1643, Fifth edition, much enlarged—1642, with portrait and frontispiece. Nassau, pt. I. 2105, 3s.—1601, Eighth edition, much enlarged—1676, 12mo. with portrait and frontispiece by F. H. Van Hove.—1689, with portrait of the earl. Dowdeswell, 402, 3s.—Fifteenth Impression, 1690.

MANCHESTER.—History of the Foundations in Manchester of Christ's College, Chetham Hospital, and the Free Grammar School. Manchester, 1828-33, 4to. 3 vols. portraits and plates, 8l. 13s. 6d.

Vol. I. in two parts, p. 1 to 418, besides Title, Dedication, Prefaces and Contents, 10 leaves. History of the College and Collegiate Church founded in 1422 by Lord de la Warre; drawn up from original documents by Samuel Hibbert, M.D., F.R.S.E. (These papers consisted of those collected by the Rev. Mr. Hollingworth in 1654, and Rev. J. Greswell)—Vol. 2. continuation of Part 1. pp. 5 to 194. Part 2. An Architectural Description of the Collegiate Church and College by John Palmer, Architect, pp. 185 to 366; also Title and Advertisement, 5 leaves.—Vol. 3. History of the School, with Notes and Lives of the founder, Hugh Oldham, Bp. of Exeter, pp. 1 to 124. Title, 1828, and Preface, two leaves. History of the Chetham Hospital and Library, with a Genealogical Account of the Founder, Humphrey Chetham, and family, pp. 125 to 294, besides Title, 1833, and Advertisement. LARGE PAPER, 3 vols. royal 4to. 5l. 5s.

Description of Manchester, by a Native of the Town. Manchester, 1783, 8vo.

Manchester vindicated: being a complete Collection of the Papers lately published in Defence of that Town in the Chester Courant. Together with all those on the other Side of the Question, printed in the Manchester Magazine, or elsewhere, which are answered in the said Chester Courant. Chester, 1749. 12mo. Pp. xii and 324. Lloyd, 331, 9s. Hibbert, 5053, 8s.

Curious Remarks on the History of Manchester, 1771, 8vo. 5s.

Characteristic Strictures, or Remarks on one hundred (written) portraits of the most eminent persons in the counties of Lancaster and Chester, particularly in the town and neighbourhood of Manchester, now supposed to be on exhibition. Lond. 1779, 4to.

Memoirs of the literary and philosophical Society of Manchester, 1785—1802, 5 vols.—Second Series, 1805-42, 6 vols. 8vo. 5l. 5s. These volumes 'are of higher merit than those of any other provincial institution, and are surpassed by few of our metropolitan societies.'—*Quarterly Review*.

A brief historical Description of the Towns of Manchester and Salford. March. 1804, 8vo.

History of the Siege of Manchester, by the King's Forces, 1642, under Lord Strange, with the complaint of Lieut. John Rosworm against the Inhabitants. Manch. 1876, royal 8vo. map. LARGE PAPER, royal 4to. Hibbert. 5177, 6s.

See AIKIN. WHITAKER, John.

MANCYS, Domynicke. The Myrrour of good Maners, contcyning the iiii Vertues, called Cardinall. Imprynted by Richard Pynson, n. d. fol.

Pp. 100. In the title-page is a woodcut of Barclay, the translator, presenting the work to Sir Giles Allington. Bibl. Anglo-Poet. 17, 12l. 12s. Roxburghe, 8296. Last leaf wanting, 10l. 10s. Resold Sir M. M. Sykes, 459, (at the end of Barclay's translation of Brant's Ship of Fools). 16l. 16s. Perry, pt. l. 854, morocco, 9l.—1570, folio. O, in sixes; with the Latin at the side of the English.

De quatuor Virtutibus, &c. Libellus. Excusum apud Joan. Harison, 1574, 16mo.

The Englyshe of Mancyne upon the foure cardynale Vertues. Small 4to. Hoswell, 939, 2l. 2s.

MANDELSLOE, John Albert de. Travels. See OLEARIUS, Adam.

Jo. Albert de Mandelslos's voyages and observations through the greatest part of the East Indies will be found in the first volume of Harris' Collection of Voyages and Travels.

MANDER, James. The Derbyshire Miner's Glossary, or Explanation of the Technical Terms of Mines, with the Mineral Laws and Customs of the High and Low Peak. Bakewell, 1824, royal 8vo.

MANDEVILLE, Bernard, M.D. The writings of Mandeville, though they contain many ingenious and just remarks, are little calculated to increase virtue or good morals.

Oratio de Medicina. Rot. 1685, 4to.

Æsop dressed, or a Collection of Fables writ in familiar Verse by Bernard Mandeville. Lond. 1704, 4to. 5s. Bindley, pt. iii. 335, with Typhon and the Planter's Charity. 1l. 5s. An edition in 8vo. without date.

Typhon, in Verse. 1704, 4to. Bindley, pt. iii. 335, with Æsop dressed and the Planter's Charity, 1l. 5s.

The Planter's Charity, a Poem, 1704, 4to.

The Virgin unmasked, or female Dialogues. Lond. 1709, 8vo. Sir P. Thompson, 6s.—1724, 8vo. Heath, 3s. 6d.—1731, 8vo.

The grumbling Hive, or Knaves turned honest. Lond. 1714, 8vo.

Free Thoughts on Religion, the Church and National Happiness. Lond. 1720, 8vo. Heath, 2s.—1723, 8vo. Willett, 1575, 14s. —Second edition. Lond. 1729, 8vo. Sir P. Thompson, 4s. 6d. Bindley, pt. ii. 1565, with the Virgin unmasked, 1709, and Treatise on Diseases, 1730, 1l. 2s.

The Fable of the Bees, or private Vices public Benefits; with an Essay on Charity and Charity Schools, and a Search into the Nature of Society; the first volume appeared anonymously in London, 1714, 12mo.—Lond. 1723, 8vo. 2 vols.—1724, 8vo. 2 vols. Bindley, pt. ii. 1541, 13s.— 1732, 8vo. 2 vols. Willett, 1574. 11. 3s. Williams, 1156, 1l. 14s.—Edinb. 1755, 12mo. 2 vols. 6s.—Lond. 1795, 8vo. complete in 1 vol. Bindley, 02, 6s. 6d. Dr. Johnson observed, 'the fallacy of this book is, that Mandeville defines neither vices nor benefits.' The Work was replied to by W. Hutcheson, Bp. Berkeley, and Wm. Law.

An Enquiry into the Causes of the frequent Executions at Tyburn, &c. Lond. 1725, 8vo. Bindley, pt. ii. 1591, 5s.

A Treatise on the Hypocondriack and Hysterick Diseases. The third edition. Lond. 1730, 8vo.

An Enquiry into the Origin of Honour, and Usefulness of Christianity in War. Lond. 1732, 8vo. Bindley, pt. ii. 1735, 5s. Sir P. Thompson, 6s.

A modest Defence of Publick Stews. Lond. 1740, 8vo. 10s. 6d.

A Conference about Whoring. Lond. 1725, 8vo.

The True Meaning of the Fable of the Bees. Lond. 1726, 8vo. See the DUNCIAD.

A Letter to Dion (Bishop Berkeley), occasioned by his Book 'The Minute Philosopher.' 8vo. 1732.

The World Unmasked, or the Philosopher the greatest Cheat. Lond. 1736, 8vo. attributed to Mandeville.

See LAWS' (W.) Works.

MANDEVILLE, or MAUNDEVILLE, Sir John. The Voyaige and Travaile, which treateth of the Way to Hierusalem, and of Marvayles of Inde, with other Islands and Countryes. Lond. 1725, royal 8vo.

First English edition. Stanley, 3l. 7s. Willett, 1685, 2l. 16s. Dent, pt. i. 1401, uncut, mor. 4l. 8s. Roxburghe, 7258, 2l. 9s. Heath, 2636, 2l. 8s. Reed, 5077, 1l. 11s. 6d. Towneley, pt. ii. 720, 1l. 10s. Gough, 2217, 2l. 15s. Other editions,—Westmynster by Wynkyn de Worde, 1499, 4to. This edition contains 109 chapters, exclusively of the introduction, and has several woodcuts, a 6 in eights, h i in sixes, k in four.—Lond. (by Wynkyn de Worde), 1503. One hundred and eight leaves, with 75 woodcuts and a map.— Emprented by Rychard Pynson, 4to. n. d. This edition terminates on the recto of the fourth leaf, after sig. K.—Lond. 1568, 4to.—Lond. T. Stanley, 1618, 4to. woodcuts. Black letter. Heber, pt. i. 2l. 8s.—Lond. 1657, 4to. woodcuts. Black letter.—1670, 4to. Black letter.—Lond. H. Scot, 1684, 4to.—1696, 4to. R. Chiswell.—Black letter, with woodcuts, same as used in 1684.—Bicevens, 1875, 7s.

5 A 2

1464

White Knights, 2545, morocco, 2l. 7s.—
Lond. for L. Osborne (1720-30), 12mo.
woodcuts. — 1722, 4to. with woodcuts,
Towneley, pt. II. 1117, 1l. 9s. Nassau,
pt. I. 2678, 18s.—1727, 8vo. Hibbert, 5240,
russia, 2l. White Knights, 2865, mor.
2l. 16s. Jadis, 97, 2l. 1s.— With Introduction, Notes and Glossary by J. O. Halliwell, Lond. 1839, woodcuts, 8vo. 10s. 6d.

These early Travels in the East, by an
Englishman, do not appear to have been
put into print prior to 1480, during which
year two editions appeared in French,
and one in Italian; versions in other
languages rapidly appeared of these marvellous and romantic relations. For a
list of several early and rare editions, see
BURNET, and for an account of the work,
the Grenville Catalogue.
See Retrosp. Review, iii. 269-93.

Early Travels in Palestine, including
Maundeville complete; also La Brocquiere and Maundrell. Edited by Thos.
Wright, Esq., in 1 vol. with map. Lond.
(Bohn's Antiquarian Library) 1848, post
8vo. 5s.

MANERICK, Ra. Saint Peter's
Chaine, consisting of eight golden
Linkes. Lond. 1596, 8vo.
Inglis, 1226, 10s. 'The linkes are faith,
vertue, knowledge, temperance, patience,
godliness, brotherly kindness, love.'

MANGLES, James, Capt. R.N.
The Floral Calendar, Monthly and
Daily, with details relative to
Plants and Flowers, Gardens and
Greenhouses. Lond. 1839, 12mo.
Printed for private distribution only.
See IRBY and MANGLES.

MANILIUS, Marcus. Astronomicon, ex Recensione et cum Notis
Rich. Bentleii. Lond. 1739, 4to.
Should contain a portrait of Bentley,
and a celestial chart.
A valuable edition, with excellent notes.
Roxburghe, 12s. Willett, 1602, 18s. Heath,
4044, 1l. 13s. Stanley, 201, morocco, 2l.
LARGE PAPER. Duke of Grafton, 547,
morocco, 2l. 2s. Drury, 2812, 2l. 10s. Dent,
pt. II. 717, morocco, 5l. 13s.

M. Manilii Astronomicon Libri quinque, cum Commentariis et Castigationibus Josephi Scaligeri, Jul. Cæsaris Scal.
Fil. F. Junii Biturigis et Fayi; his accedunt Bentleii quædam Animadversiones
Reprehensione dignæ; quibus omnibus
Editor sua Scholia interposuit. Operâ et
Studio Edmundi Burton. Lond. 1783,
8vo. 5s. Heath, 4045, 8s. 6d.

The Sphere, (Book the first of the As-

tronomicon) made an English Poem, with
Annotations and an astronomical Appendix, by Edw. Sherburne. Lond. 1675,
folio. A work of singular erudition, with
cuts. See Philos. Transact. no. 110.
Affixed is a catalogue of astronomers.
LARGE PAPER. A copy, formerly belonging
to K. Charles II., bound in morocco, is
marked in a bookseller's recent catalogue
at 10l. 10s.

The five Books of M. Manilius; containing the System of the ancient Astronomy and Astrology: done into English
Verse, with Notes by T(homas) C(reech).
Lond. 1697, 8vo. Heath, 4043, 6s. 6d.—
1700, 8vo.

MANIPULUS CURATORUM. See
MONTE ROCHERII, Guido de.

MANKIND.— A Dissertation on
the Numbers of Mankind in Ancient and modern Times, with an
Appendix. Lond. 1753, 8vo. 4s.
An ingenious and learned work by the
Rev. Dr. Robert Wallace. Reprinted,
Edinb. 1809, 8vo. 7s.

MANLEY, Mrs. De la Riviere.
Secret Memoirs and Manners of
several Persons of Quality of both
Sexes from the New Atalantis, an
Island in the Mediterranean. The
seventh edition. Lond. 1741,
12mo. 4 vols. 10s. 6d.
1736, 12mo. 4 vols. Willett, 1575, 19s.
This romance, which is a satire on those
who had effected the revolution, caused a
great sensation, and its printer and publisher were seized by a warrant from the
secretary of state's office.

Court Intrigues, in a Collection of original Letters, from the Island of New
Atalantis, &c. By the Author of those
Memoirs. Lond. 1711, small 8vo.

The Power of Love; in seven Novels.
By Mrs. Manley. Lond. 1720, sm. 8vo.

Lucius, the first Christian King of Britain, a Tragedy. By Mrs. Manley. Lond.
1717.

Memoirs of the Life of Mrs. Manley; to
which is added a Complete Key. Lond.
1717, 8vo.

— Sir Roger. The History
of the late Wars in Denmark,
from 1657 to 1660. Lond. 1670,
folio.
Roxburghe, 7851, 7s. 6d.
Commentariorum de Rebellione Anglicana ab anno 1640, usque ad annum 1685
Libellus. Lond. 1686. 8vo.
The History of the Rebellion in Eng-

land, Scotland, and Ireland, from the Year 1640 to the Beheading of the Duke of Monmouth in 1685. Lond. 1691, 8vo.
George Chalmers gives the authorship of this work to Sir Robert Murray.

MANLEY, Thomas. Temporis Augustiæ: stollen Houres Recreations. Lond. 1649, 12mo.
With portrait by Cross. Sotheby's in 1828, 1*l*. 9*s*. Heber, pt. iv. 11*s*.; pt. vi. no head, 3*s*. 6*d*.
Veni; Vidi; Vici. The Triumphs of O. Cromwell, &c. set forth in a Panygericke. Written originally in Latine, and faithfully done into English heroicall Verse, by Thos. Manley, Jun. Esq., whereto is added, an Elegy upon the Death of Henry Ireton, &c. Lond. 1652, 12mo. pp. 136. Nassau, pt. i. 2103, 5*s*. Lloyd, 1185, 6*s*. 6*d*. Hollis, 1427, morocco, 1*l*. 9*s*. Bibl. Anglo-Poet. 483, 1*l*. 11*s*. 6*d*. Bindley, pt. ii. 1572, with portrait of Cromwell, 2*l*. 6*s*. Heber, pt. iv. 1*l*. 8*s*. G. Chalmers, 1*l*. 14*s*.
The Affliction and Deliverance of the Saints, or the Whole Book of Job, composed into English Heroicall Verse, metaphrastically. Lond. 1652, 17mo. port. Utica, pt. ii. wormed, 2*l*. 6*s*. Heber, pt. iv. wanting the head, 6*s*.
Iter Carolinum, 1660. Reprinted in the fifth volume of the Somers Collection of Tracts.
A short View of the Lives of Henry, Duke of Gloucester, and Mary, Princess of Orange, deceased. Lond. 1661, 12mo. with a frontispiece. White Knights, 2426, morocco, 1*l*. 8*s*. Bliss, 4*s*. 6*d*.

MANLOVE, Ed. The Liberties and Customes of the Lead-Mines, within the Wapentake of Workesworth, in the County of Derby, composed in Meeter. Lond. 1653, 4to.
Five leaves. Marquis of Townshend, 2366, 1*l*. 8*s*. Heber, pt. iv. 11*s*.
Divine Contentment. Lond. 1667. In verse. Bindley, pt. iii. 80, 10. Nassau, pt. i. 2107, morocco, 1*l*. 11*s*. 6*d*. Heber, pt. iv. 4*s*.

MANN, D.D. The present State of New South Wales. Lond. 1810, 4to.
Pp. 100, with 4 coloured views and a plan, published at 3*l*. 13*s*. 6*d*.

— Elizabeth. The History of the Life and Intrigues of that celebrated Courtezan and Poetess Mistress, E. M., alias Boyle, alias Sample. Lond. 1724, 8vo.

— Nicholas. Critical Notes on some Passages of Scripture, comparing them with the most ancient Versions, and restoring them to the original Reading or true Sense. Lond. 1747, 8vo. 6*s*.
This book, published anonymously, is very well worthy of being consulted. A reply under the title of 'Objections, by E. Langford,' appeared in 1747, 8vo.
Of the true Years of the Birth and Death of Christ. Lond. 1633, 8vo. Williams, 1161, 8*s*. 6*d*.—Latine. Lond. 1742, 8vo.—Lond. 1752, 8vo.

MANNERS.— The Boke of good Maners. Lond. by W. de Worde, 1507, 4to.
This work consists of five books, that printed by Caxton (*see* LEGRAND, T.) is contained in four. Imp. by Pynson, 1499, folio.—Bliss, imperfect, wanting 6 leaves, 6*l*. 12*s*. 6*d*.—1514, 4to.—n. d. 4to.

— The Rules of Civility, or certain Ways of Deportment observed amongst all Persons of Quality. Lond. Rd. Chiswell. 1685, 12mo. *See* MANCYN.

MANNING, Edw. Astrea, or the Grove of Beatitudes, dedicated to Lady M. Bedingfield. 1665, 12mo.
With emblematical cuts. A copy in a bookseller's catalogue of 1814 is marked 1*l*. 11*s*. 6*d*. Bliss, pt. ii. 3*s*. 6*d*.

— James. Digested Index to the Nisi Prius Reports, with Notes. Second edition, with additions. Lond. 1820, roy. 8vo. 1*l*. 4*s*.
Practice of the Court of Exchequer, Revenue Branch. Second Edition, with an Appendix. Lond. 1826, roy. 8vo. 1*l*. 11*s*. 6*d*.
Report of the Case of the Serjeants at Law. Lond. 1840, 8vo. 16*s*.
MANNING and RYLAND's Reports in the K. B., from Trin. 1827 to East. 1830. Lond. 1829-37, roy. 8vo. 5 vols.
Manning and Ryland's Reports of Cases relating exclusively to the Office and Duty of Magistrates determined in the K. B. Mich. 1827 to Mich. 1830. Lond. 8vo. 2 vols. and pt 1 of vol. 3.
For Manning and Granger's C. B. and C. P. Reports, now proceeding, *see* Law Catalogues.

— Rev. Owen. The History and Antiquities of the County of Surrey, with a fac-simile Copy of Domesday, engraved on thirteen.

Plates. Continued to the present Time, by William Bray, Esq. Lond. 1801, 9, 14, folio. 3 vols. 12l. 12s.

'Compiled from the best and most authentic historians, valuable records and manuscripts in the public offices and libraries, and in private hands.' The preface to the first volume includes a biographical notice of the author. (Vol. I is now scarce, and worth two-thirds of the whole set.) Hibbert, 5215, 3 vols. russia, 15l. 15s. Hindley, pt. ii. 843, 15l. 15s. LARGE PAPER, in royal folio. Duke of York, 3133, 15l. Dent, pt. ii. 631, uncut, 18l. Sir M. M. Sykes, pt. ii. 404, russia, 19l. Nassau, pt. i. 2587, 21l. Gardner, in 1854, russia, 1 (l. 14s. Beckford, in 1817, uncut, 25l. 10s. North, pt. ii. 1251, russia, 8l. 10s. An Illustrated copy, in 7 vols, sold at Sotheby's in July 1856, 100l.

Collation.—Vol. I. Pp. i–xiv, and i–cviii; title-page, 'Surriæ Comitatus Descriptio;' the copy from Domesday Book, tab. i–xiii. 13 pages, not numbered, the table of places forming p. 14; the history, 654 pages; addenda, corrigenda, and directions to the binder, pp. 655–'670; Index, pp. 669–714. Pages 453–50 are repeated with an asterisk; p. 455, ending with the catch word 'Ewel;' pp. 669-70, containing the corrigenda and directions to the binder, are repeated with asterisks. The volume contains forty plates, and five separate pedigrees, folded. Vol. II. 1809. Pp. xvi and 915. Page xvi contains the list of the 23 plates, and 5 pedigrees. Vol. III. 1814. Pp. viii and 702; appendix, additions, corrections, and index, pp. cccxl; views and portraits illustrative of the history, 4 pages. Page viii contains the list of the 29 plates and 3 pedigrees, contained in the volume, as well as of four additional Plates for vol. 1, and of six for vol. 2; all of which are placed at the end of this volume; pp. lxiv and lxv of the appendix, are repeated with asterisks. Plate 26, at p. 557, 'Plan of Palace of Lambeth,' engraved by Basire, is not mentioned in the list of plates.

MANOJO, Fern. Newes from Spaine. A Relation of the Death of Don Rod. Calderon, 1622, 4to.

MANOIR, Julian. Armorick Grammar. Lhuyd's Archæologia Britannica.

MANOLESSO, E. Maria. Historia Nova, nella quale si contengono tutti i successi della guerra Turchesca, la Congiura del Duca de Nortfolche contra la Regina d'Inghilterra, &c. Padoua, 1572, 4to.

Gardner, in 1854, mor. 10s. Heber, pt. l. 4354, 9s.

MANSELL, Sir Richard. Algiers Voyage, 1621, 4to

A copy is in the British Museum. Lloyd, 759, 13s.

— Sir Robert, Knight. A true Report of the Service done upon certaine Gallies passing through the Narrow Seas. Lond. 1602. 4to.

Nassau, pt. i. 2579, 11s. Heber, pt. vi. 8s.

MANSION (The), of Magnanimitie; or the Strength of this Realme, in respect of situation, pleasantnees of ayre, &c. Lond. Mat. Lownes, 1608, 4to. BLACK LETTER.

Heber, pt. v. 2781, 2l. 12s. 6d. Second title, 'An Inventory of all the Goods, Excellencies, and Memorable Actions, from the first daies of the Conquerer, to the last daies of Queene Elizabeth,'

For first edition, see CROMPTON, Rich.

MANSTEIN, C. H. do. Memoirs of Russia, historical, political, and military, from the Year 1727 to 1744. Translated from the original MS. of General Manstein. Lond. 1770, 4to.

A work of authority, illustrated with maps and plans. The recommendatory address was written by David Hume. Roxburghe, 7831, 5s. Willett, 1633, 8s.—1773, 4to. Heath, 2512, 1l. 11s. 6d.—Second edition. Lond. 1773, 4to.—New edition. Lond. 1856, post 8vo. 5s.

MANT, Richard, Bishop of Down and Connor. Sermons for parochial and domestic Use. Second edition, Oxf. 1813-15, 8vo. 3 vols. Sixth edit. Lond. 1832, 2 vols. 18s.

Biographical Notices of the Apostles, Evangelists, and Saints. Ox. 1828, 8vo. 13s.

Scripture Narratives of Christ's Life. Ox. 1840, 8vo. 13s.

History of the Church of Ireland from the Reformation to the Union in 1801. With a Catalogue of the Archbishops, &c. to 1840, Lond. 1839-41, 8vo. 2 vols. 1l. 14s.

Poems. Oxf. 1806, small 8vo.

Familiar Guide to the Church Catechism, in Question and Answer. New edition. Lond. 1840, 12mo.

An Appeal to the Gospel, or an Inquiry into the Charge alleged by Methodists that the Gospel is not preached by the national Clergy. (Bampton Lectures.) Second edition. Oxf. 1812, 8vo.

MAN   MAN   1467

Sermons preached before the University of Oxford, &c. Oxf. 1818, 8vo.
The Book of Psalms in an English metrical Version, with Notes critical and illustrative. Oxf. 1824, 8vo.
The Book of Common Prayer, with Notes. 1820, 4to.—Fifth edition. Lond. Rivington, 1840, 4to. 1l. 16s. or 8vo 2 vols. 1l. 1s.—Sixth edition, Lond. 1850, in 1 vol. imperial 8vo. 1l. 4s.
The Christian Sabbath; its Institution and Obligation. Oxf. 1830.
The Clergyman's Obligations considered. Second edition. Oxf. 1830, 18mo.
Bp. Mant was author of many other works on Divinity, for which see London Catalogue.
See HAMPTON LECTURE. BIBLE, by D'OYLY and MANT.

MANTE, Thomas. The History of the late War in North America, and the Islands, including the Campaigns of 1763 and 1764, against his Majesty's Indian Enemies. Lond. 1773, 4to. plans, 1l. 16s.

MANTEL, F. Account of Cinque Port Meetings, called Brotherhoods and Guestlings. Dover, 1811, sm. 4to.
Coronation Ceremonies and Customs, relative to Barons of the Cinque Ports, as Supporters of the Canopy. Dover, 1820, sm. 4to.

MANTELL, Gideon Algernon, M.D. The Fossils of the South Downs. Lond. 1822, 4to.
Pp. xiv. and 327, with 42 plates, plain, published at 3l. 3s.; coloured at 6l. 6s.
Geology of the South-East Coast of England. Lond. 1833, 8vo. 1l. 1s.
The Natural History of Lewes and its Vicinity, (in Horsfield's History of Sussex.)
Illustrations of the Geology of Sussex, with Figures and Description of the Fossils of Tilgate Forest. Lond. 1827, royal 4to. with 21 plates, 2l. 15s.
Wonders of Geology, or a familiar Exposition of Geological Phenomena; being the Substance of a Course of Lectures. Lond. 1838, fcap. 8vo. 2 vols.—Third edit. Lond. 1839, fcap. 8vo. 2 vols.—Fourth edition. Lond. 1840, fcap. 8vo. 2 vols. LARGE PAPER, 8vo. 2 vols.—Seventh edit. revised and augmented by T. Rupert Jones, F.G.S., 2 vols. with coloured geological map of England, plates, and upwards of 200 woodcuts, post 8vo. Lond. (Bohn's Scientific Library) 1857-8, post 8vo. 2 vols. 15s.

MEDALS of CREATION, or first Lessons in Geology, and the Study of Organic Remains; including Geological Excursions. Lond. 1844, fcap. 8vo. 2 vols.—New edition, revised, with coloured plates, and several hundred woodcuts. Lond. (Bohn's Scientific Library) 2 vols. post 8vo. 15s.
Geological Excursions in the Isle of Wight and Dorsetshire. Lond. 1847, fcap. 8vo.—New edition, with prefatory Note by T. Rupert Jones, Esq., numerous woodcuts, and a geological map. Lond. (Bohn's Scientific Library) 1854, post 8vo. 5s.
Pictorial Atlas of Fossil Remains, consisting of coloured Illustrations selected from Parkinson's 'Organic Remains of a former World,' and Artis's ' Antediluvian Phytology,' with additions and descriptive letter-press by Dr. Mantell. Lond. 1850, 4to. 74 coloured plates, 2l. 5s.
Mantell's Day's Ramble in and about the ancient Town of Lewes, in Sussex. Lond. 1838, 12mo.—New edition. Lond. 1846, fcap. 8vo. woodcuts, 6s.
Petrifactions and their Teachings; an Illustrated Hand-book to the Organic Remains in the British Museum. Numerous wood engravings. Lond. (Bohn's Scientific Library) 1861, post 8vo. 6s.
THOUGHTS on a PEBBLE, or a First Lesson in Geology. Lond. 18 , sq. 12mo.—Eighth edition. Lond. 1849, sq. 12mo. coloured plates, 5s.
Thoughts on Animalcules; or a Glimpse of the Invisible World revealed by the Microscope. Lond. 1846, sq. 8vo. 10s. 6d.—Second edition. Lond. 1847, sq. 8vo. 6s.

MANTON, Thomas, D.D. Works, with Life by Harris. Lond. 1681-1725, folio, 5 vols. 7l. 7s.
Vol. I. was reprinted in 1684. Vol. V. contains the Life by Harris.
The works of this learned and eminent nonconformist divine consist principally of sermons. A portrait is attached to every volume.
A practical Commentary or an Exposition, with Notes, on the Epistle of James. Lond. 1653, 4to. Revised and corrected by the Rev. J. Sherman. Lond. 1840, imperial 8vo.—Abridged by Macdonough. Lond. 1844, 8vo. 10s. 6d.
A practical Commentary, or an Exposition, with Notes, on the Epistle of Jude. Lond. 1658, 4to.
A practical Exposition of the cxixth Psalm. Lond. 1681, folio.—1725, folio, with portrait, 1l. 10s. forms second edition of vol. 1 of the Works.—Third edition, with Life by Harris. Lond. 1845, 8vo. 3 vols. 2l. reduced 1l. 1s.
Exposition of the Lord's Prayer. Lond. 1684, 8vo.—Reprinted, Lond. 1841, 8vo.

MANTUAN, Joh. Baptist. Eglogs turned into English Verse and set forth with the Argument to every Eglogo, by Geo. Turbervile, Gent. An. 1567. Lond. by Henry Bynneman, 12mo.

Gardner, 1654, mor. 2l. 5s. A copy is in the British Museum.—Lond. 1597.

Eclogæ, cum Comment. Badii Ascensii. Lond. W. de Worde, 1519, 4to.

Adolescentia seu Bucolica, brevibus Jodoci Badii Commentariis illustrata. Lond. 1572, 16mo.—1584, 16mo.—1598, 16mo.

Bucolica à J. Murmelio. Lond. 1677, 12mo.

Bucolics, translated by T. Harvey, Lond. 1656, 12mo. Inglis, 60, 10s. 6d. According to Ant. a Wood, Harvey availed himself of Turbervile's translation, without the least acknowledgment.

The Lives of St. Margaret, St. Katharine, St. Etheldreda, St. George, &c. Translated by Alexander Barclay. Printed by Pynson. See Wood's Athen. Oxon. by Dr. Bliss, 1. 206.

Treatise shewing that Death is not to be feared, translated by John Hale. Lond. by John Daye, 16mo. From Maunsell's catalogue, p. 69.

MANUALE ad Usum Ecclesiæ Ebobacensis. Lond. Wynandum de Worde, 1509, folio.

A copy of this exceedingly rare work is in the Bodleian Library. Other editions were printed in 8vo. and 4to. All are extremely scarce.

MANUALE ad Usum percelebris Ecclesiæ Sarisburiensis.

Editions.—Rouen, Richard. Opera Olivier de Lorraine, 1500, 4to. An imperfect copy on vellum in the Douce Collection, Bodleian Library, Oxford.—Rothom. 1504, 4to. In British Museum.—Lond. R. Pynson, 1506, folio. A copy on vellum is at Stonyhurst College.—Lond. Wynken de Worde, 1509. A copy in the Library of Earl Fitzwilliam at Wentworth House.

Rothomagi. 1510, 4to. In the Bodleian. —Rothom. 1513, 4to.—Paris, Byrkman, 1515, 4to.

Mosen, Calliard, 1522, Douce Collection. —Antverpie, Endoven, 1524, folio.—Paris, Regnault, 1529, 4to.—Paris, Regnault, 1530, 4to. Bodleian, Gough.

Paris, 1532, 4to.—Antwerp, 1532, 4to.— Rothom. Hufort, 1533, 4to. Bodleian, British Museum.—Paris, Regnault, 1537, 4to. Bodleian, Gough.—Rothom. Imp. Cousin, 1537, 4to. St. John's Coll. Cambridge.

Antwerp, Vidue Buremond, 1542, 4to. Saint Cuthbert's College, Ushaw.—Antwerp, vidue Buremond, 1543. Bodleian, Gough, St Cuthbert's College.—Rouen, Bufuet. 1543, 4to. British Museum, Bamborough Castle.—Paris, 1544, 4to.—Paris, 1546, 4to.

Rouen, 1554, 4to. Oriel College, Queen's College.—Lond. Jugge and Cawood, 1554, 4to. 129 leaves. Rev. J. Horner; Maskell.— Another impression, same date, Jugge and Cawood, 1554, 4to. 168 leaves. Horner, British Museum, Dean and Chapter of Windsor, St. John's Coll. Cambridge.— Lond. ex officina Kyngston and Sutton, 1554, 4to.—Lond. J. Wayland, 1554, 4to. King's Library, British Museum.—Other editions of this date printed at London (with Grafton's mark), in Lambeth Library, 4to.—Rouen, Valentin, 1554, 4to. Bodleian, Gough Coll. Earl Spencer, Bp. Cosin's Library, Durham, &c. &c.—Same date, in 8vo.—Lond. Grafton, 1555, 4to. Bodleian Library.—Lond. without printer's name, 1556, 4to. Exeter College.— Rothom. Valentin, 1555, 4to.—In Caius College is a copy printed at Rouen in 4to. wanting the colophon, presented by Humphrey de la Poole in 1496. The Rev. Thomas Baker thought that the edition printed in 1554, being in the time of Cardinal Pole, and before the Council of Trent broke up, was probably the last of its kind in England.

Mr. Maskell says that all three editions by Kingston and Sutton, 1554, are so alike even to paper and catchwords, that only a careful comparison can detect the differences. They are 1. 'Londini, Kingston et Henricus Sutton impress.' (colophon.) 2. 'Londini, recenter impressum,' (title.) 3. 'Londini, noviter impressum,' (title.)

It was reprinted at Rouen in 1610, in 4to. 8vo. and 12mo.; the 8vo. sold at Sotheby's, April 1857, for 2l. 2s.

The Douay editions of 1604 and 1610 follow a different arrangement, and omit all after the Officers of Benediction.

Donay, 1604, 8vo.—Donay, Kellam, 1610, 8vo. Dr. Rock; Bodleian.—Donay, 1610, 12mo. Bp. Ullathorne; Rev. J. Horner. Editions without dates, Rouen, Morin, 4to. British Museum. Other editions, Rouen, 4to. without date or printer's name. Rev. Dr. Rock; J. R. Hope, Esq.

MANUCHE, Cosmo. The just General, a Tragi-Comedy. Lond. 1652, 4to.

Roxburghe, 5398, 6s. Rhodes, 1609, 11s. Bindley, pt III. 531*, 15s. 6d.

The Bastard, a Tragedy. Lond. 1652, 4to. Rhodes, 1607, 2s. 6d. This play is attributed to Manuche by Coxeter.

The Loyal Lovers, a Tragi-comedy.' Lond. 1652, 4to. Rhodes, 1608, 11s.

MANUTIUS, Aldus. Aldi Manutii Phrases Linguæ Latinæ, in Anglicum Sermonem conversæ. Lond. ex off. Vautrollier, 1579, 16mo.

Dedicated to Robert Cecil (afterwards Earl of Salisbury), then 16 years of age. Inglis, morocco, 3l. 1s. Lond. 1581, 16mo. Bliss, 7s.

MANUTIUS, Paul. Epistolarum Libri. Lond. 1573 et 1581, 16mo.

MANWARING, Edw. Stichology, or a Recovery of the Latin, Greek and Hebrew Numbers, exemplified in the Reduction of all Horace's Metres, and the Greek and Hebrew Poetry. Lond. 1737, 4to. 6s.
Of Harmony and Numbers in Prose and Poetry. Lond. 1744, 8vo.

— R. Religion and Allegiance. Two Sermons. Lond. 1667, 4to.
The Parliament suppressed these Sermons, fined the author 1000l., and also imprisoned him; but the king, to reward him, made him a bishop.

MAN-WOMAN. Hic Mulier, or the Man-Woman: being a medicine to cure the coltish Disease of the Staggers in the Masculine-feminines of the Times. Lond. 1620, 4to.
North, pt. II. 682, 2l. 9s.
Haec Vir; or the womanish Man. Lond. 1620, 4to. with a frontispiece. Gordonstoun, 1197. with Hic Mulier, 3l. 13s. 6d.
Muld'd Sacke, or the Apologie of Hic Mulier to the late Declaration against her. 1620, with portrait on the title page. White Knights, 2258, 6l. 16s. 6d.
The three Tracts. Hindley, pt. II. 1875, 2ll. resold Nassau, pt. I. 2112, 5l. Again, Heber, pt. IX. 5l. 7s. 6d. Another set, 3 vols. Heber, pt. VIII. 3546, 3l. 19s.

MANWOOD, John. Treatise and Discourse of the Lawes of the Forest; by W. Nelson. Lond. 1744, 8vo.
First edition. Black letter. Lond. 1598, 4to. This edition consists but of 20 chapters. Willett, 1604, 7s. Dent, pt. II. 718, 7s. 6d. Heber, pt. I. 5s.—1615, 4to. Herd, 4874, 9s. Roxburghe, 919, 10s. 6d.—1665, 4to.—1683, 4to.—1717 (new title, 1744), by W. Nelson, 8vo. Roxburghe, 960, 9s. 6d. See LEWIS.

MANZINIE. His most exquisite Academicall Discourses, Englished by an Honourable Lady. Lond. 1655, 4to.
Bliss, 12s. 6d.

MAPHÆUS. The Canto added by Maphæus to Virgil's 12 Books of Æneas. Lond. 1758, 12mo.

In English Hudibrastic verse, with the Latin text, and notes by John Ellis. Reed, 7118, 6s. 6d.
A Translation, with the Latin Original. Lond. 1809.
See LEADBEATER, Mary. TWYNE, Thos.

MAPLET, John. The Diall of Destiny. Lond. 1581, 16mo.
Pp. 162. A curious work, treating of the influence of the seven planets, written in a pedantic style.—Lond. 1582, imp. by Marshe.
A Greene Forest, or a naturall Historie, wherein may bee seene the most sufferaigne Vertues in all the whole kindes of Stones and Mettals; of Brute Beastes, Fowles, Fishes, &c. Lond. Denham, 1567, 12mo. Black letter, 112 leaves. Heber, pt. I. 13s. pt. VII. 5s. 6d.

MAPLETOFT, J. Select Proverbs, Italian, English, Scotch, British, &c. Lond. 1707, 8vo.
Constable, 630, 5s. Hibbert, 5070, 5s. 6d.

MAPS and Plans illustrative of Herodotus, Thucydides, and Xenophon, chiefly selected from D'Anville, Rennell, Anacharsis, and Calc. Oxf. 1824, 4to.

MAR, Countess of. Extracts from the Household Book of Lady Marie Stewart, Countess of Mar. [With biographical Notice by C. K. Sharpe.] Edinb. 1815, 4to. 1l. 1s. Fifty copies printed, with portrait and plates.

MARBECK, John. A Concordance, that is to saie, a Worke, wherein by the Ordre of the Letters of the A. B. C. ye maie redely finde any Words conteigned in the whole Bible, so often as it is there expressed or mencioned. Lond. Rich. Grafton excud. 1550, folio.
Stoger, April 1860, 4l. 16s.
The first Concordance to the English Bible: an account of it may be seen in Dr. Townley's Biblical Illustrations, III. 118-20. It contains Vvv, in sixes. Denyer, 29, 2l. 2s. A Concordance to the New Testament was compiled and printed by Thomas Gibson, about the year 1535.
The Booke of Common Prayer noted. Lond. by R. Grafton, 1550, 4to. Hibbert, 5403, 10l. 10s. A considerable extract from this work will be found in Dr. Burney's History of Music, II. 578-83. Reprinted, Lond. Pickering, 1844, sm. 4to.

1470 MAR

BLACK LETTER, ON VELLUM. Only two printed.
The Lyves of Holy Saincles, Prophets, Patriarches and others, contayned in holye Scripture. Lond. 1574, 4to. Perry, pt. II. 817. 8s. 6d. Inglis, 955, 10s. 6d. Denyer, 13, 1l. 4s. Heber, pt. ix. 21. 3s.
The Holie Historie of King David, drawne into English Meetre. Lond. 1579, 4to. Bindley, pt. III. 376, 8l. 15s.
A Ripping vp of the Popes Fardel. Lond. 1581, 8vo.
A Booke of Notes and Common Places, gathered out of divers writers. Lond. T. East, 1581, 4to. BLACK LETTER. Dedicated to the Earl of Huntingdon. Ends on p. 1194, with Table, 19 leaves. Inglis, 958, 5s. 6d. Bright, 17s.
Examples drawen out of holye Scripture, with their Application; also a briefe Conference betweene the Pope and his Secretaris, wherein is opened his great blasphemous Pride. Lond. 1582, 16mo.
A Dialogue betweene Youth and olde Age, wherein is declared, the Perswcetion of Christes Religion, since the Fall of Adam hitherto. Lond. 1584, 16mo.
MARBURY, Ch. A Collection of Italian Proverbs. Lond. 1581, 4to.
— Edw. A Commentary upon the Prophecy of Obadiah. Lond. 1649. 4to.
A Commentarie vpon the Prophecie of Habakuk. Lond. 1652, 4to. Sotheby's in 1821, 7s. 6d.
MARCEL, J. J. Alphabet Irlandais, précédé d'une Notice historique. Paris, 1804, 8vo.
One hundred copies printed. Bright, 5s.
MARCELLINE, George. Epithalamium Gallo-Britannicum, or Great Britaine's, France's, and the most Part of Europe's unspeakable Joy for the Union of Prince Charles and the Lady Henriette Maria. Lond. T. Archer, 1625, 4to.
With a large folding plate, in the centre of which are whole-length portraits of Charles I. and his Queen, surrounded with engravings of coats of arms. At the bottom are twelve verses, subscribed, ' Are to be sold by Thomas Archer, in Popes Head Alley.' Gordonstoun, 1810. 2l. 12s. 6d. Nassau, pt. II. 198, 7l. 10s. resold, after being inlaid in folio, at the Stowe sale in 1844, no. 3453, 21l. 10s.; now with the Sutherland Collection in the Bodleian Library. A copy is in the Bridgewater Collection. Copies without the plate are generally priced 1l. 1s. See HENRY IV.

MARCELLINUS, Ammianus. The Roman Historie, translated into English by Philemon Holland. Lond. 1609, folio, 1l. 1s.
A most accurate translation, according to Dr. Zach. Grey. A portion, ' Character of the Roman Nobles,' translated by Ed. Gibbon, will be found in his Roman History, ch. XXXI.

MARCELLUS, Marcus. See SHERBY, Rob.

MARCET, Alexander, M.D. An Essay on the Chemical History and medical Treatment of Calculous Disorders. Lond. 1819, 8vo.
An excellent work.
The Lady of this Physician has written Conversations on Chemistry, (1816); (Seventh edition, 1847); Natural Philosophy, (eleventh edition, 1847); Political Economy, (1839); Vegetable Physiology, 2 vols.; Mineralogy, (third edition, 1837); besides many Elementary Books, all of which have long enjoyed considerable popularity.

MARCH, John. Amicus Reipublicæ: the Commonwealth's Friend. Lond. 1651, 12mo.
Hollis, 809, morocco, 13s. resold, Heber, pt. vi. 12s. Bright, 8s.
New Cases in the time of Henry VIII. Edward VI. and Queen Mary, with a Table of the principal Matters. Lond. 1651, 12mo. 3s. 6d.
Reports in the Kings Bench; or, new Cases, with Judgments upon them, taken in the 15th, 16th, 17th and 18th Years of King Charles I. Lond. 1648, 4to. 4s. Second edition, with a Table of the principal Matters. Lond. 1675, 4to. 6s.

MARCHAND, Etienne. A Voyage round the World, 1790-2. Preceded by an historical Introduction, and illustrated by Charts, &c. Translated from the French of C. P. Claret Fleurieu. Lond. 1801, 4to. 2 vols. 18s.
Drury, 1815, 9s. Hibbert, 5186, 9s. 6d.
— Floram. The Fallacie of the great Water-drinker discovered (1650), 4to.
With a wood-cut portrait of Floram Marchand, whole length, on the back of the title. Nassau, pt. II. 610, 1l. 15s. Bindley, pt. II. 1264, 3l. 3s.

MARCHANT, John. Exposition of the Books of the Old and New

Testament. Lond. 1743, 1745, folio, 2 vols.

'Extracted from the writings of the best authors, antient and modern.'

A History of the present Rebellion. Lond. 1746. 12mo. Portrait of the Duke of Cumberland. Bindley, pt. II. 1831, 10s. 6d.

MARCHE, Oliver de la. *See* LEWKENOR, Lewis.

MARCHMONT Papers, illustrative of Events, 1685—1750. Edited by Sir George Rose. Lond. 1831, 8vo. 3 vols. pub. 1l. 16s. reduced to 15s.

MARCIANO, or the Discovery, a Tragi-comedy, acted with great Applause before his Majesties high Commissioner (Middleton), and others of the Nobility, at the Abby of Holyrud-house, on St. John's Night, by a Company of Gentlemen. [By William Clarke.] Edin. 1663, 4to.

Constable, 822, 4l. 14s. 6d.

MARCO POLO. *See* POLO, Marco.

MARCORT, Anthony. A Declaration of the Masse. Wittenberge, by Hans Lufte, M.D.XLVII. 16mo.

Heber, in a vol. pt. II. 2648. Another copy, pt. iv. in lot 5958. D, in eights.— Ipswich, by John Oswen, 16mo. U 4, in eights, including a table which is not in the original edition.

MARCUS, Moses. The Principal Motives and Circumstances that induced him to leave the Jewish, and embrace the Christian Faith. Lond. 1724, 4to.

MARDELEY, John, Clerc of the Kynges Maiesties Mynte, called Suffolke House. A short Reeytall of certaine holy Doctours, which proueth that the naturall Body of Christ is not conteyned in the Sacrament of the Lordes Supper, but fyguratyuely, collected in Mytor. Lond. Thomas Raynalde, n. d. 12mo.

Eight leaves. A copy is in Lambeth Library.

Another edition, also without date. This work appears to have been written in answer to John Aungell's Agreement of the holy Fathers and Doctors.

A Declaration of thee Power of Godes Words, concernyng the holy Supper of the Lord, confutynge all Lyers and fals Teachers, whych mayntayne theyr maskynge Masse, inuented agaynst the Woorde of God, and the Kynges Maiesties most godly proceedynges, compiled Anno Dom. M.D.XLVIII. Lond. by Thomas Raynalde, 16mo. Heber, pt. II, 3l. 4s. Contains E 4, in eights, dedicated to Edward, Duke of Somerset, after which 'A complaynt agaynst the styffnecked, made by the auethour of thys boke,' in seven-line stanzas.

A necessary Instruction for all couetous riche Men to beholde and lerne what Perel and Danger thay be brought into, yf they baue their Consolation in theyr daungerous and myserable Mammon. Lond. by Thomas Raynalde, 16mo. D iv. in eights. A copy is in Lambeth library.

MARDEN.— Collections concerning the Manor of Marden in the County of Hereford, folio.

Written by Thomas, Earl Coningsby, and printed at his own expense, 1722.7, with a view to support his right to the lands of Amberley, &c. Sotheby's in May, 1820, 8ll. Bindley, pt. iv. 1105, 24l. 3s. Resold, 1851, 12l. Dent, pt. i. 671, with a supplementary leaf, not mentioned by Upcott, also a title and introduction, russia, 25l. 14s 6d. Leigh and Sotheby's in April, 1813 (two leaves and the index, a reprint), 48l. 6s. Towneley, pt. II. 858, russia, 45l. 6s. *Collation.*—The volume commences on sign. D, thus '(I) Marden.' and continues to page 720. Pages 81—4 are erroneously paged 83—6; pp. 213—16 are misprinted 217—20, and pp. 561 and 562 are repeated with asterisks. The second part of the volume commences on sig. a, thus, 'I. Marden.' and is continued to p. xix. Then sig. B, commencing '(1) Nomina hominum,' &c. and is continued to p 300, ending with the date 1680. In this part pages 125 to 184 are repeated with asterisks; between pp. 170—1 is a leaf, marked [* A]; between pp. 174—5, two leaves, [* B]; between pp. 226—7, two leaves, [** C], two [** C], one [*** C]; and between pp. 250—1, two [* D], two [** D]. After p. 306 are seven leaves, one marked [E], two [* E], two [** E], two [*** E]. Another pagination then commences thus, '(1) From the Patent Roll,' &c. and is continued to p. 28, after which are [D*] one leaf, [E*] one leaf, [F*] two leaves, and (*) one leaf. 'An Index of the principal Matters,' consisting of 14 leaves, concludes the volume. A title-page, 'Collections concerning the Manor of Marden, in the County of Hereford. By the Right Hon. Thomas, Earl Coningsby,' was printed in

MARDEN—continued.

1813. Another *Collation* by signatures. B to U u u u u u u u, before signature D d d d d d is a leaf marked ["? D]; a to e; D to ll, * ll, ** ll, *,* ll (this latter only one leaf). K k to ll h h h. In this set of signatures will be found the following: a, one leaf, at p. 170; b, two leaves at p. 174; *e, two leaves, e 2, two leaves, e 3, one leaf, after p. 226; d, two leaves; d 2, two leaves, after p. 250. After ll h b h 2, is a leaf containing pages 305 and 306, then sign. e, one leaf; another sign. e, two leaves; e 2, two leaves; e 3, two leaves; A—G, (G only one leaf); then D, one leaf; E, one leaf; F, two leaves; a, one leaf; Index, X x x x x x x, to D d d d d d d d. The signatures consist of two leaves each, except when otherwise mentioned. This collation was made from a copy in the British Museum, which formerly belonged to Peregrine Towneley, Esq. A copy formerly in the library of P. A. Hanrott, Esq. contained the following additional sheets, &c. After the leaves numbered [*** E] one leaf (**** E]; after page 28 of the fourth set of signatures, are 13 leaves numbered [A *] to [C ****]; after [F *] 8 leaves [G *][G **].

A title; preface 2 pages, pages 1 to 8, pages 315.16, and Index 28 pages, wanting in most of the presentation copies, was printed by Jeffery, in 1812. Bindley, pt. iv. 1106, 6s. 6d. 1107, 7s.

The abstract of the Earl of Coningsby's case to Royal Franchise within his liberty of Leominster, in the county of Hereford, with references to the several Grants, folio, 8 pages, very rare.

The first Part of Earl Coningsby's Case relating to the Vicaridge of Lempster in Herefordshire. Lond. 1721, folio, pp. 27. Sykes, pt. i. 937, 10s.

Proofs to make good the Assertions in my Title-page to my Case, relating to the Vicarage of Lempster, folio, pp. 24.

The Case of Thomas Lingen, Clerk, and Edward Wetherstone, Esq. and others, in Relation to a Breach of Privilege charged on them by the Right Hon. Thomas, Earl Coningsby, in dispossessing the said Earl of a Tenement in the Parish of Marden, folio, pp. 4.

An historical account of the descent of the Manor of Marden, which develops the causes that induced Earl Coningsby to make the compilation above described, will be found in the second volume, pp. 10–11, and 119–21, of the Rev. John Duncomb's Collections towards the History and Antiquities of the County of Hereford.

MARGARET. Here begynneth the Lyfe of Saynte Margaret (in verse). Lond. R. Redman, 4to.

BLACK LETTER. A, B, C. in fours, etc. having the device of the Printer. Bliss, 82l., unique.

— History of the proceedings in the Case of Margaret, commonly called Peg, &c. Lond. 1761, 12mo. By Dr. Adam Fergusson. See SCOTT'S Prose Works, 12mo. vol. xix. p. 336.

— St., Queen of Scotland. The Idea of a perfect Princesse, in the Life of St. Margaret, Queen of Scotland. Whereunto is annexed, a Postscript, proving his Majestie's (Charles II.) Right and Title to the Crown of England. Paris, 1661, 8vo.

Reed, 4872, 3s. 6d. White Knights, 807, 5s. Roxburghe, Suppl. 636, 1l. Bright, 12s. Bliss, 1l. 11s.

L'Idée d'une Reine parfaite en la Vie de Marguerite Reine d'Escosse, avec les Eloges de ses Enfans Dauid et Matildo. Douay, 1660, 4to. Lloyd, 759, 11s.

A life of this Saint was written in Spanish by Juan de Soto, Alcala, 1617, 4to. and in Italian by Guil. Lesley. Rome, 1675, 8vo. See LESLEUS, G. L. SOTO, J. de.

— of Valois, Queen of Navarre. A godly Medytacyon of the Christen Sowle, concerning a Love towardes God and hys Chryste, compyled in Frenche by Lady Margarete, Quene of Navarre, and aptely translated into Englysh by the ryght vertuose Lady Elizabeth, Doughter to our late Soverayne, Kyng Henri the VIII. Imprinted in the yeare of our Lorde 1548, in Apryll, 12mo.

A copy is in the Malone Collection. The volume contains an 'Epystle dedycatory to the ryght vertuose and Christenly larned yonge Lady Elizabeth.' BLACK LETTER. Dent, pt. i. 734, morocco, 6l. Tyssen in Dec. 1801, 9l. 10s. 6d. Bright, wanting title, 1l. 11s. Bliss, wanting 5 leaves, 1l. 10s.—Lond. H. Denham, 1568, 12mo. BLACK LETTER, A to G iv. in eights. The Epistle dedicatory is signed JAMES, Cancellor. The title of this edition states it to be 'by the Right High and most virtuous Princess Elisabeth, of England, France, and Ireland, Queen, &c.

MAR 1473

Whereunto is added Godly Meditations, set forth after the Alphabet of the Queens Majesties name.' The Monument of Matrones, by Thomas Bentley, with the omission of the Epistle, by Bale, &c.

Heptameron, or the History of the Fortunate Lovers, translated by H. Codrington. Lond. 1654, 12mo. Strettell, 1*43, 2l. 2s. White Knights, 2591, 2l. 6s. This translation is dedicated to Tho. Stanley, Esq.

The Heptameron. By Margaret of Navarre. A Series of Tales, now first Translated from the original Text. Lond. (Bohn's extra Volumes) 1855, post 8vo. portrait, 3s. 6d.

Le Tombeau de Margueritte de Navarre, en Distiques Latins, fait par les trois Soeurs, (Anne, Margueritte, et Jane Seymour,) Princesses d'Angleterre, & traduits en Grec, Italien et Francoys. Paris, 1551, 8vo. portrait of Margaret of Valois in wood, on back of title. Heber, 2l. 2s. Sotheby's in 1818, 2l. 8s.

The first edition of this curious volume was in Latin, under the following title:— 'Annæ, Margaritæ, Joanæ, sororum virginum heroidum Anglorum in mortem divæ Margeritæ Valesiæ, Navarrorum reginæ hecatodistichon, ut aliorum carmina. Parisiis, 1550, sm. 8vo. It contains several distichs which were altered in the French edition.

The Grand Cabinet Counsels unlocked. Lond. 1658. Bliss, orig. bind. 15s. Again, with new title, as ' Memorials of Court Affairs, and growth and continuation of the Civil Wars in France, betwixt the Huguenots and the Papists. Translated by Codrington.' Lond. 1658, sm. 8vo.

The Memorials of Margaret de Valoys, first Wife to Henry the IVth, King of France and Navarre, compiled in French by her own Royal Hand, and translated into English by R(obert) C(odrington). Lond. 1650, 8vo.—Lond. 1652, 8vo.—Lond. 1662, 8vo.

The Life of Marguerite d'Angoulême, Queen of Navarre. From unpublished Sources. By Martha Walker Freer. Lond. 1854, post 8vo. 2 vols. fronts.

— of Anjou. See BAUDIER, Mich. PREVOST, A. F.

— Countess of Richmond. See FISHER, Bp., p. 799.

MARGAROT, Maurice. Histoire d'un Voyage qui a duré près de cinque Ans. Lond. 1780, 8vo. 2 vols.

MARGETTS, George. Horary Tables for shewing by Inspection the apparent diurnal Motion of the Sun, Moon, and Stars, the Latitude of a Ship, &c. corresponding with any celestial Object. Lond. fol. 5s.

Engraved on copper-plates, Longitude Tables for correcting the Effect of Parallax and Refraction. Lond. (1790), 4to.—Lond. (1793), folio.

MARIA Misera Miseranda, or, a brief Relation of the Life and Death of an unfortunate young Maid in the county of Desmond in Ireland, together with the most horrid Murder of her Lover, an Englishman, committed by the Father of the said Virgin. Lond. 1674, 4to.

Nassau, pt. II. 362, 4l.

MARIANA, R. F. F. John de. The general History of Spain, from the first Peopling by Tubal, to the Death of K. Philip III. To which are added two Supplements. The whole translated from the Spanish by Captain J. Stevens. Lond. 1699, folio.

A good translation of a valuable historical work. Roxburghe, 8157, 9s. Brockett, 2078, 12s. Marquis of Townshend, 3214, 14s. LARGE PAPER. Hibbert, 5320, 18s. Sotheby's in 1824, 2l. 3s. Steevens, 1598, russia, 2l. 15s.

MARIGNY, Abbé de. The History of the Arabians, with Notes, Tables, and an Index. Translated from the French, with additional Notes by Nugent. Lond. 1758, 8vo. 4 vols.

Steevens, 1620, 12s. Hibbert, 5088, 16s. Willett, 1550, 2l. 4s.

MARINER, William. An Account of the Natives of the Tonga Islands, in the South Pacific Ocean, with an original Grammar and Vocabulary of their Language. Compiled and arranged from his Communications, by John Martin. The second Edition, with Additions. Lond. 1818, 8vo. 2 vols. front.

A very full, accurate, and interesting picture of the manners and character of a singular people, drawn from long and attentive observation on the spot.—1817, 8vo. 2 vols. Strettell, 872, 1l. 5s. Hibbert, 5087, 1l. 6s. Drury, 2055, 1l. 6s.

MARINI, Gio. Bat. A Poem on the Slaughter of the Innocents, translated by T. R. Lond. 1675, 8vo.

Bindley, pt. II. 1788, K. Charles the Second's copy, 11s. Hibbert, 5090, 1l. 1s. Echo. See Stanley, Thomas.

Sospetto d'Herode, translated by Crashaw. (Included in the Complete Works of Crashaw, edited by W. B. Turnbull. Lond. J. R. Smith, 1858, 12mo. 6s.)

MARINUS. Vita S. S. Marini Episcopi Hiberno-Davari, Martyris, et Aniani Archidiaconi confessoris, conscripta per Joh. de Via. Monachii, 1679, 4to.
Sotheby, 1833, 3l. 1s. A copy in the Grenville Collection.

MARITI, Abbé. Travels through Cyprus, Syria, and Palestine: with a general History of the Levant. Translated from the Italian. Lond. 1791-2, 8vo. 3 vols.
On all that relates to Cyprus this work is peculiarly interesting and full. Roxburghe, Suppl. 614, 11s. Willett, 1681, 2 vols. 12s. 6d.

MARJORIBANKS, George. Annals of Scotland, from the Year 1514 to the Year 1591. Edinb. 1814, 8vo.
Edited by J. G. Dalyell, Esq. Bright, 5s. 6d. See MAJORIBANKS.

MARKHAM, Francis. The Booke of Honovr, or five Decads of Epistles of Honovr. Lond. 1625, fol.
Pp. 200, dedicated to King [Charles I.] It contains 50 Epistles, each decade of which has its separate dedication. Gordonstoun, 1605, 6s. Rood, 3350, 6s. Bright, fine, 9s.
Five Decades of Epistles of War. Lond. 1022, folio. Bright, 1s. Utter, 10s.

— **Gervase, or Jarvis, or Jervis.** Various Works.
Gervase Markham commenced author and poet in the reign of Q. Elizabeth. He appears, says Harte, 'to be the first English writer who deserves to be called a hackney writer. All subjects seem to have been alike easy to him: yet as his thefts were innumerable, he has now and then stolen some very good things, and in great measure preserved their memory from perishing.' The following is extracted from Baker's Biographia Dramatica. 'Mem. That I, Gervase Markham, of London, Gent. do promise hereafter never to write any more book or books to be printed of the diseases or cures of any cattle, as horse, ox, cowe, sheepe, swine, and goates, &c. In witness whereof I have hereunto set my hand the 24th daie of July, 1617. Gervis Markham.' His baptismal name is printed indifferently with a G, an I, or a J.

A Discovrse of Horsmanshippe. Lond. by I(ohn) C(harlewood) for Rich. Smith, 1593, 4to. L, in fours. Dedicated to his father, 'Ma. Rob. Markham of Cotham in the County of Nottingham, Esq. by Jervis Markham,' after which, 'To the Gentlemen Readers.'—1596, 4to. 5s.

The Gentleman's Academy, 1595. See BARNES, Juliana.

The most Honorable Tragedie of Sir Richard Grinvile, Knight. Lond. Printed by J. Roberts for Richard Smith, 1595, 12mo. An heroic poem, dedicated to Lord Montioy, succeeded by three sonnets. (Sold at West's sale in 1773, for 12s. 6d.) Bindley, pt. II. 1798, 40l. 19s. now in the Grenville Collection. The only other copy known is in the Malone Collection, Bodleian Library.

The Poem of Poems, or Syons Muse, contayning the divine Song of King Solomon, divided into eight Eclogues. Lond. 1596, 12mo. Dedicated to Miss Elizabeth Sidney, daughter of Sir Philip Sidney. In the Malone Collection—1599, 12mo. See Warton's History of English Poetry, iv. 143-4.

How to chuse, ride, traine and dyet both hunting and running Horses, &c. Lond. 1596, 4to.—Lond. 1599, 4to.—Lond. 1606, 4to.

Devoreux. Vertues Teares for the Losse of K. Henry III. of France: and the untimely Death of Walter Devoreux, who was slaine before Roan in France. First written in French by Madam Genevefve Petau Mauleite, and paraphrastically translated into English by Jervis Markham. Lond. by J. Roberts for Thomas Millington, 1597, 4to. Inscribed to Dorothy, Countess of Northumberland, and Lady Penelope Illich, the sisters of Walter Devoreux. Brand, 4l. 13s. Heber, pt. viii. 3l. 6s.

The Teares of the Beloved: or, the Lamentation of Saint John, concerning the Death and Passion of Christ Iesus our Saviour. Lond. by Simon Stafford, 1600, 4to. Twenty leaves. Lloyd, 187,

MARKHAM, G.—continued.
2l. 6s. Heber, pt. i. 4584, 2l. 5s.; pt. viii. 2l.; pt. viii. 3l. 6s.
How to trayne and teach Horses to amble. Lond. 1605, 4to.
Ariosto's Conclusions of the Marriage of Rogero and Rodomantho, the neverconquered Pagan; written in French by Phillip Des Portes, and paraphrastically translated by G. M. According to Ritson, licensed to Nicholas Ling in 1598. It was printed under the title of Rodomonts Furies, in 1608, 4to. and dedicated to Lord Monteagle. Printed by V. S. for Nicholas Ling, 1607, 4to. Jolley, 1844 (unique).
The English Arcadia, alluding his beginning from Sir Phil. Sydneys Ending. Lond. 1607, 4to. Steevens, 1807, 11s.
Ariosto's Satires, 1608, 4to. Claimed by Robert Tofte. See TOFTE.
The second and last Partes of the first Booke of the English Arcadia, full of various Deceptions and much interchangeable Matter of Wit. Lond. 1613, 4to. Gordonstoun, 1579, 1l. 2s.
Cavelarice, or the English Horseman. Lond. 1607, 4to. The imprint is on the title to the second book.—n. d. 4to. Inglis, 957, 8s. White Knights, 2712, 13s. —Newly imprinted, corrected and augmented, with many worthy Secrets not before knowne. Lond. 1617, 4to. This work is divided into eight books separately, and with distinct titles. The second and third books are dated 1616.
The Dumbe Knight. A pleasant Comedy, acted sundry Times by the Children of his Maiesties Reuels. Written by Jaruis Markham. Lond. 1608, 4to. A—K 1, in fours, A I blank. See MACHIN.
The famous Whore, or Noble Courtezan: containing the lamentable Complaint of Paulina, the famous Roman Courtezan, sometime Mistress unto the great Cardinall Hippolyto of Este, translated into Verse from the Italian. Lond. 1609, 4to. Bindley, pt. iv. 165, 4l. 6s. Heber, pt. iv. 2l. 13s.; pt. viii. 2l. 11s. Caldecott, 2l. 10s.
Cure for all Diseases in Horses. Lond. 1610, 4to.
Country Contentments: or, the Husbandmans Recreations. Lond. 1611, 4to. This work is inscribed to Sir Theodore Newton, Knight. The first Book treats of Horses, with two new Treatises, the Arts of Hunting, Hawking, &c. &c. The second is entitled the English Huswife. —1615, 4to.—1631, 4to.—Fifth edition, 1631, 4to.—Sixth edition. Lond. 1639, 4to. —1640, 4to.—1649, 4to. Strettell, 1256, 6s. —1653, 4to.—Newly corrected, enlarged, and adorned with many excellent additions, 1675, 4to. pp. 96.
The English Husbandman; two parts. Lond. 1613, 4to. Haworth, 939, 10s. 6d.—

1614, 4to.—Newly reviewed, corrected and enlarged, 1635, 4to. Bright, 4s.
The seconde Book of the English Husbandman. Lond. 1614, 4to.
The Pleasures of Princes, containing a Discourse on the Art of Fishing with the Angle; and of breeding the Fighting Cocke. Lond. 1615, 4to.—1635. Sotheby's in 1823, 1l. 6s.
Methode or Epitome: wherein is shewed his approved Remedies for all Diseases whatever incident to Horses, &c. Lond. 1616, 12mo.—1623, 12mo.—1641, 12mo.
The Countrey Farme, 1616. See STEVENS, Charles.
Cheap and good Husbandry, for the well ordering of all Beasts and Fowls. Lond. 1614.—1615, 4to.—1631, 4to.—1648, 4to.—1664, 4to.—Thirteenth edition, 1676, 4to. pp. 165, dedicated to Richard Earl of Dorset.
Conceyted Letters newlye lade open, or a most excellent bundle of New Wit. Lond. 1618. R. Alsop, 4to. Black letter. See LETTERS. M. G.
A Farewell to Husbandry. Lond. 1620, 4to.—1631, 4to.—1625, 4to.—1631, 4to.—1638, 4to.—1649, 4to.—Now newly the tenth time revised, &c. 1676, 4to. pp. 130, dedicated to Bonham Norton, Esq.
Hungers Prevention or the whole Art of Fowling by Water and Land. Lond. for Anne Helme, 1621, 12mo. with cuts. Strettell, 591, 6s.—1655, 12mo. White Knights, 2905, 1l. 6s. Gardner in 1854, 17s. Bindley, pt. ii. 1789, 18s.
Herod and Antipater, a Tragedy. By Gervase Markham and William Sampson. Lond. 1622, 4to. Bindley, pt. iii. 519, 6s. Reed, 8198, 10s. Inglis' Old Plays, 59, 1l. 11s. 6d. Rhodes, 1613, 13s. Heber, pt. ii. 4s. 6d.
Honovr in his Perfection; or, a Treatise in Commendation of the Vertues and renowned vertuous Vndertakings of the illvstrious and heroicall Princes Henry Earle of Oxenford, Henry Earle of Southampton, Robert Earle of Essex; and the euer prais worthy and much honoured Lord, Robert Bartve, Lord Willoughby of Eresby: with a briefe Chronology of theirs and their Auncestours Actions. And to the eternall Memory of all that follow them now, or will imitate them hereafter, especially those three noble Instances, the Lord Wriouthesley, the Lord Delaware and the Lord Mountioy. Lond. 1624, 4to. The Dedication is signed G. M. Gordonstoun, 1604, 2l. 12s. 6d. Nassau, pt. ii. 1886, 7l. 10s. Heber, pt. viii. 1l. 11s. Gardner in 1854, 3l. 4s.
The Souldiers Accidence, or an Introduction to military Discipline; also the Cavalry, or Forme of framing Horse Troops. Lond. 1625, 4to. Inglis, 948, 4s. 6d.

MARKHAM, G.—continued.

Vox Militis, in two Parts. Lond. 1625, 4to. This is chiefly taken (if not altogether a reprint) from Barnaby Riche's Alarum to England. Gordonstoun, with the Souldiers Accidence, 1660, 10s. 6d. Inglis, 9/7, 2s. Hright, 15s.

A Way to get Wealth, by approved Rules of Practise in good Husbandry and Housewiferie, &c. &c. I. The husbanding and enriching of all sorts of Grounds, &c. II. The ordering and curing, with the Natures, &c. of all sorts of Cattell and Fowle fit for the use of Man, &c. III. The Office of the English Housewife in Physicke, Surgerie, &c. &c. IV. The Office of Planting, Grafting, and Gardening, &c. &c. The first three books gathered by C. M.; the last by Mr. Wm. Lawson, for the benefit of the Empire of Great Britain. Lond. 1625, 4to. 15s.

The Way to get Wealth. Lond. 1631, 4to. Bindley, pt. III. 873, 11s.—1638, 4to. —Lond. 1668, in six Books, 4to. The first five gathered by G. M.; the last by Master W. L. (Wm. Lawson). 4to.—1653, 4to. —1637, 4to.—Fourteenth edition, 1683, 4to. 10s. 6d.

The whole Art of Husbandry, in four Bookes. Lond. 1631, 4to. Reed, 1337, 5s. 6d. Goldsmid, 543, 10s. 6d.

The Inrichment of the Weald of Kent. Lond. 1631, 4to.—1638, 4to.—1649, 4to.— 1664, 4to. Nassau, pt. II. 142*, 9s.—1688, 4to.—1675, 4to. pp. 19, dedicated to Sir George Rivers, Kat. of Chafford in Kent.

The English Housewife. Lond. 1615, 4to.—Lond. 1625, under signature of J. R. 4to.—1631, 4to.—1637, 4to.—1649, 4to.— Now the eighth time much augmented, &c. 1676, 4to. pp. 188, dedicated to Frances, Countess Dowager of Exeter.

The Countrymans Recreations. Lond. 1653, 4to — With the Art of Angling. Lond. 1654, 4to. 15s.

The Art of Archerie. Lond. 1634, 12mo, with a frontispiece. Haworth, 741, 1l. 8s. Inglis, 901, morocco, 1l. 1s. Heber, pt. vi. 15s. Gardner, in 1854, 17s.

The faithfull Farrier, discovering some Secrets not in Print before. Lond. 1635. 8vo.—1638, 8vo.—1640, 4to.—1667, 4to.

The Masterpiece of Farriery, &c. Lond. 1636, 4to.—1656, 4to. Fonthill, 264, 11s.—1669, 4to.—1675, 4to.—1710, 4to.

Masterpiece revived; containing all Knowledge belonging to the Smith, Farrier or Horse-leach, &c., with the Countryman's Care for his other Cattle, &c., and the Compleat Jockey. Lond. 1683, 4to.

Souldier's Grammar. Lond. 1639, 4to. Heber, pt. v. 9s.

The Soldier's Exercises, in three Books. Third edition. Lond. 1643, 4to. Heber, pt. v. 8s. 6d.

The Country Housewife's Garden. Lond. 1648, 4to.

The Perfect Horseman. Published by Lancelot Thetford. Lond. 1660, 4to. with a frontispiece. Nassau, pt. I. 2193, 8s.— 1684. Towneley, pt. I. 662, 4s. 6d.

The Gentleman's accomplished Jockey; with the compleat Horseman and approved Farmer. Lond. 1772, 12mo.

The Young Sportsman's Instructor. (A very diminutive volume.) Sold at the Golden Ring in Little Britain, n. d. Broderip in 1860, 1l. 2s. Reprinted (for T. Gosden, in 1829.) White Knights, morocco, &c. ON VELLUM. Six copies printed.

Le Marescale, or the Horse-Marshall: also those Secreits which I practise but never imparted to any Man. G. M. 18mo. MS. Quere, if not printed under the title of 'The faithful Farrier.'

Proceedings, Speeches, &c. relative to a Challenge sent by Gervase Markham to Lord Darcy, MS. The quarrel between Markham and Lord Darcy arose from his Lordship's dog 'Bowser' having been ' in danger to be trodden on' by Markham, in a hunting party at Sir Gervase Clifton's. On Nov. 27, 1616, Markham was censured by the Star Chamber, and fined in the sum of 500l. for sending the challenge.

MARKHAM, Capt. Robert. The Description of that ever to be famed Knight, Sir Iohn Byrgh, Colonell Generall of his Maiesties Armie; with his last Seruice at the Isle of Ree and his vnfortunate Death there when the Armie had most need of such a Pilote. Printed 1628, 4to. (in Verse.)

Fourteen leaves, with port. of Burgh by Cecil. A notice of the work will be found in Drydges' Censura Literaria. Gordonstoun, 1569, 14l. 14s. Bindley, pt. III. 834*, 15l.; resold Heber, pt. IV. 6l. 11s. Now in the Grenville Collection.

Memoirs of the Military Transactions of Sir John Burroughs (or Burgh), Knt., Col. Gen. of the King's Armies in the Expedition to the Isle of Rhee; with his Character by way of Elegie, written in 1627. Lond. 1758, 4to.

MARKLAND, Abraham, D.D. Ptery-plegia, or the Art of Shooting Flying. Lond. 1727, 8vo.

A curious Poem.—1785.—1767. Sermons preached in the Cathedral Church of Winchester. Lond. 1720, 8vo. 2 vols. 8s.

— Abraham. Poems on his Majesty's Birth and Restoration, his Highness Prince Rupert's, and the Duke of Albemarle's naval Victories, the late great Pestilence and Fire of London. Lond. 1667, 4to. Bliss, 1l. 2s. Caldecott, 1l. 6s.

MARKLAND, James Heywood. A Letter to the Earl of Aberdeen, K.T., P.S.A., on the Expediency of attaching a Museum of Antiquities to that Institution. Lond. 1829, 8vo. Pp. 19. *See* Quarterly Review, vol. xxxviii.

Remarks on the Antiquity and Introduction of Surnames into England. 1813, 4to. Archæol. vol. xviii.

Remarks on the early Use of Carriages in England, and on the Modes of Travelling adopted by our Ancestors. 1823, 4to. Archæol. xx. plates.

Remarks on English Churches. Oxf. 1842, 12mo. 6s. 6d.—Third edition. Oxf. 1843, 12mo.—Fourth edition. Lond. Murray, 1849, 12mo. 6s. 6d.

On the Reverence due to Holy Places. Lond. 1845, 12mo. 2s.—Third edition. Lond. 1846, fcap. 8vo. 2s.

See Chester Mysteries. The Introduction has been reprinted in Roswell's edition of Malone's Shakespeare, 1821.

—— Jeremiah. De Græcorum quinta Declinatione imparisyllabica, et inde formata Latinorum Quæstio grammatica. 1761, 4to.

Forty copies printed for presents. Bindley, pt. III. 562, 6s. This valuable grammatical treatise was reprinted with Markland's edition of Euripidis Supplices Mulieres, 1763, &c.

Epistola critica, in qua Horatii Loca aliquot et aliorum Veterum emendantur. Cantab. 1723, 8vo. An excellent work. Williams, 1181. morocco, 12s. Heath, 59. FINE PAPER. Dent, pt. l. 1383, russia, 6s. Williams, 1182, mor. 1l. 7s. A copy is in the British Museum, with MS. notes by R. Bentley.

Remarks on the Epistles of Cicero to Brutus, and of Brutus to Cicero, with a Dissertation upon four Orations ascribed to M. T. Cicero, viz. 1. Ad Quirites post Reditum. 2. Post Reditum in Senatu. 3. Pro Domo sua, ad Pontifices. 4. De Haruspicum Responsis, &c. with Notes, &c. Lond. 1745, 8vo. Gosset, 3349, 8s. Heath, 4170, 10s. 6d. LARGE PAPER. In this work Mr. Markland attempts to prove that all the above pieces are spurious, and the work of some sophist.

MARLBOROUGH, John Churchill, Duke of. Life and military History of. Lond. 1764, folio.

White Knights, 2774, with plates and portrait inserted, morocco, 4l. 6s.

Journal of the Duke of Marlbro's Marches, Battles, &c. By John Millner. Lond. 1733, 8vo. Roxburghe, 6523. 3s. White Knights, 2907, 16s.

The Conduct of the Duke of Marlborough during the present War, with original Papers. Lond. 1712, 8vo. Roxburghe, 6520, 6s.; 6521, with Remarks by a M.P. 11s.

The Anthem performed at the Funeral of the Duke of Marlborough, set to Music by Bononchini. folio. White Knights, 2775, 2l. 5s.

The History of John, Duke of Marlborough. Lond. 1741, 8vo.

Histoire de J. Churchill, Duc de Marlborough (composée par Madgwell, revue et rédigée par l'Abbé H. Dutens.) Paris, 1806, 8vo. 3 vols. Written by the command of Buonaparte, with a view to exalt his own victories upon the defeats of the generals of Louis XIV. Heber, pt. II. 2s.

Despatches, 1702-12, edited by Sir Geo. Murray. Lond. 1845, 8vo. 5 vols. 5l., reduced to 2l. 2s.

Military Life of, by Sir Archibald Allison. Lond. and Edinb. 1847, 8vo. 18s.

Life of, by Macfarlane, 12mo.—By C. W. Buck. Lond. (Murray's Family Library) 1839, 18mo.—red. Tegg, 1849, 3s. 6d. *See* CAMPBELL, John. COXE, William. LEDIARD, Thomas. MACQUEFF, J.

—— Sarah, Duchess of. The Opinions of Sarah, Duchess Dowager of Marlborough, published from her original MSS. Edinb. 1788, 12mo.

Edited by Sir David Dalrymple, Lord Hailes. Gough, 2072, 1l. 2s. White Knights, 2613, 1l. 10s. Constable, 581, 5s. 6d. Roswell, 2089, 5s. 6d. Hibbert, 5094, 6s. 6d. Bindley, pt. II. 1836, with her autograph inserted, 1l. 7s. Roxburghe, 6525, 18s. Bliss, 13s.

The secret History of Queen Zarah and the Zarazians. Lond. 1705. Two Parts. White Knights, 2620, morocco, 1l.—Fourth edition, Lond. 1743, 8vo.—1749, White Knights, 2621, 10s. Bliss, 6s.

Histoire secrette de la Reine Zarah et des Zarazions, ou la Duchesse de Marlborough demasquée. Imprimée dans le Royaume d'Albigion, 1708 — Oxford (Hollande), 1711-12, 12mo. 2 pts. in 1 vol. 5s. This edition has a key.

The Lives and Characters of the Duchess of Marlborough's four Daughters (viz. the Duchess of Montague, the Countess of Bridgwater, the Countess of Sunderland, and the Lady Visc. Reyalton), with their Portraits and other Grub Street Anecdotes. 1710. *See* MISCELLANIES, 1753.

The Duchess of Marlborough's Vision. 1711, folio.

5 B

MARLBOROUGH, Duch. of—*contd.*

An Account of the Conduct of the Dowager Duchess of Marlborough, from her first Coming to Court to the Year 1710. Lond. 1742, 8vo, privately printed. Laing papers. Hibb, 6s. 6d. Written by Nath. Hooke, the Roman Historian, on behalf of the Duchess, by whom he is said to have been handsomely paid.—Another edition, 1742, 8vo. Bindley, pt. l. 23, with Ralph's Answer, 7s. Hibbert, 5063, 12s. North, pt. l. 5, 8s. 6d. Drury, 2259, with Ralph's Answer, 9s. 6d. Willett, 1583, with the answer, 11s. An essay on this subject by Dr. Sam. Johnson appeared in the Gentleman's Mag. for 1742.

A Review of a late Treatise entituled An Account, &c. Lond. 1742, 8vo.

A Continuation of the Review of a late Treatise, &c. Lond. 1742, 8vo.

A full Vindication of the Duchess Dowager of Marlborough. Lond. 1742, 8vo.

The other Side of the Question. Lond. 1742, 8vo.

The Sarah-ad; or, a Flight for Fame, a burlesque Poem. Lond. 1742. White Knights, 2618, 1l.

Memoirs of Sarah, Duchess of Marlborough. 1744. White Knights, 2610, 11s.

The Life of the Duchess of Marlborough, with Remarks on her Will. Lond. 1745, 8vo.

Verses upon the late D—ss of M—, by Mr. P. Printed for W. Webb near St. Paul's, 1746. A single sheet. This character of Atossa is one of the printed lies of the day.

The Character of a certain great Duchess deceased, by a certain great Poet lately deceased (Alex. Pope). *See* his Epistle on the Characters of Women, L 115, *et seq.* This character was an insertion, added with no great honour to the poet's gratitude. It is reprinted in the eighth volume of the Harleian Miscellany.

In the Grenville Library is a Collection of Satires on the Duchess, *See* Catalogue, vol. ii. p. 307.

Private Correspondence, edited by Mrs. Thomson. Lond. 1637, 8vo. 2 vols. port. 10s. 6d.

Memoirs of the Duchess of Marlborough. By Mrs. Thomson. Lond. 1839, 8vo. 2 vols. 10s. 6d.

See Miscellanies, 1753.

MARLBOROUGH GEMS.—Gemmæ Antiquæ. Choix de Pierres antiques gravées de son Cabinet. Lond. 1781-90, folio, 2 vols.

One hundred copies printed for presents. This fine collection of Gems, made by George Spencer, third Duke of Marlborough, was formed principally of the cabinets of Lady Betty Germaine (valued at 7000l., the 'Cupid and Psyche' alone, the finest antique intaglio extant, at 500l., presented by her Ladyship to the Duke); and that collected by Wm. Ponsonby, second Earl of Besborough, who sold it to the Duke for 5000l. The plates were executed by Bartolozzi, &c. The Latin exposition to vol. l. was written by Jacob Bryant, and the French translation by Dr. Maty; that to vol. ii. by Dr. William Cole, and the translation into French by Louis Dutens. Dent, pt. ii. 759, morocco, 63l. Hibbert, 5323, mor. 7ll. 8s. Sotheby's in May, 1820, 73l. 10s. Sotheby's in Dec. 1823, 22l. 9s. Combe, 4462, morocco, 28l.

MARLBOROUGH GARLAND, a real Anecdote from common Life. 1795, 4to.

White Knights, 2713, 7s.

MARLEBURGH, James, Earl of. Fair Warnings to a careless World; with the last words of 140 of the most learned Persons of England, &c. Lond. 1665, 4to.

Bliss, 1s. 6d.

MARLIN. *See* **MERLIN.**

MARLOE, C. *See* **MARLOWE.**

MARLORAT, Augustin. Propheticæ et Apostolicæ, id est, totius diuinæ ac canonicæ Scripturæ Thesaurus, Ordine alphabetico digestus. Ex Augustini Marlorati Aduersariis a Guliel. Feuguereio in Codicem relatus. Lond. 1574, folio.

This work hath the approbation of Abp. Parker, and the Queen's privilege. The works of this eminent protestant divine, who is classed among the reformers of the church, are now in little estimation.

A catholike and ecclesiasticall Exposition of the holy Gospell after S. Mathewe, translated out of Latine into Englishe by Thomas Tymme Mynister. Lond. 1570, folio. Dedicated to 'Sir William Brooke, Lord Cobham, Lorde Warden of the Cinque Portes.'

Prayers on the Psalmes, translated by Rodolph Waterup. Lond. 1571, 18mo.

A catholike Exposition vpon the Revelation of Sainct Iohn. Lond. Byneeman, 1574, 4to. Dedicated to Sir Walter Mildmay, Knyghte.' Fol. 318, besides title, Table, Faultes, 15 leaves. *See* CALVIN.

A catholike and ecclesiasticall Expostion of the holy Gospell after S. John. Lond. 1575, folio. Dedicated to 'Lord Thomas Earle of Sussex,' &c.

A catholike and ecclesiasticall Exposition of the holy Gospell after S. Marke and Luke, translated by Thomas Timme. Lond. 1583, 4to. pp. 341, 1l. 1s.

A catholicke and ecclesiasticall Exposition on S. Jude, translated by J. D., Minister. Lond. 15s4, 8vo. Inglis, 9O2, 2s.

A Treatise of the Starre against the Holy Ghost. Translated out of French. Lond. by John Allde, 1565, 16mo. C, in eights.

Enchiridion Locorum communium theologicorum ex Marloratii Thesauro, &c. Lond. 1568, 8vo.

MARLOW, ISAAC. Controversie of Singing brought to an End. Lond. 1696, 8vo.

Sotheby's in 1824, 15s.

Truth soberly Defended, in a Reply to Benjamin Keach, concerning Psalm Singing. Lond. 1692, 8vo. 5s.

— Jeremiah. A Book of Cyphers or Letters reversed; very pleasant and usefull for Engravers, Chacers, and Others. Engraved by N. Glascock. Lond. 1683, 8vo.

MARLOWE, Christopher. Works (edited by George Robinson, Esq.) Lond. Pickering, 1826, post 8vo. 3 vols.

Works, with Notes, and some Account of his Life and Writings, by the Rev. Alex. Dyce. Lond. Pickering, 1850, post 8vo. 3 vols. LARGE PAPER, 17 printed. An entirly new Text, formed on a Collation of the early Copies.

'Kit Marlowe is beyond comparison the finest of the neglected dramatists.'

Tamburlaine the Greate, who, from the state of a Scythian shepheard, became a most puissant and mightye monarque, and (for his tyranny and terrour in warre) was tearmed 'The Scourge of God,' devided into two tragicall discourses. Lond. by Richard Jones, 1590, 8vo. A to I, in eights. In the Malone Collection at Oxford. Roxburghe, 5l. 15s.; bought by Kemble, now in the Devonshire Collection.—Another edition, two parts, Lond. 1605-6, 4to. Inglis' Old Plays, 9l. 12s. Roxburghe, 1805, pt. 1. only, 12s. Part II. date 1605. Heber, both parts, 4l. 10s. Jolley, 2 pts. 5l. 15s. In the British Museum Catalogue, Tamburlaine the Great, 1605, is attributed to John Marston.

The Tragedie of Dido, Queene of Carthage. Written by Christopher Marlowe and Thomas Nash. Lond. by the Widowe

Orwin, for Thomas Woodcocke, 1594, 4to. Dr. Wright, in 1787, 16l. 16s., purchased by Mr. Malone, and now in the Bodleian. A copy, purchased by Henderson the actor of Yardley the bookseller for four-pence, in the Kemble Collection, Steevens in 1800, (presented to him by Is. Reed, Esq.) 17l.; resold, Roxburghe in 1812, 17l. 17s.; purchased by Sir E. Brydges, resold Heber, in 1834. 35l. A copy is in the Bridgwater Collection. A transcript made by Henderson, afterwards Steevens', then Forsters', Sotheby, 1860, russia.

The true Tragedie of Richards Duke of Yorke, and the Death of good King Henrie the Sixt, with the whole Contention betweene the two Houses Lancaster and Yorke, as it was sundrie Times acted by the Right Honourable the Earl of Pembroke his Servants. Lond. by P. S. (Peter Short), 1595, 8vo. G. Chalmers, unique, 131l. See RICHARD III. SHAKSPEARE.

The troublesome Raigne and lamentable Death of Edward the Second, King of England. &c. As it was publickly acted by the Earle of Pembroke his Servauntes. Lond. by Richard Bradocke for William Jones (1598), 4to. Copies in the British Museum and Malone's Collection.—1604. —1612, for Roger Barnes, 4to. Heber, pt. II. 1l. 8s.—1622, 4to. Rhodes, 1814, 16s. Roxburghe, 5407, 1l. 6s.

The tragical History of the Life and Death of Doctor Faustus. Lond. 1604, 4to. FIRST EDITION, in the Malone Collection. Lond. by G. E. for John Wright, and are to be sold at Christ Church Gate.—1609, 4to. BLACK LETTER (unknown to Mr. Dyce in 1850), 14 leaves. A copy in the Hamburg Public Library.—Lond. for J. Wright, 1611, 4to. Heber, pt. II. 7l. 10s. These two differ materially from after editions. —Lond. 1616, 4to. BLACK LETTER.—Lond. 1619, 4to. Inglis' Old Plays, 60, 9l. 14s. In the title-page is a woodcut of Mephostophilus (played by Edward Alleyn) in his dramatic costume.—With new additions. By Ch. Mar. Lond. 1624, 4to. A —ll 3, in fours. BLACK LETTER—1631, 4to. Roxburghe, 5401, 1l. 16s.—Printed with new Additions, with several new Scenes, together with the Actors Names, Lond. 1663, 4to. with a frontispiece. Hibbert, 5192, 10s. Rhodes, 1616, 2l. 16s.

Hero and Leander, begunne by Christopher Marloe and finished by George Chapman. Lond. 1606 (third edition), 4to. pp. 68. Sir M. M. Sykes, pt. II. 400, 94.9s. Bright, cropped, 2l. 4s. Hibl. Anglo.Poet. 487, 15l.—1609, 4to. Reed, 6976, 17s.—1613. Heber, pt. IV. 1l. 15s. Caldecott, 1l. 2s. —1629, 4to. Heber, pt. IV. 10s.—Midgley, 3l. 5s. Utterson, 2l. 9s. Heber, pt. IV. 17.5s.; pl. VIII. 1l. 16s.—1637, 4to. pp. 90. Heber, pt. VIII. 18s. Hibbert, 5197, 2l. 18s. Inglis,

MARLOWE, Chris.—*continued*.
958, with plates by Faithorne inserted, morocco, *£*. 13s. 6d. Bibl. Anglo-Poet. 488, 4*l*. 4s.—The first two Sestiads only were written by Marlowe, and these were first printed, Lond. E. Blount, 1598, 4to. Heber, pt. viii. 4*l*. 6s. This edition has no divisions or arguments, as afterwards when completed by Chapman, and printed in 1606, 4to.; a copy of which is in the Malone Collection.—New edition, revised and corrected, with a critical preface by S. W. Singer, Esq. Chiswick, 1821, 12mo.

The famous Tragedy of the Rich Jew of Malta. Written by Christopher Marlo. Lond. 1633, 4to. Field, 291, 10s. 6d. Boswell, 1962, 10s. 6d. Roxburghe, 5403, 15s. Bindley, pt. iii. 524, 16s. Rhodes, 1815, 1*l*. 1s.—With a preface by W. Shone. Lond. Reynell and Son, 1810, 8vo. 2s. 6d.

Lust's Dominion, or the Lascivious Queen, a Tragedie. Written by Christofer Marlow, Gent. Lond. 1657, 12mo. Rhodes, 1617, 3s. Field, 292, 8s. 6d. Nassau, pt. i. 2106, 9s. Roxburghe, 5404, 9s. 6d. Bindley, pt. ii. 1062, 1*l*. 9s.—1661, 12mo. Rhodes, 1618, 6s.

The Massacre at Paris, with the Death of the Duke of Guise. Lond. by E. A. for Edward White, 12mo, no date. A–D 6, in eights, A 1 blank. Inglis' Old Plays, 62, 10*l*. 10s. Bindley, pt. ii. 1061, 8*l*. 13s. Perry, pt. ii. 722, 11*l*. 5s.; resold Heber, pt. ii. 2*l* 3s. A copy in the Malone Collection, Bodleian Library. A MS. transcript by Ritson, with an account of Marlowe and his works, Roxburghe, 5405, 4*l*. 4s.

Marlowe's Plays (6) were printed, with some few introductory notices, by Oxberry, in his 'Theatre,' between 1818 and 1829, and were afterwards collected into one volume, with a general title, undated.

Marlowe's Poems have recently been edited by Mr. Rob. Bell, in his annotated edition of the British Poets.

Epigrammes and Elegies by J. D. and C. M. *See* DAVIES, John.

See COLUTHUS, LUCAN, M. C.; OVID.

MAR-MARTIN. *See* MARTIN MAR-PRELATE.

MARMET, M. de. Entertainments of the Court at Paris, englished by Thomas Sainterf. Lond. 1658, 8vo.
Boswell, 1803, 5s. 6d. G. Chalmers, 6s.

MARMION, Shackerley. Cupid and Psyche, an epick Poem. Lond. 1637, 4to.
With an engraved title-page Nassau, pt. ii. 143, 11s. Heber, pt. viii. 2*l* 16s.—

1638, 4to, with a frontispiece. Sotheby's in March 1817, 6*l*. 16s. 6d.—New edition, edited by S. W. Singer, Esq. Chiswick, 1820, 12mo. In this reprint several passages are omitted.

Hollands Leaguer, an excellent Comedy. Lond. 1634, 4to. Bindley, pt. iii. 525, 6s. Roxburghe, 5410, 7s. 6d. Inglis' Old Plays, 63, 14s. Heber, pt. ii. 7s. 6d.—1632, 4to.

A fine Companion, a Play. Lond. 1633, 4to. Boswell, 1698, 5s. Roxburghe, 5409, 6s. 6d. Heber, pt. ii. 6s. 6d.

The Antiquary, a Comedy. Lond. 1641, 4to. Boswell, 1694, 6s. Roxburghe, 5408, 6s. Heber, pt. ii. 6s. 6d. Reprinted in Dodsley's Collection of Old Plays. Ant. à Wood mentions an edition of the date of 1633.

Cupid's Courtship; or, the Celebration of a Marriage between the God of Love and Psiebe. By S. M. Lond. 1666, 16mo. A 4 leaves, B to F, in eights.

MARMONTEL, J. F. Memoirs, written by himself; containing his literary and political Life, and Anecdotes of the principal Characters of the eighteenth Century. Lond. 1805, 12mo. 4 vols. 12s.—Second edition, 1806.

Moral Tales, translated by C. Dennis and R. Lloyd. Lond. 1781, 8vo. 3 vols.—Lond. and Perth, 1792, 12mo. 4 vols.—Lond. Cadell, 18*l*0, 12mo. 3 vols. 10s. 6d.

New Moral Tales, translated from the French, 1792, 12mo. 2 vols.—Second edition improved. Lond. 1794, 12mo. 4 vols. 10s.

Tales of an Evening, followed by the Flemmel Breton. 1792, 12mo. 2 vols.

The Incas, or the Destruction of Peru, 1777, 12mo. 2 vols.—Second edition, 1814, 18mo. 2 vols.

Belisarius, translated by F. Ashmore. Lond. 1769, 8vo.—Lond. 1820, 12mo. 3s.; with plates, 6s. Frequently reprinted in small forms.

MARMOR NORFOLCIENSE. *See* JOHNSON, Samuel, LL.D.

MARMOR Sandvicense cum Commentario et Notis a J. Taylor, LL.D. Cantab. 1743, 4to.
Gough, 3786, mor. 1*l*. 11s. 6d. Heath, 4661, 10s. 6d.

MARMORA Arundelliana, &c. *See* OXFORD.

MARMYUN FAMILY. *See* BANKS, T. C., p. 109.

MARNIX, Phil. de. The Beehive of the Romish Church, translated by George Gilpin. Lond. 1578, 12mo.

Reprinted, Lond. 1623, 24mo.

MAROCCUS EXTATICUS, or Bankes Bay Horse in a Trance; a Discourse set downe in a merry Dialogue betweene Bankes and his Beast: anatomizing some Abuses and bad Tricks of this Age, &c. By John Dando, the Wiredrawer of Hadley, and Harrie Runt, Head Ostler of Bosomes Inne. Lond. for Cuthbart Burby, 1595, 4to.

With a woodcut. Gordonstown, 1596, 13/. 2s. 6d., resold Saunders' in 1818, 10/. 10s. Bindley, pt. i. 745, 13/. 5s., resold Perry, pt. i. 335, 9/. 9s. Jolley, 16/. 16s. Reprinted for the Percy Society, No. 47, q. v. In Appendix. A notice of this curious tract will be found in Reed's edition of Shakespeare, vol. vii.

MAROTTES A VENDRE, ou Tribouliet Tabletier. Lond. 1812, fcp. 8vo. 10s. 6d.

Selected from many works of great rarity. On PINK OR COLOURED PAPER. Six copies printed. Goldsmid, 490, 1/. 11s. 6d. White Knights, 2620, 13s. Heber, pt. vi. 9s.

MAR-PEOPLE, Sir Martin. His Coller of Essex, 1590, 4to.

In verse. King and Lochée's in March, 1810, bt. 6d.

MARPRELATE. See MARTIN MARPRELATE. PENRY, John.

MARRIAGE.—The Fyftene Joyes of Maryage. Lond. by W. de Worde, 1509, 4to.

One hundred and forty-one leaves, exclusive of the title-page and fly leaf at the end. Heber, pt. iv, 10/. 5s.

The Payne and Sorrowe of euyl Maryage. Lond. by W. de Worde, (1509), 4to. Four leaves. Heber, pt. iv. 4/. 10s. Reprinted for the Percy Society, No. 3. See APPENDIX.

A Complaynt of them that be to soone maryed. Lond. by W. de Worde, (1535), 4to. Thirteen leaves; unique. Heber, pt. viii. 11/.

A Complaynte of them that ben to late maryed. Lond. by W. de Worde, (1535), 4to. Eight leaves. Heber, pt. iv. 4/. 2s. 6d.

The Marriage of Wit and Wisdom, an ancient Interlude, edited by J. O. Halliwell, Esq. for the Shakespeare Society, No. 31. See APPENDIX.

L'Abus du Marriage. 1641, oblong 4to. 51 plates by Crispin de Pas. With metrical descriptions in French, Dutch, and English; the preface is signed by the engraver. Heber, pt. iv. 1422, mor. 1/. 13s.

Marriage à la Mode, in six Cantos, being an Explanation of Hogarth's Prints. Lond. 1746, 8vo. Field, 1607, 5s.

The Married Men's Feast to all who master their Wives. 1671, 4to. Bindley, pt. iii. 368, 1/. 12s.

A Treatise concerning the Use and Abuse of the Marriage Bed. 1727. See DEFOE, Daniel.

Hymen, or the Ceremonies used in Marriage by every Nation in the World, shewing the Oddity of some, the Absurdity of others, and the Drollery of many. Lond. 1760, 12mo. 5s.

Marriage and Wiving. See TOFTE, R. A Description of the Land of Wedlock. Lond. 1603, 12mo.

See GAYA, Louis de. LIGNAC, M. MATHMONY. NICCHOLES, Alex.

MARRIOT, John. The great Eater of Grayes-Inne, or the Life of Mr. Marriot the Cormorant; with many pleasant Stories of his Travels into Kent and other Places. By G. F., Gent. Lond. 1652, 4to.

Pp. 41, with title, frontispiece, and To the Reader, two leaves. Bindley, pt. ii. 1631, 14/. 1s. resold Hibbert, 5196, 4/.

A Letter to Mr. Marriot, from a Friend of his: wherein his Name is redeemed from that Detraction G. F. Gent. hath indeavoured to fasten upon him, by a scandalous and defamatory Libell, intituled The great Eater of Grayes Inne, or the Life of Mariot the Cormorant, &c. Lond. 1652, 4to. Four leaves, including a woodcut, representing G. F. Gent. asking pardon of Marriot, under which are six lines commencing 'Oh I confesse my fault, forgive therefore,' &c.

The English Mountebank: or, a physical Dispensatory. By J. Marriot, of Gray's-Inn, Gent. Lond. 1652, 4to. Four leaves, including a woodcut of Marriot, with four verses, commencing 'If thou observ'st these Rules, and tak'st my Physick,' &c.

The above articles relative to 'the Cormorant' are in the British Museum. Two copies of verses on him will be found in the works of Charles Cotton, Esq.

MARRIOTT, Rev. William. The Antiquities of Lyme and its Vicinity. Stockport, 1810, small 4to.

Pp. xii and 699, Index 3 pages, also 15 plates at pp. 154, 200, 202, 217, 224, 231, 253, 303, 306, 308, 318, 324, 334, 304 and 373.

MARRYAT, Frederick, Capt. R.N.
Code of Signals for the use of Vessels employed in the Merchant Service. Lond. 1837, 8vo. 10s. 6d.—
Eighth edition, entirely revised and corrected. Lond. 1841, 8vo. 10s. 6d.

This admirable invention is now in use in the royal and mercantile service, not only of this country but of foreign nations. Captain Marryat twice received the public thanks of the Shipowners' Society for it, and upon its being translated into French, Paris, 1840, was complimented by Louis Philippe with the cross of the Legion of Honour.

— Frank Mildmay, or the Naval Officer. Lond. 1829, post 8vo. 3 vols. 1l. 11s. 6d.—Colburn's Standard Novelists, 1836, 12mo. 6s. Reissued 1860, 8s. 6d.—Cheap edit., Routledge, 1s. 6d.

— King's Own. Lond. Colburn, 1830, post 8vo. 3 vols. 1l. 11s. 6d.—Bentley's Standard Novels, 1838, 12mo. 6s. Reissued, 1849, at 3s.6d.—Cheap edit., Routledge, 1s. 6d.

— Newton Forster. Lond. Bentley, 1832, post 8vo. 3 vols. 1l. 11s. 6d.—Bentley's Standard Novels, 1838, 12mo. 6s. Reissued, 1849, 3s. 6d.—Cheap edit., Routledge, 1s. 6d.

— Peter Simple. Lond. Saunders & Otley, 1833, post 8vo. 3 vols. 1l. 11s. 6d.—Bentley's Standard Novels, 1838, 12mo. 6s. Reissued, 1849, 3s. 6d.—Cheap edit., Routledge, 1s. 6d.

— Jacob Faithful. Lond. Saunders & Otley, 1835, post 8vo. 3 vols. 1l. 11s. 6d.—Bentley's Standard Novels, 1838, 12mo. 6s. Reissued, 1849, 3s. 6d.—Cheap edit., Routledge, 1s. 6d.

— Pacha of Many Tales. Lond. Saunders & Otley, 1835, post 8vo.
3 vols. 1l. 11s. 6d. — Bentley's Standard Novels, 1839, 12mo. 6s. Reissued, 1849, 3s. 6d.—Cheap edit. Routledge, 1s. 6d.

— Japhet in Search of a Father. Lond. Saunders & Otley, 1836, post 8vo. 3 vols. 1l. 11s. 6d.—Bentley's Standard Novels, 1839, 12mo. 6s. Reissued, 1849, 3s. 6d. — Cheap edit., Routledge, 1s. 6d.

— Midshipman Easy. Lond. Saunders & Otley, 1836, post 8vo. 3 vols. 1l. 11s. 6d. — Bentley's Standard Novels, 1838, 12mo. 6s. Reissued, 1849, 3s. 6d. — Cheap edit., Routledge, 1s. 6d.

— Pirate and Three Cutters, illustrated with 20 engravings, from drawings by Clarkson Stanfield, R.A. Lond. Longman, 1836, 8vo. 1l. 11s. 6d.—Fourth edition. Lond. Bohn, 1851, 15s.— Fifth edition, same plates, 1854, 8vo. 10s. 6d.— New edition, with same plates, and Life of the Author. Lond. (Bohn's Illustrated Library), 1860, 5s.

— Snarley Yow, or the Dog-Fiend. Lond. Colburn, 1837, post 8vo. 3 vols. 1l. 11s. 6d.—Bentley's Standard Novels, 1839, 12mo. 6s. Reissued, 1849, 3s. 6d. — Cheap edit., Routledge, 1s. 6d.

— Phantom Ship. Lond. Colburn, 1839, post 8vo. 3 vols. 1l. 11s. 6d. — Bentley's Standard Novels, 1840, 12mo. 6s. Reissued, 1849, 3s. 6d.—Cheap edit., Routledge, 1s. 6d.

— Diary in America, with Remarks on its Institutions. Two Series. First Series. Lond. Longman, 1839, post 8vo. 3 vols. 1l. 11s. 6d.—Second Series. Lond. Longman, 1839, post 8vo. 3 vols. 1l. 11s. 6d.

— Olla Podrida. Lond. Longman, 1840, post 8vo. 3 vols. 1l. 11s. 6d.—Bentley's Standard

MARRYAT, Capt.—*continued.*
Novels, 1841, 12mo. 6s.—New edition, Bohn, *in the Press.*
— Poor Jack, illustrated with 46 fine wood engravings, after the designs of Clarkson Stanfield, R.A. Lond. Longman, 1840, 8vo. 14s.—Second edition (stereotyped). Lond. Bohn, 1842, 9s.—New edition, same plates. Bohn, 1859, 8vo. 6s.
— Joseph Rushbrook, or the Poacher. Lond. Colburn, 1841, post 8vo. 3 vols. 1l. 11s. 6d.—Bentley's Standard Novels, 1842, 12mo. 6s. Reissued, 1849, 3s. 6d.—Cheap edit., Routledge, 1s. 6d.
— Percival Keene. Lond. Colburn, 1842, post 8vo. 3 vols. 1l. 11s. 6d.—Bentley's Standard Novels, 1843, 12mo. 6s. Reissued, 1849, 3s. 6d.—Cheap edit., Routledge, 1s. 6d.
— Travels and Adventures of Monsieur Violet, in California, Sonora, and Western Texas. Lond. Longman, 1843, post 8vo. 3 vols. 1l. 11s. 6d.—Bentley's Standard Novels, 1844, 12mo. 6s. Reissued, 1849, at 3s. 6d.—Cheap edit., J. Hodgson, 1s. 6d.
— Masterman Ready, or the Wreck of the Pacific. Written for young people (for his own children). Lond. Longman, 1841, 12mo. 3 vols. 1l. 2s. 6d.—New edition, with 92 wood engravings. Lond. 1853, 12mo. 3 vols. 12s.—New edition, in 1 vol. 93 wood engravings. Lond. Bohn, 1857, 12mo. 6s. Reissued, with the same engravings, in Bohn's Illustrated Library, 1860, post 8vo. 5s.
— Privateer's Man, one hundred years ago. Adventures by Sea and Land, in civil and savage Life, one hundred years ago. Lond. Longman, 1844, 12mo. 2 vols. 12s.—Second edition, with 8 plates, in 1 vol. Lond. Bohn, 1859, 12mo. 6s. Reissued in Bohn's Illustrated Library, 1860, post 8vo. 5s.
— Settlers in Canada. Written for young people. Lond. Longman, 1844, 12mo. 2 vols. 12s.—New edition, with 10 engravings on steel, in 1 vol. Bohn, 1854, 6s. Reissued in Bohn's Illustrated Library, 1860, post 8vo. 5s.
— Mission, or Scenes in Africa. Written for young people. Lond. Longman, 1845, 12mo. 2 vols. 12s.—New edition, with Illustrations by John Gilbert, in 1 vol. Lond. Bohn, 1856, 12mo. 6s. Reissued in Bohn's Illustrated Library, 1860, post 8vo. 5s.
— Children of the New Forest. Lond. Hurst, 1847, 12mo. 2 vols. 10s.—New edition, in 1 vol. Routledge, 12mo. 5s.
— Little Savage. Lond. Hurst, 1847, 12mo. 2 vols. 10s.—New edition, in 1 vol. Routledge, 12mo. 5s.
— Valerie; an Autobiography. Lond. Colburn, 1849, post 8vo. 2 vols. 1l. 1s.—Cheap edition, in 1 vol. Routledge, 12mo. 1s. 6d.

Captain Marryat, who died in 1848, was one of the most pleasing of our romance writers, and especially excelled in Naval Stories. Among his later works worthy of especial notice is his Masterman Ready, which has all the charm of Robinson Crusoe, and will ever be a prime favourite with young people. It was the first of a series of books especially designed for the rising generation, and with which he is known to have taken more pains than with any of his previous writings. He was editor of the METROPOLITAN MAGAZINE (which had been commenced by the poet Campbell) from 1832 to 1836 inclusive, during which period some of his most popular Novels were first published in its pages.

MARS and VENUS.—The Loue and Complayntes betwene Mars and Venus. Westmoster for me Julianus Notarii, 4to.

Blank letter. Fourteen leaves. Roxburghe, 3283, 60l. resold Sir M. M. Sykes, pt. II., 40l. 42l. 10s. 6d. resold Heber, pt. II. 1383, 22l. 10s.

The Diversions of Mars and Venus, consisting of several Love Stories, as told by little Cupid to divert Venus his Mother, being chiefly real Intrigues, with some modern Amours of Greenwich Parks, Tunbridge, Bath, &c. 1710, 12mo. With woodcut frontispiece.

MARSDEN, William, D.C.L., F.R.S., &c. The History of Sumatra. Third Edition, revised and enlarged. Lond. 1811, 4to. with maps and plates in atlas folio, published at 3l. 13s. 6d. reduced 1l. 11s. 6d.

'A perfect model for Topographic and Descriptive composition: but as we had little or no intercourse with the north-eastern coast of Sumatra, his account could only be very general and imperfect.'—Quart. Rev. First edition, 1783, 4to. Fonthill, 754, 10s. Willett, 1808, 17s. Heath, 2649, 1l. 15s.—Second edition, 1784, 4to. Hibbert, 5197, 16s.

A Catalogue of Dictionaries, Vocabularies, Grammars and Alphabets. In two Parts. Lond. 1796, 4to. pp. 154, with title, &c. Only 50 copies, privately printed. Heber, pt. vi. 1l. 12s. Dent, pt. ii. 720, 2l. 11s.

A Dictionary of the Malayan Language; in two Parts; Malayan and English and English and Malayan. Lond. 1812, 4to. 2l. 2s.

A Grammar of the Malayan Language, with an Introduction and Praxis. Lond. 1812, 4to. 1l. 1s.

The Dictionary and Grammar have been translated into German and French, by C. P. J. Elout, Harlem, 1824, 4to.

Numismata Orientalia Illustrata. The Oriental Coins of his own collection described and historically illustrated. Lond. 1823-5, 4to. 2 vols. plates, 8l.

Miscellaneous Works. Lond. 1834, 4to. Bibliotheca Marsdeniana Philologica et Orientalis. A Catalogue of Books and Manuscripts collected with a View to the General Comparison of Languages, and to the Study of Oriental Literature. This extremely valuable Collection, with other Works, was bequeathed to King's College, London. Privately printed. Lond. 1827. Heber, pt. vi. 1l. 12s.

Memoirs of a Malayan Family, written by themselves. Translated. Lond. 1830, 4to.

A Brief Memoir of his Life and Writings, drawn up by himself, with Notes from his Correspondence only. To which is usually attached: Maon and Moriat, a Tragedy, written at Sumatra. Lond. 1838, 4to. Eyton, 1l. 6s. Printed for private distribution only; edited by his widow (a daughter of Sir Ch. Wilkins, now Mrs. Col. Leake).

See also MARCO POLO.

Several curious treatises by Marsden will be found in the Publications of the Oriental Fund, in Appendix; Philosophical Transactions of the Royal Society; Royal Society of Literature; Asiatic Society of Calcutta; Archæologia; Asiatic Researches.

MARSH, H. A new Survey of the Turkish Empire and Government. Lond. 1633.

White Knights, 2632, morocco, 15s.

— Herbert, Bishop of Peterborough. A Course of Lectures, containing a Description and systematic Arrangement of the several Branches of Divinity; with an Account of the principal Authors who have excelled at different Periods in theological Learning. Camb. 1809-23, 8vo. pts. i. to vii.

An important work, indispensably necessary in every theological library. It embraces almost every topic of biblical criticism and interpretation, and also the genuineness, authenticity and credibility of the Scriptures; and is particularly valuable for its biographical and critical notices of the principal writers who have treated on these subjects.—New edition. Lond. 1838, 8vo. in one vol. 12s.

An Essay on the Usefulness and Necessity of Theological Learning to those who are designed for Holy Orders. 1792, 4to.

The Authenticity of the five Books of Moses considered: being the Substance of a Discourse lately delivered before the University. Camb. 1792, 4to. 1s. 6d.

Letters to Mr. Archdeacon Travis, in Vindication of one of the Translator's Notes to Michaelis's Introduction and in Confirmation of the Opinion, that a Greek Manuscript now preserved in the Public Library of the University of Cambridge, is one of the Seven which are quoted by R. Stephens at 1 John v. 7. With an Appendix, containing a Review of Mr. Travis's Collation of the Greek MSS

MARSH, Bp.—*continued.*
which he examined in Paris; an Extract from Mr. Pappelbaum's Treatise on the Berlin MS.; and an Essay on the Origin and Object of the Vatican Readings. Leipzig, 1795, 8vo. Sotheby's in 1824, 1l. 9s.

An Examination into the Conduct of the British Ministry relative to the late Proposal of Buonaparte. 1800, 8vo.

History of the Politics of Great Britain and France, from the Time of the Conference at Pillnitz to the Declaration of War against Great Britain. With an Appendix and Postscript. Lond. 1800, 8vo. 2 vols. 10s. 6d.

The History of the Politics of Great Britain and France vindicated from a late Attack by Wm. Belsham. Lond. 1801, 8vo 8s.

A Dissertation on the Origin and Composition of the three first canonical Gospels. Camb. 1801. 8vo. 5s. [Incorporated in the second edition of Marsh's translation of Michaelis.]

Letters to the anonymous Author of 'Remarks on Michaelis and his Commentator.' 1802, 8vo.

The Illustration of the Hypothesis proposed in the Dissertation on the Origin and Composition of our three first Canonical Gospels; with a Preface and Appendix, being a Rejoinder to the anonymous Author of 'Remarks on Michaelis and his Commentators.' Lond. 1803, 8vo. 4s.

A Defence of the Illustration of the Hypothesis. 1804, 8vo.

A Letter to the Conductor of the Critical Review on the Subject of Religious Toleration. Camb. 1810, 8vo. 1s. 6d.

The National Religion the Foundation of National Education; a Sermon preached at the yearly Meeting of the Children educated in the Charity Schools in and about London. Lond. 1811, 4to. Frequently reprinted.—Sixth edition. Lond. 1813, 8vo.

Vindication of Dr. Bell's System of Tuition. Lond. 1811, 8vo.

A History of the Translations which have been made of the Scriptures, from the earliest to the present Age, throughout Europe, Asia, Africa and America. Lond. 1812, 8vo. 4s.

A Letter to the Rt. Hon. N. Vansittart, being an answer to his second Letter on the British and Foreign Bible Society. Lond. 1812, 8vo. 2s.

An Inquiry into the Consequences of neglecting to give the Prayer Book with the Bible. Camb. 1812, 8vo. 2s. 6d.

Letter of Explanation to the Dissenter and Layman, who has lately addressed himself to the Author on the Views of the Protestant Dissenters. 1813, 8vo.

Letter to the Rev. P. Gandolphy in Confutation of the Opinion that the Vital Principles of the Reformation have lately been conceded to the Church of Rome. 1813, 8vo.

A Reply to the Strictures of the Rev. Isaac Milner, D.D. Camb. 1813, 8vo. 3s. 6d.

A Sermon preached before the University of Cambridge. 1813, 4to.

Two Letters to the Rev. Chas. Simeon on Baptism. 1813-14, 8vo.

Primary Charge at Landaff. 1817, 8vo. 2s.

A comparative View of the Churches of Rome and England. Camb. 1814, 8vo. 6s.—The second edition, with an Appendix. 1816. 8vo. 8s. 6d.—Third edition. Lond. 1841, 12mo. 6s.

Primary Charge at Peterborough. 1820, 8vo. 1s. 6d.

Horæ Pelasgicæ. Part the first. Containing an Inquiry into the Origin and Language of the Pelasgi, or the ancient Inhabitants of Greece; with a Dissertation on the Pelasgic or Æolic Digamma, as represented in the various Inscriptions in which it is still preserved; and an Attempt to determine its genuine Pelasgic Pronunciation. Camb. 1815, 8vo. 7s. 6d.

LXXXIII Questions to Candidates for holy Orders, with Illustrative Replies in the Form of Essays. Lond. 1831, 8vo. 6s.

Lectures on the Criticism and Interpretation of the Bible, with two preliminary Lectures: to which are now added two Lectures on the History of Biblical Interpretation. Lond. 1838. 8vo.

Lectures on the Authenticity and Credibility of the New Testament, and on the Authority of the Old Testament; with an Appendix of Tracts. Lond. 1840, 8vo.

See MICHAELIS.

MARSH, John. His Mickle Monument raised on Shepherds Talkings, in moderate walkings, in divine expressions, in human transgressions (in verse). Anno Dom. 1645, 4to.

Lloyd, 790, 2l. 4s. Heber, pt. iv. 1l. 1s.

— John. Memoranda of the Parishes of Hurstley and North Baddesley, in the County of Southampton. Winchester, 1808, royal 8vo.

NOT PUBLISHED. *Collation.*—Title, half-title and dedication, 3 leaves; advertisement, 2 leaves, memoranda, 63 pages; half-title and dedication, 2 leaves; memoranda, 32 pages, also 4 plates by J. Powell.

MARSHAL, Rev. Ebenezer. The History of the Union of Scotland and England, stating the Circumstances which brought that Event forward to a Conclusion, and the Advantages resulting from it to the Scots. Edinb. 1794, 8vo. 6s.

— Humphry. Arbustum Americanum; the American Grove, or an alphabetical Catalogue of Forest Trees and Shrubs, Natives of the American United States, arranged according to the Linnæan System. Philadelphia, 1788, 8vo. 3s.

— Joseph. Travels through Holland, Flanders, Germany, Denmark, Sweden, Lapland, Russia, the Ukraine, and Poland, in the Years 1768-70. Lond. 1772, 8vo. 3 vols.
Fonthill, 2043, 19s.

MARSHALL, John. Royal Naval Biography, or Memoirs of the Services of all the Flag-Officers, Rear-Admirals, retired Captains, Commanders, &c., from 1760 to 1835, written by themselves; with Historical and Explanatory Notes, 8vo. 12 vols. Lond. 1823-35, pub. at 8*l.* 8s. reduced 3*l.* 3s.

— Rev. Charles. A plain and easy Introduction to the Knowledge and Practice of Gardening, with Hints on Fish Ponds. Fifth Edition, enlarged. Lond. 1814, 8vo. 9s.
First edition. Lond. 1796, 8vo.

— Charles. Reports of Cases in the Court of Common Pleas from Michaelmas Term 54 George III. to Michaelmas Term 57 George III. Lond. 1814-18, royal 8vo. 2 vols. 2*l.* 10s.

— George. A compendious Treatise in Metre, declaring the first originall of Sacrifice, and of buylding Aultars and Churches and of the first Receiving the Christen Fayth here in England. Lond. J. Cawoode, 1554, 4to.
A Poem of the greatest rarity. It is a severe attack on the Reformers. A copy is in the Lambeth library. Evans, March 7, 1841, 20*l.* 6s. resold, Bright, 21*l.* 10s.

MARSHALL, II. History of Kentucky, its Discovery, Settlement, &c. Frankfort (Kentucky), 1824, 8vo. 2 vols. 1*l.* 1s.

— John. The Life of General George Washington. Lond. 1804-7, 4to. 5 vols. maps and plans.
Prefixed is a compendious view of the colonies planted by the English in North America. Sir M. M. Sykes, pt. II. 482, 2*l.* Hibbert, 5108, 2*l.* 8s. Drury, 4589, 2*l.* 18s. Duke of York, 3162, 3*l.* 3s.—Lond. 1804-7, 8vo. 5 vols. 1*l.* 5s.—New edition, in 2 vols. 8vo. Philadelphia, 1830, 1*l.* 5s.

— Nathaniel, D.D. On the Penitential Discipline of the Primitive Church for the first 400 years after Christ. Lond. 1714, 8vo. 9s.
New edition. Oxford. 1844, 8vo. 8s.

— Serj. Samuel. Treatise on the Law of Insurance, in four Books. Third Edition, with Corrections and Additions by C. Marshall. Lond. 1823, royal 8vo. 1*l.* 15s.
A valuable and well-digested work.

— Stephen, B.D. The Godly Man's Legacy to the Saints upon Earth, exhibited in the Life of Mr. S. Marshall. Lond. 1670, 4to.
This divine published many sermons.

— Walter. The Gospel Mystery of Sanctification opened, in sundry practical Directions. Lond. 1692, 12mo.
A posthumous work, frequently reprinted.

— William. Agricultural Works. Lond. 1778-1817, 4to. and 8vo.
Formerly in considerable estimation. Minutes of Agriculture, made on a Farm of 300 Acres of various Soils, near Croydon, Surrey. To which is added, a Digest, with Drawings of new Implements, &c. Lond. 1778, 4to.
Experiments and Observations concerning Agriculture and the Weather. Lond. 1779, 4to.

MARSHALL, Wm.—*continued.*
Planting and Ornamental Gardening; a practical Treatise. Lond. 1785.—Planting and Rural Ornament. Being a second Edition, with large Additions, of 'Planting and Ornamental Gardening, a practical Treatise.' Lond. 1796, 8vo. 2 vols. — Third edition, improved, 1803.

The rural Economy of Norfolk. Lond. 1787, 8vo. 2 vols.—The second Edition. Lond. 1795.—1796, 8vo. 2 vols. Vol. I. pp. 424. Vol. II. pp. 412.

The rural Economy of Yorkshire. Lond. 1788, 8vo. 2 vols.

The rural Economy of Glocestershire; including its Dairy; together with the dairy Management of North Wiltshire; and the Management of Orchards and Fruit Liquor in Herefordshire, &c. Gloucester, 1789, 8vo. 2 vols.

The rural Economy of the Midland Counties; including the Management of Live Stock in Leicestershire and its Environs; together with Minutes on Agriculture and Planting, in the District of the midland Station. Lond. 1790, 8vo. 2 vols.

A Review of 'The Landscape; a didactic Poem (by R. P. Knight);' also an Essay on the Picturesque; together with practical Remarks on rural Ornament. Lond. 1795, 8vo.

The rural Economy of the West of England; including Devonshire, and Parts of Somersetshire, Dorsetshire, and Cornwall; together with Minutes in Practice. Lond. 1796, 8vo. 2 vols. 12s.

The rural Economy of the southern Counties; comprising Kent, Surrey, Sussex; the Isle of Wight; the Chalk Hills of Wiltshire, Hampshire, &c.; and including the Culture and Management of Hops, in the Districts of Maidstone, Canterbury, and Farnham. Lond. 1798, 8vo. 2 vols. 15s. To the second edition, in 1799, was prefixed a Sketch of the Vale of London, in an outline of the rural economy.

Minutes, Experiments, Observations, and General Remarks, on Agriculture, in the Southern Counties. A new Edition, to which is prefixed a Sketch of the Vale of London, and an Outline of its rural Economy; now first published. Lond. 1799, 8vo. 2 vols.

Proposals for a Rural Institute, or College of Agriculture, and other Branches of rural Economy. Lond. 1799, 8vo.

On the Appropriation and Enclosure of commonable and intermixed Lands; with Heads of a Bill for that Purpose. Together with Remarks on the Outline of a Bill, by a Committee of the House of Lords for the same Purpose. Lond. 1801, 8vo.

The Landed Property of England, an elementary and practical Treatise; concerning the Purchase, the Improvement, and the Management of landed Estates. Lond. 1804, 4to.

The Management of Landed Estates; a general Work, for the Use of professional Men: being an Abstract of the more enlarged Treatise of Landed Property, recently published. Lond. 1806, 8vo.

A Review and complete Abstract of the Reports of the Board of Agriculture, from the several Departments of England. Lond. 1817, 8vo, 5 vols. Published in separate volumes, commencing in 1808.

MARSHAM, Sir John. Chronicus Canon Ægyptiacus, Ebraicus, Græcus, cum Disquisitionibus historicis et criticis. Lond. 1672, folio.
Heath, 2286, 10s. 6d. Willett, 1523, 16s. 6d. A learned work, frequently reprinted abroad, written to induce the belief that all the Jewish rites were of Egyptian origin. Witsius, in his Ægyptiaca, controverts this opinion.

— Thomas. Entomologia Britannica, sistens Insecta Britannia indigena, secundum Methodum Linnæanum disposita. Lond. 1802, 8vo. vol. i. all printed. 14s.
Pp. xxiv and 548.

New title. Coleoptera Britannica. Lond. 1803, 8vo. divided into 2 vols. 80 coloured plates. Vol. I, pp. 214, with 12 coloured plates. Vol. II, pp. 235—547, with plates coloured, 13—30.

MARSHMAN, J., D.D. Clavis Sinica, or Elements of Chinese Grammar, with a preliminary Dissertation, and an Appendix containing the Ta-Hyoth of Confucius, with a Translation. Serampore, 1814, royal 4to.
A valuable and beautifully printed work. Heber, pt. i. 4584, 1l. 1s.

A Dissertation on the Characters and Sounds of the Chinese Language. Serampore, 1809, 4to, pp. 116. Heber, pt. ii. 1s.
The first plain, simple, and intelligible introductory treatise to the Chinese language.—*Quart. Review.*

See CONFUCIUS.

MARSILIUS of Padua. The Defence of Peace, translated out of Latin into English by Wyllyam Marshall. Lond. R. Wyer, 1535, fol.
Heber, pt. ix. 5l. 10s. A copy of this apology for the defence of Ldowyke, Emperour of the Romaynes, is in the British Museum. In the preface is a Prayer for Anne Boleyn.

MARSOLLIER, Jacques. Histoire
de Henry VII. Roi d'Angleterre.
Paris, 1697-8, 12mo. 2 vols. 5s.
This work is esteemed the master-piece
of this entertaining historian.—Paris,
1724, 12mo. 2 vols.
The Life of S. Francis de Sales, translated by W. H. Coombes, D.D. Shepton-
Mallett, 1812, 8vo. 2 vols. 10s. 6d.

MARSTON, John. Dramatic and
Poetical Works.
The Scourge of Villanie: three Bookes
of Satyres. Lond. by J. R(oberts), 1598,
16mo. First edition, published anonymously. To sig. V 8. Bright, mor. 9l. 9s.
Reprinted in Pieces of ancient English
Poesie, 1764, 12mo. edited by the Rev.
John Bowle.
The Scourge of Villanie, corrected, with
the addition of newe Satyres. Three
Bookes of Satyres. Lond. printed by J.
R(oberts), 1599, 16mo. pp. 120. A tenth
satire is added to this second edition.
Bibl. Anglo-Poet. 486, 6l. 10s. Bindley,
pt. ii. 1803, 8l. 10s. Geo. Chalmers, pt. i.
8l. 10s. 6d. This was Major Pearsons'
copy. Heber, pt. iv. 3l. 1s. Bright, made
up with manuscript, 2l. 10s. An Answer
to Marston and his Scourge of Villanie was
printed under the title of 'The Whipper
of the Satyre, his Penance in a White
Sheet, or the Beadle's Computation.' Lond.
printed for Thomas Pavier, 1601, 16mo.
Heber, 6l. 6s.
The Metamorphosis of Pigmalion's
Image, and certaine Satyres. Lond. 16mo.
(published anonymously), printed for Edmond Matts, and are to be sold at the
Signe of the Hand and Ploogh in Fleete
Streete, 1598. At the end of the Satyres
(to which a second title is prefixed) is
'Printed by James Roberts,' 1598. This
volume is dedicated 'To the Worlds
mightie Monarch Good Opinion,' by W.
K(insayder), the now de plume under
which Marston published some of his
early productions. Bright, 3899, wanting
all after p. 70, and the title, 1l. 16s. Perry,
pt. ii. 698, with the Scourge of Villanie.
1598, 8l. 10s. 6d. Heber, pt. iv. 1498,
with the Scourge of Villanie, 1599, 4l. 14s.
A copy is in the Malone Collection. The
first poem is printed in 'Aldilla,' a Collection of Poems, 1598. It is also given in
the volume edited by Bowle in 1764. The
rarity of Pigmalion's Image may be accounted for, as, from its licentious character, the prelates Whitgift and Bancroft
ordered its suppression and destruction
soon after its appearance.
Antonio and Mellida. The first part.
Lond. 1602, 4to. Hibbert, 5199, 1l. Roxburghe, 55, 1l. 11s. 6d. Heber, pt. ii. 1l. 7s.
Bright, 12s. Reprinted in the second volume of 'Old Plays,' edited by Dilke, 1816,
8vo.
Antonio's Revenge. The second part
of Antonio and Mellida. Lond. 1602, 4to.
Inglis' Old Plays, 64, 1l. 7s. Roxburghe,
5414, 1l. 11s. 6d. Bright, 16s. Rhodes,
1625, with Antonio and Mellida, 2l. 5s.
Heber, pt. ii. 17s.
The Malcontent. First edition, printed
at London by V. S., for Wm. Aspley,
1604, 4to. Dedicated to Ben Jonson. The
leaf at the end containing the Prologue
is often wanting. Roxburghe, 5417, 1l. 10s.
Rhodes, 1629, 1l. 19s. Heber, pt. ii. 17s.
Second edition, (but not so marked), at
London. Printed by V. S., for Wm. Apsley,
1604, 4to. Rhodes, 1677, 2l. 10s. Heber,
pt. ii. 17s. Augmented by Marston, with
the Additions, played by the King's Servants, written by Iohn Webster. See
WEBSTER. Reprinted in Dodsley's Collection of Old Plays, and a modernized
edition in Mr. Dyce's Edition of Webster's
works.
Eastward Hoe, by G. Chapman, B. Jonson, and I. Marston. Lond. 1605, 4to.
Three editions the same year. See CHAP-
MAN, Geo. JONSON, Ben. A modern text
of this Play is given in Dodsley's collection. It was altered by Tate in 1685, to
the 'Cuckold's Haven: or, an Alderman
no Conjuror.' Again, in 1752, as 'Eastward Hoe: or, the Prentices;' and again,
1775, by Mrs. Lennox, as 'Old City Manners.'
The Dutch Courtezan, a Comedy. Lond.
1605, 4to. Roxburghe, 5415, 16s. Hibbert, 5900, 1l. 4s. Inglis' Old Plays, 65,
1l. 10s. Rhodes, 1630, 1l. 15s. Heber, pt.
ii. 19s. Revised in 1850, under the title
of 'The Revenge, or, a Match in Newgate,' and again, about 1748, as 'The Vint-
ner tricked.'
Parasitaster, or the Fawn, a Comedy,
Lond. 1606, 4to. Roxburghe, 5413, 1l. 5s.—
Corrected of many Faults, which by reason of the Author's absence were let slip
in the first edition. Lond. 1606, 4to.
Rhodes, 1629, 1l. 13s. Inglis' Old Plays,
66, 1l. 18s. Heber, pt. ii. 1l. 12s. A modern Text of the Parisitaster is printed in
'Old Plays,' vol. ii. edited by Dilke, 1816,
8vo.
The Wonder of Women, or the Tragedie
of Sophonisba, as it hath beene sundry
Times acted at the Blacke Friers. Lond.
1606, 4to. Fisher, pt. ii. 1l. 14s. A—G 3,
in fours. In the Malone Collection. Mr.
Gifford observes, 'It is not very probable
that Mr. M. G. Lewis ever looked into
Marston, yet some of the most loathsome
parts of the Monk are to be found in this
detestable play.'
What you will. Lond. for T. Thorpe,
1607, 4to. Hibbert, 6201, 7s. 6d. Rhodes,
1631, 1l. 5s. Roxburghe, 5419, 1l. 14s. He-

MARSTON, John—continued.
ber, pt. ii, 1l. 8s. A modern text of this play is printed in 'Old Plays,' edited by Dilke, 1816, 8vo.

The Insatiate Countesse, a Tragedy. Lond. 1613, 4to. Rhodes, 1029, 13s. Heber, pt. ii. 19s.—1616, 4to. Inglis' Old Plays, 67, 1l. 18s.—1631, 4to. Boswell, 1967, 5s. Rhodes, 1633, 11s. Roxburghe, 6416, 1l. 1s. Bindley, pt. iii. 628, 1l. 11s. Heber, pt. ii. 15s. Reprinted, Lond. by F. Marshall, 1820, 8vo, 2s. for Mr. J. Boaden, to complete the 'Workes' issued in 1633, with a reprint of the dedication to Lady Elizabeth Faulkener prefixed to that volume, which is often wanting.

Workes.—Sir Tragedies and Comedies. Lond. 1633, 12mo. This volume contains Antonio and Mellida, Antonio's Revenge, Parisitaster, Wonder of Women, What you will, and The Dutch Courtezan. It was issued twice in the same year, the titles differing; for 'The Puritans and Prynne' had brought so great an odium on the Stage, and everything connected with it, that the very name of Tragedy or Comedy was offensive; and Sheares, the publisher, found it a bad speculation to offer it under the obnoxious title, so changed it to 'Workes, being Tragedies and Comedies collected into one Volume.' The introduction to Lady Eliz. Carie, Viscountess Favrkland, is printed in the Introduction of Mr. Halliwell's edition of the Works. Roxburghe, 3092, 1l. 1s. Bindley, pt. ii. 1967, 2l. 16s. Jadis, 38, morocco, 1l. 19s. Lloyd, 640, 1l. 3s. Bishop of Ely, 1803, 1l. 16s. White Knights, 2633, 1l. 15s.; 2634, 1l. 11s. Nassau, pt. i. 2199, 2l. 10s. Heber, pt. iv. 1l. 9s.

Spectacle presented to the sacred Majesty's of Great Britain and Denmark, as they passed through London in 1606. 4to. MS. in the British Museum, admitted into Halliwell's edition. Printed in the second number of 'The Crypt,' edited by P. Hall.

The Lords and Ladye Huntingdon's Entertainement of their right Noble Mother Alice, Countesse Dowager of Darby, the firste Nighte of her Honor's arrivall at the House of Ashby. MS. Printed in Mr. Halliwell's edition of the Works. Published in part, in Nichols' History of Leicestershire, the Progresses of King James I., and in Todd's edition of Milton's Poetical Works.

A Sermon 'preached at St. Margaret's in Westminster,' Feb. 1642. 4to. Unquestionably by a different author. See Collins's Peel. Decam. i. 269.

The Newe Metamorphosis or a Feaste of Fancie, or Poeticall Legends. 1600, 4to. MS. See Brathwait's Barnabee's Journal, 1820, l. 96. Doubtful.

The Mountebank, a Masque. See second part of Gesta Grayorum, in Nichols' Progresses of Queen Elizabeth, edition 1823, iii. p. 320; also the vol. on Inigo Jones, edited by Collier for the Shakspeare Society in 1848.

Workes, Dramatic and Satirical. Reprinted from the original editions, with Notes, and some Account of his Life and Writings, by J. O. Halliwell, Esq. Lond. 1856, post 8vo. 3 vols. 15s. LARGE PAPER.

Gifford, in his edition of Ben Jonson, styles Marston 'the most scurrilous, filthy, and obscene writer of his time;' on the other hand, the Rev. P. Hall styles him 'a poet of distinguished celebrity in his own day, no less admired for the versatility of his genius in tragedy and comedy, than dreaded for the poignancy of his satire; in the former department the colleague of Jonson, in the latter, the antagonist of Hall.'

Notices of Marston and his writings will be found in Wood's Athen. Oxon. by Dr. Bliss, l. 763 & iv. 656-7; Warton's History of English Poetry, 8vo. iv. 364, &c. Ritson's Bibl. Poet. 277-8; the Retrospective Review, vi. 113-39; and in the second volume of C. Lamb's Works.

MARSTON, Robert. Tam Martis quam Artis Nenia; or the Soldier's Sorrow and Learning's Loss; an elegiacall Poem on the Death of Thomas, Lord Grey of Wilton. Lond. 1822, 4to.

Presented to the members of the Roxburghe Club by Lord Morpeth. Dent, pt. ii. 1223, 1l. 5s. Sir M. M. Sykes, pt. i. 1643, 6l. 6s. The MS. from which this piece was printed is in the Granville Collection.

MARSYS, F. de. Histoire de la Persecution presente des Catholiques en Angleterre. 1646, sm. 4to. three Parts, 16s.

MARTEL, Peter. An Account of the Glaciers, or Ice Alps in Savoy. Lond. 1744, 4to. plates, 4s.

MARTEN, Anthony. An Exhortation to stirre up the Minds of all her Majesty's faithfull Subjects to defend their Countrey in this dangerous Time, from the Invasion of Enemies. Lond. 1588, 4to.

BLACK LETTER. Pp. 22, F, in form. Reprinted in the first volume of the Harleian Miscellany.

The seconde Sounde or Warning of the Trumpet unto Judgement. Lond. 1589, 4to. Inglis, 989, 2s. 6d.

MARTEN, Col. Henry. Familiar
Letters to his Lady of Delight, also
her kinde Returnes, with his Rivall
B. Pettingalls heroicall Epistles.
Published by E. Gayton. Oxford,
1663, 4to.
Pp. 68. Jadis, 291, 1l. 8s. Townsley,
pt. ii. 1129, 11. 6s. Bred. 2210, 8s. White
Knights. 7616, 4s. Nassau, pt. ii. 145,
date 1663, 10s. This trash was written by
one of the Parliamentary generals, who
was chiefly instrumental in publishing
King Charles's private Letters.
The familiar Epistles of Coll. Henry
Martin, found in his Misses' Cabinet. The
second Edition. Lond. 1685, 4to. Pp. 88,
besides a sheet containing the title and
dedication.

— Tho. A Reconciliation of all
the Pastors and Clergy of this
Church of England. Lond. 1590,
4to.

MARTENS, G. F. von. Compendium of the Law of Nations, with a
List of all the Treaties, Conventions, &c. 1731-88. Translated,
and the Treaties brought down to
1802, by W. Cobbett. Lond. 1802,
8vo. 6s.

MARTIALIS, M. V. Epigrammata,
a Th. Farnabio. Lond. excud.
Kingston, 1615, 12mo. 2s. 6d.
Cum notis Farnabii, editio nova. Lond.
excudebat Robertus Junius. Impensis Philemonis Stephani at Christophori Meredith, 1633, 12mo. 3s. 6d. On vellum. A
copy is in Earl Spencer's Library. Reprinted 1655, 1676, 1677.
Martialis Epigrammata, a Ric. Bushelo,
D.D. Lond. 1601, 12mo. 2s. 6d. In this
edition the obscenities are expunged. Reprinted 1670 and 1689.
Martialis Epigrammata, Interpretationes
et Notis illustr. Vincent Collesso, ad Usum
Delphini. Lond. 1701, 8vo.—Lond. 1720.
Frequently reprinted.
Martialis Epigrammata (edente M.
Maittaire). Lond. Tonson and Watts,
1716, 12mo. 3s. A neat and correct edition,
with a valuable index. LARGE PAPER,
Heath, 3110, 1l. Hibbert, 5131, with MS.
notes, &c. by Turnbull, morocco, 2l. 2s.
Stanley, 196, mor. 2l. 6s. Dent, pt. i. 816,
morocco by Roger Payne, 3l.
Martialis Epigrammata, in Usum Scholæ
Westmonasteriensis. Lond. 1721, 8vo. 3s.
Edited by Tho. Fitzgerald. Frequently
reprinted.

Martialis Epigrammata. Glasg. 1759,
12mo. 3s. Foulis edition, in little request.
Martialis Epigrammata. Birm. 1773,
12mo. Baskerville's edition.
M. Val. Martialis Epigrammata in XII
Libros digesta; ut uni eloquomnibus Poetis
facem præferente Jacobo Elphinstonio.
Lond. 1782, 8vo. with a frontispiece by
Bartolozzi. Hibbert, 5110, 3s. Dent, pt. i.
1369, 3s. 6d.
M. Valerii Martialis Epigrammata ex
optimarum Editionum Collatione emendata. (ed. Carey.) Lond. 1816, 12mo. Called the Regent edition.

TRANSLATIONS.

Flowers of Epigrams, from Martial and
others, by Timothy Kendall. Lond. 1577.
See KENDALL.
Select Epigrams of Martial, translated
by Tho. May. Lond. 1629. Bindley, pt. ii.
date 1620 (prob. an error), with epigrams
in MS. 2l. 12s. 6d. Bindley, pt. ii. 1064,
date 1629, 5l. 12s. 6d.
Ex Otio Negotium: or, Martiall his Epigrams translated. With sundry Poems and
Fancies by R. Fletcher. Lond. 1656, 8vo.
pp. 276, with port. of Martial by Vaughan,
1l. 11s. 6d. Garrick, 900, 13s. Nassau, pt.
i. 2200, 16s. Bibl. Anglo-Poet. 277, 1l. 1s.
Sotheby's in 1857, 1l. 16s.
Select Epigrammatum. Fourteen Bookes
of Epigrams made English by J. Wright.
Lond. 1663, 12mo. Sotheby's in 1853, 2l. 7s.
Select Epigrams of Martial translated
into English. Lond. 1689, 8vo. with a
frontispiece by Hollar. Bindley, pt. ii.
1989, 15s.
Epigrams of Martial (select), translated
into English by Cotton. Lond. 1695, 8vo.
with an engraved title by Hollar, 10s. 6d.
Select Epigrams of Martial, translated
and imitated, by William Hay, Esq.;
with an Appendix of some translated by
Cowley and other Hands. Lond. 1755,
12mo. In these imitations Mr. Hay has
generally preserved the sense, and often
the spirit and turn of Martial. (There
are two editions printed at same time,
one with the Latin text in 12mo., the
other without it in 8vo.) Dent, pt. i. 1320,
10s. Nassau, pt. i. 2201, 16s.
Epigrams from Martial (select), with
Mottos from Horace, translated, imitated,
adapted, and addressed to the Nobility,
Clergy, and Gentry. With Notes, moral,
historical, explanatory, and humorous (by
the Rev. W. Scott). Lond. 1773, 12mo.
Bindley, pt. ii. 1750, 5s. 6d.
The Epigrams of Martial, twelve Books,
with a Comment, by Jas. Elphinston.
Lond. 1782, 4to. A wretched translation,
much more difficult to understand than
the original; nor are the whole given;
the translator having omitted whatever he
could not mystify. Roxburghe, 2373, 11s.

Imitations of some of the Epigrams of Martial. In four Parts. By N. B. Halhed. 1793-4. 4to. 10s.

Marziale, fedelmente tradotto in Italiano da Ginepano Graglia. Lond. 1782, royal 8vo. 2 vols. 12s. With the Latin text and notes. Hibbert, 5117, ll. 6s.

Martial's Epigrams (the whole fifteen books) literally translated into English Prose, each accompanied by one or more Verse translations selected from the works of English Poets, and various other sources. With a copious Index. Lond. (Bohn's Classical Library) 1860, post 8vo. 7s. 6d. The first attempt ever made to give Martial complete in an English form.

Some Account of an ancient MS. of Martial's Epigrams, illustrated by an Engraving. By John Graham Dalyell, Esq. Edinb. 1811, 8vo. 7s. There were several copies printed ON VELLUM.

MARTIAL.—The British Martial; or an Anthology of English Epigrams; being the largest Collection ever published. With some Originals. Lond. 1806, crown 8vo. 2 vols. 10s.

MARTIAL, John. A Treatyse of the Crosse, gathered out of the Scriptures, Councells, and auncient Fathers of the primitiue Church. Antwerp, J. Latius, 1564, 8vo.
Dedicated to Queen Elizabeth.

A Replie to M. Calfhill's blasphemous Answer, made against the Treatise of the Crosse. Louaine, by John Bogard, 1566, 4to. See CALFHILL, J. FULKE, W.

MARTILOGE, or Martyrology.— The Martiloge in Englysshe after the Vse of the Chirche of Salisbury, and as it rodde in Syon [monastery near London], with Addicyons. Lond. by W. de Worde, 1526, 4to.

One hundred and fifty four leaves. Prefixed is an epistle to the devout readers by the wretch of Syon, R. Whytford, wherein we learn that he translated it out of Latin, &c. Maunsell, in his Catalogue, p. 71, mentions an edition of this work without date or printer's name. Copies are in the British Museum; Bodleian among Gough's Books; Stonyhurst College and Lambeth Libraries.
See MARTYRS.

MARTIN, Antonie. Exhortation to stirre up the Mindes of all her Mayestie's faithfull Subjects to defend their Countries in this dangerous Time. 1588, 4to. 2l. 12s. 6d.

MARTIN, Benjamin. The Natural (and Topographical) History of England. Lond. 1759-63, 8vo. 2 vols.

With a map of each county. Nassau, pt. l. 2236, 8s. Towneley, pt. l. 743, 5s. 6d.

Bibliotheca technologica; or, a philological library of literary arts and sciences. Lond. 1776, 8vo.

Philosophia Britannica; a system of the Newtonian Philosophy, Astronomy, and Geography. Lond. 1759, 8vo. 3 vols.

Young Gentlemen and Lady's Philosophy, in a Survey of the Works of Nature and Art. Lond. 1781, 8vo. 3 vols.

This author was an eminent optician, and published many other works in philosophy and mathematics, formerly in much estimation.

— David. The Genuineness of 1 John v. 7, demonstrated by Proofs which are beyond all Exception. Translated from the French. Lond. 1722, 8vo. 4s.

'We must applaud the zeal, though we cannot always approve the wisdom, of this worthy defender of Christianity.'—Orme.

A critical Dissertation upon the seventh Verse of the fifth Chapter of St. John's first Epistle. Translated from the French. Lond. 1719, 8vo.

An Examination of Mr. Emlyn's Answer to the Dissertation. Lond. 1719, 8vo.

A second Dissertation by Mr. Martin in Defence of the Testimony given to our Saviour by Josephus. Lond. 1719, 8vo.

Mr. Martin was the editor of a French translation of the Bible, which appeared at Amsterdam in 1707, folio.

— Edward, Dean of Ely. Five Letters. Lond. 1662, 8vo.

Nassau, pt. l. 2303, 5s. These letters consist of 1. The Difference between the Church of England and Geneva. 2. The Pope's Primacy, as pretended Successor to St. Peter. 3. The Authority of the Apostles' Constitutions and Canons. 4. The Discovery of the genuine Works of the primitive Fathers. 5. The false Brotherhood of the French and English Presbyterians. Geo. Chalmers, 6s.

— Gregory. A Treatise of Schisme, shewing that all Catholics ought in any Wise to abstaine altogether from heretical Conuenticles, &c. Draci, 1578, 10mo.

Bindley, pt. ll. 1943, 13s. 6d. resold, Heber, pt. ll. ll. 11s. Geo. Chalmers, 1l. This work was reprinted under the title of 'Reasons that Catholickes ought in any wise to abstain from Heretical Con-

MARTIN, Gregory—*continued.*
venticles,' in London (though said to be at Doway, by Wm. Carter), in 1580, under the name of John Howlet, (i.e. Robert Parsons), and dedicated to Q. Elizabeth, for which he was tried, cast, and condemned at the Sessions-house in the Old Baily, 10 Jan. 1584; and on the next morrow was drawn from Newgate to Tyborne, and there hanged, bowelled and quartered. *See* Holinshed's Chronicle.

A Discoverie of the manifold Corruptions of the Holy Scriptures by the Heretikes of our Daies. Rhemes, Fogny, 1582, small 8vo. Heber, pt. iv. 8s. 6d. This work was refuted by W. Fulke, D.D. 8vo. 1583. Bliss, 17s. See Lewis' History of the Translations of the Bible, 272—4.

A Treatyse of Christian Peregrination. Whereunto is adioined certen Epistles, written by him to sundrye his Frendes Anno Domini 1583, 16mo. Bright, title torn, 1l. 14s. The peregrination occupies E 1, in eights, with a blank leaf following; the letters are on 42 leaves, without signatures or numbers.

An account of this eminent Catholic, who 'was the chief man that translated the New Testament printed at Rhemes, 1582,' will be found in Wood's Athen. Oxon.

MARTIN, Isaac. The Trial and Sufferings of Mr. Martin, who was put into the Inquisition in Spain for the sake of the Protestant Religion. Lond. 1723, 8vo. plates.
Hibbert, 5124, 4s. Nassau, pt. i. 2205, 5s. Also in French. Lond. 1723, 8vo.

— James. Disputatio de prima Generatione Corporum simplicium & concretorum, per Jac. Martinum, Scotum. Cantab. 1584, 8vo.
A copy is in the Bodleian Library.

— James. Translations from ancient Irish MSS., with other Poems. Lond. 1811, crown 8vo. 5s.

— John. An Inquiry into the State of the legal Polity of Scotland. Lond. 1791, 8vo. 5s.
Horne Tooke, 459, with MS. notes, 4l. 4s. Another edition, enlarged, with the Judicial Polity. Lond. 1792, 8vo. Horne Tooke, 460, with MS. notes, 6l. 6s.

— John. Bibliographical Catalogue of privately printed Books. Lond. 1834, 8vo. 1l. 1s. front. and cuts.

LARGE PAPER. Imperial 8vo. the frontispiece in colours, 2l. 2s. Second edition, enlarged and continued. Lond. 1854, 8vo.
This edition was intended to be in two volumes, but the death of the author interrupted the second volume. It therefore covers only to page 814 of the first edition, (of course with the necessary additions), and omits, among other things, all the Club Books. The two editions are therefore necessary to form a complete work.

— M. A Description of the Western Isles of Scotland: a particular Account of the Second Sight: a brief Hint of Methods to improve Trade in that Country by Sea and Land. To which is added, a brief Description of the Isles of Orkney and Shetland. Lond. 1703. 8vo. Map.
Pp. 392, besides the dedication, preface and contents. This is the book which, having been put into the hands of Dr. Johnson, when very young, by his father, is supposed to have infused into him the first desire of visiting the Hebrides, of which he has given so interesting and humorous an account. Bishop of Ely, 616, 13s. 6d. Townshend, 2041, 14s. 6d. Roxburghe, 8781, 1l. 5s.—Lond. 1716, 8vo. Second and best edition. Dent, pt. i. 1294, 9s. Nassau, pt. i. 2304, with MS. notes, 12s. Bishop Randolph, 854, 16s. Heath, 4730, 1l. 1s. Bindley, pt. ii. 1810, 1l. 2s. Mr. Heber had two copies of this vol.; one with original MS. notes by J. Toland and Lord Molesworth (pt. ii. 6668, 3l. 10s.); the other with the same notes transcribed by Sir P. Thompson, (ii. 8668* 2l.). The book is reprinted in the third volume of Pinkerton's Collection of Voyages and Travels.

A late Voyage to St. Kilda, the remotest of all the Hebrides, or Western Isles of Scotland. Lond. 1698, 8vo.
Pp. 158, and six leaves of introductory matter, with map and plate. This work, according to 'The History of the Works of the Learned,' vol. v., was very agreeable to the curious, especially to such as have any true taste for natural and experimental philosophy. Willett, 1682, 17s. 6d. Bindley, 1l. 2s. Jadis, 98*, 7s.—Lond. 1753, 8vo. Best edition. Dent, pt. i. 1392, 5s. Heath, 4733, 13s. Fonthill, 2577, 10s. It will be found printed in the third vol. of Pinkerton's Collection of Voyages and Travels.

— Matthew. The Aurelian' Vade Mecum, containing an English alphabetical, and Linnæan systematical, Catalogue of Plants affording Nourishment to Butterflies, Hawkmoths, and Moths, and Moths in the State of Caterpillars, with the Linnæan and some of the best approved English Names of Insects. Exeter, 1785, 12mo. 6s.

MARTIN, R. Montgomery. History of the British Colonies. Lond. 1834-5, 8vo. 5 vols. maps, 4l. 4s.

The first volume was reprinted in 1835, without alterations. — Second edition, abridged and compressed into one volume, royal 8vo. (double columns.) Lond. 1839, pub. 2l. 2s. red. 15s. The work was afterwards recast, with additions, and published under the following title:—

BRITISH COLONIAL LIBRARY; comprising a popular and authentic Description of all the Colonies of the British Empire; founded on official and public Documents, furnished by Government and the Hon. East India Company. Maps and plates. — Lond. 1843, fcap. 8vo. 10 vols. 3l. red. to 1l. 10s. Each volume was sold separately, as follows :—

Vol. 1. The Canadas, Upper and Lower.
Vol. 2. New South Wales, Van Diemen's Land, Swan River, and South Australia.
Vol. 3. The Cape of Good Hope, Mauritius, and Seychelles.
Vol. 4. The West Indies, Vol. I. — Jamaica, Honduras, Trinidad, Tobago, Granada, the Bahamas, and the Virgin Isles.
Vol. 5. The West Indies, Vol. II. — British Guiana, Barbadoes, St. Lucia, St. Vincent's, Demerara, Essequibo, Berbice, Anguilla, Tortola, St. Kitt's, Barbuda, Antigua, Montserrat, Dominica, and Nevis.
Vol. 6. Nova Scotia, New Brunswick, Cape Breton. Prince Edward's Isle, the Bermudas, Newfoundland, and Hudson's Bay.
Vol. 7. Gibraltar, Malta, the Ionian Islands, &c.
Vol. 8. The East Indies: Vol. I. — containing Bengal, Madras, Bombay, and Presidencies.
Vol. 9. Ditto, Vol. II.
Vol. 10. British Possessions in the Indian and Atlantic Oceans, viz. Ceylon, Penang, Malacca, Singapore, Sierra Leone, the Gambia, Cape Coast Castle, Accra, the Falkland Islands, St. Helena, and Ascension.

The History, Antiquities, Topography, and Statistics of Eastern India. Lond. 1833, 8vo. 3 vols. pub. 3l. 12s. red. 1l. 1s.

CHINA, political, commercial, and social; an official Work by order of Her Majesty's Government. Lond. 1847, 8vo. 2 vols. with 6 maps, statistical tables, &c. 1l. 4s. red. 10s. 6d.

— Richard. A Speech in the Name of the Sheriffs to K. James I. Lond. 1603, 4to.

A copy is in the British Museum. It is reprinted in Nichols' Progresses of K. James I. An edition reprinted at Edinburgh in 1603, in 4to, was priced in a bookseller's late catalogue at 4l. 4s.

— Thomas, LL.D. A Traictyse declaryng and plainly proving that the pretended Marriage of Priestes and professed Persons is no Marriage but altogether unlawful. Lond. by Robert Caly, 1554, 4to.

M m in fours, dedicated to Q. Elizabeth. Heyne Tooke, 461, 11s. 6d. Inglis, 942, 15s. Caldecott, 18s. Heber, pt. v. 9s.; pt. viii. 3l.

A Confutation of Dr. John Poynet's Book, entit. A Defence for the Marriage of Priests, &c. Lond. 1555, 4to. Heber, pt. v. both pieces, 1l.

See POYNETT, John. WILLIAM of Wykeham.

— Thomas, of Palgrave. The History of the Town of Thetford, in the Counties of Norfolk and Suffolk, from the earliest Account to the present Time. Lond. 1779, 4to.

Edited by Richard Gough, who has affixed a life of the author. Heath, 4624, 1l. 5s. Willett, 1611, 1l. 10s. Sir M. M. Sykes, pt. ii. 483, 19s. Marquis of Townshend, 2180, 1l. 13s. Towneley, pt. ii. 1121, 12s. Dent, pt. ii. 721, 13s. Bindley, pt. iii. 302, 14s. Collation.—Pp. 1-10, and xi-xviii; history, pp. 320; appendix, index, errata, and list of (9) plates, pp. 186; list of books printed by J. Nichols, one page. Prefixed is a presumed portrait of the author.

— Thomas. A Circle of the Mechanical Arts. Lond. 1813, 4to. plates.

Now of little repute.

— William. The Historie and Lives of the Kings of England, from William the Conqueror, unto the End of the Raigne of King Henry the Eight. By William Martyn, Esquire, Recorder of Exeter. Lond. 1615, folio.

5 c

Reed, 8351, 6s. Googh, 2569, 8s. *Collation.*—Title and complimentary verses, two leaves; contents, 10 leaves: 'The Historie,' pp. 1-420: 'The Successions of the Dukes and Earles, &c.' 29 leaves, including the title; The table, — leaves. —With the Historie of K. Ed. VI. Q. Mary, and Q. Elizabeth, by B. R.—Second edition. Lond. 1638, folio. Engraved title by Marshall, and portraits by Elstracke, &c. from the coppers originally used for The Heroiologia, of course much worn. Lloyd, 520, 1l. 2s. Hibbert, 5223, morocco, 2l. 2s. Marquis of Townshend, 2217, 2l. 8s.

Youth's Instruction. Lond. 1612, 4to. Bliss in a volume. — Lond. 1618, 4to. Bright, 18s. In this 'book is shewed a great deal of reading,' says Ant. à Wood.

MARTIN, Wm. Petrificata Derbiensia: or, Figures and Descriptions of Petrifactions collected in Derbyshire. Wigan, 1809, 4to. 2l. 2s.

With 52 plates, etched and coloured by the author. Roscoe, 3l. *Collation.*—Half title and title, 2 leaves; preface, 6 pages; dedication to Sir Jos. Banks, one leaf; addenda and corrigenda, 2 pages; an arrangement of the petrifactions, &c. 2 pages; half title 'Plates and Descriptions,' one leaf; letter-press descriptions of 52 coloured plates, A—2 B; half title, 'A systematical arrangement,' one leaf; Petrifacta Derbiensia, 28 pages.

Outlines of an Attempt to establish a Knowledge of extraneous Fossils on scientific Principles. In two Parts. Macclesfield, 1809, 8vo. pp. 250, 34. Rosson, 1780, 9s. 6d.

MARTINE, Bishop of Dumience. The Rule of an honest life, written by the holy Man Martine, Bishop of Dumience, unto King Mito, King of Galilia in Spain: whereunto is added, the Enchiridion of a spiritual Life. St. Albans by me Jo. Herford, 1538, 8vo.

— George. Reliquiæ divi Andreæ, or the State of the venerable and primatial See of St. Andrews. St. Andr. 1797, 4to.

Pp. 253. This work, though for the first time printed in 1797, was written in 1683. Bindley, pt. III. 320, 6s. 6d. Roxburghe, 8742, 17s.

MARTINELLI, Vincentio. Istoria d'Inghilterra. Lond. 1774, 4to. 3 vols. 10s. 6d.

An abbreviated translation of Rapin, addressed to Sig. Luke Corsi. Istoria critica della Vita civile. Lond. 1752, 4to. 6s. Lettere familiari e critiche. Lond. 1758, 8vo. 5s.

MARTINENGO, Earl Nestor. *See* MALIM, Wm.

MARTINIERE, Bruzen de la. A new Voyage to the Northern Countries. Lond. 12mo. 1674.

MARTIN-MARPRELATE. Tracts. 'There was not only one *Martin Marprelate*, but other venomous books daily printed and dispersed; books that were so absurd and scurrilous, that the graver divines disdained them an answer. And yet these were grown into high esteem with the common people, till *Tom Nash* appeared against them all; who was a man of a sharp wit, and the master of a scoffing Satyricall merry pen, which he imployed to discover the absurdities of those malitious senseless pamphlets, and sermons as senseless as they; *Nash* his answers being like his Books; which bore them or like Titles, 'An Almond for a Parrot,' 'A Fig for my God-son, Come crack me this Nut,' and the like, so that his merry list made some sport, and such a discovery of their absurdities as (which is strange) he put a greater stop to their malicious pamphlets than a much wiser man had been able.'—*Iz. Walton.* The libels of Martin Marprelate are attributed to four persons named Penry, Throgmorton, Udal, and Fenner. Copious notices of them will be found in Fuller's Church History, Wood's Athenæ Oxon. by Dr. Bliss, Collier's Ecclesiastical History, Ames' Typogr. Antiquities, by Herbert, and Beloe's Anecdotes of Literature.

Theses Martinianæ. Printed by the Assignes of Martin Junior, without any Priviledge of the Catercaps. [1589]. B, in eights. Heber, pt. vi. 5s. 6d. A second and finer copy in pt. vi. 2263, 1l. 11s.

Anti-Martinus, sive Monitio cujusdam Londinensis contra Martin Marprelat. Lond. 1589, 4to. pp. 60. Bindley, pt. I. 644, 3s. Burstell, 188, 8s. 6d.

Martins Months Minde, that is, a certaine Report and true Description of the Death and Funeralls of olde Martin Marre-prelate, the great Makebate of England, and Father of the Factions. 1589, 4to. II, in fours. Strettell, 1255, 1l. 1s. Saunders' in 1818, 4l. 10s. Heber, pt. VIII. 10s. Bright in a volume, with 7 other tracts, in fine condition, 21l. This and the previous piece are attributed to Thos. Nash; but this last is subscribed 'Marphorius.' It is dedicated 'to Pasquin of England,' a name given to Nash.

MARTIN MARPRELATE—*contd.*
The Returne of the renowned Cavaliero Pasquill of England. 1589, 4to. D, in fours. Roman letter. *See* Nash, Thomas.
A Countercuffe given to Martin Junior; by the venturous, hardie and renowned Pasquill of England, Cavaliero. Printed betwene the Skye and the Grounde, &c. 1589, 4to. Heber, pt. viii. 4s. Four leaves, including the title. Roman letter. Generally ascribed to Thos. Nash. *See* Brydges' British Bibliographer, ii. 124-7.
A Dialogue wherein is plainly laide open the tyrannicall dealing of L. Bishops against Gods children: with certaine Points of Doctrine, wherein they approoue themselues (according to D. Bridges his judgement) to be truely Bishops of the Diuell. 12mo, D in fours, very neatly printed in roman letter. No pagination.—1589, 4to.—1640. Heber, pt. vii. 6s. Another edition with new title, 'Character of a Puritan and his Gallimaufrey of the Anti-Christian Party; prepared with D. Bridges' Sance for the present time to feed on, with a description of a Puritan in verse.' Printed in the time of Parliament. 1641, sm. 4to. Utter, pt. ii. 2214, 1L 5s.
The Protestatyon of Martin Marprelat, wherein he maketh known that he feareth neither Proud Priest, Antichristian Pope, tirannous Prelat, nor godlesse Catercap. n. d. 16mo. D in fours, or 32 pages, printed 23 by mistake. Roman letter. Heber, pt. vi. 10s.—1590, 16mo. Bindley, pt. i. 1836, with Certaine demonstrative conclusions, 2L 10s.
A Whip for an Ape, or Martin displaied. 4to. BLACK LETTER. In 21 six-line stanzas, on 4 leaves, the last page blank. Caldecott, 8L 4s. [Reprinted in D'Israeli's Quarrels of Authors.]
Pappe with an Hatchett; or, a Counter Cuffe to the Idiott Martin to hold his Peace. (1589), 4to. E iij. in fours. No pagination. Roman letter. [Reprinted, Lond. Petheram, 1845, post 8vo. 5s.]
The last Censure and Reproofes of Martin Junior. n. d. 12mo. D, in fours. No pagination. Small Roman letter. Bindley, pt. iii. 423, 1L 19s. Heber, pt. vi. 4s. In the Grenville Collection.
Sacred Decretal, or Hue and Cry for the Apprehension of Rev. Young Martin Marpriest. 1645, 4to. woodcut. Bright, 10s. 6d.
An Almond for a Parrat; or Cutbert Curry-knaves Almes. Fit for the knave Martin. 4to. Black letter. contains P, in fours, the last leaf blank, pp. 20. Midgeley, G, 1L Strettell, 175, 2L 2s. Heber, pt. viii. 18s. Bright, 1L 5s. [Reprinted, Lond. Petheram, 1844, post 8vo. 5s.]

Oh read over D. John Bridges, for it is a worthy Worke. Compiled by Martin Marprelate. Printed oversea in Europe, &c. 4to. (1588). [by John Peury]. Black letter. A to O in fours, pp. 54. Inglis, 561, 6s. Boswell, 1533, 12s. Gordonstoun, 1761, 1L 1s. White Knights, 3151, morocco, 1L 10s. Bright, 1L 8s. *See* Ames' Typog. Antiq. by Herbert, iii. 1683-5.
There are two works with nearly the same title; one, *the Epistle* as above, 'dedicated to the Confocation house,' 52 pages. The other, *the Epitome*, 'dedicated by a second Epistle to the terrible Priests,' 46 pages, also 4to. black letter, but without pagination; collates G 2, in fours, the last leaf blank. Both were published in 1588, [and reprinted, Lond. Petheram, 1843, post 8vo. 3s. each.]
Mar-Martin. 4to. n. p. or d. In verse. Three leaves. Reprinted in Brydges' Censura Literaria, vi. 236.
Marre-Mar-Martin; or Marre-Martin's Medling in a Manner misliked. 4to. n.p. or d. Black letter. In verse. Bright, 4L 6s.
Rhythmes against Martin Marre-Prelate. 4to. Bindley, pt. iii. 1638, 2L 15s.
Martin's Minerals. Certain Minerall and Metaphisical School points to be defended by the Reverend Bishops and the rest of my Cleargie, Masters of the Convocation House, against bothe Universities, and all the Reformed Churches in Christendome. Wherein is layd open the very Quintessence of all Catercorner divinitie, &c. An unique folio broadside, in the Lambeth Library.
Martin's Epistle sent from Scotland.
Hay any Worke for Cooper: Penned and compiled by Martin the Metropolitane. Printed in Europe, not farre from some of the bouncing Priestes. 4to. n. d. H 4, in fours. Pp. 48. Black letter. Strettell, 1L 1s. Inglis, 960, 14s. Caldecott, 8s. Saunders' in 1818, 1L 7s. An attempt to ridicule Bishop Cooper's meritous confutation. Also with a different title, 'Reformation no Enemie.'—1641. 4to. 6s. [Reprinted. Lond. Petheram, 1845, post 8vo. 3s.]
Hay any more Worke for the Cooper. While printing this, the press was discovered and seized at Manchester, with several pamphlets unfinished, as 'Epistle (Episco) Mastix, Paradoxes, Dialogues, Miscellanea, Versi Lectiones, Martin's Dream, the Lives and Doings of English Popes, Itinerarium or Visitationes, Lambethismes.'
History of the Martin Marprelate Controversy, by Rev. W. Maskell. Lond. Pickering. 1845, post 8vo.
'In the early part of the Rebellion against Charles I. several of the old Marprelate tracts were reprinted, and diligently dispersed.'—*Maskell.*

See Bridges, John, p. 270. Cartwright, Thomas. Cooper, Thomas, p. 519. Dialogue, p. 639. Lilly, John, p. 1351. Nash, Thomas. Pasquil. Penry, John. Some, R. T. T. Wright, Leonard.

Martin Mar-People (Sir). His Collar of Esses. 1590, 4to. In verse.

King and Lochée's, in March, 1810, 5s. 6d.

Martin Mar-sixtus. A second Replie against the Defensory and Apology of Sixtus the fifth, late Pope of Rome, defending the execrable Fact of the Iacobine Frier, vpon the Person of Henry the Third, late King of France, to be both commendable, admirable and meritorious. Wherein the saide Apology is faithfully translated, directly answered, and fully satisfied. Lond. 1592, 4to.

Twenty-three leaves. In the Preface to this little Work is an attack on the unfortunate Robert Green. It is inscribed 'To the right worshipful and vertuous Gentleman Master Edmund Bowyer, Esquiler,' and signed R. W. Gordonstoun, 1471, 4s. 6d. Bright, 3s. 6d.

Martyn, John, F.R.S. Historia Plantarum rariorum, Decades quinque. Lond. 1728-37, folio. 1*l.*1s.

With 50 plates, printed in colours by Kirkall. White Knights, 2776, russia, 2*l.*

Tabulæ synopsicæ Plantarum officinalium ad Methodum Ralamum dispositæ. Lond. 1726, folio.

Methodus Plantarum circa Cantabrigiam nascentium. Lond. 1727, 12mo.

Dissertations and critical Remarks upon the Æneids of Virgil, containing, among other interesting Particulars, a full Vindication of the Poet from the Charge of Anachronism with Regard to the Foundation of Carthage. To the Whole is prefixed, some Account of the Author and his Writings. Lond. 1771, 12mo. 5s. 6d. *See* Virgil.

— Joseph. New Epigrams (60) and a Satyre. Lond. 1621, 4to.

Sixteen leaves. Sir M. M. Sykes, pt. II. 498, 6*l.* 10s. Bindley, pt. III. 829, 4*l.* 7s. Gardner in 1854, 1*l.* 4s. Heber, pt. iv, 1*l.* 10s. Bright, 2*l.* 12s. A notice of this volume will be found in Brydges' British Bibliographer, ii. 65—7.

— Thomas. Flora Rustica, exhibiting Figures of such Plants as are either useful or hurtful in Husbandry; with scientific Characters, popular Descriptions and useful Observations. Lond. 1792—4. 8vo. 4 vols. often bound in one.

Each volume contains 36 coloured plates, with their corresponding descriptions. White Knights, 2646, 1*l.* 11s.

Plantæ Cantabrigienses: or a Catalogue of Plants which grow wild in the County of Cambridge. Lond. 1763, 8vo.

The English Connoisseur: containing an Account of whatever is curious in Painting and Sculpture, &c. in the Palaces and Seats of the Nobility and Gentry of England, both in Town and Country. Lond. 1766, 12mo. 2 vols. 5s. Published anonymously.

Catalogus Horti Botanici Cantabrigiensis: a Catalogue of the Botanic Garden at Cambridge. Camb. 1771, 8vo. with a plan.

Elements of Natural History. Camb. 1775, 8vo. vol. I. pt. I. Mammalia, 3s.

A Tour through Italy. Lond. 1791, 8vo. with a coloured chart. Edwards, 500. 4s. Fonthill, 2055, 15s.

The Language of Botany: being a Dictionary of the Terms made Use of in that Science, principally by Linnæus; with familiar Explanations, and an Attempt to establish significant English Terms. The whole interspersed with critical Remarks. Lond. 1793, crown 8vo. —1795, 8vo.—1807, 8vo.

Thomas Martyn, who succeeded his father, John Martyn, F.R.S., as Regius Professor of Botany at Cambridge, published an improved edition of Miller's Gardener's Dictionary, and a translation of Rousseau's Botany, which see.

— Thomas. The Universal Conchologist: exhibiting the Figure of every known Shell, many of them nondescript, from the South Seas, accurately drawn and painted after Nature; with a new systematic Arrangement in English and French. Lond. 1784, &c. folio, 4 vols. 160 coloured plates, comprising 322 figures of shells.

Roscoe, 1785, red morocco, 34*l.* 2s. 6d. North, pt. II. 704, the first 2 vols. morocco, 8*l.* 8s. This superb work, published at different periods, is seldom found complete. Vols. I. and II. pp. 27, with 80 plates. Vols. III. and IV., 80 plates; all beautifully coloured.

Collection of 79 Paintings of nondescript Shells, collected in the different

Voyages to the South Seas. Lond. 1789, imp. 4to. (Probably the first two volumes of the preceding work.) Duke of York, 3164, morocco, 10l. 10s.

The English Entomologist, exhibiting all the coleopterous Insects found in England, including upwards of 500 different Species, arranged and named according to the Linnæan System. Lond. 1792, royal 4to. Pagus, English, 33; French, 41, with 42 plates, painted, and two plates representing the medals the author received for his Conchology. White Knights, 2722, morocco, 3l. Dent, 722, 3l. Duke of York, 3165, 4l. 4s. Beckford in 1817, no. 147, with the original drawings on vellum, and a portrait of the author, morocco, 17l. 17s.

Aranei; or, the Natural History of Spiders, including the principal Parts of the well-known work on the English Spiders, by Eleazar Albin; and also the whole of the celebrated Publication on Swedish Spiders, by Charles Clerk. Lond. 1793, royal 4to. Pp. 1-70, and 1-31, with plates, 1-11, and 1-17, coloured. Townsley, pt. ii. 1125, morocco, 3l. 5s. Beckford in 1817, 2l. 12s. 6d.

Psyche; Figures of nondescript lepidopterous Insects, or rare Moths and Butterflies from different parts of the World. Lond. 1797, royal 4to. with coloured plates. Townsley, pt. ii. 1133, 1l. 1s.

MARTIN, W. See MARTYN, W.
— Wm. Frederick. A new Dictionary of Natural History. Lond. 1784-5, folio, 2 vols. plates, 10s.

Copies occur with the plates coloured 2l. 4s.

Compiled by the Rev. W. Mavor, LL.D.

MARTYR, Peter, of Angleria. The Decades of the newe Worlde, or West India, &c. Wrytten in the Latine tounge. Translated into Englyshe by Rycharde Eden. Lond. G. Powell, 1555, 4to.

BLACK LETTER. This volume contains by signatures A A A a a 8, besides the prefaces on 21 leaves. Nassau, pt. ii. 748, 13s. Hibbert, 5368, with the five rem. decades, 1612, russia, 2l. 11s. Inglis, 963, with De Novo Orbe, by Lok, 1612, 4l. 14s. 6d. Caldecott, 2l. 1s. Heber, pt. ii. 1l. 19s.; vi. 5l. 15s. Bright, 3l. 10s. For second edition, 1577, see Eden, Richard.

De Orbe novo Decades VIII. cum Apoc. Rich. Haklvyt. Paris, 1587, 8vo. with a map. A copy is in the British Museum. Heber, pt. ix. 1l. 6s.

De Novo Orbe, or the History of the West Indies, translated by R. Eden, and enlarged by M. Lok. Lond. 1612, 4to.

Gordonstoun, 1637, 1l. 7s. Roxburghe, 7347, 3l. 7s. Heber, pt. vi. 17s. Bright, slightly damaged, 16s.

MARTYR, Peter, Vermilius. Commentries on the Book of Judges. Lond. 1564, folio.

Goldsmid, 683, 2l. 15s. Heber, pt. v. 5371, 10s. 6d. This volume, consisting of fol. 284, is dedicated to the 'Earle of Leicester,' by the printer, John Daye. At the end are the tables and index.

Tractatio et Disputatio de Sacramento Eucharistiæ et Disputatio de eadem, Oxonii habitæ A.D. 1549, 4to. A copy is in the Lambeth library.

A Discourse or Tractise, wherin he openly declared his whole and determinate judgemente of the Sacramente of the 'Lordes Supper (translated by Nic. Udall). Lond. by Robert Stoughton, n. d. 4to. pp. cx. Sotheby's in 1824, 10s. Heber, pt. vii. 11s.

Diatribe de Hominis Justificatione contra Pet. Martyrem. Lovain, 1550, 8vo.

An Epistle written to the Duke of Somerset, anone after his deliverance out of trouble. Translated by Thomas Norton. Lond. 1550, 16mo. From Maunsell's catalogue, p. 66. In the Grenville collection, and Lambeth library.

A Treatise of the Cohabitacyon of the Faithfull with the Vnfaithfull, translated by Miles Coverdale: whereunto is added, a Sermon made of the Confessyng of Chryste and his Gospell and of the Denyinge of the same. Made in the Convocation of the Clergie at Zuricke, the 28th Jan. 1555, by H. B. [Henrie Bullinger]. Printed in angular Gothic type, probably at Zurich, 16mo.), . 6. in eights. Caldecott, 16s. 6d. Horner, 1834, mor. 1l. 18s.

Commentaries on the Epistle of S. Paul to the Romanes, translated by H. B. [ullinger]. Lond. 1568, folio. Sotheby's in 1824, 19s.

Most Godly Prayers compiled out of Davids Psalmes. Translated into English by Charles Glemham. Imprinted by Peres, 1569, 16mo. Heber, pt. v. 6s. 6d. Sir M. M. Sykes, pt. ii. 337, 11s. resold Sotheby, June, 1836, 1l. 5s.

A briefe and most excellent Exposition of the xij Articles of our Fayth, translated by T. P. Lond. 1576, 10mo. K 4, in eights.—n. d. 16mo.

Loci communes ex variis ipsis Auctoribus Libris collecti, et in quatuor Classes distributi. Lond. 1576, fol. 10s.

Common Places. Translated by A. Marten. Lond. 1583, folio. 16s.

An account of Peter Martyr will be found in Wood's Athen. Oxon.

MARTYRS and Martyrology.

Novitates quædam ex diversorum præstantium epistolis desumptæ. De Sancto-

MARTYRS, &c.—*continued.*
rum in Regno Angliæ persecutione ac
Martyrii constantia Joannis Roffensis
Episcopi, Thomæ Mori Cancellarii, com-
nullorum aliorum tum religiosorum tum
secularium, sine loco et anno (1536), 12mo.
12 leaves.

Historia aliquot nostri Sæculi Martyrum in Anglia, cum pia, tam Lecta jucun-
da, nun quam antehac Typis excusa. Mo-
guntiæ, 1550, 4to. a, b, and D to E, in fours.
The running title of this book is 'Historia
Martyrum Angliæ.' Bindley, pt. ii. 1927,
1l. 10s. Stewart, W. and A. in Feb. 1828,
1l. 13s. Bright, 15s.—Ed. altera, Brugis,
apud Philippum Juntam, 1583, 8vo. To this
edition is subjoined an Epistle from the
Editor, Thelesinus a Urageuns, titular
Bishop of York, not in the former edition.

Illustria Ecclesiæ Catholicæ Trophæa,
1573. S-1 Ecclesiæ, p. 709.

Acta Martyrum, eorum videlicet qui hoc
Sæculo in Gallia, Germania, Anglia, Flan-
dria, Italia, constans dederunt Nomen
Evangelio, idque Sanguine suo obsigna-
runt, ab Wiclefo et Husso ad hunc usque
diem. Genev. 1556, 12mo. 9s.

Actiones et Monumenta Martyrum,
eorum qui a Wicleffo et Husso ad nostram
hanc ætatem, in Germania, Gallia, Britannia, &c. veritatem Evangelicam sanguine suo obsignaverunt. Genevæ, Jo.
Crispinus, 1560, 4to. 1l. 1s.

De Persecutione Anglicana Epistola
qua explicantur afflictiones et acerbissima
martyria quæ Catholici nunc Angli pa-
tiuntur [par R. Parsons]. 12mo. Bononiæ,
1581. Ingolstad, 1582, 12mo.—In French,
Paris, 1582, 8vo. Bright, 17s.—Rom. 1582.
Bindley, 5l. 16s. 6d. 8 plates. Bright, 15s.
See Parsons, R.

Historia del glorioso Martirio di sediei
Sacerdoti martirizati in Inghilterra l'Anno
1581-3, trad. dall' Inglese. Macerata,
1583, 8vo. With six plates copied from
the Latin edition. Hibbert. 3835, morocco,
2l. Sotheby's in July 1831, 3l. 9s. Bindley,
pt. ii. 825, 4l. 10s. Heber, pt. ii. 3098,
2l. 2s.—1583, with six plates. Bindley,
pt. iii. 84, 2l. 3s. Heber, pt. iv. 1l. 11s.
Copies of both editions are in the British
Museum.—Altra edizione, s'è aggiunto il
Martirio di due altri Sacerdoti e uno seco-
laro Inglesi martyrizati l'anno 1577 e
1578. Milano, 1584, sm. 8vo. pp. 206, with
two woodcuts, copied from the last two in
the editions previously noticed.

Relacion de algunos Martyres que de
nuevo han hecho los Hereges en Ingla-
terra, traduzida do Ingles en Castellano
per Robert Persono. Madrid, 1590, 12mo.
6s. Rob. Parsons the Jesuit was probably
the author as well as the translator of
those several editions.

A briefe Historie of the Martyrdom of
12 reverend Priests, executed within these
twelve Moneths for Confession and Defence of Catholicke Faith, but under false
Pretence of Treason, a Note of sundrie
Things that befel them in their Life and
Imprisonment, and a Preface declaring
their Innocence. Printed An: 1582, sm.
8vo.—The same in Latin, under the title
Brevis Narratio felicis Agonis, &c. Pragæ,
1583, sm. 8vo. Gardner, 1l.

Vera Relazione del Martirio di due
Rev. Sacerdoti (Nicol e Yaxley) a due
Laici seguito l'anno 1589, in Oxonio citta
di Studio in Inghilterra. Roma con li-
cenzia de' Superiori, e ristampata in Firenze l'anno 1590, sm. 8vo. Four leaves.
—In French. Paris, 1590. Bright, 7s. 6d.

Relatio Incarcerationis et Martyrii P.
Joannis Ogilbei Scoti, e Soc. Jesu Presbyteri, ex autographo ipsius Martyris in
carcere exarato Glasguæ octiduo ante
mortem. Duaci, 1615, 12mo. Heber, pt. vi.
6s. 6d. (Reprinted in Miscellaneous Papers principally illustrative of Events in
the reigns of Queen Mary and King
James VI. Glasg. 1834, 4to. See Maitland Club, Appendix.)

Coppie d'une Lettre envoyee d'Angleterre au Seminaire des Anglois à Douay,
contenant l'Histoire du Martyre de quatre
autres Prestres de mesme College, les-
quels ont esté condamnez et mis à Mort
en Angleterre en ceste presente Année
1616, pour avoir esté recognues Prestres.
Douay, 1616, 8vo. 7s.—Douay, 1618, 8vo.

Martyrium Corn. Doveelli, 1614. See
Ireland.

The English Martyrologie, (by John
Wilson, or Watson), Douay, 1640, 8vo.
Bindley, pt. i. 2122, 18s. 6d.—Douay, 1671.
Hazlewood, in 1876. See Watson, John.

The Theatre of Catholique and Protestant Religion, by I. C. 1620, 8vo. At
the end of this work will be found a complete Catalogue of those persons that suffered death for the Catholick faith, as
well under King Henry VIII. as Queen
Elizabeth and James, i.e. from A.D. 1535
unto 1618; and the pages following to
596 give much curious matter relating
to the Martyrs and Confessors of Ireland
under Queen Elizabeth.

The Palme of Christian Fortitude, or
the glorious Combats of Christians in
Japonia, taken out of Letters of the Society of Jesus, from thence, anno 1624
—permissu superiorum, 1630, 12mo. Jadis, 93, 18s. (In this is 'a curious and
faithful narration of the numerous Jesuits who suffered martyrdom in Japan,'
Dec. 1623 to Nov. 1624.) See Japan.

La Mort glorieuse de plusieurs Prestres
Anglois, seculieres et religieux, qui ont
souffert le Martyre pour la Defense de la
Foy en Angleterre, 1645, 4to.

MARTYRS, &c.—continued.
Brachy-martyrologia, 1657. See BRINKLEY, Nicholas.
The Royal Martyrs from 1641 to 1658. Lond. 1660, folio.
The State Martyrologie from 1613 to 1670, Lond. 1680, folio.—Lond. 1700, folio.
The Roman Martyrologie, set forth by the command of Pope Gregory XIII., and reviewed by the authority of Urban VII., translated out of Latin by G. K. (George Keynes), of the Society of Jesus. S. Omers, 1627, sm. 8vo. front. by De Jode.—Nassau, pt. ii. 262, 9s.—Second edition, with divers saints put on the calendar not in the former edition. S. Omers, 1667, sm. 8vo. pp. 376, besides title and prefatory matter, 9 leaves.
A New Martyrology, 1680, 8vo. 5s.
History of the English Martyrs who suffered Death for opposing the Romish Religion. Lond. 1720, 8vo.
A Select History of the Lives and Sufferings of the principal English Protestant Martyrs. Lond. 1740, 8vo.
The Spirit of Antichrist displayed in the History of the English Martyrs, 1740. 5s.
Western Martyrology. See JEFFREIES.
The Book of Martyrs. Lond. 1765, 12mo. 5 vols. 1l. 1s.
Memorial of ancient British Piety, or a British Martyrology. Lond. 1761, 12mo. 5s.
See ANDREWS, W. BUTLER, Alban, Cartesian Triplex. CHAUNCEY, M., p. 430. FOX, John, p. 820. HAVENSIUS, H., p. 1012. Martiloge. WORTHINGTON, Thomas. Wright, Peter. VERSTEGAN, R. YEPEZ.

MARVELL, Andrew. The Works of Andrew Marvell, Esq. Poetical, Controversial, and Political, containing many original Letters, Poems, and Tracts, never before printed; with a new Life of the Author, by Capt. Edward Thompson. Lond. 1776, 4to. 3 vols. Portrait by Basire, 4l. 4s.
Marquis of Townshend, 21l. 3s, 2l. 15s. Heath, 1707, 2l. 17s. Hollis, 707, morocco, 4l. 7s. A notice of Marvell will be found in the Retrospective Review, x. 828—43, and xi. 174—95; and a Life, in H. Coleridge's Northern Worthies.
The Works of Andrew Marvell (to which is prefixed, an Account of the Life and Writings of the Author, by Mr. Cooke). Lond. 1772, 12mo. 2 vols. This selection contains only the Poems and Letters.—Lond. 1776, 12mo. 2 vols. fine portrait.—1726, 12mo. 2 vols. Hollis, 615, morocco, 17s. 6d.
The Rehearsal transprosed, or Animadversions upon a late work intituled 'A Preface showing what grounds there are of Fears and Jealousies of Popery,' by Dr. Sam. Parker, Bishop of Oxford. Lond. 1672-3, 12mo. 2 vols. 7s. 6d. Swift observed, that this was the only instance of an answer which could be read with pleasure, when the publication which occasioned it was forgotten. A second impression of vol. i., dated 1672, appeared, with additions and amendments. On the back of the title is an advertisement, stating that a counterfeit impression had already appeared under the Title and Pretence of a second edition, 'whereas in truth, it is corrupt in the sense and words of the copy;' signed N. P. (Nathaniel Pond, the Publisher).—Throughout the work I. O. stands for Dr. J. Owen; Mr. D., Mr. Baxter; Mr. Hayes, Dr. Parker.
Mr. Smirke, or the Divine in Mode; being certain Annotations upon the Animadversions written by Dr. Fran. Turner, on a late Pamphlet, entitled The Naked Truth (by Bishop Croft); together with a short historical Essay concerning general Councils, Creeds, and Impositions in Matters of Religion, 1674, 4to. The essay was reprinted 1680, 4to.—1687, 4to.—1680, 8vo.
An Account of the Growth of Popery and arbitrary Government in England; more particularly from the long Prorogation of Parliament of Nov. 1675, ending the 15th of Feb. 1676, till the last Meeting of Parliament the 16th of July, 1677. Lond. 1678, folio. Reprinted in State Tracts, 1689, folio. This pamphlet, which traces the intrigues of the Court of England with that of France, made a great impression on the nation. A reward of 100l. was offered in the Gazette, for the discovery of the author.
Miscellaneous Poems. Lond. 1681, folio, with an octagon portrait of A. Marvell. Roscoe, 1880, 1l. 16s.
(Marvell's Poems are included in several Collections.)
Flagellum Parliamentarium; being sarcastic Notices of nearly 200 Members of the first Parliament after the Restoration, A.D. 1661 to 1678. Lond. 1877, 8vo. 4s. Edited by Sir Harris Nicolas, from a contemporary MS. in the British Museum. This bitter article was originally published, with some variations, under the title of 'A seasonable Argument.' Another copy occurs in the additional MS. No. 4106, in the Museum, and the same was also printed under the title of 'A List of the principal Labourers in the Design of Popery,' &c. For the discovery of the author, 50l. were offered by the government.

MARY, The Virgin. The Myracles of our Lady. Lond. by Wynkyn de Worde, 1514, 4to.
A copy is in the British Museum.— 1530, 4to. Twenty-four leaves printed by W. de Worde. Horne Tooke, 474, 13*l.* 10*s.* —Printed in Caxton's House by Wynkin de Worde, 4to. A copy is in Dr. Hunter's library at Glasgow.

The song of Mary the Mother of Christ; containing the Story of his Life and Passion, the Tears of Christ in the Garden, with the Description of heavenly Jerusalem. Lond. 1601, 4to. Pp. 46. In this work are six poems. Reed, 7438, 1*l.* 2*s.* Inglis, 1363, 2*l.* 9*s.*

MARY Magdalen's Lamentations for the Losse of her Maister Iesvs. Lond. 1601, 4to.
Twenty-seven leaves, by N. Breton. —1604, 4to. pp. 62. Bibl. Anglo-Poet. 938, 10*l.* 10*s.* Nassau, pt. II. 143, 8*l.* 1*s.* Midgeley, 495, 3*l.* 13*s.* 6*d.* Heber, pt. IV. 6*s.* Another, ll. 16*s.* Caldecott, 2*l.* 10*s.*
Saint Marie Magdalen's Conversion. Printed with licence (1603), 4to. A Poem written by a Romen Catholic—the second stanza of which contains some curious allusions to several of Shakspeare's works. Caldecott, 3*l.* S— C. J., p. 342.
The Soules Pilgrimage to heavenly Hierusalem. In three severall Dayes Journeyes. By three severall Wayes; Purgative, Illuminative, Unitive. Expressed in the Life and Death of Saint Mary Magdalen. Printed in the Yeare 1650, 4to. Saunders' in 1818, 3*l.* 3*s.*
Mary Magdalens Pilgrimage to Paradise, wherein are lively imprinted the Footsteps of her excellent Vertues for Sinners to follow, who desire to accompany her thither, by J. S., of the Society of Jesus. [Douay] permissu superiorum, 12mo. pp. 142. Interspersed with poetry.
Mary Magdalens Tears wip't off, or the Voice of Peace to an unquiet Conscience. By a Person of Quality [T. Martin.] Lond. 1659, 12mo. with frontispiece by Gaywood. Nassau, pt. I. 9210, 3*s.* Towneley, pt. I. 549, with front. by Hollar, 6*s.* 6*d.* Bliss, 2*s.*
See SOUTHWELL, Robert.

MARY MAGDALENE of Pazzi, Saint, The Life of. Lond. 1687, 4to.

MARY of the Holy Cross. A short Account of the Life and Virtues of the Abbess of the English Poor Clares at Rouen. Lond. 1767, 8vo.

MARY, S. of Egypt.—A sacred Poeme, describing the miracvlovs Life and Death of the gloriovs Convert S. Marie of Ægypt, who passed fortie-seauen Yeares in the Desarts, leading a penitentiall Life, to the Astonishment of all succeeding Ages. (Douay, circa 1650), 4to.
Pp. 66. Bibl. Anglo-Poet 690, 10*l.* 10*s.* Sotheby's in 1821, 19*s.* 6*d.* Heber, pt. VIII. 2*l.* 3*s.* Bright, 2*l.* 7*s.*

MARY of Nemmegen.—A lyttell Story that was of a trewthe done in the Lande of Gelders of a Mayde that was named Mary of Nemmegen, yt was the Dyuels Paramoure by the Space of vij Yere longe. Antwerpe by me John Duisborowgho, n. d. 4to.
Twenty leaves without signatures. Roxburghe, 6378, 67*l.*, resold White Kuights, 2724, 42*l.*, resold Inglis, 964, 24*l.*, resold Hibbert, 5369, 14*l.* 13*s.* 6*d.*; again, Heber, pt. IX. 16*l.*

MARY, Daughter of King Henry VII.
The Solempnities and Triumphes doon and made at the Spousellz and Mariage of the Kinge's Doughter the Lady Marye, to the Prynce of Castyla, Archduke of Austrige. 4to. Eight leaves, printed by Pynson. This very curious tract alludes to an intended marriage of Mary to the Emperor Charles V., which match, for reasons of state, was broken off. In 1513 the union was again proposed, and failed also: in the same year Mary became the wife of Lewis XII. of France, after whose decease she married Charles Brandon, Duke of Suffolk. A detailed account of this tract (a copy of which is in the British Museum) is given by Sir H. Ellis, in the Archæologia, xvIII. pt. I. p. 33.— 1818, 4to. Presented to the members of the Roxburghe Club by the late John Dent, Esq. Dent, pt. II. 1205, 1*l.* 13*s.* Roswell, 5083, 3*l.* 19*s.* Sir M. M. Sykes, pt. I. 1627, 4*l.* ON VELLUM, one copy struck off.
L'Ordre des Joustes faites a Paris a l'Entree de la Reine, Femme de Lovis XII. Ecrit par Montjole, Hel d'Armes. (1512) 8vo.
L'entre de la tres-excellente Princesse Mad. Marie d'Angleterre, Reine de France, en la noble Ville de Paris le 6 Novembre 1513. Paris, 1514, 8vo.
Epitre au Nom d'illustre Dame Mad. Marie, Reine Douairiere de France, qu'elle resrit au Roy d'Angleterre son frere, Henri VIII. touchant le Trepas du Roy Lovis XII. son Espoux.

Bernardini Rincii Mediolanensis Epistalamion in Nuptiis Francisci Gallarum Delphini et Mariæ Britannorum Regis Filiæ. (Paris) 1518, sm. 4to. A—C, twelve leaves.—Sylva Bernardini Rincii, Apparatum, Ludos, Convivium explicans, &c. (Paris) 1518, sm. 4to. A—B. in fours.— Oratio Rich. Parei in pace superrime composita et federe percusso inter Anglim regem et Francorum regem, in æde Divi Pauli Londini habita. Paris, 1518, sm. 4to. A and B in fours.

These three tracts are bound together in the British Museum.

The Illustrious Lovers, or Princely Adventures in the Courts of England and France; containing sundry Transactions relating to love Intrigues, noble Enterprises, and Gallantry; being an Historical Account of the famous Lovers of Mary, sometime Queen of France, and Charles Brandon, the renowned Duke of Suffolk. From the French. Lond. 1680, 8vo. The running title of this volume is 'English and French Adventures;' it was issued a second time, with title, 'The English Princess, or the Duchess Queen, in two Parts.'

MARY I., Queen of England, daughter of K. Henry VIII.

Coronatione de la Regina d'Inghilterra fatta li di primo d'Ottobre, 1553. 8vo. 4 leaves. Hibbert, 6868, in a vol. In the Grenville Collection.

This and other rare foreign tracts relating to Queen Mary and her husband, Philip of Spain, are in the Grenville Collection. See that Catalogue, pp. 446, 447, pt. i.; p. 809, pt. ii.

A Declaration of Q. Mary of her Profession of the true Religion, and forbidding the Names of Distinction (Papists and Hereticks) among her Subjects. Gyven at Rychmond, xviii. Aug. Regni f. Excusum in Ædibus Johannis Cawodi (1553).

A godlie and devout Prayer for the Quenes Hyghnes Delyveraunce, and for the Quietnes and Wealth of this Realme. Excudit J. Cawodus. A broadside.

Tractatus matrimonialis inter Mariam Angliæ Reginam et Philippum. Bibl. Cott. Vitellius, 116, in British Museum.

The Ballad of Joye vpon the Publication of Q. Mary, Wife of King Philip, her being with Child, Anno Do. 1554. Lond. by Wyllyam Ryddnell (1554). Reprinted in Dr. Dibdin's edition of Ames' Typogr. Antiquities, vol. iv. 407-8, from a copy in the Pepysian Library, Cambridge.

Copie of a Letter sent from the Councill to E. (Bonner) Bp. of London, concerning Q. Mary's conceiving with Child. A Broadside dated from Westminster, Nov. 27, 1554, printed by J. Cawood. Jolley, 653, 7l. 2s. 6d. See Strype's Life of Cranmer, folio, p. 307. It is reprinted in Fox's Martyrs, edit. 1562, p. 1014.

Vera Expositio Disputationis institutæ mandato D. Mariæ Reginæ Angliæ, &c. in Synodo Ecclesiastica. Londini. In Comitiis Regni ad 16 Octob. Anno 1553. Romæ, 1554, 8vo. A copy in a bookseller's recent catalogue was priced 5l. 5s. Bright, with another piece, 1l. 18s.

Il Felicissimo Ritorno del Regno d'Inghilterra alla Catholica Unione et alla Obedientia della sede Apostolica. Roma, 1554, 4to. Heber, pt. i. 4510, 1l. 14s.

Lettere del Re d'Inghilterra (Philip II.) a del Card. Polo al Papa Julio III., sopra la reduttione di quel regno alla unione della santa madre Chiesa et obedienza della sede Apostolica. Roma (1554), 4to. This rare piece concludes with the Pope's absolution of England from heresy. A copy was in Lord Guildford's collection, pt. iii., and another, with the previous piece, in part ii.

Gratulatorium in Philippi II. Adventum in Belgium, et in Nuptias cum Maria Angliæ. Colon. 1555, 4to. Bindley, pt. II. 1658, 10s. Heber, pt. vii. 4828, 19s.

A Supplication to the Queen's Majestie. Imp. for J. Cawoods, 1555. BLACK LETTER. This piece is dated 1555, but internal evidence proves it to be of the year 1555. A and B, in eights, C, 4 leaves. Sotheby, 1832, f.L.12s. Puttick, June. 1858, 17l. 5s.

The Epitaphe upon the Death of the most excellent and our late vertuous Queue Marie deceased. Augmented by the first Author. Lond. by Richd. Lant (1558). In Verse. Reprinted in the tenth volume of the Harleian Miscellany from a copy, supposed unique, in the library of the London Society of Antiquaries.

Memoirs of Queen Mary's Dayes; wherein the Church of England and all the Inhabitants may plainly see (if God hath not suffered them to be Infatuated) as in a Glass, the sad Effects which follow a Popish Successor enjoying the Crown of England. Printed in the Year 1681, folio. pp. 4. Reprinted in the first volume of the Harleian Miscellany.

The History of the Life, bloody Reign, and Death of Queen Mary, eldest Daughter to Henry VIII. The third Edition corrected; to which is now added, an Account of the remarkable Judgements of God on many of the Persecutors. Lond. 1682, 12mo. A—I, in twelves, with a front. Nassau, pt. i. 1587, 7s.

New Lights thrown upon the History of Mary Queen of England, eldest Daughter of Henry VIII. Lond. 1771, 8vo. 8s. Addressed to David Hume.

Household Book of the Princess Mary, Daughter of Henry VIII., afterwards Queen Mary. Edited by Sir F. Madden.

Lond. 1830, 8vo. 1l. 1s. LARGE PAPER, only twelve printed.
See DICKES, Thomas, p. 608. DEWES, Giles, p. 635. ELDER, John. GUIDUS, F. A., p. 955. JUNIUS, Hadrian. NIGER, F. P. PALGGRAVE, John. PHILIP II., King of Spain. TUNSTALL, Cuthbert.

MARY STUART, Queen of Scots.

The Ceremonial of the Marriage of Mary Queen of Scots with the Dauphin of France (1557). Lond. 1818, 4to. BLACK LETTER. Printed by Wm. Bentham, Esq. for presentation to the members of the Roxburghe Club. Dent, pt. II. 1210, 1l. 8s. Boswell, 3051, 3l. 13s. Sir M. M. Sykes, pt. I. 1632, 4l. 11s. *See* ROXBURGHE CLUB, Appendix.

A Declaration of the triumphant Marriage of the two maist nobill Prince and Princesse, Francis de Valoys and Mary Stuart, by the Grace of God King and Quene of Scotland, and Dolphine and Dolphin of France. Paris, 1558, 8vo.

In Francisci Illustrias. Francisce Delphini et Mariæ serenism. Scotorum Reginæ Nuptias, Viri cujusdam amplis Carmen. Paris, apud Morell. 1558, 4to. A poetical tract by Michael Hospitalius. Heber, pt. vii. with other pieces, 1l.

Oratio quam ipsa Sponsallum die Regina Scotiæ ad Henricum regem habuit. Paris, 1558, 4to. Heber, pt. vii. in a vol.

Carmen Nuptiale in Delphicum et Mariam, a Renato Guillonio. Paris, 1558, 4to. Heber, pt. vii. 4108, in a vol. with several other pieces, ejusd. generis, 1l.

Other pieces were also produced in honour of this marriage; those by George Buchanan were translated and printed in English, 1711, 4to. eleven leaves. Reprinted, Edinb. 1845. Sixty copies on paper, one on vellum. A more elegant version from the pen of Archd. Wrangham has been printed.

Elegie sur le despart de la Royne Marie retournant à son Royaume d'Escosse. Lyon, 1561, 12mo. G. Chalmers, 8s.

Allegations against the surmised Title of the Queen of Scots and the Favourers of the same. 1565, 4to. A copy is in the British Museum.

Proditionis ab aliquot Scotiæ Perduellibus adversus serenissimam suam Reginam non ita pridem perpetratæ brevis et simplex Narratio. Lovanii, 1566, 8vo. A copy in a bookseller's recent catalogue was marked 6l. 6s.

De Maria Scotorum Regina, totaque ejus contra regem conjurationes, fædo cum Bothwellio adulterio, &c. Historia. (By George Buchanan.) 12mo. s. a. Illibert, 5131, 6s. 6d. A translation in French appeared, Edinb. 1572, 12mo.

De Maria Scotorum Regina, Historia

à Gall. Mov etlo, 1571, 16mo. Steevens, 1789, 12s. 6d.

A Discourse touching the pretended Match betwene the Duke of Norfolke and the Queene of Scottes. (1571), 16mo. Roxburghe, 8728, title wanting, 17s. 6d. resold Heber, pt. v. 4s. 6d. Written, as supposed, by one Sampson a preacher. It is reprinted by Anderson in his collections relating to Mary Queen of Scots.

A Letter vindicating the Queen (Elizabeth) in the Case of the Duke of Norfolk and Queen of Scots. By R. G. Lond. by Richard Grafton, 1571, 10mo. BLACK LETTER, five leaves. Roxburghe, 6737, in a vol. with the two previously-named pieces, and others by Buchanan, 12l. 12s.

The Copie of a Letter, written by one in London to his Friend, concerning the Credit of the late published Detection (by G. Buchanan) of the Doynges of the Ladie Marie of Scotland (1572), 16mo. BLACK LETTER, 8 leaves. This tract is reprinted in the second volume of Anderson's Collection, and in the third volume of the Harleian Miscellany. A copy is in Trinity College Library, Cambridge. For the Detection, *see* BUCHANAN, Geo. p. 301.

L'Innocence de Marie Royne d'Escosse. Imprimé l'An. 1572, 8vo. Written by Francis de Dellaforest. Bp. of Ely, 559, 3l. 13s. 6d. Bindley, pt. II. 1080, 3l. 4s. Chalmers, 18s. Steevens, 1781, 1l. 7s. Bright, mor. 1l. 7s. Printed in Jebb's Collection.

Discours contre les Conspirations pretandues entre feltes sur l'Estat d'Angleterre, avec les Responses a celui qui defend la Cause et Innocence de la tras illustre Royne d'Escosse. Imprimé l'An. 1572. 8vo. A translation, with some additions, of an attack upon Queen Elizabeth, Lord Keeper Bacon, and Secretary Cecil, printed under the ironical title of 'A Treatise of Treasons against Q. Elizabeth,' &c. 1572. *See* THROCKMORTON, Francis.

A Proclamation concerning the Sentence against Mary Queen of Scots, dated Richmond, Dec. 4, 1586. Printed by Christ. Barker. Roxburghe, 8747, in a vol. with others, 21l.

Il Compassionevole et Memorabil caso della morte della Regina di Scotia. Vicenza, 1587, 4to. Heber, pt. vii. 12s.

Epitaphium Mariæ Scotiæ Reginæ, Lat. et Gall. Regale Monumentum. Discours de la Mort de Marie Stouard, Royne d' Escosse. 1587, 8vo.

Narratio Mortis Mariæ Stuartæ, Germanice. München, 1587, 4to. Heber, pt. vii. 8s.

Histoire de la Royne d'Escosse, Douairiere de France, prochè heritiere de la Royne d'Angleterre, avec un petit livr. de sa Mort — (with the following title: — 'La Mort de la Royno d'Escosse, Douai-

MARY, Q. of Scots—continued.
rière de France.') Paris, 1569, 8vo. Roxburghe, 6746, 5l. 15s. 6d.—Paris, 1589, sm. 8vo. Constable, 699, morocco, 19s. Dibdley, pt. II. 1751, 4l. 6s. Boswell, 1915, 2l. 16s. Heat, pt. i. 1896, 1l. 16s. Hibbert, 2l. 1s. Jadis, 79, with four folding woodcuts representing her execution, erroneously supposed to be unique, 4l. 10s. See Dibl. Westiana, no. 4553, 1l. 5s. Heber, pt. i. 4477, 2l. 1s. Reprinted in the second volume of Jebb's Collection. The two parts, being separately paged, are sometimes transposed, but are really only one work, the second being mentioned on the title of the first.

A Defence of the honorable Sentence and Execution of the Queene of Scots, with the Opinions of learned Men, and Answers to certaine Objections. Lond. by John Windet, 1587, 4to. By Maurice Kyffin. King and Lochée's in 1816, 5l. 5s. White Knights, 2725, morocco, 6l. 6s. Hibbert, 5364, morocco, 5l. 1s.—1588. Col. Stanley, 4l. 8s.

Apologie, ou defense d' l'honorable Sentence et tres-juste Execution de defuncte Marie Stenard, derniere Royne d'Escoss, avec les Copies des Lettres, Actes et Articles, qui servent à descouvrir et à bien verifier la Trahison de la dite Royne. (Paris) 1689, 8vo. Steevens, 1782, 1l. 9s. Bright, stained, 8s. 6d. At the end should be found two leaves of errata.

Summarium de Morte Mariæ Stuartæ, opera Romualdi Scoti. Ingolst. 1588, sm. 8vo. Nassau, pt. i. 120, with a portrait, and Barnestaple's Life of Mary, Queen of Scots, 1588, 6l.—Colon. 1627. Bp. of Ely, 1337. See BARNESTAPLE.

Vera e Compita Relatione del successo della Morte della Regina di Scotia, con la dichiarazione dell' essequie fatte in Parigi dal Christianissimo Re, suo cognato, e nomi de' personaggi intervenutivi. s. a. 4to. An Italian account of the execution; very interesting from the names being given of those attending the funeral honours paid to her memory at Paris. Heber, pt. v. in a volume, 1l. 9s.

Eat Natura Hominum Novitatis avida. The Scottish Queens Buriall at Peterborough, upon Tuesday beeing Lammas day, 1587. Lond. by A. J. (Abel Jeffes) for Ed. Venge, 1589, 16mo. four leaves. Roxburghe, 6744, 9l. 9s.

Collections relative to the Funerals of Mary, Queen of Scots, 1588. Containing 'The Scottish Queen's Buriall at Peterborough, upon Tuesday, being Lammas day, 1587,' with other contemporary Accounts from MSS. and early printed copies. Edited by Robert Pitcairn, Esq. Edinb. 1822, post 8vo. One hundred and twenty-five copies printed. Brockett, 1949, 6s. Hibbert, 5123, 17s. THICK PAPER, only 12 printed. Constable, in 1828, 2491, 17s.

Mariæ Stuartæ Scotorum Reginæ nuper ab Elizabetha Regina et Ordinibus Angliæ Supplicium et Mors pro Fide catholica constantissima, &c. Colonia, 1587, 8vo. Heber, pt. iv. 8s.; another, pt. v. 6s. 6d. A copy in a bookseller's recent catalogue was marked 4l. 4s.

The first Catholic publication on the execution of Mary.

Ode sur la Mort de Marie Royne d' Escosse, mort pour la Foy, par la Cruauté des Anglois Hereticques, Ennemys de Dieu, avec l'Oraison funebre prononcée a Notre Dame de Paris, au jour de ses obsequies. Paris, 1588, 8vo. Sir M. M. Sykes, pt. ii. 338, with Discours de la Mort de Maria. Anvers, 1589, 5l. 10s.

Discours de la Mort de Marie Steward. Anvers, 1589, 8vo. four leaves. Sir M. M. Sykes, pt. ii. 338, 8vo. with the Ode 1588. 5l. 10s. Another edition, without place or date.—Edinb. 1689, with Oraison Funebre, 12mo. Hibbert, 5123, 5s.

Oraison funebre de Marie Reyne d'Escosse, par Renauld de Beaulieu, Archevesque de Bourges. In Jebb's Collection.

Stuarta Tragœdia. Duaci, 1593, 4to. See HOULBATUS, Anton.

History of the Life and Death of. 1624, folio. See STRANGUAGE.

La Reina di Scotia. Tragedia di Federigo della Valle. Milano, 1628, 4to.

Maria Regina di Scotia, Poema heroico del Bassiano. Bologna, 1633, 4to. front. representing the execution. Hibbert, 5367, portraits inserted, morocco, 2l. 2s.

Marie Stuard, Reyne d'Escosse, de M. Regnault. Paris, 1639, 12mo. Heber, pt. vi. portraits of Mary and Elizabeth, 11s.

Maria Stuart of Gemarteide Majesteit. Treurspel. Keulen, 1646, 4to. with portraits on title-page.

La Maria Stuarda, Opera scenica, del Archidiacono Savaro, di Mileto. Milano, 1662, 12mo. Hibbert, 7128, 5s.

Mariæ Stuartæ Vivenlis ac Morientis Acta. (Anctore J. Dinselio.) Ambergæ, 1675, 12mo. Heber, pt. vii. 8s.—l'ermissu superiorum, 1723, with portrait.

Marie Stuart, Reyne d'Escosse, Nouvelle historique. Paris, 1675, 12mo. 3 pts. in 1 vol. From the Elzevir press. Streittell, 913, 9s. Lloyd, 844, 12s. Bindley, pt. ii. 1752, date 1645? 14. 7s. Roxburghe, 6748, date 1674, 8s.—Amst. 1712, 12mo. Hibbert, 5088, 1s. 6d.

A brief History of the Life of Mary, Queen of Scots, 1681, folio. By F. Walsingham. Roxburghe, 8751, 4s. 6d. G. Chalmers, 7s. 6d.

The Island Queen: or, Death of Mary,

MARY, Q. of Scots—*continued.*
Queen of Scotland. A Tragedy, by J.
Banks. Lond. 1684, 4to.—1704, 4to. This
edition is entitled the Albion Queens.

Vindication of Mary, Queen of Scotland,
from the vile Reflections and foul Aspersions of Buchanan. Lond. (circa 1715)
8vo.

The Genuine Letters of Mary, Queen of
Scots, to James, Earl of Bothwell, translated from the French Originals by Edw.
Simmonds. Westminster, 1781, 8vo. —
Second edition, 1726, 8vo. 6s.

De Vita & Rebus gestis Mariæ Scotorum Reginæ, quæ scriptis tradiderunt Auctores sedecim, recensuit a Sam. Jebb.
Lond. 1725, folio, 2 vols. 1l. 16s. With a
portrait of the Queen by Vertue, and a
genealogical table. Fonthill, 1378, 2l. 9s.
LARGE PAPER. Roxburghe, 6753, 3l. 10s.
Heath, 4718, 4l. Hibbert, 4353, 3l. 3s.

The History of the Life and Reign of
Mary, Queen of Scots, and Dowager of
France; extracted from original Records
and Writers of Credit. Written by Dr.
Sam. Jebb. Lond. 1725, 8vo. portrait of
the Queen by Vertue. Bindley, pt. (l.
1308, 9s. 6d. Heath, 4720, 8s. 6d. Brockett, 1502, 15s. LARGE PAPER, 18s.—Dublin, 1753, 8vo.

Life of Mary, Queen of Scots, translated
from the French (of P. le Pesant de Bois
Guilbert), with Notes, by James Freebairn. Edinb. 1725, 8vo.

The secret History of Mary, Queen of
Scots, and the real causes of her misfortunes. Translated from the French by
Eliza Haywood. Lond. 1725, 8vo. Brockett,
1484, 7s. Dowdeswell, 252, 9s.—Second
edition. Lond. 1726, 8vo.

Marie Stuart, Reyne d'Escosse, Tragedie. Paris, 1735, 8vo.

Vida e Morte tragica de Maria Stuart,
Rainho de França e Escocia par F. de
Sousa da Sylva Alcoforado Itebello. Lisboa, 1737, 4to.

Histoire de Marie Stuart, Reine d'Ecosse, avec les Pieces justificatives et des
Remarques (par M. M. de Marsy et Faron). Londres (Paris), 1742, 12mo. 2 vols.
with half-length portrait. Bindley, pt. II.
709, 1l. 8s.

Prejudice detected by Facts; or, a candid and impartial Enquiry into the Reign
of Q. Elizabeth, so far as it relates to
Mary, Q. of Scots. Lond. (1753), 8vo.

An Historical and critical Enquiry into
the Evidence produced by the Earls of
Murray and Morton against Mary, Queen
of Scots. With an Examination of the
Rev. Dr. Robertson's Dissertation, and Mr.
Hume's History, with Respect to that
Evidence. Edinb. 1772, 8vo. 3s.

Recherches sur Marie Stuart. Paris,
1773, 12mo. Brockett, 2494, 11s.

Critical Observations concerning the
Scottish Historians, Hume, Stuart, and
Robertson; including an Idea of the Reign
of Mary, Queen of Scots, as a Portion of
History; Specimens of the Histories of
this Princess by Dr. Stuart and Dr. Robertson; and a comparative View of the
Merits of these Historians; with a literary Picture of Dr. Robertson, in a contrasted Opposition with the celebrated
Mr. Hume. Lond. 1782, 8vo. 2s. 6d.

Miscellaneous Remarks on 'The Inquiry
into the Evidence against Mary, Queen of
Scots.' 1784, 8vo. Lloyd, 646, 10s.

History and Antiquities of Fotheringay; with some Account of the Execution
of Mary, Queen of Scots. Lond. 1787, 4to.
See Nichols' Bibl. Topog. Brit.

Mary, Queen of Scots, a Tragedy, by
the Hon. John St. John. Lond. 1789, 8vo.
2s.

A Sonnet, supposed to have been written by Mary, Queen of Scots, to the Earl
of Bothwell, previous to her marriage with
that Nobleman. Translated into English
by Mr. Shillito. To which is subjoined, a
Copy of the French Sonnet, written, as is
said, with the Queen's own Hand, and
found in a Casket, with other secret Papers. Lond. 1790, 8vo. 2s. 6d.

Mary, Queen of Scots, an historical Tragedy, by Mrs. Mary Deverell. Lond. 1792,
8vo. 2s. 6d.

History of Mary, Queen of Scots, including an Examination of the Writings
which are ascribed to her, by Dr. Thos.
Robertson. Edinb. 1793, 4to.

Mary Stewart, Queen of Scots. An historical Drama. Edinb. 1801, 8vo. By
James Grahame. Constable, 835, 4s. 6d.

Effusions of Love, from Chatelar to
Mary, Queen of Scotland. Translated
from a Gaelic Manuscript in the Scotch
College, at Paris, interspersed with Songs,
Sonnets, and Notes explanatory, by the
Translator. Lond. 1806, 12mo. 5s. An
undoubted forgery by W. H. Ireland; with
a frontispiece and portrait of Mary.
Brockett, 1181, morocco, 1l. 7s.

Lettres de Marie Stuart, Reine d'Ecosse; et de Christine Heine de Suède.
Paris, 1807, 12mo. 3 vols.

The Legend of Mary, Queen of Scots,
and other ancient Poems, from a MS. of
the 16th Century. By John Fry. Bristol,
1810, 8vo. 8s. 6l. LARGE PAPER, in 4to.
6s.

Mary, Queen of Scots, a Poem, by Margaretta Wedderburn. Edinb. 1811, 8vo.

The Queen's Wake, a legendary Poem,
by James Hogg. Edinb. 1813, royal 8vo.

Marie Stuart, Tragédie en cinq Actes,
par M. Pierre Le Brun. Paris, 1863, 8vo.

The Royal Exile; or Poetical Epistles of
Mary, Queen of Scots, during her Captivity in England. By a young Lady. Also,

MARY, Q. of Scots—*continued.*
by her Father, the Life of the Queen. Lond. 1822, 8vo. 2 vols. LARGE PAPER.

Mary Stuart, a dramatic Representation, by Miss Macauley. Lond. 1823, 8vo.

Love Letters of Mary, Queen of Scots, and Earl Bothwell. By Hugh Campbell, LL.D. Lond. 1825, 8vo. 6s.

The Case of Mary, Queen of Scots, and of Elizabeth, Queen of England, drawn from the State Papers, and most authentic Sources. By Hugh Campbell, LL.D. Lond. 1825, 8vo. 13s.

Mary, Queen of Scots, a Drama, taken from Sir Walter Scott's Novel of the Abbot. Edinb. 1825, 12mo.

Mary, Queen of Scots: her Persecutions, Sufferings and Trials, from her Birth till her Death. Glasg. 1836, 12mo. 7s. 6d.

James Maitland of Lethington's Narrative of the principal acts of the Regency, during the minority; and other papers relating to the History of Mary, Queen of Scotland. Ipswich, no date (1833). Fifty copies printed for private circulation, from Mr. Fitzh's MS.

Lettres Inédites de Marie Stuart, accompagnées de diverses Dépêches et Instructions, 1558-1587, publiées par le Prince Alex. Labanoff. Paris, 1839, 8vo. Copies printed on vellum paper for Members of the Society of the Bibliophiles Français.

Letters of Mary, Queen of Scots, and Documents connected with her Personal History, now first published, with an Introduction by Miss Agnes Strickland. Lond. 1843. post 8vo. 3 vols.— Second edition. Lond. 1843, post 8vo. 2 vols. 15s.

A Life of Mary, Queen of Scots, is in Miss Strickland's Lives of the Queens of Scotland. Edinb. 1850-1856, post 8vo. 6 vols. 3l. 8s.

Lettres, Instructions et Mémoires de Marie Stuart, Reine d'Ecosse, publiés sur les originaux et MSS. et accompagnés d'un résumé chronologique par le Prince Alex. Labanoff. Lond. 1844, 8vo. 7 vols. 4l. 4s. reduced to 1l. 1s. LARGE PAPER, only 50 printed.

Letters of Mary Stuart, Queen of Scotland, selected from the 'Recueil des Lettres de Marie Stuart,' together with the Chronological Summary, &c. by Prince Alexandre Labanoff. Translated, with notes, by W. Turnbull. Lond. 1845, 8vo.

Catalogue of the Antiquities, Works of Art, and Historical Scottish Relics exhibited in the Museum of the Archæological Institute, during their Annual Meeting, held at Edinburgh, July, 1856; comprising Notices of Mary, Queen of Scots, &c. &c. Edinb. 1859, 8vo. portrait of the Queen, and other plates. [Edited by Albert Way, Esq.]

Life of Mary, Queen of Scots, by H. G. Bell. Lond. (Constable's Miscellany), 1838, 18mo. 2 vols. 7s.—Lond. Whittaker, 1840, roy. 8vo. 3s. 6d.

The Life and Tragedy of the heroicall Lady, Mary Queen of Scotts. A MS. English poem, by John Woodward, in the Advocates' Library at Edinburgh. Another memoir, in Italian, by Francisco Marsaldi, in MS., is mentioned by Nicolson in his Scottish Historical Library. Old copies of it are not very uncommon. In a catalogue published by Rivingtons and Cochran in 1824, was a curious MS. relating to the proceedings against Mary.

In the Bodleian Library are sundry broadsides relating to Mary Queen of Scots, with portraits. See Dr. Dibdin's Libr. Comp. p. 267; and in a valuable little publication entitled 'The Crypt,' is a chronological list of publications, 168 in number, relative to this unfortunate princess. The question of Queen Elizabeth's real intentions, as to the execution of Mary, is minutely discussed in Mr. Nicolas's Life of Secretary Davison, 1823, 8vo.

See ANDERSON, James. BANNATYNE, Richard. BARNESTAPLE, Oberius. BENGER, Miss. BIRRELIUS, J. BLACKWOOD, Adam. BOIS-GUINBERT, l'e le Pesant de. Bos, L. V. BUCHANAN, George. CAUSSIN, Nicholas. CHALMERS, George. CHAMBER, David. COKE, George. CRYFT, (he. FLEETWOOD, Wm. GOODAL, Walter. GRÆVIUS, J. G. GRAHAME, James. HERRERA, Ant. KAMP, Wm. LAING, Malcolm. LEYI, A. M. LESLEY, John. MONTCHRESTIEN, Ant. de. PLUMPTRE, Rev. James. ROBERTSON, William. ROUERIUS, Anth. RUTHVEN, Lord. SANDERSON, W. SCHILLER, F. SCOTUS, Romoaldus. SPOTSWAET, Gul. A. STRANGUAGE, Wm. STRADA, Fam. TYTLER, Wm. UDALL, W. VEGA, Lope de. VERSTEGAN, Michd. WHITAKER, John. WINZET, Ninian.

MARY, Daughter of K. James I.
A Funeral Sermon on the Princess Mary's Grace. By J. Leech. Lond. 1607, 12mo.

A copy is in the British Museum. *See* LEECH, John.

—, Daughter of K. Charles I., afterwards Princess of Orange. Verses on the Birth of the Princess Mary. Camb. 1631, 4to.
Bindley, pt. ii. 256, &c.

Academiæ Oxoniensis Epicedia in Obitum Mariæ Principissæ Arausionensis. Oxon. 1661, 4to. Lindley, pt. ii. 522, &c.

MARY II., Queen of England.
Epithalamia Cantabrigiensia in Nuptias Principis Arausii et Mariæ Britanniæ. Cantab. 1677, 4to.
Lachrymæ Cantabrigienses in Obitum serenessimæ Reginæ Mariæ. Oxon. 1694-5. 4to.
The Form of the Proceeding to the Funeral of Queen Mary II., 1695, folio.
Orationes et Carmina in ejus Obitum. 1695, 4to.
A Collection of Poems on the Death of Mary Queen of England, 1695, folio. Bindley, pt. III. 2084, 1l. 1s.
A brief History of the pious and glorious Life and Actions of Mary Queen of England, &c. Faithfully done by J. S. The Second Edition. Lond. 1695, 12mo. A—F, in twelves, with port. of Mary by J. Drapentier. Nassau, pt. I. 2006, 6s.
Grutori Funeralia Mariæ II. Britann. Reginæ Gulielmi III. Conjugis. Amst. 1695, folio, plates. Sir M. M. Sykes, pt. I. 1863, 12s.

MARYLAND.—The Laws of Maryland, with Indexes, Notes, &c. To which is prefixed the Charter; with an English Translation by Tho. Bacon. Annapolis, 1765, fol. 2l. 2s.
A former edition, 1727, folio.
Acts of Assembly passed in the Province of Maryland, from 1692 to 1715. Lond. 1723, folio.
A Relation of Maryland, together with a Map of the country. The condition of the Plantation, his Majesty's Charter to Lord Baltimore, translated, &c. 1635, 4to. Geo. Chalmers, pt. III. J. 1s. Only three known with the Map. Sir Hans Sloane's copy is in the British Museum.
Proceedings of the Conventions of the Province of Maryland, held at the City of Annapolis in 1774-6. Baltimore, (U. S.) 1836, 8vo.
History of the first Years of its Settlement, by Doxman. Baltimore, (U. S.) 1811, 8vo.
History of Maryland from 1634 to 1848, by James M'Sherry. Baltimore, (U. S.) 1849, 8vo.
Sketches of the early History of Maryland, by Thos. W. Griffith. Baltimore, (U. S.) 1821, 8vo.
Digest of Reports of Decisions, by Harris and M'Henry, 8vo. 1700—1799, 4 vols. By Harris and Johnson, 8vo. 1800—1826, 7 vols. By Harris and Gill, 1826—1829, 2 vols. By Gill and Johnson, 1829—1843, 8vo. 12 vols. By Gill, 1843—1850, 8vo. 9 vols. 1851—1857, 8vo. 10 vols.
Dorsey's Digest of Laws to 1839, inclusive. 1840, 8vo. 3 vols.

MASANIELLO.—The Rebellion of Naples, or the Tragedy of Masaniello. Lond. 1662, 12mo.
With frontispiece by Marshall. A copy is in the British Museum. Hibbert, 5145, 1l. 1s.—1649, 4to. With a frontispiece by Marshall. Rhodes, 325, 11s.—1651. Roxburghe, 4267, 5s. 6d.
The second part of Masaniello, his Body taken out of the Town-Ditch, and solemnly buried, with Epitaphs upon him. Lond. 1652, 12mo. with portraits by Cross. Hibbert, 5141, 5s.
The remarkable History of the Rise and Fall of Masaniello, the Fisherman of Naples. Lond. 1769, 12mo. 2s. 6d.
See HOWEL, JAMES. MIDON, F.

MASCALL, Leonard. A Booke of Fishing with Hooke and Line, and of all other Instruments thereunto belonging. Another of sundrie Engines and Trappes to take Polcats, Buzards, Raites, Mice and all other Kindes of Vermine & Beasts whatsoever. Lond. John Wolfe. 1590, 4to.
BLACK LETTER. The first part, containing the treatise of Fishing, (taken from Juliana Barnes) ends on 50, the second part on p. 83. This part has a folding leaf between pp. 86-7, of 'the Crow-Net set or bent.' A copy is in the British Museum. Haworth, 947, imperfect, 1l. 7s. Brand, 3l. 8s.—1596, 4to—1600. In this edition p. 23 is marked 91. 4to. Haworth, 948, 1l. 19s. 849, 1l. 19s. 6d. King and Lochée's in Feb. 1808, 2l. 13s.—1606, 4to.
The Art of Planting and Grafting, 4to. Many editions. First edition. 1l. Denham, for John Wright, 1572, 4to. Black letter.—1569, 4to. Townsley, pt. I. 706, 8s. 6d.—T. Este, 1580, 4to. Caldecott, 11s.—1592, 4to. Reed, 1341, 8s.—1596, 4to. Bindley, pt. III. 875, 2s. 6d.
The Government of Cattle. Lond. 1662, 4to. In the title-page is a portrait of Mascall by Robt. Gaywood. Dowdeswell, 578, russia, 18s. 6d. This work was frequently printed.—1587, 4to. Bindley, pt. III. 874, 1l. 1s.—1596, 4to. Reed, 1340, 7s.
The husbandlie Ordring and Government of Poultrie. Lond. 1581, 8vo.

MASCARDI, Augustin. Relation of the Conspiracy of J. L. Count de Fieschi against Genoa; out of the Italian, by Hugh Hare. Lond. 1693, 8vo. 4s.

MASCOU, J. J. History of the ancient Germans and other Northern Nations, translated by Thomas Lediard. Lond. 1738, 4to. 2 vols. 10s. 6d.

MASERES, Francis, Curaitor Baron of the Exchequer. Scriptores Logarithmici. Lond. 1791-1807, 4to. 6 vols. 3l. 3s.

A valuable collection.

The Principles of the Doctrine of Life Annuities. Lond. 1783, 4to. 2 vols.

Baron Maseres published other mathematical treatises, and likewise edited several valuable historical works. See CANADA, p. 354. CHARLES I. Tracts on the Civil Wars. DUCHESNE, A. LUDLOW, Edm. MAY, Tho. MILTON, John. QUEBEC. TEMPLE, Sir John, &c.

MASKELYNE, Nevil, D.D. Astronomical Observations made at Greenwich, from 1765 to 1810. Lond. 1776, &c. folio, 4 vols.

The works of this eminent astronomer and mathematician are much esteemed.

The British Mariner's Guide. Lond. 1763, 4to. 5s.

Tables requisite to be used with the Nautical Almanac. Several editions.

An Account of the going of Mr. Harrison's Watch, at the Royal Observatory, from May 6, 1766, to March 4, 1767, together with the original Observations and Calculations of the same. Lond. 1768, 4to. 2s. 6d.

Tables for computing the apparent Places of the fixed Stars, and reducing Observations of the Planets. Lond. 1774, folio, 15s.

Answer to a Pamphlet, entitled, A Narrative of Facts, lately published by T. Mudge, Jun. Lond. 1792, 8vo.

Many articles by Maskelyne will be found in the Philosophical Transactions.

MASON, Ab. A wonderful Relation of his cursed Design to give himself to the Devil. Lond. folio.

A copy is in the British Museum.

— Rev. Francis. Of the Consecration of the Bishops in the Church of England: with their Succession, Jurisdiction, &c.: as also of the Ordination of Priests and Deacons. Lond. 1613, folio.

This work is highly praised by Ant. à Wood, who states that the author is worthily styled 'Vindex Ecclesiæ Anglicanæ.'—Secunda, priori Editio Anglicana, auctior. Lond. 1626, folio. Williams, 1418, mor. 2l. 5s. Hibb, mor. probably Dedication copy to James I., 4l. 10s.—Ed. alt. Lond. 1638, fol. Heber, pt. II. De Thou and Colbert's copy, 5s.—Translated by John Lindsay. To which is prefixed by the Translator, a Series of the succession of our Bishops since the Reformation. Lond. 1728, folio, 10s.—Lond. 1734, folio.

The Authority of the Church in making Canons and Constitutions concerning Things indifferent. Oxf. 1634, 4to. *A former edition*, Lond. 1607, 4to.

The Validity of the Ordination of the Ministers of the reformed Churches. Oxford, 1641, 4to.

See CHAMPNEY, Ant.

MASON, George. An Essay on Design in Gardening. Lond. 1795, 8vo.

Originally published anonymously in 1768.

The Life of Richard Earl Howe. Lond. 1803, 8vo. 4s.

— George and John Earsden. The Ayres that were sung and played at Brougham Castle, Westmorland. Lond. T. Snodham, folio.

Reprinted in Stafford Smith's Musica Antiqua.

— Henry. The new Art of Lying, covered by Jesuites under the Vaile of Equivocation, discovered and disproved. Lond. 1624, 4to. 7s.

This divine published several other works.

— James. The Anatomie of Sorcerie, wherein the wicked Impiety of Charmers, Inchanters and such, is considered and confuted. Lond. 1612, 4to. 3s. 6d.

— John, M.A. The Turke, a worthie Tragedie. Lond. 1610, 4to.

Inglis' Old Plays, 63, 15s. Roxburghe, 5421, 16s. Rhodes, 1637, 1l. 15s. Heber, pt. II. 13s.—1632, entitled Mulcasses The Turke, 4to. Roxburghe, 5422, 8s. Suppl. 676, 5s. Rhodes, 1638, 12s. Heber, pt. II. 7s. 6d.

The School Moderator. Lond. 1648, 4to. *A copy is in the British Museum.*

— John. A briefe Discourse of the New-found-land, with the situation, temperature, and commodities

thereof. Edinb. Andro Hart, 1620, 4to. Seven leaves.
G. Chalmers, 2l. 1s.

MASON, John, of Fordham. The History of the young converted Gallant, or Directions to the Readers of that divine Poem, written by Benjamin Keach, intituled, Warre with the Devil. Lond. 1676. 8vo.
Pp. 164, with a frontispiece. Bindley, pt. ii. 1792, 11s. 6d. Nassau, pt. i. 2l. 12s. Bibl. Anglo-Poet. 4896, 1l. 1s. Heber, pt. iv. 7s.

— Rev. John, of Water Stratford. Songs of Praise to Almighty God, or Spiritual Songs; together with Solomon's Song of Songs, in English verse. Lond. R. Northcott, 1683, 12mo.
FIRST EDITION (only two known). Bliss, 3l. 12s.—SECOND EDITION, with the addition of Dives and Lazarus, a sacred Poem (printed here for the first time). Lond. H. Northcott, 1685, 12mo.—THIRD EDITION, with Dives and Lazarus, and Penitential Cries in three decades, begun by the author of the Songs of Praise, &c., and carried on by another hand (the Rev. Timothy Shepherd of Braintree). Lond. T. Parkhurst, 1693, 12mo. licensed Feb. 23, 1691-2.—TENTH EDITION. Lond. 1708, 12mo. the Penitential Cries being dated 1701. Bliss, presentation copy in morocco, 1l. 15s.
With the exception of George Wither, Mason was the earliest English writer of Hymns. Dr. I. Watts borrowed whole lines from him.

The Angel's Oath—Time is no longer; a prophecy from Mr. Mason's People, 1694, 8vo.
Some remarkable passages in the Life and Death of J. M., to which are added Letters, Poems and Hymns. Lond. John Dunton. 1694, 4to. Puttick, May, 1859, 14s.
An impartial Account of J. M. and his sentiments, by H. Maurice. Lond. 1695, 4to. Puttick, May, 1859, 16s.—Second edition, with a Letter giving an Account of the Doctrine and manner of the behaviour of Mr. Mason, with the Hymns they usually sing. Lond. Randal Taylor, 1694, 4to. Reprinted (verbatim et literatim), by S. Manning, Newport Pagnel, 1823, 12mo. (only 50 copies printed).
The Midnight Cry, a Sermon on the Parable of the Virgins. Lond. 1690.—Lond. 1694, 4to.

Remains, in Two Sermons (published by the Rev. Timothy Shepard of Braintree). Lond. T. Parkhurst, 1698, 12mo.
Select Remains collected by his grandson, the Rev. John Mason, of Dorking. Lond. 1742, 12mo.—Lond. 1743, 12mo.

MASON, John, A.M., of Dorking. A Treatise on Self-Knowledge. Lond. 1745.—First edition, revised and corrected from the earlier and more perfect editions, with a Life of the Author prefixed, by John Mason Good. Lond. 1811, 12mo.
This excellent work has gone through numerous editions and several translations.

The Lord's Day Evening Entertainment. Lond. 1752, 8vo. 4 vols. Gosset, 3378, with Christian Morals, 1l. 6s. Williams, 1186*, 2l. 2s.

Christian Morals. Lond. 1761, 8vo. 2 vols.
This eminent Nonconformist Divine published other works.

— John Monk. Comments on the several Editions of Shakespeare's Plays, extended to those of Malone and Steevens. Dublin, 1807, 8vo. 10s. 6d.
Comments on the last Edition of Shakespear's Plays. Lond. 1785, 8vo. Steevens, 1285, 15s. Field, 519, 4s.—Dublin, 1785, 8vo.
Comments on the Plays of Beaumont and Fletcher, with an Appendix, containing some further Observations on Shakespeare, extended to the late edition of Malone and Steevens. Lond. 1798, 8vo. 3s. 6d. Steevens, 1386, 16s. 6d. Hoxburghe, Suppl. 615, 3s. 6d. Bindley, pt. ii. 1573, 5s.

— John M., A.M. First ripe Fruits; being a Collection of Tracts; to which are added, two sermons, with a short Memoir of the Author. Lond. 1803, 8vo.
Williams, 1185*, 6s.
A collective edition of the works of this eminent Presbyterian Divine, of New York, edited by his son, was printed at New York, 1849, 8vo. 4 vols. 2l. 2s.

— Thomas. Christ's Victorie over Sathan's Tyrannie. Lond. G. Eld. 1615, folio. BLACK LETTER. 10s. 6d.
Chiefly abstracted out of Fox's Book of Martyrs.

A Revelation of the Revelation. Lond. 1619, 8vo.
Noble Par. or the Funeralls of the Earle of Hertford, and the Ladie Marie, his worthie Sister. According to Ant. à Wood, very few copies were printed.

MASON, W. Handful of Essaies or imperfect Offers. Lond. 1621, 12mo.
Dudley, pt. II. 1812, 10s. 6d. Geo. Chalmers, lt. is. Bliss, 6s. Heber, pt. vi. 8s.

— William. Arts Advancement, or exact short Writing. Lond. 1682, 12mo. 4s.
With portrait of Mason engraved by Ben. Rhodes.
La Plume volante, or the Art of Shorthand improved. Lond. 1707, 12mo.—Lond. 1719, 12mo. Caldecott, 6d.
Aurea Clavis, or a golden Key to the Cabinet of Contractions, unlocking all the Mysteries (or seeming Difficulties) of an Engraved Sheet of Short Hand lately published, entituled A regular and easy Table of natural Contractions, &c. Lond. 1696, 12mo.
A Pen pluck't from an Eagle's wing; or, the most swift, compendious and speedy Method of Short-writing. 1672, 12mo. Bliss, 12s.

— William. The Works of William Mason, M.A. Lond. 1811, 8vo. 4 vols.
Sir M. M. Sykes, pt. II. 829. 1l. 5s. Drury, 2664, 1l. 10s.—Lond. 1816, 8vo. 4 vols.
Poems by William Mason, M.A. Lond. 1764, 8vo. Two portraits. First complete edition, LARGE PAPER, 1l. 1s.—York, 1771, 12mo.—York, 1774, 8vo.—York, 1779, 8vo. —York, 1797, 8vo.
Caractacus, a dramatic Poem. Lond. 1759, 4to.—Third edition, Lond. 1762, 8vo.
Caractacus, Græco Carmine redditus, cum Versions Latina, à G. H. Glasse. Oxon. 1781, 8vo. 'One of the most extraordinary efforts in Greek literature that has appeared since the revival of letters.' —*Tytler.* Drury, 2267, 6s.—In verso Italiano, da T. J. Mathias. Napoli, 1823, 8vo.
Elfrida, a dramatic Poem. Lond. 1752, 4to.—Ninth edition. Lond. 1773, 8vo.
The English Garden; a Poem, in four Books. A new Edition, corrected; to which are added, a Commentary and Notes, by W. Burgh, LL.D. Lond. 1778-79, 4to.—Lond. 1785, 8vo. 4s. Roscoe, 1453, 3s. 6d.—York, 1783. Drury, 2666, 2s.
Essays, historical and critical, on En-

glish Church Music. York, 1795, 12mo. 3s. 6d. Fourhill, 3546, 11s.
Religio Clerici; a Poem, in two Parts. 1810, 8vo.
Saffo, Drama Lirico in tre atti sul Modello Toscano, dall' Inglese di G. Mason, da T. J. Mathias. Napoli, 1827, crown 8vo. *See* SATIRE, School for.

MASON, Wm. Monck. The History and Antiquities of the Cathedral Church of St. Patrick near Dublin, from its Foundation in 1190 to 1819. Dublin, 1820, 4to. L. P. 1l. 1s.
An elaborate work, displaying much antiquarian research. It contains some new and interesting matter relative to the life and writings of Swift, with portrait, &c. Hibbert, 1l. 2s. LARGE PAPER, in imp. 4to. proofs on India paper, 1l. 11s. 6d.

— William Shaw. A Statistical Account, or Parochial Survey of Ireland, drawn up from the Communications of the Clergy. Dublin, 1814, 18, 19, 8vo. vols. i, ii. iii. 1l. 5s.
A valuable work. It proceeded no further.
A Survey, Valuation, and Census of the Barony of Portnahinch, compiled in the Year 1819. Dublin, 1821, folio.
Bibliotheca Hibernica; or, a descriptive Catalogue of a select Irish Library, collected for the Right Hon. Robert Peel, &c. &c. Dublin, 1823, 8vo. 9s., only fifty printed. Pp. vii. and 51, with a facsimile of a page in MS. of Sir John Davies' tract on Ireland. LARGE PAPER, in 4to. 12s.

MASQUES.—The Masque of Flowers. Lond. 1614, 4to.
Fifteen leaves. The last of the court solemnities exhibited at Whitehall in honour of the marriage of Carr, Earl of Somerset, with the Lady Frances, daughter of the Earl of Suffolke. Roxburghe, 4370, 1l. 5s. Rhodes, — 2l. 6s. Sotheby's in Nov. 1826, 2l. 19s.; in Feb. 1824, 6l. Heber, pt. II. 1l. 8s. A copy is in the British Museum. It is printed in Nichols' Progresses of K. James I.
Masque at Kenilworth, before Q. Elizabeth. *See* KENILWORTH.
The true Description of a royall Masque at Hampton Court. Lond. 1604, 4to. Copies are in the British Museum and Bodleian.
The King and Queen's Entertainment at Richmond, in a Masque, after their departure from Oxford, presented by Prince Charles. Oxf. 1636, 4to. Copies are in the British Museum and Bodleian. Heber, pt. II. 1l. 11s. 6d.

5 D

Lumiualis, or the Festival of Light. Lond. 1637, 4to. Heber, pt. ii. 18s.

See CORONA MINERVÆ and MULIER MINERVÆ, p. 1721. ELIZABETH, Q., pp. 717, 719. ELIZABETH, daughter of James I., p. 720; and SHAKESPEARE SOCIETY, Appendix.

MASS.—The Interpretacyon and Sygnyfycacyon of the Masse. Imprynted by me Robert Wyer, 1532, 8vo.

This volume has neither running titles, catchwords, nor the leaves numbered, but contains to sig. E 4 in the second alphabet. The first alphabet begins with a f, and proceeds regularly in half sheets.

The Duryinge of the Masse. Imp. at Wesell, 1548, 17mo. Roxburghe, 11l. 0s. 6d. Another edition, Roxburghe, 13l. 13s.

This is Roy's Satire, but placed under this heading in the Roxburghe Catalogue. See ROY, W.

Answere that the Preachers of the Gospel at Basil made for the Defence of the true Administration and Use of the Holy Supper of our Lord, agaynst the Abhominations of the Popyshe Mass, translated out of Latin by George Bancrafte. Imp. by Day and Seres, 1548, 8vo. BLACK LETTER. Sotheby, 1855, 2l. 8s. Heber, pt. vi. 17s.

The V. abominable Blasphemies conteined in the Masse. Lond. H. Powell, 1548, 16mo.

A new Dialogue, wherein is conteyned the Examination of the Mass, and of that kind of Priesthode that is to saye Masse. Lond. John Daye, n. d. (1550).

The Dateris of the Popes Botereulx, commonly called the High Aultare, compiled by W. J. Lond. R. Crowley, 1550, 16mo.

Newes from Rome concerning the blasphemous Sacrifice of the Papisticale Mass, with divers other Treatises. Canterbury, by J. Mychell, n. d. (1554), 17mo.

A lewde Apologie of pryvate Masse againste certaine Sermons by the Bishop of Salisburie (Jewell). Lond. 1562. 12mo. BLACK LETTER. Heber, pt. i. 4l. 12s. 6d. Horner, 18s.

An Answere in Defence of the Truth, against the Apologie of Private Masse. Lond. T. Powell, 1562, 12mo.

A plaine and godlye Treatise concernynge the Masse and blessed Sacraments of the Aulter, for the Instruction of the symple and unlerned People. BLACK LETTER. Pottick, Dec. 1855, 2l. 7s. Horner, 1l. 1s.

A Treatise of the holy Sacrifice of the Altar, called the Masse. Translated out of the Italian into English by Thomas Butler, Doctor of the Canon and Civil Lawes. 1570, 16mo.

An Answer to a certain godly Maiden Letters, desiring his Freendes Iudgement, whether it be lawfull for a Christian man to be present at the Popishe Masse, and other supersticious Churche Servies. 1557, 16mo. 8 leaves. Sotheby, 1854, 2l. 2s.

The Doctrine of the Masse Booke, truly translated into Englyshe, Anno Dom. M.D.LIII. 16mo. C, in eights.

A new Dialoge called the Endightment agaynste Mother Masse. Lond. by Wm. Hill and Wm. Seres, 1549, 16mo. Heber, in lot 8149, pt. i.; pt. ii. 1l. 11s. 6d. A copy in the Lambeth Library.

The Dysclosyng of the Canon of ye Popysh Masse, with a Sermon annexed vnto it, of ye famous Clerke of worthy Memorye, D. Martyn Luther. Imprynted beside al Papistes, by me Hans Hytpryche, (1543), 8vo. Contains C, in eights. The pages are misplaced, especially in the form of signature D.

The Vpcheringe of the Messe. Lond. by John Daye & Wilyam Seres, 16mo. Accordyng to Ritson, in black letter and in Skeltonic verse. Roxburghe, 3306, Suppl. 6l. 6s. 10s.; resold Heber, pt. iv. 5l. 5s.

Patheos, or an inward Passion of the Pope for the Loss of hys Daughter the Masse. Lond. by John Daye and Wm. Seres, 8vo. In English metre.

The Vertes of ye Masse. Lond. by W. de Worde, 4to. A vi. j. D iiij. A copy is in the Public Library at Cambridge.

The Resurrection of the Masse. With the wonderful Vertues of the same, newly set forth unto the harties ease, joye, and comforte of all the Cathoiykes, by Hugh Hilarie. Strauburgh, in Elsas, 1554, 16mo. BLACK LETTER. A to G v, in eights. Geo. Chalmers' copy from Bright's sale (4l. 15s.), now in the Grenville Collection, is the only copy that can be traced of this rare piece, which is in Verse. See HILARIE, Hugh, p. 1069.

A Liturgical Discourse of the Holy Sacrifice of the Mass. By A. F., the least of Friar Minours. Printed Anno Dom. 1639, 8vo. Two parts in one volume.

A famous Conference between Pope Clement the XIth. and Cardinal de Monte Alto concerning the Discovery of the Masse in Holy Scripture, made by the worthy Father Patrick. Lond. 1674, 4to. This tract exposes a fraud of the Roman church, which, in an edition of the New Testament printed at Paris in 1672, 12mo. introduced the word Mass into the text; on its being discovered, the Papists destroyed the edition. It was again put forth, under the sanction of the Theologians of Louvain, at Bordeaux in 1686, 12mo. Only seven or eight copies are known. One sold at

Sotheby's (Bp. Daly's books), June, 1858, for 82l.

The Funeral of the Mass, &c. Lond. 1677, 18mo. *See* Howson.

Several excellent Methods of hearing Mass, with Fruit and Benefit, according to the Institution of that Divine Sacrifice, and the Intention of our Holy Mother the Church; with Motives to induce all good Christians, particularly religious Persons, to make Use of the same. Collected together by the Right Honourable Lady Lucy Herbert of Powis, Superioress of the English Augustin-Nuns. Bruges, 1743, 8vo. 114 pages.

MASSACHUSETTS. — The General Laws and Liberties of the Massachusetts Colony. Cambridge, N. E. 1672, folio.

First edition, very rare. A copy, with additional Laws made at Boston, May 1672, to May 1674, sold at Puttick's, May 1850, 10l. One leaf, D11, in facsimile. A copy is in the British Museum.

Acts and Laws passed by the General Assembly of the Province of Massachusetts Bay, from 1692 to 1719. Lond. 1724, folio.

The Perpetual Laws of the Commonwealth of Massachusetts. Boston, 1789, folio.

A brief State of the Services and Expenses of the Province of. Lond. 1785, 8vo.

Proceedings of the Court of Assembly of Massachusetts Bay. Boston, 1769, 4to.

Original Papers relative to the History of the Colony of Massachusetts Bay. Boston, 1769, 8vo.

Massachusettensis, a Series of Letters, containing an Account of the Troubles in Massachusetts Bay. Lond. 1776, 8vo. (By — Leonard.)

Debates, &c. of the Convention of the Commonwealth of Massachusetts, for the Purpose of ratifying the Constitution. Boston, 1788, 8vo.

History of Massachusetts Bay. By G. R. Minot. Boston, 1798, 8vo.

History of, from 1775 to 1789, by Bradford. Boston, 1825, 8vo.

Massachusetts Reports, from 1804—1822, by Williams and Tyng, 17 vols. From 1822—1840, by Pickering, 24 vols. From 1840—1845, by Metcalf, 13 vols. From 1849—1853, by Cushing, 12 vols. From 1854—1855, by Gray, 8 vols.; together, 74 vols. 8vo. Boston (U.S.), 1824-55.

Chronicles of the Pilgrim Settlers of Massachusetts. By Alex. Young. Boston, 1840, 8vo.

Transactions of the Historical Society of. *See* APPENDIX.

See HUTCHINSON. MACDUFF, Is. PLYMOUTH.

MASSECETH REBACOTH, Titulus Talmudicus, in quo agitur de Benedictionibus, Precibus et Gratiarum Actionibus, Heb. adjecta Versione Latina. Oxon. 1667, 8vo.

MASSEY, William. The Origin and Progress of Letters. Lond. 1763, 8vo. in two Parts.

In this volume will be found a curious account of early English Writing-Masters. Gossett, 8361. 11s. Dilke, 10s. 6d. Sir P. Thompson, 444, 14s. 6d.

On Alphabetic Writing. Lond. 1772, 8vo.

Corruptia Latinitatis Index, or a Collection of barbarous Words and Phrases. Lond. 1735, 8vo. Gossett, 8293, 6s. 6d.

Remarks upon Milton's Paradise Lost. Lond. 1761, 12mo. 2s. 6d.

MASSIE, Wm. Sermon at the Marriage of the Daughter of Sir Edm. Trafforde. Oxf. 1586, 16mo.

A copy is in the British Museum.

MASSILLON, J. B., Bishop of Clermont. Sermons selected and translated by William Dickson, LL.D. Lond. 1798, 8vo. 3 vols. 15s.

Reprinted, with Life by D'Alembert, Edinb. 1816, 8vo. in 1 vol.—Lond. 1828, 8vo.—Again, Lond. 1840, 8vo. 6s.

Sermons on the Duties of the Great, translated from the French by Wm. Dodd, LL.D. Lond. 1769, 8vo. 4s. LARGE PAPER. Garrick, 1524, 7s. 6d. Williams, 1166, morocco, 13s.

The Charges of Massillon, Bishop of Clermont, with two Essays:—I. On the Art of Preaching. II. On the Composition of a Sermon. Translated from the French by Theophilus Saint-John (the Rev. S. Clapham). Lond. 1805, 8vo. 6s.

Massillon's Thoughts on different Subjects, moral and religious, extracted from his works, and arranged under Heads. Translated from the French by Hulton Morris. 1824, 12mo. 5s.

A Defence of the Worship of Jesus Christ, taken from the Discourses of Massillon, with a Preface by A. Crichton. Lond. 1824, 8vo.

Selections from the Works of Massillon. Lond. 1828, 8vo.

Select Sermons, translated by Dulten Morris. Lond. 1830, 8vo.

A Sermon on Almsgiving; translated from the French. Lond. 1847, 8vo.

Sermons on Death (translated in Winbolt's Sermons). Lond. 1800, 8vo.

Ecclesiastical Conferences, Synodical Discourses, and Episcopal Mandates, on

1510 MAS MAS

the principal Duties of the Clergy. Translated by C. H. Boylan, of Maynooth College. 1825, 8vo. 2 vols.

MASSINOBERD, Henry. Council and Admonition to his Children. Lond. 1656, folio, with portrait by Cross.
Very scarce. A copy was at Strawberry Hill.

MASSINGER, Philip. Plays, with Notes critical and explanatory, by William Gifford. Lond. 1813, 8vo. 4 vols.
Best edition, but not perceptibly different from the previous one of 1805, of which it has been said, 'that a more perfect edition of an old poet than this never issued from the press.' 4l. 4s. LARGE PAPER, 5l. 5s. Drury, 2569, morocco, 8l. 8s. Foothill, 534, 2l. 7s. 6d. Sir M. M. Sykes, pt. II. 540, russia, 4l. 6s. Strettell, 877, morocco, 8l. 8s.—First edition, 1805, 8vo. 4 vols. Dent, pt. I. 1393, 1l. 16s. Reed, 8286, 1l. 19s. Marquis of Townshend, 2047, 2l. Goldsmid, 455, 2l. 3s. Stanley, 482, 2l. 4s.
Other Editions.—By Thomas Coxeter. Lond. 1759, 8vo. 4 vols. Bindley, pt. II. 1533, 1l. 3s.—Lond. 1761. 8vo. 4 vols. with portrait. The edition of 1759, with a new title-page, and an essay on the old English dramatic writers by G. Colman. Reed, 8265, 1l. Steevens, 1251, 11. 5s. Willett, 1684, 2l. 14s.—By John Monck Mason. Lond. 1779. 8vo. 4 vols. Steevens, 1252, 1l. 2s. Heath, 1942, 2l. 2s.
Plays (castrated edition), Murray's Fam. Lib. Lond. 1830, 12mo. 3 vols. 10s. 6d.
Plays, by Gifford, (without the Notes.) Third edition. Lond. 1840, med. 8vo. 18s.—1842. 8s. 6d.—Lond. 1845, 10s. 6d.
Massinger and Ford's Dramatic Works, by Hartley Coleridge. Lond. Moxon, 1840, med. 8vo. 16s. port.—Reduced, 1860, 12s.
The Virgin Martir, a Tragedie; written by Philip Messenger and Thomas Decker. Lond. 1622, 4to. Rhodes, 1640, 16s. Field, 297, 9s.—1631, 4to.—1651, 4to. Rhodes, 1641, 8s. Field, 298, 14s.—Fifth edition, 1661, 4to.—New edition. Lond. 1845, 8vo. with 6 designs by Pickersgill.
The Duke of Millaine, a Tragedie. Lond. 1623, 4to. A very correct edition. Rhodes, 1643, 18s. Heber, pt. II. presentation copy, with verses to Sir W. Foljambe in the hand-writing of Massinger, the only autograph known to be extant, 2l. 8s.—1638, third edition, 4to. Of little value. Roxburghe, 5427, 5s. Rhodes, 1644, 7s.
The Bond-Man, an antient Storie. Lond. 1624, 4to. Rhodes, 1647, 10s.—1638, 4to. A very incorrect edition. Rhodes, 1648,

7s. Roxburghe, 5425, 5s. 6d. Another edition same year.—1719, 8vo.
The Roman Actor, a Tragedie. Lond. 1629, 4to. Roxburghe, 5437, 7s. Rhodes, 1645, 11s.—1722, 8vo. Roxburghe, 5438, 4s.
The Renegado, a Tragaecomedie. Lond. 1630, 4to. Roxburghe, 5435, 8s. 6d. Rhodes, 1649, 8s. 6d.
The Picture, a Trage-comedie. Lond. 1630, 4to. Roxburghe, 5434, 8s. Rhodes, 1650, 8s. 6d.
The Emperour of the East, a Tragecomedie. Lond. 1632, 4to. Roxburghe, 5428, 11s. Rhodes, 1652, 7s. 6d.
The Fatall Dowry, a Tragedy, written by P(hilip) M(assinger) and N(ath). F(ield). Lond. 1632, 4to. Roxburghe, 5429, 11s. 6d. Rhodes, 1653, 12s.
The Maid of Honour, a Tragi-comedy. Lond. 1632, 4to. Roxburghe, 5431, 5s. Bindley, pt. III. 534, with the Unnatural Combat, 1639, and Old Law, 1656, 1l. 15s. Rhodes, 1651, 7s.
A New Way to pay Old Debts, a Comedy. Lond. 1633, 4to. Reed, 8194, 5s. Roxburghe, 5432, 7s. 6d. Rhodes, 1654, 7s. 6d.
The great Duke of Florence, a Comical History. Lond. 1636, 4to. Roxburghe, 5430, 6s. 6d.—1639 ? 4to. Rhodes, 1655, 7s.
The Unnatural Combat, a Tragedie. Lond. 1639, 4to. Roxburghe, 5439, 8s. 6d. Rhodes, 1656, 7s. Bindley, pt. III. 534, with the Maid of Honour, 1632, and Old Law, 1656, 1l. 15s.
Three Playes, viz. the Bashful Lover, the Guardian, and the very Woman. Lond. 1655, 8vo. with portrait by Cross. Sir M. M. Sykes, pt. II. 341, 18s. Jadis, 42, 1l. 1s. Dowdeswell, 408, 1l. 12s. Rhodes, 1659, 1l. 1s. Bindley, pt. II. 1632, 2l. 15s. Also printed separately in 4to. same date.

The excellent Comedie called the Old Law, or a new Way to please you. By P. Massinger, T. Middleton, and W. Howley: together with an exact and perfect Catalogue of all the Playes, with the Authors Names, more exactly printed than ever before (often wanting). Lond. 1656, 4to. Roxburghe, 5433, 1l. 2s. Rhodes, 1657, 9s. 6d. Bindley, pt. III. 534, with the Maid of Honor, 1632, and the Unnatural Combat. 1639, 1l. 15s.

The City-Madam, a Comedie. Lond. 1658, 4to. Roxburghe, 5426, 7s. 6d. Rhodes, 5s. 6d.—1659, 4to.

Believe as you List, a Play; licensed on the 6th of May, 1631, by Sir Henry Herbert. Printed for the first time by the Percy Society, from the original MS. (recently discovered), under the editorial care of Crofton Croker, Esq. See PERCY SOCIETY, No. 60, in Appendix; also SHAKESPEARE PAPERS.

Fourteen Plays by P. Massinger, in 1 vol. 4to. Jadis, 179. 9l. 19s. 6d. 16 separate, in one lot, at Heber's, pt. II. 4l. 2s.
Critical Reflections on the old English dramatic Writers; intended as a Preface to the Works of Massinger (by George Colman). Lond. 1761. 8vo. 2s.
Some Account of the Life and Writings of Philip Massinger (by Thomas Davies). Lond. 1779. 8vo. Reed, 8287, 5s.

MASSON, Francis. Stapeliæ novæ; or, a Collection of several new Species of that Genus discovered in the Interior Parts of Africa. Lond. 1796, folio.
FASC. I—IV. pp. 24, with 41 coloured plates. White Knights, 2779, miss. 4l. 10s. Roscoe, 1765, 8l.

MASSOUL, Constant de. A Treatise on the Art of Painting and the Composition of Colours. Translated from the French. Lond. 1797, post 8vo. 4s.

MASSY, Isaac. Massy's Midsummer's Prognostication of Pacification and Unity betwixt the King and Parliament, to the Joy of the two twin Sisters, London and Westminster. Lond. 1642, 4to. 6s.
In verse.

MASTER, Martin. Surveyours Perambulation. Lond. 1661, 12mo.
With portrait by Gaywood. Grave. 729, 2l. Bindley, pt. II. 1571, 5l. 15s. 6d. North, 4l.

— Thos. Mensa lubrica, seu ludus vulgo Shovel-board, carmine heroico descripta, &c. Oxon. 1658, 4to.
'A poem in Latin and English, describing the game call'd shovel-board play, published with Sir Henry Savile's Oratium to Queen Elizabeth, 1658, and again 1690.'—*Anf. à Wood.*
Monarchia Britannica sub Elizabetha, et Jacobo: Oratio. Oxon. 1661, 4to.—1681, 8vo.
Iter Boreale. 1675, 4to. 5s. In prose and verse.

MASTERS, Robert, B.D. The History of the College of Corpus Christi and the B. Virgin Mary, (commonly called Bene't) in the University of Cambridge, from its Foundation to the present Time. In two Parts. Camb. 1753, 4to.

A valuable work. Nassau, pt. II. 150, rmsia, 13s. Bindley, pt. III. 317, 1l. 8s. Towneley, pt. II. 1122. 1l. 11s. 6d. LARGE PAPER. Printed for presents. Dent, pt. II. 725, 16s. Heath, 4521, 1l. 6s. Sir M. M. Sykes, pt. II. 487, 2l. 13s. A copy in the Grenville Collection. *Collation.*— Title and dedication, 2 leaves; preface, with directions to the binder, 4 pages; the history, 212 pages; title to part II. sig. *Dd*; dedication to Abp. Secker, 1 page; preface, 2 pages; historical part, pp. 213-428; appendix, 115 pages; index, 19 pages; a list of the names, &c. *A—G 3*, 54 pages. The volume contains six plates and a folded plan, designed by R. Masters.
New edition, with additions and continuation to 1830, by John Lamb, D.D., Master of the College. Camb. 1831, 4to. 1l. 11s. 6d.
In this edition the appendix is incorporated. Pp. 504, besides title and preface, 2 leaves; front., one plate of Seals, and three of the Arms of the Masters of the College.
Memoirs of the Life and Writings of the late Thomas Baker, B.D. of St. John's College, Cambridge, from the Papers of Dr. Zachary Grey. With a Catalogue of his MS. Collections. Cambridge, 1764, 8vo. 4s.—New edition. Camb. 1834. 8vo.
A short Account of the Parish of Waterbeach, in the Diocese of Ely, by a late Vicar. 1795, 8vo. Twenty-five copies printed for presents. Pp. 56, with a Plate of the Remains of Denny Abbey. Stevens, 1656, 6s. 6d. Bindley, pt. III. 29, 1l. 13s. Hibbert, 5239, 2l. 1s. Gardner in 1854, 18s. Heber, pt. vi. 11s.

MASTIN, Rev. John. The History and Antiquities of Naseby, in the County of Northampton. Cambridge, 1792, 8vo.
Nassau, pt. I. 2207, 7s. Bindley, pt. II. 1564, 9s. 6d. Dent, pt. I. 1388, 10s. 6d. *Collation.*—Pp. 81 and 206, not including title and half-title, with a folding plate of the battle of Naseby, fought the 14th of June, 1645, copied from one in Sprigge's England's Recovery.

MASTIVE, The. See GODDARD, Wm. PARROT, Henry.

MATELIFE, Cornal. Voyage into the East Indies. Lond. 1608, 4to.
A copy is in the British Museum.

MATERIAL WORLD.—An Essay on the Nature and Existence of the Material World. Lond. 1781, 8vo.
'The reader who has a taste for metaphysical disquisitions may consult the above essay, together with the correspondence of Price and Priestley.'—*Bp. Watson.*

MATHER, Cotton, D.D. Magnalia Christi Americana, or the Ecclesiastical History of New England. Lond. 1702, folio, with a Map delineated in 1620-30, 5l. 5s. LARGE PAPER, 8l. 8s.
Roxburghe, 7843, 1l. 8d. Puttick, May 1859, with the map, 5l.; and March 1860, 5l. 7s. 6d. The map has been very closely copied in lithography, and attached to many copies.—'One of the most singular books in this or in any other language. Its puns and its poems, its sermons and its anagrams, render it unique in its kind.'—*Quart. Rev.* (Southey.)—Hartford, N. E., 1820, 8vo.—Again. Hartford, N. E. 1853, with Notes by T. Robbins, D.D. port. but without the map.
Reply to. *See* WHITING.
Peslierium Americanum. *See* PSALMS.
Late memorable Providences relating to Witchcrafts and Possessions. 1689, 12mo. Inglis, 004, morocco, 14s.—The second Impression. Lond. 1691, 12mo. Puttick, May 1854, 2l. 14s. Loscombe, 1854, 2l. 8s. One of the earliest American works referring to the witchcraft frenzy. *See* MATHER, Increase.

The Triumphs of the Reformed Religion in America, in 1690. 12mo.

The Life and Death of the Rev. John Eliot, who was the first Preacher of the Gospel to the Indians in America, with an Account of the many strange Customs of the Pagan Indians in New England. Lond. John Dunton, 1691. (*published at one shilling.*) Bliss, 1374, 19s.—Boston, 1685, 12mo.—Lond. 1694, 12mo. Puttick, May 1854, 1l. 2s.—Lond. 1812, 12mo.—Lond. 1820, 12mo. 8s.

Remarks on a pretended Answer to a Discourse concerning the Common-Prayer Worship, with Exhortation to the Churches in New England. Lond. 1712, 12mo.

Several Sermons (concerning Walking with God, and that in the days of Youth,) preached at Boston, in New England. Lond. Dunton, 1689, 12mo. Puttick, with the Life of N. Mather, May 1850, 1l. 9s.

Early Piety exemplified in the Life of Mr. N. Mather, who having become, at the Age of nineteen Years, an Instance of more than common learning and virtue, changed Earth for Heaven, Oct. 17, 1688. Lond. John Dunton, 1689, 12mo. pub. at 1s. Sotheby, 1800, 1l.

Elegy on the much-to-be-deplored Death of the Rev. Nathaniel Collins. Boston, N. F., R. Pierce for O. Gill, 1685, 12mo. Puttick, May 1859, 6l. 11s.

Military Duties recommended to our Artillery Company. Boston, N. E. 1687, 12mo. Puttick, May 1859, 2l. 6s.

Souldiers Counselled and Comforted; a Discourse to the Forces engaged in the just War of New England against the Northern and Eastern Indians. Boston, by Samuel Green, 1689, 12mo. Puttick, May 1859, 2l. 14s.

Right Thoughts in sad Hours; a Sermon, at Charlestown, on the untimely Death of Children. Lond. 1689, 12mo. Puttick, May 1859, 1l. 6s.

Meditations upon the Ark as the Type of the Church. Boston, 1689, 12mo.

Small Offers towards the Service of the Tabernacle, in four Discourses, at Boston. Boston, 1689, 8vo. Puttick, May 1859, 2l. 10s.

Speedy Repentance urged; a Sermon preached at Boston, Dec. 29, 1640, at the Request of Hugh Stone, under Sentence of Death for Murder; to which are added, certain memorable Providences relating to other Murders, &c. Boston, 1690, rare. Sotheby, 1850, 10l.

A little History of several very astonishing Witchcrafts and Possessions, which partly from my ocular observations, and partly my undoubted information, hath enabled me to offer unto the publick notice of my Neighbours. 12mo. pp. 75.

The wonderful Works of God commemorated in a thanksgiving Sermon, Dec. 19, 1689. Boston, 1690, 12mo.

A Sermon preached unto the Convention of the Massachusetts Colony, May 23, 1689. Boston, 1690, 12mo. Puttick, May 1859, with the previous article, 4l. 17s.

The Wonders of the Invisible World; an Account of the Tryals of several Witches lately executed in New England. Lond. J. Dunton, 1683, 4to. First edit. ends p. 98.—Second edit. same year, ends p. 62, 4to.—Third edit. same year, ends p. 64, 4to. Puttick, May 1859, 2l. 18s. Sotheby, 1860, 2l. 12s. 'A work which may be regarded as official.'—*Perrior.*

The Life of the rev. and excellent Jonathan Mitchell, a Pastor of the Church, and glory of the Colledge in Cambridge, in New England. Massachusets, 1697, 12mo. Heber, pt. vi. 12s. 6d.

Kakuttohkaouk Papsume Kuhquttamooouk, &c.: a Discourse on the Institution and Observance of the Lord's Day. Indian and English. Boston, N. E. reprinted by B. Green, 1707, 12mo. Puttick, May 1854, 2l. 8s.

The grand Point of Solicitude, a Sermon. Boston, B. Green, 1715, 12mo.

Fair Dealing between Debtor and Creditor, a very brief Essay upon the Caution to be used about coming into Debt, and getting out of it; offered at the Boston Lecture. Boston, 1716, 16mo.

A Year and a Life well concluded; a Sermon preached the last Day of the Year 1719. Boston, 1719-20, 12mo.

MATHER, Colton—continued.
Coheleth, a Soul upon Recollection. Boston, 1720, 12mo.

India Christiana; a Discourse delivered unto the Commissioners for the Propagation of the Gospel among the American Indians. Boston, 1721, sm. 8vo. Sotheby, 1850, 2l.

Pastoral Letter to Families visited with Sickness. Boston, 1721, third impression, 12mo.

Silentiarius. [Contains a funeral Sermon for Mrs. Abigail Willard.] Boston, 1721, 12mo.

Bethiah, The Glory which adorns the Daughters of God. Boston, J. Franklin, 1722, 12mo.

Reasonable Religion, or the Truths of the Christian Religion demonstrated; together with the Religion of the Closet. Lond. 1713, 12mo. Puttick, May 1854, 9s. 6d.

Discourse upon the gracious and wondrous Restraints laid by the Providence of God on the sinful Children of Men. Boston, 1713, 12mo.

Present of Summer Fruit; a brief Essay to offer some Instructions of Piety. Boston, 1713, 12mo.

A Desirable Man described. [A funeral Sermon for Mr. Keith, Minister at Bridgewater.] Boston, S. Kneeland, 1719, 12mo.

Elizabeth in her Holy Retirement; an Essay to prepare a pious Woman for her Lying-in. Boston, N. Boone, 1710, 12mo. Puttick, May 1854, 7s.

A true Account of the Tryals, &c. of divers Witches, at Salem in New England. Lond. for J. Conyers, 1697, 4to.

The Order of the Churches in New England Vindicated. [Boston, 1700,] 12mo.

The Curbed Sinner; a Sermon occasioned by a Sentence of Death passed upon a poor young Man for the Murder of his Companion. Lond. 1713, 12mo.

Columbanus; or the Doves flying to the Windows of their Saviour. Boston, 1722, 12mo.

Honesta Parsimonia; or Time spent as it should be. Boston, [1722,] 12mo.

The Minister; a Sermon offered unto the Anniversary Convocation of Ministers. Boston, 1722, 8vo.

Pia Desideria; or the Smoaking Flax raised into a Sacred Flame. Boston, 1722, 12mo.

A remarkable Relation of certain Pirates, with a Sermon preached at their Execution. Boston, 1726, 12mo. Puttick, May 1859, 2l.

Manuductio ad Ministerium. Directions to a Candidate for the Ministry. Boston, 1726. 12mo. FIRST EDITION. Puttick, May 1859, with another edition of the celebrated Latin Preface, and a translation of it by H. Welford, 8l. 4s. It was reprinted under the title of 'STUDENT AND PREACHER,' by John Ryland. Lond. 1781. Again, with a translation of the Preface, and an abridgment of Ryland's Preface, in 1789, 5s.

Life; by his Son, Samuel Mather, M.A. Boston, 1729, 8vo. In this volume is given a list of THREE HUNDRED AND EIGHTY-TWELVE separate works written by Dr. Cotton Mather, (1685—1727,) many of which are in the British Museum. Sotheby, 1860, 2l.

Life, abridged by David Jennings. 1744, sm. 8vo. 10s. 6d.

See ELIOT. PULPIT. PRAYERS. PSALMS.

MATHER, Increase, D.D. An Essay for the Recording of illustrious Providences. Boston, N. E., 1684, 12mo.

First edition, rare. Nassau, pt. 1. 2216. A copy is in the Greenville collection.

Republished as Remarkable Providences of the Earlier Days of American Colonisation. With Introductory Preface by George Offor. Lond. 1856, 12mo. port. 6s.

The Wicked Man's Portion; a Sermon preached 1674, when two Men were executed who murther'd their Master. Boston, 1765, 4to. Probably the first book printed at Boston. Sotheby, 1860, 3l.

The Mystery of Israel's Salvation. Boston, 1669, 12mo. Puttick, May 1859, 18s. Sotheby, 1860, 2l.

A brief History of the War with the Indians in New England, June 1675 to Aug. 1676. Lond. 1676, 4to. Heber, pt. viii. 17s. Bright, 13s. Puttick, May 1859, uncut, 5l.

The first Principles of New England concerning the Subject of Baptism and Communion of Churches. Cambridge, N. E., by S. Green, 1675, 4to.

The Divine Right of Infant Baptism asserted. Boston, by John Foster, 1680, 4to.

Returning unto God the great Concernment of a Covenant People. Boston, 1680, 4to.

Diatriba de Signo Filii Hominis, et de Secundo Messiæ adventu. Amst. 1682, 12mo. Puttick, May 1856, 10s.

Kometographia, or a Discourse concerning Comets. Boston, N. E. 1683, 12mo. Puttick, 1859, 1l. 16s. Reprinted, 1811, 10s.

The Mystery of Christ, opened and applied, in several Sermons. Boston, N. E. 1690, 12mo. Puttick, May 1859, portrait inserted, 2l. 5s. Sotheby, 1860, 2l. 5s.

Testimony against several superstitions Customs, now practised by some in New England. 1687, 8vo. Puttick, May 1859, uncut, 3l.

History of the Wars with the Indians, 1688 to 1698. Lond. 1699, 4to. Puttick, May 1854, 1l. 10s.

1514 MAT

MAT

MATHER, Increase—*continued.*
De Successu Evangelii apud Indos Occidentales in Nova Anglia, Epistola ad Johannem Leusdenum. Lond. 1688. Puttick, May 1854, 10s.—Ultraj. 1699, 12mo.

A further Account of the Tryals of the New England Witches. Lond. J. Dunton, 1693, 4to. Puttick, May1859, 2l. 18s. Sotheby, 1860, 2l. 12s.

A brief Discourse concerning the unlawfulness of the Common-Prayer Worship, and of laying the Hand on, and kissing the Book in Swearing. *Published anonymously* (Boston, 1686). Puttick, 1859, 4l. 6s. There is a fac-simile reprint of this executed in London. It was answered, in 1691, in 'A brief Discourse concerning the lawfulness of worshipping God by the Common Prayer (by John Cotton). 1694, 4to.' 1l. 1s.

Angelographia; or a Discourse concerning the Nature and Power of the Holy Angels. Boston, 1696, 8vo. portrait.

Two Discourses, on Hardness of Heart, and on the Sin of Disobedience to the Gospel. Lond. 1699, 12mo. 10s. 6d.

The Duty of Parents to pray for their Children; and the Duty of Children whose Parents have prayed for them. Two Sermons. Boston, 1703, 12mo. Sotheby, 1860, 3l. 3s.

Meditations on the Glory of the Lord Jesus Christ, in several Sermons. Boston, 1705, 16mo.

A Discourse concerning the Maintenance due to those that preach the Gospel. Boston, 1706, sm. 8vo.

Doctrine of Singular Obedience as the Duty of the true Christian. Boston, 1707, 12mo, 7s.

Some Remarks on a pretended Answer to a Discourse concerning the Common-Prayer Worship. Lond. N. Hiller, &c. 1711, 12mo. Puttick, May 1859, 2l. 12s.

Several Sermons, wherein is shewed that Jesus Christ is a mighty Saviour. Boston, N. E. 1715. Puttick, May 1859, 1l. 9s.

Practical Truths plainly delivered. Boston, 1718, 8vo.

Sermons on the Beatitudes; in fifteen Discourses. Boston, 17—, 8vo.—Dublin, 1721, 8vo. Puttick, May 1859, 9s.

Parentalia; or Memoirs of the Remarkables in the Life of Dr. Increase Mather. 1724, sm. 8vo, portrait.—New edition, with a Preface by Dr. Ed. Calamy. Lond. 1725. 8vo. 2 portraits, 1l.

MATHER, Nath., D.D. Twenty-three select Sermons at Pinner's Hall. Lond. 1701, 8vo.

Pietas in Patriam; or Life of Sir Wm. Phipps, Governor of Massachusetts Bay.

Lond. 1697, small 8vo. Heber, pt. v. 2s. Bright, Cs. 6d.—Lond. 1699, 12mo.
Fast-Day Sermon. Lond. 1711, 8vo.

MATHER, Rd. A modest and brotherly Answer to Mr. Chas. Herle, his Book against the Independency of the Churches. Lond. 1644, 4to.
Sotheby, 1860, 16s.
Reply to Mr. Rutherford, or a Defence of the Answer to Mr. Herle's Booke against the Independency of Churches. Lond. 1647, 4to.

— Samuel, M.A. The Figures or Types of the old Testament explained and improved in sundry Sermons. Dublin, 1673, 4to.
An esteemed work.—1683, 4to.—1705, 4to. 10s. 6d.

Early Piety exemplified; or the Life and Death of Mr. Nathaniel Mather. Lond. 1689, 12mo. (Qy. by Cotton Mather?)

A Vindication of the Holy Bible, wherein the Arguments for, and Objections against the divine original Purity and Integrity of the Scriptures are proposed and considered. Lond. 1723, 8vo. In this work, which contains much useful information, the author, who was an English dissenting minister at Witney, defends the Masorets and Buxtorfs with a good deal of keenness.

An Apology for the Liberties of the Churches in New England. Boston, 1738, 8vo.

Life of his Father, Dr. Cotton Mather. *See* MATHER, Cotton.

MATTHEW, Edward. The most glorious Star or celestial Constellation of the Pleiados; or Charles Waine. Lond. 1661, 12mo.
Brockett, 1874, russia, 1l. 4s.—1660, 8vo. With a whole-length portrait and print of his giving thanks to God, May 29, 1660. Towneley, pt. i. 490, 6s. Bindley, pt. ii. 1774, 3l. 4s.—1662. Olles, with plate, 2s.—1664. In the Grenville Collection.

— Francis. A mediterranean Passage by Water from London to Bristol, and from Lynn to Yarmouth, and so consequently to the City of York, for the great Advancement of Trade and Traffique. Lond. 1670, small 4to.
Pp. 12. Reed, 2224, with portrait of Charles II. by Hertocha, 11s.

A mediterranean Passage by Water between the two Sea Towns Lynn and Yarmouth, upon the two Rivers the Little

Ouse and Waveney. With further Results, producing the passage from Yarmouth to York. Lond. 1830, sm. 4to. pp. 15, the title-page within a border.

MATHEWS, Francis. Regularis observantiæ et aliorum ordinum mendicantium Regni Hiberniæ. Lovanii, 1632, 4to.

A copy is in the Grenville Collection.
For other works by this writer, who assumed the name of Edmundus Ursulanus, see HARRIS's edition of Ware's History of Irish Writers.

— Le, A.M., à suera domest. A Pindarique upon the Death of Jeremye (Taylor), late Lord Bishop of Doune (sic) Connor and Dromore. Dublin, 1667, 4to. pp. 14.

— Sir Tobie. A Collection of Letters made by Sir T. Mathews, with a Character of Lucy, Countess of Carlisle. Lond. 1660, sm. 8vo.

In this volume (edited by Dr. John Donne) will be found a free Account of the trial of Sir Walter Raleigh. Prefixed is a portrait of Sir Toby by J. Gammon. Reed. 2599, 4s. Bishop of Ely, 1311, 9s. 6d. Bindley, pt. II. 1368, 16s.—1686, with portrait.

The penitent Bandito; or, the History of the Conversion and Death of Trollo Sabelli. 1663, 12mo.

An account of Sir Toby Mathews will be found in Wood's Athen. Oxon., and several of his letters are in the Cabala and the Scrinia Sacra.

MATHIAS, T. J. Componimenti Lirici de' più illustri Poeti d'Italia, scelti da T. J. Mathias. Lond. 1802, post 8vo. 3 vols.

White Knights, 2558, 1l. 6s. Hibbert, 5236, 13s. 6d.
Aggiunta al Componimenti lirici de' più illustri Poeti d'Italia. Lond. 1808, post 8vo. 3 vols. White Knights, 2559, unive. 1l. 10s.
Runic Odes, imitated in the Norse Tongue in the Manner of Mr. Gray. Lond. 1781, 4to.
An Essay on the Evidence relating to the Poems attributed to Rowley. Lond. 1783, sm. 8vo.
Odes, English and Latin. 1798, 12mo. Privately printed. Combe, 1293, 7s. 6d. Marquis of Townshend, 2051, 17s.
Canzoni Toscani, 1805, 4to.
Canzuole Prose Toscane. 1808. White Knights, 2660, 5s.

Poesie di Scrittori Illustri Inglesi, recate in verso Italiano. Napoli, 1830, sm. 8vo. Contains Italian versions of Milton's Lycidas, Thomson's Castle of Indolence, Spenser's Mutabilitie, &c.
Poesie Liriche e Prose Toscane. Lond. 1810, 4to. Privately printed. Hibbert, 5378, 4s.—Napoli, 1830, 12mo.
The Pursuits of Literature, a Satirical Poem in Four Dialogues, with Notes. To which are added, an Appendix, the Citations translated, and a complete Index. Sixteenth edition. Lond. 1812, 4to. LARGE PAPER in folio, for illustration.
(The First Dialogue was published in 1794; the Second and Third, 1796; the Fourth, 1797. All the editions are anonymous; those previous to the 16th in 8vo.)
Observations on the Writings and on the Character of Mr. Gray, originally subjoined to the second Volume of Mathias's complete Edition, in 1814, of Gray's Works in two vols. 4to. Lond. 1815, sm. 8vo, 7s.

See CHRISCIMBENI. GRAVINA. GRAY, T. MAMIN, W. MENZINI. MILTON, John. MORTI. PURSUITS OF LITERATURE, HEND, ROWLEY. SPENSER, Ed. THOMSON, J. TIRABOSCHI.

MATHIEU, Pet. History of Henry IV. of France, translated by Ed. Grimston. Lond. 1612, 4to. port.

This history contains some curious anecdotes communicated to the author by Henry himself. Sir M. M. Sykes, pt. II. 489, 12s. White Knights, 2750, 16s. At the end are the Trophies of Henry the Great, translated by Jos. Sylvester).
The History of Lewis XI. translated by E. Grimston. Lond. 1614, folio. Roxburghe, 7996, 5s.
Unhappy Prosperitie, expressed in the History of Æl. Sejanus and Philippa the Catanian, with Observations on the Fall of Sejanus. Translated by Sir T. Hawkins. Lond. 1632, 4to. Bindley, pt. III. 365, 5s. 6d. White Knights, 2731, 7s.—1639, 12mo. See M. P.

MATHISON, Gilbert. Notices respecting Jamaica in 1808, 1809, 1810. Lond. 1811, 8vo. 5s.

— G. F. G. Narrative of a Visit to Brazil, Chili, Peru, and the Sandwich Islands in 1821-2. Lond. 1825, 12mo.

Journal of a Tour in Ireland during October and November, 1835. Lond. 1836, 8vo. (Printed for private circulation only.)

MATHO, or the Cosmotheoria puerilis. See BAXTER, Andrew.

MATON, Robert. Israel's Redemption, with a Discourse of Gog and Magog. Lond. 1642, 12mo.

A Treatise on the fifth Monarchy; or Christ's personal Reign on Earth one thousand Years with his Saints, &c. Lond. 1655, 4to. with portrait by Cross.

A notice of Maton will be found in Wood's Athenæ Oxonienses.

—— William George, M.D. Observations relative chiefly to natural History, picturesque Scenery, and Antiquities of the western Counties of England, made in the Years 1794 and 1796. Salisbury, 1797, 8vo. 2 vols.

Illustrated by a mineralogical map and sixteen views in aquatinta by Alken. Duke of York, 3347, 14s. Edwards, 632, 1l. 8s. Fonthill, 2172, 3l.

Descriptive Catalogue of the British Testacea. Lond. 1804, 4to. plates. *See* Linnean Transactions, vol. viii.

Memoir of the Life of. (By Dr. Paris.) Lond. colombier 8vo. with a portrait. Privately printed.

MATRIMONY.—The Pleasures of Matrimony, intermix'd with a Variety of merry and delightful Stories. Lond. 1688, 8vo.

Reed, 2763, 9s. 6d. Lloyd, 238, 15s.

Spirituall Matrimonie betweene Christ and his Church. Worcester, by John Oswen, 1548, 16mo.

The spirituall Matrimonye betweene Chryste and the Soul. Canterbury, by John Mychell, n. d. 24mo.

The Order of Matrimony. Lond. by Anthony Scholoker, 16mo. Heber, pt. iv. 1l. 5s. Contains B 4, in eights, half-sheets.

An Admonition for the Necessity of the present Time, till a further Consultation, to all such as shall intend hereafter to enter the State of Matrimony godly and agreeable to Law. Lond. by Reg. Wolfe, 1550. A broadside. *See* Strype's Life of Abp. Parker, p. 87. In Bp. Sparrow's collection is a copy from an edition of 1553, with some omissions in the title-page. Mr. Hearne thought it set forth about 1571, that probably being the date of the copy he saw.

An admonition to all such as intend hereafter to enter the State of Matrimony, godly and agreeable to the Laws. Lond. by Peter Short, for John Harrison, 1594. A broadside. *See* Strype's Life of Abp. Parker, p. 87, &c.

The Fifteen Comforts of Matrimony. 1683. Perry, pt. i. 1612. M. 9s. Boswell, 1057, 5s.—1791. White Knights, 2663, 7s.—1700, with an addition of three Comforts more.

The Mistake of Matrimony, wherein is clearly set out the shamefull Craftincess as well by Men as Women, 1641, oblong 4to. plate of the Frolick Waggon, and 5 oval heads of Wanton Women and Men, by Crispin de Pass. Sotheby's in 1823, 2l. 12s.

Matrimonial Customs. 1697, 12mo. Stanley, 601, 15s.

The Levellers: a Dialogue between two young Ladies concerning Matrimony; proposing an Act for enforcing Marriage, for the Equality of Matches, and taxing single Persons; with the Danger of Celibacy to a Nation. Dedicated to a Member of Parliament. Lond. 1703, 4to. pp. 32. Reprinted in the fifth volume of the Harleian Miscellany.

The present State of Matrimony. 1739. White Knights, 2562, 5s.

Matrimony made easy; or, a new System of Marriage. Lond. 1764, 8vo.

Matrimonial Ceremonies displayed. Lond. 1768, 12mo. Heber, 1s.

Curtain Lectures, or Matrimonial Misery displayed. 1770, 6s.

See GAYA, L. de. MARRIAGE. WARD, E.

MATRONS, The. Six short Histories. Lond. 1762, 12mo. 5s.—Dublin, —— 12mo.

With a frontispiece, edited by Thomas Percy, Bp. of Dromore. *Contents*.—1. The Ephesian Matron, from Petronius. 2. The Chinese Matron, from Du Halde. 3. The French Matron, from a letter from Sir Geo. Etherege to the Duke of Buckingham. 4. The British Matron, (an abstract of ' The Widow of the Wood,' published in 1755. *See* VICTOR, Benj.] 5. The Turkish Matron, from a MS. 6. The Roman Matron, from ' The seven wise Mistresses of Rome.' Dublin, 12mo. front.

MATTHEW, Saint, the Evangelist. Evangelium secundum Matthæum, ex Codice rescripto in Bibliotheca Collegii S. Trinitatis juxta Dublin: descriptum Opera et Studio Joh. Barret. Cui subjungitur Appendix Collationem Codicis Montfortiani complectens. Dublini, 1801, 4to.

An excellent critique on this fac-simile will be found in the Eclectic Review,

MATTHEW, St.—*continued.*
vol. iii. pp. 193 and 580. *See* also Horne's Introduction to the Scriptures, vol. iv. pt. i. ch. iii. sect. iii. § 4. The prolegomena occupy 52 pp., the fac-simile plates, 64, which are also exhibited in as many pages, in the common Greek type; and the collation of the Codex Montfortianus, 35 pages. Gomet, 1050, 14s. Gough, 1548, 1l. 13s.

An Exposition upon the Vth, VIth, and VIIth Chapters of Matthew. No place or date, 12mo. Printed for Wm. Tyndal while he was in Holland in 1537, by N. Grafton, for which he was thrown into the Fleet for six weeks.

The Gospel according to Saint Matthew, with part of the First Chapter of Saint Mark, translated from the Greek by Sir John Cheke, (circa 1550), with an account of the Translation by J. Goodwin. Lond. Pickering, 1843, 8vo.

A new Version of the Gospel according to St. Matthew, with a literal Commentary on all the difficult Passages; to which is prefixed, an Introduction to the Reading of the Scriptures. By M. Beausobre and M. Lenfant. Lond. 1727, 4to.—Cambridge, 1788, 8vo.—Lond. 1808, 8vo. 10s. 6d.—Lond. 1816, 8vo.—Lond. 1819, 8vo.

A new Version of St. Matthew's Gospel, with select Notes, wherein the Version is vindicated, and the Sense and Purity of several Words and Expressions in the original Greek are settled and illustrated; to which is added, a Review of Dr. Mill's Notes on this Gospel. By D. Scott, J.U.D. Lond. 1741, 4to. 4s. 6d. An esteemed version by the compiler of the Appendix to Stephens's Greek Thesaurus, a learned dissenter of the Baptist denomination.

A Paraphrase on the fifth, sixth, and seventh Chapters of St. Matthew. 1764.

A new Translation of the Gospel of St. Matthew, with Notes, critical, philological, and explanatory, by Gilbert Wakefield, B.A. Lond. 1782, 4to. 10s.

The Gospel according to Matthew, translated from the original Greek, and illustrated by Extracts from the theological Writings of the Hon. Eman. Swedenborg, together with Notes and Observations of the Translator annexed to each Chapter. Lond. 1805, 8vo.

The Gothic Gospel of Saint Matthew, from the Codex Argenteus of the fourth Century; with the corresponding English or Saxon, from the Durham Book of the eighth Century, in Roman Characters; a literal English version of each; and Notes, Illustrations, and Etymological Disquisitions on organic Principles. By Samuel Henshall, M.A. Lond. 1807, 8vo. 7s. 6d.

An Inquiry concerning the canonical Authority of St. Matthew. Lond. 1732, 8vo.

A Letter to a Lady in Defence of the canonical Authority of St. Matthew's Gospel. 1732, 8vo.

A free Enquiry into the Authenticity of the first and second Chapters of St. Matthew's Gospel. Lond. 1771, 8vo.

Free Thoughts upon a free Enquiry into the Authenticity of the first and second Chapters of St. Matthew's Gospel. Addressed to the anonymous Author. With a short prefatory Defence of the Purity and Integrity of the New-Testament Canon. By Theophilus. Lond. 1771, 8vo.

The Authenticity of the first and second Chapters of St. Matthew's Gospel vindicated. Lond. 1771, 8vo. *See* MATTHIAS.

MATTHEW OF WESTMINSTER. Flores Historiarum per Matthæum Westmonasteriensem collecti, præcipuè de Rebus Britannicis ab Exordio Mundi usque ad Annum Domini 1307. Lond. 1570, folio.

First edition. Published by Abp. Parker. The copy in the Cracherode collection is the identical one presented by the Archbishop to Queen Elizabeth. Bp. of Ely, 1041, 1l. 6s. Gough, 2773, 2l. 10s. Roscoe, 459, 3l. Roxburghe, 8130, 3l. 19s. LARGE PAPER.—Lond. 1567, fol. Gough, 2772, 2l. 15s.—Francof. 1601, folio. This edition, though incorrect as regards English words, is held to be the best, as it contains an Index, and also Chronicon ex Chronicis, ab initio Mundi ad Ann. Dom. 1118, Auctore Florentio Wigorniensi Monacho, etc. Heath, 4501, 2l. 4s. FINE PAPER. Dent, pt. ii. 763, morocco, 6l.

The Flowers of History, especially such as relate to the Affairs of Britain. From the beginning of the World to the Year 1307. Collected by Matthew of Westminster. Translated from the original by C. D. Yonge, B.A. Lond. (Bohn's Antiq. Lib.) 1853, post 8vo. 2 vols. 10s.

MATTHEW PARIS. *See* PARIS, M.

MATTHEWS, A. N. Mischkat-ul-Masabih: a Collection of Traditions regarding the Actions and Sayings of Muhammed; with a Translation by Capt. Matthews. Calcutta, 1809-10, roy. 4to. 2 vols. Foulhill, 1769, 1l. 17s.

— Col. John, of Herefordshire. Eloisa en Dishabille, done into familiar English metre by a Lounger. Lond. 1801, imp. 8vo. 10s. 6d.

According to Moore, in his Life of Byron, this is erroneously ascribed to Prof.

Porson. Often reprinted in 18mo. 8s.
Copies on vellum.
This writer printed a Letter to Dr.
Madan on Polygamy, and a Letter to
Price on the Picturesque.

MATTHEWS, H. The Diary of an
Invalid, being the Journal of a Tour
in Portugal, Italy, Switzerland, and
France, 1817-19. Lond. 1820, 8vo.

Light and pleasant sketches of manners,
and other popular information on Portugal,
Italy, Switzerland, and France. Drury,
2674, 10s.—Second edition, 1820.—1822, 2
vols. post 8vo. Combe, 1291, 9s.—Fifth
edition, Lond. Murray, 1835, fcap. 8vo.
front. and vignette title, 7s. 6d.

— John. A Voyage to the River
Sierra-Leone on the Coast of Africa.
Lond. 1788, 8vo.

Pp. 4, and 185, with a chart and a view
of the Bananas. Drury, 2672, 8s. Fonthill,
2644, 17s.—1791, 8vo. Fonthill, 2845, 15s.

— Thomas. Advice to a young
Whist-Player. 12mo.—Eighteenth
edition, Bath, 1828, 12mo.

A very popular treatise.

— William. See QUAKERS.

MATTHIE, Augustus. The Greek
Grammar translated into English,
by the Rev. E. V. Blomfield. Cambridge, 1818, 8vo. 2 vols.

An admirable work. Williams, 1187,
1l. 13s. Drury, 2675, russia, 2l. 1s.—Second edition, with Index. Lond. 1820, 8vo.
2 vols. Hibbert, 6235, 16s.—Third edition,
(with an additional Index of Ancient Authors referred to in the Grammar). Lond.
1824, 8vo. 2 vols.—Fourth edition, revised
by the Rev. John Kenrick. Lond. 1829,
8vo. 2 vols. (also with additions and Index
of Authors).—Fifth and last complete
edition. Lond. 1837, 8vo. 2 vols.—Seventh
edition, abridged by Blomfield and revised
by Edwards. Lond. 1841, 12mo. 8s. frequently reprinted.

Index of Quotations from Greek Authors contained in the Grammar. Lond.
1833, 8vo.—Second edition. Lond. 1841,
8vo. 7s. 6d.

Manual of the History of Greek and
Roman Literature, translated from the
Third Edition of the German. Oxford,
1841, fcap. 8vo. 6s.

MATTHIAS, the Apostle. The
true Time of keeping St. Matthias's
Day in Leap Years, &c. Lond.
1712, 12mo. See MATTHEW, Saint.

MATTHISON, Frederick. Letters
written from various parts of the
Continent, between the Years 1785
and 1794; containing a variety of
Anecdotes relative to the present
State of Literature in Germany,
and to celebrated German Literati.
With an Appendix. Translated from
the German by Anne Plumptree.
Lond. 1799, 8vo. 6s.

In the appendix are included three letters of the poet Gray's never before published in this country.

MATY, Matthew, M.D. Journal
Britannique. La Haye, 1750-7,
12mo. 24 vols.

An account of the productions of the
English Press. Osmont, 3394, 17 vols.
2l. 12s. 6d. Willett, 1625, 18 vols. 10s 6d.
Heber, pt. II. 18 vols. 1l.

— Paul Henry. New Review,
with Literary Curiosities and Intelligence. Lond. 1782-6, 8vo. 9 vols.
Gough, 2515, 1l. 2s. Hollis, 819, 1l. 7s.
Reed, 2558, 2l. 3s.

Sermons preached in the British Ambassador's Chapel, at Paris, in the Years
1774, 1775, 1776. Lond. 1788, 8vo. Bindley, pt. II. 1565, 6s.

Maty, who was librarian at the British
Museum, published a General Index to
the Philosophical Transactions, &c. Lond.
1787, 4to.

MAUDE, John. Visit to the
Falls of Niagara in 1800. royal 8vo.
With engravings. 10s.

MAUDIT, John. ANTIPOBAAH, or a Defence of the Minister of Pensherst, in a case between
him and the Earl of Leycester, in
Michaelmas Term, 1657. Lond.
by T. R. for the author, 1660,
12mo. pp. 51, with title.

The Practises of the Earl of Leycester
against the Minister of Pensherst, laid
open in a Narrative sent to his late Highness, Oliver, Lord Protector, August, 1656.
Lond. by T. R. for the author, 1660, 12mo.
pp. 52, with title and 2 leaves at end.

Mr. Bindley possessed both the preceding, bound in one volume (now in the
British Museum), in which he had written, "The only copy I ever saw." See J.
R. Smith's Bibl. Cantiana, p. 254. Puttick. June 10, 1858, 8l. 8s. Heber, pt. v. 1l.

MAUDUIT, Isr. A short View of
the History of the Colony of Mas-

MAU 1519

sachusetts Bay, with Respect to their Charter and Constitution. Lond. 1774, 8vo.—Fourth edition, Lond. 1776, 8vo.

MAULE, George. Reports in the K. B. from Hilary, 53 Geo. III., to Trinity Term, 58 Geo. III., 1813-17. By G. Maule and W. Selwyn. Lond. 1814-19, royal 8vo. 6 vols. 2l. 12s. 6d.

Continued by Barnewall, &c.

— Henry, of Melgum. History of the Picts. Edinb. 1706, 12mo.

Inserted in Miscellanea Scotica, vol. iv. Heber, pt. v, 6s.

— John. An historical Account of the royal Hospital at Greenwich. Lond. 1789, 4to. plate.

MAUND, B. The Botanic Garden, consisting of representations of hardy ornamental flowering Plants cultivated in Great Britain. Lond. 1824-50, fscap. 4to. 13 vols.

Published in numbers at 1s. each, with the plates partly coloured, (17l. 11s.); or FINE PAPER in post 4to., the plates wholly coloured, at 1s. 6d. each (25l. 15s.)

MAUNDEVILLE. See MANDEVILLE.

MAUNDRELL, Henry, M.A. A Journey from Aleppo to Jerusalem, at Easter, A.D. 1697. The seventh Edition, to which is now added an Account of the Author's Journey to the Banks of the Euphrates at Beer, and to the Country of Mesopotamia. With an Index to the whole Work. Oxford, 1749, 8vo.

Pp. (xii) and 171, also fifteen plates. Best edition. Bishop Newton, in speaking of Maundrell, observes, ' whom it is a pleasure to quote as well as to read, and whose Journal from Aleppo to Jerusalem, though a little book, is yet worth a folio, and is so accurately and ingeniously written, that it might serve as a model for all writers of travels.' Marquis of Townshend, 2053, 11s. LARGE PAPER. Towneley, pt. II. 784, 11s. 6d. Steevens, 1880, 18s. 6d. Williams, 1198, morocco, 19s. Bp. Randolph, 820, 1l. 5s.—Oxford, 1703, 8vo. 5s. LARGE PAPER. Sir M. M. Sykes, pt. II.

344, 1l. 13s.—Oxford, 1707. 8vo.—Oxford, 1714, 8vo. 5s. LARGE PAPER. Hibbert, 5341. 15s.—Oxford, 1721, 8vo. 5s.—Oxford, 1732, 8vo. Roxburghe, 7263, 6s. 6d. Hindley, pt. II. 1734. 6s. 6d. LARGE PAPER. Dent, pt. L 1402, morocco, 1l. 1s. Edwards, 521, 9s.—Oxford, 1740, 8vo. Fonthill, 2386, 1l. 6s. Reed, 5076, 12s. Willett, 1637, 11s.—Oxford, 1743, 8vo. 8s. LARGE PAPER. Heath, 2637, 1l. 19s.—Dublin, 1749, termed the Sixth Edition, 8vo.—Perth, 1800, 12mo.—Lond. 1810, 8vo. Drury, 2676, 14s. Foothill, 630, 1l. 1s. LARGE PAPER. Earl of Kerry, 857, 17s. 6d. This edition has Bp. Clayton's Journey to Mount Sinai, and Jos. Pitt's Account of the Mahometans, attached to it. Maundrell's Journey will be found in Harris's, Moore's, and Pinkerton's Collections of Voyages and Travels ; and it is completely reprinted from the best edition, in Bohn's collection of the ' Early Travels in Palestine ;' which also contains Maudeville, De la Brocquiere, Benjamin of Tudela, and others. Lond. 1848, post 8vo. 5s.

MAUNSELL, Andrew. Catalogue of English Bookes. Lond. 1595, folio, 2 parts.

Hibbert, 5430, 1l. 8s. Bindley, pt. II. 1236, 1l. 18s. Geo. Chalmers, 1l. 18s. Dibdin, 62, 2l. 8s. Heber, MS. notes by the Rev. Tho. Baker, 2l. 12s. 6d. Bliss, 1l. 18s. Collation.—Part I. printed by Windet, pp. 123, besides title and 3 dedications, 4 leaves. Part II. printed by James Roberts, pp. 27, besides titles and 3 dedications, 3 leaves. Herne calls this catalogue ' a very scarce and yet a very useful book,' and it is curious on many accounts, particularly as registering many works and authors long since lost or forgotten. It is to be regretted that Maunsell did not proceed to his third collection.

MAUPERTUIS, P. L. M. de. On the Figure of the Earth ; translated from the French. Lond. 1738, 8vo. 3s. 6d.

MAURICE, of Nassau. A briefe Relation of what hath happened unto Counte Maurice of Nassau, since the taking of Rynbark. Lond. 1601, 4to.

Ireland in 1601, 571, 9s. 6d. Inglis, 967, russia, 12s. Bindley, pt. II. 1856, 1l. 10s.

A Discourse, more at large, of the late overthrowe given to the King of Spaine's Armie at Tournehout by Count Maurice of Nassau. Lond. 1597, 4to. BLACK LETTER.

A True relation of the famous Victorie latelie atchieved by the Count Maurice of Nassau, neere to Newport, in Flan-

1520 MAU MAV

ders, against the Archduke Albertus. Lond. for C. B. a. d. 4to. BLACK LETTER.

The Battails fought betweene Count Maurice and Albertus, Archduke of Austria, nere Newport, in Flaunders, 22nd June, 1600. Lond. Andrew Wise, 1600, 4to.

MAURICE, Rev. Thomas. Indian Antiquities: or, Dissertations relative to the Geography, Theology, Laws, &c. of Hindostan. Lond. 1793-1800, 8vo. 7 vols. 2l. 2s.

Bindley, pt. ii. 1536, 1l. 11s. 6d. Earl of Kerry, 331, 2l. 15s. 'I recommend, in the most earnest manner, both the dissertations and the history of this writer to the attention of all those who are desirous of seeing strong additional light thrown upon some of the most important doctrines of the holy scriptures.'—*Bishop Townlias.*

The (Antient) History of Hindostan; its Arts, and its Sciences, as connected with the History of the other great Empires of Asia, during the most ancient Periods of the World. With numerous Illustrative Engravings. Lond. 1795-8, 4to. 3 parts in 2 vols. Bindley, pt. iii. 313, 15s. Fonthill, 3137, 6l. 6s. Duke of York, 3169, 1l. 15s.

The Modern History of Hindostan; comprehending that of the Greek Empire of Bactria, and other great Asiatic Kingdoms, bordering on its western Frontier: commencing at the Period of the Death of Alexander, and brought down to the Close of the Year 1798. Lond. 1802-10. 4to. 5 parts in two vols. Earl of Kerry, 400, with the Ancient History, 4l. 6s. Duke of York, 3169, 1l. 13s.

Grove Hill (Camberwell); a rural and horticultural Sketch (with a Catalogue of Fruit Trees and Plants in the Garden). Lond. 1804, 4to. pp. 47, with six plates.—1799, 4to. pp. 82, including the title, preface, and argument, also fifteen woodcuts, by J. Anderson, from drawings by G. Samuel, exclusive of the vignette in the title-page. This edition contains 'an Ode to Mithra.' Bindley, pt. iii. 315, 9s. 6d.

Richmond Hill; a descriptive and historical Poem: illustrative of the principal Objects viewed from that beautiful Eminence. Lond 1807, 4to. 5s. Pp. 178, including the two titles, dedication to Lord Sidmouth, advertisement and list of subscribers, also two folding views.

Westminster Abbey: with other occasional Poems, and a free Translation of the Œdipus Tyrannus of Sophocles. Lond. 1813, royal 8vo. 4s. pp. 217, with three plates.—1784, 4to. 10s. 6d.

Memoirs of the Author of Indian Antiquities. 1819, 8 parts. Combe, 1296, 10s. 6d.

MAURIER, Baron. The Lives of all the Princes of Orange from William the Great, Founder of the Commonwealth of the United Provinces, including the Life of William III. to the time of his landing in England, translated by Thos. Brown. Lond. 1693, 8vo. 5s.

MAURITIUS.—A Voyage to the Island of Mauritius, (or Isle of France), the Isle of Bourbon, the Cape of Good Hope, &c. with Observations and Reflections by a French Officer. Translated from the French by John Parish. Lond. 1775, 8vo.

An Account of the Conquest of the Isle of France, or Mauritius and Bourbon; with some Notices on the History, &c. of those Islands, 1812, 8vo. 2 vols.

A Catalogue of the exotic Plants cultivated in the Mauritius at the Botanic Garden, Montplaisir, Hedmit, and other Places. Mauritius, 1816, 4to., See GRANT.

MAUROCORDATUS, J. N. A. Liber de Officiis, Gr. et Lat. Londini, 1724, small 8vo. 3s.

MAURUS, Abbot. Of the Sacrament. *See* GUILD, William, p. 955.

MAURY, The Abbé. The Principles of Eloquence, adapted to the Pulpit and the Bar. Translated from the French, with additional Notes, by J. N. Lake, A.M. Lond. 1793, 8vo.

Williams, 1189, 5s.

MAYER, John. *See* ZUÑIGA, M. de.

MAVERICKE, Radford. Saint Peter's Chaine, consisting of eight Golden Linckes, most fit to adorne the neckes of the greatest States, Nobles, and Ladies, in this land, as the chiefest Jewell of True Nobilitie, and not unfit for the meaner sort. Lond. J. Windet, 1596, 4to. Bright, soiled copy, 12s.

MAVOR, William, LL.D. Universal History, ancient and modern, to the Peace of 1801. Lond. 1802 & 1813, 18mo. 25 vols. Maps, &c. 2l. 10s.

" A useful work. FINE PAPER, 4l. 4s.

Historical Account of the most celebrated Voyages, Travels, and Discoveries, from the Time of Columbus to the present Period. Lond. 1796-1802, 18mo. 25 vols. plates.—1910, 18mo. 25 vols.—New edition, adding the Travels of Lord Valentia, 1813-15, 18mo. 29 vols. 2l. 2s.

The British Tourists. Lond. 1798-1800, 18mo. 6 vols.—1807, 18mo. 6 vols. 10s. 6d. Miscellanies, two parts:—I. Prose. II. Verse. Oxf. n. d. (1829) 8vo. portrait.

Dr. Mavor published a variety of other works, principally for the use of schools. His Spelling Book is extremely popular. *See* MARTYN, W. F. TUMER, Thomas.

MAWE, John. Travels in the Interior of Brazil; including a Voyage to the Rio de la Plata, and an historical Sketch of the Revolution at Buenos Ayres. Lond. 1812, 4to. plates, 1l. 1s.

Fonthill, 8vo. 2l.—Second edition. Lond. 1821, 8vo. with coloured plates and a map, 18s.

The Mineralogy of Derbyshire; with a Description of the most interesting Mines in the North of England, in Scotland, and in Wales; and an Analysis of Mr. Williams's work intitled 'The Mineral Kingdom.' Subjoined is a Glossary of the Terms and Phrases used by Miners in Derbyshire. Lond. 1802, 8vo. Nassau, pt. I. 2222, 10s. *Collation.*—Pp. 211, besides title; preface and errata, 8 pages; contents, 6 pages, also three plates and a map of Derbyshire.

The Linnæan System of Conchology. Lond. 1823, 8vo. pp. 207, with 37 plates, plain, 1l. 1s.; coloured, 2l. 12s. 6d.

Shell Collector's Pilot, or Voyager's Companion. Fourth Edit. Lond. 1825, 4s.

Instructions for the Management of the Blow Pipe. Fourth Edition. Lond. 1825, 12mo. 4s.

A Treatise on Diamonds and precious Stones. Lond. 1913, 8vo.—Second edition. Lond. 1822, 8vo. 15s.

Amateur Lapidary's Guide, containing Instructions for cutting, polishing, and setting precious Stones. Third edition. Lond. 1823, 12mo. 1s. 6d.—Lond. 1827, 12mo. 1s. 6d.

Description of Lapidaries' Apparatus. 12mo.

Familiar Lessons on Mineralogy and Geology. Eighth edition. Lond. 1828, 12mo. coloured plates, 7s.—Ninth edition. Lond. 1828, 7s. 3s.

Catalogue of Minerals for Learners. Lond. 1815, 12mo. 4s.

A new descriptive Catalogue of Minerals, arranged for the Use of Students, with Diagrams of their simple Forms from Dr. Clarke's Syllabus. Second edition. Lond. 1816, cr. 8vo. plate.—Fourth edit.

entirely rewritten. Lond. 1821, 7s.—Eighth edition. Lond. 1829, 12mo. 7s.

Introduction to the Study of Conchology. Lond. 8vo. 7 plates, 9s.; coloured plates, 14s.—Fifth edition. Lond. n. d. plates, 9s.; coloured plates, 14s. *See* WODARCH.

— Thomas. Universal Gardener and Botanist, or a general Dictionary of Gardening and Botany. By Thomas Mawe and John Abercrombie. Lond. 1797, 4to.

Every Man his own Gardener. By Thos. Mawe and John Abercrombie. The twenty-third edition, edited by J. Main, F.L.S. Lond. 1829, 12mo. 6s.—Twenty-sixth edit. by Main and Glenny. Lond. 1857, 12mo. 6s.—New edition, by Gowans. Lond. 1849, 12mo. 5s.

MAWMAN, Joseph. An Excursion to the Highlands of Scotland, and the English Lakes, with Recollections, Descriptions, and References to Historical Facts. Lond. 1805, 8vo. map, and 3 plates from early Drawings by J. M. W. Turner, 7s.

Picturesque Tour through France, Switzerland, on the Banks of the Rhine, and through Part of the Netherlands; in the Year 1816. With maps. Lond. 1817, 8vo.

Mr. Mawman was a London bookseller and publisher.

MAXEY, Anth. Five Sermons before the King [James I.]. Lond. 1614, 4to.

The Golden Chain of Man's Salvation. Lond. 1606, sm. 8vo. Bright, 18s.

MAXIMS, Characters, and Reflections, critical, satyrical, and moral. Lond. 1756, 8vo.

An ingenious work by F. Greville, published anonymously. Bindley, pt. II. 904, 6s.

MAXIMUS TYRIUS. Dissertationes. Gr. et Lat. ex Recens. Jo. Daviii; edit. emendata; accedunt Jer. Marklandi Annotationes. Lond. 1740, 4to.

An excellent edition. Hibbert, 5384, 9s. Steevens, 292, 9s. 6d. Willett, 1614, 11s. 6d. Drury, 2338, russia, 1l. Duke of Grafton, 152, 1l. 3s.

Maximi Tyrii Dissertationes, Gr. et Lat. Oxon. 1677, 12mo. A neat and correct edition. Drury, 2338, 3s. 6d.

Maximi Tyrii Dissertationes, Gr. et Lat. ex Interpretatione D. Heinsii, recensuit et Notis illustravit Jo. Davisius, Cantab. 1703, 8vo. 8s.

The Dissertations of Maximus Tyrius, translated from the Greek by Thomas Taylor. Lond. 1804, crown 8vo. 2 vols. 15s.

MAXWELL, James, M.A. The laudable Life and deplorable Death of Prince Henry. Together with some other Poems, in Honour of King James, Prince Charles, and Princess Elizabeth. Lond. E. Allde. 1612. 4to.

A, two leaves, B—F. in fours. Nassau, pt. II. 161, 2l. 11s. Bindley, pt. iv. 712, 3l. 9s. Bibl. Anglo-Poet. 459, morocco, 10l. 10s. resold Midgley, 5l. 2s. 6d. Several of the stanzas (13 to 39) are printed in Cornwallis' History of Prince Henry.

The Golden Art, or the right Way of Enriching. Lond. 1611, 4to.

The Golden Legend; or Mirrour of religious Men and goodly Matrons, concerning Abraham, Isaac, and Jacob, and their Wives. Lond. 1611, 8vo.

Queen Elizabeth's Looking-Glasse of Grace and Glory. 1612, 12mo. Geo. Chalmers, 1l. 11s.

A speedy Passage to Heaven, or the Christian's Practice; being an Exposition upon the ten Commandments, Creed, and Lord's Prayer. Lond. 1612, 8vo.

A Monument of Remembrance, erected in Albion, in Honor of the magnificent Departure from Brittanie, and honorable Receiving in Germanie of the two most noble Princes Fredericke and Elizabeth. Lond. N. Okes, 1613, 4to. In all, 24 leaves. In verse. Gordonstown, 1571, 2l. 16s. Bindley, pt. III. 591, 2l. Nassau, pt. ii. 152, with portraits by Visscher inserted, 3l. 6s. Heber, pt. iv. 10s. 6d. Jolley, 2l. 10s.

Carolanna, that is to say, a Poeme in Honour of our King, Charles-James, Queene Anne, and Prince Charles. By Iames Anneson. Lond. Edw. Allde, (1614) 4to. pp. 48. Sir M. M. Sykes, pt. I. 256, mor. 4l. 17s. Gordonstown, 1570, 2l. 2s. Bindley, pt. iv. 1074, 4l. 14s. 6d. Bibl. Anglo-Poet. 5l. 5s.

Admirable and Notable Prophecies uttered in former times by Twenty-four Romain Catholickes, concerning the Church of Rome's defection, tribulation, and reformation. Lond. 1615, 4to. Bright, 15s.

MAXWELL, John, Bp. of Ross. Sacro-sancta Regum Majestas, or the sacred Prerogative of Christian Kings. Oxford, 1644, 4to.

An answer to this tract forms part of Rutherford's Lex Rex. Lond. 1644. See LEX.

The Burden of Issachar, or the Tyrannicall Power and Practises of the Presbyteriall-Government in Scotland. Printed in the yeare 1646, 4to.

— John. A Discourse concerning God, with a short Account of the Cape of Good Hope. Lond. 1715, 12mo.

MAY, Edward, M.D. A Relation of a strange Monster, or Serpent found in the left Ventricle of the Heart of John Pennant, a Gentleman, of the age of 21 Years. Lond. 1639, 4to. with two cuts.

Twenty-three leaves. Reed, 1343, 4s. Nassau, pt. ii. 153, 7s. Roxburghe, 1809, 8s. 6d. Reprinted in the fifth volume of the Somers' Collection of Tracts.

— Edward. Epigrams Divine and Morall, two centuries. Imp. by T. B. for John Grove, 1633, sm. 8vo. Bindley, pt. ii. 1964, 5l. 12s. 6d. Heber, pt. iv. 2l. 5s. Sotheby, May 1856, 10l. 17s. resold Halliwell, May, 1857, 16l. 10s.

— George. The White-Powder Plot discovered; or a prophetical Poeme. 1662, 4to.

Lloyd, 782, with Answer of Walter's Painter to his many new Advisers, 1687 16s. resold, Heber, pt. iv. 1s.

— R. The Accomplisht Cook. Lond. 1671, 8vo. portrait by Gaywood. Bliss, 4s.

— Thomas. Works.

The Heire, a Comedy. Lond. 1622, 4to. Boswell, 1968, 12s.—1633, 4to. Boswell, 1970, 7s. Roxburghe, 6412, 12s. North, 2l. Heber, pt. ii. 6s. Reprinted in Dodsley's Collection of Old Plays.

Antigone, a Tragedy. Lond. 1631, 8vo. Caldecott, 1l. 18s.

Cleopatra, a Tragedy. Lond. 1639, 12mo. Roxburghe, 6441, 11s. Caldecott, 7s. Bindley, pt. ii. 1579, with Agrippina, 1639, 2l. 4s. Field, 820, with Agrippina, 1639, 7s.

Julia Agrippina, Empresse of Rome, a Tragedy. Lond. 1639, 12mo. Reed. 6232, 2s. 6d. Roxburghe, 6443, 11s. Hibbert, 4918, 2s. 6d.

Two Tragedies, viz. Cleopatra, Queene of Egypt, and Agrippina, Empress of Rome. Lond. 1654, 12mo. Nassau, pt. i. 2245, 1l. 3s. Rhodes, 1867, 1l. 5s.

The Old Couple, a Comedy. Lond. 1658, 4to. Roxburghe, 8444, 2s. Boswell, 1979, 8s. 6d. Rhodes, 1606, 6s. Bindley, pt. iii. 523, 2s. Heber, pt. ii. 6s.

In the year 1744, Coxeter circulated proposals for printing this author's Plays. Gents.' Mag. May, 1781. An article 'on the comedies of Thomas May' will be found in the New Monthly Magazine, n. s. ii. 70-6.

The History of the Parliament of England, which began Nov. 3, M.DC.XL.: with a short and necessary View of some pre-

MAY, Thos.—*continued.*
endent Years. Lond. 1647, folio. Hibbert, 5431, 10s. 6d. Hollis, 772, 11s. Gordonstoun, 1617, 14s. Roxburghe, 1119, 16s. Marquis of Townshend, 2637, 14s. Brockett, 2079, 1l. 1s. Drury, 2354, 1l. 18s. There are copies on LARGE PAPER.—Lond. 1812, 4to. 15s. pp. xxxi, including titles, and 337, with a portrait of May, by Middiemist, and a view of the two houses of the parliament. Edited by Baron Maseres, who has added a preface, and in the margins of the pages of the work has given short abstracts of its contents, and likewise an appendix containing the declarations, &c., of both houses of parliament, with the king's answers. 'This history is written with much temper, moderation, and judgment, and with great vigour of style and sentiment.'—*Bishop Warburton.* Though highly praised by the Earl of Chatham for its honesty, it cannot by any means be considered an impartial work.—New edition, Oxford, University Press, 1854, 8vo. 6s. 6d.

The Reigne of King Henry the Second, written in seven Bookes. Lond. 1633, small 8vo., written by command of King Charles I., pp. 208, and portrait of the King by Vaughan. Hibbert, 5251, morocco, 11s. Sir M. M. Sykes, pt. ii, 848, 1l. 10s. Inglis, 905, 2l. 2s.

The victorious Reigne of King Edward the Third, written in seven Bookes. Lond. 1635, 8vo. Written in verse by the special command of K. Charles I. Roscoe, 1631, 10s. Hibbert, 5252, morocco, 14s. Jadis, 82, 1l. 14s. Bibl. Anglo-Poet. 471, 2l. 5s. Inglis, 906, 2l. 12s. 6d. *Collection.*—A, including portrait of the king, 4 leaves; B—N, 6 leaves each, and O 2 leaves.—1638? Bindley, pt. ii. 1966, 2l. 10s.

An Epitome of English History, wherein Arbitrary Government is displayed to the Life, in the illegal transactions of the late times under Oliver Cromwell, but now happily delivered by the means of King William and Queen Mary. Lond. —Third Edition, 1690, 12mo. with copperplate. Mitford, April, 1860, 3s.

Supplementum Lucani. Lug. Bat. 1640, 12mo. Dr. Johnson, according to T. Warton, prefers the Latin poetry of May and Cowley to that of Milton, and thinks May to be the first of the three.

A Continuation of Lucan's Historical Poem, till the Death of Julius Cæsar, in Seven Books. Lond. for James Boler, 1630, 12mo. engraved title; first edition, B to K in eights, with Dedication to King Charles. Latin verses by Sulpitius; Complaint of Calliope against the Destinies, 2 leaves.

A Discourse concerning the Success of former Parliaments. Lond. 1642, 4to.

The Character of a right Malignant. 1644, 4to.

The changeable Covenant. Lond. 1650, 4to.

Historiæ Parliamenti Angliæ Breviarium. Lond. (1650), 12mo. 3s.

A Breviary of the History of the Parliament of England, in three Parts. Lond. 1650, 12mo.—1655, with a portrait of May by Cross. Gordonstoun, 1618, 18s. Bindley, pt. ii. 1762, 1l. 10s. Towneley, pt. i. 428, morocco, 2l. 11s.

The Life of a satirical Puppy, called Nim, who worrieth all those Satyrists he knows, and barkes at the rest. Lond. 1657, 12mo. Pp. 118, with a frontispiece containing portraits of Nim and his man Oliver Bungs in the dress of the times. Nassau, pt. i. 2007, russia, 2l. 13s. Heber, pt. viii. 2l. Hodgson, April, 1830, 1l. 18s. Bindley, pt. ii. 1836, without the frontispiece, 13s.

May translated the Georgics of Virgil, Lucan's Pharsalia, some of Martial's Epigrams, Barclay's Argenis, and his Icon Animorum. *See* MARTIAL.

MAYANS i SISCAR, D. Greg. The Life of Michael de Cervantes Saavedra, translated by Mr. Ozell. Lond. 1738, 4to.

MAYDMAN, Henry. Naval Speculations, or Maritime Politicks. Lond. 1667, 8vo. port. ætat. 52, by Van Hove. pp. 348, 6s.

MAYER, John, D.D. A Commentary upon the Bible; wherein the divers Translators and Expositions, literall and mysticall, of the most famous Commentators, both antient and modern, are propounded and examined. Lond. 1653, folio. 5 vols. 4l. 14s. 6d.

—— Luigi. Views in Egypt, from Drawings in the Possession of Sir Rob. Ainslie, taken during his Embassy to Constantinople, by Luigi Mayer, with a History of the Country (in English and French). Lond. R. Bowyer, 1801, imp. folio, 12 Nos. containing 48 finely-coloured Plates.

Gough, 2277, 12 nos. 5l. 5s., Willett, 1639, morocco, 6l. 6s. White Knights, 2782, morocco, 8l. 10s. Earl of Kerry, 639, with Views in Caramania and in Palestine, 16l. 16s. Nassau, pt. i. 2583, with Views in Caramania and in Palestine, russia, 18l. 6s. 6d. Evans, 1846, with Views in Caramania, Palestine, and Turkey, morocco, 25l.

Views in Palestine, from the original

MAYER, Luigi—continued.
Drawings of Luigi Mayer, with an historical and descriptive Account of the Country and its remarkable Places, in English and French. Lond. R. Bowyer, 1804. imp. folio, 24 coloured plates. Earl of Kerry, 633, 3l. 13s. 6d. Marquis of Townshend, 2221, 4l. Gough, 7275, 4l. 6s.

Views in the Ottoman Empire, chiefly in Caramania, a Part of Asia Minor hitherto unexplored, with Descriptions in English and French. Lond. R. Bowyer, 1803, imp. folio, 24 coloured plates. Gough, 2378, 6 nos. 3l. 13s. 6d.

Views in Turkey in Europe and Turkey in Asia, comprising Roumelia, Bulgaria, Wallachia, Syria, and Palestine, and in some of the Mediterranean Islands, from the original Drawings taken for Sir Rob. Ainslie by Luigi Mayer. Lond. R. Bowyer, 1810, folio, 2 pts. in 1 vol. 71 coloured plates.

The first edition of this work was published in four Parts by the engraver, W. Watts, Lond. 1810, and has only 54 plates, four of which serve as frontispieces.

MAYER, Michael. Lusus serius, or serious Pastime, a philosophical Discourse concerning the Superiority of Creatures under Man. Translated by J. De la Salle. Lond. 1654, 12mo.

White Knights, 2870, 4s. 'Put out in English by John Hall: Half of which was done in one afternoon, over a glass of wine in a tavern.'—Ant. à Wood.

— Tobias. Tabulæ Motuum Solis et Lunæ novæ et correctæ, quibus accedit Methodus Longitudinum promota. Lond. 1770, 4to. 10s. 6d.

Published by Dr. Maskelyne. The parliament granted 3000l. to the widow of this astronomer for his excellent tables.

Theoria Lunæ juxta Systema Newtonianum. Lond. 1767, 4to.

Lunar Tables improved by C. Mason. Lond. 1789, 4to.

MAYHAM, Randulph. His Travels, containing a true recapitulation of all the remarkable passages which befell in the Author's Peregrinations and Voyages, in severall employments in the space of Forty Years. Lond. T. H. for Rd. Harper, 1638, 16mo. woodcuts.

The Author's employments were a Voyage to Ireland for Queen Elizabeth, at Breda, to Cales, to the Isle of Rhe, &c.; the details are given in verse and prose. Heber, pt. iv. 3l. 4s., now in the Grenville Collection. Caldecott, wanting title, 1l. 6s.

MAYERNE, Patrike. The Patterne of all Pious Prayer; a paraphrasticall Meeter upon the Pat.r-noster, Ave Maria, and Credo, &c., also a Divine Panigyre on Maryland, in America. Doway, 1636, small 8vo.

Anonymous, but the Author (a Roman Catholic) discovers his name in the anagram 'Marke prayer in't.' Bright, wanting the last portion, 1l. 15s.

— Sir Thomas. Excellent and approved Receipts in Cookery. Lond. 1658, 8vo.

Bliss, russia, 1l.

— TURQUET, Lewis de. A general Historie of Spaine, in thirty Books, translated by E. Grimestone. Lond. 1612, folio.

Reed, 4833, 12s. 6d.

MAYHEW, Experience. Indian Converts, or some account of the Lives and Dying Speeches of a considerable number of the Christianized Indians of Martha's Vineyard in New England. Lond. 1727, 8vo.

Williams, 1191, 7s. 6d.

— R. Death of Death in the Death of Christ. Lond. printed by T. Snowden for the Author, in the Year 1600 [? 1680].

Poema Mortuale; or an Elegy upon Death; in Verse, by R. M., no Poet, nor the Son of a Poet. 2 vols. in 1, Anno Prædicto, 1600 [? 1680].

MAYNARD, Sir John. Reports temp. Edward II. See in Year Books. 1679, vol. 1.

— Sir John, Serjeant-at-Law. The Royall Quarrell, or England's Lawes and Liberties vindicated, against the tyrannical usurpation of the Lords. Lond. 1647, 4to.

— John. Lutenist at the most famous Schools of St. Julians in Hartfordshire. The XII Wonders of the World. Set and composed for the Violl de Gambo, &c. Lond. T. Snodham, 1611, folio.

Heber, pt. ii. 9s.

Copies of this curious work are in the Bodleian Library and British Museum. Of the Songs only, 16 copies were reprinted by Mr. Utterson at his private press, Isle of Wight, 1842, sq. 12mo. Bliss, 5s.

MAYNE, Jasper, D.D. Two Plaies, the City Match, a Comoedy, and the Amorous Warre, a Tragi-Comedy, both long since written. Oxford, 1658, 4to.
Bindley, pt. iv. 143, 3s. Rhodes, 1663, 6s. 6d. Roxburghe, 5287, 10s. 6d.—1869. Hibbert, 5032, 5s.
The Citye Match, a Comedye. Oxford, 1639, folio. Roxburghe, 5395, 5s. Rhodes, 2626, 4s. Reprinted in Dodsley's Collection of old Plays.
The Amorous Warre, a Tragi-comedy, 1648, 4to. Roxburghe, 5395, 6s. 6d.
Certaine Sermons and Letters of Defence and Resolution to some of the late Controversies of our Times. Lond. 1653, 4to.

MAYNWARING. See MANWARING.

MAYO, Charles, LL.D. A compendious View of universal History from the Year 1753 to the Treaty of Amiens in 1802, with Notes. Bath, 1804, 4to. 4 vols.
Little esteemed. Sir M. M. Sykes, pt. ii. 491, 16s. Duke of York, 5363, 1l. 11s. Hibbert, 5365, russia, 1l. 14s. Heber, pt. vii. 4s. 6d.
A Chronological History of the European States, with their Discoveries and Settlements, from the Treaty of Nimeguen in 1678, to the close of 1792. Bath. 1793, folio. Roxburghe, 7423, 5s. 6d. Heber, pt. x. 5s.

— John. The Pope's Parliament. Whereunto is annexed, an Anatomie of Pope Joane. Lond. 1591, 4to.
Dedicated to Sir George Trenchard, Knight.—Lond. 1594, 4to.

MEAD, Richard, M.D. Medical Works. Lond. 1762, 4to. portrait.
Bindley, pt. iii. 810, 6s.—Edinb. 1763, 1765. 8vo. 3 vols.—Dublin, 1767, 8vo. 3 vols.
Medica Sacra, sive de Morbis Insignioribus qui in Bibliis, etc. Lond. 1748, 8vo. 2s. 6d.
Medica Sacra; or a Commentary on the most remarkable Diseases mentioned in Holy Scripture. Translated from the Latin by Thomas Stack, M.D. Lond. 1755, 8vo. 5s. In this work Dr. Mead contends that the demoniacal possessions were a species of disease.

A Mechanical Account of Poisons, in several Essays. Third edition, with large additions. Lond. Brindley, 1745, 8vo. 5s. LARGE PAPER, 10s.—4th edition, 1747, 8vo.
A Discourse on the Plague. Ninth edition. Lond. 1744, 8vo. 3s. 6d. LARGE PAPER, 7s.
Authentic Memoirs of the Life of R. Mead, M.D., by Dr. Maty. Lond. 1755, 8vo.
Some Memoirs of the Life and Writings of Dr. R. Mead. Lond. 1755, 8vo.
Life of Dr. Richard Honeywater. 8vo. Lond. 8vo. (satirical).
Museum Meadianum. Lond 1755, 8vo. Bibliotheca Meadiana. Lond. 1754-5, 8vo.

MEAD, Robert, M.D. The Combat of Love and Friendship, a Comedy. Lond. 1654, 4to.
Rhodes, 1669, 2s. Roxburghe, 5445, 5s. Inglis' Old Plays, 69, 10s. 6d. Reed, 8196, 11s.
The costlie Whore, a comical Historie. Lond. 1633, 4to. Sotheby's in 1824, 10s. 6d. Roxburghe, 5446, 9s. Attributed to Mead by Phillips without foundation.

MEADLEY, George Wilson. Memoirs of William Paley, D.D. Second Edition, revised and corrected; to which is added an Appendix. Edinb. 1810, 8vo.
Bindley, pt. iv. 65, 5s. 6d.—Sunderland, 1869, 8vo.
Memoirs of Algernon Sydney. Lond. 1813, 8vo. with a portrait, 12s. FINE PAPER, 18s.

MEARA, Dermitius. Ormonius: sive, D. Tho. Butleri Ormoniae Comitis, etc. Commemoratio, heroico carmine conscripta. Lond. 1615, 12mo.
An Historical Poem on Thomas, Earl of Ormond and Ossory, with some matters relating to that noble family, temp. Queen Elizabeth. A copy is in the British Museum, and another in the Bodleian library. Heber, pt. ix. 1890, 3l. 6s.
Pathologia hereditaria, sive de Morbis hereditariis. Dublin, 1619, 12mo.

MEARES, John. Voyages made in the Years 1788 and 1789, from China to the North-west Coast of America. To which are prefixed, an introductory Narrative of a Voyage performed in 1786, from Bengal, in the Ship Nootka; Observations on the probable Existence of a

North-West Passage; and some Account of the Trade between the North-West Coast of America and China, and the latter Country and Great Britain. Lond. 1790, 4to.
Townley, pt. II. 1132, 11s. Roxburghe, 7171, 13s. Willett, 1615, 14s. Drury, 2983, russia, 1l. 6s. Fonthill, 3111, 4l. Baker, 467. morocco, 4l. 4s,—1791, 8vo. 2 vols.—1796, 8vo. 2 vols.

Remarks on the Voyages of John Meares, by Capt. George Dixon. Lond. 1790, 4to. 2s. 6d. Fonthill, 1906, 14s.

An Answer to Capt. George Dixon, by John Meares. Lond. 1791, 4to. 2s. 6d.

Farther Remarks on the Voyages of John Meares, by Capt. George Dixon. Lond. 1791, 4to. 2s. 6d.

MEARS, William. Lives of the Princes of the illustrious House of Orange. Lond. 1734, 8vo.
With portraits. Williams, 1192, morocco, 1l. 1s.

MEASON, Gilbert Laing. The Landscape Architecture of the great Painters of Italy. Lond. Carpenter, 1828, 4to.
With 55 lithographic plates on India Paper. 150 copies printed for private circulation, but sold at 4l. 4s. Mitford, 1560, 1l. 6d.

MECHANICS' Magazine from its Commencement in 1823, to Dec. 1859. Lond. 8vo. 71 vols. woodcuts, still continued.

MECKLENBURGH.—The History of Mecklenburgh, from the first Settlement of the Vandals in that Country, to the present Time, including a Period of about three thousand Years. Lond. 1762, 8vo. 6s.
Written by Mrs. Sarah Scott.

MEDALS.—The Knowledge of Medals, translated from the French of Mons. Jonbert, [by Roger Gale, the Antiquary]. Lond. 1715, 12mo. 3s.

Hollis, 730, 7s.—1697, 8vo.

A critical Essay on modern Medals. Lond. 1704, 8vo.

Catalogue of Medals from Julius Cæsar to the Emperor Heraclius. Lond. 1716, 8vo.

The Medallic History of England. 1790. See PINKERTON, John.

The Medallic History of Napoleon, with Supplement. By James Millingen. Lond. 1819-21, roy. 4to. 60 plates. Combe, 1844. 3l. Brockett, 2026, 2l. 12s. 6d.—Supplement. Lond. 1821, roy. 4to. 14 plates.

Medallic History of N. Bonaparte, translated by Miss Ann Mudie Scargill from the original MS. Lond. 8vo.
See ADDISON, Joseph. LASKEY, J.

MEDBURNE, E. Saint Cecily, a Christian Tragedy. Lond. 1666, 4to.
Bliss, 18s.

MEDE, Joseph, B.D. Works, with a general Preface and an Account of his Works by J. Worthington. Lond. 1672, folio.
Bindley, pt. II. 844, 1l. 1s. These esteemed works, which were originally published in detached parts, contain much elaborate criticism. 'Modern expositors of the prophecies contained in the Revelation and in the book of Daniel, have very properly availed themselves of the lights held out to them by this great divine.'—Bp. Watson. The examination of Mede's Clavis Apocalyptica occupies the chief part of Bishop Hurd's tenth sermon on the study of the prophecies.—Second edition, 1664, folio, 2 vols. LARGE PAPER. Duke of Grafton, 104, russia, 1l. 15s. Heber, pt. vii. russia, 5l. 5s.—1677. Gough, 2220, 12s. Bishop of Ely, 1036, 15s.

Clavis Apocalyptica ex Innatis et insitis Visionum characteribus eruta et demonstrata. Cantab. 1627, 4to.

The Key of the Revelation; with a Comment. Translated by Richd. More' whereunto is added a Conjecture concerning Gog and Magog. Lond. 1643, 4to.—1650, 4to.

The Apostasy of the Latter Times, Lond. 1641, 4to.—With an Introduction by T. D. Gregg. Lond. 1836, 8vo.—With an Introduction by the Rev. J. H. Birks, Lond. 1845, 18mo.

Translated by R. Bransby Cooper. Lond. 1833, 8vo. 9s.

MEDICI, Lorenzo de'. Poesie del magnifico Lorenzo de' Medici e di altri suoi Amici contemporanei. Lond. 1801, 4to.
Drury, 2578, russia, 9s.—1791, 8vo. Twelve copies printed.
See Roscoe, William. TENHOVE. Nic.

MEDICINE.—Anonymous Publications on Medical Science, &c.
Medicina curiosa, or a Variety of new Communications. Lond. 1684-85, 4to.

Medical Essays and Observations, revised and published by a Society in Edin-

MEDICINE—*continued.*
burgh. Edinb. 1733-44, 8vo. 5 vols. In 6.
The merits of these transactions were
acknowledged by Haller.—Third edition,
enlarged. Edinb. 1747, 8vo. 5 vols,—
Fourth edition, enlarged. Edinb. 1752,
8vo. 5 vols.

Essays and Observations physical and
literary. Edinb. 1754—71, 8vo. 3 vols.

Bibliotheca Collegii regalis Medicorum
Londinensis Catalogus. Lond. 1757, 8vo.

Medical Observations and Inquiries.
By a Society of Physicians in London.
Lond. 1757-84, 8vo. 6 vols. 18s. Willetts,
1625, 6 vols. 1769-84, 2l. 2s.

Medical Transactions published by the
College of Physicians in London. Lond.
1768—1820, 8vo. 6 vols.

Medical Register. Lond. 1778-9, 8vo.

London Medical Journal. 1781—90, 8vo.
11 vols.

Medical Communications. Lond. 1784
—90, 8vo. 2 vols.

Memoirs of the Medical Society of London; instituted in the Year 1773. Lond.
1787-1805, 8vo. 6 vols.

Medical Facts and Observations. Lond.
1791-1800, 8vo. 8 vols. Edited by Dr.
Simmons.

Transactions of a Society for the Improvement of medical and chirurgical
Knowledge. Lond. 1793—1812, 8vo. 3 vols.

Medical and Chirurgical Review, 1795
—1807, 8vo. 15 vols. 'A useful work, but
rather too theoretical.'—*Dr. Young.*

Medical Extracts, on the Nature of
Health, with practical Observations: and
the Laws of the nervous and fibrous Systems. By a Friend to Improvements.
[Dr. Thornton]. Lond. 1796, 8vo. 3 vols.
with plates.

Medical Commentaries by Duncan and
others. Edinb. 1773—95, 8vo. 20 vols.
Duncan's Annals of Medicine. Edinb.
1797—1805, 8vo. 8 vols.

The London Medical Review and Magazine. By a Society of Physicians and
Surgeons. Lond. 1799-1806, 8vo. 8 vols.

The (London) Medical and Physical
Journal, from March, Lond. 1799 to 1825
inclusive, 55 vols. 8vo. New Series, Lond.
1826—33, 14 vols. (vols. 56-69) 8vo.—Index to vols. 1-40. Lond. 1820, 8vo.

The London Medical Review, 1808-12,
8vo. 5 vols. 'Respectable, but occasionally too severe.'—*Dr. Young.*

Catalogue of the Library of the Medical
and Chirurgical Society of London. Lond.
1816—19, 8vo. 3 parts.—New edition, Lond.
1856, 8vo.

Catalogue of the Library of the Medical
Society of London. Lond. 1829, 8vo.

Catalogue of the Library of the Royal
College of Surgeons. Lond. 1831-50, 8vo.
4 vols. and Index of Subjects.

Medico-chirurgical Transactions. Lond.
1826-59, 8vo. 41 Vols. (Index to vols.
1-33). Still continued, annually, at from
12s. to 21s. per vol.

The London Medical, Surgical, and
Pharmaceutical Repository. Vols. 1, 2,
(continued under the title of The London
Medical Repository, Monthly Journal,
and Review. By G. M. Burrows, W.
Royston, and A. T. Thomson; subsequently edited by D. Uwins, H. Palmer,
and S. F. Gray; and after vol. 17 by J.
Copland and R. Dunglison, vols. 8-20), 20
vols.—New Series, edited by J. Copland
and R. Dunglison, 3 vols.—New Series
[the Third], edited by J. Copland, J. Darwall and J. Conolly, &c. Lond. 1814-24,
8vo. 6 vols.

The London Medical and Surgical Journal, by J. Davies, J. Epps, and J. Houlton. Lond. 1828-9, 8vo. 2 vols.—Continued as The London Medical and Surgical Journal, including the London Medical Repository, edited by Ryan, vols. 6-7.
Lond. 1829-31, 8vo.—New Series, edited by
Dr. Ryan. Lond. 1832-36, 8vo. 8 vols.—
[New Series, the Fourth, edited by Dr.
Ryan, 1832-37.] Lond. 1832-37, 8vo. 11
vols. No more published; the work being
at this point incorporated with the
'Medical News.'

The Medical Intelligencer, comprising
an Analysis of the whole of Medical Literature. Lond. 1820-3, 8vo. 4 vols.

Medical Botany; or History of Plants
in the Materia Medica of the London,
Edinburgh, and Dublin Pharmacopœias,
arranged according to the Linnæan System. Lond. 1821, royal 8vo. 2 vols. Vol.
I. pp. 228, with coloured plates 1-72. Vol.
II. pp. 218, and plates 73-138. *By* BARTON. BIGELOW. CHURCHILL. STEPHENSON. WOODVILLE.

New London Medical and Physical Review. Lond. 1810-15, 8vo. 10 vols.

Medico-Chirurgical Journal and Review. Edited by Dr. James Johnson.
Lond. 1815-20, 8vo. 11 vols. Continued
under the title of Medico-Chirurgical Review, 1820-44, 8vo. 40 vols.—New Series.
Lond. 1844-47, 8vo. vols. Merged in
the British and Foreign Medico-Chirurgical Review. Lond. Churchill, 1847-50,
8vo. 24 vols. Still continued quarterly,
at 6s.

Edinburgh Journal of Medical Science.
Edinb. 1826-7, 8vo. 3 vols.

Edinburgh Medical and Surgical Journal. Edinb. 1805-55, 8vo. 82 vols. (Index to first 20 vols.)

London and Edinburgh Monthly Journal of Medical Science, continued as the
Monthly Journal of Medical Science.
Edinb. 1841-55, 20 vols.—Continued as the
Edinburgh Medical Journal, 1855-60, 8vo.
5 vols. Still continued, monthly, at 2s.

1528

MEDICINE—*continued.*
London Medical Gazette. Lond. 1827-48, 8vo. 36 vols.—New Series, 1845-51, 13 vols. Merged in the Medical Times, under the title of Medical Times and Gazette, at the end of 1852.
Medical Times. Lond. 1839-50, 4to. 21 vols.—New Series, 1850-52. Continued as the Medical Times and Gazette, 1853-59, 4to. 19 vols. Still continued weekly at 7d. or 1l. 10s. per ann.
Glasgow Medical Journal. Glasg. 1828-32, 8vo. 5 vols.—New Series. Glasg. 1854-59, 6 vols. Still continued quarterly, at 3s. per No.
Dublin Journal of Medical Science. Dub. 1832-45, 8vo. 28 vols. and a General Index. Continued as the Dublin Quarterly Journal of Medical Science, 1846-60, 29 vols. Still continued quarterly, at 5s.
Dublin Medical Press. Dub. 1839-60, sm. 4to. 43 vols. Still continued weekly, at 5d.
Dublin Hospital Gazette. Dub. 1843-8, royal 8vo. 9 vols.—New Series, 1854-9, 6 vols. Still continued bimonthly, at 6d. or per ann. 10s.
British and Foreign Medical Review. Edited by Dr. Forbes. Lond. 1836-47, 8vo. 24 vols. and Index. Merged in the British and Foreign Medico-Chirurgical Review. Lond. 1847-59, 8vo. 24 vols. Still continued quarterly, 6s. per No.
Provincial Medical and Surgical Journal. Lond. 1840-52, 8vo. 16 vols. Continued as the Association Medical Journal. Lond. 1853, and continued since 1857 as the British Medical Journal. Edited by Dr. Wynter. Lond. 1853-9, sm. 4to. 7 vols. Still continued weekly, at 6d.
Retrospect of Medicine. Edited by W. Braithwaite. Lond. 1841-59, post 8vo. 40 vols. Still continued biennially, at 8s.
Abstract of the Medical Sciences. Edited by W. H. Ranking. Lond. 1845-59, post 8vo. 30 vols. Still continued biennially, at 6s.
Journal of Psychological Medicine. Edited by Forbes Winslow, M.D. Lond. Churchill, 1848-59, 8vo. 12 vols. Still continued quarterly, at 3s. 6d.
Medical Circular. Lond. 1852-59, 4to. 15 vols. Still continued weekly, at 4d.
London Medical Examiner. Edited by Edward Crisp. Lond. 1851-2, 2 vols.
See EDINBURGH. LANCET. STEVENSON.

MEDICINE OF LIFE.—The Medicine of Life, whereunto is added, certaine Gatherings of Scripture called Patrickes Places. Lond. by Wm. Copland. 16mo.
From Maunsell's Catalogue, part. I. p. 72. *See* HAMILTON.

MEDICIS, Catherine de. *See* KATHERINE DE.

— Mary de. A true Discourse of the whole Occurrences in the Queenes Voyage, from her Departure from Florence, untill her Arrivall at the Citie of Marseilles, together with the Triumphs there made at her Entrie: whereto is adjoined her Receiving and Entrie into Lyons. All faithfully translated out of French by E. A. Lond. 1601.
Reprinted in the second volume of Nichols' Progresses of Queen Elizabeth. *See* BRABB, J. P.
Life, by Miss Pardoe. Lond. 1852, 8vo. 3 vols.

MEDINA, The Duke of. Orders set downe by the Duke of Medina, Lord General of the King's Fleet, to be observed in the Voyage toward England. Translated out of the Spanish into English by T. P. Lond. 1588, 4to.
Eight leaves. Reprinted in the first volume of the Harleian Miscellany.

— Peter de. The Arte of Navigation, translated out of Spanish by John Frampton. Lond. 1581, folio.
A curious treatise with schemes and tables.—Lond. 1595, 4to.

MEDITATIONS.—Certayne devout Meditations very necessary for Christian Men, &c., concerning Christ his Life and Passion, and the fruits thereof, with two Hymns. Duaci, per Joan Bogardum. 1576.
A very diminutive volume, being only 4 inches by 3. BLACK LETTER. Bliss, 4l. 10s.
A Pitious Platforme of an oppressed Mynde, set downe by the extreme Surmizes of sundrye distressed Meditations. By G. C. Imprinted by T. Gardiner, n. d. 12mo.
These poems are sometimes attributed to George Chapman, but without sufficient reason. Heber, pt. iv. 258, 1l. 17s.

MEDYTACION of the VII. Shedynges of the blood of our Lorde Jhesu Cryste. Lond. Wynkyn de Worde. n. d. 4to.
Heber, pt. v. 2820, in a volume.
See BUSCONES, II.

MEDLEYS.—The Medleys for 1711. To which are prefixed the five Whig Examiners. Lond. 1712, royal 8vo.

A periodical paper principally directed against Swift and his party, conducted by Mr. Maynwaring, assisted by Oldmixon. They commenced Oct. 5, 1710, and were continued until Aug. 6, 1711, extending to 45 numbers, and were resumed March 3, 1712, and expired on Aug. 4, 1712, having likewise reached to 45 numbers. A selection from the first Medley was published in 1769, by Mr. Nichols, together with the Lover and Reader of Steele. Bright, 6d.

MEDOWS, Sir Philip. Observations concerning the Dominion and Sovereignty of the Seas, being an Abstract of the marine Affairs of England. Lond. 1689, 4to.

A curious and excellent treatise, highly commended by Lord Chief Baron Parker.

MEDWALL, Henry. A goodly Interlude of Nature. (Lond. by J. Rastell. 1538), folio.

A copy is in the Garrick collection now in the British Museum. A MS. copy at the sale of the library of the Duke of Roxburghe, no. 5448, produced 2l. 8s.

MEDWIN, Captain Thomas. The Angler in Wales. Lond. 1834, 8vo. 2 vols.

Lady Singleton; a Novel. Lond. 1843, post 8vo. 2 vols.

The Shelley Papers: Memoirs of Percy Bysshe Shelley, with original Poems and Papers. Lond. 1833.—Lond. 1847, post 8vo. 2 vols.

See BYRON, Lord, page 340.

MEEN, Rev. Henry, B.D. Successive Opera; or, Selections from ancient Writers, sacred and profane, with Translations and Notes. 1815, 5s.

This writer likewise published an excellent volume of remarks on Lycophron (1800), and a translation of Coluthus.

— Miss. Exotic Plants at Kew. 1791. 2 nos. *See* BAUER.

MEERMAN, Gerard. Conspectus Originum Typographicarum a Meermanno proxime in lucem edendarum, in usum amicorum typis descriptus. Lond. 1761, 8vo.

MEETING (The) of Gallants at an Ordinarie, or the Walkes in Powles. Lond. 1604, 4to.
George Chalmers, II. 470, 15l. 15s.
Reprinted in 12mo. for the Percy Society.

MEG OF HEREFORDSHIRE.—Old Meg of Herefordshire for a Mayd Marian, and Hereford Towne for a Morris Daunce; or twelve Morris Dancers in Herefordshire of twelve hundred Years old. Lond. 1609, 4to.

Hibbert, 5908, morocco, 1l. 12s. Bibby's in Dec. 1830, morocco, 5l. 7s. 6d. Bright, 2944, 20l. 6s. Reprinted 1814 as no. I. of Miscellanea Antiqua Anglicana.

MEG OF WESTMINSTER.—The Life of Long Meg of Westminster: containing the mad merry Prankes she played in her Life time, not onely in performing sundry Quarrels with divers Ruffians about London: but also how valiantly she behaved her selfe in the Warres of Bolloiugne. Lond. W. How for Abraham Veale, 1582, 4to.

Heber, pt. v., part of title inlaid, 1l. Nassau, pt. I. 2041, morocco, 5l. 7s. 6d. Jolley, 7l. 7s.—Lond. R. Bird, 1636, 4to. Heber, pt. ix. 1962, fine copy, 2l. 12s. 6d. Reprinted 1814 as no. III. of the Miscellanea Antiqua Anglicana.

MEHEGAN, Wm. Alex. A View of universal modern History, from the Fall of the Roman Empire. Translated by Henry Fox. Lond. 1779, 8vo. 3 vols. 10s. 6d.

MEIBOMIUS, Herm. Diet. In Historiam Anglicanam Programma. Helmst. 1689, 4to.
Programma in Notitiam Regnorum et Rerumpublicarum in qua De Anglicanae Historiae Periodis et praecipuis Scriptoribus, &c. Helmst. 1702, 4to.

— John Henry, M.D. A Treatise of the Use of Flogging in physical and venereal Affairs: also of the Office of the Loins and Reins. Made English from the Latin Original by a Physician. To which is added, a Treatise of Hermaphrodites (by — Jacob). Lond. 1718, 12mo.

Published by Edmund Curll. Fonthill,

1296, 15s.—Latine. Lond. 1665, 16mo. White Knights, 9676, morocco, 6s.—Lond. 1770, 12mo. Heber, pt. ii. 4s. 6d.

MEIER, Geo. Fred. The merry Philosopher, or Thoughts on Jesting, transl. into English from the German original. Lond. 1764, 12mo. 3s.

MEINERS, C. History of the Female Sex, translated from the German by Fred. Shoberl. Lond. 1808, 12mo. 4 vols. 12s.

MEISTER, Henry. Letters during a Residence in England. Translated from the French, together with a Letter from the Margravine of Anspach to the Author. Lond. 1799, 8vo.
Fonthill, $100, 6s.

MELA. *See* POMPONIUS MELA.

MELA Britannica. *See* KELSALL, C.

MELAMPUS. The Contemplation of Mankinde, englished by Thomas Hyll. Lond. 1671, sm. 8vo.
A curious treatise on physiognomy, &c. White Knights, 2879, morocco, 16s.

MELANCHOLY. — An Antidote against Melancholy made up in Pills compounded of witty Ballads, jovial Songs, and merry Catches. Lond. 1661, 4to.
Lloyd, £16, 2l. 12s. 6d.
Pills to purge State Melancholy. Lond. 1715, 12mo.
The Melancholy Cavalier, or Fancy's Master Piece, by J. C. Lond. printed for C. R., in the year 1654, 8vo. Heber, pt. iv. 259, 1l. 7s. *See* DAIGHT. BOSTON. DURFEY, Tom.

MELANCTHON, Philip. Epistolæ, accedunt Tho. Mori et Lud. Vivis Epistolæ. Lond. 1642, folio. 18s.
The works of this distinguished reformer are admired for their learning and moderation.
The Apologie that is to say the Defense of the Confession of the Germans made by Philip Melancthon, and translated by Richard Tanermer at the Commaundement of his Mayster, the ryght honorable Master Thomas Cromwell chefe Secretarie to the Kyngis Hyghnes. Impr. by me Rob. Redman, 1536, 8vo. Contains Z 6, in eslaves.

A verie godlie Defence, ful of Lerning, defending the Marriage of Priests, translated oute of Latyne vnto Englyshe by Lewis Beuchame. Lond. 1541, 8vo.
A newe work discerning both partes of the Sacrament to be receyved of the lay people as well under the kind off wine as under the kind off bread, with certen other articles concerning the Masse, &c. Newly translated out of Latyn. No Place or Printer, 1548, small 8vo. To E in eights. A copy is in the Lambeth Library.—Lond. R. Jugge, (1566), 8vo.
Epistle to Henry the VIII. for the revoking and abolishing of the six Articles, set forth and enacted by the craftie meanes of our Prelates of the Clergie, newly translated out of Latyn into Englishe by L. C. Wessel, 1547. BLACK LETTER. B in eights. Hibbart, 6267, 1l. 3s. White Knights, 2260, 2l. 12s. Sotheby (Bp. Daly), June 25, 1858, 2l. 2s.
A Waying and Considering of the Interim. Translated by John Rogers. Lond. 1548, 16mo.
The Justification of Man by Faith only, englished by Nich. Lesse. Lond. W. Powell, 1548, 8vo. Reed, 631, 10s. Inglis, 1021, 12s.
Of the trewe Auctoritie of the Churche, newly translated out of Latyn into Englyshe. Ipsw. 1548, 16mo.
A famous and godlie Historie; containing the Lyues and Actes of Martine Luther, John Ecolampadius, and Huldericke Zuinglius: the Declaration of Martin Luthers Faythe, wyth an Oration of hys Dethe all set forthe in Latin by Ph. Melancthon, Wolfangus Faber, Capita, Simon Grineus, and Oswald Miconius; newelie euglyshed by Henry Bennet Callesian. Lond. John Awdely, 1561, 8vo. Inglis, 1025, 2l. 10s. Sotheby, (Bp. Daly), June 25, 1858, 1l. 19s.
The Miseries of Schoole Masters, vttered in a Latine Oration, made by the famous Clearke Ph. Melancthon. Lond. 1569, 8vo.
Formulæ de Arte Concionandi et discendæ Theologiæ Ratio. Lond. 1570, 8vo.
Praiers, translated by Richard Robinson. Lond. 1579, 8vo.
Two wonderful Popish Monsters to wyt, of a Popish Asse which was found at Rome in the River of Tyber, and of a monkish Calfe, calved at Friberge in Misne, &c. Witnessed and declared by Philip Melancthon, the other by Martyn Luther. Translated out of French into English by John Brooke. (Lond.) T. East, 1579, 4to. With woodcuts of the monsters. Gordonstoun, 1785, 2l. 12s.
A godly and learned Assertion in Defence of the true Church of God and of his Worde, translated by R(ichard) R(obinson). Lond. 1580, 8vo.

MELANCTHON—continued.
The Confessyon of Fayth delyvered to the Emperoure Charles the Vth, by the Lordes of Germanye. Translated into Englyshe by Rob. Byngylton. Canterbury. 8vo. *See* CONFESSIONS of Augsburg.
Whether it be mortall Sinne to transgresse civil Lawes of civil Magistrates. Lond. by Richard Jugge, 8vo. (1566). Inglis, 10*s*. 2*s*. n. d.
A godlye Treatyse of Prayer translated into Englishe by John Bradforde. Lond. by John Wight, 8vo. Roxburghe, Suppl. 597. Inglis, 10*s*. 6*d*.
The Life of, comprising an Account of the most important Transactions of the Reformation, by Francis Augustus Cox, A.M. Second edition, with considerable additions. Lond. 1817, 8vo.
Life of. Edinh. 1837, 16mo.—Philadelphia (1829). 12mo.
Observations upon the Handwriting of Philip Melancthon, illustrated with Facsimiles from his marginal Annotations, his Common-place Book, and his Epistolary Correspondence. By S. L. Sothaby. Lond. 1839, folio, 2*l*. 12*s*. 6*d*.

MELANTHE, Fabula pastoralis, acta Cantabrigiæ, coram Rege Jacobo. Cantab. 1615, 4to. 6*s*.

MELBANCKE, Brian. Philotimus. The Warre betwixt Nature and Fortune. Lond. R. Warde, 1583, 4to.
A close imitation of Lilly's Euphues, in which mention is made of the tale of Romeo and Juliet long before the appearance of Shakspeare's Play. It consists of 226 pages, besides four leaves of introduction. Bolland, in 1840, 8*l*. 12*s*. Bliss, 2*l*. 6*s*. Heber, pt. vi. 2*l*. 19*s*.

MELDRUM, Squire. *See* Pinkerton's Scottish Poems, vol. 1. LYNDESAY, Sir D.

MELINTHUS.—The History of the Amours and Gallantry of the several noble and polite Persons at Rome and Syracuse; being the Adventures of Malinthus. Lond. 1728, 8vo. 2 vols.

MELISH, John. Travels through the United States of America in the Years 1806—11, and Travels through various Parts of Britain, Ireland, and Canada. Philadelphia, 1818, 8vo.

MELISMATA, Musicall Phansies fitting the Court, Citie, and Countrhy Humours, to 3, 4, and 5 Voices. 1611

MELLIS, John. A briefe Instruction and manner how to kerpe Bookes of Accompts after the Order of Debtor and Creditor. Lond. 1588, 8vo.
BLACK LETTER. Sir P. Thompson, 454, 10*s*. Bright, 8*s*. 6*d*.

MELMOTH, Courtney, *i. e.* PRATT, S. J.

— William, K.C., of Lincoln's Inn. The Great Importance of a Religious Life considered. First edition. Lond. 1711, 12mo. port.
A valuable little work, erroneously attributed by Horace Walpole to John Perceval, Earl of Egmont. There have been numerous editions, exceeding 100,000 copies.—A new edition, under the patronage of the late Queen Adelaide, was in the press at the time of her lamented decease. It would have contained The Life, by his son, from the edition of 1796, and four appendices. I. Miscellaneous Notes. II. Notices of remarkable persons buried in the cloister under Lincoln's Inn Chapel. III. Short notices of Prelates and eminent Divines who have been Preachers to the Society of Lincoln's Inn. IV. A List of Sermons preached at the Warburtonian Lecture in Lincoln's Inn Chapel, which have been printed. By C. P. Cooper, Esq., Q.C. Lond. Roworth, 1849, royal 8vo. It has not been published. The index ceases at Le Clerc, p. 408.

— William, of Bath. Letters on several Subjects, by Sir Thomas Fitzosborne. Lond. 8vo. 2 vols. 6*s*.
These letters are highly admired, and contain just and liberal remarks on various topics, moral and literary. They have been frequently reprinted.
Memoirs of a late eminent Advocate, [Wm. Melmoth, K.C.] and Bencher, of the Honourable Society of Lincoln's Inn, temp. Geo. I. & II. Lond. 1796, 8vo. pp. 72, with portrait.
Melmoth's Translations of Pliny and Cicero are considered masterpieces.

MELODINO. Relics of Melodino, a Portuguese Poet. Translated from an unpublished MS. dated 1640. Lond. 1815, 8vo.
Shegg, mor. 11*s*.

MELPOMENE, or the Muses Delight, being new Poems and Songs written by several of the great Wits of our Age. Lond. for H. Rogers, 1678, 8vo.
Bindley, pt. ii. 1374, 4l. 4s. resold, Heber, pt. iv. 1l. 5s.

MELROS Papers. See BANNATYNE CLUB, *Appendix*.

MELROSE.—A Description of the Parish of Melrose; in Answer to Mr. Maitland's Queries, sent to each Parish of the Kingdom. Edinburgh, 1743, 8vo.
By the Rev. Adam Milne. Edinb. 1764. —Edinb. 1769, 12mo.—Kelso, 1782, 12mo.

MELTON, Edward. *Engelsch Edelman's*, [i. e. English Nobleman]. Zee-en Land Reizen door Egypten, West Indien, Perzien, Turkeyen, Oost-Indien, &c., 1660, 1677. Amst. 1681, 4to. plates by Luyken.—Amst. 1702, 4to.

— John. Astrologaster, or the Figvre-caster. Rather the Arraignment of artlesse Astrologers and Fortune-tellers. Lond. 1620, 4to.
Towneley, pt. i. 705, 5s. 6d. Gordonstoun, 1563, 11s. Heber, pt. i 10s.
A Sixe-folde Politician, together with a six-folde Precept of Policy. Lond. 1609, 4to. This work has been erroneously attributed to Milton's father. Bindley, pt. iii. 1087, 9s. Gordonstoun, 1526, 19s. Reed, 2613, 2l. 14s. Bliss, wormed, 1l. 4s. A copy, said to be on LARGE PAPER, is in the Grenville Collection.

— William. Sermo exhortatorius Cancellarij Ebor. hijs qui ad sacros Ordines pciunt promouer̄i. Lond. per Wyn. de Worde. 4to.
It concludes on the reverse of sig. A viij. Inglis, 1350, 1l. 18s.

MELVILLE, MELVIL, or MELVIN, Andrew. ΣΤΕΦΑΝΙΣΚΙΟΝ ad Scotiæ Regem habitum in Coronatione Reginæ, 17 Maij 1590. Edinb. Waldegrave, 1590, 4to. 10s. 6d.
Five leaves.
Principia Scoti Brit. Natalia. Edinb. 1594, 4to. A copy is in the British Museum.
Satyra Menippæa 'uncimus quid Vesper serus vehat.' 1619, 4to—1620, 4to.

(This tract is by Scioppius, and erroneously attributed to Andrew Melville. Copies of both editions are in the British Museum.)
A. Melvini Musæ et P. Adamsoni Vita et Palinodia. No place, 1620, 4to. Gordonstoun, 1515, 1l. 7s. Heber, pt. i. 18s.; pt. vi. 7s.; pt. viii. 15s. Bright, 7s. 6d. Gardner, in 1854, 4s. 6d.
Gathelus, sive de Origine Gentis Scotorum origines Fragmentum. Amst. 1602. See JOHNSTONI Inscriptiones, p. 1272.
Life of Andrew Melville. *See* M'CRIE.
— James. Cartamen cum Lutheranis Saxoniæ habitum. Bononiæ, 1530, sm. 8vo.
Fifteen leaves. Heber. pt. i. 13s. The name of the writer of this piece was unknown until Mr. Heber purchased his copy at the Lucas sale. It is reprinted in the first volume of the Wodrow Miscellany, Edinb. 1854, 8vo.

— Sir James, of Halhill, Memoirs of his own Life, published from the original MS. by George Scott. Lond. 1683, folio.
An excellent historical work, particularly relating to the reigns of Queen Elizabeth, Mary Queen of Scots, and King James. Roxburghe, 5757, 3s. 6d. Bright, 2s. Marquis of Townshend, 2729, 10s.—Edinb. 1735, 8vo.—Glasg. 1751, 12mo. 2s. Lond. 1752, 8vo. Hibbert, 5577, 2s.
Ad Jacobum I. Ecclesiæ Scoticanæ Libellus supplex. Lond. 1645, 4to.
A copy is in the British Museum.
Memoirs of his own Life, 1549—1593. Edinb. 1827, 4to. Edited from the original MS. under the superintendence of Thomas Thomson, Esq., for the members of the Bannatyne club. Hanrott, 6l. 2s. 6d. Caley, 5l. 18s. Bright, 2l. 11s.
This edition was reprinted in 1833 by the MAITLAND CLUB, which see in *Appendix*.

— James, Minister of Kilrenny. Diary, 1556-1601. Edinb. 1829, 4to.
Bright, 1l. 11s.
Autobiography and Diary of the Rev. James Melville, Minister of Kilrenny, 8vo. Edinb. 1842. Printed by the Wodrow Society.
The Black Bastel, or a Lamentation in Name of the Kirk of Scotland, composed by M. James Melvil, when he was confined at Berwick, Anno 1611. Abridged by N. Acme Domini 1634. small 8vo.
Jolley, 1844, 3l. Pp. 16, reprinted in 'Various Pieces of fugitive Scottish Poetry,' edited by David Laing.

A Dream, &c&c., printed in Laing's series of Fugitive Scottish Poetry. (Edinb. 1853), from a MS. volume of the Author's Poems in the Advocates' Library, Edinburgh.
See Bannatyne Club. 1829. Appendix.

MELVILLE, Elizabeth. *See* CULROS, Lady.
— John. Meditations. Lond. 1659, 12mo.

MEMES, S., M.A. Memoirs of Antonio Canova, with a critical Analysis of his Works, and an historical View of modern Sculpture. 1825.

This is a book (say the Quarterly Reviewers) of some merit and more pretension; it contains much useful information concerning art, many just remarks on sculpture, is written with an anxious regard to truth, and displays abundance of enthusiasm about the person and productions of its hero.

MEMNON. *See* AGATHARCIDES.

MEMOIRS, British and Foreign, of the most illustrious Persons who dy'd in the Years 1711 and 1712. Lond. 1712-18, 8vo. 2 vols.
Hibbert, 5298, vol. 1, 3s. Roxburghe, 9288, vol. 1, 8s.

Memoirs for the Ingenious, containing several curious Observations in Philosophy, Mathematicks, Physicks, and other Arts and Sciences, in miscellaneous Letters, by J. De la Crose, E.A.P. (Eccl. Angl. Presb.) Jan. 1693 to Dec. 1693; with an alphabetical Table. Lond. H. Rhodes for J. Harris, 1693, 4to. 11f continued later.

Memoirs for the Ingenious; or, the Universal Mercury. By several Hands. This work commenced in January, 1694, and was published monthly by Randal Taylor, near Stationers' Hall.

Memoirs for the Curious, containing an Abstract of the most valuable Things that have been published both at home and abroad, in relation to Arts and Sciences. With the Lives of the most eminent Men deceased. The whole interspersed with several Discourses on Trade, Botany, Mathematicks, &c. By several Hands. Lond. 1710, 4to. 2 vols. Vol. I. pp. 404, with a general index. Vol. II. pp. 324. A periodical monthly work published by the celebrated James Petiver in sixpenny 4to. numbers, throughout the years 1707 and 1708.

Memoirs of the Antiquities of Great Britain, relating to the Reformation. Lond. by H. Tracey, at the Three Bibles on London Bridge, 1723, 18mo. cuts. Dilos, 10s. 6d.

Memoirs of an Unfortunate young Nobleman, returned from a Thirteen Years' Slavery in America. Lond. 1743, 12mo. 3 vols. The last volume is often wanting. (This is the case of James Annesley, Esq., who obtained the Annesley Peerage.)

The Memoirs of a Protestant condemned to the Gallies of France for his Religion. Written by himself. Translated from the Original, published at the Hague. Lond. 1758, 12mo. 2 vols. Dr. Goldsmith's earliest performance. *See* REFORMATION.

Memoirs of the Bedford Coffee-House. Lond. 1763, 12mo. 2 vols. 8s.

Moral and Historical Memoirs. Lond. Dilly, 1779, 8vo. (By Henry Constantine Jennings, Esq.) published anonymously. *See* JENNINGS.

Memoirs of a Pythagorean. Lond. 1785, 3 vols.

MEMORIALS.—A proper Memorial for the 29th of May. Lond. 1715, 8vo.
A curious pamphlet. *See* Savage's Librarian, ii. 139-40.

Memorials for the Ingenious. [Edited by Henry Fulthorpe and J. Kersey.] Lond. 1683, 4to.

Memorials of the Bagot Family. Lond. 1824, sm. 4to. Compiled by the second Lord Bagot. Privately printed.

MEMORY.—The Art of Memory, translated out of French into English by Rob. Coplande. Lond. by W. Myddylton, 12mo.

MEN before Adam, a theological Systeme. Lond. 1656, 12mo.
Nassau, pt. i. #234, 10s. Roxburghe, 520, 2s. 6d.

MENANDER. Fragments.
Translations of some of the Fragments of Menander, by Jos. Warton, will be found in the Adventurer, No. 105; also in Fawkes's Poems, 8vo. 1761, and Colman's Version of Terence.

Emendationes in Menandri et Philemonis Reliquias ex nupera edit. Clerici, anctore Phileleuthero Lipsiensi (J. C. de Panw) accessit Epist. crit. R. Dentieri de J. Malala Antiocheni. Cantab. 1713, 8vo.

MENASSEH BEN ISRAEL. Anglo-Judæus, or the History of the Jews whilst in England. Lond. 1656, 4to.
Several other pieces by this Jewish Rabbi have appeared in the English language.

1534   MEN   MEN

MENCE, Richard. The Law of Libel. Lond. 1824, 8vo. 2 vols. in 1.

A work of considerable merit.

MENDELSSOHN, Moses. Memoirs, with his Correspondence with Lavater, by M. Samuels. Lond. 1837, 6s.

Jerusalem, translated by M. Samuels. Lond. 1838, 8vo. 2 vols. 1d. 1s.

MENDEZ, Moses. A Collection of the most esteemed Pieces of Poetry that have appeared for several Years, with Variety of Originals. Lond. 1767, 12mo. 4s.

Intended as a supplement to Dodsley's Collection of Poems.

MENDHAM, Joseph, A.M. Clavis Apostolica; or a Key to the Apostolic Writings. Lond. 1821, 12mo.

A series of papers which originally appeared in the sixth volume of the Christian Observer, in opposition to the principles of Dr. Taylor's Key to the Epistle of the Romans.

Account of the Indexes, both prohibitory and expurgatory, of the Church of Rome. Lond. 1826, 8vo. 5s.

Essay on Church Reform. Lond. 1834, 8vo. 10s. 6d.

Index Librorum Prohibitorum a Sixto V. Lond. 1835, 4to. 5s.

Literary Policy of the Church of Rome exhibited in an Account of her damnatory Catalogues or Indexes, both prohibitory and expurgatory; with illustrative Extracts, Anecdotes and Remarks. Second edition. Lond. 1830, 8vo. Supplement, 1836.—Third edition, including Supplement. Lond. 1844, 8vo. 7s.

The Life and Pontificate of St. Pius the 5th, with a historic Deduction of the Episcopal Oath of Allegiance to the Pope. Lond. 1832, 8vo.—Second edition, with Supplement. Lond. 1844, 8vo. 6s.

Memoirs of the Council of Trent. Lond. 1834, 8vo. Supplement. Lond. 1836, 8vo.—New title to both, 1844, 7s.

The Declaration of the Fathers of the Councell of Trent concerning the going unto Churches at such Time as hereticall Service is said, &c. Edited, with a Preface, by Espator (Rev. J. Mendham). Lat. and Eng. Lond. 1850, 8vo.

Paleotti Historia Acta Concilii Tridentini, an. 1562 at 1563, cum aliis multis circa dictum Concilium. Lond. 1842, 8vo. red. (Bohn) to 8s.

Index of Books prohibited by the Command of Pope Gregory XVI. in 1835, being the latest specimen of the literary Policy of the Church of Rome. Lond. 1840, 12mo. 2s., portrait.

Venal Indulgences and Pardons of the Church of Rome examplified. Lond. 1839, 12mo.

The Spiritual Venality of Rome—Taxæ Sacræ Penitentiariæ Apostolicæ; preceded by a historical and critical Account of them; as also of the Taxæ Cancellariæ Apostolicæ. By Emanelpatas (Rev. J. Mendham). Second edition, enlarged. Lond. 1836, 12mo. 5s.

Mr. Mendham has written and edited several other pieces against the Church of Rome.

MENDIBIL, Don Pablo de. Resumen histórico de la Revolucion de los Estados Unidos Mejicanos. Lond. 1828, 8vo. with plates.

MENDOÇA, Gonçalez de. History of China, translated from the Spanish by Parke. Lond. 1588, 4to.

Undertaken at the request of Rd. Hakluyt. Bright, title inlaid, 1l.—New edition, edited by Sir Geo. T. Staunton, Bart. with an Introduction by R. H. Major, Esq. Lond. 8vo. 2 vols. Printed for the Hakluyt Society. See CHINA, page 437. HAKLUYT SOCIETY, Appendix.

MENDOZA, Andrew de. Two Royal Entertainments given to Prince Charles by Philip IV. Lond. 1623, 4to.

A copy is in the British Museum.

— Don Antonio de. Querer por solo querer: To love only for Love Sake; a dramatick Romance. Written in Spanish in 1623. Paraphrased in English, Anno 1654 (by Sir R. Fanshawe). Together with the Festivals of Aranwhez. Lond. 1671, 4to.

Collation.— A, a, and b, ten leaves; Querer par solo, B—Y; Flestas de Arauja, Z—Dd 3, not including a title, dated 1670. Dindley, pt. III. 513, 17s. 6d. Heber, pt. IV. 19s. Bright, 6s. 6d. THICK PAPER.

— Don Bernard de. Theorique and Practise of Warre. Translated out of the Castilian Tonge by Sir Edwarde Hoby, Knight. Lond. 1597, 4to.

Dedicated to Sir George Carew, Knight. Gordonstoun, 1857, 7s. 6d. Inglis, 675, 8s. 6d. Bright, 9s.

— Hurtado de. See LAZARILLO DE TORMES.

— Lopez de. See LOPEZ.

MENDOZA RIOS, Joseph de. A complete Collection of Tables for Navigation and nautical Astronomy; with simple, concise, and accurate Methods for all Calculations useful at Sea; particularly for deducing the Longitude from Lunar Distances, and the Latitude from two Altitudes of the Sun and the Interval of Time between the Observations. Lond. 1805, 4to.
Tables for facilitating the Calculation of nautical Astronomy. Lond. 1801, 4to.
Forms for the ready Calculations of the Longitude with the Tables. 1814, folio.
MENELAUS. Sphæricorum Libri III. edidit. Edm. Hallcius, LL.D. Præfationem addidit G. Costard, A.M. Oxon. 1758, 8vo. 8s.
Constable, 207, 6s. Bliss, 6d.

MENEWE, Gracious. A plain Subversyon or turning up syde down all the Arguments that the Pope Catholykes can make for the maintenance of Auricular Confession; also a Confutacyon, &c. made Dialogue-wyse, betweene the Priesto and the Prentyce, 12mo. n. d.
Printed about 1554. Sotheby, June, 1856, 1l. 2s.

MENGS, Sir Ant. Raphael. Works on the Fine Arts, translated from the Italian. Lond. 1796, 8vo. 2 vols. 12s.

MENIN, M. A Description of the Coronation of the Kings and Queens of France; with an historical Account of the Institution of that august Ceremony in France, and in other Kingdoms in Europe. Lond. 1723, 8vo.
Pp. 383, with a frontispiece by J. Clark, representing the coronation of Louis XV.
—A new edition. Lond. 1775, 8vo. 6s.

MENNIS, Sir John. Musarum Deliciæ; or the Muses Recreation, containing several Pieces of poetique Wit. The second Edition. By Sir J(ohn) M(ennis) and Ja(mes) S(mith). Lond. 1656, 12mo.
Pp. 101. Hibbert, 5320, 1l. Bibl. Anglo-Poet. 475, 6l. 6s. Lloyd, 555, 4l. 14s. 6d. Nassau, pt. I. 2239, 16s. Sir M. M. Sykes, pt. II. 426, morocco, 1l. 2s. Bindley, pt. II.

1859, 5l. Gardner, in 1854, 1l. 8s.—1656. Hibbert, 5319, with a portrait, a pen and ink drawing, russia, 1l. 2s. Reed, 7131, 12s. Stanley, 293, 1l. 10s. White Knights, 2285, 1l. 6s. Heber, pt. iv. 1l. Mitford, fine, 1l. 16s. In some copies a cancelled leaf (reprinted in the new edition) is found, in which are the lines—
'But he that fights and runs away, May live to fight another day,'
which have been often quoted as occurring in Hudibras. See a long note on the subject in Bohn's edition of Hudibras, p. 403.
Facetiæ. Musarum Deliciæ; or, the Musæ Recreations, containing severall Pieces of Poetique Wit, by Sir J. M. and Ja: S. 1656.—Wit Restored, in severall select Poems, not formerly publish't, by Dr. J. Smith. 1658.—Witt Recreations, selected from the finest Fancies of moderne Muses, with a thousand Out-landish Proverbs. 1640.—To which are now annexed Memoirs of Sir John Mennis and Dr. James Smith, with a Preface (by Edward Dubois.) Lond. 1817, post 8vo. 2 vols. with woodcuts, 1l. 6s. Brockett, 2151, morocco, 3l. 10s.

MENJET de Salmonet, R. See MONTETH, Robert.

MENU. Menu Dhārma Sāastra. The Institutes of Manu, edited by G. C. Haughton, M.A., F.R.S. Lond. 1824, 4to.
A valuable work. See Jones, Sir Wm.

MENZIES, John. Papismus lucifugus, or a faithfull Copie of the Papers exchanged betwixt him and Francis Demster, a Jesuite, surnamed Rin or Logan. Aberdeen, 1668, 4to.
Gordonstoun, 1500, 6s.

MENZINI, Benedetto. L'Arte Poetica Italiana, in cinque Canti. Lond. 1804, post 8vo. 4 vols. 5s.
A very neat edition, edited by Mathias.

MERBURY, Charles. A briefe Discourse of Royall Monarchie, with a Collection of Italian Proverbs. Lond. Vautrollier, 1581, 4to.
This book appears to have been printed only to be presented by the author to his friends. Reed, 5163, 7s. Heber, pt. ix. russia, 17s. Bright, imperfect, 6s.

MERCATOR, or Commerce retrieved. Lond. 1703, folio.
A character of this paper will be found in Wilson's Life of Defoe.

MERCER, Major James. Lyric Poems. Second Edition, with some

additional Poems. Lond. 1804, 12mo. 4s.

The first edition of these highly-finished poems was published anonymously.—With life by Lord Glenbervie. Lond. 1806, 12mo. portrait.

MERCER, Lieut.-Col. William. Anglia Speculum, or England's Looking Glasse. Divided into two Parts. Lond. 1646, 4to.

Sig. Q 2. Part I. ending with sig. F, contains one long poem: part II. consists of 58 short poems. Prefixed is a portrait of the Earl of Essex by Marshall. Nassau, pt. II. 158, with additional portrait of the Earl of Essex by Glover, 6l. 8s., now in the Grenville Library. Bibl. Anglo-Poet. 484, 10l. 10s. Constable, 763, with two engravings of the Earl of Essex, 2l. 15s. 6d. Dindley. pt. iii. 834, 8l. Brand, M. 9s. Bolland, 3l. 19s. Gardner, 3l. 13s. 6d. Bright, 2l. 4s. Skegg, 2l. 5s.

Funeral Elegy on Rob. Devereaux, Earl of Essex. Lond. 1646, folio, a broadside.

Edinburgh Vertues, and other Poems. Edinb. Wreittoun, 1632, 12mo. BLACK LETTER, only one copy known, and that wanting the title.

News from Parnassus. Lond. 1682, 8vo. In this volume Mercer announces a rhyming 'Chronicle of the Three Kingdoms,' which never appeared.

The Moderate Cavalier; or the Soldier's Description of Ireland, and of the Country Disease, with Receipts for the same (in Verse.) Printed A.D. 1675, 4to. The copy in the Grenville Collection is the only one of this historical poem that has been seen.

A Welcome to Jo. Lord Roberts, Baron of Truro, Lord Lieutenant of Ireland, his royal Entrie into the Castle of Dublin. Dublin, 1669, 4to. Bright, wanting all after D iii. 1l. 2s.

No other copy known. From the tail of the 9 being cut off by the binder, the date has been mistaken for 1660.

MERCHANTS.—The Book of Merchauntes. Lond. Jugge, 1547, 12mo.
BLACK LETTER. G. Chalmers, pt. I. 302, 3l.

MERCHISTON, Lord. *See* NAPIER, John.

MERCKS, Thomas, Bishop of Carlisle. Speech in Parliament concerning the deposed King Richard II. Lond. 4to.

MERCURIO ITALICO, IL. The Italian Mercury. Lond. 1789-90, 8vo. 2 vols.

By Baretti. Marquis of Townshend, 2078. 2 vols. and part I. of vol. iii. 18s. Bindley, pt. II. 1935, 2 vols. 8s.

MERCURIUS.

In Chalmers' Life of Ruddiman will be found a list of newspapers published under the titles of Mercurius ———— &c., &c. *See* also Brydges' British Bibliographer, vol. I. Catalogue of the British Museum Library, Timperley's Ency. of Literary Anecdote, and Bibl. Reed. nos. 2297 to 9231.

Wine, Beer, and Ale, together by the Eares. A Dialogue written first in Dutch by Gallobelgicus, and faithfully translated out of the original Copie, by Mercurius Britannicus, for the Benefits of his Nation. 1629, 4to. Roxburghe, 434, 16s. Rhodes, 429, 16s.

Mercurius Britannicus, or the English Intelligencer; a Tragi-Comedy as acted at Paris. Lond. 1641, 4to. A political play on the subject of Ship-money, in which several of the Members of Parliament are attacked under feigned names. Mitford, in 1860, 10s.

Mercurius Britannicus; his welcome to Hell. 1647, 4to.

Mercurius Hibernicus; or a discourse of the Insurrection of Ireland, displaying the true causes, &c., (by Dr. Hewell) Bristol, 1644, 4to. Chalmers, 2s.

The Levellers levelled, an Interlude, by Mercurius Pragmaticus. 1647, 4to. Lloyd, 774. 5s. 6d.

Mercurius Rusticus. 1647. *See* RYVES, Bruno.

Mercurius Psittacus, No. 1.; or the Parroting Mercurie, communicating the affairs of the Kingdom. Lond., 1648, 4to.

Craftie Cromwell, or Oliver ordering our new State. A Tragi-Comedie. Written by Mercurius Melancholicus. Printed in the Year 1648, 4to.

Mistris Parliament her Gossipping. By Mercurius Melancholicus. Printed in the Year of the Downfall of the Sectaries. 1648, 4to.

Mistris Parliament presented in her Bed, &c. By Mercurius Melancholicus. Printed in the Year of the Saint's Fear, 1648, 4to. four leaves.

The Cuckow's Nest at Westminster, or the Parliament between the two Ladybirds Queen Fairfax and Lady Cromwell, &c. By Mercurius Melancholicus. Printed in Cuckow-time in a Hollow-tree, 1648, 4to. Reprinted in the fifth volume of the Harleian Miscellany. (The author's real initials seem to have been J. H.)

Ding Dong, or Sir Pitifull Parliament on his Death-bed. By Mercurius Melancholicus. Printed in the Yeare 1648, 4to. Four leaves.

Mercurius Anti-mechanicus, or the simple Cobler's Boy, with his lapful of Caveats. 1648, 4to. Bindley, pt. iv. 117, 2s. Lieber, pt. iv. 5s. 6d.

Mercurius Propheticus, or a Collection of some old Productions. Of May they

grove built empty Fictions. 1648, 4to. Nassau, pt. ii. 809, 10s.
Mugals for Cerberus and his three Whelps, Mercurius Elenticus, Bellicus and Melancholicus. Lond. 1648, 4to.
A Pacquet of Popish Delusions, false Miracles, and lying Wonders by Mercurius Hibernicus. Lond. 1681, 4to. with a frontispiece. Hibbert, 6040, russia, 10s.
Mercurius Menippeus. The loyal Satyrist, or Iludibras in Prose. Printed in the Year 1682, 4to. North, pt. iii. 635, 5s. Heber, pt. i. 4s. Reprinted in the seventh volume of the Somers' Collection of Tracts.
Athenian Mercury. *See* DUNTON.
Lacedemonian Mercury. *See* DUNTON.
Mercure Britannique, a Journal edited by Mallet du Pan.
See BIRKENHEAD, Sir John. BRATHWAIT, Rich. BUTLER, Sam – p. 536. HALL, Joseph. Lacedemonian. NEEDHAM, Marchmont. RYVES, Bruno. TAYLOR, John, the Water-Poet.

MERCURY GALLANT, pleasant Relations of what passed at Paris till the King's Departure. 1673, 8vo.
Strettail, 994, 6s. Nassau, pt. i. 2237, 7s.

MERDON. *See* IMBER, Mat.

MEREDITH, Henry. Account of the gold Coast of Africa, with a brief History of the African Company. Lond. 1812, 8vo. 9s.
A lucid and valuable account.
— Walker. The Fidelity, Obedience and Valour of the English Nation. Lond. 1642, 4to.
— Sir William. Historical Remarks on the Taxation of free States. Lond. 1788, 8vo.
Of this pamphlet, which is mentioned in Junius's Letter to Sir Wm. Blackstone, only 12 copies were originally printed, in 4to. privately, without date. *See* Walpole's Correspondence, vol. vi. p. 34. Mitford, in 1860, 14s.
— William George, A.M. Memorials of Charles John, King of Sweden and Norway. Lond. 1829, 8vo. port. 5s.
A valuable historical work.

MERES, Francis, M.A. Palladis Tamia. Wits Treasury, being the second Part of Wits Common Wealth. Lond. P. Short, 1598, 12mo.
'A noted school book, set forth chiefly for the benefit of young scholars.'—*Ant. à Wood.* It consists of one hundred and seventy-four leaves. Boswell, 1851, 3l. 12s. 6d. Bindley, pt. iv. 284, 2l. 10s. Jadis, 51, morocco, 2l. 3s. Gordonstoun, 1684, 2l. 12s. 6d. Heber, pt. ii. 6s. Inglis, 1027, 2l. 2s. Sir M. M. Sykes, pt. iii. 1073, with Politeuphuia, 1598, 2l. 6d. A portion of this work, a Comparative Discourse of our English Poets with the Greeke, Latine, and Italian Poets, was reprinted in 1815. *See* Poetry. Wit's Commonwealth (the first part) was written by John Bodenham. Republished as Wits Academy, a Treasurie of goulden Sentences, Similies, and Examples. Sot forth cheefely for the Benefiti of young Schollers. Lond. 1634, 12mo. Prefixed is an engraved title by Jo. Droeshout, bearing date 1636. Inglis, 1029, date 1635, 10s. Nassau, pt. i. 2238, with Wits Commonwealth, 1689, 1l. 6s. Bright, 1l. 12s. [Contains at p. 289 the earliest printed list of Shakspere's Plays.]
God's Arithmeticke. Lond. Ed. Jones, 1597, 12mo. Twenty-five leaves, in the Grenville Collection.
The Sinners Guide. 1598. *See* LEWIS of Grenada.

MERIGOT, J. Select Collection of Views and Ruins in Rome and its Vicinity, executed from Drawings made upon the Spot, in 1791. (Letter-press in French and English.) Lond. Edwards, 1797-99, 4to. 2 pts. in 1 vol. 61 aquatinta plates. LARGE PAPER, sm. folio, the plates coloured.
This work has been twice reprinted; first, by White and Cochrane, about 1805; subsequently, by Mr. Hearne, about 1819; both with very inferior impressions of the plates, the last the worst.

MERITON, George. Anglorum Gesta: or a brief History of England. Lond. 1675, 12mo. Portrait of King Charles II.
Nassau, pt. i. 2239, 5s.—1678, 12mo.
The Praise of Yorkshire Ale, with the Humours of all sorts of Drunkards, and a Dialogue in the Yorkshire dialect. Lond. 1684, 12mo.—York, 1683, 12mo.—York, 1685, 12mo.—York, 1697, 8vo. Reed, 7917, 5s. 6d. Perry, pt. ii. 1157, 6s. Nassau, pt. ii. 61, 9s. Bindley, pt. ii. 2474, 12s. Skegg, 6s.
— Thomas. Love and War, a Tragedy. Lond. 1658, 4to.
Roxburghe, 5451, 3s. 6d. Rhodes, 1878, 6s. Heber, pt. ii. 4s. 6d. Mitford, in 1860, 7s.
The Wandering Lover, a Tragi-comedy, acted several Times privately at sundry Places by the Author and his Friends, with great Applause. Lond. 1658, 4to. Rhodes, 1879, 3s. 6d. Roxburghe, 5455.

6s. Reed, 1198, with Love and War, 1836, 10s. 6d. Heber, pt. II. 4s. 6d.

MERIVALE, J. H. Orlando in Roncesvalles, a Poem in five Cantos. Lond. 1814, 8vo.
Hibbert, 5326, morocco, 10s. On vellum. One or more copies struck off.
The Minstrel, Book III. In Continuation of Dr. Beattie's Poem. 4to.
Poems, Original and Translated, now first collected. Pickering, Lond. 1836-44, 12mo. 3 vols. 1L 1s. Vol 3, containing the Translation of Schiller's Poems, is very scarce.
Reports of Cases in Chancery, 1815-17. Lond. 1817-19, royal 8vo. 3 vols. 4l. 4s.
For continuation, see SWANSTON, C. T.

MERLIN, Ambrose. Life and Prophecies. See HEYWOOD, Thos.
'The true name, according to Humph. Lluid, is Merdhyn, so called from Caermarthen (Maridunum) where he was born.'—Nicolson.
Here begynneth a lytel treatyse of the Byrth and Prophecys of Merlin. Lond. Wynkyn de Worde, 1510, 4to. Forty-four leaves. Heber, pt. iv. unique, 1l. 15s. This poetical Romance differs in many respects from the MS. copies. See Drydens Censura Literaria.
Merlin, a Romance. An abstract from two MSS. will be found in the first volume of Ellis' Specimens. There were several French and Italian versions published about the commencement of the sixteenth century, a full description of which will be found in Brunet, Manuel du Libraire.
Prophetia Anglicana, Latine a Galfrido Monumetensi, cum explanat. Alani de Insulis. Francof. 1603, 12mo. Steevens, 1679, 3s. 6d.—Francof. 1608, 8vo.
See ABBOTSFORD CLUB, in Appendix.

MERRETT, Christopher, M.D. Pinax Rerum naturalium Britannicarum, continens Vegetabilia, Animalia, et Fossilia in hac Insula reperta. Lond. 1667, 12mo. 4s.
'Rather a short catalogue of our national curiosities than a just treatise of them.'—Nicolson. It is the first publication which gives an account of British insects exclusively. See NASH.

MERREY, Walter. Remarks on the Coinage of England; to which is added, an Appendix, containing Observations upon the ancient Roman Coinage, and a Description of some Medals found near Nottingham. Nottingham, 1789, 8vo.
An excellent tract. Brockett, 2098, &c.

MERRICK, James, M.A. Annotations, critical and grammatical, on the Gospel according to St. John. Reading, 1764-7, 8vo. 2 pts. 5s.
This little work abounds with classical illustrations, and was designed for the use of young persons as an introduction to the study of the New Testament.
Several poems by Merrick are included in Dodsley's Collection.
See PSALMS. TRYPHIODORUS.
— Rice. A Book of Glamorganshire's Antiquities. 1578, folio.
First printed (privately) from the original MS. by Sir Thomas Phillipps at his seat, Middle Hill, Worcestershire, in 1825. The title bears this imprint, Typis Medio-montanis una Labienaei.

MERRIE-MAN, Doctor. 1609. See ROWLAND, Samuel.

MERRY DEVIL, The, of Edmonton, as acted at the Globe. Lond. 1617, 4to. 1l. 11s. 6d.—1631, 4to.
Reprinted, Milford, 6s.

MERRYLAND.—A new description of Merryland, containing a topographical, geographical, and natural History of that Country. Bath, 1741, 8vo. 7s.
A meretricious piece, attributed to Thomas Stretzer.
Merryland displayed; being Observations upon a new description of Merryland. Bath, 1741, 8vo. 5s.
The potent Ally, or Succours from Merryland. Lond. 8vo. 5s.
Merryland Miscellany. Lond. 1742, 8vo. Printed for Curll. Nassau, pt. 1. 2242, 13s.
Description of the Roads which lead to Merryland. Lond. 1745, 8vo. 5s.
The whole of the above belong to the class 'Facetiae.'

MERRYMAN, Thomas. The matchless Rogue; or an Account of the Cheats and Amours of Tom Merryman, commonly called Newgate Tom. Lond. 1725, 8vo.

MERRY MUSICIAN, (the), or Cure for the Spleen; being a Collection of diverting Songs and Pleasant Ballads set to Musick. Lond. 1716, 3 vols. 8vo.
Heber, pt. iv. 1l. 2s.—Lond. Walsh, 1730, 8vo. 3 vols. Utterson, in 1852, 2l. 19s.

MERVINE.—The most famous and renowned Historie of that woorthy and illustrious Knight,

Sonne to Oger the Dane, by L M.
Lond. 1612, 4to.
Black letter. 176 leaves. Steevens.
1177, 14. Roxburghe, 6364. 1l. 17s. Nassau, pt. ii. 161, 3l. 15s. Bright, 6l. 7s. 6d. Bliss, 5l. 17s. 6d.

MESNAGER, Nicholas. Minutes of his Negociations at the Court of England. Translated from the French. Lond. 1717, 8vo. 4s.
By Daniel Defoe.

MESSALINA. — The Amours of Messalina, late Queen of Albion. Lond. 1689, 12mo.
Nassau, pt. i. 33, 6s. Perry, pt. i. 44, 8s. 6d. An account of the intrigues of the last four years of the reign of King James II. Several editions with Paris imprint have appeared; also translations into French at Paris, Cologne, &c.

The Royal Wanton, or Gallick Intrigues, being the second volume of the Amours of Messalina. Lond. 1690, 12mo. [Previously with title, Love Letters between Polydorus, the Gothick King, and Messalina, late Queen of Albion. Par. 1689, 8vo.]

MESSIA. See MEXIA.

MESSINGER. See MASSINGER.

MESSINGHAM, Thomas. Florilegium Insulæ Sanctorum; seu, Vitæ et Acta Sanctorum Hiberniæ. Paris, 1624, folio, 5l. 5s.
Pp. 441, with a cut in the title-page of whole-length figures of saints Columba, Patrick, and Bridget. Townsley, pt. ii. 1161, 3l. 18s. Hibbert, 5447, 2l. 6s. Heber, pt. i. 4l. 1s.

See OFFICIA.

MESTERS, M. de. Souvenirs d'un Voyage en Angleterre. Paris, 1791, 16mo.

MESTON, William, A.M. Poetical Works. Edin. 1767, 12mo.
Contains "Mother Grimm's Tale." Though the title-page bears 'the sixth edition,' the writer of the biographical sketch observes that the whole was never before collected into one volume, nor published in a uniform manner. Nassau, pt. i. 2714, 9s. See Retrosp. Review, pt. iii. 318-35.

METALS.—A Collection of Valuable Treatises upon Metals, Mines, and Minerals. Lond. 1738, 12mo. 4s.
This volume contains, 1. A. A. Barba's Art of Metals. 2. G. Plattes' Discovery of all sorts of Mines. 3. Houghton's Complete Miner. — 1740, 12mo. See BARBA.

METAPHRASTES, Symeon. Vitæ sanctorum Evangelisi. Johannis et Lucæ, Gr. et Lat. a Rich. Brotto. Oxon. 1597, 16mo.

METASTASIO, Abate Pietro. Opere, illustrate di Note e Dilucidazioni grammaticali da Romualdo Zotti. Lond. 1813, 12mo. 6 vols.
A neat edition, with portrait of Metastasio by Minasi. Sotheby's in 1821, 2l.

Scelta delle Opere dell' Abate Pietro Metastasio, da Fracc. Sastres. Lond. 1767, 12mo. 2 vols. 5s.

Opere scelte, riveduto da Leonardo Nardini. Seconda Edizione. Lond. 1807, 12mo. 3 vols. 7s.

Dramas and other Poems of the Abate Pietro Metastasio, translated from the Italian by John Hoole. Lond. 1800, 8vo. 3 vols. This edition contains eighteen plays. Rhodes, 1327, 10s. 6d. LARGE PAPER. Nassau, pt. ii. 1452, 1l. 6s. Fonthill, 1301, 1l. 10s. — 1767, sm. 8vo. 2 vols. This edition contains only six plays. Heath, 3482, 9s. 0d. LARGE PAPER. Garrick, 1443, 1l. 3s.

Three Dramatic Pieces of Metastasio, the Dream of Scipio, the Birth of Jupiter, and Astrea appeased. Translated from the Original by Francis Olivari. Dublin, 1767, 8vo. 3s. 6d.

A Translation of the Canzonettes of Metastasio, with original Poems to complete the Series, dedicated to the Countess of Effingham, by W. Kelso. Privately printed. Sotheby's in May, 1823, in morocco, 12s. Heber, pt. iv. 64.

Ariaserxes; an Opera. Translated from the Italian, and set to Musick by Dr. T. A. Arne. Lond. 1761, 8vo.—Artaxerxes, an English Opera [in three Acts, and in Verse]. Lond. 1763, 8vo.—Dublin, 1761, 8vo.—Lond. 1787, 8vo.—[In two Acts.] Lond. 1818, 8vo. Reprinted in vol. i. of Duncombe's British Theatre. Lond. 1823, &c. 12mo.

Conspiracy; a Tragedy [altered from the Clemenza di Tito] by R. Jephson. Lond. 1796. 8vo.

The Clemency of Titus. Liverp. 1828, 8vo.

Endimione; Serenata [in three Acts, and in Verse]. Ital. and English. Dub. 1758, 8vo.

The Patriot; a Tragedy [altered from Metastasio], by Charles Hamilton. Lond. (1784) 8vo.

The Desert Island; a Dramatic Poem, in three Acts, [in Verse, altered from Metastasio] by A. Murphy. Lond. 1780, 8vo.

The Royal Shepherd; an English Opera, [altered from Metastasio] by R. Rolt. Lond. (1764) 8vo.—1765, 12mo,

Translations, chiefly from the Italian of Petrarch and Metastasio, [by the Rev. Thos. Le Mesurier]. Oxf. 1795, sm. 8vo. Ullas, 6s. 6d.

Miscellaneous Translations from Metastasio and Lamartine, by J. S. Morrit. Lond. 1853, 8vo.

Some translations of minor pieces will be found in—

Pieces selected from the Italian Poets by Ag. Isola. Camb. 1778, small 8vo.— Capel Loft's Laura. Lond. 1814, 12mo. 5 vols.—Strong's (Rev. C.) Specimens of Sonnets. Lond. Murray, 1827, 8vo.

For Life of Metastasio, see BURNEY, Charles, Mus. D.

METCALFE, John of Knaresborough, commonly called Blind Jack. Life of. York, 1795, 12mo. port.
Fonthill, 22, 6s.

METCALFE, Theophilus. Short Writing. Lond. 1660, 12mo. 5s.

With portrait of Metcalfe. This essay, which is said to have passed through thirty-five editions, had never, in reality, more than one. The editions, as they are called, were only small numbers taken from the same plates at different times, and the dates as often altered in the title.

METELLUS. See LEWKENOR, J.

METEORS, The. Lond. 1800, sm. 8vo. 2 vols.
A Collection of Poems Boxburghe, 3182, 6s.

METHUEN, Emanuel. Historia Belgica. See CHURCHYARD, Thos.

METRES. See SEALE, J. B.
An Introduction to the Metres of the Greek Tragedians. By a Member of the Univ. of Oxford (Dr. J. Burton), 8vo. 3s.

METRICAL Miscellany. Lond. 8vo. 1803. Edited by Mrs. Riddle.

METRICAL Romances. See ABBOTSFORD CLUB. ELLIS, GEO. RITSON, Joseph. WEBER, Henry.

METRONARISTON. See WARNER, J.

METROPOLITAN MAGAZINE, a Journal of the Fine Arts, Literature, &c. from its Commencement in 1831 to the end of 1849 (then discontinued). Lond. Saunders and Otley, 244 pts. pub. at 3s. 6d. each, and forming 56 vols. 8vo. 10l. 10s.

This serial was at first edited by Thos. Campbell, the poet, afterwards by Capt. Marryat, then by Edw. Howard and others.

METZ, Conrad Mart. Imitations of Ancient and Modern Drawings from the Restoration of the Arts in Italy to the present Time. Lond. 1798, fol.

A collection of 100 plates in aquatinta, containing about 139 figures. Fonthill, 1258, 157 plates (including the Parmegiano), 6l. 10s. 6d.

Imitation of Drawings by Parmegiano, engraved by C. M. Metz. Lond. 1790, oblong folio, 1l. 5s.

Imitations of Drawings by Caravaggio, in the possession of Sir Ab. Hume. Lond. 1791, imp. folio, 64 plates. 1l. 10s.

Studies from Drawings, chiefly from the Antique. Land. for the author, 1785. imp. fol. 80 plates.

METM, John de. The Dodechechedron of Fortvne; or, the Exercise of a quick Wit, Englished by Sir W. D. Knight. Lond. 1613, sm. 4to. BLACK LETTER.

Pp. 170. A string of prose questions with metrical answers in couplet verse. Bibl. Anglo-Poet. 900, 8l 3s., Stevens, 960, 11s. * Sotheby's in 1823, 11s. Perry, pt. i. 1492, 9s. Freeling, 18s.

MEURSII Elegantiæ Latini Sermonis, seu Aloisiæ Sigeæ Satyræ Sotadicæ de arcanis Amoris et Veneris. Lond. a. a. 12mo. 1l. 1s.

There are at least two editions printed in England without any designation of place or date; also one printed with Baskerville's types in 2 vols. 18mo. dated 1757; and another, Birminghamiæ, ex typis nomullius, 1770, 2 vols. 18mo. containing Fragmenta Kroticα.

Delights of the Nuptial Bed, laid open in luscious Dialogues. (An abridgment). Printed in the island of Paphos, n. d. 12mo, price 1l. 10s. plates.

This elegantly written, but licentious work is by some attributed to Nicholas Chorier, an advocate at Grenoble, author of a History of Dauphiny; by others to Westrenen, an advocate of Copenhagen. See the Bibliotheca Parriana, p. 508.

MEXIA, Pedro. The Treasurie of auncient and moderne Times. Translated out of Pedro Mexia and M. Franc. Sansovino; as also of Anthonie Du Verdier, Lord of Vauprivaz; Louys Guyon, Sieur de la Nauche; Claudius Gruget, &c. [Translated by Thomas Milles.] Lond. 1613-19, folio, 2 vols.

This work contains much curious matter, the result of various and extensive

reading, related in the quaint style of that age. Reed, 3353, 1l. 2s. Gordonstoun, £59, some leaves MS. 1l. 7s. Nassau, pt. 1. 2594, 1l. 9s. Hibbert, 11s.
The Forest or Collection of Histories. See Fortescue, Tho.
History of all the Roman Emperors. 1654, folio. G. Chalmers, 4s.—Imperial History, or Lives of the Roman Emperors, translated by W. T. [Traheron.] Enlarged by Edw. Grimstone. Lond. 1623, folio. 9s.
Rarities of the World, translated into English by Jos. Baildon. Lond. 1651, 4to.

MEXICO (New), otherwise the Voyage of Anthony of Espeio, who in the yeare 1583, with his company, discovered a Lande of 15 provinces, replenished with Townes and Villages, with House of four or five stories height. Translated out of the Spanish. Lond. T. Cadman, n. d. (1587), 12mo.
Hebar, pt. vi. 6l. 5s. 6d.

— The present State of Mexico: as detailed in a Report presented to the General Congress, by the Secretary of State for the Home Department and Foreign Affairs, at the Opening of the Session in 1825. With Notes, and a Memoir of Don Lucas Alaman. 1825.

MEYRICK, Samuel Rush, LL.D., &c. A critical Inquiry into Ancient Armour, as it existed in Europe, but particularly in England, from the Norman Conquest to the reign of K. Charles II. with a Glossary of Military Terms, &c. (First edition.) Lond. 1824, folio, 3 vols.
A valuable work, with 80 plates, 72 of them coloured.
SECOND GREATLY-IMPROVED EDITION, corrected and enlarged throughout by the Author, with the assistance of literary and antiquarian friends (Albert Way, &c.), the plates illuminated in gold and silver, with an additional plate of the Tournament of Locks and Keys. Lond. Bohn, 1844, Imperial 4to. 3 vols. 10l. 10s.
Sir Walter Scott justly describes this collection as 'the incomparable Armoury.'
'This most superb archæological work is animated with numerous novelties, curious and historical disquisitions, and brilliant and recondite learning.—Learn-

ing going to Court in the full, rich costume of the Order of the Garter.—Plates as fine as the monuments of Westminster Abbey. Really and truly the work is admirably executed, and deserves every eulogy.'—Edinburgh Review.

MEYRICK'S ENGRAVED ILLUSTRATIONS OF ANCIENT ARMS AND ARMOUR, a Series of 154 very highly-finished Etchings of the Collection at Goodrich Court, Herefordshire, engraved by Joseph Skelton; accompanied by Historical and Critical Disquisitions by the possessor, Sir Samuel Rush Meyrick, LL.D., &c. Oxf. 1830, imp. 4to. 2 vols. portrait. Published at 12l. PROOFS ON INDIA PAPER, 20l.—Second edition, corrected by the Author. Lond. Bohn, 1854, imperial 4to. 2 vols. portrait and 154 plates, 4l. 14s. 6d.
'We should imagine that the possessors of Dr. Meyrick's former great work would eagerly add Mr. Skelton's as a suitable illustration. In the first they have the History of Arms and Armour; in the second work beautiful engravings of all the details.'—Gentleman's Magazine.

The History and Antiquities of the County of Cardigan, together with the mineralogical and agricultural State of the County, &c. Lond. 1810, 4to. With twenty engravings. Drury, 3008, russia, 1l. 7s.

The Costume of the original Inhabitants of the British Islands, from the earliest Periods to the sixth century; to which is added, that of the Gothic Nations on the western Coasts of the Baltic, the Ancestors of the Anglo-Saxons and Anglo-Danes. Lond. 1815, 4to. 24 coloured plates.

Dr. Meyrick contributed many Papers to the Archæologia, Gent's. Mag., &c.
See CARTER, John. SMITH, Charles Hamilton. SKELTON, Jos. WELCH VISITATIONS, under WALES.

MEZERAY, F. E. Sr. de. A general chronological History of France, beginning before the Reign of King Pharamond, and ending with the Reign of K. Henry IV. Translated by John Bulteel. Lond. 1683, folio, 6s.

MICHAELIS, John David. Introduction to the New Testament, transl. from the German, and considerably augmented with Notes, and a Dissertation on the Origin and Composition of the three first Gospels, by Herbert Marsh, [Bishop of Peterborough]. Camb. 1793-1801, 8vo. 6 vols.

MICHAELIS, J. D.—*continued.*
An invaluable work on biblical literature.—Camb. 1802. 8vo. 6 vols. Drury, 2714, 2l. 11s. LARGE PAPER, 6l. 6s.—1839, 8vo. 6 vols. Williams, 1197, bound in 4 vols. 2l. 12s.
Remarks on Michaelis's Introduction to the New Testament, vols. iii. iv., translated by the Rev. Herbert Marsh, and augmented with Notes, by way of Caution to Students in Divinity. Second Edition, with a Preface and Notes, in Reply to Mr. Marsh, 8vo. 2s. 6d. Attributed to Dp. Randolph.
Letters to the anonymous Author of Remarks on Michaelis and his Commentator, relating especially to the Dissertation on the Origin and Composition of our three first canonical Gospels. By Herbert Marsh, 1802, 8vo.
The Evidence for the Authenticity and divine Inspiration of the Apocalypse, stated and vindicated from the Objections of the late Professor F. D. Michaelis; In Letters addressed to the Rev. Herbert Marsh. Lond. 1802, 8vo. 6s.
St. Luke's Preface to his Gospel examined: with reference to Mr. Marsh's Hypothesis respecting the Origin of the three first Gospels. Bath, 1802, 8vo.
Illustration of the Hypothesis proposed in the Dissertation on the Origin and Composition of our three first canonical Gospels. With a Preface, and an Appendix containing miscellaneous Matters. The whole being a Rejoinder to the anonymous Author of the Remarks on Michaelis and his Commentator. By Herbert Marsh. 1803, 8vo. 4s.
Supplement to Remarks on Michaelis's Introduction to the New Testament, &c. in Answer to Mr. Marsh's Illustrations of his Hypothesis, 8vo. 2s.
A Defence of the Illustration of the Hypothesis proposed in the Dissertation on the Origin of the Gospels; being an Answer to the Supplement of the anonymous Author of the Remarks on Michaelis and his Commentator. By Herbert Marsh. 1804, 8vo. 2s.
Introductory Lectures to the sacred Books of the New Testament, by J. D. Michaelis. Lond. 1761, 4to. 'Much information may be gleaned from this work.' —*Rp. Watson.* Drury, 3012, 2s. 6d. Edwards, 781, 6s.—1780.
J. D. Michaelis in E. Lowth Praelectiones de sacra Poesi Hebraeorum Notae et Epimetra. Oxon. 1763, 8vo. *See* LOWTH, p. 1408.
A Dissertation on the Influence of Opinions on Language, and of Language on Opinions, with an Enquiry into the Advantages and Practicability of an universal learned Language. Lond. 1769, 4to. 6s. Horne Tooke, 467, 18s.

Epistolae de LXX Hebdomatibus Danielis. Lond. 1773, 8vo. These letters, addressed to Sir John Pringle, contain some ingenious but rather singular views of the celebrated prophecy of Daniel.
Select Discourses. I. Of the Correspondence of the Hebrew Months with the Julian, from the Latin of J. D. Michaelis. II. Of the Sabbatical Year. From the same. III. Of the Years of Jubilee, from an anonymous Writer, in M. Masson's Histoire critique de la Republique des Lettres, vol. v. art. ii. p. ix. &c. Translated by Wm. Bowyer. Lond. 1773, 12mo.
Commentaries on the Laws of Moses translated from the German by Alexander Smith, D.D. Lond. 1814, 8vo. 4 vols. Williams, 1196, 2l. 8s. 'The spirit of the political and ceremonial law, contained in the writings of Moses, is copiously investigated in this work. Valuable as these commentaries of Michaelis are in many respects, it is much to be regretted that they are not free from that licentiousness of conjecture and of language, as well as tendency to scepticism, which are the too frequent characteristics of some distinguished modern biblical critics in Germany. Great caution, therefore, will be necessary in consulting this work.' —*Rev. T. H. Horne.* Prefixed to Dr. Boothroyd's Family Bible is a well-executed abridgment of this work.
The Burial and Resurrection of Jesus Christ, according to the four Evangelists (from the German, by Sir George Dockett). Lond. 1827, 12mo. 6s. 6d. *See* MARSH, Bishop.

MICHAELIS, Sebastian, D.D. The Admirable History of the Possession and Conversion of a penitent Woman converted, who was seduced to become a Witch by a Magician in the Country of Provence in France, and of the end of the said Magician. Translated by W. B. Lond. William Aspley, 1613, 4to. Pp. 418. A l. to G g l.—after, on G g ll. new title, 'A Discourse of Spirits, containing whatsoever is necessarie for the more full understanding and resolution of the difficult Argument of Sorcerers,' pp. l to 154, and Table; ending on T t l*v. Dright, 33s.

MICHAUX, J. A., M.D. Travels to the Westward of the Allegany Mountains, in the States of the Ohio, Kentucky, and Tennessee, and Return to Charlestown, through the Upper Carolinas. Translated from the French by B. Lambert. Lond. 1805, 8vo.

These travels are instructive regarding the manners, commerce, soil, climate, and especially botany. Prefixed is a map of the states in the centre, west, and south of the United States. Drury, 2715. 4s. 6d.

North American Sylva; or a Description of the Forest Trees of the United States, Canada, and Nova Scotia, considered with respect to their Use in the Arts, and their Introduction into Commerce. Translated from the French by A. L. Hillhouse. Paris, 1819, royal 8vo. 3 vols. Vol. I. pp. 286, with 50 plates. Vol. II. pp. 247, and plates 51 to 100. Vol. III. pp. 223, and plates 101-156.—Second edition. To which is added, a Description of the most useful European Trees, with Notes by J. J. Smith. Philad. 1850, roy. 8vo. 3 vols.— New edition, 1854, roy. 8vo. 3 vols. 7l. 7s.

North American Sylva; or a Description of the Forest Trees of the United States, Canada, and Nova Scotia, not described in the work of F. A. Michaux; containing all the Forest Trees discovered in the Rocky Mountains, the Territory of Oregon, down to the Shores of the Pacific, and into the confines of California, as well as in various Parts of the United States. By Thomas Nuttall, F.L.S. Philad. 1848-49, royal 8vo. 3 vols. 121 coloured plates. —Second edition. Philad. 1854, roy. 8vo. 3 vols. 122 coloured plates. 6l. 6s.

MICHE, M. L. The English Courtoisy. Amsterdam, 1636, sm. 8vo. Bright, 5s.

MICHELBURNE, Col. John. Ireland preserved, or the Siege of Londonderry, in two Parts. Lond. 1705, folio, with a folding plate.

A singular dramatic history, each part in five acts. The only copy known is in the British Museum. Account of Transactions in Ireland, 1689. See IRELAND, p. 1166.

MICHELL, James. History of St. Neots, Co. Cornwall. Bodmin, 1833, 8vo.

— John. A Treatise of artificial Magnets. Camb. 1751, 4to.

An ingenious essay, containing many curious observations and particulars.

MICKLE, Wm. Julius. Poetical Works, with his Life by J. Sim. Lond. 1806, 12mo.

Best edition. Fonthill, 3494, 9s.—1794, 4to. Roxburghe, 3974, 7s. Fonthill, 655, 12s. See CAMOENS.

MICKLETHWAIT, —. History of

Olivares of Castile and Arthur of D'Algarve. Lond. 1695, 4to.
Goldsmid, 16s. Nassau, pt. I. 2247, 11s. See OLIVES of CASTILE.

MICMAKIS.—An Account of the Customs and Manners of the Micmakis and Maricheets Savage Nations, now dependent on the Government of Cape Breton. Lond. 1758, 8vo.

A translation from the French, to which are annexed several pieces relative to the savages, to Nova-Scotia, and to North America in general. Fonthill, 2798, 15s.

MICQUELLUS, J. L. Aureliæ urbis memorabilia ab Anglis obsidio, Anno 1428, et Joannæ virginis Lotharingæ res gestæ. (Joan of Arc.) Paris, 1560, small 8vo.
Sir M. M. Sykes, pt. II. 430, 2l.—Lot. Par. 1631, 24mo. Boswell, 1859, 4s. 6d.

MICRO-CHRONICON, or Chronology of Battles between his Majestie and the Parliament. 1647, 12mo. 7s.
Forms a part of, and is attached to Bruno Ryves' 'Mercurius Rusticus,' 1647. See under Charles I., p. 416.

MICROCYNICON, Six Snarling Satyres. Lond. 1599, 12mo.
Reprinted at Mr. Utterson's private press, 1842, sq. 12mo. See M. T., page 1431.

MICROCOSM, The, a periodical Work, by Gregory Griffin, of the College of Eton. 1787, 8vo. 7s.
Written by four young gentlemen of Eton College; viz. Mr. John Smith, Mr. George Canning, Mr. Robert Smith, and Mr. John Frere, with the occasional assistance of other Etonians.-Windsor, 1788, 8vo. Drury, 2714, a presentation copy from the Rt. Hon. G. Canning, mor. 2l. Fonthill 87*, 10s.-1790, 12mo. 2 vols.—Fifth edition. Lond. 1825, post 8vo. 1 vol.—and 18mo. 2 vols.

MICROCOSM of London. Lond. Ackermann, 1811, impl. 4to. 3 vols. 104 coloured plates (the architecture by Pugin, the manners and customs by Rowlandson). Pub. at 13l. 13s., now 6l. 6s.

MICROCOSM, or a Picturesque Delineation of the Arts, Agriculture, Manufactures, &c. of Great Britain. See PYNE, W. W.

MICROCOSMOGRAPHY. See EARLE, John, p. 707.

MID

MICRON, Martin. Instruction for the Edifyenge and Comfort of the symple Christians which intende worthely to receyue the holy Supper of the Lord.
Dated 6 Dec. 1552.

MICROSCOPICAL SOCIETY, Transactions. *See* Appendix.

MIDDIMAN, Sam. Select Views in Great Britain, engraved from Pictures and Drawings by the most eminent Artists; with Descriptions. Lond. 1784, oblong 4to. 53 plates.

Consists of 13 nos. Fonthill, 1069, 2l. 2s. Grave, 873, 2l. 2s. PROOFS. PROOFS BEFORE LETTERS.—Reissued in 1813, inferior impressions, oblong 4to.

Picturesque Castles and Abbeys in England and Wales. Lond. 1805-6, 16 plates, oblong folio, 16s.

MIDDLESEX.—A Description of the County of Middlesex. Lond. 1775, 8vo. 3s. 6d.
Pp. 199, with 8 plates.

The Antiquities of Middlesex, 1705. *See* BOWACK, John.

Customs and Privileges of the Manors of Stepney and Hackney, in the County of Middlesex. Lond. 1587, 4to. BLACK LETTER. Heber, pt. vii. 13s.—In the Savoy, 1736, 12mo. pp. 128, and two pages of contents.—Several editions of recent date.

The Visitation of Middlesex begun in the Year 1663, by Wm. Ryley, Esq., Lancaster, and Henry Dethick, Rouge Croix, Marshals and Deputies to Sir Edward Byshe, Clarencieux King of Arms. Salisbury, 1820, folio; pp. 51, index not included, 15s. This Haraldic Visitation contains 64 pedigrees. One hundred and fifty copies printed.
See LYSONS.

MIDDLETON, Charles. Plans, Elevations, and Sections of the House of Correction for the County of Middlesex. Lond. 1788, folio, 9s.
Fifty-three copper-plates, with title and 12 pages of letterpress.

— Christopher. The Legend of Humphrey Duke of Glocester. Lond. for Nicolas Ling, 1600, 4to.
A metrical legend, consisting of 184 stanzas, written on the plan of the Mirror for Magistrates, and dedicated to Sir Jarvis Clifton, Knt. Steevens, 981, 1l. 12s. (now in the Grenville Collection.) Sotheby's in 1821, 2l. 2s. Bindley, pt. iv. 702, 2l. 14s. Bibl. Anglo-Poet. 460, 10l. 10s.

Heber, pt. iv. 2l. 2s. It is reprinted in the tenth volume of the Harleian Miscellany.

The Historie of Heaven: containing the Poetical Fictions of all the Starres in the Firmament; gathered from amongst all the Poets and Astronomers. Lond. 1596, 4to. A Poem, in six-line stanzas. Caldecott, 2l. 15s. Reed. 5862, 4l. 4s. A copy is in the Malone Collection.

The famous History of Chinon of England, with his strange Adventures for the Love of Celestina, daughter to Lewis, King of France. Lond. 1597, 4to. Roxburghe, 6303, 7l. 7s. resold Heber, pt. vi. 3217, 2l. 9s.

A short Introduction for to learn to Swimme. *See* DIGBY, Everard.

MIDDLETON, Christopher. *See* DOBBS, Arthur.

— Conyers, D.D. The History of the Life of Marcus Tullius Cicero. Lond. 1741, 4to. 2 vols.
A work of authority, and considered a model of elegant composition. The accuracy of some of the translations from Cicero's writings have been questioned. Gough, 2467, 1l. 4s. Bindley, pt. iii. 812, 12s. 6d. Roscoe, 264, 1l. 5s. LARGE PAPER. Heath, 1545, 2l. 12s. 6d. Marq. of Townshend, 2191, 2l. 12s. 6d. Stanley, 49, 3l. 3s. Williams, 1025, 8l. 19s.—1742, 8vo. 3 vols. Gosset, 3514, 13s. 6d. Willett, 1705, 1l.— 1755, 8vo. 3 vols.—1757, 4to. 2 vols. Roxburghe, 9177, 1l. 6s.—1787, 8vo. 3 vols. Marquis of Townshend, 2361, 1l. 9s.—1804, 8vo. 3 vols. Drury, 2717, 1l. 1s.—1810, 8vo. 3 vols.—1837, 8vo. in 1 vol. 12s.—Royal 8vo. double columns. Lond. Moxon, 1845, 9s.—Reprinted, Bohn, 1854, 5s.

Bibliothecæ Cantabrigiensis ordinandæ Methodus quædam. Cantab. 1723, 4to.
A Dissertation concerning the Origin of Printing in England; shewing that it was first introduced and practised by our Countryman William Caxton, at Westminster, and not, as is commonly believed, by a foreign Printer at Oxford. Camb. 1735, 4to. 4s. Written chiefly in refutation of Atkyns' pamphlet, *see* p. 84. A French translation by D. G. Imbart was published Lond. 1775, 8vo.

Germana quædam Antiquitatis eruditæ Monumenta, quibus Romanorum veteran Ritus varii, tum sacri quam profani tum Græcorum atque Ægyptorum, nonnulli, illustrantur: Romæ olim maxima ex parte collecta, ac Dissertationibus jam singulis instructa. Lond. 1745, 4to. Bindley, pt. iii. 508, 2s. 6d. Townley, pt. ii. 1281 5s. 6d. This collection of Antiquities was purchased by Horace Walpole, afterwards Earl of Orford, and dispersed at the Strawberry Hill Sale in 1842.

A Letter from Rome; shewing an exact

Conformity between Popery and Paganism. Fourth edition, with a prefatory Discourse and Appendix. Lond. 1741, 8vo.— New edition. Lond. 1824, 12mo.—Dublin, 1841, 12mo.

Treatise on the Roman Senate. Lond. 1747, 4to.—1748, 8vo.—1778, 4to.

A free Inquiry into the Miraculous Powers which are supposed to have subsisted in the Christian Church, from the earliest Ages through several successive Centuries. To which is added, the Author's Letter from Rome.—1749, 4to. Drury, 3015, 5s. 6d.—Lond. 1824, 8vo. 13s. —New edition. Lond. Boone, 1844, 12mo. This work produced one of the most remarkable controversies of the last century.

Miscellaneous Works. Lond. 1752, 4to. 4 vols. Portrait by Ravenet, and 22 plates. Roscoe, 285, 1l. 16s. Marquis of Townshend, 2192, 2l. 8s. Willett, 1622, 3l. LARGE PAPER, Baker, 471, 5l. 18s. Duke of Grafton, 407, russia, 2l. 7s. Heath, 1713, 5l. 5s.—With the Life of Cicero, 1741, also on LARGE PAPER. 6 vols. Fonthill, 2449, 4l. 4s. Reed, 2234, with MS. notes, &c. 7l. 10s. Brockett, 2063, 5l. 12s. 6d. Dent, pt. ii. 729, 3l. 3s.—1755, 8vo. 5 vols. Gosset, 3315, 2l. 14s. Bindley, pt. ii. 1607, 2l. 2s. Towneley, pt. ii. 726, 1l. 3s. Garrick, 1556, 1l. 2s.

MIDDLETON, Rev. Erasmus. Biographia Evangelica; or, an historical Account of Authors or Preachers, both British and Foreign, in the several Denominations of Protestants, from the Beginning of the Reformation to the present Time. Lond. 1779-86, 8vo. 4 vols. portraits.

Williams, 1199, 4l. 1s.—1816, 8vo. 4 vols. 18s.

— Sir Henry. Voyage to Bantam and the Malucco Islands, being the second Voyage set forth by the Governor and Company of Merchants of London trading to the East Indies. Lond. T. P. for Walter Burre, 1606, 4to.

The Last East Indian voyage, containing much varietie of the state of the several kingdoms where they have landed, with the letters of three severall kings to the king's Majestie of England, begun by one of the voyage and since continued by the faithfull observations of them that are come home. Reprinted, with annotations, &c. by Bolton Corney, Esq. for the Hakluyt Society, Lond. 8vo. 1857. See APPENDIX.

MIDDLETON, Sir Hugh, Bart. the "Undertaker" or Projector of the New River.

For an account of the Ceremonies, &c. at the Opening on Michaelmas Day, see "The Triumphs of Truth" at his brother's inauguration to the office of Lord Mayor that year, page 1548, also Stowe's London, Matthew's Hydraulis, where a short biography, with portrait, of this benefactor to London will be found.

— John. Practical Astrology. Lond. 1679, 8vo.

With portrait of the author.

— Richard, of Yorke, Gentleman. Epigrammes and Satyres. Lond. 1608, printed by N. Okes, sm. 4to.

In the Drummond Library, Edinburgh. Unique. 40 copies reprinted, Edinb. 1840, sq. 17mo. Bright, 6s. 6d. Sotheby, April, 1866, 5s. 6d.

See RITSON's Bibl. Poet.

— Richard. The Key of David. Lond. 1619, 12mo. front. with portrait by R. Elstracke.

The Carde and Compass of Life. Lond. 1613, 8vo. Bright, 8s.

The Heavenly Progress. Lond. 1617, 8vo.

— Thomas. Dramatic Works, now first collected, with some Account of the Author, and Notes by the Rev. Alex. Dyce. Lond. 1840, 5 vols. post 8vo. portrait, 2l. 2s. LARGE PAPER, 4l. 4s.

Bright, 1l. 6s.

Middleton, a very voluminous writer, lived in the time of K. Charles 1st, and is supposed to have died soon after the publication of the Pageant for 1626. See HAZEN's Biog. Dram. C. LAMB's Works, vol. ii. Retrosp. Review, viii. 125-45.

The Wisdom of Solomon Paraphrased. Lond. Valentine Sims, 4to. no place or date, but 1597. Bliss, 3l. 15s. The only two other copies known are the one in the Malone Collection, and that sold in Geo. Chalmers, pt. ii. 475, for 11l. 16s. Reprinted in the Works, vol. V.

Blurt, Master-Constable, or the Spaniard's Night-Walke, a Comed . Lond. 1602, 4to. Roxburghe, 5450, 2l. 2s. Bindley, pt. iii. 628, 3l. Rhodes, 1689, N. 7s. 6d. Heber, pt. ii. 2l. 5s. In Chetwoo I's Collection, 12mo. 1750.

Part of the Entertainment to King James, 1604. Given in vol. V. of the Works. See DECKER, Thomas.

Michaelmas Terme. Lond. 1607, 4to. Inglis' Old Plays, 73, 2l. Bindley, pt. iii.

1546 MID MID

MIDDLETON, T.— *continued.*
530, 2*l*. 11*s*.—1630, 4to. Rhodes, 1653, 11*s*.
Heber, pt. II. 5*s*. 6d. Roxburghe, 5463,
14*s*.—16*s*.0, 4to.
The pleasant Comedie of Patient Grissel. 1607. *See* DEKKER, Thomas.
The Phœnix. Lond. 1607, 4to. Rhodes,
2*l*. 2*s*. Inglis' Old Plays, 7*l*, 18*s*. Heber,
pt. II. 7*s*.—1630, 4to. Rhodes, 1684, 8*s*.
Roxburghe, 5463, 9*s*. Burettall, 1859, 7*s*.
Heber, pt. II.3*s*. 6d.
Your Five Gallants. (1607), 4to. Roxburghe, 5474, 1*l*. 6*s*. Rhodes, 1685, 1*l*. 18*s*.
Inglis' Old Plays, 7*l*, 2*l*. 11*s*. Heber, pt. II.
1*l*. 3*s*.
The Familie of Love, a Comedy. Lond.
1608, 4to. Roxburghe, 5463, 3*l*. 11*s*. Inglis' Old Plays, 74, 3*l*. 6*s*. Rhodes, 1687,
2*l*. 15*s*. Sotheby's in April, 1821, 4*l*. 11*s*.
Heber, pt. II. 1*l*. 13*s*.
A Mad World, my Masters, a Comedy.
Lond. 1608, 4to. Inglis' Old Plays, 75,
1*l*. 6*s*. Rhodes, 1688, 1*l*. 9*s*. Gordonstoun, 1572, 1*l*. 6*s*. Hibbert, 5419, mor. 19*s*.
Heber, pt. II. 1*l*. 7*s*.—1640, 4to. Rhodes,
1689, 11*s*. North, pt. III.523, 4*s*. Roxburghe,
5165, 8*s*. Heber, pt. II. 6*s*. 6d. Reprinted in
Dodsley's Collection of Old Plays.
A Tricke to Catch the Old-one, a Comedy. Lond. printed by G. E[ld]. 1609,
4to. Roxburghe, 5471, 1*l*. 11*s*. 6d. Rhodes,
1686, 1*l*. 13*s*. Sotheby's in 1821, 2*l*. 12*s*. 6d.
Heber, pt. II. 8*l*. 8*s*.—1608, 4to. G. Eld, and
are to be sold at his house in Fleet Lane.
This edition, unnoticed by Mr. Dyce,
differs from that previously noted, though
bearing the same date. Halliwell, May,
1856, 5*l*. 10*s*.—1616, 4to. Hibbert, 5461, 13*s*.
Reprinted in the fifth vol. of 'Old Plays,'
1818.
Account of Sir Robert Sherley, sent
Ambassador by the King of Persia to the
King of Poland and other Princes, his
royal Entertainment into Cracovia, and
his pretended Comming into England;
also the hon. Praises of the same Sir R.
Sherley given unto him in that Kingdom.
Lond. 1609, 4to. A copy in a bookseller's
recent catalogue was priced 4*l*. 14*s*. 6d.
The Roaringe Girle, or Moll Cut-Purse.
By T. Middleton and T. Dekkar, Lond.
1611, 4to. Sotheby's in Nov. 1826, 2*l*. 15*s*.
Rhodes, 1690, 3*l*. 6*s*. Jolley, 3*l*. 6*s*. Heber, pt. II. 2*l*. 2*s*. Reprinted in Dodsley's
Collection of Old Plays.
The Triumphs of Truth: a Solemnity
at the Confirmation and Establishment of
Sir Thomas Middleton, Knight, in the
honourable Office of his Majesties Lieutenant, the Lord Major of the thrice famous Citty of London. Lond. N. Okes, 1613,
4to. A—D, in fours, sixteen leaves. In
the British Museum. Hibbert, 5420, 7*l*.
Dent, pt. I. 1143, 10*l*. 10*s*. Nassau, pt. II.
164, 8*l*. 8*s*. Bindley, pt. III. 391, 6*l*.; pt. iv.
821, 6*l*. Garrick in a vol. lot 477. Reprinted in Nichols' Progresses of King
James I., vol. II. pp. 679-701, and in
vol. V. of the Works.—Another issue,
Lond. by N. Okes, same date, 1613, with
the following added, 'showing also his
Lordship's Entertainment at the New
Riverhead upon Michaelmas Day last,'
&c. &c.
The Triumphs of Honor and Industry, a
Solemnity performed at the Confirmation
of the Rt. Hon. Geo. Bowles into the Office of Mayor. Lond. 1617, 4to. Garrick
in a vol. 2610, now in the Duke of Devonshire's Collection. *Unique*. Given in vol.
V. of Dyce's edition of the Works.
Civitatis Amor; the City's Love: an
Entertainment by Water at Chelsea and
Whitehall. Lond. 1616, 4to. With a
portrait of Charles Prince of Wales by
Delaram. Nassau, pt. I. 840, morocco,
6*l*. 12*s*. 6d. Gordonstoun, 610, 3*l*. 13*s*. 6d.
Rhodes, 1691, 5*l*. 5*s*. White Knights,
1650, mor. 4*l*. 4*s*. Reprinted in Nichols'
Progresses of King James I., and in vol. V.
of the Works.
A Fair Quarrel, a Comedy. By T.
Middleton and W. Rowley. Lond. for
J. T. 1617. — Again, with new Additions of Mr. Chaugh's and Trimtrams
Roaring, and the Baud's Song. Lond.
1617, 4to. Roxburghe, 5462, 1*l*. 2*s*. Rhodes,
1692, 1*l*. 5*s*. Heber, pt. II. 18*s*.—Lond.
1622, 4to. Field, 829, 1*l*. Rhodes, 1693,
1*l*. 10*s*. Heber, pt. II. 5*s*.
The Triumphs of Love and Antiquity,
an honourable Solemnity, performed at
the Confirmation and Establishment of
Sir William Cockayn, Knt. in the Office
of Lord Mayor. Lond. 1619, 4to. This
pageant was at the expense of the Stationers' Company. Bindley, pt. iv. 155,
1*l*. resold Rhodes, 1694, 4*l*. 4*s*. - Reprinted
in Nichols' Progresses of King James I.,
and in Works, vol. V.
The Inner Temple Masque, or the
Masque of Heroes, presented as an Entertainment for many worthy Ladies, by
the Members of that Society. Lond. 1619,
4to. Roxburghe, 5468, 2*l*. 16*s*. Heber,
pt. II. 1*l*. 17*s*. In the Devonshire Collection. Reprinted in vol. V. of the Works.
A Courtly Masque; the Device called
The World tost at Tennis, as it hath
been divers Times presented to the Contentment of many noble and worthy Spectators. By Thomas Middleton and Wm.
Rowley. Lond. 1620, 4to. With a woodcut. Field, 828, 1*l*. 1*s*. Rhodes, 1695,
1*l*. 11*s*. Read, 8204, 1*l*. 13*s*. Roxburghe,
5473, 2*l*. 2*s*. Heber, pt. II. 12*s*. In vol. V.
of the Works.
The Sunne in Aries. A noble Solemnity, performed at the Confirmation and
Establishment of Edward Barkham in
the high Office of Lord Mayor of London.
Lond. 1621, 4to. Mr. Kemble's copy is

MIDDLETON, T.—*continued.*
now in the possession of the Duke of Devonshire. Reprinted in Nichols' Progresses of James I. vol. iii. pp. 724-31, and in Works, vol. V.

The Triumphs of Honor and Virtue; a noble Solemnity performed through the City at the sole Cost and Charges of the Honourable Fraternity of Grocers, at the Confirmation and Establishment of their most worthy Brother, the Right Honourable Peter Proby, in the high office of his Majesties Lieutenant; Lord Mayor and Chancellor of the famous City of London on the 29th of October, 1622. Lond. by Nicholas Okes, 1622, 4to. *Unique.* Its existence was unknown to Mr. Dyce when editing Middleton's Works in 1840. Reprinted entire in the second volume of the Shakespeare Society Papers.

The Triumphs of Integrity in the Entertainment of Sir Martin Lumley, 29th Oct. 1623. Lond. N. Okes, 1623, 4to. *unique.* In the Duke of Devonshire's Collection. Reprinted in vol. V. of the Works.

A Game at Chesse as it hath bene sundrey Times acted at the Globe on the Banck Side. No date (1624), 4to. Heber, pt. ii. 1l. 16s.—Lond. n. d. (1625) A—I, in fours. The title is engraved, and contains figures of a fatte Bishop, the Black Knight and the White Knight (qy. portraits of Gondomar and Loyola.)—4to. n. d. For writing this play the author was committed to prison. Sir M. M. Sykes, pt. ii. 507, 6l. 2s. 6d. Inglis' Old Plays, 70, 2l. 14s. Hibbert, 5413, 18s. Heber, pt. ii. 1l. 1s. resold Jolley, 51. 7s. 6d. Garrick, 1013, 4l. 4s. Gordonstoun, 1573, 8l. 8s. Towneley, pt. i. 839*, 4l. 15s. Strettell, 1252, 3l. 5s. Rhodes, 1696, 4l. 14s. 6d. Bindley, pt. iii. 529, 3l. 10s. Roxburghe, 5464, 8l. 1s.

The Triumphs of Health and Prosperity at the Inauguration of the Rt. Hon. Cuthbert Hacket, Draper, in 1626. Lond. N. Okes, 1626, 4to. Garrick, 764, in a vol. Heber, pt. iv. 1l. 5s. In Works, vol. V.

A chast Mayd in Cheape-side, a pleasant conceited Comedy. Lond. 1630, 4to. Hibbert, 5422, 1l. Roxburghe, 5461, 2l. 11s. Rhodes, 1697, 2l. 5s. Heber, pt. ii. 1l. 11s.

The Widow, 1652. *See* JONSON, Ben.

The Changeling, a Tragedy. By T. Middleton and W. Rowley. Lond. 1653, 4to. Roxburghe, 5450, 5s. Heber, pt. ii. 5s. Rhodes, 1700, 6s. Inglis' Old Plays, 74, 7s. 6d.—1668, 4to. Reprinted in the fourth volume of 'Old Plays,' 1816.

The Spanish Gipsie, a Comedy. By T. Middleton and W. Rowley. Lond. 1653, 4to. Bindley, pt. iii. 531, 3s. Roxburghe, 5470, 1l. 2s. Rhodes, 1698, 1l. 4s. Heber, pt. ii. 5s. 6d.—1661, 4to. Rhodes, 1699, 4s. 6d. Heber, pt. ii. 9s. Reprinted in the fourth volume of 'Old Plays,' 1816.

The Old Law. 1656. *See* MASSINGER, P.

Two new Playes, viz. More Dissemblers besides Women—and Women beware Women. Lond. 1657, 8vo. Nassau, 6774, 12s.—Lond. 1657, with general title and portrait of the author crowned with laurel in 'Marshall's manner.' Gardner, 1l. 11s. Garrick, 1555, 2l. 11s. Bindley, pt. ii. 1l. 1s. 6d. resold, Heber, pt. ii. 3l. Reprinted in the fourth and fifth volumes of 'Old Plays,' 1816.

No { Wit } like a Woman's, a Comedy. { Help } Lond. 1657, 4to. In the Duke of Devonshire's and Malone Collections.—1657, 8vo. Rhodes, 1703, with 'Two new Playes,' 8vo. 1657, no head, 1l. Reprinted with new title, 'The Counterfeit Bridegroom, or the defeated Widow.' Lond. 1677, 4to.

The Mayor of Quinborough, a Comedy. Lond. 1661, 4to. Roxburghe, 5467, 6s. 6d. Rhodes, 1701, 7s. 6d. Heber, pt. ii. 7s. Reprinted in Dodsley's Collection of Old Plays.

Any Thing for a quiet Life, a Comedy. Lond. 1662, 4to. Rhodes, 1702, 1l. 10s.

A Tragi-Comœdie called the Witch, written by Tho. Middleton. Lond. 1778, 8vo. Shakespeare was greatly indebted to this play for his witchery in Macbeth. One hundred and four copies were printed at the expense of Is. Reed, Esq. Roxburghe, 8473, 5s. Strettell, 876, 5s. 6d. Nassau, pt. i. 2250, 6s. Hibbert, 8346, 7s. FINE PAPER. Twenty copies printed. Bindley, pt. ii. 1639, 10s. Dent, pt. i. 1418, 14s. Rhodes, 1704, 1l. The original MS. at the sale of G. Streevens' library, no. 1256, produced 7l. 10s., and is now in the Malone Collection.

See M. T. MICROCYNICON. The Black Book. FATHER HUBBURD'S TALES.

MIDDLETON, Thomas Fanshaw, Bp. of Calcutta. The Doctrine of the Greek Article, applied to the Criticism and the Illustration of the New Testament. Lond. 1808, 8vo.

A book of profound learning and most masterly criticism.—Second edition, edited by the Rev. James Schofield. Camb. 1828, 8vo. 16s.—Third edition. Lond. 1833, 8vo.—Fourth edition, edited by H. J. Rose, D.D. Lond. 1841, 8vo.

Life, by the Rev. C. W. Le Bas. Lond. 1831, 8vo. 2 vols. portrait.

Sermons and Charges, with Life by H. K. Bonney. Lond. 1823, 8vo.

The Country Spectator. Gainsborough, 1793, 8vo. 6s.

MIDLTON, Capt. William. Bardoniaeth neu Brydvaeth y Hyfr. Kynaf. Llunden, 1593, 4to.

An account of Capt. Midleton will be found in Wood's Athen. Oxon.

MIDON, Francis. History of the Rise and Fall of Masaniello the Fisherman of Naples. Lond. 1729, 8vo.
Roxburghe, 5s. 0d. 7s. 6d.—1747, 12mo. *See* MASANIELLO.

MIDWIFE, The; or old Woman's Magazine. Lond. 12mo. 3 vols. 12mo. fronts.
Dent, pt. I. 1419, 1l. Nassau, pt. I. 2251, 1l. 18s. White Knights, 2801, 2l. Reed, 2559, 3l. Bindley, pt. II. 1591, 1l. 6s.

MIEGE, Guy. The great French Dictionary, in two Parts. Lond. 1688, folio.
Reed, 222, 5s. Roxburghe, 2155, 5s. 6d.
A Dictionary of barbarous French. Lond. 1679, 4to.
Delight and Pastime; a pleasant Diversion for both Sexes, consisting of witty Jests, smart Repartees, &c. French and English. Lond. 1697, 8vo. Sotheby, June, 1856, 1l. 8s. *See* JESTS, p. 1203.
The present State of Great Britain and Ireland. Lond. 1711, 8vo. 'A work every way instructive and commendable.'—*Nicolson*.
Miege published several other works, chiefly elementary.

MIERS, John. Travels in Chile and La Plata. Lond. 1826, 8vo. 2 vols. Maps and Views.
A work containing much valuable information strangely huddled together.

MIGNAN, Capt. Rob. Travels in Chaldea. Lond. 1820, 8vo.

MIGNOT, Abbé. The History of the Turkish, or Ottoman Empire, from its Foundation in 1300, to the Peace of Belgrade in 1740; to which is prefixed an historical Discourse on Mahomet and his Successors. Translated from the French by A. Hawkins. Exeter, 1787, 8vo. 4 vols.—Lond. 1788, 8vo. 4 vols.
— Stephen, D.D. Histoire des Démélés de Henry II. avec St. Thomas de Canterbury. 1756, 12mo.

MIHIL MUMCHANCE. *See* GREENE, Robert, p. 938.

MILANO, Giovanni de. *See* SCHOLA SALERNITANA.

MILBOURNE, Luke. Notes on Dryden's Virgil. Lond. 1698, 8vo.
This writer is called by Pope the fairest of all critics, for having subjoined his own version of certain parts, that they might be compared with that which he censured. Milbourne published other works, now forgotten. *See* KEMPIS, Thomas à. PSALMS.

MILBURN, Wm. Oriental Commerce, or a Guide to the Trade of the East Indies and China. Lond. 1813, royal 4to. 2 vols.
Duke of York, 3376, 2l. 11s.—Improved by Tho. Norton. Lond. 1824, royal 8vo. 1 vol. 1l. 16s.

MILDMAY FAMILY.—Pedigree of the Families of Mildmay of Moulsham Hall, Essex, and St. John of Farley, Hampshire. Lond. 1803, 4to.
Privately printed. Dent, pt. II. 731, 18s.

MILES and Clericus. 4to.
A Poem.

MILFORD, John. Observations moral, literary, and antiquarian, made during a Tour through the Pyrenees, France, Switzerland, the whole of Italy, and the Netherlands, in the Years 1814 and 1815. Lond. 1817-18, 8vo. 2 vols. 1l. 1s.
Norway and her Laplanders in 1841; with a few Hints to the Salmon-Fisher. Lond. 1842, 8vo. 10s. 6d.

MILFORD HAVEN.—Observations on Milford Haven. Lond. 1812, 4to.
Dent, pt. II. 35, 6s. 6d. LARGE PAPER. 4to, Sir M. M. Sykes, pt. II. 636, 2s.—Second edition with considerable additions, 1817, 8vo.

MILITARY.—The A, B, C of Armes, or an Introduction Directorie, whereby the Order of Military Exercises may be understood and readily practised. By J. T., Gent. Lond. 1616, sm. 4to.

MILITARY ART, The, of Trayning; with a Description of all martial Officers, their Places, Duties, and honorable Ceremonies, from a Generall to an inferior Soldier; with the Discipline of Drilling both for the Musket and Pike, all in lively Portraitures setting out the particular Postures, in 74 whole-length costume Figures. Lond. by C. Alide, and are to be sold by Roger Daniell, 1622, sm. 4to.
Lond. 1623. Brand, 2l. 8s. Probably an early edition of the following.

MILITARY DISCIPLINE, wherein is martially shown the Order for drilling the Musket and Pike set forth in Postures, with the Word of Command. Lond. T. Jenner, 1642, small 4to.

Seventy-seven plates, very neatly engraved. Nassau, pt. II. 166, 7s.—n. d. 8vo. White Knights, 2l. 2s., morocco, 1l. 1s.

The ancient Code of Military Laws, for the Government of the English Army, under King Henry V., enacted at Manues, with some additional Ordinances made by the Earl of Salisbury. Lond. 1784, 4to. 2s. 6d. A separate publication from the second edition of Grose's Antiquities of England and Wales.

The Military Mentor. Second edition. Lond. 1804, crown 8vo. 2 vols. 6s.

A Treatise on Military Finance. 2 vols. 12s. 6d.

MILITARY CLASSICS; or Corpus Historicum; a Series of Translations, comprising—
Anacharsis' Travels in Greece, 8 vols.
Arrian, by Rooke.
Cicero, 4 vols. viz.—
  Orations, by Guthrie.
  Letters to his Friends, by Melmoth.
  Letter to Atticus, by Guthrie.
  Cato and Lælius, by Melmoth.
  Life, by Dr. Middleton.
Comines (P. de.) Memoirs.
Diodorus Siculus, by Booth, 2 vols.
Froissart's Chronicles, by Lord Berners, 2 vols.
Livy, with Freinsheim's Supplement, 3 vols.
Plutarch's Lives, by the Langhornes, 3 vols.
Polybius, by Hampton.
Tacitus, by Murphy, 2 vols.
Thucydides, by Smith.
Xenophon's Anabasis, by Spelman.
—— Cyropædia, by Ashley.
Zosimus, by Smith.

Together 26 vols. royal 8vo. Lond. J. Davis, 1814, &c., 10l. 10s.

MILITARY LIBRARY, and Journal of Military Knowledge. Lond. 1799, 4to. 2 vols. 15s.

Military Antiquities. See GROSE, F. MAURICE, S. R.

Military Miscellany. 1793, 8vo. 2 vols. Contains several curious pieces.

Military Exercise, and Manœuvres with the Lance, by Lieut. Col. N. H. de Montmorency. Lond. 1820, 4to. 20 outlines.

Many works on the Exercise, Manœuvres, Discipline, &c., of the British Army, are published by authority of the War Office, and sold there.

MILIZIA, Francesco. The Lives of celebrated Architects, ancient and Modern. Translated from the Italian by Mrs. E. Cresy. With Notes and additional Lives. Lond. 1826, 8vo. 2 vols. pub. 1l. 8s.

MILL, Humphry. Poems occasioned by a melancholy Vision; or, a melancholy Vision upon divers Theames enlarged, which by severall Arguments ensuinge is shewed. Lond. 1639, small 8vo.

The title is in the centre of a leaf, engraved in compartments by John Droeshout, opposite are some verses giving 'the minde of the frontispiece,' with 14 other leaves preliminary. B to Q in eights. On II is a title, 'Poems, Pleasant and Profitable,' dated 1639, and on M 3 another, 'Poems concerning Death,' 1639. Bindley, pt. III. 11s., wanting dedication and preface, 19s. Nassau, pt. I. 2253, imperfect, 8s. Bibl. Anglo-Poet. 470, 8l. 8s. Bindley, pt. II. 1807, 7l. 7s. Heber, pt. iv. 2l. 18s. resold, Gardner in 1854, 1l. 6s. G. Chalmers, 2l. 10s. Caldecott, 2l. 15s.

A Nights Search, discovering the nature and condition of all sorts of Night Walkers; with their associates; digested into a Poem. In two Parts. Lond. 1640–6, small 8vo. 2 vols. Bindley, pt. III. 11s., wanting the frontispiece to the second part, 6l. resold Nassau, pt. I. 2257, M. 8s. Bindley, pt. II. 1806, 18l. 7s. 6d. Hibbert, 3360, 4l. Townsley, pt. I. 493, 2 pts. with fronts 6l. 10s. Heber, fronts. fine, 6l.—Part I. R. Bishop, 1640, 148 leaves, with an emblematical frontispiece and a poetical illustration, dedicated to the Earl of Essex. Bibl. Anglo-Poet. 468, 5l. 5s. Midgeley, 3l. 15s.—The second Part, II. Shepard, 1646, pp. 150, dedicated to Robert Earl of Warwick, and divided into twenty-six sessions, frontispiece and leaf of explanation. Bibl. Anglo-Poet. 469, 5l. 10s.

—— James. The History of British India. Lond. 1818, 4to. 3 vols. pub. 6l. 6s.

A valuable work.—Second edition, 1820, 8vo. 6 vols. Drury, 2719, 4l. 18s.—Fourth edition, with continuation and Notes by H. H. Wilson. Lond. Madden, 1840–8, demy 8vo. 9 vols. 6l. 6s.—Fifth edition, post 8vo. Lond. 1858, 10 vols. 3l.

The Elements of Political Economy. Lond. 1821, 8vo. 8s.

Essays on Government, Jurisprudence, Liberty of the Press, Prison and Prison-discipline, Colonies, Law of Nations, and Education. Lond. 8vo. 7s. Reprinted from the Supplement to the Encyclopædia Britannica, for private distribution.

The principles of Toleration. Lond. 837, 12mo.

MILLAR, James, M.D. The Elements of Chemistry. Lond. 1822, 8vo.

— John. Historical View of the English Government, from the Settlement of the Saxons in Britain, to the Revolution in 1688. To which are subjoined, some Dissertations connected with the History of the Government, from the Revolution to the present Time. Lond. 1803, 8vo. 4 vols.—Second edition, 1812, 8vo. 4 vols.—Fourth edition, 1818, 8vo. 4 vols. (verbatim reprints), 1l.—Lond. 1787, 4to.

The Origin of the Distinction of Ranks in Society. Fourth edition, with the Life of the Author by John Craig, Esq. Edinb. 1806, 8vo. Best edition, 9s.—1771, 4to. Roxburghe, 8s., &c.—Third edit. 1761, 8vo.

— Robert. The History of the Propagation of Christianity and Overthrow of Paganism. Edinb. 1723, 8vo. 2 vols.
Roxburghe, 7800, 14s. 6d.—Lond. 1731, 8vo. 2 vols.
History of the Church under the Old Testament, from the Creation of the World. Edinb. 1730, folio, 10s. 6d.

MILLER, Edmond. An Account of the University of Cambridge, and the Colleges there. Second edition. Lond. 1717, 8vo.
This useful work appears in form of a proposition to both Houses of Parliament. Pp. 200 (A 2—N 4). Bishop of Ely, 617, 5s. Towneley, pt. II. 736, 3s.

— Edward, Mus. D. The History and Antiquities of Doncaster and its Vicinity; with Anecdotes of eminent Men. Doncaster (1804), 4to.
Nassau, pt. II. 167, 1l. 7s. Duke of York, 3376, 1l. 1s. Sir M. M. Sykes, pt. II. 510, 19s. LARGE PAPER. Bent, pt. II. 739, 15s. Collation.—Title and dedication, 2 leaves; list of subscribers, 6 pages; contents, introduction, and errata, 6 pages; historical part, 328 pages; appendix and addenda, at beginning a half-title, pp. i—xlv. The volume contains 10 plates, at pp. 1, 71, 140, 145, 159, 259, 265, 303, 312, and 359. There are also several cuts in the letter-press, and a map of the environs of Doncaster, as a frontispiece.

Dr. M. also wrote Institutes of Music, Elements of Thorough Bass and Composition, and set the Psalms of David to music. See PSALMS.

— Fred. Cimelia Physica. Figures of rare and curious Quadrupeds, Birds, and Plants, with Descriptions by George Shaw. Lond. 1796, imperial folio.
The volume contains 60 coloured plates. Fonthill, 679, 4l.; 776, 4l. 17s.—Hibbard, same title, but the plates not so carefully finished, 1l. 16s.

— George, D.D. Lectures on the Philosophy of Modern History. Dublin, 1816-28, 8vo. 8 vols.
Second edition, under the title of History Philosophically Illustrated. Lond. Murray, 1832, 8vo. 4 vols. (In this edition the form of lectures is abandoned, and many alterations and additions made.) —Third edition, revised by the author, with Memoir and Index. Lond. Bohn, 1853-4, post 8vo. 4 vols. portrait, 14s.
Dr. Millar also wrote a considerable number of Sermons and Tracts, which will be found enumerated in the Memoir prefixed to vol 4 of the edition last mentioned.

— Jos. See JESTE, page 1203.

— General John. Memoirs while in the Military Service of the Republic of Peru. Lond. 1828, 8vo. 2 vols. portrait, 9s.
An interesting description of the War of Independence of the Spanish colonies in South America.

— John. An Illustration of the sexual System of the Genera Plantarum of Linnæus (in Latin and English.) Lond. 1777, imp. folio, 2 vols.
This work obtained the approbation of Linnæus himself. No. 1 appeared in 1775, the last, No. 20, in 1777, published at 1l. 1s. each. The work should contain 117 plates, viz. an engraved frontispiece, 104 plates numbered, 7 supplementary ones published in 1780, one ditto not numbered, and 4 others of leaves. Copies with the plates not coloured are of little value. Hibbert, 6452, with coloured plates, 2l. 14s. —With two sets of plates, one plain, the other coloured. Garrick, 1815, 6l. 10s. Bent, pt II. 778, russia, 4l. 10s. Towneley, pt. II. 1023, morocco, 10l. 15s. Edwards, 725, 14l. 8s. 6d. North, pt. II. 878, russia, 19l. 6s. 6d. Willett. 1856, 7l. 10s.
Proposals for publishing Prints of Plants and Insects. Lond. 1759, folio.
An Illustration of the sexual System of Linnæus. Lond. 1779, 89, 8vo. 2 vols. With

coloured plates, 1l. 11s. 6d. Copies with plain plates are of no value.

MILLER, John Frederick. Various Subjects of Natural History, wherein are delineated Birds, Animals, and many curious Plants; with the Parts of Fructification of each Plant, all of which are drawn and coloured from Nature. Lond. 1785, imp. folio.

Pp. 176, 12 plates, and 2 leaves of tabulæ. Published in numbers.

— J. S. A Natural History of the Crinoidea ; or lily-shaped Animals. Bristol, 1821, 4to.

Pp. 150, with 50 tinted plates. Sotheby's in 1855, 1l. 13s.

— Mrs. M. Letters from Italy, describing the Manners, Customs, Antiquities, Paintings, &c. of that Country, in the Years 1770 and 1771, to a Friend residing in France. By an English Woman. Lond. 1777, 8vo. 3 vols. 10s. 6d.

Fonthill, 2054, 1l. 9s.

— Philip. The Gardener's and Botanist's Dictionary, corrected and newly arranged, with Additions by Thomas Martyn. Lond. 1803-7, roy. folio, 4 vols. plates, 8l. 8s.

White Knights, 2971, russia, 15l. 15s. Roscoe, 1772, [ll. 11s. Sir M. M. Sykes, pt. ll. 408, russia. 13l. Nassau, pt. l. 2300, 9l. 9s. Duke of York, 541B, 6l. 15s. *First Editions*. Lond. 1731-7, folio, 2 vols.— 1737, folio, 2 vols. LARGE PAPER, 2l. 2s. —1752, folio.—Heventh edition, 1759, folio. 2 vols. Steevens, 1470, 1l. 3s. Willett, 1651, 6l.— Eighth edition, 1768, folio. The last edition published by the author, Garrick, 1617, with the figures of the plants coloured, 1771, 5l. 17s. 6d.—1798, folio, 2 vols. *See* Don, George.

The Gardener's Dictionary abridged. Lond. 1735, 8vo. 3 vols.—1748, 8vo. 3 vols.

Figures of the most beautiful, useful, and uncommon Plants, described in the Gardener's Dictionary. Exhibited on three Hundred Copper-plates, accurately engraven after Drawings taken from Nature. With the Characters of their Flowers and Seed Vessels, drawn when they were in their greatest Perfection. To which are added, their Descriptions, and an Account of the Classes to which they belong, according to Ray's, Tournefort's, and Linnæus's Method of classing them. By Philip Miller. Lond. 1760, folio, 2 vols. Published in numbers, no. l. appeared in 1755. Dent, pt. ll. 772, russ. 10l. 10s. North, pt. ll. 679, morocco, 16l. 10s. Roxburghe, 1757, 7l. 7s.—1771, folio, 2 vols. Garrick, 1617, with the Gardener's Dictionary, 1778, 5l. 17s. 6d. Nassau, pt. l. 2801, 4l. 4s.

Catalogus Plantarum officinalium quæ in Horto Botanico Chelseyano aluntur. Lond. 1730, 8vo. pp. 152 (U—U 4), exclusive of the dedication, and explanation of the abbreviations, with a front. of the entrance gate to the Garden.

The Gardener's Calendar. Twelfth edition. Lond. 1760, 8vo.

— Samuel, A.M. A brief Retrospect of the eighteenth Century. New York, 1805, 8vo. 6 vols.

A sketch of the revolutions and improvements in sciences, arts, and literature during that period.—Lond. 1805, 8vo. 3 vols.

— Vincent. The Man-plant : or, Scheme for increasing and improving the British Breed. Lond. 1751, 8vo. 4s.

— William. Pamphlets: *See* LAYCOCK, Wm. TOOKER, Chas.

— Wm. Biographical Sketches of British Characters deceased since the Accession of George IV. [1820], comprising 230 Subjects chronologically arranged, with a List of their engraved Portraits. Lond. 1826, 4to. 2 vols. 1l. 1s.

LARGE PAPER, elephant folio, printed for illustration, to admit the largest size whole-length engraved portraits. Twenty-five copies printed at 10l. The greater part of the impression was wasted. Present value, 3l. 3s.

MILLERS, Geo. A Description of the Cathedral Church of Ely; with some Account of the conventual Buildings. Lond. 1808, royal 8vo.

Townley, pt. ll. 716, 12s. 6d. Dent, pt. l. 1421, 3s. 6d. Dent, pt. l. 1422, russia, 4s. Hibbert, 5355, 4s. *Collation.*—Title and dedication to the Bp. Ely, 2 leaves; preface, 5 pages; table of contents and errata, 2 pages; introduction, description, and appendix, 175 pages. The volume contains ten plates, a list of which will be found on the reverse of the table of contents.—Third edition, 1834, royal 8vo, 1l. LARGE PAPER, 1l. 5s.

MILLES, Isaac, Rector of Highcleer, Hants. An Account of his Life and Conversation, with his Funeral Sermon. Lond. 1721, 8vo.

By Tho. Milles, Bishop of Waterford. Gough, 5337, 6s. 6d.

— Jer. Inscriptiones antiquæ a J. Milles et E. Pococke editæ. 1752, folio. See POCOCKE, E.

— Thomas. The Catalogve of Honor, or Treasvry of trve Nobility, pecvliar and proper to the Isle of Great Britaine. Wherevnto is prefixed, a Treatise of Nobility politicall and civill. Lond. 1610, folio.

An elaborate and judicious work, compiled from the collections of Robt. Glover, Somerset Herald. Folles 493-494. In most copies, are mutilated or supplied in manuscript—the following passage being cut out of the page relating to Charles Blount, Earl of Devonshire: 'Naturall children, which he had by Penelope, daughter to Walter Devereux Earle of Essex, and sister to Robert Earl of Essex, she being wife to Robert Baron Rich. Charles, Montjoy, Saint John, Elizabeth and another daughter.' Heber, 2355, 1l. 1s. Gough, 2478, 14s. 6d. Nassau, pt. i. 2607, with many of the arms coloured, 2l. 12s. 6d. LARGE PAPER. Sir M. M. Sykes, pt. ii. 276, russia, 21l. Collation.—Title, engraved by H. Elstracke, one leaf; epistle dedicatory, to the reader, and a table, sign. A, 4 leaves. 'Of Nobility political and civill,' sign. B to K, in sixes, after which is a single leaf, p. 241. Many of the pages are occupied by engravings, page 70 is blank, page 99 is erroneously marked 97, and page 100 contains 'Commilitonum Garteriani Ordinis habitus.' The Catalogue, A a–V v, in sixes, after which is a single leaf, page 241; Bbb–Aaaaaa, then Bbbbbb, 4 leaves, the last of which contains the errata. After sign. Qqqqq is a leaf containing duplicate pages 1029 and 1030. The paging throughout the volume is very inaccurate.

Nobilitas politica vel civilis. Lond. 1608, folio. Bindley, pt. ii. 1474, 2l. 2s. Brockett, 2087, 2l. 6s. Lloyd, 892, 19s. LARGE PAPER. Sir M. M. Sykes, pt. ii. 977, 2l. 3s. Heber, pt. i. 1l. 7s. Hibbert, 5454, 2l. 16s. Collation.—A. 4 leaves, A 1 blank; B–R, in sixes, after which is a single leaf commencing 'Efficienti.' Sign. G, 1, G 8, H 1, H 8, I 3, I 6, L 3, M 5, and R 3, are plates.

The Cvstomer's Alphabet and Primer, containing their Creed; with the Cvstomer's Apology. Lond. 1604, folio. Heber, pt. ii. with MS. notes by the author, 17s.

An Out-port Cvstomer's Account of all his Receiptes to a Shilling, without Concealment. Lond. 1608, folio. Heber, with MS. notes, 16s.

The Cvstomer's Replie, or second Apologie; that is to say, an Answer to a confused Treatise of publicke Commerce, printed and dispersed at Midlebourghe and London, in Favour of the private Society of Merchants-Adventurers. Lond. J. Roberts, 1604, folio. B—F 7, besides title and dedication to Lord Buckhurst, &c. 5 leaves. Puttick, June 10, 1858, 1l. 18s. See Cvstomer's Apology, CUSTOMS.

The Mysterie of Iniquitie, whereby the World may see, read and vnderstand the proud and vaine Comparison of a Cardinalles red Hat and a King's golden Crowne. No date (1618), folio. This tract was privately printed in the reign of K. James I. Bindley, pt. iii. 334, morocco, 10s. 6d. Hibbert, 5637, 17s.

The History of the Holy War, begun Anno 1095 by the Christian Princes of Europe against the Turks, for the Recovary of the Holy Land, and continued to 1294. Lond. T. Malthus, 1604, 16mo. plates.

MILLINERS.—The intriguing Milliners and Attornies Clerks, a mock Tragedy. Lond. 1738, 12mo.

An anonymous burlesque, written by — Robinson of Kendal. White Knights, 2091, 3s. Hibbert, 6089, 3s.

MILLINGEN, J. G., M.D. Curiosities of Medical Experience. Lond. 1837, 8vo. 2 vols.—Second edition, 1839, 8vo. 1 vol. 16s.

History of Duelling. Lond. 1841, 8vo. 2 vols. 16s.

There are several other works by this author, mostly on medical subjects.

— James, F.A.S. Ancient unedited Monuments, comprising Painted Greek Vases, Statues, Busts, Bas-Reliefs, and other Remains of Grecian Art. Two Parts, with 62 plates, mostly coloured. Lond. 1822, imp. 4to. pub. 9l. 9s. red. Bohn, 4l. 14s. 6d.

Recueil de quelques Medailles Grecques Inedites. Rome, 1812, 4to. 4 plates, 7s. 6d.

Peintures Antiques et Inedites de Vases Grecs. tirees de diverses Collections. Rome. 1813. Atlas folio, 63 plates in outline, 4l. 4s.

Peintures Antiques des Vases Grecs de la Collection de Sir John Coghill. Imp. folio. Rome, 1817, 52 plates, 4l. 4s.

Ancient unedited Coins of Greek Cities and Kings from various Collections principally in Great Britain. Lond. 1837, roy. 4to. 4 plates, 1l. 1s.

Considerations sur la Numismatique de l'Ancienne Italie. Florence, 1841, 8vo. 10s. 6d.

This learned and esteemed Antiquary has several papers in the Archæologia and other English Periodicals; he printed many pamphlets, &c., on early Art, principally abroad, where he resided on account of ill health.

See NAPOLEON MEDALS.

MILLOT, Abbé C. X. Elements of the History of England from the Invasion of the Romans to the Reign of George II. Translated by Mrs. Brooke. Lond. 1771, 12mo. 4 vols. 12s.

Two other translations appeared the same year, one by a Lady, in 12mo. 3 vols. the other by Kenrick, 8vo. 2 vols. Nassau, pt. I. 2256, &c.

Elements of general History, translated from the French of the Abbé Millot. Part I. Ancient History. Part II. Modern History.—1778, 8vo. 9 vols. Nassau, pt. I. 2257, 4s.—1779, 5 vols. Nassau, pt. I. 2258, 6s.—A new edition. Edinb. 1803, 12mo. 5 vols. 1l. 1s.—Edinb. 1823, 8vo. 6 vols. 15s.

MILLS, Charles. The Travels of Theodore Ducas, in various Countries in Europe, at the Revival of Letters and Arts. Edited by Chas. Mills. (Part the first, Italy, *all published*.) Lond. 1822, 8vo. 2 vols.

An amusing 'voyage imaginaire,' written with considerable spirit. Drury, 1256, 14s.

A History of Mohammedanism; comprising the Life of the Arabian Prophet, and succinct Accounts of the Empires founded by the Mahommedan Arms. Lond. 1817, 8vo. 12s.

History of the Crusades for the Recovery and Possession of the Holy Land. Lond. 1818, 8vo. 2 vols.—Second Edition. Lond. 1821, 8vo. 2 vols.—Fourth Edition. Lond. 1828, 8vo. 2 vols.

Traduit par Mons. Paul Tiby. Paris, 1835, 8vo. 5 vols.

History of Chivalry; or, Knighthood and its Times. Lond. 1825, 8vo. 2 vols. Hibbert, 5362, 17s.—Lond. 1828, 8vo. 2 vols.

— Henry, A.M. An Essay of Generosity and Greatness of Spirit. The Builders of Colleges, Hospitals, and Schools prais'd and commended. The invaluable Blessing of a sound, useful, and pious Education, especially that of School Learning: with a particular View to Archbp. Whitgift's Foundation at Croydon, Surrey. Lond. 1732. 8vo. 6s.

Pp. 1—lxiii (not including two title-pages); 1—xvi; table of contents, 4 pages, and the essay, 220 pages.

— Nicholas. The History of Mexico, also Observations as to working the Mexican Mines by British Capital, &c. 1824, 8vo. 10s. 6d.

MILMAN, Rev. Henry Hart, Dean of St. Paul's. Poetical and Dramatic Works. Lond. 1839.—1840, fscp. 8vo. 3 vols. 18s.

The Belvidere Apollo; a prize Poem, recited in the theatre. Oxf. 1812, 8vo.

Alexander tumulum Achillis invisens; poema cancellarii præmio donatum, et in theatro Sheld. recitatum, 1813. Oxf. 1813, 8vo.

Fazio: a Tragedy. Oxf. 1815, 8vo.—Second Edition.—Oxf. 1816, 8vo.

In Historia scribenda quænam præcipua inter auctores veteres et novos sit differentia? Oratio cancellarii præmio donata et in theatro Sheld. recitata, 1816. Oxf. 1816, 8vo.

A Comparative Estimate of Sculpture and Painting: a prize Essay, recited in the theatre, 1816. Oxf. 1816, 8vo.—Again, Lond. 1818.

Samor, Lord of the bright City. An heroic Poem. Lond. 1818, 8vo. pp. 374.

The Fall of Jerusalem, a dramatic Poem. Lond. 1820, 8vo.—Again, 1853.

The Martyr of Antioch. Lond. 1822, 8vo. pp. 168.

Belshazzar, a dramatic Poem. Lond. 1822, 8vo.

Poems; comprising the Belvidere Apollo; Fazio, a Tragedy, and other Poems. Lond. 1821. 8vo. 8s. 6d.

Anne Boleyn, a dramatic Poem. Lond. 1826, 8vo.

The Office of the Christian Teacher considered, in a Visitation Sermon on 1 Cor. xiv. 3. Oxf. 1826, 8vo.

History of the Jews. Lond. 1829–30, 12mo. 3 vols. In Murray's Family Library, 15s. The first edition contains some passages afterwards suppressed. Lond. Tegg, 1853, 10s. 6d.

Nala and Damayanti, and other Poems, translated from the Sanscrit. Oxf. 1834, 8vo. 12s.

Life of Edward Gibbon. Lond. 1839,
8vo. 9s.

History of Christianity, from the Birth
of Christ to the Abolition of Paganism in
the Roman Empire. Lond. 1840, 8vo.
3 vols. 1l. 16s.

History of Latin Christianity; including
that of the Popes to the Pontificate
of Nicolas V. Lond. 1854-5, 8vo. 6 vols.
3l. 16s.—Second edition, 1857, 6 vols. 3l. 12s.

Character and Conduct of the Apostles
considered as an Evidence of Christianity
(eight sermons preached at the Hampton
Lecture for 1827). Lond. 1828, 10s. 6d.

Dean Milman has written other Sermons,
and contributed articles to the
Quarterly Review, &c.

See GIBBON, Ed. HOBACE.

MILNE, Colin. A Botanical Dictionary.
Third edition, revised,
corrected, and very considerably
enlarged, illustrated by twenty-five
new plates. Lond. 1805, 8vo. plain
10s. coloured 15s.

Indigenous Botany; or Habitations of
English Plants; containing the Results
of several botanical Excursions chiefly in
Kent, Middlesex, and the adjacent Counties,
in 1790, 1791, and 1792. By Colin
Milne, LL.D. and Alexander Gordon.
Lond. 1793, 8vo. vol. i. 4s.

This divine also published some Sermons.

— Joshua. A Treatise on the
Valuation of Annuities and Assurances,
&c. Lond. 1815, 8vo. 2
vols. 1l. 10s.

MILNER, J. A practical Grammar
of the Greek Tongue. Lond.
1740, 8vo. 5s.

Best edition.

— John. Church History of
Palestine, from the Birth of Christ
to Diocletian. Lond. 1688, 4to.

— John, D.D. The History
civil and ecclesiastical, and Survey
of the Antiquities of Winchester.
Winchester (1798), 4to. 2 vols.

A performance which, notwithstanding
the Roman Catholic bias of the author,
will always keep its place among the few
standard works in English topography.
This first edition must claim the preference
as regards quality of paper and impressions
of the plates. Libbert, 5425, russia,
3l. 4s. Sir M. M. Sykes, pt. ii. 511, 2l. 12s.
Duke of York, 3579, 2l. 12s. Nassau, pt. ii.
163, russ. 3l. 6s. Towneley, pt. ii. 1124, with
some additional plates, 4l. 7s. 6d. LARGE
PAPER. Twelve copies printed. The se-

cond appendix, 1801, was never printed on
large paper. Dent, pt. ii. 733, uncut, 6l. 12s.
Baker, 473, russia, 13l. 2s.6d. Fonthill, 3352,
morocco, 13l. 13s. *Collation*.—Vol. I. Engraved
title-page, by J. Pass, after T. H.
Turner; dedication to the Countess Chandos Temple,
dated Ap. 6, 1798, 4 pages;
preface, pp. 5—19; contents, 5 pages;
history, part i. 451 pages. This volume
contains 4 plates, at pp. 41, 303, 433*, and
449. Vol. II. Engraved title-page, by J.
Pass after J. Cave; preface, 6 pages;
contents, 4 pages; part II. including appendix,
270 pages; index and errata, 5
pages. This volume contains 6 plates at
pp. 23, 59, 147, 177, 229, and 249.—The
SECOND EDITION corrected and enlarged.
Winchester, 1809, 4to. 2 vols. 3l. 6s. LARGE
PAPER. Beckford in 1817, 161, 3l. 6s.
Collation.—Vol. I. Engraved title-page;
dedication, 4 pages; advertisement and
direction for placing the plates, 2 pages;
preface, 16 pages; contents, 5 pages; description
of the plans, 1 page; history,
451 pages. This volume contains 5 plates.
Vol. II. Pp. 312, not including the title,
and 8 plates. Pages 137 to 144 are repeated,
and follow p. 174 for 172.—The
THIRD EDITION. Winchester, 1839, royal
8vo. 2 vols. 1l. 4s. LARGE PAPER, India
proofs, 2l. 4s.

Letters to a Prebendary; being an Answer
to Reflections on Popery, by the Rev.
J. Sturges, LL.D., with Remarks on the
Opposition of Hoadlyism to the Doctrines
of the Church of England, and on various
Publications occasioned by the late civil
and ecclesiastical History of Winchester.
By the Rev. John Milner. Winchester,
1800, 4to. Gosset, 3063, 10s.

A Letter to the Rev. John Milner, occasioned
by his false and illiberal Aspersions
on the Memory and Writings of Dr.
Benjamin Hoadly, formerly Bishop of
Winchester. By Robert Hoadly Ashe,
D.D. Lond. 1799, 8vo. 2s. 6d.

Reflections on the Principles and Institutions
of Popery, &c., &c., occasioned by
the Rev. John Milner's History of Winchester.
By John Sturges, D.D. Second
Edition, with Corrections and Additions.
Lond. 1800, 8vo. 6s.—1799, 4to. 5s.

End of Religious Controversy; or a
Friendly Correspondence between a Religious
Society of Protestants, and a Roman
Catholic Divine. Second edition,
revised and corrected. Lond. 1818, 8vo. 3
parts.—1824. Fifth Edition. This tract
was answered by Dr. Parr.

An historical and critical Inquiry into
the Existence and Character of Saint
George, Patron of England, of the Order
of the Garter, and of the Antiquarian Society;
in which the Assertions of Edward
Gibbon, Esq., History of Decline and Fall,
cap. 23; and of certain other modern

Writers, concerning this Saint, are discussed. Lond. 1795, 8vo.

A Dissertation on the modern Style of altering antient Cathedrals, as exemplified in the Cathedral of Salisbury. Lond. 1798, 4to. pp. 54, with a view of the monument of Bishop Poore, by J. Carter. Fonthill, 1258, 11s. Dent, pt. II. 734, 18s.—Lond. 1811, 8vo. 89 pp. with two plates.

An Inquiry into certain vulgar Opinions concerning the Catholic Inhabitants and the Antiquities of Ireland. Lond. 1808, 8vo. xl and 278 pp. also errata 1 leaf. Horne Tooke, 4701, date 1810, 12s. 6d.

A Treatise on the Ecclesiastical Architecture of England, during the Middle Ages. Lond. 1811, royal 8vo. with ten plates. An excellent and admirable little work. Drury, 2772, date 1810, russia, 12s. LARGE PAPER in 4to.

MILNER, Joseph. History of the Church of Christ. Lond. 1794, &c. 8vo. 5 vols.

An esteemed work.—1810, 8vo. 5 vols. Edwards, 763, 2l. 8s.—With Additions by Isaac Milner. 1819, 8vo. 5 vols.—1824, 8vo. 5 vols.—1834. Cadell, 8vo. 4 vols. 2l. 8s.—New edition, revised, with additional Notes, by the Rev. T. Grantham, D.D. Lond. 1847, 8vo. 4 vols. 2l. 12s. Red. Bohn, 1l. 1s.

For Continuations, see SCOTT, J. STEBBING, H.

There are several abridgments, of which the principal are: Lond. 1834, with continuation by the Rev. T. Hawels. Edinb. 1834, 8vo. in 1 vol. 10s. 6d. And one published in Seeley's Family Library, fcap. 8vo. 6s.

Practical Sermons; second edition, revised, with Life by the Rev. J. Milner, 1801-23, 8vo. 3 vols. 1l. 1s.

Tracts and Essays, theological and historical. Lond. 1810, 8vo. 12s.

MILNER OF ABINGDON.—A ryght pleasant and merye Historie of the Mylner of Abyngton, with his Wife and his fayre Daughter; and of two poore Scholers of Cambridge. Lond. by Rycharde Ihones. 4to.

A copy, consisting of eight leaves, is in the Bodleian Library. By Ant. à Wood attributed to Andrew Borde.

MILTON, John. The POETICAL WORKS of John Milton; with Notes of various Authors. The third Edition. With other Illustrations, and with some Account of the Life and Writings of Milton; derived principally from Documents in his Majesty's State-Paper Offices, now first published. By the Rev. H. J. Todd. Lond. 1826, 8vo. 6 vols.

This edition does not contain the Verbal Index to Milton's poetry, which is in that of 1809.—Todd's first edition. Lond. 1801, 8vo. 6 vols. LARGE PAPER. Bindley, with Life and Verbal Index by Todd added, 2l. 17s. White Knights, 2806, mor. 5l. 10s. Earl of Kerry, 834, with the Prose Works, 1806, together 14 vols. russia, 11l. 15s.—Lond. 1809, 8vo. 7 vols. (including the Verbal Index). Combe, 1333, 1l. 14s. LARGE PAPER, in imperial 8vo. Duke of York, 3567, 7l.—1842, 8vo. 4 vols. including a Glossarial, but not the Verbal Index.—Fifth edition. Lond. 1852, 8vo. 4 vols. 2l. 2s.

Other Editions of the Poetical Works.

Lond. Tonson, 1688, folio, (Par. Lost, Regained, and Samson Agonistes), portrait and plates. Christie's, July 1860, mor. 4l. 14s. 6d.—The same (with the Minor Poems). Lond. Tonson, 1695, folio. 2 vols. (sometimes in one) portrait by White, and plates. Bindley, pt. II. 539, 15s. A copy described as LARGE PAPER, is valued in a recent catalogue at 8l. 16s. 6d. See PARADISE LOST.

Lond. Tonson, 1705, royal 8vo. 2 vols. plates. The letter of Sir H. Wotton is given in this and the subsequent editions.

Lond. Tonson, 1707, 8vo. 2 vols. plates.

Lond. Tonson, 1711, 1715, 18mo. 2 vols. port. Utterson, mor. 16s. Much esteemed; contains an Index of principal matters, and rectifies some errors in the handsome editions of 1705, 1707.

Lond. 1720, 4to. 2 vols. Tickell's edition, with Addison's criticism on the Paradise Lost, and an Index of the principal matters. Splendidly printed. Edwards, 130, 17s. Roxburghe, 3391, 1l. Marquis of Townshend, 2369, 18s.

Lond. 1721, 12mo. 2 vols. With Addison's criticism on the Paradise Lost.

Lond. 1727, 8vo. 2 vols. Fenton's edition. Bindley, pt. II. 1541, 16s. Sotheby's in 1858, old morocco, 2l.

Lond. 1720, 8vo. 2 vols. Fenton's, with Addison's Criticism.

Poetical Works, with Addison's Notes, collected from the Spectator (136 pages, placed at end of the first volume), and an Index of Subjects; also 'a new set of handsome cuts.' Lond. printed in the year 1720 (apparently in Holland), 12mo. 2 vols. portrait, frontispiece, and 12 plates by Coster. 10s. 6d.

Lond. Tonson, 1746, 12mo. 4 vols. (Paradise Lost, 2 vols. Par. Regained, &c. 2 vols.) Very correct.

With Notes of various Authors, by Thomas NEWTON, Bp. of Bristol. Lond. 1749-52, 4to. 3 vols. Bindley, pt. III. 843, 2l. Dent, pt. II. 736, with Milton's prose Works, 1753, 2 vols. (together 5 vols.)

MILTON, John, POETICAL WORKS. morocco, 15l. 15s. Nassau, pt. ii. 16s, with Milton's Prose Works, 1753, 5 vols. russia, 13l. 13s. Williams, 102s. with Milton's Prose Works, 1753, 5 vols. morocco, 26l. 5s.—Lond. 1753, 8vo. 4 vols.—Third edition. Lond. 1734. 4to. 3 vols. plates, 2l. 2s. Sotheby, 1857, with Prose Works, 5 vols. old blue morocco, 10l. 10s. Another copy of same edition. Books 1. to ix. interleaved in 3 vols. and filled with MS. notes by Rcbt. Lord, Bp. Newton's nephew, (who died 1793), was sold at Lady Dacre's sale in 1835, 5l. 5s.—Lond. 1757, 8vo. 4 vols.—Lond. Tonson, 1761, 4to. 2 vols. Roxburghe, 5283, 2l. 12s. 6d. Stanley, 401, russia, 4l. 14s. 6d. Steevens, 905, with Milton's Prose Works, 1753, 5 vols. in blue turkey, 14l. 15s.

Poetical Works by Newton. New Edition. Lond. 1763, 8vo. 4 vols.—Lond. 1766, 8vo. 4 vols.—Lond. 1770, 8vo. 4 vols.—Lond. 1773, 8vo. 4 vols.—Lond. 1775, 4to. 3 vols. Heath, 1644, 2l. 5s.—Eighth edition, Lond. 1778, 8vo. 4 vols. White Knights, 2604, 1l. 16s.—Ninth edition. Lond. 1790, 8vo. 4 vols. 2l. 2s.

Dublin, 1752, 8vo. 2 vols.

With a Glossary, Edinb. 1732, 8vo. 2 vols. Lond. 1753, 12mo. 2 vols.

With a Critique on Paradise Lost by Addison, a Preface, in which are inserted Characters of the several Pieces, a Glossary, and a Life of Milton. Edinb. 1755, small 8vo. 2 vols.

Birmingham, Baskerville, 1758, royal 8vo. 2 vols. Bindley, pt. ii. 1562, russia, 2l. 16s. Baker, 417, 2l. 5s. Willett, 1708, 2l. 11s. Utterson, in 1852, 2l. 4s.

Birmingham, Baskerville, 1759, 4to. 2 vols. Roxburghe, 3393, morocco, 2l. 10s. White Knights, 2754, morocco, 5l. 4s.

Birmingham, Baskerville, 1760, 8vo. 2 vols. Marquis of Townshend, 2068, 1l. 2s. Garrick, 1821, ruled with red lines, and bound in morocco, 5l. 10s.

Edinburgh, Donaldson, 1762, 8vo. 2 vols. with Life and Glossary; plates by Phinn, 1l. 1s.—Edinb. 1767, 12mo. 2 vols.—Edinb. 1772, sm. 8vo. 2 vols.

With Life and Glossary. Lond. 1778, 12mo. 4 vols.

Poetical Works of John Milton, with a Life of the Author by William Hayley. Lond. 1794, 5, 7, imp. folio, 3 vols. Boydell's magnificent edition, with plates after Westall, published at 15l. 15s. By many thought to be the finest production of Mr. Bulmer's press. Duke of York, 3419, morocco, 6l. 15s. Bindley, pt. ii. 833, 7l. 7s. Willet, 1553, morocco, 11l. Dent, pt. ii. 774, morocco, 12l. 12s. Marquis of Townshend, illustrated, russ. 42l. Foot, bill, 3018, 32l. 11s. Pacori. Roxburghe, 5396, morocco, 21l.

London, 1796, 8vo. 2 vols. 18s. Elegantly printed by Bensley, Bindley, pt.

ii. 1544, 1l. 5s. LARGEST PAPER, Stanley, 402, morocco by Roger Payne, 8l. 12s. 6d. With additional plates from Westall's edition, &c. 2 vols. 8vo. blue morocco. Sotheby's, 1829, 3l. 13s. 6d.

The Poetical Works, from the Text of Newton, with a critical Essay by J. Aikin, M.D. London, 1801, small 8vo. 4 vols. with portrait and plates. — 1805, am. 8vo. 2 vols.—1805, 18mo. 3 vols.

Poetical Works, from the Text of the Rev. H. J. Todd, with a critical Essay by J. Aikin. Lond. Cadell, 1808, 12mo. 4 vols. port. and plates after Rigaud, 1l. 1s.

Poetical Works, edited by Thomas Park. Lond. 1803. 18mo. 4 vols. Sharpe's pocket edition, with engravings after Westall.

The Poetical Works, with his Life by Samuel Johnson, Ll.D., and Remarks by John Aikin, M.D. Lond. Sharpe, 1820, fcap. 8vo. 3 vols. LARGE PAPER.

With Notes by W. Cowper; edited by Hayley. Chichester, 1810, 4 vols. post 8vo. with portraits. Hollis, 841, 1l. 11s.

With Westall's Plates, (including the Latin Poems and Translations). Lond. 1816-17, 4 vols. 16mo. 1l. 2s.; or LARGE PAPER, 4 vols. 12mo. 1l. 8s. (Published separately: Paradise Lost, 2 vols. Paradise Regained and Minor Poems, 2 vols.) Lond. 1817, 8vo. 2 vols. With Stothard and Westall's Plates.

Poetical Works (Paradise Lost, with Fenton's Life and Dr. Johnson's Criticism; Paradise Regained and Minor Poems, with Notes adjoined). Lond. 1817, 8vo. 2 vols. plates by Fittler and Heath, 1l. 1s.

With biographical Sketch by John Byerley. Paris, Lefevre, 1822, 24mo. 3 vols. 9s.

With Notes of various Authors, selected and edited by Edward Hawkins. M.A.; to which is added, Newton's Life of Milton. Oxford, 1824, 8vo. 4 vols. 1l. 12s.

Poetical Works, with Cowper's Translations of the Latin and Italian Poems, and Life of Milton by his nephew, E. Phillips (with an Introduction by J. F., i.e. Joseph Parkes, Esq.). Lond. Pickering, 1826, crown 8vo. 3 vols. portrait, 1l. 7s.

Edited by J. H. Lake, Esq. Paris, 1827, 24mo. 3 vols.

Lond. Pickering, 1832, 12mo. 3 vols. portrait. The Aldine edition, with Life by the Rev. John Mitford, 15s.—Again, Pickering, 1851, 3 vols. 12mo. 15s.

With Notes and Translations by W. Cowper, and Life by W. Hayley. Lond. 1835, post 8vo. 4 vols.

Edited, with Notes and a Life, by Sir Egerton Brydges. Lond. 1835, &c., fcap. 8vo. 6 vols. port. and 12 engravings after J. M. W. Turner, 1l. 10s.—New edition, in 1 vol. 8vo. Lond. Tegg, 1842, with portrait and 6 plates after Turner, 16s.—Reprinted, 1849, 16s.

MILTON, John, POETICAL WORKS.
By Sir John Egerton Brydges; a small
edition, with portrait and 12 engravings
after Turner, but without notes. Lond.
Tegg, 1839, 12mo. 8s. 6d. Frequently reprinted.

Poetical Works, with a Memoir, and 7 Embellishments by Fuseli, Westall, and Martin. Lond. Charton, 1841, 8vo. 12s. Reprinted Lond. Bohn, 1853, and since, 6s.

With Memoir and critical Remarks by James Montgomery, illustrated with 120 engravings on wood by Thompson, Williams, and Orrin Smith. Lond. Tilt and Bogue, 1843; and again, 1858, 8vo. 2 vols. pub. 1l. 4s. red. Bohn, 14s. Of this beautiful edition (1843) two copies were printed on INDIA PAPER, at 10l. 10s.

With Life and Notes by Dr. Stebbing; to which is prefixed Dr. Channing's Essay on Milton. Lond. Bohn, 1840, fcap. 12mo. 3s. 6d.

Poetical Works, with Notes and a Life of the Author. Boston, U. S. 1845, royal 8vo. 2 vols. 1l. 1s. This is a verbatim reprint of Pickering's Aldine edition of 1832.

Poetical Works, printed from the original editions, with a Life of the Author by the Rev. John Mitford. Lond. Pickering, 1851, royal 8vo. 2 vols. (The first two volumes of Mitford's edition of the works printed off separately on LARGE PAPER.)

With Life of the Author, Preliminary Dissertation on each Poem, Notes critical and explanatory, and Index, by C. J. Cleveland. Philadelphia, 1853, post 8vo. 10s. 6d.

Poetical Works, with Notes by Thomas Keightley. Lond. 1859, 8vo. 2 vols. 1l. 4s. To this may be added, Keightley's Life of Milton, 1859, which are under *Miltoniana*.

There are various other editions, of which several are published in Series of the British Poets; among the more recent is that edited by Gilfillan. Edinb. 1853, 8vo. 2 vols.

— Paradise Lost. A Poem Written in TEN BOOKS. By *JOHN MILTON*. Licensed and Entred according to Order. London; Printed, and are to be sold by *Peter Parker* under *Creed* Church, near *Aldgate*. And by *Robert Boulter* at the *Turks Head* in *Bishopsgate Street*, and *Matthias Walker*, under *St. Dunstons* Church, in *Fleet street*, 1667, 4to.

MILTON, John, PARADISE LOST.
FIRST TITLE-PAGE OF THE FIRST EDITION, 171 leaves. The author's name is in *italic* capitals. The Poem immediately follows the title-page, without the 7 preliminary leaves containing the arguments, list of errata, etc. which were afterwards added. Some of these errata appear to have been corrected in a few sheets while they were passing through the press, and probably some leaves were cancelled and reprinted. Bibl. Anglo-Poet. 449, russia, 5l. 5s. Libbert, 557l, with Paradise Regained, 1631, and Poems, 1645 and 1673, 4 vols. russia, 8l. 10s. Dent, pt. II. 735, with portrait of Milton by Faithorne inserted, in morocco by Roger Payne, 4l. Hindley, pt. III. 244, with an extra title-page dated 1668, original binding, 8l. 8s. Hemble. Utter, 134. Sotheby, Aug. 1858, 5l. 5s. Puttick, July, 1860, 9l. 5s.

Second title-page (1667). In this the name " JOHN MILTON" is much smaller than in the preceding.

It should be observed, that although this variation is placed as the second state, it is just as likely to be the first, as there is no evidence to the contrary. The sale prices, therefore, which are quoted to what we describe as the first title may in some instances belong to the second; as before Lowndes pointed out the distinctions no particular attention had been paid to them.

Third title-page (1668). Paradise Lost. A Poem in TEN BOOKS. The Author J. M. (*initials only*). Licensed and Entred according to Order. Lond.; Printed and are to be sold by *Peter Parker*, &c. as before. 4to. 1668. Hollis, 921, 14. 2s. Nassau, pt. II. 170, 1l. 1s. Freeling, 8l. 13s. 6d. Holland, July, 1860, 4l. 10s. Mitford, ll. 2531, portrait by Faithorne inserted, 9l. 15s.

Fourth title-page (1668). Paradise Lost, a Poem in ten Books. The Author *JOHN MILTON*. Lond.; Printed by S. Simmons, and are to be sold by S. Thomson, at the Bishop's Head, in Duck Lane, H. Mortlack, at the White Hart, in Westminster Hall, M. Walker, under St. Dunston's Church, in Fleet Street, and R. Boulter, at the Turk's Head, in Bishopsgate Street, 1668, 4to. In this variation there is a fleur-de-lis ornament of four lines under the author's name. Immediately after the title are prefixed, for the first time, 7 preliminary leaves, containing: the address of the Printer (S. Simmons), to the Reader *in three lines*, the Arguments, the Verse, and Errata. Stanley, 403, with the Paradise Regained and Samson Agonistes, 1671, first edition, morocco, 4l. 14s. 6d. Singer, 1860, 4l. 10s.

MILTON, John, PARADISE LOST.
Fifth title-page (1668). Paradise Lost, a Poem in ten Books, the Author ,*, John Milton. ,*, London, printed by S. Simmons, &c. 1668. 4to. Prefixed are the address of The Printer to the Reader, the Argument, and errata, 7 leaves.

Sixth title-page (1669). Same as the fifth, excepting that there are no stars on the title-page, and the printer's address to the reader consists of five lines instead of three. Bibl. Anglo-Poet. No. 450, 3l. 3s.

The following prices apply equally to the variations dated 1668: Bibl. Anglo-Poet. 431, 3l. 3s. Sir M. M. Sykes, pt. II. 513, with 2 portraits inserted, 1l. 2s. Hollis, 925, 1l. 5s. Stanley, 404, 2l. 14s. Bindley, pt. III. 345, 1l. 1s. Sir M. M. Sykes, pt. III. 83, 1l. 10s. Reeves, 1353, 3l. 7s.

Seventh title-page (1669). Paradise lost, a POEM, IN TEN BOOKS. The Author JOHN MILTON. LONDON. Printed by S. Simmons, and are to be sold by T. Helder, at the Angel in *Little Britain*. 1669. Date at foot of page, in centre, instead of at end of previous line. Contains the address of the Printer to the Reader (in some copies the *three line* address, in others the *five line*), Arguments, Errata, etc. as before. Gancia, at Sotheby's, June, 1860, unbound, 4l. 6s.

In some copies bearing what we here distinguish as the seventh title there are three variations in the last page of Book 8, viz., I. having the top line numbered 740, and *will* instead of *is* in the penultimate line. II. Having the top line numbered 740, but the correct word *is*. III. The top line not numbered, the penultimate line numbered 750, and the word *is* correct.

Eighth title-page (1669). The same as before, excepting that the word *Angel* on the title-page is in italic, and there is a comma instead of a full stop after the word Brittain. It contains the 7 preliminary leaves, but without the Printer's Address to the Reader. All these leaves, as well as the last two of the poem, appear to have been reprinted. The penultimate line of the Errata has lib. 2 instead of lib. 6.

The following prices apply equally to the variations dated 1669:—Hollis, 926, 1l. 5s. Towneley, pt. II. 1116, 16s. 6d. Hibbert. 5540, 1l. Bindley, pt. III. 346, 10s. Sir M. M. Sykes, pt. III. 84, 1l. 4s. Caldecott, 1f. 17s. Dilke, 3l. 3s. Utterson, in 1852, morocco, 4l. 10s. Gardner, 4l. 6s. Skegg, 1l. 10s. Bright, 1l. 13s. Bibl. Anglo-Poet. 451, 2l. 6s. Pickering, with autograph, a verse in Latin by Milton, and facsimile of Agreement, 18l.

PARADISE LOST, a Poem in twelve books. The Author John Milton. THE SECOND EDITION, Revised and Augmented by the same Author. Lond. S. Simmons, &c., 1674, small 8vo. *Portrait by Dolle, and the commendatory verses of Barrow and Marvell.* The First Edition in which the poem was divided into XII Books. Bindley, pt. II. 1545, 1l. Hollis, 842, 1l. 1s.—New title. 1675, 8vo. Hollis, 843, 18s. 6d.

Third Edition, augmented by the same author. Lond. 1678, 8vo. Bindley, pt. II. 1546, 8s. Caldecott, 7s. Pickering, morocco, 18s. Singer, portrait inserted, 2l. 16s.

Fourth Edition. Lond. Tonson, 1688, folio. THE FIRST ILLUSTRATED EDITION. Portrait by White, and other plates. Published by subscription under the patronage of Lord Somers and Bishop Atterbury. Prefixed is a list of more than 500 subscribers, among whom are all the most distinguished characters of that period. The Paradise Regained and Samson Agonistes of same date often accompany this edition, and have a title of Poetical Works. Roscoe, 1384, 2l. 12s. Bindley, pt. II. 634, 1l. 10s.

Paradise Lost [and Regained.] Lond. 1692, folio. with cuts. Lond. Tonson, 1696, folio, with cuts.

Paradise Lost. Lond. 1695, folio. With copious and learned notes or commentary by P[atrick] H[ume] and with a table of the most remarkable parts of the poem, under the three heads of Descriptions, Similes, and Speeches. Sir P. Thompson, 586, 10s. 6d. To this Commentary subsequent editors, "apprehending no danger of detection from a work rarely inspected, and too pedantic and cumbersome to attract many readers, have been often amply indebted, without even the most distant hint of acknowledgment." This volume of annotations has a distinct title, and sometimes occurs as a separate volume. Lond. Tonson, 1695.

The Paradise Regained, with Samson Agonistes, of same date or 1668; and Poems on several Occasions, of same date, sometimes accompany this edition of the Paradise Lost, and with it form ' the Poetical Works,' under a general title. *See* p. 1555.
Lond. 1705, 8vo. A handsome, but incorrect edition. LARGE PAPER. Williams, with the Paradise Regained, same date, morocco, 4l. 14s. 6d.

Lond. Tonson, 1711, 18mo. portrait and plates. This pocket edition is much esteemed. Annexed is an index of the principal matters. Stanley, 405, 3l. 3s. White Knights, 2906, Addison's copy, 3l. Williams, 1201, on thick paper, morocco, 8l. 10s.—With the ' Paradise Regained, &c., 1718. Bindley, pt. II. 1547, 2 vols. 1l. 11s. 6d. Reed, 7038, 2 vols. 13s. 6d. Dent, morocco by Roger Payne, 2l. 6s.

Lond. Tonson, 1719, 12mo. portrait and plates.

MILTON, John, PARADISE LOST.
Dublin, Grierson, 1784, 8vo. portrait and plates. White Knights, 2807, morocco, 13s. Bindley, pt. ii. 1546, 10s. 6d. Hollis, 844, with the Paradise Regained, 1l. 2s.

Lond. Tonson, 1725, 8vo. Elijah Fenton's first edition, to which is prefixed a life, and portrait. Hollis, 845, 12s. 6d.

Edited by Richard Bentley, D.D. Lond. 1732, 4to. Portrait by Vertue. The text of this edition is interpolated, but there are some notes which render it valuable. It was severely attacked by Bp. Pearce and others. Bindley, pt. III. 847, 5s. 6d. Hollis, 927, 10s. 6d. LARGE PAPER, royal 4to. Lond. Tonson, 1737, 8vo.

Lond. Tonson, 1738, with Life by Elijah Fenton, plates. A copy, with autograph of S. Rogers, "presented to his early friend and schoolfellow, W. Maltby." Sotheby, 1755, 1l. 10s.

Lond. Tonson, 1746, 12mo. 2 vols. An edition printed with great correctness.

Dublin, 1747, royal 8vo. Hawkey's edition, very handsomely printed, and highly valued for its accuracy. Bindley, pt. ii. 1542, with the Paradise Regained of 1752, 2 vols. 15s. LARGE PAPER? Sir M. M. Sykes, pt. ii. 439, russia, 2l. Stanley, 408, russia, 1l. 6s.

Compared and revised by John Hawkey. Dublin, 1748, 8vo. 'Printed on Irish paper.'

With Notes of various Authors, by Thomas Newton, Bishop of Bristol. Lond. 1749, 4to. 2 vols. With cuts designed by Hayman. Published at the expense of the Earl of Bath. To this edition is usually added Bp. Newton's edition of Paradise Regained, and other Poems, 1752, forming together 3 vols. 4to. 3l. 8s. —1750, in 8vo. 2 vols.—Dublin, J. Exshaw, 1751, 8vo. 2 vols.—Lond. 1753, 8vo. 2 vols. or with the Paradise Regained, &c., of same date, 4 vols. 8vo. 2l. 2s. For other of Newton's editions, see Poetical Works, pp. 1555-6.

Book the first (of Paradise Lost). Glasgow, 1750, 4to. With notes and references to the Ancient Poets. This excellent publication has been attributed by some to Dr. Gillies, by others, more justly, to Mr. Callander. It is to be lamented that no more appeared. Bindley, pt. iii. 848, 7s. 6d. Hollis, 928, 17s. See MILTONIANA, p. 1568.

Paradise Lost, Glasgow, 1750, 12mo. Lloyd, 863, 4s. White Knights, 2808, 10s. Stanley, 407, 1l. 11s. 6d.

Lond. Tonson, 1751, 8vo. Life by Fenton, portrait and plates, 8s.

With Notes selected from Bentley, Pearce, Addison, Newton, and others, by John Marchant, Gent. Lond. 1751, 12mo. 2 vols. plates.

Lond. Tonson, 1753, 24mo.
Lond. Griffiths, 1760, 12mo.

1763, 12mo. An edition edited by the famous John Wesley, M.A., 'curtailed of its proportion,' but with a very good intention.

With Notes of various Authors, by John Ross. Lond. 1766, 8vo.

Glasgow, Robert and Andrew Foulis, 1770, folio. pp. 484. Bibl. Anglo-Poet. 452, russia, 2l. 2s. A copy was sold at Sotheby's in 1856, "with a MS. interlinear translation into Italian by Guido Sorelli, for Tommaso Lillington," russia, 8l. 8s.

Lond. 1770, 12mo.

Paradise Lost and Paradise Regained, with Notes translated from the French of Raymond de St. Maur, and various critical Remarks from Addison, &c. 1755, 8vo. Lieber, pt. i. 7s. A new Edition. Lond. 1775, small 8vo. 2 vols.

Paradise Lost, illustrated with Texts of Scripture, by John Gillies, D.D. Lond. 1762, small 8vo. 3s. 6d.—Second edition, with additions. Lond. 1793, small 8vo.—Third edition. Lond. 1804, 12mo.

Several small editions of Paradise Lost, without any particular merit, appeared about this date.

Lond. 1790, 18mo. Stanley, 408, morocco, 1l. 8s.

Paradise Lost, printed from the first and second Editions collated. The original System of Orthography restored; the Punctuation corrected and extended. With various Readings; and Notes, chiefly rhythmical. By Capel Lofft, Esq. Books i and 2. Bury St. Edmund's, 1792-3, 4to. A learned preface, and an appendix are prefixed to the first book. Lieber, pt. i. 4664, 3s.

Lond. 1794, 4to. An elegant edition with portrait and 24 plates by Richter, of which 12 are vignettes on the letter-press. Pub. 4l. 4s. Roxburghe, 8394, 1l. 16s.

Lond. 1795, 8vo. FINE PAPER. Dent, pt. 1424, morocco, by Roger Payne, 2l.

Lond. 1796, with notes and Life by Johnson, port. and 12 plates by Heath, from designs by Corbould, 2 vols. in 1, roy. 8vo. 15s.

Paradise Lost, to which is prefixed the celebrated Critique by Samuel Johnson, LL.D., with a Sketch of the Life and Writings of Milton by the Rev. John Evans, A.M. Lond. 1799, royal 8vo. with engravings.

Lond. 1803, crown 8vo. 2 vols. Dorovetay's edition with plates. LARGE PAPER, in royal 8vo. with proof plates. Sir M. M. Sykes, pt. ii. 434, morocco, 2l. 10s. Strettell, 860, with additional proof plates from Westall's designs, morocco, 3l. 13s. 6d.

Lond. 1802, royal 8vo. Hepplestall's elegant edition, with plates by Bartolozzi, from pictures by Fuseli and Hamilton, 1l. 11s. 6d.

MILTON, John, PARADISE LOST.
Lond. Cundee, 1804, with an abridgment of the Notes of Bishop Newton, additions and Life by the Rev. John Evans. 12mo. 2 vols. plates. FINE PAPER, post 8vo.
Lond. 1809, post 8vo. with fine plates.
Paradise Lost, with Illustrations by John Martin. Lond. S. Prowett, 1825-7. Colombier 8vo. 2 vols. with 24 engravings (8 in. by 5½), published in numbers at 6l. 6s. Another edit. in imp. 4to. 2 vols. with 24 engravings on a larger scale (10½ in. by 7½), pub. at 10l. 10s. Of this edit. 50 copies were taken off in imp. fol. with proof plates. Pub. at 25l. 4s. Stowe, (in 1 vol.) 8l. 10s. The large plates were also pub. separately in a portfolio. Prints, 5l. 5s.; proofs, 10l. 10s.; now sold for less than half.
Martin's 24 Illustrations were subsequently used in a one-volume edition. Lond. Washbourne, 1849, 1853, imp. 8vo. and imp. 4to. The plates retouched.
'Lond. Pickering, 1830, 48mo. frontis. by Stothard, smallest edition ever printed.
Lond. 1840, 8vo. with copious notes, partly selected and partly original, by J. Prendeville, M.A.—17l. Esteemed.
Paradise Lost, and other Poetical Works, 7 engravings on steel, after Martin, Westall, and Fuseli. Lond. Charton, 1841, 8vo. 12s.—New edit. Bohn, 1848, 5s.
Milton's Paradise Lost, with notes critical and explanatory, selected and original, for Schools, by the Rev. J. R. Major, D.D. Lond. 1843, post 8vo. 7s. 6d.
Paradise Lost, with Memoir by James Montgomery, and variorum notes, selected by H. G. Bohn, and a complete Index. 1850, post 8vo. nearly 100 wood engravings, 5s.
Par. Lost, the first four Books, with Notes for Schools, by C. W. Connon. Lon. 1859, 5s.
Selections from Par. Lost, with Notes for Schools, by R. Dawson. Edinb. 1859, 18mo. 1s. 6d.

Imitations, Paraphrases, &c. of Par. Lost.
Paradise Lost imitated in Rhyme, in the 4th, 6th, and 9th Books, by John Hopkins. Lond. 1699, 8vo.
A Paraphrase in Verse, on Part of the first Book of Milton's Paradise Lost, by W. Howard. Lond. 1738, 4to. The titlepage was varied, as the author, an aged and infirm man, in order to relieve his wants, circulated his paraphrase by printing on every titlepage an address to some distinguished person.
Paradise Lost, attempted in Rhime. Book I. Lond. 1740, 8vo.
The State of Innocence, and Fall of Man, described in Milton's Paradise Lost. Render'd into Prose, with Notes, &c., from the French of Raymond de St. Maur, by a Gentleman of Oxford. Lond. 1745, 8vo.
A new Version of (the first Book of the) Paradise Lost; or Milton paraphrased with Annotations. By a Gentleman of Oxford (G. Smith Green). Lond. 1756, 8vo. For a criticism on this version, see D'Israeli's Curios. of Lit., under 'Literary Follies.'
The first six Books of Paradise Lost, rendered into grammatical Construction by James Buchanan. Edinb. 1773, 8vo. Heber, pt. I. 4s.
Paradise Lost, illustrated in a series of 54 fine outlines, by J. Flaxters, sculptor. Lond. 1851, royal fol. pub. 5l. 5s. reduced 1l. 5s.
Martin's Illustrations of the Paradise Lost, 24 plates. See previous column.

Translations, &c. of Paradise Lost.
Paradisus Amissus, Poema heroicum. Liber primus. Lond. T. Dring. 1686, 4to. Heber, pt. I. 1s. 6d. A dedication to Sir Thomas Mompesson is prefixed, signed J. C. The imprim. Nov. 18, 1685.
Paraphrasis Poetica in tria Johannis Miltoni, Viri clarissimi, Poemata, viz. Paradisum Amissum, Paradisum Recuperatum, et Samsonem Agonisten. Auctore Gulielmo Hogæo. Lond. 1690, 8vo. Roth. 1699, 8vo.
Paradisi Amissi Liber primus, ex Anglicana Lingua in Latinam conversus. Cantab. 1691, 4to. The dedication is signed by T. P., who is said to be Thomas Power of Trin. Coll. Cambridge. His translation into Latin verse of the remaining books exists in manuscript. See Peck's Memoirs of Milton, p. 68.
Paradisus Amissus, Poema Anglicè scriptum à Johanne Milton, nunc autem ex Auctoris Exemplari Latine redditum, per M. B(old, Aul. Trin. Cant. Soc.). Liber primus. Lond. 1702, 8vo. Of this specimen two other title-pages were printed of the dates 1708 and 1717. It was reprinted in 1736, 4to. Bright, 4s. 6d.
Paradisus Amissus interprete Jos. Trapp. 1740—44, 4to. 2 vols.
Part of the fourth Book of Paradise Lost, translated into Latin Hexameters by John Theobald, dedicated to Francis Douce, M.D., grandfather of the late Fr. Douce, Esq. Lond. n. d., 4to.
Paradisus Amissus, Poema Latine redditum à Guilielmo Dobson, LL. B. Oxon. 1750—1753, 4to. 2 vols. This admirable translation was encouraged by Mr. Benson, who had erected in Westminster Abbey the monument to the Poet. Oldys, in his manuscript notes on Langbaine's Dramatick Poets, says that Dobson's reward was to be a thousand pounds, when the translation should be finished, with the interest of that sum while he was performing it. 'It is more to the original, both in sense and spirit, than any other poetical version of length I have seen.'—Dr. Beattie.
Paradisi Amissi Liber primus, Græcè, a Stratford; cum celebri Versione Latinâ Rev. Gulielmi Dobson. Dublin, 1770.

MILTON, John, PARADISE LOST. 4to. Dindley, pt. III. 858, 2s. Dedicated to the then Bishop of Derry. Proposals for printing a Greek version were put forth by Richard Dawes in 1736, but he never proceeded with the undertaking.

Il Paradiso perduto, tradotto in versi sciolti da Paolo Rolli. Lond. 1735 or 1736, folio, pp. 397, besides, Varie Lezioni et Emendazioni, 4 pp. also title, dedication to Frederick, Prince of Wales, and Life of Milton, 13 leaves; portraits of John Milton, Paoli Rolli and Frederick Prince of Wales. Some copies on large blue paper. —Paris, 1760, 12mo. 2 vols.—Verona, 1742, folio. LARGE PAPER. A copy on VELLUM is said to be preserved in England.

Il Paradiso Perduto, tradotto in Versi Italiani da Felice Mariottini. Lond. 1794, 8vo. The first book only, with the life of Milton, and Addison's criticism; to both which, additions are subjoined: and copious annotations.

Il Paradiso Perduto, tradotto in Versi Italiani da Felici Mariottini. Lond. 1796, 8vo. The whole Poem, in two parts. Heber, pt. II. 2s. 6d. Other editions.

Paradiso Perduto, recato in versi Italiani da Mich. Leoni. Pisa, 1817, 8vo. 3 vols.

There are several other Italian translations, e. g.: By Papi, Lucca, 1811, 8vo. 3 vols.—Reprinted, Lucca, 1817, 18mo. 2 vols; and Milan, 1827, 74mo. 3 vols.—In verse, with the English text, by G. S. Martinengo. Venez. 1801.—In verse, by L. A. Corner. Venez. 1818, 2 vols.—By G. C. Cunso. Roma, 1822.—By Polidori. Lond. 1812, 12mo. 3 vols. 16s.—By Sorelli. Lond. 1832, 8vo. 1l. 1s.

Le Paradis Perdu, traduit par J. Delille. avec le Texte Anglais. Paris, 1804, 8vo. 3 vols. plates. LARGE PAPER, 3 vols. royal 4to. Two copies on VELLUM.

Le Paradis Perdu de Milton, avec des Notes et des Remarques d' Addison, trad. par Racine fils. Paris, 1755, 12mo. 3 vols. Very literal.

Le Paradis Perdu, en Anglais et en Français (la traduction par Nic. F. Dupré de St. Maur). Paris, 1799, 4to. 2 vols. coloured plates. First published, Paris, 1729, 12mo. 3 vols. Another edition, in 4 vols. Both frequently reprinted. The translation is by some attributed to the Abbé de Boismorand. It is less exact but more elegant than that by Racine.

There are several other French translations, e.g.: By Mouneron. Paris, 1804, 12mo. 2 vols. (first pub. 1788).—By M. Salgues. Paris, 1807, 8vo.—In verse, by M. Daloynes d'Autroche, 1808, 8vo. — In verse, by J. V. A. Delatour de Pernes. Paris, 1813, 8vo. — By Chateaubriand. Paris, 1836, 8vo. 2 vols. By Pongerville, Paris, Charpentier, 1850, 12mo.

Paradise Lost, translated into Welch by Pughe. 1819, 12mo. 7s.

Das Verlustige Paradies, in Teutsch durch E. G. von Berge. Zerbst, 1682, 8vo. Printed at the author's own expense.

Milton's Verlornes Paradies, übers. von Zacharia. Altona, 1762, 8vo. 2 vols.

Milton's Verlornes Paradies, ein episches Gedicht übersetzt von Rodmer. Zurich, 1769 and 1780, 8vo. 2 vols.

Verl. Parrdies, übers. von Bürde. Berl. 1702, 8vo. 2 vols.—Again, Breslau, 1823.

Milton's Paradys Verlooren. (In Dutch blank verse, translated by Theod. Haak.) Haarlem, 1729, 4to.

Het Paradys Verlooren, door L. P. (A translation into Dutch rhyme.) Amst. 1730, 8vo.

El Paraiso Perdido, trad. por D. Ramon de Hermida. Madrid, 1814, 8vo. 2 vols.

Paraiso Perdido, trad. en verso castellano por J. D. Escoiquiz. Bourges, 1812, 8vo. 3 vols.

Paraizo Perdido, traduzido em vulgar (portug.) por Jose Amaro de Silva, com o Paraiso restaurado. Lisboa, 1789, 8vo. 2 vols.

Paradise Lost, in Armenian, by Dr. P. Aucher. Ven. 1824, 8vo.

It has also been translated into Russian, Swedish, and Icelandic.

See TODD'S Milton, 1812, at end of vol. 4.

— PARADISE REGAIN'D, a Poem in four Books. To which is added SAMSON AGONISTES. The Author John Milton. Lond. printed by J. M. for John Starkey, 1671, 8vo. with a leaf preceding title, "Licens'd July 2, 1670."

FIRST EDITIONS of both pieces. White Knights, 9755, 1l. 1s. Heath, 1839, 1l. 5s. Roscoe, 1385, 1l. 5s. Hollis, 851, 14s. 6d. Heber, pt. v. 12s. Skegg, port. by Marshall inserted, 1l. 18s. Pickering, mor. 2l. 12s. 6d. Singer, port. inserted, 2l. 12s. A copy described as THICK PAPER, but Query, as they are all thick. Sotheby's, Aug. 19, 1856. Gardiner, 1l. 8d. no port.

Lond. 1680, 8vo. Bindley, pt. II. 1654, 6s. Jadis, 127, 7s. Nassau, pt. 1. 2268, 7s. Hollis, 852, 11s. Sotheby, Aug. 19, 1858, 19s. Pickering, mor. 17. Singer, 1736, 1l. 11s.

Lond. 1688, folio. This edition generally accompanies the Paradise Lost of the same date.

Paradise Regained, Samson Agonistes and the smaller Poems. Sixth edition, with explanatory notes upon each Book, and a table never before printed. Lond. 1695, folio. This volume generally ac-

MILTON, J., PARADISE REGAINED. companion to the Paradise Lost of the same date.
Lond. 1705, 8vo. LARGE PAPER. Dent, pt. l. 1425, morocco, 10s.
Lond. 1707, 8vo. A handsome, but incorrect edition.
Lond. 1713, Tonson, 12mo. This edition generally accompanies the Paradise Lost of 1711. Prefixed is a portrait by Vandergucht, copied from Marshall's print, with the Greek inscription intended by Milton as a satire on the engraver. Bibl. Anglo-Poet. 456, 9s.—With Paradise Lost, 1711. Bindley, pt. ii. 1547, 2 vols. 1l. 11s. 6d. Some copies have title-pages of the dates of 1713 and 1721, and as printed for W. Taylor.
Lond. 1725, 8vo. Fenton's edition.
Lond. 1742, royal 8vo. A beautifully printed edition.
Lond. 1747, 12mo. See Poetical Works.
Paradise Regained, and other Poems, with Notes of various Authors, by Thomas Newton, D.D., Bp. of Bristol. Lond. 1752, &c.—1763, 8vo. 2 vols. These editions generally accompany the Paradise Lost of 1749 and 1750.
Dublin, 1752, 8vo. Hawkey's elegant edition, highly valued for its accuracy. It generally accompanies the Paradise Lost of 1747.
Edinb. 1770, 12mo.
Lond. 1773, 12mo.
With Notes of various Authors, by Charles Dunster, M.A. Lond. 1795, 4to. A valuable edition, with judicious and elegant observations. Bindley, pt. iii. 350, 6s.
Paradise Regained, Samson Agonistes, and the smaller Poems. Printed by Bensley. Lond. 1796, 8vo. A copy on VELLUM was sold by auction in 1804 for 17l. 6s. 6d.
Numerous later editions have been printed with the Paradise Lost.

Versions and Translations of Paradise Regained.

The Recovery of Man, or Milton's Paradise Regained, in Prose, after the Manner of the Archbishop of Cambray, Author of Telemachus. To which is prefixed, the Life of the Author. 1771, 12mo.

Paradis Terrestre imité par Madame D. B * * * (Du Bocage). Lond. Par. 1760, 12mo. Biles, mor. 2s.

See an article on the Bibliography of Milton's Poetical Works in Retrospective Review, vol. xiv.

— A Maske (COMUS) presented at Ludlow Castle, 1634, on Michaelmasse Night, before the Earls of Bridgewater, Viscount Brocly, Lord President of Wales, and one of his Majesties most honourable privie Counsell. Lond. Humphrey Robinson at the signe of the Three Pigeons, in Paul's Church Yard. 1637, 4to. 30 pages. Printed without Writer's name.

Rhodes, 1711, 2l. 8s. Bindley, pt. iii. 522, 6l. Jadis, 148, 1l. 8s. Steevens, 972, with view of Ludlow Castle inserted, 1l. 3s. Hollis, 911, with Justa Edovardo King, Cantab. 1638, 2l. 10s. Caldecott, 1l. 14s. Bright, title dirty, 4l. 15s. Cranford, morocco, 10l. 10s. Sotheby, Aug. 19, 1858, title laid down, and D 4 from another copy, 11l. Loscombe, 26l.

From a letter to Milton, written by Sir H. Wotton, it would seem that a previous edition of Comus, attached to a copy of Randolph's Poems, had come into his hands, but there is else no evidence of it.

Comus, a Mask, &c. With Notes critical and explanatory, by various Commentators, and with preliminary Illustrations: to which is added a Copy of the Mask, from a MS. (in the handwriting of M. Lawes, dated Sept. 29, 1634), belonging to his Grace the Duke of Bridgewater. By the Rev. H. J. Todd. Canterb. 1798, 8vo. Hollis, 287, 7s.

Comus, a Mask, adapted to the Stage by Dr. Dalton. Lond. 1785, 12mo. A judicious and elegant performance. The songs were set to music by Dr. Arne.

Comus, &c., with Warton's Account of its Origin, also L'Allegro and Il Penseroso. Lond. Bensley for E. Harding, 1799, 12mo. Plates by N. II. Cromek, designed by T. Stothard. LARGE PAPER. Post 8vo. A very neat edition.

Comœdia Joannis Miltoni (quæ agebatur in Arce Ludensi) paraphrastice reddita à Gulielmo Hogæo. Lond. 1698, 4to.

Il Como, Favola boscherreccia, trad. da Gaetano Polidori. Lond. 1802, crown 8vo.

Comus, Masque. Traductions litterales (en vers François par M. de Bintenaye, et en vers Italiens par Gaetano Polidori) Paris, 1804, 4to. An edition printed at the expense of, and edited for the Hon. Francis H. Egerton (afterwards Earl of Bridgewater.) Heber, pt. ii. 10s. 6d.

See PUTEANUS.

Miltoni Fabula Samson Agonistes et Comus, Græce interp. est Edv. Greswell. Oxon. 1832, 8s.

— ARCADES, Part of a Masque, or Entertainment presented to the Countess Dowager of Derby, at

MILTON, John, MINOR POEMS. Harefield, by some noble Persons of her Family; who appear on the Scene in pastoral Habit, moving towards the Seat of State, with Songs.
First printed in Milton's Miscellaneous Poems, 1645, 12mo.

— LYCIDAS.

This poem first appeared at the end of the second portion of a Cambridge collection of verses on the death of Mr. Edward King, fellow of Christ's College, printed at Cambridge, 1638, 4to. Holland, July 1860, fine, 13/. Sotheby, Aug. 1858, facsimile title, 2l. 16s. See King, Edw. p. 1272. The original MS. is still at Trinity College, Cambridge. It appeared for the second time in the Poems, 1645, small 8vo.

Paraphrasis Latina in duo Poemata (quorum alterum à Miltono, alterum a Clievlando, Anglicè scriptum fuit) quibus deploratur Mors Juvenis praeclari et eruditi I.D. Edvardi King, qui Nave, quà vectabatur, saxo illisâ, in Oceano Hybernico submersus est. Auctore Guilielmo Hogaeo. Londini, pro Antbore, 1694, 4to. This contains the original as well as the Latin paraphrase. Sotheby, Aug. 19, 1858, 2l.

Miltonis Poema Lycidas. Gracè redditum (a Job. Plumptre), 1797, 4to.

Licida di Giovanni Milton, da T. J. Mathias (with the English text). Londra, 1812, 12mo. Nuova edizione, Napoli, 1830, 8vo. See MATHIAS, T. J.

— SAMPSON AGONISTES. Lond. Printed and sold by Randal Taylor, 1686, fol. It first appeared with the Paradise Regained in 1671.

Samson Agonistes. Lond. printed by R. E., and are to be sold by John Whitlock. 1696, folio, pp. 57 besides Title, What is called Tragedy,' and arguments, 3 leaves. (Reprinted from edition of 1688.)

Samson Agonistes, Graeco Carmine redditus, cum Versione Latina a G. H. Glasse, A.M. Oxon. 1788, 8vo. An excellent version. LARGE PAPER. Heath, 4365, 11s. Drury, 2725, 13s. Williams, 1202, russia, 1l. 5s.

MINOR POEMS.

Poems by Mr. John Milton, both English and Latin, compos'd at several Times. Printed by his true Copies. The Songs were set in Music by Mr. Henry Lawes, Gentleman of the King's Chappell, London. Printed by Ruth Raworth, for Humph. Moseley, &c., 1645, sm. 8vo.

FIRST COLLECTIVE EDITION, and the first work bearing Milton's name. With an oval portrait, ætat 21, by W. Marshall, with a Greek inscription, intended by the poet as a satire on the engraver for representing him as of middle age. Nassau, pt. i. 2767, 18s. Bindley, pt. ii. 1853, 2l. 10s. Towneley, pt. i. 484. 4l. Bibl. Anglo-Poet. 453, 6l. Roscoe, 1390, 1l. 2s. Hollis, 854, 2l. 1s. Lloyd, 885, 2l. 10s. Inglis, 1038, morocco, 2l. 6s. Caldecott, 1l. 5s. Heber, iv. 2l. 2s. Another, 4l. 1s. Craufurd, 6l. Gardner, very fine, 11l. 10s. Hibbert, no port. 3l. 10s. Singer, copy of port. 2l. 19s. Mitford, port. 6l. 10s. Sotheby's, Aug. 1858, no portrait, 1l. 15s.

Sonnet to Henry Lawes, prefixed to Choice Psalms, set to Musick by H. and W. Lawes. Lond. II. Moseley, 1648, 4to.

Poems, &c. upon several Occasions. By Mr. John Milton; both English and Latin, &c. Compos'd at several Times. With a small Tractate of Education to Mr. Hartlib. Lond. printed for Thomas Dring, 1678, small 8vo. port. by W. Dolle. To the English Poems in this edition were first added, I. Ode on the Death of a fair infant. II. At a Vacation Exercise in the College. III. On the new Forcers of Conscience under the Long Parliament. Iv. Horace to Pyrrha. v. Nine Sonnets. vi. All the English Psalms. To the Latin poems, I. Apologus de Rustico at Hero. II. Ad Joannem Rousium, &c. In this edition the Dedication of Comus to Lord Brackley, and the epistle from Sir Henry Wotton, are omitted. The volume consists of pp. 352. Nassau, pt. i. 2768, 5s. Bibl. Anglo-Poet. 455, 1l. 4s. Roscoe, 1381, Warton's copy, 2l. 8s. Hollis, 855, 7s. Caldecott, 7s.

Poems, upon several Occasions, composed at several Times, by Mr. John Milton. Third edition. Lond. 1695, folio, 60 pages, besides title and table of contents. (This generally accompanies the Paradise Regained of 1688 or 1695.)

Poems upon several Occasions, English, Italian, and Latin, with Translations, by John Milton: viz. Lycidas, l'Allegro, Il Pensaroso, Arcades, Comus, Odes, Sonnets, Miscellanies, English Psalms, Elegiarum Liber, Epigrammatum Liber, Sylvarum Liber. With Notes critical and explanatory, and other Illustrations, by Thomas Warton. Lond. 1785, 8vo. Hibbert, 5459, 6s. Fonthill, 84, 14s. Roscoe, 1382, 1l. 5s.

Second Edition, with many Alterations and large Additions. Lond. 1791, 8vo.

MILTON, John, MINOR POEMS.
Edwards, 15*l*. 6*s*. 6*d*. Foothill, 70, 10*s*.
This does not entirely supersede the
former, inasmuch as many of the notes
are omitted, their place being supplied by
references to Paradise Regained and Samson Agonistes, of which it would seem
Mr. Warton contemplated an edition.

Milton's Italian Poems translated, and
addressed to a Gentleman of Italy. By
Dr. Langhorne. Lond. 1776, 4to. 16 pp.

Latin and Italian Poems of Milton,
translated into English verse, with the
originals; and a Fragment of a Commentary on Paradise Lost, by the late
William Cowper. With a Preface by the
Editor (William Hayley). Chichester,
1808, 4to. Bindley, pt. I. 1629, 6*s*. 6*d*.
Sir M. M. Sykes, pt. 737, 17*s*. Hollis,
972, 18*s*. Nothing can be more musical
and finished than Cowper's Translation
of the Latin and Italian poetry of Milton.
—*Dr. Drake.*

A Translation of the Latin and Italian
Poems of Milton, by J. G. Strutt. Lond.
1811, 8vo. See also in Poetical Works.
Lond. Pickering, 1826, 3 vols.

L'Allegro, Il Penseroso, et Il Moderato.
In 3 Parts. Set to Music by Mr. Handel.
Lond. Tonson, 1740, 4to.

L'Allegro and Penseroso. German and
English. Mannheim, 1782, 8vo.

L'Allegro and Il Penseroso. With 30
Plates, designed expressly for the Art
Union of London, and engraved on wood
by principal artists. Lond. 1838, imp. 8vo.
3*l*. 3*s*. Proofs, royal 4to. morocco, 6*l*. 6*s*.

L'Allegro et le Penseroso, traduit en
Vers François par Ribouville. Lond.
1788, 4to.

L'Allegro, trad. da Gaetano Polidori.
Lond. 1805, 12mo.

Miltoni Poema. L'Allegro, Latine redditum à Car. Marsh, 1811, 4to.

L'Allegro and Il Penseroso, Illustrated
by engravings on steel after designs by
Birket Foster. Lond. 1860, imp. 8vo.
1*l*. 1*s*.

Il Penseroso. Lond. 1844, folio. With
designs by J. E. G.; etched by J. E. G.
and H. P. O., on India paper.

—— **PROSE WORKS**, with a Life
of the Author, interspersed with
Translations and critical Remarks.
By Charles Symmons, D.D. Lond.
1806, royal 8vo. 7 vols.

An excellent edition. Bright, boards,
4*l*. 6*s*. LARGE PAPER. Earl of Kerry,
834, with Milton's Poetical Works, 6 vols.
1801, russia, 15*l*. 15*s*. Sir M. M. Sykes,
pt. II. 440, bds. 4*l*. 14*s*.

Works, Historical, Political, and Mis-

MILTON, John, PROSE WORKS.
cellaneous, Latin and English. Amst.
1698, (but really printed in London), folio,
3 vols. With a portrait of Milton by
Faithorne. This edition was collected and
published by John Toland, but through
error or ignorance he printed from the
first editions of some tracts to which the
author had afterwards made considerable
additions. Roxburghe, 6962, 2*l*. 2*s*. Boswell, 1708, 1*l*. 8*s*. Hollis, 941, 1*l*. 5*s*.

Lond. 1738, folio, 2 vols. Edited by
Birch, with portrait of Milton, a bust,
by Vertue, from a drawing by J. Richardson. Hollis, 942, 1*l*. 6*s*. Marquis of
Townshend, 2239, 1*l*. 14*s*. Bindley, pt. II.
837, 3*l*. Roscoe, 1832, 3*l*. LARGE PAPER.
A few copies printed. Duke of Grafton,
405, 5*l*. Williams, 1490, russia, 7*l*. 17*s*. 6*d*.

Prose Works. To which is prefixed, an
Account of his Life and Writings (by
Thomas Birch, M.A.) Lond. 1753, 4to. 2
vols. With portrait of Milton, a bust, by
Vertue. A very correct edition, carefully
read through the press by Richd. Baron.
Heath, 1845, 4*l*. 7*s*. Hollis, 905, with the
Poetical Works, 1761, 8 vols. (together 5
vols.), russia, 6*l*. 6*s*. Garrick, 1580, with
the Poetical Works, 1754, 5 vols. 5*l*. 16*s*. 6*d*.
Nassau, pt. II. 189, with the Poetical
Works, 1749, 5 vols. russia, 13*l*. 13*s*. Steevens, 962, with the Poetical Works, 1761,
5 vols. blue morocco, 14*l*. 15*s*. Dent,
pt. II. 738, with the Poetical Works, 1749,
5 vols. mor. 16*l*. 16*s*. Williams, 1027, with
the Poetical Works, 1749, 5 vols. morocco,
26*l*. 5*s*.

Prose Works, a Selection, containing
his principal Political and Ecclesiastical
Pieces, with new Translations, and an Introduction by George Burnett. Lond. 1809,
12mo. 2 vols. 10*s*. 6*d*. Hollis, 858, 1*l*. 10*s*.

Works (Prose and Verse), printed from
the original editions, with a Life of the
Author by the Rev. John Mitford. Lond.
Pickering, 1853, 8vo. 8 vols. port. pub.
4*l*. 4*s*.

Works (Verse and Prose), with Introduction by Fletcher. Lond. 1833, 1 vol.
Imperial 8vo. A stereotype edition
(printed by Messrs. Childs, of Bungay),
frequently reprinted.

Milton's Prose Works complete, edited
by J. A. St. John, including the Christian
Doctrine, revised by Bp. Sumner. Lond.
Bohn, 1848-53, post 8vo. 5 vols. part and
2 from *l*. 17*s*. 6*d*.

'There is much reason for regretting
that the Prose works of Milton, where
passages of such beauty occur, should be
in the hands of so few readers, considering the advantages which might be derived to our literature from the study of
their original and nervous eloquence.'—
Bishop Sumner. This want has been sup-

MILTON, John, PROSE WORKS, pubd by the publication of the preceding article.

Separate Prose Works.

Of Reformation touching Church Discipline in England, in Two Books. Lond. 1641, 4to.

Of Prelatical Episcopacy, and whether it may be deduced from the Apostolical times by Virtue of those Testimonies which are alleg'd for that purpose in some late treatises, one whereof goes under the name of James (Usher), Bishop of Armagh. Lond. 1641, 4to. 24 pp.

See HALL, Bishop, p. 981.

The Reason of Church Government urged against Prelaty, in two Books. Lond. 1641, 4to. title and 65 pages.

Animadversions upon the Remonstrant's Defence against Smectymnus. Lond. 1641, 4to. In reply to Bishop Hall's Defence of the Humble Remonstrance. *See* p. 981.

An Apology for Smectymnus; against a 'pamphlet called 'A modest Confutation of the Animadversions.' [Supposed to be by Bp. Hall]. Lond. 1642, 4to.

Observations upon some of his Majestie's (Charles I.) late Answers and Expresses. Lond. 1642, 4to. [An Answer to the same was printed by his Majestie's command. Oxford, 1642, (? the Author).] Reply to the Answer, by J. M. Lond. 1642, 4to.

An Argument or Debate in Law of the great Question concerning the Militia, as it is now settled by Ordinance of both Houses of Parliament, by J. M. Lond. 1642, 4to.

Tyrannical Government Anatomized; or A Discourse concerning evil Counsellors: Being the Life and Death of John the Baptist. 1642, 4to. A translation from Buchanan's Baptistes, ascribed by Peck, but on slender grounds, to Milton, and reprinted by him as such, with his Life of the Poet, in 1740. *See* PROS.

The Doctrine and Discipline of Divorce. Lond. 1643, 4to.—Second edition (augmented and divided into Chapters). Lond. 1644, 4to. A presentation copy, "*ut dono auctoris*," with corrections by the author. Sotheby, Aug. 19, 1836, 2l. 2s. —Second edition. Lond. 1645, 4to. A reprint of that of 1644 on better paper, with inferior type. This work called forth 'An Answer to a Book entitled "The Doctrine and Discipline of Divorce, or a Plea for Ladies, and Gentlewomen, and all other Women, against Divorce." Lond. 1644, 4to. pp. 41.' Replied to by Milton. *See* his Colasterion, post.

The Judgment of Martin Bucer concerning Divorce; englished by John Milton. Lond. 1644, 4to.

Letter to Master Hartlib on Education. 1644, 4to. A single sheet, reprinted at the end of 'Poems, edit. 1673, 8vo.'—and in Blackburne's Remarks on Johnson's Life of Milton, pub. 1780, 12mo.

Mr. Warton observes that 'Milton's plan has more of show than value.' Dr. Johnson remarks, 'Education in England has been in danger of being hurt by two of its greatest men, Locke and Milton. Milton's plan is impracticable, and I suppose has never been tried.' This treatise was translated into French, and appended to "Lettres sur l'Education des Princes." Paris, 1746, 12mo.

Areopagitica; a Speech to the Parliament of England for the Liberty of unlicensed Printing. Lond. 1644, 4to.—FIRST EDITION, pp. 40, besides title. 'The most close, conclusive, comprehensive, and decisive vindication on the liberty of the press that has yet appeared.'—*Warton*. 'The most splendid of his Prose Works in English.'—*W. Godwin*. Bindley, pt. ii. 355, with Eiconoclastes, 1650, 1l.— Lond. 1738, 8vo. with preface by Thomson the Poet.—Lond. 1772, 8vo. with a smart ironical dedication to C. Jenkinson, the late Lord Liverpool, and a preface, by some ascribed to Arch. Blackburne.—Lond. 1780, 12mo. with Blackburne's remarks on Johnson's Life of Milton.—Lond. 1791, 8vo. edited by James Losh, Esq.—Lond. 1809, edited and printed by Baron Maseres, in his volume of 'Occasional Essays,' 8vo.—New edition, with prefatory Remarks, copious Notes, and cursive Illustrations, by T. Holt White, Esq. To which is subjoined, A Tract sur La Liberté de la Presse, imité de l'Anglois de Milton, par le Comte de Mirabeau. Lond. 1819, 8vo. A notice of the Areopagitica will be found in the Retrospective Review, ix. 1-19. It was abridged and printed in 1693, sm. 4to. under the title of 'Reasons humbly offered for the liberty of Unlicensed Printing, with the Just and true Character of Edmund Bohun, the Licencer of the Press.'

See Retrospective Review, vol. ix. p. 1.

Tetrachordon; or Expositions upon Passages of Scripture, which treat of Marriage, or Nullities in Marriage. 1645, 4to.

Colasterion: a Reply to a nameless Answer against the Doctrine and Discipline of Divorce. Lond. 1645, 4to. The Doctrine, &c., ante.

Among other opponents whom Milton met with for promulgating his Doctrines of Divorce, were Dr. Featley, Herbert Palmer, and others; his doctrines gave rise to a sect called *Miltonists*. *See* in Pagitt's Haresiography, &c., Lond. 1654, p. 129.

A Treatise of Magistracy: showing the Magistrate hath been, and for ever is to

MILTON, John, PROSE WORKS.
be, the chiefe Officer in the Church, out of
the Church, and over the Church. Lond.
1647, 4to. Sotheby's, Aug. 19, 1856, 10s.

The Tenure of Kings and Magistrates;
proving that it is lawful for any to have
the power to call to account a Tyrant or
Wicked King, and after due conviction
to depose and put him to death. Lond.
1648-9, 4to. Pickering. 3s. Two editions
same date. Lond. 1650, with additions,
4to. Omitted in every edition of Milton's
Prose Works, until that of Symmons.

Observations on the Articles of Peace
between James Earl of Ormond, for King
Charles I. on the one hand, and the Irish
Papists and Rebels on the other, &c.
1649, Animadversions on the Scotch Presbytery at Belfast.

EIKONOKAASTHS (the image-breaker),
in Answer to Εικων Βασιλικη (The King's
Image). Lond. Matt. Simmons, 1649, 4to.
pp. 242, besides title and preface, 6 leaves,
Bindley, pt. III. 553, 8s.—Lond. 1650, with
additions, 4to. Heber, pt. vi. a presentation
copy, with inscription in Milton's autograph; 'To be presented to the Right Hon.
the Earle of Carbery.' 1l. 11s. 6d. Bindley,
pt. III. 556, with Areopagitica, 1644, 1l.—
Amst. 1690, 12mo. Bliss, 2s.— With enlargements by R. Baron. Lond. 1756, 4to.
Bindley, pt. III. 556, 3s. 6d.—1770, 8vo.
Bindley, pt. II. 1566, 6s. 6d. See MILTONIANA.

Eikonoclastes, traduit de l'Anglois.
Lond. Du Gard, 1652, 12mo.

A Treatise of Civil Power in Ecclesiastical Causes, shewing that it is not lawfull to compell in matters of Religion.
Lond. 1859, 18mo.—Lond. 1790, 8vo.

' Considerations touching the likeliest
Means to remove Hirelings out of the
Church. Lond. 1659, 12mo. Bliss, 2s.—
Lond. 1723, 8vo.

A Letter to a Friend concerning the
Ruptures of the Commonwealth. Published from the Manuscript. Lond. 1659.
Written upon the dissolution of the parliament by the army, with a view to prevent the restoration of kingly government.

The present Means and brief Delineation of a free Commonwealth, easy to be
put in Practice and without Delay. In a
Letter to General Monk. Published from
the Manuscript. Lond. 1660, 4to.

The readie and easie Way to establish
a free Commonwealth. Lond. 1660, 4to.—
1791, 8vo. This piece was replied to in
'The Dignity of Kingship asserted,' by
G. S., probably George Searle. 1660, 12mo.
Bliss, 2s. 6d. Pickering. pt. III. 3s. 6d.

Brief Notes upon a late Sermon preached
and since published by Matthew Griffith,
D.D., and Chaplain to the late King.
Wherein many notorious Wrestlings of
Scripture and other Falcities are observed. This pamphlet was occasioned
by a sermon on 'The Fear of God and
the King;' preached March, 1659-60, by
Dr. Matthew Griffith. The notes were immediately answered by L'Estrange in a
pamphlet insultingly denominated 'No
Blind Guides.'

A cadence commenc't Grammar. Lond.
1669, 12mo. Hollis, 829, 15s. Bright, unset,
8s. resold Gardiner in 1854, 10s. Todd
states it was first printed in 1661.

The History of Britain, that Part especially now called England; from the first
traditional Beginning, continued to the
Norman Conquest. In six Books. Lond.
1670, 4to. Prefixed is a portrait of Milton by
Faithorne, ætat. 62, 1670. Dent, pt. II. 737,
11s. Hollis, 921, 2l. 8s. Pickering, mor.
2l. 8s. Jadis, 133*, 1l. 11s. 6d.—Skegg,
13s.—Lond. 1671, 4to. with portrait by
Faithorne. Bindley, pt. III. 551, 1l. 5s.—
Lond. 1677.—Lond. 1695, 8vo. Roxburghe,
8418, 2s. 6d. Of this history the first printed
copies were mutilated; for the licenser expunged several passages, which reprobating the pride and superstition of the monks
in the Saxon times, were understood as a
concealed satire upon the bishops in the
reign of the second Charles. Milton, however, presented a copy of the unlicensed
passages to the Earl of Anglesey: which
were published in 1681, with a preface,
stating that they originally belonged
to the third book of his history. They
have since been restored in all editions.

Reprinted, Lond. 1818, royal 8vo. with
preface by Baron Maseres.—Lond. 1820,
8vo. See Retrospective Review, vol. ix.
p. 87.

Of True Religion, Heresy, Schism, Toleration, and what best Means may be used
against the Growth of Popery. Lond. 1673,
4to.—New edition, with Preface by Dp.
Burgess. Lond. 1826, 8vo.

A Declaration or Letters patent for the
Election of John III., King of Poland.
Translated by J. Milton. Lond. 1674,
4to.

Character of the Long Parliament and
Assembly of Divines, never before Printed. Lond. H. Brome, 1681, 4to. Bliss,
pt. II, 2s.

A brief History of Moscovia. Lond.
1682, 12mo. Heber, pt. v. 8s.

Oliver Cromwell, Letters (7) to Foreign
Princes and States for Strengthening and
Preserving the Protestant Religion and
Interest; with an Appendix. Lond. 1700,
4to. Translated from the Latin of Milton.

Original Letters and Papers of State,
addressed to O. Cromwell, concerning the

MILTON, John, PROSE WORKS.
Affairs of Great Britain, 1649-58. Found among the political Collections of Mr. John Milton. Now first published from the Originals, by John Nickolls, Jun. Lond. 1743, folio, 12s. These State Papers were probably collected by Milton, with a view to some particular or general history of his times.
Original Papers illustrative of the Life and Writings of John Milton, including sixteen letters of State written by him, now first published from MSS. in the State Paper Office. With an appendix of documents relating to his connection with the Powell family. Collected and edited by W. Douglas Hamilton. Lond. (for the Camden Club), 1859, 4to.

OPERA LATINA, WITH THEIR TRANSLATIONS.

POEMATA LATINA, with a separate title. See POEMS ENGLISH and LATIN, 1645, ante.
Defensio pro Populo Anglicano contra Claudii Salmasii Defensionem Regiam. 1650, 12mo.—1651, 4to. LARGE PAPER. Lond. 1651, folio. Bright, 6s. The best apology, says T. Warton, that ever was offered for bringing kings to the block. Roscoe, 1833, 8s. 6d.—1651, 18mo. Second edition. Roscoe, 1854, 5s.—Cum Indice. Lond. 1651, 12mo.—Lond. 1652, 12mo.—Lond. 1657, 12mo.—Defence of the People of England, translated into English. (Amst.) 1692, 8vo. Translated by Mr. Washington of the Temple. See SALMASIUS.
On the 13th of June, 1660, it was ordered by the restored House of Commons that this Book and the Iconoclastes of Milton should be burnt by the common hangman. A proclamation issued for his apprehension, see it printed in Bp. Kennett's Register, fol. 1728, and in Chalmers' Supplemental Apology for the believers in the Shakspere Papers. 1799, 8vo.
Britannierum Rex, a Securi et Calamo Miltoni vindicatus. Dublini, apud Liberum Correctorem Via Regia, sub signo Scuti Fascis, 1652, sm. 12mo. pp. 118. Bright, 1198, 17s. The scarcest volume in the Controversy between Milton and Salmasius. See CHARLES. I.
Defensio pro se contra Alex. Mori libellum "Regii Sanguinis Clamor," cui adjungitur Joannis Philippi Responsio ad Apologiam anonymi cujusdam Tenebrionis pro Rege et Populo Anglicano infamissimam. Lond. 1855, 12mo.
Defensio secunda pro Populo Anglicano contra infamem Libellum cui titulus, Regii Sanguinis Clamor adversus Parricidas Anglicanos. Lond. 1654, 12mo. Hag. Com. 1654—1658, 12mo. See MOULIN, Peter du. MORE, Alex.

Literæ pseudo—Senatus Anglicani, necnon Cromwelli, &c. nomine et jussu conscriptæ. Lond. 1676, 12mo. 8s.—Lips. 1690, quas nunc primum in Germania recondidecit M. J. G. Pritius, 12mo. Best edition.
—In English, under the title of ' Letters of State to most of the Sovereign Princes and Republics of Europe during the administration of the commonwealth, and the Protectors Oliver and Richard Cromwell.' Lond. 1694, 12mo. Translated by Edward Philips, Milton's youngest nephew. A very interesting volume, containing a short biography of the Poet, which subsequent writers on Milton have made much use of, without acknowledgment. This has been reprinted in Pickering's edition of 1826.
Scriptum Domini Protectoris contra Hispanos. Lond. 1655, 4to. A translation under the title of 'A Manifesto of the Lord Protector of the Commonwealth,' appeared in 1738, with James Thomson's "Britannia" attached to it, two editions in 8vo. same year.
Epistolarum familiarum (31) Liber unus; quibus accesserunt ejusdem, (jam olim in Collegio Adolescentulis,) Prolusiones quædam oratoriæ. Lond. 1874, 12mo. Nassau, pt. I. £2 2s, 7s. Singer, 5s. 6d.
Epistola ad Polionem cum nolis F. S. Lond. 1738, folio.
Artis Logicæ Institutio ad P. Rami Methodum concinnata. Adjecta est Praxis analytica, et P. Rami Vita, Libris duobus. 1670, 12mo. Prefixed is a portrait of Milton by W. Dolle.—Lond. 1671, 12mo.—Lond. 1673, 12mo.
J. Miltoni Angli, de Doctrina Christiana. Libri duo posthumi. Cantab. 1825, 4to. pub. at 3l. 3s. Edited by Dr. Sumner, Bp. of Winchester, from a MS. discovered in the State Paper Office. Some copies on LARGE PAPER, royal 4to. 5l.
A Treatise on Christian Doctrine, translated by Dr. Sumner. Cambridge, 1825, 4to. pub. at 2l. 3s. 'A manly, close, and generally accurate translation, with valuable notes.' A few copies, LARGE PAPER, royal 4to. 5l.
New edition, revised and corrected by Dr. Somner, Bishop of Winchester. Lond. Bohn, 1852-3, post 8vo. 2 vols. 7s. being vols. 4 and 5 of Bohn's edition of Milton's Prose Works, 5 vols. post 8vo.

Miltoniana.

A Perspective of the Impudence, &c., in a libell, entitled Eikonoklastes, written by John Milton (by J. Lane). 1645, 4to. Singer, 8s.
Remarks on the Life of Milton, as published by J. T[oland] with a Character of the Author and his party. Lond. 1699, 8vo.

MILTON, John, MILTONIANA.
Milton's Sublimity asserted. Lond. 1719, 8vo.
Emendations on the twelve Books of Milton's Paradise Lost. By Richard Bentley, D.D. Lond. 1732, 4to.
Milton restor'd and Bentley depos'd. Numb. I. Lond. 1732, 8vo. Lloyd, 908, 10s.
A friendly Letter to Dr. Bentley, occasioned by his new Edition of Paradise Lost, by a Gentleman of Christ-Church College, Oxon. Lond. 1732, 8vo. The author is said to be Dr. Pearce, Bishop of Rochester.
A Review of the Text of the twelve Books of Paradise Lost, in which the chief of Dr. Bentley's Emendations are considered, &c. Lond. 1733, 8vo. 3s. Hollis, 899, 6s. 6d. By Bishop Pearce. First printed in separate parts in 1732. According to Bp. Newton, 'The review of the text of the Paradise Lost, by Dr. Pearce, the present Bishop of Bangor, is not only a complete answer to Dr. Bentley, but may serve as a pattern for all future critics, of sound learning and just reasoning, joined with the greatest candour and gentleness of manners.'
Richardson (J.). Explanatory Notes and Remarks on Milton's Paradise Lost; with a Life of the author and Discourse on the Poem. Lond. 1734, 8vo. 7s.
Paterson (James), Complete Commentary, etymological explanations, critical and classical notes on Milton's Paradise Lost. Lond. 1744, sm. 8vo. portrait, 7s.
A Critical Essay on the (Musical) Numbers of Paradise Lost will be found in "Poems on several occasions," &c., by Mr. Samuel Say. Lond. 1745, 4to. pp. 115—160.
Critical Dissertation on Paradise Regained, by the Rev. Mr. Meadowcourt. Lond. 1732, &c.—1748, 8vo.
An Essay upon Milton's Imitations of the Ancients in his Paradise Lost, with some Observations on the Paradise Regain'd. Lond. 1741, 8vo. 62 pp. and one leaf of advertisement.
A verbal Index to Milton's Paradise Lost, adapted to every edition but the first, which was published in ten Books only. Lond. 1741, 12mo. 5s.
The best verbal Index is contained in Todd's Life of Milton, 1809.
Il Tasso, a Dialogue: the Speakers John Milton and Torquato Tasso. In which new Light is thrown on their poetical and moral Characters. 1761, 8vo.
A familiar Explanation of the Poetical Works of Milton. To which is prefixed

Mr. Addison's Criticism on Paradise Lost. With a Preface, by the Rev. Mr. Dodd. Lond. 1762, 12mo. 2s. 6d.
The Poetry of Milton's Prose. Lond. 1827, 12mo.
A Letter to the Rev. Mr. T. Warton, on his late Edition of Milton's Juvenile Poems. Lond. 1785, 8vo. Said to be written by Samuel Darby, M.A. Rector of Whatfield in Suffolk.
Narrative of the Disinterment of Milton's Coffin, by Philip Neve, Esq. Lond. 1790, 8vo. See Neve, Ph.
Saggio di Critica sul Paradiso Perduto. (del Filippo Scolari) e sulla annotazioni a quelle di Giuseppe Addison, aggiungovi "L'Adamo, sacra rappresentazione" di Gio Bat. Andreini. Venezia, 1818, royal 8vo. portrait, 10s. LARGE PAPER, 15s.
Milton is said to have taken the first idea of his Paradise Lost from the Adamo of Andreini, first printed at Milan in 1613.
The Story of our first Parents, in one continued Narrative, selected from Milton's Paradise Lost. By Mrs. Siddons. Lond. 1822, 8vo. 6s. 6d.
Report on the unpublished MSS. of Callander's Notes on Milton, by D. Laing, 1826.' In Archæologia Scotica, or Transactions of the Scottish Antiquaries, vol. 3, pt. 1. 1828, 4to.
Dunster, Rev. Charles. Considerations on Milton's early Reading, and the prima Stamina of his Paradise Lost. Lond. 1800, 8vo. 3s. 6d.
The Student's Practical Grammar, with a Commentary on the First Book of Paradise Lost, by T. Goodwin. Lond. 1835, 8vo. 4s. 6d.
Milton, a Poem; at the End of "the Siamese Twins," by Sir E. L. Bulwer. Lond. 1831, 8vo.
Flowers of Milton, by Miss Giraud. Lond. 1830, 4to. 30 plates, 1l. 11s. 6d.
An Essay on the Paradise Lost, considered with reference to its theological Sentiments and moral Influence, by the Rev. F. A. Cox, D.D. In the Journal of Sacred Literature for April, 1848, pp. 236-257.
Some unrecorded passages in the Life of John Milton, by Edward Taylor, Professor of Music; in the Christian Reformer for 1840.
Seven Lectures on Shakespeare and Milton, by S. T. Coleridge, edited by J. Payne Collier. Lond. 1856, 8vo. 12s. (The authenticity of these lectures is questioned.)
An Historical Memoir of the political Life of John Milton. By Charles Edward Mortimer, Esq. Lond. 1805, 4to. Bright, 2s.
Todd's (H. J.) Account of the Life and Writings of Milton; with a verbal Index

MILTON, John, MILTONIANA.
to the whole of his Poetry. Lond. 1809, 8vo. portrait, 10s. LARGE PAPER, roy. 8vo. 1l. 1s.
This forms vol. 1 of the 1809 edition of Todd's Milton; a certain number of copies being printed off with a distinct title-page, and sold separately.
Life of John Milton, interspersed with Translations and critical Remarks, by Dr. Symmons. Lond. 1806, 8vo.—Again, 1810 and 1822, 7s. LARGE PAPER, roy. 8vo. 12s.
Life and Times of Milton, by Joseph Ivimey. Lond. 1833, 8vo. 10s.
Life and Times of Milton, by Carpenter. Lond. 16 , 17mo. 3s. 6d.
An Account of the Life, Opinions, and Writings of John Milton, with an Introduction to Paradise Lost, by T. Keightley. Lond. 1855, 8vo. pp. 484. 14s. 6d.
Life, narrated in connection with the Political, Ecclesiastical, and Literary History of his Time, by David Masson. Lond. 1859, vol. 1, portraits.
Life of Milton, with Amyntor, by John Toland. See TOLAND.
Life of Milton, by Dr. Johnson, see in Lives of the Poets.
Remarks on the Life by Dr. Johnson. See BLACKBURNE.
A Bibliographical Account of Milton's Poetical Works will be found in the Retrospective Review, vol. 14, pp. 222-304.
A Complete Concordance to Milton's Poetical Works, by G. Lushington Prendergast. Madras, 1857-9, 4to. in 12 parts, 416 pages, 2l. 5s.
See DENSON, William. BLACKBURNE, Fr. DOUGLAS, Bp. DUNSTER, Charles. HAYLEY, William. HUME, Patrick. IVIMEY, Jos. JOSTIN, John, D.D. KIRKPATRICK, J. LAUDER, William. LAWRENCE, Henry. MASSEY, W. NEVE, Philip. PATERSON, James. PECK, Francis. RICHARDSON, R. ROWLAND, David. SALMASIUS, Claude. SCHALLER, J. SYMMONS, C. THOMSON, James. TODD, H. J. TOLAND, J. VOLTAIRE, M. ZEIGLER, Caspar.
A very copious list of the various editions and translations into various languages, many printed abroad, of Milton's poetical works, and of detached pieces of criticism, and *Miltoniana* generally, will be found in Todd's Life of the Poet; and at the end of the 4th volume of Todd's Milton, 1852.

MILTON, Richard. London's Miseric. The Countryes crueltie with God's Mercie, explained by remarkable observations of each of them during this last Visitation. Lond. N. Okes, 1625, 4to.
Heber, pt. iv. 3l. 19s.

MILTON, Thos. Views of Seats in Ireland, with an Account of each. Dublin, 1783-93, oblong 4to. 5 pts. in 1 vol. 24 plates, 2l. 2s. PROOFS, —Again, 1821.
Duke of York, 1820, 1l. 12s. Graves, 830, 2l. 14s.

MILWARD, Edward, M.D. Trallianus reviviscens; an Account of Alexander Trallian, one of the Greek Writers that flourished after Galen, &c. Lond. 1734, 8vo.
Intended as a supplement to Friend's History of Physick. Constable, 653, 4s. 6d.

MINADOI, John Thomas. The Historie of the Warres betweene the Turkes and the Persians, translated by Ahr. Hartwell. Lond. 1595, 4to.
Bindley, pt. iii. 394, 5s. 6d. Reed, 5171, 6s. Nassau, pt. ii. 171, 7s. Heber, pt. i. 4ms, 16s.

MIND, Will and Understanding, a Morality. See ABBOTSFORD CLUB. Appendix.

MINES. See CORNWALL. HAUGHTON. MANDER. MANLOVE, Ed. PETTUS, Sir John. PRYCE, Wm.

MINIATURE, The. A periodical Paper, by Solomon Grildrig, of the College of Eton. In 40 Numbers. Windsor, 1806, 8vo. 6s.
The second periodical work which issued from the College of Eton: the joint production of Dr. Rennell, Mr. Knight, Mr. Canning, and the sons of the Marquis of Wellesley.—1805, 12mo. 2 vols. For the former, see MICROCOSM.

MINNESINGERS.—The Lays of the Minnesingers, or German Troubadours of the 12th and 13th Centuries. Lond. 1825, post 8vo. plates.
An elegant selection, with valuable notes by Edgar Taylor, Esq.

MINORITY.—The History of the Minority. 1765, 8vo.
Only twelve copies printed.

MINOT, Lawrence, Poems. See RITSON, Joseph.

MINSHEU, John. Doctor in Linguas. The Guide into the (11) Tongues, viz. English, Welsh, Low

Dutch, High Dutch, French, Italian, Spanish, Portuguez, Latine, Greeke, Hebrew, &c. Lond. 1617, folio.

'Minshen's Guide is a very important work, and has furnished great assistance to subsequent lexicographers.'—*Todd.* It contains the first printed list of Subscribers to any Book. Roxburghe, 2l. 12s. 6d. Bindley, pt. II. 1048, 1l. 10s. Towneley, pt. II. 1021, 1l. 3s. LARGE PAPER. A copy is in the British Museum, which formerly belonged to K. James I., to whom the work is dedicated.—Second edition, containing only nine languages, viz. English, Low Dutch, High Dutch, French, Italian, Spanish, Latine, Greeke, Hebrew, &c. Lond. 1626, 6 or 7. This edition is by some preferred for its additions and corrections, but as it omits the Welsh and Portuguese languages, it is less valuable commercially. Boswell, 1707, 8s. Roxburghe, 2l. 63, 10s. 6d. Bindley, pt. II. 1049, 18s. Marquis of Townshend, 2233, 1l. 2s. Boswell, 1703, 1l. 6s. Horne Tooke, 471, 1l. 11s.

Pleasant and Delightful Dialogues in Spanish and English. Lond. by M. Bollifant, 1599, folio. This forms a portion of Minshen's improved edition of PERCIVAL's Spanish Grammar.

Vocabvlarivm Hispanico-Latinvm et Anglicvm copiosissimvm. Lond. 1617, folio. This is generally found at the end of Minshen's Dictionary of eleven Languages.

See PERCIVALE's, Richard, Spanish Dictionary and Grammar.

MINSHULL, R. Proposals for printing an exact and ample account of all the Books printed by William Caxton, who was the first printer in England, &c., &c., 8vo. 2 leaves.

In the Grenville Collection.
— *See* PARIS and VIENNA.

MINSTRELSY.—English Minstrelsy: being a Selection of fugitive Poetry, from the best English Authors; with some original Pieces hitherto unpublished. Edinb. 1810, sm. 8vo. 2 vols. 10s. 6d.

An excellent selection, made by John Ballantyne, under the guidance of Sir Walter Scott. *See* MOTHERWELL, William.

MINTE, the, of Deformity. Lond. 1600, 4to. (in verse).
Bindley, 2l.

MINUCIUS FELIX, Marcus. Octavius, ex iterata Recensione Joan. Daviaii, LL.D. Cum Animadversionibus Des. Heraldi et Nic. Rigaltii, necnon selectis aliorum. Accedit Commodianus, ævi Cyprianici scriptor. Cantab. 1712, 8vo. 4s.

An excellent edition, with valuable notes. Drury, 2779, morocco, 7s. 6d. LARGE PAPER. 10s. 6d. Sir M. M. Sykes, pt. II. 444, russia, 1l. 10s. Williams, 1205, morocco, 1l. 10s. Dent, pt. I. 1428, morocco. 1l. 11s. 6d. Mac-Carthy, 86 fr.—1707, 8vo. 2s. 6d. LARGE PAPER. Williams, 1203, morocco, 1l. 6s.

Octavius: Cæcilius Cyprianus de Idolorum Vanitate, cum Observationibus Nic. Rigaltii; & Julius Firmicus de profana ac vera Religione, cum Notis Ioan. Wower. Oxon. 1662, 12mo. 2s. 6d.—Oxon. 1627, 12mo.—Oxon. 1631, 12mo.

Octavius, ex Recensione J. Daviaii. Glasg. Foulis, 1750, 12mo. Duke of Grafton, 77, morocco, 2s. 6d. LARGE PAPER. QUARTO. Mac-Carthy, 51 fr.

Octavius, translated into English (with the Latin Version) by Richard James of C. C. C. Oxford. Oxon. 1636, 12mo. Inglis, 1039, 8s. 6d.

Octavius, translated by P. Lorrain. Lond. 1695, 18mo. 3s. 6d.

Octavius, englished by E. Combe. Lond. 1703, 8vo.

Octavius, with Tertullian's Apology for the primitive Christians. Lond. 1708, 8vo. &c.

Octavius: a Dialogue (translated by Sir David Dalrymple, Lord Hailes). Edinb. 1781, 12mo. 4s. A faithful translation with valuable notes, in which are strictures on Gibbon's Roman History.—New edition, Cambridge, 1854, 8vo.

Octavius. The text newly revised from the original MS. with an English Commentary, Analysis, Introduction, and Copious Indices. Edited by H. A. Holden, M.A. Cambridge University Press, 1853, 9s. 6d.

See REEVES, William.

MINUTIUS, Cassid. Aureus. Colloquium Davidis cum Anima sua (accinente Paraphraseim in 104 Psalmum) de Magnalibus Dei. Lond. 1670, folio.

MIRABAUD, John Baptist. The System of Nature: or, the Laws of the moral and physical World. Translated from the French by Hodgson. Lond. 1797, 8vo. 4 vols. 18s. Lond. 1817, royal 8vo. 2 vols.

MIRABEAU, Honoré Gabrielle, Count, President of the French National Assembly in 1791. Secret History of the Court of Berlin. Translated from the French. Lond. 1789, 8vo. 2 vols.

Mirabeau's Letters during his Residence in England. Lond. 1832, 8vo. 2 vols.

Memoirs, biographical, literary, and political. Lond. 1835-36, 8vo. 4 vols. 2l. 2s.

MIRACLE PLAYS (5), or Scriptural Dramas. Privately printed under the care of J. P. Collier, Esq. F.S.A. Lond. 1836, post 8vo.

ONLY TWENTY-FIVE COPIES PRINTED. The volume consists of a title and introduction, 2 leaves; The Harrowing of Hell, 16 pages; The Sacrifice of Abraham, 18 pages; The Marriage of the Virgin, 24 pages; The Adoration of the Shepherds, 44 pages; The Advent of Antichrist, 36 pages; Glossary, 4 pages. The four last pieces are here printed for the first time. Bliss, 1. 1l. 4s.

A Fragment of an ancient York Miracle Play, viz. "The Incredulity of Saint Thomas," will be found in "Excerpta Antiqua," York, 1797, 8vo. edited by J. Croft. See ante, p. 555. In the late Mr. Wright's sale was a fine folio MS. of the York Miracle Plays, on vellum, which produced 30l. It had formerly belonged to Sir Henry Fairfax, who presented it to the Antiquary Thoresby, at the dispersion of whose Museum it was purchased by H. Walpole, and at the Strawberry Hill sale in 1842, sold for 23l.

See Harrowing of Hell. HONE, Wm., MYSTERIES. SURTEES' SOCIETY, WRIGHT, Thomas.

MIRANDULA, Earl of. See PICUS, John.

— Scipio. Cynthia Coronata: seu serenissima Maria Austriaca inclytissimo Principe Carolo Sole suo Auricomo cincta. Sine loco ao Anno. 4to.

Pp. 187, likewise five leaves of introductory matter. Prefixed is a curious print representing P. Charles joining hands with the Infanta, also figures of James I., the Duke of Buckingham, and the King of Spain. Heber, pt. ii. 10s. 6d.

MIRROR, The, a periodical Paper published at Edinburgh in the Years 1779 and 1780. Edinb. or Lond. folio.—Again 1782, 12mo. 3 vols.—Lond. 1801, 12mo. 3 vols.

Frequently reprinted, and forming one of the series entitled ESSAYISTS (British).

MIRROR FOR MAGISTRATES, in 5 parts. Edited by Joseph Haslewood. Lond. 1815, 4to. 3 vols.

Best edition of this popular production of the reign of Elizabeth. Collated with the various editions and historical notes. 150 copies printed. In it 'are several things of note to be consulted by those who write of the English history.'—Hearne. Duke of York, 3381, 2l. 4s. Strettell, 1246, morocco, 7l. Heber, pt. i. 1l. 19s. Hibbert, 5583, 2l. 13s. Nassau, pt. ii. 173, 4l. 4s. ON VELLUM. Four copies printed. The substratum of this work was Lydgate's Fall of Princes. See HOCHAS, JOHN.

A Myrroure of Magistrates. Anno 1559. Londini in Ædibus Thomæ Marshæ. 4to. 92 leaves. BLACK LETTER. First edition, edited by William Baldwin, containing 19 legends. The leaves are erroneously numbered, p. 48 being followed by p. 50. Steevens, 758, 3l. 1s. Bibl. Anglo-Poet. 437, 25l. Resold, Heber, pt. iv. 9l. 12s.

A Myrrovr for Magistrates. Anno 1563. Lond. by Thomas Marshe. 4to. BLACK LETTER. 178 leaves. Second edition (of Part 1), edited by W. Baldwin, containing 27 legends. Steevens, 759, 1l. 2s. Saunders' in 1818, 1l. 11s. 6d. Reed, 6881, date 1565, 2l. 2s. Sir M. M. Sykes, pt. ii. 516, 4l. 9s. Nassau, pt. ii. 827, 4l. 14s. 6d. Bibl. Anglo-Poet. 438, 14l. 14s. Roxburghe, 8313, morocco, 16l. 5s. 6d. sold at White Knights as the first edition, 846, 5l. 5s. resold, Heber, pt. iv. 9l. 1s.

A Myrrovr for Magistrates. Newly corrected and augmented. Anno 1571. Lond. by Thomas Marshe. 4to. 164 leaves. Folios 130 to 139 are misused. This edition (first part only) contains 27 legends. Bibl. Anglo-Poet. 826, 16l. 16s. Heber, pt. iv. part of title in MS. 3l. 1s.

The first Parte of the Mirovr for Magistrates, contayning the Falles of the first Infortunate Princes of this Lande: from the comming of Brute to the Incarnation of our Saulour and Redemer Iesu Christe. Imprinted by Thomas Marshe, 1574. 4to. in eights, to sig. K. ii. fol. 74, and introduction, 6 leaves. This Part contains 16 legends, and was edited by J. Higgins. The Poem on "Lord Hastings" differs from that printed in the editions of 1571-3. Bibl. Anglo-Poet. 439, with the preceding article, 10l. 10s. Nassau, pt. ii. 179, 18s. Inglis, 136, (with Blennerhassett's second part), 3 pts. 1574-8, morocco, 6l. 2s. 6d.

The last (or third) Parte of Mirovr for Magistrates. Lond. by Thomas Marsh, 1574. 4to. 108 leaves. The contents are the same as that of 1571. Bibl. Anglo-Poet. 439, (with the previous article, and Blennerhassett's second portion). Heber, pt. iv. 11s.

The first Parte of the Mirovr for Magistrates. Lond. by Thomas Marshe, 1575,

MIRROR, &c.—continued.
4to. BLACK LETTER. 80 leaves. A reprint of the first edition, with an addition of eleven stanzas at the end of Nennius, another legend concluding the volume, viz. 17. Irenglass.'
The last (or third) Part of the Mirour for Magistrates. Lond. by Thos. Marshe, 1578, 4to. The edition of 1574, the first sheet being reprinted.
The first Parte of the Mirour for Magistrates. Imprinted for Thomas Marshe, 1578, 4to. This edition, says Ritson, contains 17 legends.
The last (or third) Part of the Mirour for Magistrates. Newly corrected and enlarged. Lond. by Thomas Marshe, 1578, 4to. The edition of 1571, with new title. The Table recites 29 legends, but only 27 were printed. Bibl. Anglo-Poet. 440, short copy, and four leaves MS. 5l. 5s.
The seconde Part of the Mirrour for Magistrates, containing the Falls of the infortunate Princes of this Lande: from the Conquest of Cæsar unto the comming of Duke William the Conqueronr. Imprinted by Richard Webster, 1578, 4to. pp. 144. This portion, published by Tho. Blenerhasset, contains 12 legends. Bibl. Anglo-Poet. 441, 10l. 10s. Only one edition of this part. Heber, pt. iv. fine, 1l. 11s.
'The Mirour for Magistrates. Newly imprinted, and with the Addition of diuers Tragedies enlarged. Lond. by Henry Marsh, 1587, 4to. 253 leaves. Baldwin and Higgins's editions, with several additions to each part, published by Higgins. It contains 73 legends. Bibl. Anglo-Poet. 442, 8l. 8s. 443. 6l. Sir M. M. Sykes, pt. 517, 3l. 1s. Lloyd, 788, 5l. 10s. Stanley, 381, russia, 12l. 12s. Heber, pt. iv. 3l. 16s. Utterson, 1852, 12l. 15s. Gardner, 7l. Bliss, fine, 8l. 10s.
A Mirovr for Magistrates. Newly enlarged, with a last Part, called A Winter Night's Vision, being an Addition of such Tragedies, especially famous, as are exempted in the former Historie, with a Poem annexed, called England's Eliza. Lond. F. Kyngston, 1610, 4to. pp. 596. In this edition many of the legends are curtailed and modernized. The volume was formed from the labours of Higgins, Blennerhasset and Baldwin, by Richard Niccols, contains, according to contents, 91 legends. In Malone's copy there is a dedication of the Winter Night's Vision to the Earle of Nottingham, but this being suppressed is seldom found in the volume. Sir M. M. Sykes, pt. ii. 518, russia, 5l. 10s. Hibbert, 5564, 19s. Bibl. Anglo-Poet. 444, 5, 6, 12l. 10s. 10s. 15l. Roscoe, 1433, 6l. 6s. Bindley, pt. iii. 576, 8l. 8s. Crawfurd, 7l. 2s. 6d. Heber, pt. iv. 4l. 6s. Bliss, 2l. 4s. Hibbert, 3994, date 1620, russia, 1l. 18s.

Dowdeswell, 423, 8l. Nassau, pt. ii. 379, 1l. 11s. North, pt. iii. 762. russia, 3l. 7s.
The Falles of vnfortunate Princes. Lond. F. Kingston for T. A. Jones, 1619, 4to. The edition of 1610 with a new titlepage, pp. 596. Sotheby's in 1823, russia by Roger Payne, 2l. 17s. Steevens, 762, 1l. 1s. Bibl. Anglo-Poet. 443. 7l. 7s. Heber, pt. iv. 2l. 1s.—1620, 4to. North, pt. iii. 769, russia, 2l. 11s. Reed, 6323, 1l. 12s. —1621, 4to.
The Mirrour of Mirrovrs; or, all the Mirrour of Magistrates abbreuiated in hreefe Histories in Prose. Lond. for James Roberts, 1598, 12mo.

MIRROR OF GOLD.—The Mirroure of Gold for the Synfull Soule, translated out of the Frenche into Englishe by the ryght excellent Princesse Margaret, Moder to our Soverayne Lorde King Henry the VII. 4to.
Printed by Richard Pynson. On vellum. Nw Bibl. Harleiana, vol. iv. p. 525, no. 10198. Other editions.—Lond. by W. de Worde, 1522, 4to. J in sixes. A copy is in the public library at Cambridge. Duke of Sussex (wanting a coat of Arms), 8l.—Lond. by John Skot, 1522, 4to. A copy is in the British Museum.—Lond. by W. de Worde, 1526, 4to. A copy is in the Lambeth Library.

MIRROR OF OUR LADY.—The Boke callyd the Myrroure of oure Lady very necessary for all relygyous Persones. Lond. by me Richarde Fawkes, 1530, folio.
This Mirror consists of three parts. Pt. 1 treats of the proper behaviour at divine service. Pt. 2, begins on fol. xxxii. and consists of the service for each day of the week, which the author termeth 'vil stories,' and ends on folio Clxliii, with a colophon, the next leaf blank. Pt. 3, printed with a fresh set of signatures, commences on fol. Clavi. and concludes on folio Clxxxiii., without colophon or device, and six leaves ending with a colophon. It has two prologues and a table of the chapytres, xxliii in number, for the first part. A copy is in Lambeth Library.

MIRROR OF THE WORLD.—The Mirrour of the World. Printed in the Abbey of Westmestre by William Caxton, 1481, folio.
First edition, printed on excellent paper. Supposed to be the first book printed in this country with wood-cuts. Spaces are left for the introduction of capital initials. W. Knights, 2977, four leaves wanting, morocco, 15l. Roxburghe, 1752, 831l. 16s. now in the Devonshire collection. Sir M. M. Sykes, pt. ii. 519, 57l. 15s.

Collation.—The volume contains sign. a to n f in eights, a 1 blank. The full page contains 39 lines. A copy is at Ham House. See Ames's Typog. Antiq. by Dibdin, i. 101—13. Bibl. Spencer. iv. 231—5.

— The Myrrour of the World. Caxton me fieri fecit, n. d. (1491), folio.

Second Edition, with printed capital initials. White Knights, 2978, morocco, 65*l*. 13*s*. Inglis, 1205, damaged, 11*l*. 15*s*. Willett, 1672, morocco, 13*l*. 10*s*. Hibbert, 5663, morocco, 56*l*. 4*s*. 6d. Culwich Hall, 1444, 75*l*. resold, Hurt, 1853, 97*l*. *Collation.*—The signatures extend to L inclusively in eights, and a full page contains 81 lines. On fol. lvii. Caxton me deri fecit, lviii. recto blank, the reverse having Caxton's large mark only. See Ames's Typog. Antiq. by Dibdin, i. 101—13. Bibl. Spencer. iv. 235—44.

— The Myrrour and Dyscrypcyon of the Worlde with many Mcruaylles. Enpr. by me Laurence Andrewe, folio.

This chef-d'œuvre of Andrewe's press is a reprint of Caxton's edition, having his prologus and several of his cuts introduced. A copy at the sale of Woodhouse's library produced 23*l*. Sent, pt. ii. 764, 6*l*. 10*s*. Geo. Chalmers, ii. 947, 6*l*. Gardner in 1854, last leaf repaired, 7*l*. 7*s*. Singer in 1860, imparfect, 2*l*. 4*s*. *Collation.*—The volume contains y in fours, having four leaves, between sign. f and g, marked K.

MIRROR, MIRROUR, or MYRROUR; various works.

The Mirror of Compliments. 1650. *See* Compliments.

The Myrrour or Glasse of Christes Passion. Lond. by me Robert Redman, 1534, folio. Contains fol. CIX. The preface is dedicated to the Hon. Lord Lisney. 'From Syon the vi. Day of December, 1534. Your dayly oratour Johan Fewterer.' Towneley, pt. i. 774, 8*l*. Heber, pt. vii. 4*l*. 4*s*.

A Trewe Mirrour or Glase, wherein we may beholde the woful state of this our Realme of Englonde, set forth in a dialogue of communication between Eustinus and Theophilus. Imprinted in 1556, 16mo. BLACK LETTER. A—C iv. in eights, 20 leaves. In Lambeth library.

The Mirror, or Glasse of Health. *See* MOULTON, Thomas, D.D.

The Mirror of Honor, 1597. *See* NORDEN, John.

The Mirror of Humilitie. *See* FRESTON.
Mirror of Good Manners. *See* MANCYN Domynicke.

Mirror of Love. *See* HOGARD, M.

The Mirrour of Madnes; or, a Paradoxe mainteyning Madenes to be most excellent; done out of French into English by Ja(mes) San(ford) Gent. Lond. by Tho. Marshe, 1576, 16mo. This work is somewhat similar in its design to Erasmus's Praise of Folly. In Trinity College Library, Cambridge.

The Mirrour of Majestie, or Badges of Honour conceitedly emblasoned with Emblems annexed, poetically unfolded. 1619, 4to. White Knights, 2524, morocco, 16*l*. with reprinted title. Resold, Perry, 17*l*. 17*s*. Resold, Heber, 7*l*. 10*s*. Halliwell, May, 1857, 20*l*. 10*s*.

The Mirror of Man's Life, englished by H. Kerton. Lond. 1580. 16mo. Dedicated to Anne Countess of Pembroke, K, in eights. — 1576. 16mo. Inglis' 822, 1*l*. 2*s*. —1583, 16mo. Lloyd, 50*l*, 11*s*. 6d.

The Mirrour of Mans Miseries, or a brief Summarie of the first Parte of the Resolution, in Verse. Lond. 1684, 8vo.

Mirror of the Church. *See* AUGUSTIN or AUSTIN, St.

Mirror of Martyrs. *See* OLDCASTLE.

The Mirror of Mirth, by R. D. 4to. A Story Book. In BLACK LETTER. In the Capel Collection. *See* D. H. p. 574.

Mirror for Monsters. *See* HAKETE, Wm.

The Mirror of Mutabilitie, 1679. *See* MUNDAY, Ant.

Mirrovr of the new Reformation, wherein Reformers, by their own Acknowledgement, are represented ad vivum. The Beauty also of their Handy-warke is displayed. Second Edition, augmented. Paris, by John Couaturier, 1634, 8vo. pp. 138. A collection of satirical epigrams on Luther, Calvin, Melancthon, Bullinger, and others. Sotheby's in 1821, 14*s*. Inglis, 1040, 6*s*. Bibl. Anglo-Poet. 940, 5*l*. 5*s*. Hibbert, 5468, 1*l*. 3*s*. Bindley, pt. ii. 1966, 6*l*. 16*s*. 6d. Perry, pt. ii. 725, *l*. 18*s*. 6d. Heber, pt. iv. 1*l*.

A princelie Mirrour of peerless Modestie. 16mo. C 5 in eights. The story of Susannah wrought into a novel, [by B. Greene. Imp. for R. Warde, 1584.] *See* GREENE, R. p. 935. SALTAR, Thomas.

The Mirrour of princely Deedes and Knighthood, wherein is showed the Worthinesses of the Knight of the Sunne, and his brother Rosicleer, with the strange Love of the beautiful Princess Briana and the valiant Actes of other noble Princes and Knights, translated out of the Spanish by Margaret Tyler and H. F. Imprinted by Tho. Este, &c. 1585—1601, 4to. 9 parts. BLACK LETTER. Heber, parts 1 and 2, 1*l*. 15*s*.; pt. viii. the nine parts, 7*l*. 10*s*. Steevens, 1158, 5*l*. 5*s*. Goldsmid, 544, 7 vols. imparfect, 14*l*. resold Utterson, 1852, 6*l*. 4*s*.

The Mirrour of Policie. A Worke no lesse profitable than necessary for all Magistrates, and Governers of Estates and Commonweals. Lond. A. Islip, 1594, 4to. A curious and amusing book, full of entertaining observations on the customs of different nations, and on social duties, interspersed with poetry and quotations. Date 1599. Gordonston, 1800. Hindley, pt. iii. 340, 5l. 5s. Nassau, pt. ii. 174, 2l. 16s. Perry, pt. ii. 999, 1l. 17s. Inglis, 982. Herbert notices an edition of the date of 1598. The title says from the French of Guil. de la Perriere, 1567.

MIRROR OF LITERATURE, Amusement, and Instruction. Lond. Limbird, Nov. 1822-1840, 36 vols. woodcuts. Published weekly at 2d.— New Series. Lond. Cunningham, 1841-44, 6 vols.—Lond. Burstall, 1845-6, 4 vols. — Fourth Series, published monthly. Lond. 1847-49, by Hurst; Ollier; Kent and Richards, successively. 6 vols.—In all, 46 vols. 8vo.

This once popular periodical was originally edited by Mr. Thomas Byerly, the Reuben of the Percy Anecdotes. At his decease, it was edited for about six months by a Mr. Ray, but, falling off under him, it was transferred to Mr. John Timbs, who continued editor until Mr. Limbird relinquished the proprietorship in 1840. From 1841 to 1844 it was edited by Mr. D. M. Aird; from 1844 to 1846, by Mr. Gaspey; and from 1847 to the close, by Mr. J. B. St. John.

MISACMOS, i. e. Sir John HARINGTON.

MISCELLANEA, by J. G. (James Glassford.) Edinb. 1818, 4to.

Privately printed. Contains translations of Addison's Machinæ Gesticulantes et Sphæristerium, lines from Metastasio, Italian Sonnets, &c. Eyton, 9s. 6d.

MISCELLANEA ANTIQUA ANGLICANA: or, a select Collection of rare and curious Tracts, illustrative of the History, Literature, Manners, and Biography of the English Nation, during the 16th and part of the 17th Centuries. Lond. Smeeton, 1814-22, 4to.

Of this work, of which 250 copies were printed, only eight numbers were published. Burstall, 1847, 1l. 15s. Nassau, pt. ii. 175, 2l. Gardner, in 1854, 17s. CONTENTS: "Life and Death of David Illuzio." "Account of a Quarrel between A. Hall and M. Mallerie, 1579." "Account of the Christmas Prince, as exhibited in 1607." "Old Meg of Herefordshire, 1609." "The Cold Years, 1614." "Life of Long Meg of Westminster. 1635." "Historie of Fryer Bacon." "Rules and Orders for the Government of the House of an Earle, by M. Brathwait."—The first seven numbers are often found in a volume with Title as Volume I., and list of Contents.

MISCELLANEA SACRA. See BARRINGTON, Lord.

MISCELLANEA SCOTICA. See SCOTLAND.

MISCELLANIES on several curious Subjects: now first publish'd from their respective Originals. Lond. Curll, 1714, 8vo.

Pp. xxx. and 58. On the title-page is a portrait of Ant. à Wood. Edited by Dr. Rawlinson. In this volume are the proceedings against Anthony à Wood, in 1692, for insinuations of bribery and corruption against Edward Hyde, Earl of Clarendon, when Chancellor of the kingdom, with the author's defence. Geo. Chalmers, 8s.

Miscellaneous Letters, giving an Account of the Works of the Learned both at Home and Abroad. 4to. Vol. I. 578 pp. besides a copious Index. Vol. II. consists of only 7 numbers. The first number of this work, published weekly, price 3d. each, appeared on the 17th October, 1694.

Miscellanies, Historical, and Philological. A curious Collection of private Papers: (chiefly relating to English History and Heraldry) found in the Study of a Nobleman lately deceased (by some said to be by John, Duke of Lauderdale, Marq. of Halifax). Lond. 1703, 8vo. 6s. Contains the Secret Transaction of Sir John Bowring. temp. Charles I. at p. 78 to 182.

Mirth and Wisdom in a Miscellany of different Characters. Lond. B. Draggs, 1708. Blim, 7s. Reprinted, Lond. 1708, 8vo. with new title, 'Hickiety Pickelty, or a Medley of Characters.' Blim, 2830, 4s. 6d.

Miscellanea Aurea, or the golden Medley. Lond. 1720, 8vo. Nassau, pt. i. 2276, 5s.

Miscellanies in Prose and Verse (by Lord Suffolk). 1725, 8vo. 5s. LARGE PAPER. Lloyd, 670, 8s.

Miscellany on Taste, by Mr. Pope, &c. Lond. 1752. With frontispiece by Hogarth. Field, 1557, 12s.

Miscellany, a, consisting of the following particulars:—I. The Duke of Buckingham's Epitaph, translated into English. II. Epitaph on the Duke of Marlborough, &c. III. Reflections with regard to Dr. Atterbury, the Duke of Buckingham, Earl of Sunderland, and others. IV. The Characters of the Duke of Marlborough's Four Daughters. Printed in the Year 1753, 12mo.

Miscellanea Curiosa. Edited by W. Derham. Lond. 8vo. 3 vols. 5s.

Miscellaneous and Fugitive Pieces. Lond. 1774, sm. 8vo. 3 vols. 10s. 6d. These miscellanies, published by Tho. Davies, without Dr. Johnson's concurrence or knowledge, contain many things in which the Doctor had no concern whatever.

Miscellanies in Prose and Verse. Intended as a Specimen of the types at the Logographic Printing-Office. Lond. J. Walter, 1785, 12mo.

Miscellanies in Prose and Verse. Edinb. 1787, 2 vols. Gosset, 3559, 11s. *See* PAOET, Lord.

Miscellany of the DAFFNAYTNE CLUB, and of other Printing Clubs. *See* APPENDIX.

MISCHEAT-ul-Masabih. *See* MATTHEWS, A. N.

MISCHIEFS.—Strange and wonderfull Account of the great Mischiefs sustained by the late dreadful Lightning, Thunder, and Land-Floods. 1683, 8vo.
Nassau, pt. ii. 617, 17s.

MISCHNA.—Misnæ Pars; Ordinis primi Zeraim Tituli vii. Latine vertit et Commentario illustravit Gul. Guisius. Accedit Mosis Maimonidis Præf. in Misnam, Edv. Pocockio Interprete. Oxon. 1690, 4to.

Eighteen Treatises from the Mischna, translated by the Rev. D. A. de Sola and the Rev. M. J. Raphall. Lond. 1843, 8vo. 7s. 6d.

MISERERE, The. Panegyrical Essays upon the Lord's Prayer. Lord pity the people. Lond. 1717, 12mo.
Heber, pt. v. old mor. 16s.

MISERERE MEI DEUS.—A lytell Treatyse in Englysshe called the Exposycyon of Miserere mei Deus, translated by me P. Bushe, Preest & Bonehomme of Edyngton. 4to.

In verse. Herbert mentions two editions, 1501 and 1525, both printed by W. de Worde.

MISERIES of Human Life; or the Groans of Samuel Sensitive and Timothy Testy. With a few supplementary Sighs from Mrs. Testy. In *twelve* Dialogues (forming vol. 1 of the Work as afterwards published). Lond. Miller, 1806, 12mo. folding coloured frontispiece by W. H. Pyne.

Fifth edition. Lond. Miller, 1806, 12mo. folding coloured front.—Sixth edition (in which the name of the author, James Beresford, is first given).—Seventh edition. Lond. Miller, 1807, 12mo. front.

This humorous publication, written by the Rev. James Beresford, was exceedingly popular, and ran through five editions in one year. It was reviewed in the Edinb. Rev. No. 17, 1806.

Miseries of Human Life, &c. with which are now, for the first time, interspersed Varieties incidental to the principal Matter, in Prose and Verse. *In sex additional Dialogues*, as overheard by James Beresford, A.M., Fellow of Merton College, Oxford. Lond. Miller, 1807, 12mo. with folding frontispiece after Beresford, by Scriven.

This is the first edition of vol. 2, and was published in conjunction with the eighth edition of vol. 1 of same date. It was republished three times in 1807, by Miller, and a fourth time in 1810, by Tegg.

Miseries, &c. Tenth edition; to which are now, for the first time added, Posthumous Groans by T. T. and S. S. In twenty-one Dialogues. Lond. P. Wright, 1825, 12mo. 2 vols. the frontispiece reduced to size of book.

Eleventh edition. Lond. P. Wright and Son, 1826, 12mo. 2 vols. frontispiece reduced.

The Miseries of Human Life. An old Friend in a new Dress. New York, Putnam's Popular Library, 1853, 8vo. with alterations.

More Miseries, by Sir Fretful Murmur. Lond. 1807, 12mo.

Sixteen Scenes taken from the Miseries of Human Life, by one of the Wretched (J. A. Atkinson). Lond. 1807, oblong 8vo.

The Comforts of Human Life; or Smiles and Laughter of Charles Chearful and Martin Merryfellow. In seven Dialogues. Second edition. Lond. Oddy, 1807, coloured front. by Green.

The Pleasures of Human Life, or 'the Miseries' turned topsy-turvy, by Hilarius Benevolus (John Dritton). Lond. 1807, 12mo. plates by Rowlandson, 10s. 6d.

An Antidote to the Miseries of Human Life, in the History of the Widow Placid and her Daughter Rachel. Fifth edition. Lond. 1809. sm. 8vo. [By Harriet Corp]. —Sequel to second Edition, corrected, Lond. 1806, 12mo. Of a different character to the 'Miseries,' being a connected story.

MISSALE ad Usum Ecclesiæ Eboracensis, optimis Caracteribus recenter impressum. (Rouen, Olivier) 1516, folio.

THE YORK MISSAL.— Of this edition only four copies are known. Two of which are in the Bodleian (Gough and Douce col-

lections), the Third in the Univ. Library,
Camb., the Fourth at Stonyhurst College. A fragment exists in the British
Museum.—Rouen, Cousin, 1517, 4to. Imperfect copies are in the Bodleian and
Queen's Coll. Oxford.—Rouen, Bernard
and Cousin, opera Olivier. In the Maskell
Coll. British Museum.—Sine loco, Gachet,
1530, 4to. In the Gough Coll. Bodleian
Library.—Paris, Regnault, 1533, 4to. St.
John's Coll. Camb.; Bodleian, Douce, and
Gough Collections; Rev. J. Mendham.
Dr. Rawlinson had a copy of this edition,
in which he had written 'The monks of
Scotland, who allowed a dependance on
this metropolitan see, rejected its use, and
followed that of Sarum.'—Rouen, Violette,
n. d. folio. In the Gough Collection,
No. 31. See Gough's Account of York
Missals.

MISSALE ad Usum Ecclesiae Herefordensis. Rothom. P. Olivius
et Johannis Mauditier, 1502, folio.

THE HEREFORD MISSAL.—A copy, formerly T. Hearne's, ON VELLUM, minus a
small woodcut, is in the Bodleian Library,
and another on paper, but wanting the
title and part of the Syllabus. In the library of St. John's College, Oxford, is also
an imperfect copy.

MISSALE ad Usum Ecclesiae Sarisburiensis. Lond. R. Pynson, Impensis Card. Morton, Jan. 1. 1500
folio.

THE SALISBURY MISSAL.—A copy ON
VELLUM is in Earl Spencer's library. See
Dibdin's Ædes Althorp. ii. 193. Mss.
Carthy, i. p. 67, no. 256, 172 fr. Bodleian.
Emmanuel College.

A fac-simile of an advertisement for
the publishing of Missals 'in usum Ecclesiae Sarisburiensis, in the price letter,'
printed by Caxton, is to be found in Dr.
Dibdin's edition of Ames' Typog. Antiq.
i. p. cli. and in the Bibl. Spenc. iv. 349-50.

Other editions.—Rothom. Morin, die 12
Oct., 1492, folio. Coll. A—A a in eights.
A—D in eights. E. F. G. in sixes. Last
leaf contains device of printer. A copy
on VELLUM has been lately sold to the
British Museum, it is said, for 200l. Bodleian, partly on VELLUM, and imperfect.
—Venetiis, Raynoldus de Noviomagio,
1493, sic 8vo. ON VELLUM. FIRST KNOWN
EDITION. Mac-Carthy, 81 fr.—Venet. 1494,
12mo.—Venet. Hertzog. Impensis Egmont
et Barrevelt. Kal. Sep. 1494, fol.—Venet.
Hertzog. Impensis Egmont, 12mo. 1494.
Douce and Gough; in Bodleian; King's
Coll. and Univ. Lib. Cambridge.—Rothomagi, Morin, 1497, folio. Duke of Devonshire, ON VELLUM. A fine copy is in the
Royal Lib. Windsor Castle. Another, also

on VELLUM, at St. Edmund's College,
Herts.—Lond. apud Westmonasteriam
per Julianum Notarie et Johannem Barbier. Impensis W. de Worde, 1498, folio.
THE FIRST EDITION IN ENGLAND. cclxxxvi
leaves. University Library, Cambridge.
British Museum, imperfect. Duke of Sutherland.—Paris, Higman and Hopyl, 16
Julii, 1500, fol. marked in Bodleian Catalogue as 1510.—Ilanyn, s. l. Sep. 4, 1501,
fol. Bodleian.—Paris, J. de Prato, folio.
1502.—Paris, typis J. de Prato, seu. Jo. du
Pré, fol. 1502. Dean and Chapter of Ely.—
Paris, Kerver, 1503, 8vo. Bodleian. ON
VELLUM. St. Cuthbert's College, Ushaw.
—Lond. par Rich. Pynson, 1504, Kal. Jan.
folio. Emmanuel College, Cambridge, ON
VELLUM, Lord Spencer; British Museum,
but imperfect. The work begins at fol. x.
(preceded by a calendar) opposite the regal
arms and portcullis, with a Latin subscription of four leaves. On the reverse of fol.
cxviii. we have 'finit temporale.' Leaves
renumbered as far as fol. liii. On the reverse 'Explicit sanctuarale'; renumbered
again as far as fol. xxxvii. On the reverse follows a table; and 'Finis' in red,
concludes the volume.—Another edition,
in 1504, differing from all the other folios
of Pynson, ON VELLUM, is in St. John's
Coll. Oxford.—Paris, Verard, Jouii 29, 1504,
fol. University Library, Cambridge, no
title.—Paris, Hopyl, for Cloer de Ammerfoort and Byrkman, Sept. 13. 1504, folio.
Univ. Lib. Trinity College, Dublin; Earl of
Ashburnham.—Rouen, 1508, 8vo, ON VELLUM. Queen's College, Oxford. — Rouen,
1508, Mail xii. Morin, Impensis R. Richard, J. Iluayn, P. Coste, et W. Bernard,
4to.—Sine loco (Rouen), Ap. 27, 1508, folio.
Bodleian.—Rothomagi, impensis Hannin et
Bernard, Aug. 6, 1508, 4to. British Museum.
—Rouen, Sep. 27, 1508, 4to. Gough, in
Bodleian.—Rouen, Violletie, Aug. 2, 1509,
4to. British Museum, Sir R. S. Adair.—In
alma Parisiorum Academia, Morin, 1510,
folio.—Paris, Byrkman, 1510, fol. Chapter
Library, York.—Paris, Hopyl. Impensis
Byrkman, 10 Cal. April of Feb. 7, 1510-11,
folio. A. J. B. Hope, Esq. Bodleian, ON
VELLUM. Abp. Laud's copy, in University
Library, Trinity College, Dublin.—Lond.
per R. Pynson, 1512, folio. Bodleian, Balliol, and Christ's College. Inglis, 1014, one
leaf wanting, 2l. 5s.—Paris, Kembolt, Jan.
21, 1513, folio. St. John's College, Cambridge.—Paris, Hopyl, Impensis Byrchman, 1514, fol. Bodleian, University Lib.
Cambridge. Earl of Ashburnham—Rouen,
28, 1514, fol. Bp. Cosin's Library, Durham.
—Paris, apud Fr. Byrkman, 1515, 8vo.
Brit. Mus. Bodleian, Douce, and Gough,
Dr. Bloch—Paris, apud Joh. Petit et Joh.
Dieuaysa, 1516, 8vo. British Museum.—
Paris, 1516, 8vo. University College, Cam-

MISSALS—continued.
bridge.—Rouen, Danbet, impensis Guerin, 1517, 8vo.—Paris, Impensis Fran. Regnault, Mar. 20, 1519, folio. Bodleian, Trin. Coll. Dublin, Queen's Coll. Camb.—Paris, Higman, impensis Regnault et Byrkman, Oct. 29, 1519, 4to. Bodleian, Gough's Coll. two copies; St. Peter's Priory, Hinckley.—Paris, per Nichol. Higman, Oct. 50, 1519, 4to. Stonyhurst Coll.—Paris, Olivier, expensis Jacobi Cousin, Dec. 24, 1519, fol. Dean and Chapter of Salisbury, Sir H. Hoare, Trin. Coll. Camb.—Sine loco, Cousin, ? 1519. Bodleian, Gough, 109.—Lond. per Rich. Pynson, 1520, Kal. Jan. folio. According to Ames, this fine book, with musical notes, is curiously printed in red and black ink, and has the English arms quartered with the French. Bodleian Library, Douce, Gough, Emmanuel College. Copies on VELLUM are in the Bodleian Library, University Library, Camb.; St. John's College, Oxford, Abp. Land's copy.—Rothomagi, Caillard, 1521, 4to, Bodleian Library.—Rouen, Olivier, impensis Cousin, Sept. 5, 1521, 4to. Bodleian.—Paris, Petit, 1521, fol. British Museum, imperfect.— Paris, Impensis Franc. Regnault Parisien, 1526, folio. Bodleian, Maynooth College, Chapter Lib. York; Univ. Lib. Camb.—Paris, Fr. Regnault, 1527, Juill. 27, 4to. British Museum, Bodleian, imperfect.— Antwerp, Rnremond, impensis Byrkman, Mar. 28, 1527, folio. In the Spencer Collection, Bodleian, National Library. Paris.—In alma Parisi Acad. Opera Nic. Prevost, impensis Franc. Byrckman, 1527, folio. Bishop of Ely, 1258, 2l. Bodleian, Douce, and Gough Collections; Salisbury Cathedral, National Lib. Paris. ON VELLUM, from the McCarthy Collection, two leaves wanting. Sir M. M. Sykes, 22l. 1s. Brit. Museum, imperfect.—Opera atque Impensis Christ. Suremund. Ap. 14, 1528, folio. Bodleian. Imperfect—Parisiis, Regnault, 1529, folio or 4to. Bodleian Lib. Christ's College, Oriel College, Oxford; University Library and Queen's Coll. Cambridge.—1530, Paris, Remboldt. Utterson in 1852, pura, 47l. 10s.—Paris, Regnault, 1531, fol. Douce Collection. Bodleian.—Paris, 1532, folio. Univ. Lib. Cambridge.—Paris, 1533, 4to. University Library, Cambridge.—Parisiis, May 27, 1533, 4to. Bodleian, Gough.—Paris, 1534, folio. British Museum, Bodleian, imperfect. Constable, 23l, 1l. 1s.—Paris, Regnault, 1534, folio. St. Edmund's Coll. Herts.—Paris, 1535, 8vo.—Parisiis, 1539, 4to. A copy ON VELLUM, formerly belonging to Queen Mary, is in Eton College Library.—Venet. 1541, 8vo. Rob. Valentini ex officina R. Hamiltonis, typog. [Collation.—161—78—68].—Paris, Kerver.—1663, folio, ON VELLUM, St. Cuthbert's College, Ushaw.—Rouen,
Valentin, 1554, 4to. Pickering, sheets G and H wanting, 3l. 5s.—Rouen, Hamilton, sold by Valentin, 1554, 4to. Gough and Douce Collections, Bodleian Library, British Museum.—1555. Lond. per Joh. Kyngston and Henry Sutton, 4to. A copy is in the British Museum, Bodleian, C. Fynton, Esq.—Paris, impensis Merlin, 1555, folio, probably the finest edition of the Sarum Missal, with woodcuts, initials, &c., Sotheby, Dec. 1857, 16l. 5s. Heber, pt. 1. 4970, imperfect, 13s.—Paris, 1555, fol.—Paris, Amazeur, 1555, fol.—Paris, Amazeur pro Merlin, 1555, fol.—Paris, Amazeur, impensis Merlin, 1555, fol. Copies are in the British Museum, Bodleian, Queen's College, Oxford, Canterbury Cathedral, &c. 17 copies of this date have been seen with varied imprints, but they appear to be of the same edition; for difference between copies, see Herbert's Ames, page 1580.—Lond. Kyngston and Sutton, 1555, 4to. Bodleian, Gough, 198; C. Fytton, Esq.—Rouen, Valentin, 1555, 4to. British Museum.—Rouen, Hamilton, sold by Valentin, 1555 (in colophon 1554), 4to. Bodleian, Douce.—Sine loco, Valentin, 1555, 4to. Rev. J. Horner.—Lond. 1555, Dean and Chapter of Ely.—Lond. 1557, folio (? by John Day). Contains fol. CC. xliiii. besides the table and calendar prefixed, 21 copies are known. This edition is in the British Museum, Bodleian, Stonyhurst College, University Library, Cambridge; Balliol College, and New College, Oxford, &c., &c.—Editions without dates: Paris, Regnault, folio. Advocates' Library, Edinb.; Sir D. Dundas, &c. An imperfect copy ON VELLUM is in St John's College, Cambridge.—Lond. Pynson, folio. Without date or place, folio. Bodleian, Rev. J. Horner.—Small 8vo. An imperfect copy at Saint Cuthbert's College, Ushaw, containing Prayers for Henry VIII.

Although there are so many different editions of the Missals and other ancient Service books of the Ancient English Church, they but rarely occur for public sale, and therefore we are unable to guess prices. It may be taken as a general rule that they are all extremely valuable, and worth many times as much as they were a few years ago. A good account of them will be found in Maskell's Monumenta Ecclesiæ Anglicana, vol. 1 ; and in [Dickinson's] Account of the Service Books. Lond. Masters, 1860, 8vo. 8s. 6d.

MISSALE parvum pro Sacerdotibus in Anglia, Scotia et Ibernia itinerantibus, ex Missale Romano reformato Sine loco, 1615, 4to.

Formerly in the Harleian Collection. See Cat. vol. i. art. 1645; then of A. W. Pugin, Esq., the Architect.

Antwerp, 1626, 4to. Maskell. Sotheby's,

April, 1857, 8d. British Museum, J. Horner, Trinity College, Dublin; Bodleian and Queen's College, Oxford; Earl Spencer.

MISSALE aliquot pro Sacerdotibus, &c. Sine loco et imprim. 4to.
A copy in Sion College Library.

MISSALE Romanum ex decreto Sacrosancti Concilii Tridentini restitutum Pii V. jussu editum, et Clementis VIII. primum, nunc denuo Urbani Papæ VIII. auctoritate recognitum, et novis Festorum missis huonsque concessis auctum. IIis accedunt Festa quæ ex indulto Apostolico in Regno Hiberniæ celebrantur. Dublinii ex typog. R. Coyne, 1822, 8vo. also Keating and Brown, Lond.

Editions in 8vo. and 12mo. printed by authority of the Roman Catholic Church, either in Dublin or London, are always in print.

MISSAL. the Roman, for the use of the Laity, Lond. n.d. 12mo. Various editions and sizes kept in print.

Missale Romanum, Latin and English, with Supplement by F. C. Husenbeth. Lond. 1845, 12mo. 2 vols.

MISSELDEN, Edward, Merchant. The Circle of Commerce: or, the Ballance of Trade, in Defence of free Trade. Lond. 1623, 4to. 5s.

A curious tract of eighty leaves, written in opposition to the treatises by Gerard Malynes, an old Dutch merchant. Heber, pt. iv. 16s.

Free Trade: or, the Means to make Trade flourish. Lond. 1622, 8vo. Inglis, 1011, 6s.

MISSIONARIES.—Edifying and curious Letters of some Missionaries, 1707, 8vo. 2 vols.

Describing the labours of the Jesuits in the East. See JESUITS.

Propagation of the Gospel in the East; being an Account of the Success of two Danish Missionaries, sent to the East Indies, for the Conversion of the Heathens in Malabar; rendered into English from the High-Dutch. Lond. 1709-10, 8vo. two parts.

Thirty-four Conferences between the Danish Missionaries and the Malabarian Bramins (or Heathen Priests) in the East Indies, concerning the Truth of the Christian Religion, &c.; translated out of High-Dutch by Mr. Phillips. Lond. 1719, 8vo.

Several Letters relating to the Protestant Danish Mission at Tranquebar, in the East Indies. Lond. 1720, 8vo.

MISSON, F. M., Voyage to Italy. Lond. 1739, 8vo. 4 vols.

Highly praised by Addison. It was the first general account of Italy that appeared, but is in many places incorrect and prejudiced. Dent. pt. I. 1429, 6s. Heath, 2284, 1l. 6s. — London, 1699, 8vo. 2 vols.—Lond. 1714, 8vo. 4 vols. Bindley, pt. II. 1522, 9s. Misson's travels will be found in the second volume of Harris's Collection.

Memoirs and Observations in his Travels through England, englished by I. Ozell. Lond. 1719, 8vo. 3s. 6d. Willett, 1719, 6s.

MISSY, Cæsar de. Les Paraboles ou Fables, et autres petites Narrations du Sieur Issemedrases de Serdnol, Citoyen de la République Chrétienne du 18 Siècle : Mises en Vers. Et suivies d'un Appendice. Lond. 1769, 8vo. 3s. 6d.

Prefixed is a portrait of C. de Missy; a small oval, by G. Powle.

MIST, ——. Miscellany Letters. A Selection from Mist's Journal. Lond. 1722, 12mo. 2 vols.

Heber, pt. vii. 1s.

A republication of essays originally printed in a newspaper established to oppose the government of K. George I. and the claims of the Protestant succession.

Mist's Weekly Journal, folio. Bindley, pt. II. 1059. For 1725-6-7-8. Heber, in a vol. folio, 19s.

MITCHEL, James. Ravaillac redivivus : being a Narrative of the late trial of Mr. J. Mitchel, a Conventiclo-preacher, for an attempt on the sacred Person of the Archbishop of St. Andrews. To which is annexed, an Account of the Tryal of Major Thomas Weir, executed for Adultery, Incest and Bestiality. Lond. 1678, 4to.

Dr. George Hickes is said to be the author of this tract. It is reprinted in the eighth volume of the Somers Collection of Tracts. Nassau, pt. II. 1394, 6s.

MITCHELL, Hugh. Scotticisms, vulgar Anglicisms, and grammatical Improprieties corrected. Glasgow, 1799, 8vo.

— John, D.D. An Essay on the best Means of civilizing the Subjects of the British Empire in India, and of diffusing the Light of the Christian Religion throughout the Eastern World. 1806, 4to. 15s.
For this essay the University of Glasgow adjudged Dr. Buchanan's prize.

— Joseph. Poems. Lond. 1729, royal 8vo. 2 vols.
Now in little estimation. Mitchell was patronised by Sir Robert Walpole, and was distinguished by the title of Sir Robert Walpole's poet.

MITCHELL, Robert. Plans and Views in Perspective, with Descriptions of Buildings erected in England and Scotland; and also an Essay to elucidate the Grecian, Roman, and Gothic Architecture; accompanied with Designs. Lond. 1801, imperial folio, 1l. 1s.
Some copies have coloured plates.

MITCHELL (T.) Index Græcitatis Platonicæ, Oxonii, 1832, 8vo. 2 vols. See ARISTOPHANES. ORATORES GRÆCI. PLATONIS OPERA.

MITFORD, Rev. John. Agnes, the Indian Captive. A Poem. Lond. 1811, 12mo.
Poems. Lond. 1810.—Second edition, Lond. 1814, fcap. 8vo.
Christina, Maid of the South Seas. Lond. 1811, 8vo.
Narrative Poems on the Female Character in the various Relations of Life. Lond. 1812, vol. 1, 8vo.
Miscellaneous Poems. Lond. 1858, 12mo.
This well-known book collector and accomplished scholar edited the works of Gray, Milton, &c., and was, from 1834 to 1850, twice editor of the Gentleman's Magazine. He died, 1859, and a Memoir of him is given in the July number of the Gent.'s Mag.

— Mary Russell. Our Village; Sketches of Rural Character and Scenery. Lond. (Vol. 1, 1824, rep. 1825; vol. 2, 1826; vol. 3, 1828; vol. 4, 1830; vol. 5, 1832), &c. post 8vo. 5 vols.
New edition, revised. Lond. 1835, post 8vo. 3 vols. woodcuts.—New edition. Lond. Bohn, 1848, post 8vo. 2 vols. woodcuts, and fronts. on steel after Harvey, 10s.—Again, 1852, and since. A very amusing and sterling work.

American Stories for Young People; intended for children above ten years of age. Edited by Mary Russell Mitford. Lond. 1832, 17mo. 3 vols. fronts. The same book was re-issued in 1835, under the title of "Tales for Young People above ten Years of Age, selected from American writers."

Stories for Little Boys and Girls: intended for children under ten years of age. Selected from American writers by Mary Russell Mitford. Lond. 1833, 12mo. 3 vols. Re-issued in 1835 and 1840.

Lights and Shadows of American Life. Lond. 1832, post 8vo. 3 vols.

Country Stories. Lond. 1837.—Again, Lond. Parlour Library, 1847, post 8vo.

Belford Regis, or Sketches of a Country Town. Lond. Bentley, 1835, post 8vo. 3 vols. 1l. 11s. 6d. Reprinted in one volume in Bentley's Standard Novels, 1846, post 8vo. 6s.

Atherton and other Tales. Lond. 1854, post 8vo. 3 vols. 1l. 11s. 6d.

The Fresh-water Fisherman, Country Town Life, Christmas Amusements, Scenes and Charades, Old Master Green, are reprinted from Miss Mitford's "Village," by consent, for an edition of Johnstone's Edinburgh Tales. 1845-6, roy. 8vo. 3 vols. 13s. 6d.—Reissued from the same stereotype plates. Lond. Chapman and Hall, n. d. the 3 vols. bound in one, 8s. 6d.

Dramatic Works. Lond. 1854, 12mo. 2 vols.
Julian, a Tragedy, in five Acts, (verse). Lond. 1823, 8vo.
Scenes, Sonnets, &c. Lond. 8vo.
Foscari, a Tragedy. Lond. 1826, 8vo.
Rienzi, a Tragedy. Lond. 1828, 8vo.
Charles the First, an historical Tragedy in 5 Acts.

Wallington Hill: a Poem. Lond. 1819, 8vo.

Recollections of a Literary Life, or Books, Places, and People. Lond. 1851, post 8vo. 3 vols. port.—Second edition, Lond. 1853, post 8vo. 3 vols. port.—Third edition, Lond. 1858, post 8vo. 1 vol. 6s.

Miss Mitford also contributed to the following:

Finden's Tableaux; a series of picturesque scenes of national character, beauty, and costume. Lond. 1838, 4to.

Finden's Tableaux of the Affections; a series of picturesque illustrations of the womanly virtues. Lond. 1839, fol.

Finden's Tableaux; the Iris of prose, poetry, and art, for 1841. Lond. 1841, folio,

MITFORD, Wm. The History of Greece, with the Author's last Additions and Corrections; and a Life of the Author by Lord Redesdale. Lond. 1829, 8vo. 8 vols.
First edition, 5 vols. 4to. (vol. 1, Lond. 1784; vol. 2, 1790; vol. 3, 1795, vol. 4, 1808; vol. 5, 1818). Lond. 1784—1818, 4to. 5 vols. Vol. 1 was reprinted with additions and corrections in 1789. These additions were also printed separate, 4to. 2s.
Second quarto edition. Lond. 1808—1818, 4to. 5 vols.
First octavo edition, 10 vols. (vols. 1 to 8, Lond. 1795-7, vols. 9 and 10, 1818).
Second octavo edition, (vols. 1 to 8, Lond. 1814. Vols. 9 and 10, 1818).
Third octavo edition. Lond. 1818, 10 vols.
Fourth octavo edition. Lond. 1822, 10 vols.
Fifth octavo edition, with the author's last corrections and additions, (edited by W. King), to which is added a memoir by his brother, Lord Redesdale. Lond. 1829 8vo. 8 vols.
Sixth edition, edited by W. King. Lond. 1835, 12mo. 10 vols. pork. pub. at 2l. 10s.
Seventh and last edition, re-edited by W. King. Lond. 1838, 8vo. 8 vols. port. pub. at 4l. 4s.
With Continuation by R. A. Davenport. Lond. 1835, 12mo. 8 vols. An unauthorised reprint of the first half of Mitford's work, of which the copyright had expired, with an inferior Continuation in lieu of that portion which was still protected by copyright.

Observations on the History and Doctrine of Christianity. Lond. 1823, 8vo.

Treatise on the Military Force, and particularly the Militia of this Kingdom. Lond. 18, 8vo.

An Essay upon Harmony in Language, intended principally to illustrate that of the English Language. Lond. 1774, 8vo. Heath, 5s. 6d.—1804, 8vo. Drury, 2l 4s, 7s. Nassau, pt. i. 2284, 8s.

MITRE, The, a Poem.
Printed without a title. Galeb, in 1838. The writer's copy, with suppressed passages and additional stanzas, 6s. 6d.
See PERRONETT, E.

MITRE, The, and Crown. By George Osborn. Lond. 1748, and 8vo. 3 vols.
Reber, i. 4596, 1s.
The Mitre and the Crown; or a real Distinction between them: In a Letter to a reverend Member of the Convocation. Lond. 1711, 8vo.

A Continuation of the Mitre and the Crown; In a second Letter. Lond. 1712, 8vo.

The History of the Mitre and Porse; in which the first and second Parts of the secret History of the White Staff are fully considered, and the Hypocrisy and Villanies of the Staff himself are laid open and detected. Lond. 1714, 8vo.
(For 'The secret History of the White Staff,' see DEFOE, p. 619.)

MOALLAKAT, The. See JONES, Sir William.

MOCKETT, Richard, D.D. De Politia Ecclesiæ Anglicanæ. Lond. 1683, 8vo.
'A learned and useful system.'—Nicholson.—Lond. 1818. 4to. This edition was 'condemned to the flames and burnt.' —Nicholson. See also Wood's Athen. Oxon.

Deus et Rex—God and the King. 1615, &c. Frequently printed both in Latin and English by Royal Proclamation for the instruction of his majesty's subjects. Dedicated to the Immortal Memory of K. Edward VI. and the Stability of the English Church. See FULLER's Church History, by Brewer, vol. v. pp. 446. Heylin, Life of. Lond. pp. 76.

MOCQUET, John. Travels and Voyages into Asia, Africa, and America, the East and West Indies, Syria, Jerusalem and the Holy Land. Translated from the French by Nath. Pullen. Lond. 1696, 8vo.
Hibbert, 5479, russia, 8s. 6d. Roxburghe, 7121, 7s. White Knights, 2232, 10s.

MODENA, Leo. The History of the rites, customs and manner of life, of the present Jews throughout the world. Translated from the Italian, by Edmund Chilmead. Lond. 1650, 12mo. 4s.
An excellent work, consisting of pp. 249 and 23 leaves of introductory matter. —1707, 12mo.

MODERATE INTELLIGENCER, The. Lond. 1645, 4to. 2 vols.
Bindley, pt. iii. 364, 1l. 9s.

MODERATION—The History of, with her Nativity, Country, Pedigree, &c. Lond. 1669, 12mo. 2s. 6d.

MODERN TRAVELLER.—A Popular Description of the various Countries of the Globe. Edited by Josiah Conder. Lond. 1828, &c. 12mo. 30 vols. maps and woodcuts.

MODES.—A Treatise upon the modes: or, farewell to French Kicks. Lond. 1715, 8vo.
Written by Bishop Hains. Read, 2823, 4s. 6d. Hindley, pt. III. 1843, with the names of the persons satirically alluded to, filled up in MS, 11s. 6d.

MODUS tenendi Unum Hundredum, sive Curiam de Recordo. Lond. per W. de Worde, 4to.
Ten leaves. — Impr. per Rich. Pynson (1510). 4to.—Lond. R. Redman, 1528, 12mo. 4d. This treatise was frequently reprinted in the fifteenth century.

MODUS tenendi Curiam Baronum, cum Visu Francplegii. Impr. per Rich. Pynson. 1516, 4to.
Fourteen leaves. Frequently reprinted.

MORRIS ATTICISTA. De Vocibus Atticis et Hellenicis, Græce. Gregorius Martinus de veteri et vera Græcarum Litterarum Pronuntiatione. Oxon. 1712, 8vo. 4s.

MOFFATT, Rev. J. M. The History of the Town of Malmesbury, and of its ancient Abbey: together with Memoirs of eminent Natives, &c. and an Appendix. Tetbury, 1805, 8vo.
Nassau, pt. 1. 2287, 6s. Fonthill, 2111, 16s. FINE PAPER. Fifty copies printed. Baker, 425, 6s. 6d. Collation.—Pp. 1—xx. 1—250, and 4 plates.

MOFFET, William (Schoolmaster). The Irish Hudibras, in eight Cantos. Lond. 1755, 8vo.
In little estimation. The design is to ridicule the manners of the country people of Ireland; the humour is very low, and the poetry lower than the humour. See Retrospective Review, III. 318-35.

MOGUL.— A true Relation of the Kingdom of the great Magor or Mogul. Lond. 1622, 4to.
Title and seven leaves, the last blank. Reprinted in the first volume of the Harleian Miscellany.

MOGUL TALES, or the Dreams of Men awake; being Stories told to divert the Sultanas of Guzerat. Written in French by the celebrated Mr. Guelette, author of the Chinese Tales, &c. Now first translated into English. Lond. 1743, 12mo. 2 vols. copper-plates.

MOHAMMED. See KORAN. PRIDEAUX, H. IRVING, Washington.
Life of Mohammed, translated from the Arabic of Abulfeda, with an Introduction, &c., by the Rev. W. Murray. Elgin, n. d. 8vo. pub. 10s.

MOHUN.—Trial of Lord Mohun for killing the Duke of Hamilton in a Duel. Lond. Folio. See HAMILTON.

MOHS, Frederick. Treatise on Mineralogy; or, the Natural History of the Mineral Kingdom. Translated from the German, with considerable Additions, by William Haidinger, F.R.S.E. 1825, post 8vo. 3 vols. 12s. pub. 1l. 16s.
The characters of the classes, orders, genera, and species; or the characteristic of the natural history system of mineralogy. Ed. 1820, 8vo.

MOISES, Edward, M.A. The Persian Interpreter, in three Parts. 1. Grammar of the Persian Language. 2. Persian Extracts in Prose and Verse. 3. A Vocabulary, Persian and English. Newcastle, 1792, 4to.
According to Dr. Adam Clarke, 'this grammar, which is founded on the model of that by Sir Wm. Jones, and which professes to be an introduction to it, is a work of considerable merit. Brockett, 2263, 7s.

MOIVRE. See DE MOIVRE.

MOLANUS, John. Idea Togatæ Constantiæ sive Francisci Tailleri Dubliniensis prætoris in persecutione congressus, et Religionis Catholicæ defensione interitus. Paris, 1629, 12mo. title engraved.
Harris, in his edition of Ware, III. p. 205, says he had never seen this small volume. Heber, pt. I. 4534, 4l. 4s. Now in the Grenville Collection.

MOL

HOLDSWORTH, Robert, Lord Viscount. An Account of Denmark in 1692. Lond. 1738, 8vo.
Best edition of this elegant work. Heath, 2491, 10s. 6d. Foothill, 2675, 12s. —1694, 8vo. Three editions appeared in this year.
Animadversions on a pretended Account of Denmark. Lond. 1694, 8vo. Written by Dr. Will. King, of Ch. Ch. Oxford.
The Commonwealth's Man unmasqued, or a Rebuke to the Author in his Account of Denmark, in two Parts. Lond. 1694, 12mo. According to Ant. à Wood, written by Thomas Rogers.
Denmark vindicated: being an Answer to a late Treatise called an Account of Denmark as it was in the year 1692. Lond. 1694, 8vo.

— R. Poems and Translations. Lond. 1716, 8vo.

MOLIÈRE, J. B. P. de. Œuvres avec des Remarques par M. Bret. Londres, 1809, 12mo. 8 vols.
Plays, translated by John Ozell. 1714. 12mo. 6 vols. Rhodes, 1875, 6s. 6d.
Select Comedies in French and English (interpaged). Lond. Watts, 1732, 12mo. 8 vols. with cuts by Hogarth, &c. Reed, 2292, 1l. 18s. Dent, pt. L 1434, 2l. 4s.
The Works of Molière, French and English (interpaged). Lond. Watts, 1739, 12mo. 10 vols. port. and plates. A complete translation, attributed to Mr. Henry Baker, F.R.S., and the Rev. Mr. Miller. This is a reprint of the previous edition of 1732, with the same plates, and the addition of about 15 Plays; but the Life and Dedications are different. Marquis of Townshend, 2103, 10 vols. 2l. 2s.—1748, 12mo. 10 vols. Roswell, 1892, 1l. 18s. Nassau, pt. II. 1457, 1l. 11s. 6d.—1755, 12mo. 10 vols. White Knights, 2537, 2l. 2s.
Works translated into English. Berwick, 1770, 12mo. 6 vols. 12s.
Tartuffe, or the French Puritan, a Comedy, translated by Matthew Medbourne. Lond. 1670, 4to. Rhodes, 1672, 6s. 6d. Roxburghe, 5477, 5s.—1707, 4to.
The Metamorphosis; or the old lover outwitted, a farce, translated by John Cary. Lond. 1704, 4to.
Monsieur de Pourceaugnac; or Squire Trelooby, done into English. Lond. 1704, 4to.
Tales from (sixteen of) Molière's Plays by Dacre Barrett Lennard. Lond. Chapman and Hall, 1869, post 8vo. 10s. 6d.

MOLIÈRE, H. S. Memoirs of the Life and Rare Adventures of Henrietta Sylvia Molière, a Romance translated from the French,
in 7 pts. Lond. 1672-7, 12mo. 2 vols. in 1. Hibbert, 4s. 6d.

MOLINA, Don Juan Ignatius. The geographical, natural and civil History of Chili. To which are added, Notes from the Spanish and French Versions, and two Appendices by the English Editor. Lond. 1809, 8vo. 2 vols. 12s.—Lond. 1817, 8vo. 2 vols.
An excellent work.

MOLINÆUS, Anglicè MOULIN.

MOLL, Herman. A new Description of England and Wales and the adjacent Islands. Lond. 1724, folio. Heber, pt. ix. 1l. 2s.
System of Geography. Lond. 1701, folio. Heber, pt. x. 8s.
Moll published many maps, which are attached to various works.

MOLLESON, William, and John LANE. The Reports of the Commissioners appointed to examine, take, and state the Public Accounts of the Kingdom; presented to his Majesty, and to both Houses of Parliament: with the Appendices complete. Lond. 1783-7, 4to. 3 vols. 1l. 1s.

MOLLIEN, M. G. Travels in the Interior of Africa to the Sources of the Senegal and Gambia. Edited by T. E. Bowdich. Lond. 1820, 4to. With a Map and Plates. pub. 2l. 2s.
Travels in the Republic of Colombia in the Years 1822 and 1823. Translated from the French. Lond. 1824, 8vo.

MOLLOY, Charles. De Jure Maritimo et Navali. Ninth Edition, with Additions. Lond. 1769. 8vo. 2 vols. 8s.
Best edition of a work originally published in 1676.
Holland's Ingratitude, or a serious Expostulation with the Dutch. Lond. 1666, 4to. With a Frontispiece by Gaywood, and explanatory leaf in verse. Lloyd, 799, 1l. 15s. Dowdeswell, 562, 1l. 8s. Hollis, 1080, 1l. 15s. Heber, pt. II. 2s. Bindley, pt. iv. 348, 11s. Dilae, pt. II. 2345, 2l. 10s.

— Franciscus, Grammatica Latino-Hibernica compendiata. Romæ, Prop. fide, 1677, 12mo. 10s. 6d.

A copy of this and both the following are in the British Museum.
Speculum Vitæ vel Desiderius, Hibernice. Lond. 1676.
Lucerna Fidelium, Hibernicè. Rom. 1676, 8vo. Heber, pt. i. 4540, uncut, 9s.

MOLYNEUX, T., M.D. Observations on the Danish Mounts, Forts and Towers in Ireland. Dublin, 1725, sm. 4to.
See BOATE, Gérard.

MOLYNEUX, William. The Case of Ireland's being bound by Acts of Parliament in England, stated. Dublin, 1698, sm. 8vo.
Roxburghe, 8887, 4s. Frequently reprinted. LARGE PAPER. 10s. 6d. — 1720, 8vo. — 1725, 8vo. — 1770, 8vo.
Answers to this work, by William Atwood and John Cary, appeared in 1698.
See REILLY, Hugh.

MOLYNEUX Family.—The Pedigree of the Family of Molyneux, of Castle Dillon, in the County of Armagh, Ireland. Evesham, 1819, fol.
A single sheet, arranged and printed for private distribution by Sir Thomas Phillipps, Bart.
A History of the Family of Molyneux, 1821, 12mo. Fifty copies printed for private distribution by Sir Thomas Phillipps, Bart.

MONARDUS, Nicholas, M.D. of Seville. Joyfull Newes out of the newe founde Worlde, wherein is declared the Vertues of diuerse and sundrie Herbes, Trees, Oyles, Plantes and Stones, &c. Three Bookes. Englished by Jhon Frampton. Lond. 1577, 4to.
Hibbart, 5601, morocco, 11s. Inglis, 565, morocco, 1l. 9s. White Knights, 1723, morocco, 2l. 2s.—1580, 4to. Bliss, 1l. 9s.—1596, 4to. Newly corrected and amended, and as by conference with the old copies may appeare, whereunto are added three other bookes treating of the Beaar Stone, the herb Escuerçonera, the properties of Iron and Steele in Medicine, and the benefit of Snow. A second title occurs at page 111, but the paging continues to 187. Gardner, in 1854, 1l. 15s. North, pt. iii. 571, morocco, 2l. 10s. Towneley, pt. i. 529*, 1l. 5s. Bindley, pt. ii. 1002, 13s. Caldecott, 12s.

MONBODDO, James Burnet, Lord. Ancient Metaphysics; or, the Science of Universals. Edinb. 1779-99, 4to. 6 vols.

Of the Origin and Progress of Language, Edinb. 1773-92. 8vo. 6 vols. Horne Tooke, 477. Vol. 1. only with MS. notes by Tooke, 5l. 7s. 6d. resold. Heber, pt. vii. 2l. 15s. Edinb. 1774-92, 8vo. 6 vols. Edwardes, 2l. 9s. Heath, 3, 4l. Roscoe, 90, 3l. 6s.
Monboddo, among other strange fancies, considered that men were originally monkeys, and that a nation still existed with tails.

MONCRIEFF, W. Thomas. Poems. Lambeth, at his private press, for private distribution only. 1829, 12mo.
Eyton, mor. 10s.
This gentleman's name originally was Thomas, but he assumed that of Moncrieff on writing for the Stage; he was most famous for his Burlesques. "Giovanni in London," " Tom and Jerry," with others have been printed, as also many popular Songs, Dramas, &c., written before he became blind. The Amatory Poems of Thomas Shuffleton, Esq., 12mo. is attributed to him.

MONEY.—The Pleasant Art of Money Catching. 1705, 12mo. reprinted, Lond. 1840.
Nassau, pt. ii. 59, 7s. — 1737, 12mo. —1684, 12mo.
The Massacre of Money (a Poem by T. A.). Lond. T. Creed, 1602, 4to. Attributed to Thomas Achelly or Achellou; but only on the ground of the correspondence of initials. Heber, pt. iv. 112, 2l.
All for Money.—An old moral Play. *See* Collier's History of Dramatic Poetry, vol. ii. p. 347. Reprinted by Mr. Halliwell in his privately printed volume, "The Literature of the xvith and xviith Centuries." 4to.
A Search for Money, or the Lamentable Complaint of the Wandering Knight, Mons. l'Argent. *See* Percy Society, No. 2, Appendix.
Money masters all Things, or satyrical Poems. 1696, sm. 8vo. Inglis, 1042, 4s. —1698, sm. 8vo. Nassau, pt. ii. 1480*, 5s. White Knights, 2344, 11s.
Money does master all Things, a Poem. York, 1696, sm. 8vo. Hibbert, 5433, 2l. 6s. Bliss, pt. ii. 3486, 1l.

MONFART, Henry de. An exact and curious Survey of all the E. Indies, even to Canton, all duly performed by Land. Wherein also are described the huge Dominions of the great Mogor. Lond. 1615, 4to.
A copy is in the British Museum. Inglis, 964, 1l. 11s. 6d. Gordonstoun, 1628.

2l. 7s. Weber, pt. vi. 1l. 5s. It is reprinted in the third volume of the Somers Collection of Tracts.

MONIER, P. The History of Painting and Engraving. Lond. 1699, 8vo. 5s.

Hoscoe, 1839, 8s.

MONINGS, Edward. The Landgravine of Hessen his princelie Receiving of her Magesties Embassador (Henry Clinton, second Earl of Lincoln). Lond. by Robert Robinson, 1596, 4to.

Bindley, pt. ll. 2530, 1l. 1s. Hibbert, 5604, morocco, 2l. White Knights, 1644, morocco, 3l. 15s. Reynold, Heber, pt. ix. 2l. 11s. Reprinted in Nichols' Progresses of Queen Elizabeth.

MONIPENNIE, John. The Abridgment or Summarie of the Scots Chronicles, with a short Description of their Originall, &c. (Lond.) Printed at Brittaine's Burse, by John Budge, 1612, 4to.—Another edition. Lond. 1612, 12mo.

Lond. 1612, 12mo.—Nassau, pt. ll. 17, 11s. Reed, 5245, 13s. Roxburghe, Supplement, 674, 2l. 4s. Gordonstoun, 1600, 1l. 1s. Hibbert, 5495, 10s. Nassau, pt. l. 2291, 6s. This edition is reprinted in Misc. Scotica, vol. l. 1818, 12mo.—Edinb. J. W(reitton), 1633, 12mo. Bindley, pt. ll. 1778, 19s.— Edinb. 1662, 18mo.—1671, 18mo.

See SCOTLAND, Certayne Matters, 1597.

MONITOR.—The Monitor; or British Freeholder, Aug. 9, 1755, to July 3, 1759, Nos. 208. Lond. 1756-9, 8vo. 4 vols.

A popular political paper, originally planned by Alderman Beckford.
The Monitor, or Green-Room laid open, 1767, folio. Eighteen numbers, all published. A periodical theatrical paper. Field, 1005, 12s.

MONK, George, Duke of Albemarle. Observations upon military and political Affairs. Lond. 1671, fol. portrait.

Bindley, pt. l. 172, 5s.—1796, 8vo. Illustrated with plates, 6s.

The Pedegree and Descent of General Monck, setting forth how he is descended from Edw. III. and Richard, King of the Romans, Lond. 1659, 4to. 5s.

Five Tracts relating to General Monk. 1659-70, 4to. Gough, 2263, 1l. 10s.

The Cloud opened; or, the English Heros. By a loyal and impartial Pen. Lond. 1670, 4to. A scurrilous pamphlet consisting of 48 pages. It is reprinted in the fourth volume of the Harleian Miscellany.

The Christian's Victory over Death, preached at the Funeral of George, Duke of Albemarle, in the Collegiate Church of Westminster, 30th Apr. 1670; on 1 Cor. xv. 57. By Seth Ward, Bishop of Salisbury. Lond. 1670, 4to. Prefixed is a portrait of Monk. Bright, 8s. 6d.

Musarum Cantabr. Threnodia. Cantab. 1670, 4to. Bindley, pt. lll. 653, 2s.

Epicedia Universitatis Oxoniensis in Obitum Georgii DucisAlbemarliæ. Oxon. 1670, folio.

A Collection of his Letters relative to the Restoration of the royal Family. Lond. 1714, 8vo.

The Order and Ceremonies used at the Funeral of his Grace George Monk, Duke of Albemarle. Lond. 1722, 4to. Bindley, pt. iv. 98.

Monk; or the Fall of the Republic and the Restoration of the Monarchy in England in 1660, by M. Guizot; translated from the French by Andrew R. Scoble. Lond. Bohn, 1851, post 8vo. 1s. Gd.

See GUIZOLE, Thomas. LLOYD, David. PRICE, John. SANDYOAN, Francis. SKINNER, Thomas. Also Granville Catalogue, il. p. 8id. In the British Museum are many tracts relative to Monk, Duke of Albemarle.

— John. An Agricultural Dictionary. Lond. 1794, 8vo. 3 vols.

Consisting of extracts from the most celebrated authors and papers.

— James Henry, Bishop of Peterborough.

See BENTLEY, Richard. EURIPIDES, Porson, Richard.

MONK.—The Monk's Hood pull'd off; or, the Capvchin Fryar described. In two parts, translated out of French. Lond. 1671, 8vo.

With a frontispiece. The first part was written by Du Moulin, the second by M. Clovet. Reed, 2636, 4s.

MONMOUTH, James Scot, Duke of. An historical Account of the heroic Life and magnanimous Actions of James, Duke of Monmouth, &c. By S. T. Lond. 1683, 12mo. Portrait by Van Hove.

Lloyd, 121, 4s. 6d. Nassau, pt. l. 2008, 5s. Dowdeswall, 385, 6s. 6d. Roxburghe, 6371, 1l. 16s. Several tracts relating to this unfortunate Prince are reprinted in the Harleian Miscellany and the Somers' Collection of Tracts.

— Robert Cary, Earl of. Memoirs of the Life of Robert Cary, Baron of Leppington, and Earl of

Monmouth. Written by himself. With some explanatory Notes. Lond. 1759, 8vo. frontispiece.
Sir M. M. Sykes, pt. ii. 423, 10s. Gough, 2110, 10s. 6d. Willett, 850, 10s. Bindley, pt. ii. 1726, 10s. Garrick, 1512, 10s. Heath, 1875, 1l. 1s. Fonthill, 1470, 1l. 2s. Roxburghe, 8452, 13s. LARGE PAPER. 1l. 1s. —New edition, edited by Sir Walter Scott. Edinb. 1809, 8vo. 6s. LARGE PAPER. Duke of York, 8495, 13s.

MONMOUTHSHIRE.— Lamentable News out of Monmouthshire, occasioned by the Overflowing of Waters in the said County. Lond. 1607, 4to. frontispiece.
A copy is in the British Museum. Perry, pt. ii. 501, 1l. 10s.
Memoirs of Monmouthshire, 1708, 18mo. See Rooses, N. Heber, pt. ii. 3 copies, 2s. each; pt. v. 6s. 6d.
A Gentleman's Tour through Monmouthshire and Wales (by Joseph Cradock, Esq.] Lond. 1794, 12mo. 5s. Fonthill, 2558, 15s.
A Tour in Monmouthshire and Part of Glamorganshire. Halesworth, 1807, 12mo. Fonthill, 2664, date 1817, 8s.
See Coxe, Archdeacon. WILLIAMS.

MONRO, Alexander, M.D. The Works, with the Life of the Author. Edinb. 1781, 4to. 10s. 6d. plates.
Published by the author's son, with a portrait of the doctor, after A. Ramsay, by J. Basire, 1776.
Essay on Comparative Anatomy. Lond. 1744, 8vo.—New edition, with additions. Edinb. 1783.
Osteology; or a Treatise on the Anatomy of the Bones. To which are added, a Treatise on the Nerves, &c. Sixth edition, corrected and enlarged. Edinb. 1758, 8vo.—Again, Edinb. 1763.—Edinb. 1785.
Translated into French, with plates by Cl. Sue. Paris, 1759, folio.

— Alexander, M.D., son of the preceding. The Structure and Physiology of Fishes explained, and compared with those of Man and other Animals. Edinb. 1785, royal folio.
Pp. 128, with 44 plates.
Observations on the Structure and Functions of the nervous System, illustrated with Tables. Edinburgh, 1783, royal folio. Willett, 1655, 1l.
A Description of all the Bursæ Mucosæ of the Human Body; their Structure explained, and compared with that of the capsular Ligaments of the Joints, and of those Sacs which line the Cavities of the Thorax and Abdomen; with Remarks on the Accidents and Diseases which affect those several Sacs, and on the Operations necessary for their Cure. Illustrated with Tables. Edinb. 1788, folio.
A System of Anatomy and Physiology, with the Comparative Anatomy of Animals. Edinb. 1795, 8vo. 3 vols.

MONRO, ALEX., M.D., son of the preceding. Elements of the Anatomy of the Human Body in its sound State, with occasional Remarks on Physiology, Pathology, and Surgery. Edinb. 1825, 8vo. 2 vols.
Outlines of the Anatomy of the Human Body in its sound and diseased State. Edinb. 1813, 8vo. 4 vols. (vol. 4 being plates.)

— Donald. Description of the Western Isles of Scotland called Hybrides. Edinb. 1774, 12mo.
The following is the title of this curious work, 'Description of the Western Isles of Scotland, called Hybrides; by Mr. Donald Monro, High Dean of the Isles, who travelled through most of them in the Year 1549, with the Genealogies of the chief Clans of the Isles. Now first published from the MS. To which is added, 1. An Account of Hirta and Rona, by the Lord Register, Sir George M'Kenzie, of Tarbat, never before published. 2. A Description of Saint Kilda, by Mr. Alexander Duchao, late Minister there. 3. A Voyage to Saint Kilda, in 1697, by M. Martin, Gentleman.' The volume consists of pp. 64 and 156, with title and contents. The tracts have separate titles, dated 1773. Only 50 copies printed. Heber, pt. ix. 6s.

— Donald, M.D. A Treatise on Medical and Pharmaceutical Chemistry. Lond. 1788-90, 8vo. 4 vols. and appendix to vol. iii.

— Colonel Robert. Expedition with the worthy Scots Regiment (called Mac-Keyes Regiment) levied in August 1626, and reduced after the Battaile of Narling to one Company, in September 1634, at Wormes in the Paltz. To which is annexed the Abridgement of Exercise, &c. Lond. 1637, folio.

1586 MON MON

Roxburghe, 7955, 19s. Bindley, pt. II. 1053, 1l. 11s. Dowdeswell, 613, 1l. 14s. Bright, 10s. 6d. LARGE PAPER. Gordonstoun, 1803, 2l. 12s. 6d. Now in the Grenville Collection. Constable, 865, 7l. 12s. 6d. *Collation.*—Title, epistle dedicatory to the 'Prince Elector Palatine of Rhine,' to the reader, and Latin verses, 8 leaves; part I. pp. 89, also table, &c. 11 leaves; part II. pp. 724, and table, 9 leaves.

MONROE, James, President of the United States. A Tour of Observation through the north-eastern and north-western States in 1817. Philadelphia, 1818, 8vo.

MONSON, W. J. Extracts from his Journal during a Tour in Istria and Dalmatia in 1817. Lond. 18 , 8vo. not published.

— Sir William. Megalopsychy: being a particular and exact Account of the last XVII Years of Queen Elizabeth's Reign, both military and civil. The first written by Sir W. Monson; the second by H. Townshend. Lond. 1682, folio.

'To this work Camden was greatly indebted.'—*Nicolson.* Dent, pt. II. 775, 1l. 3s. Bright, 3s. An enlarged edition of Monson's Account of the English and Spanish Fleets during the War with Spain in Queen Elizabeth's Time, with five other treatises by the same author, (referred to as "Monson's Tracts,") published from original MSS., will be found in the third volume of Churchill's Collection of Voyages and Travels.

MONSTRELET, Eng. de. Chronicles, translated from the most approved Originals, with Notes by Col. Thomas Johnes. Hafod, 1809, 4to. 5 vols. the fifth consisting entirely of plates in outline.

An excellent translation. Strettell, 1244, 8l. 10s. Duke of York, 5387, 18l. 10s. LARGE PAPER in folio, twenty-five copies printed at 25l. 5s.; a few of them with the plates coloured under the inspection of Col. Johnes, 521. 10s.—Second edit. Lond. 1810, 8vo. 19 vols. with the 51 original plates in 4to. pub. at 7l. 4s.—New edition, with notes, and upwards of 100 woodcuts (uniform with Froissart). Lond. 1839, super-royal 8vo. 2 vols.—Again, Lond. 1853, 2 vols. 1l. 4s.

Les Chroniques de France, &c. Paris, Ant. Verard (1494), folio. 2 vols. two editions. —Paris, 1512, folio. 2 vols.—Paris, 1518, folio. 3 vols.—Paris, 1572, folio. 3 vols.

Best edition. Thuanus's copy on LARGE PAPER is in the Grenville Collection. It produced at Col. Stanley's sale 13*l*. Sir M. M. Sykes, 48*l*. 6s.—Paris, 1595, folio. 3 vols.—Paris, 1603, folio. 2 vols. And several recent editions in 8vo.

MONSTERS.—Of Two wonderful Popish Monsters, to Wyt; of a Popish Asse which was found at Rome, and a Monkish Calfe, calved at Friberge, witnessed and declared by Luther and Melancthon, translated by John Brook, of Ash, next Sandwich. Lond. T. East, 1579, 4to. two woodcuts.

MONTACUTIUS. *See* MONTAGU.

MONTAGU, Basil. Selections from the Works of Taylor, Hooker, Barrow, South, Latimer, Brown, Milton, and Bacon. Third Edition. Lond. 1829, crown 8vo. 12s.

An excellent selection.—First edition, 1805. 12mo. 5s.—Second edition, 1807, 12mo. 2 vols. Duke of York, 3603, 14s.

A Summary of the Law of Set-off, with an Appendix of Cases on that Subject. Lond. 1801, 8vo. 6s.—1827, 8vo.

Precedents and Orders in Bankruptcy. Lond. 1807, royal 8vo. 10s. 6d.

Selection of Opinions of different Authors upon the Punishment of Death. Lond. 1809, 1813, 15. 8vo. 3 vols. 1l. 1s.

Inquiry concerning the Expediency of limiting the Creditor's Power to refuse a Bankrupt's Certificate according to the Alterations now proposed in Parliament. Lond. 1809, 8vo. 2s.

The Debates during the last Session of Parliament upon the Bills for abolishing the Punishment of Death for Stealing to the Amount of 40s. in a Dwelling-house; for Stealing to the Amount of 5s. privately in a Shop, and for stealing on navigable Rivers. Lond. 1811, 8vo. 5s.

Inquiries into the Effects of fermented Liquors. By a Water-drinker. Lond. 1814, 8vo. plates.—Third edition, Lond. 1841, 10s. 6d.

Inquiry into the aspersions upon the late Ordinary at Newgate, with observations on Newgate and the Punishment of Death. Lond. 1815, 4to.

Digest of new Decisions in Bankruptcy, with Suggestions for Improvement of the Bankrupt Laws. Lond. 1820-5, royal 8vo. pts. 1. to v. 1l. 13s.

Reports of Cases in Bankruptcy, 1831 and 1832. Lond. 1832, continued by Montagu and Bligh's Reports, 1832-33; Mon-

MONTAGU—*continued*.
tagu and Ayrton, 1833-37; Montagu and
Chitty, 1839-40; Montagu, Deacon, and
De Gex, 1841-44, in all 9 vols. royal 8vo.
18*l*. 15*s*.
— Summary of the Law of Lien, with an
Appendix of Cases. Lond. 1821, 8vo. 12*s*.
— Digest of the Laws of Partnership. Second Edition. Lond. 1822, royal 8vo. 2
vols, 1*l*. 10*s*.—First edition, 1815, 2 vols.
16*s*.
— On the Law of Composition with Creditors. Lond. 1823, 8vo. 6*s*.
— Digest of Pleadings in Equity, with
Notes of the Cases decided in the different
Courts of Equity. Lond. 1824, royal 8vo.
2 vols.
— Inquiries respecting the Courts of Commissioners of Bankrupts and Lord Chancellor's Court. Lond. 1825, 8vo. 3*s*. 6*d*.
— Arrangement of the new Bankrupt Act,
6 Geo. IV. c. 16. Lond. 1825, 8vo. 4*s*.
— Evidence in Bankruptcy. Lond. 1826,
8vo. 6*s*.
— Letter on the Report of the Chancery
Commission. Lond. 1826, 8vo. 2*s*.
— A Digest of the Bankrupt Laws, as
altered by the new Statutes. Third Edition, with considerable Additions. Lond.
1827, royal 8vo. 2 vols. 2*l*. 12*s*. 6*d*.—First
edition, 1804-5, royal 8vo. 2 vols.—Second
edition, 1819-20, royal 8vo. 3 vols. 1*l*. 1*s*.
— Thoughts on Laughter, by a Chancery
Barrister. Lond. 1830, 18mo. on vellum,
unique. Eyton, mor. 1*l*. 2*s*. On yellow
paper, unique. Eyton, mor. 10*s*. 6*d*.
Mr. Montagu is author of various other
Juridical Works. *See* BACON, Francis.

MONTAGU, Mrs. Elizabeth. Letters, with some of the Letters of her
Correspondents, in two Parts. Lond.
Bulmer, 1809-13. crown 8vo. 4
vols. portrait, 12*s*.
Hindley, pt. II. 1587, II. 1*s*. LARGE PAPER, in demy 8vo. 2*l*. 2*s*. Mrs. Montagu
was the founder of 'The Blue Stocking
Club.'

— Essay on the Genius and Writings of
Shakspeare, compared with the Greek and
French dramatic Poets; with Remarks
upon the Misrepresentations of M. de Voltaire. 8vo. According to T. Warton, the
most elegant and judicious piece of criticism this age has produced.—1769, 8vo.
Roxburghe, 3881, 7*s*.—1770, 8vo. Garrick,
1630, 6*s*.—1772, 8vo. Willett, 1719, 3*s*. 6*d*.
—1785, 8vo. Edwards, 143, 3*s*. 6*d*.—1810,
8vo, 7*s*.

— Col. George. Ornithological
Dictionary; or, Alphabetical Synopsis of British Birds, 2 vols.
Lond. 1802. Supplement, 1 vol.—
Exeter, 1813, 8vo. together 3 vols.
An esteemed work. Sotheby's in 1826,
2*l*. 4*s*. Collation.—Vol. I. A to L. Pages
xiii of Introduction, and a plate coloured of
Cirl Bunting. Vol. II. M to Z. Appendix,
List of British Birds, Explanation of technical Terms, and Catalogue of Authors.
Supplement. A to Y, and Appendix A to
8, Definitions, Directions, and a Catalogue
of Additions and Alterations to be made
in the original list of British Birds, also
23 plates.
— New Edition, edited by Rennie. Lond.
1831, 8vo. in one volume, 1*l*. 1*s*. woodcuts.
— Testacea Britannica: or natural History of British Shells. With Supplement.
Romsey, 1823. Exeter, 1808, 4to. 2 vols.
2*l*. 2*s*. Vol. I. pp. 606 and index, with 16
plates. Vol. II. (Supplement) pp. 183, with
plates 17-30. FINE PAPER, with coloured
plates, 3*l*. 13*s*. 6*d*. (Reprinted, under same
date, by Nattali.)
— Observations on some Peculiarities observable in the Structure of the Gannet
(Pelicanus Bassanus), and an Account of a
new and curious Insect inhabiting the
cellular Membrane of that Bird. 8vo. 6*s*.
pp. 13 and 7, with a plate.
Several papers by this esteemed naturalist will be found in the Transactions
of the Linnean Society.

— Magdalena, Viscountess. Vita
Dominæ Magdalenæ Montis-Acuti
in Anglia Vicecomitissæ, per R.
Smitheum. Romæ, 1609, 12mo.
Heber, pt. vii. 1*l*. 1*s*.

MONTAGUE, Edward Wortley.
Reflections on the Rise and Fall of
the antient Republics. Lond. 1778,
8vo.
Willett, 1720, 5*s*. Roscoe, 678, 7*s*. According to a note in 'An authentic Detail
of Particulars relative to the late Duchess
of Kingston,' 1788, this book was in reality
the work of the Rev. Mr. Foster, the private tutor to this eccentric character.—
1760, 8vo.—1769, 8vo.
— Memoirs of the late Edward Wortley
Montague, Esq., with Remarks on the
Manners and Customs of the Oriental
World; collected and published from his
posthumous Papers. Lond. 1778, 12mo.
2 vols. 10*s*. 6*d*. A mere novel.—Reprinted, Dublin, 1779, 12mo. 2 vols.

— Lady Mary Wortley. Works,
including her Correspondence,
Poems, and Essays, with Memoirs
of her Life. Lond. 1803, crown
8vo. 5 vols. portrait and facsimiles.
Edited by Mr. Dallaway from papers in

1588 MON

MON

the possession of John, first Marquis of Bute. Bindley, pt. II. 1529, 1l. 5s. White Knights, 2846, 2l. 2s. LARGE PAPER. Bindley, pt. II. 1530, 2l. 2s.—New edition, (called the sixth), 1817, crown 8vo. 5 vols. portrait and facsimiles, 1l. 10s.

MONTAGUE, Lady Mary Wortley. Letters and Works, edited by her great-grandson, Lord Wharncliffe. Lond. 1837, 8vo. (Two editions in the same year, the second with a few additional notes), 3 vols, portraits, 1l. 16s. A new and much improved edition is in the press.

Letters written during her Travels in Europe, Asia, and Africa. Lond. 1783, 12mo. 3 vols. A surreptitious edition edited by Cleland.—An additional volume [with Verses written in the Chiask at Pera]. Lond. 1767, 8vo.—A new edition. Lond. 1778, 12mo. 2 vols. 4s.—Lond. 1784, 12mo. 2 vols.—With her Poems. Lond. Cadell, 1789, 12mo. 3 vols. portrait.—Paris, 1790, 18mo. 2s. 6d. Didot's stereotype edition. On VELLUM, two copies printed. Junot, 15, 4l. 17s.

Letters from the Levant, edited by J. A. St. John. Lond. 1838, fcap. 8vo. 5s.

Lady Montague's Letters are clever, spirited, and easy, and invaluable for the traits of manners they have preserved of her own times.

Poetical Works (edited by Isaac Reed). Lond. 1768, 12mo. 2s. 6d.

— Ralph, Duke of. Life, containing his Travels abroad; his marriages, children, and other actions at Home, with his Death, &c. Lond. 1709, 8vo.

— Richard, successively Bishop of Chichester and Norwich. De Originibus Ecclesiasticis Commentationes. Lond. 1636-40, folio. 2 vols. in 1. 14s.

The writings of this prelate are not in much repute. The second part only, on LARGE PAPER, is in the Grenville collection.

Diatribæ upon the first Part of the History of Tithes. Lond. 1691, 4to. 3s. Written, according to Moore in his Memoirs of Captain Rock, in a tesselated style.

Analecta Ecclesiasticarum Exercitationum. Lond. 1622, folio. 7s.

A Gagg for the new Gospell? No, a new Gagg for an old Goose. Lond. 1624, 4to. Boswell, 1618, 6s.

Appello Cæsarem, a just Appeale from two unjust Informers. Lond. 1625, 4to. By proclamation, dated 17th Jan, 1625, called in and suppressed. Roswell, 1617, 5s.

Treatise of Invocation of Saints, &c. Lond. 1624, 4to.

Antidiatribæ ad priorem Partem Diatribarum J. Hulsengeri adversus Exercitationes Is. Casauboni. 1625, folio, 5s.

Apparatus ad Origines Ecclesiasticas. Oxon. 1635, folio.

The Acts and Monuments of the Church before Christ incarnate. Lond. 1642, folio. Bp. Montague edited the Works of King James I. See page

— Walter. The Shepherds Paradise, a Pastoral Comedy. Lond. 1629, 8vo.

This piece, acted before K. Charles I. by the Queen and her ladies of honour, is ridiculed by Sir John Suckling in his Session of Poets. Bindley, pt. II. 1786, 7s. Rhodes, 1578, 7s.—1659, 8vo. Roxburghe, 5498, 6s. Reed, 8296, 7s. 6d. Rhodes, 1751, 4s. Nassau, pt. I. 2314, 7s.

Miscellanea Spiritualia, or devout Essays. Lond. 1648, 4to. with a frontispiece by Marshall. Bindley, pt. III. 538, 15s.—1649. Heber, pt. II. 10s. 6d. Gordonstoun, 1430. 7s. 6d.—Part 2. Lond. 1654, 4to.

— William. The Delights of Holland, or three Months Travel about that and other Provinces. Lond. 1696, 8vo.

Fonthill, 2754, 15s. Heber, pt. v. 1s.

MONTAIGNE, Michel, Sr. de. Les Essais, avec Remarques par P. Coste. Lond. 1724, 4to. 3 vols.

Garrick, 1586, 16s. Reed, 2428, 17s.—Avec des additions, Lond. 1739, 12mo. 6 vols.—Lond. 1745, 12mo. 7 vols.

Supplement, avec sa Vie, par Mr. le President Bouhier, et la Charactere de Montaigne par Mr. Pascal. Lond. 1740, 4to. This supplement includes the additions made by Coste in his edition of 1739.

The Essays of Michael, Lord of Montaigne, done into English by John Florio. Lond. 1603, folio. Archæologia XXVII. two leaves of "Errors and Omissions." A copy with an undoubted autograph of Shakspere, sold at Evans's, May 1839, for 100l. The interest of this autograph was increased by its having been shewn that Shakspere used Florio's translation of Montaigne in Tempest, Act II. Sc. 1.—Second edition, Lond. 1613, folio, with portrait of Florio by Hole, 7s.—Third edition. Lond. 1632, folio, with index, frontispiece, and page of verses.

Essays of Michael Seigneur de Montaigne, made English by Charles Cotton, Esq. First edition. Lond. 1693, 8vo. 8 vols.—Fourth Edition. Lond. 1711, 8vo. 3 vols.—1738, 8vo. 3 vols. 10s. 6d.—1743, 8vo. 3 vols. 15s.

Essays, translated into English from the Edition of Peter Coste. Lond. 1776, 8vo. 3 vols. Nassau, pt. I. 2292, 17s. Williams, 1910, morocco, 4l. 4s.—Lond. Miller, 1811, 8vo. 3 vols. portrait. An elegantly printed edition, 2l. 2s.

Works, viz., his Essays, Letters, and Journey through Germany and Italy; with Notes from all the Commentators, Biographical and Bibliographical Notices, &c. by William Hazlitt. Lond. 1841, royal 8vo. portrait.—Second edition, 1845, 15s.
Essays, selected from Montaigne, with a Sketch of the Life of the Author. Lond. 1800, 12mo. 8s.
A notice of Montaigne's Essays will be found in the Retrosp. Review, ii. 208-27.

MONTALTE, L. do. *See* PASCAL, Blaise.

MONTALVAN, Don F. Balthas de. The Naked Truth; or Discovery of the Intrigues of Amorous Fops. Lond. 1678, 12mo. 10s. 6d.

— Perez do. The Spanish Bawds. Lond. 1631, folio; attached to Aleman's Spanish Rogue.

MONTANUS, Arnoldus. 'Atlas Chinensis et Japanensis. *See* OGILBY, John.

— Fabritius. An Oration wherby he teacheth that Christian Men cannot resorte to the Councel of Trent without committing an haynous offence. Euglyshed by L. A. Lond. 1562, 12mo.
Black letter. Heber, pt. iv. 1*l*. 11s.

— Joh. Ferrarius A Woorke touchynge the good Orderynge of a Common Weale, englished by W. Bavande. Lond. 1559, 4to.
In this volume, dedicated to Q. Elizabeth, are interspersed several poetical translations from classic authors. Bindley, pt. ii. 1018, 2*l*. 1s.

— Reg. Gonsal. A Discovery and playne Declaration of sundry subtill Practices of the Holy Inquisition of Spayne, newly translated. Lond. by Jhon Day, 1568, 4to.
BLACK LETTER, translated by V. Skinner. Saunders' in 1818, 5s. Another edition, with some additions appeared in 1569, 4to.

MONTCRESTIEN, Ant. de., Sieur de Vasteville. Escossoisse, ov le Desastre. Tragedie. Seconde Edition. Rouen, 1603.
A copy is in the British Museum. Collation.—A, C, and E, eight leaves, B, and D, 4 leaves, and F, 3 leaves.

MONTEFIORE, J. An authentic Account of the late Expedition to Bulam, on the Coast of Africa; with a Description of the present Settlement of Sierra Leone and the adjacent Country. Lond. 1794, 8vo. 2s.

Fonthill, 2557, 1*l*.

— Joshua. Commercial Dictionary. Lond. 1803, 4to. 1*l*. 16s.
Commercial and Notarial Precedents. Lond. 4to.
This author published other esteemed works relative to trade and commerce.

MONTEITH, Robert, M.A. A Theater of Mortality; or the Illustrious Inscriptions extant upon the Monuments in the Gray Friars Church Yard, &c., in Edinburgh and its Suburbs. Edinb. 1704. A further Collection of Funeral Inscriptions over Scotland. Edinb. 1713, small 8vo. 2 vols. generally bound in one.
Hibbert, 5504, 16s. Towneley, pt. ii. 740, 1*l*. 7s. Nassau, pt. i. 293, russia, 1*l*. 10s. *See* Retrosp. Review, xii. 213-20. Buchanan's Fratres Fraterini. Three Books of Epigrams and Book of Miscellanies in English Verse. Edinb. 1704, small 8vo. Bright, 9s. 6d. Heber, pt. iv. 11s.
Description of the Islands of Orkney and Zetland. Edinb. 1711, 8vo. with two maps.
Published by Sir Robt. Sibbald.—Reprinted, Edinb. 1845, 8vo. facsimilies of the scarce maps; only 144 printed. Eyton, 7s. on VELLUM, unique. Eyton, 1*l*. 9s.

— Robert. The Forester's Guide and profitable Planter. Second Edition. Edinburgh, 1824, 8vo.—Again, 1836, 8vo.
An excellent article on planting waste lands, with a notice of this 'useful and interesting treatise,' will be found in the Quarterly Review, vol. xxxvi.

MONTEITH, Robert. History of the Troubles of Great Britain, containing an Account of the most remarkable Passages in Scotland, from 1633 to 1650. To which is added, a Continuation to the favourable Restoration of Charles II. by D. Riordan de Musery. Translated by J. Ogilvie. Lond. 1735, folio. 1*l*. 1s.

MONTELION.—The famous Historie of Montelyon, Knyghte of the
Oracle. Lond. 1633, 4to.
By Emanuel Foord.—Steevens, 117, 4s.
—166s, 4to. Nassau, pt. II, 179, 6s.—1637,
4to. Bliss, 12s.—1625, 4to. with a frontispiece. Hibbert, 5605, 7s. 6d. Roxburghe, Suppl. 676, 8s. 6d.—n. d. for S.
Tracy, 4to. White Knights, 2043, 10s.
Goldsmid, 409, 11s. Bliss, 1l.

MONTELION. See LAMBERTO.
PHILLIPS, John.

MONTEMAYOR, George of. Diana
of George of Montemayor, translated by Bartholomew Yong. Lond.
1598, folio.
This pastoral Spanish romance, dedicated to the Lady Rich, and like Sydney's
Arcadia, full of poetry, has been assigned
as the original of the Two Gentlemen of
Verona. Bindley, pt. II. 1058, 1l. 3s.
Reed, 5442, 19s. Bibl. Anglo-Poet. 684,
4l. 4s. Bright, 13s.

MONTENAY, Georgette. A Booke
of Armes, or Remembrance, wherein
are 100 godly Emblemata first in-
vented and elabourated in the
French Tongue: but now in severall Languages. Franck. 1619, 8vo.
Heber, 1l. 15s.

MONTE-ROCHERII, Guido de.
Manipulus Curatorum. Lond. per
Winandum de Worde, 1502, 16mo.
A work very popular at the close of the
fifteenth century. This edition contains,
including the title, fol. cxxxv besides the
table at the end. A copy is in the Bodleian library.—Lond. per Wln. de Worde,
1506, 16mo—Imp. per Rich. Pynson. 1508,
4to. folios cxxvii.—(Lond. per Rich. Pynson), 16mo. Inglis, 670, 13s. There is a
copy in the British Museum, wanting the
title-page, at the end of which is the
mark of Pynson. Collation.—A—Z in
eights, after which are three other sheets,
each containing 8 leaves.—Impr. per
Jullanum Notarium, 1508, 16mo. 133
leaves, besides a title at the end.—Lond.
per Wynandum de Worde, 1509, 16mo.
A copy in Lambeth library.

MONTESQUIEU, M. de. The complete Works of M. de Montesquieu.
Translated from the French. Lond.
1777, 8vo. 4 vols.
Reed, 7029, 1l. 15s. Nassau, pt. I. 2295,
1l. 13s. Marquis of Townshend, 3115, 2l. 8s.
Dublin, 1777, 8vo. 4 vols.
Considérations sur les Causes de la Grandeur des Romains et de leur Decadence.
Edinb. 1751, small 8vo. LARGE PAPER.
Williams, 1811, morocco, 1l. 3s. This work
was highly praised by Gibbon.
Reflections on the Causes of the Rise
and Fall of the Roman Empire. Lond.
1754, 12mo.—Lond. second edition, 1752,
12mo, 2 vols.
De l'Esprit des Loix. Londres, 1749,
8vo. 2 vols. First edition printed in England of this work. It was at one time
highly esteemed throughout Europe, but
has of late lost much of its popularity.
Montesquieu is indebted to Aristotle for
whatever is most excellent in his Spirit
of Laws.—Edinb. 1751, 8vo. 2 vols. Copies
on LARGE THICK PAPER.
Spirit of Laws, translated by Nugent.
Lond. 1756, 12mo. 2 vols. 7s. 6d.—Aberd.
1756, 8vo. 2 vols. Lond. 1758, 8vo. 2 vols.
—1766, 8vo. 2 vols.—Sixth edition, with
an index. Lond. 1793, 8vo. 10s. 6d.—
Edin. 1778, 12mo. 2 vols.—A new Edition, to which are prefixed an Account
of the Author, and an Analysis of the
Work, by M. D'Alembert. Lond. 1829,
8vo. 2 vols. 14s. That part (book vi. ch.
11.) which relates to the Constitution of
England has been translated and published separately by Baron Masères. 1781,
8vo. 4s.
Miscellaneous Pieces of M. de Secondat,
Baron de Montesquieu, translated from
the new Edition of his Works in 4to
printed at Paris. Lond. 1759, 8vo. 6s.
Persian Letters, translated from the
French by Mr. Floyd. The fourth Edition with several new Letters and Notes.
Lond. 1762, 12mo. 2 vols. 6s. These Letters
were intended as a satire upon French
manners. There are several other editions.
The Temple of Gnidus, a Poem, from
the French Prose of M. Secondat, Baron
de Montesquieu, by John Sayer, M.A.
Lond. 1765, 4to. Several other English
versions of this voluptuous love-story
have appeared.
Fugitive pieces by M. de Montesquieu,
consisting of the Temple of Gnidus, and
Arsaces and Ismenus. Lond. 1769, 12mo.
2s. 6d.
This work was originally published in
French, Paris, 1661, folio. See SALMONEY,
Mentel de.

MONTFART. See MONFART.

MONTFAUCON, Bern. de. Anti-
quity explained and represented in
Sculptures. Translated by David
Humphreys. With a Supplement.
Lond. 1721-5, folio, 7 vols. plates,
copied from the original work.
Goldsmid, 573, 7l. 15s. LARGE PAPER,
7 vols. royal folio. Sotheby's, 1835, 12l. 12s.

Travels from Paris through Italy. Lond. 1712. 8vo. Willett, 1723, 9s. 6d.

Diarum Italicum: the Antiquities of Italy, being the Travels of M. de Montfaucon from Paris through Italy; made English by J. Henley. Lond. 1725, folio, 10s. 6d.

Regal and Ecclesiastical Antiquities of France. Lond. 1750, folio, 2 vols. with 300 plates, reduced from the 'Monumens de la Monarchie Française.' Towneley, pt. II. 1010, 4l. 14s. 6d.

MONTGOMERY, Capt. Alex. The Poems, now first published from several ancient MSS., with biographical Notices by David Irving, LL.D. Edinb. 1821, post 8vo.

The Cherrie and the Slaye. Composed into Scottish meeter. Edinb. printed by Robert Walde-grave, printer to the King's Majestie. Anno Domini 1597, 4to. first edition. A copy marked 15l. 15s. in a London bookseller's catalogue.

The Cherrie and the Slaye. Printed according to a copie corrected by the Author himselfe. Edinb. printed be Robert Walde-grave, prenter to the King's Majestie, anno 1597, 4to. In the Advocates' Library.—Edinb. 1699. R. Heber, pt. iv. 7l.—Glasgow, 1751, 12mo.

Edinb. 1615, 12mo. An edition sought for by Lord Hailes, Ritson, G. Chalmers, and Laing, but not found.—Edinb. 1636, 16mo. — Aberd. 1645, 12mo.—Glasgow, 1668, 12mo.—Edinb. 1675, 12mo.—Edinb. 1722, 12mo.—Glasgow, 1754, 12mo.

Glasg. 1751. Hibbert, 6619, 10s. Sotheby's in May, 1823, 9s. 6d.—Glasgow, Urie, 1754.—1786, 12mo. Read, 7186, 13s.

Cerasum et Sylvestrum Prunum, in Latinos Versus translatum per T. D. S. P. M. B. P. P. (Thomam Dempsterum, Scotum,) Aretauni Francorum Typis Fleischmannidæ, 1631, 12mo. Chalmers, pt. III. 155, 15s. Heber, pt. iv. 7s.

The Mindes Melody. Edinb. R. Charteris, 1605, small 8vo. 16 leaves. See PSALMS.

The flyting betwixt Montgomerie and Polwart. Edinb. by the heires of Andro Hart, 1629, 4to. In Verse. Bright, 9l. 15s. —Edinb. heirs of Finlayson, 1639, 4to. G. Chalmers, 8l. 8s. Reprinted in edition of Poems, 1821. It is inserted in Watson's Choice Collection of Poems, Edinb. 1711. See HUME, Alex. p. 1136, col. 2.

— James. Poetical Works. Lond. 1819, 12mo. 3 vols. 1l. 8s. 6d.— Lond. 1836, 12mo. 6 vols.—New edition, collected by himself, with additions and notes. Lond. 1841, and again 1855, 12mo. 4 vols. portrait and plates, 14s.—Lond. 1850, and again 1853, sq. 8vo. in 1 vol. port. and engraved title, 10s. 6d.

The Wanderer of Switzerland and other Poems. Lond. 1806, 12mo.—1811, 12mo. —1813, 12mo.

The World before the Flood, in ten Cantos, with other Pieces. Lond. 1813, 1814, and since, 12mo.

Greenland, and other Poems. Lond. 1819, 8vo. pp. 250.

Songs of Zion, being Imitations of Psalms. Lond. 1822, foolscap 8vo, 5s.

Poems on the Abolition of the Slave-trade, written by James Montgomery, James Graham, and E. Benger. Lond. Bowyer, 1809, royal 4to. 13 plates.

The West Indies, and other Poems. Lond. 1810, 12mo. pp. 160. (This is Mr. Montgomery's portion of the "Poems on the Slave Trade.")

Verses to the Memory of the late Richard Reynolds of Bristol. Lond. 1817.

The Chimney-sweeper's Friend, and Climbing-boy's Album. (Edited by Mr. Montgomery, and containing several of his poems.) Lond. 1824.

The Pelican Island, in nine cantos, with other Poems. Lond. 1827 and 1828, fscap. 8vo.

Lectures on Poetry and general Literature, delivered at the Royal Institution in 1830 and 1831. Lond. 1833, post 8vo. 10s. 6d.

A Poet's Portfolio; or minor Poems, in three Books. Lond. 1835, 12mo. 6s.

The Christian Poet, or Selections in Verse on sacred Subjects. Glasgow, 1825. Second edition. Glasgow, 1827.

Christian Psalmist, or Hymns selected and original. With an Instructory Essay. New edition. Lond. W. Collins, 1852, 24mo. 2s.—Tenth edition. Lond. Griffin, 1827, 18mo. pp. 500, 2s.

Poems (select) by James Montgomery, edited by the Rev. R. A. Willmott. Lond. Routledge, 1849, sm. 4to. portrait and 100 illustrations on wood, 1l. 1s.

Original Hymns for Public, Private, and social Devotion. Lond. Longman, 1853, 12mo. 5s. 6d.

Lives of the most eminent Literary and Scientific Men of Italy, Spain, &c. By Mrs. Shelley, Sir D. Brewster, J. Montgomery, &c. Lond. (Lardner's Cab. Cy.), 1835-7, fcap. 8vo. 8 vols.

Christian Correspondence; a Collection of Letters, with preliminary Essay by James Montgomery. Lond. 1837, fcap. 8vo. 3 vols. 18s. reduced 12s.

James Montgomery; a Memoir, Political and Poetical. By J. W. King. Lond. Partridge, 1858, 12mo. pp. 400, 5s.

Memoirs, including Selections from his Correspondence, Remains in Prose and

1592 MON — MON

Verse, and Conversations on various Subjects. Edited by John Holland and Jas. Everett, post 8vo. 7 vols. with port. and fronts. (in all 14 plates.) Lond. 1854-56, (pub. 5l. 13s. 6d.) reduced, Bohn, 1l. 1s.

Mr. Montgomery conducted the *Sheffield Iris* for thirty-one years, from 1794 to 1825, and underwent several prosecutions and two imprisonments.

MONTGOMERY, Rev. Robert. Omnipresence of the Deity. Lond. 1828, 12mo.—Twenty-first edition. Lond. 1841, 12mo. 4s.—Twenty-eighth edition. Lond. Chapman and Hall, 1855. 18mo. 4s.—Maunder's School edition. Lond. 1845, 18mo. 2s. 6d.

This, the author's first poem, was written in his 20th year.

Satan; or Intellect without God. Lond. 1830, 8vo.—Again, Lond. Hogue, 1841, roy. 8vo. 1s.; and 12mo. (Baisler) 4s. After the publication of this poem the author received the sobriquet of Satan Montgomery.

A Universal Prayer; Death; a Vision of Heaven; and a Vision of Hell. Lond. 1828, 4to.—Fourth edition with additions. Lond. 1829, 8vo. 7s. 6d.—Again, 1840, 12mo. 5s. 6d.

Oxford; a Poem. Second edition. Oxf. 1831, 8vo. 7s. 6d.—With Illustrations by J. Skelton. Oxford, 1831, 8vo.—Lond. Whittaker, 1840, 12mo. 7s. 6d.

The Messiah; a Poem. Second edit. Lond. 1832, 8vo.—The Sacred Annual; being the Messiah, a Poem, Lond. 1834, 8vo.—Eighth edition, Lond. Baisler, 1842, fcap. 8vo. 6s.

Woman, the Angel of Life; a Poem. Lond. 1833, 8vo.—Woman, and other Poems. Fifth edition. Lond. Baisler, 1841, fcap. 8vo. 4s.

Luther, or the Ideal of the Reformation, a Poem. Second edition. Lond. 1842, 12mo. 6s.—Third edition. Lond. 1843. 6s.—Fourth edition. Lond. Simpkin, 1846, roy. 8vo. 1s. 6d.—Sixth edition. Lond. J. Blackwood, 1851, 12mo. 5s.

The Gospel in advance of the Age. Second edition. Lond. Baisler, 1844, 8vo. 10s.—Third edition, revised and rearranged. Edinb. Clark, 1848, 8vo. 12s. Fourth edition. Lond. Routledge, 1855, 8vo. 6s.

Christ our all in all. Second edition. Lond. 1845, fcap. 8vo. 5s.—Third edition. Lond. Hatchard, 1846, 4s. 6d.—Lond. 1828, 12mo.—Second edition, revised and enlarged. Lond. 1828, 8vo.

The Ideal of the Christian Church. Lond. 1845, 8vo. 2s. 6d.

Scarborough, a poetic glance. Lond. 1845, 8vo. 1s. 6d.

The Great Salvation, and our sin in neglecting it. A religious essay, in 3 Parts. Lond. 1846, 8vo.

The World of Spirits. Lond. 1847, 8vo.

Sacred Meditations and Moral Themes in verse. Third edition. Lond. 1847, 12mo. 5s.

The Christian Life; a Manual of Sacred Verse. Lond. 1848, 12mo.—Second edition. Lond. Hall, 1849, 12mo. front. 7s. 6d.—Third edition. Lond. Rivington, 1850, 32mo. 5s.—Fourth edition. Lond. Brough, 1851, 32mo. 5s.—Sixth edition. Rivington, 1853, 24mo. 4s.

Reflective Discourses. Second edition. Lond. Baisler, 1844, 8vo. 10s. 6d.

Religion and Poetry. Second edit. Lond. Nisbet, 1847, 12mo. 5s.

Sacred Gift. Lond. P. Jackson, 1842, roy. 8vo. 1l. 1s.

The Scottish Church and English Schismatics. Third edition, with documentary evidence. Lond. Masters, 1849.

Sermons. Lon. Baisler, 1843, 8vo. 10s. 6d.

World of Spirits. Lond. Bentley, 1847, post 8vo. 7s. 6d.

Spiritual Discourses on Important Texts. Third edition. Lond.

God and Man. Lond. Longman, 1850, 8vo. 12s.

Church of the Invisible. Fourth edit. Lond. Darling, 1851, 32mo. 8s. 6d.

Lyra Christiana: Poems selected. Lond. G. Bell, 1851, 32mo. 5s. 6d.

Sanctuary, a Companion to the English Prayer Book. Lond. Chapman and Hall, 1855, 18mo. 5s. 6d.

Lyric Christian Poems on Christianity and the Church; Original and Selected from the Works of Robert Montgomery. Lond. G. Bell, 1857, 32mo. 2s. 6d.

Poetical Works. New edition. Lond. Bell, 1639-40, 18mo. 6 vols. 18s.—New edit. in 1 vol. Lond. Chapman and Hall, 1853, 8vo. 1l.

Robert Montgomery and his Reviewers. With some remarks on the present state of English poetry and on the laws of Criticism. By Edward Clarkson. Lond. 1830, 8vo.

This author was extremely anxious to make his books appear very popular, and therefore constantly changed his title pages, and even cancelled or sold off almost as waste one edition for the sake of printing another. He was severely reviewed by Lord Macaulay, in the Edinb. Review, of 1830.

MONTGOMERY FAMILY.—Memorables of the Montgomeries, a Narrative in Rhyme, composed before the present Century. Glasg. 1770, 4to. 5 leaves.—Reprinted, Edinb. 1822, 4to. Only 75 copies printed. See REILLY.

The Montgomery Manuscripts; containing Memoirs of the Viscounts Montgomery; also a Description of the Barony of Ards, composed by Wm. Montgomery, between the Years 1698 and 1704. Belfast, 1830, 12mo.

The Montgomery Manuscripts; containing Accounts of the Colonisation of the Ardes in the Co. of Down, temp. Elizabeth and James; Memoirs of the Viscounts Montgomery, &c. By William Montgomery. 1832, 12mo. 10s. 6d. Only a small number printed, chiefly for presents.

MONTHLY REVIEW, The, from its Commencement in May, 1749, to December 1789. 81 vols. Second Series, from 1790 to 1825, 108 vols. [Edited, until 1803, by R. Griffiths.] Third or 'New Series,' Jan. 1826-1830, 15 vols. Fourth, or 'New Third,' or 'New Series,' Jan. 1831—Jan. 1845, 45 vols. After which it was discontinued. A General Index, 1749-84, by the Rev. S. Ayscough, 2 vols. Continued, 1784-9, by the same, 1 vol. Another, 1790-1816, by J. C., 2 vols. Lond. 1749, &c. 8vo. 206 vols.

Fonthill, 1749-1822, 175 vols. 44l. 12s. 6d. Reed, 1749-89 and index, also N.S. 1t01-6, 36l. 10s. Heber, 1749-1826 and index, 4l. 16s. Mr. Heber also possessed the Publisher's and Proprietor's (Dr. Griffith and his son's) copy from 1749 to May 1808, in which, up to 1815, the initials or names of the writers were noted at the close of each article. This very interesting set, with indexes, 8 vols.—in all 201 volumes. Sold (in part viii.) for 42l.

Monthly Mercuries, 1688.

Monthly Miscellany, or Gentlemen's Journal, 1691-4, 4to. 4 vols. Reed, 2431, 1l. 2s.

Monthly Miscellany, or Memoirs for the Curious. Lond. 1707-9, 4to. 3 vols. This work was conducted by James Petiver, a celebrated botanist. A copy is in the British Museum, Gough, 2225, with the Muses' Mercury, both of 1707, 1l. 6s.

The Monthly Amusement. A periodical publication projected by Ozell, and consisting principally of translations from French novels or plays. It was commenced in Nov. 1709, by Hughes, assimilating to the form originally established by Steele in the Tatler.

The Monthly Chronicle for the Years 1728, 1729, 1730, 1731, 4to. 4 vols. A copy is in the Royal Institution.

The Monthly Magazine from the Commencement in February, 1796 to 1825, commenced by Sir Richard Phillips, 60 vols.—New Series from 1826 to 1834, 18 vols. Lond. 8vo.—New Series, 1835 1 vol. vol. 19.) Continued as Monthly Magazine of Politics, Literature, and the Belles Lettres. Lond. 1836-8, forming vols. 20-26. —Continued as the Monthly Magazine, edited by J. A. Heraud (B. E. Hill, &c.) Lond. 1839-43, 9 vols.

(Vols. 7-9 of the last series are described on the title-pages as vols. 95-97, in reference to the collective numeration of the entire work.)

New Monthly Magazine, and Universal Register. Lond. 1814-20, 8vo. 14 vols.—Continued as The New Monthly Magazine and Literary Journal. Lond. 1821-3d, 8vo. 34 vols. forming vols. 15-48. [Vols. 15-30 edited by T. Campbell.]—Continued as The New Monthly Magazine and Humorist. [Vols. 49-62, edited by T. Hook; vols. 63-8, edited by T. Hood; vols. 78 and after, by W. H. Ainsworth.] Lond. 1837—July 31, 1860, vols. 49 119.—Continued monthly at 3s. 6d.

Monthly Masks of Vocal Music. See MUSIC.

Monthly Mirror from the Commencement in 1796 to the year 1806, 22 vols, New Series, 1807-11, 6 vols. Lond. 8vo. 31 vols. with portraits. Thomas Bellamy was the original projector of this periodical and its editor Ed. Du Bois, Esq. Reed, 3564, 1795-1808, 5l. 7s. 6d.

Monthly Epitome, or Catalogue of new Publications, 8vo. Fonthill, 784, from Jan. 1797 to 1804, 8 vols. 18s. Townley, pt. ii. 717, 9 vols. in 10, 11s.

Monthly Repository of Theology and general Literature. Lond. and Hackney, 1806, &c. 8vo. Hollis, 957, 11 vols. 1806-16 5l. 2s. 6d.

Monthly Censor. Lond. 1823. A short-lived publication.

MONTI, Vincenzo. La Rivoluzione Francese, Visione alla Dantesca in quattro Canti, de Vincenzo Monti; l'Anno 1793, in Occasione della Morte di Ugo Bassevilla. Londra, 1804, crown 8vo. 5s.

An elegant edition, edited by Mathias. The Penance of Hugo, a Vision on the French Revolution. In the manner of Dante. In four Cantos. Written on Occasion of the death of Nicola Hugo de Basseville, Envoy from the French Republic at Rome, January 14, 1793. Translated from the original Italian into English Verse, with two additional Cantos, by the Rev. Henry Boyd. Lond. 1805, 12mo. 5s.

MONTLUC, Blaise de. Commentaries, translated by Charles Cotton. Lond. 1674, folio.

Marquis of Townshend, 2438, 17s.

MONTMORENCY FAMILY. — Genealogical Memoir of the Family of Montmorency, styled De Marisco, or Morres, ancient Lords de Marisco in the Peerage of England and Ireland. Paris, 1817, 4to. plates.

— Les Montmorency de Franco, et les Montmorency d'Irlande. Precis Historique. Par Mons. H. de Montmorency-Morres. Paris, 1828, 4to. plates.

BOTH WORKS PRIVATELY PRINTED.

MONTOLIEU, Mrs. Enchanted Plants, Fables in Verse. Lond. 1800, 8vo.

Printed by Bensley. ON VELLUM. Two copies struck off.

The Festival of the Rose, and other Poems. Lond. 1802, 4to. ON VELLUM. One copy struck off.

MONTROSE, Graham of. Pietas illustrissimi Domini, Principis generosæ Graemorum Familiae, Comitis Montis-rosarum, in Patrem à Vita placidè docendentem 9 Novemb. 1608, qui Regis Vices in Britannia septentrionali foeliciter gesserat, et in supremo Regni foro Senatorum Principem integerrimè egerat pioque Filij mærentis Dolori adhibita Consolatio. Edinburghi, 1609, 4to.

Six leaves. A copy is in the British Museum.

Tracts relating to the Marquis of Montrose, 1641, &c. 4to. Townsley, pt. i. 703, 5l.

A Declaration of the Marquis of Montrose to settle Charles the Second in all his Dominions, &c. 1649, 4to. One sheet, reprinted in the third volume of the Harleian Miscellany.

A Relation of the Execution of James Graham, late Marquis of Montrose, at Edinburgh, on the 21st of May instant. Lond. 1650, 4to. pp. 8. Reprinted in the fifth volume of the Harleian Miscellany.

De Rebus anno 1644, et dumbus sequentibus ab Illust. Jacobo Marchione Montisrosarum in Scotia gestis. 12mo. 1647. Heber, pt. ii. 6s.—pt. vi. portrait inserted, 4s. Paris, 1648, 12mo. and copies in 8vo. ON LARGE PAPER. Heber, pt. vii. 14s.—

pt. ix. 8s. 6d. Said to be written by Dr. George Wishart, Bp. of Edinburgh.

The History of the King's Majestie's Affairs in Scotland under the Conduct of James Marquis of Montrose, in the years 1644-45-46. Printed in the year 1648, 4to. —At the Hague, n. d. Called the second edition. 8vo. Portrait by Matham.— Again, with a second part, never before published, and an Appendix. Edinb. 1720, post 8vo.; and again, 1750, post 8vo.— With same additions. 1756.—Edinb. 1819, 8vo. port.

Montrose redivivus, or the Portraiture of James late Marquess of Montrose. Lond. 1652, 8vo. port. Nassau, pt. i. 2294, russia, 9s. Baker, 681, 9s. 6d. Reed, 5218, 1l. 11s. 6d. Heber, pt. ix. 1l. 3s.

The Exclamas of Rhodopæ. To the Lamentable Death of the most noble Marquis of Montrose. Written formerly and now published at his honourable Interment. By J. M. O. 8vo., 1651. Fourteen pages. Reprinted from the only known copy (belonging to J. F. Collyer, Esq.), in the second series of Scottish Fugitive Poetry, edited by Mr. D. Laing.

A Relation of the true Funerals of the Lord Marquis of Montrose, with that of Sir William Hay of Delgity. Printed in the year 1661, 4to. pp. 24. A copy in the Grenville Collection. It is reprinted in the seventh volume of the Harleian Miscellany. See WISHART, George.

Montrose and the Covenanters, their Characters and Conduct. Illustrated from private Letters and other original documents hitherto unpublished. By Mark Napier, Esq. Lond. 1838, 8vo. 2 vols. port. 12s.

The Life and Times of Montrose, by Mark Napier. Lond. 1840, 8vo.

Memoirs of the Marquis of Montrose by Mark Napier. Edinb. 1856, 8vo. 2 vols. with portraits and plates, 1l. 16s. This is the fourth performance of Mr. Napier respecting Montrose; the third being that published, in two quarto volumes, by the MAITLAND CLUB, which are Appendix.

Memoirs of James, Marquis of Montrose, by James Grant. Lond. Routledge, 1858, 12mo. portrait and wood cut, 5s.

MONTS, M. de. Nova Francia; or, the Description of that Part of New France which is one Continent with Virginia. Lond. 1609, 4to. Translated by P. Erondelle. It is reprinted in the second volume of the Oxford Collection of Voyages and Travels.

MONTSERRAT.—Code of Laws from 1668 to 1778, 1790, folio, 18s.

Printed by order of the Assembly.

Acts of Assembly passed in the Island of Montserrat, from 1668 to 1740. Lond. 1740, folio.

MOODIE, A. Scotiæ indiculum; or the present State of Scotland. Together with divers Reflections upon the ancient State thereof. Lond. 1682, sm. 8vo.

MOON.—The Man in the Moone, discovering a Worlde of Knavery under the Sunne. Lond. 1638, first edition.
titles, 4s. 6d. Lond. 1657, 12mo.
Man in the Moone, telling strange Fortunes; or the English Fortune-teller. See M. W.
The Man in the Moon. Lond. 1783, 12mo. 2 vols.

— Lord.—The whole Life and History of Lord Moon, and the Earl of Warwick. With the comical Frolicks that they play'd. Lond. 1711, 4to.
A copy is in the British Museum.
See DRAYTON, M. MAN. WILKINS, Bp.

MOONE, Peter. A shorte Treatyse of certayne Thinges abused in the Popish Church, long vsed; but now abolyshed to our consolation, and God's word advaunced, the Lyght of our salvation, 4to. In Verse.
Eight leaves, printed at Ipswich by John Oswen, about the year 1548. See Warton's History of English Poetry. Dright, 4l. 11s.

MOONSHINE: Curious, Satyrical, Facetious, and Descriptive Sketches in Poetry and Prose, with Appendix of unconnected Trifles. Lond. 1832-5, 8vo. 5 vols. port. of J. Thorpe, M.D., Oxon.
Privately printed, for presents only. These curious pieces were written by Mrs. E. M. Potts of Sloane Street.

MOOR, Edward, Major. The Hindu Pantheon. Lond. 1810, royal 4to. 105 plates of Hindoo deities in outline.
White Knights, 1945, russia, 4l. 14s. 6d.
A Narrative of the Operations of Captain Little's Detachment, and of the Mahratta Army, commanded by Puserum Bhow; during the late Confederacy in India, against the Nawab Tippo Sultan Bahadur. Lond. 1794, 4to. 6s. Fonthill, 344, 1l. 1s.
Hindu Infanticide; or Account of the Measures adopted for suppressing the Practice of the systematic Murder by their Parents of Female Infants, and other Customs peculiar to the Natives of India; with Notes and Illustrations. Lond. 1811, 4to.
Oriental Fragments. Lond. 1834, post 8vo. plates. 7s. 6d.
Suffolk Words and Phrases; or an Attempt to collect the lingual Localisms of that County. Woodbridge, 1823, 12mo. Bright, 10s.

— James, LL.D. Essays read to a Literary Society at the Weekly Meeting within the College of Glasgow. Glasgow, 1759, 12mo.
Essay on the End of Tragedy, according to Aristotle; read to a Literary Society in Glasgow. In two parts. Glasgow, 1763, 12mo.
Addison's Cato, done into Latin Verse, without the Love Scenes. Glasgow, 1764, 12mo.
Elementa Linguæ Græcæ. Glasg. 1770, 12mo.; G. 1766.—Edinb. 1798, 1800, 1809. —Glasg. 1817; G. 1843, &c. 12mo.
An Introductory Essay on the Prepositions of the Greek Language; read to a Literary Society in Glasgow. Glasg. 1766, 12mo.
Moor was Greek professor at the university of Glasgow, and his Elementa Linguæ Græcæ has continued in general use in the universities and schools of Scotland to the present time. The more recent editions have been edited by Dunbar, Neilson, Tate, and Rowlatt. His merit is conspicuous as a philologer, but his English style is very indifferent.

MOORE, And. History of the Turks. Lond. 1660, 8vo. 4 vols.
A translation of the Alcoran occupies vol. 4 of the work.

— Ann. A full exposure of Ann Moore, the pretended fasting Woman of Tetbury. Lond. 1813, 8vo.
A relation of her extraordinary Abstinences. Birm. (1813) 8vo.
Examination of the Imposture of Ann Moore. By Alexander Henderson, M.D. Lond. 1813, 8vo. 2s.
Statement of Facts relative to the supposed Abstinence of Ann Moore. By the Rev. Leigh Richmond, 1813, 8vo.

— Charles, M.A. A full Inquiry into the Subject of Suicide. To which are added, two Treatises on Duelling and Gaming. Lond. 1790. 4to. 2 vols. 10s. 6d.
An excellent work.

MOORE, Edward. Poems, Fables and Plays. Lond. 1756, 4to.
Bindley, pt. II. 815, 4s.
Fables for the Female Sex. Lond. 1744, 8vo. With cuts by Hayman. Bindley, pt. II. 1724, 6s.—1766. Bindley, p. ii. 1882, 5s. 6d.
Dramatic Works. Lond. 1788, 12mo. With portrait of the author by Neagle after Worlidge, and plates. Reed, 5294, 5s.

Moore was principal contributor to a periodical publication entitled The World.

— Sir Francis. Reports in the Reigns of Henry VIII., Elizabeth and James. Lond. 1675 or 1688, folio, 18s.
'Moore is a very accurate reporter.'—Ld. Ellenborough.—1683, folio, with portrait by Faithorne, 15s.

— Francis. Travels into the inland Parts of Africa. To which is added Captain Stibb's Voyage up the Gambia in 1723. Lond. 1738, 8vo.

A valuable work, introducing the reader to many parts and tribes of Africa even yet but little known, partly drawn from the accounts of an African prince, who came to England. A notice of the volume will be found in Hugh Murray's valuable work on Africa. Heath, 2710, 14s. 6d. Nassau, pt. I. 2301, 7s. Willett, 1729, 8s. Roxburghe, 7297, 12s.

Voyage to Georgia. Lond. 1744, 8vo. Fonthill, 2785, 18s.

— George. The History of the British Revolution of 1688-9. Lond. 1817, 8vo. 6s.

— George. Lives of Cardinal Alberoni and the Duke of Ripperda, Ministers of Philip V. King of Spain. Lond. 1806, 8vo.
Second edition, with Life of the Marq. de Pombal. Lond. 1814, 8vo. See POMBAL.

— Rev. Henry. The Life of the Rev. John Wesley, A.M., including the Life of his Brother the Rev. Charles, A.M., and Memoirs of their Family. 1824, 8vo. 10s. 6d.

— J. Twenty-five Views in Scotland, engraved by J. Landseer. Lond. 1794, 4to. 10s. 6d.

— James. A List of the principal Castles and Monasteries in Great Britain. Lond. 1798, 8vo. 5s. Hibbert, 5523, russia, 5s. See PARKYNS, G. J.

— James. A Narrative of the Campaign of the British Army in Spain, commanded by Lieut.-Gen. Sir John Moore, K.B. Lond. 1809. 4to.
With a portrait of Sir John Moore, &c. Edwards, 704, 12s. Nassau, pt. II. 181, 6s. ON VELLUM. Duke of York, 3294, morocco, 6l. 8s. 6d.

— John, successively Bishop of Norwich and Ely. Sermons, published by Dr. Sam. Clarke. Lond. 1715, 8vo. 2 vols. 10s. 6d.
With portrait of the author by Vander Gucht.

— Lieut.-Gen. Sir John. Life and Letters, edited by his Brother, James Carrick Moore. Lond. 1833, 8vo. 2 vols. port. pub. at 1l. 1s.

— John. Columbarium, or the Pigeon-House, being an Introduction to a natural History of tame Pigeons. Lond. 1735, 8vo. 8s.

— John, M.D. Works, with Memoirs of his Life and Writings, by Robert Anderson. Edinb. 1820. 8vo. 7 vols. portrait.

A View of the Society and Manners in France, Switzerland and Germany: with Anecdotes relating to some eminent Characters. Lond. 1779, 8vo. 2 vols. 10s. 6d. Fonthill, 2088, with the View of Italy, 1l. 11s.—Second edition, 1789, 8vo. 2 vols. Edwards, 481, 15s. 6d.

A View of Society and Manners in Italy; with Anecdotes relating to some eminent Characters. Lond. 1781, 8vo. 2 vols. 8s.

A Journal during a Residence in France, from the Beginning of August to the Middle of December 1792. To which is added, an Account of the most remarkable Events that happened at Paris from that time to the Death of the late King of France.—Lond. 1793, 8vo. 2 vols. 10s. 6d. Edwards, 629, 13s. Fonthill, 2790, 1l. 4s.

A View of the Causes and Progress of the French Revolution. Lond. 1795, 8vo. 2 vols. 7s.

Zaluco. Various Views of Human Nature, taken from Life and Manners, foreign and domestic. Lond. 1789, 8vo. 2 vols. 8s.

Edward. Various Views of Human Nature, taken from Life and Manners, chiefly England. Lond. 1796, 2 vols. 7s.

MOORE, John, M.D.—*continued*.
Mordaunt. Sketches of Life, Characters, and Manners, in various Countries: including the Memoirs of a French Lady of Quality. Lond. 1800, 8vo. 8 vols. 10s. 6d.

Moore's various Works, collected. 8vo. 15 vols. Williams, 1213, 4l. 16s.

Medical Sketches; in two parts. Lond. 1786, 8vo. Edwards, 301, 5s. 6d.

Mooriana; or Selections from the moral, philosophical, and miscellaneous Works of the late Dr. John Moore. Illustrated by a new biographical and critical Account of the Doctor and his writings; and Notes, historical, classical, and explanatory. By the Rev. F. Prevost and F. Blagdon, Esq. Lond. 1803, 2 vols. fcap. 8vo. port.—New edition, [entitled Beauties of Dr. John Moore] corrected and augmented. In one vol. Lond. 1813, post 8vo. port. 5s.

MOORE, John. Collections for a topographical, historical and descriptive Account of the Hundred of Aveland. Lincoln, 1809, small 4to.
Part I. (Bourn), 5s. Pp. 48, with two plates. LARGE PAPER. 7s. 6d.

— John Bayley. Reports of Cases in the Courts of C. P. and Exchequer, 1817-24. Lond. 1818-31, royal 8vo. 12 vols.
A digested Index to the Term Reports in K. B. 1785—1819, in C. P. 1788—1819, and in the Exchequer, 1792—1818. Lond. 1821, royal 8vo. 2 vols. 1l. 16s.
Supplement to Moore's, Manning's and Hammond's Digests. By J. B. Moore. Lond. 1824, royal 8vo. 18s.

— J. B., and Payne's, J. Reports in the C. P. and Exchequer Chamber, from Mich. 1827 to East. 1830. Lond. 1828-32, royal 8vo. 5 vols.

— J. B., and Scott's, J. Reports in the C. P., Exch. C., and in the House of Lords, from Mich. 1831, to Trin., 1834. Lond. 1833-4, royal 8vo. 4 vols.

— John Hamilton. The new practical Navigator. The 19th Edition, enlarged and carefully improved by Joseph Dessiou. Lond. 1814, 8vo.
The first edition of this useful work appeared in 1772.

— Sir Jonas, Knt. A new System of the Mathematics. Lond. 1681, 4to. 2 vols.
Willett, 843, 10s. 6d. This eminent mathematician was, according to Granger, the first Englishman that composed a 'System of the Mathematics.'

England's Interest; with the profitable framing of Fish Ponds, &c. Lond. 18mo.

Mapp of ye Great Levell of the Fenns. Folio. Sixteen half sheets. Lond. 1665.

The History or Narrative of the Great Level of the Fennes, called Bedford Level. Lond. 1685, 12mo. with a map. Duke of Grafton, 699, 17s. Dent, pt. I. 201, 8s. Hibbert, 5525, 10s. 6d. Heber, pt. II. 3s. 6d.

— Robert. Diarium historico-Poeticum. Oxon. 1595, 4to.
Heber, pt. vii. 10s. 6d. Bright, with autograph of Dr. Donne, 1l.

— Samuel. The Yearnings of Christ's Bowels towards his languishing Friends. Lond. 1648, 8vo. 7s. 6d.
With portrait of the author by W. Marshall.

— Rev. Thomas. History of Devonshire from the earliest period to the present time, 1829, 8vo. 3 vols. Plates by Deebla.

— Sir T. *See* MOORE, Sir Thomas.

— Thomas. Return made by the Governors of the bounty of Queen Anne, 1736, folio.
Marquis of Townshend, 2436, 1l. 7s.

— Thomas. Observations on the first and second Visions of St. John. Lond. 1750-2, 8vo.
An Enquiry into the Nature and Causes of our Saviour's Agony in the Garden. Lond. 1769, 8vo. Published by Dr. Nath. Lardner and the Rev. Caleb Fleming.

MOORE, Thomas. POETICAL WORKS, collected by himself. (*First collective edition.*) Lond. Longman, 1840-1, 12mo. 10 vols. port. and 19 plates, 2l. 10s.
In respect to this edition, the Literary Gazette, December, 1840, says: 'From among the earlier productions the most prurient have been expurgated; and upon others the author has laid the hand of exclusion and improvement.'

MOORE, Thos.—*continued.*
Reissued as *Cabinet* Edition. Lond.
Longman, 1859, 12mo. 10 vols. port. and
19 plates. 1*l.* 15*s.*
Library Edition, complete in 1 vol. medium 8vo. Lond. Longman, 1843, portrait by Richmond, vignette view of Sloperton Cottage by Creswell.—Again, 1857, 1*l.* 1*s.*
Traveller's Edition, complete in 1 vol. crown 8vo. *printed in Ruby Type.* Lond. Longman, 1858, 12s. 6d.
People's Edition. Lond. Longman, 1860, square 8vo. port. 10 parts, published at one shilling each. This contains exactly the same as the 1*l.* 1s. edition, but on rather smaller paper.
The next two editions are *non-copyright,* and do not contain any poems published since 1819.
Poetical Works, with Life of the Author, illustrated by Corbould. Lond. Routledge, 1859 (pp. 550), 12mo. 5s.
The Poetical Works, with Life. Edinb. Gall and Inglis, 1859 (pp. 520), 12mo. 6 plates, 3s. 6d.

The Poetical Works of the late THOMAS LITTLE, Esq. Lond. 1801, first edition, fcap. 8vo. (The Preface signed T. M.)—
Second edition. Lond. Carpenter, 1802, 12mo. — Third edition, 1803. — Eleventh edition, 1813.—Fifteenth edition, 1822, 7s.

IRISH MELODIES. [The words only.]
With an Appendix containing the original Advertisement, and the prefatory Letter on Music. Lond. J. Power, 1821, 12mo.—Again, 1822, 1839. Lond. Longman and Co. 1843, fcap. 8vo. with plates, 10s.
New edition, vignette title, Lond. Longman and Co. 1858, post 8vo. (or sq. 16mo.) 5s. Reduced, 1859, 2s. 6d.
With 161 Designs by D. MACLISE, R.A., and the Letter-press engraved on Steel by F. P. Becker. Lond. Longman and Co. 1846, super-royal 8vo. Printed on a fine thick paper, 3*l.* 3s. Reprinted in 1850 on a thinner paper, at 1*l.* 11s. 6d.
With 18 highly-finished steel Plates, from original Designs by Cope, Creswick, Egg, Frith, W. E. Frost, J. C. Horsley, Maclise, Millais, Mulready, Sant, F. Stone, and Ward. Lond. Longman and Co. 1856, sq. crown 8vo. 21s.
Printed in *Ruby Type,* with the Preface and Notes from the collective Edition of Moore's Poetical Works, the Advertisements originally prefixed, and a portrait of the Author. Lond. Longman and Co. 1856, 32mo. 2s. 6d.—Reduced, 1858, to 1s.
Other editions: Lond. Field, 1859, 32mo. 1s. 6d. — Lond. Hall, 1859, 32mo. 6d.—Lond. Routledge, 1859, 32mo. 6d.—Lond. Allman, 1859, 32mo. 1s.

Cantus Hibernici, Latine redditi a Nob.
Iao Torre. Lond. 1835, post 8vo.—Editio nova, aucta (nonnullis Graece redditis). Leamington, 1856-9, 8vo. *three series.*

LALLA ROOKH.

LALLA ROOKH, an oriental Romance; containing the Veiled Prophet of Khorassan; Paradise and Peri; the Fire-Worshippers, and the Light of the Harem. Lond. Longman and Co. 1817, 4to. Hibbert, 5849, with Westall's plates, proofs, morcc. 1*l.* 1s. Burstlell, 1851, with Westall's plates, proofs, morocco, 5*l.*
Sixth edition, with plates after Westall. Lond. 1817, 8vo.
Lond. 1818, 8vo. Drury, 3783, 10s. 6d.
Lond. 1839, fcap. 8vo. with four plates after Westall.
Lond. 1839, royal 8vo. with numerous beautiful plates, 1*l.* 1s. INDIA PROOFS, 2*l.* 2s.
Lond. Longman, 1848, fcap. 8vo. plates, 10s. 6d.
Lond. Longman, 1850, post 8vo. (or sq. 16mo.) vignette title, 5s. Reduced, 1860, 2s. 6d.
With 13 highly-finished steel Plates, from original Designs by Corbould, Meadows, and Stephanoff, engraved under the superintendence of the late Chas. Heath. Lond. Longman, 1851, sq. crown 8vo. 15s.
—Again, 1856, 1858.
Lalla Rookh. New edition, printed in *Ruby Type;* with the Preface and Notes from the Collective Edition of Moore's Poetical Works, and a Frontispiece from a Design by Kenny Meadows. Lond. Longman, 1859, 32mo. 2s. 6d. Reduced 1s.
With Illustrations by Evans, after Thomas, Pickersgill, Birket Foster, E. H. Corbould. Lond. Routledge, 1859, 4to. pp. 320, 15s.
Lond. Routledge, 1859, 12mo. 1s.
Lond. (Edinb.) Nicolson, 1859, 12mo. 1s.
Lond. Field, 1859, 32mo. 1s. 6d.
Lond. Allman, 1859, 32mo. 1s.
With woodcut Illustrations by Tenniel.
Lond. Longman, fcap. 4to. (In the press.)

Translations.

Lalla Rukh in den Sylbenmaassen des originals uebersetzt von F. Baron de la Motte Fouqué (*anhang,* Das Paradies und die Peri uebers. von Breuer). Wien. 1825, 16mo. 2 vols. (Forming vols. 12 and 13 of the Classische Cabinet—Bibliothek.)
Laleh Rukh nach dem englischen bearbeitet von Wollheim. Hamb. and Leip. (1846), 16mo. (Forming vol 1 of the Classische Bibliothek des In-und Auslandes.)
Il Profeta Velato, poema orientale, tradotto da Giov. Fiecchia. Torin. 1838, 12mo.
De Vuur aanbidders. Naar het Engelsch,

MOORE, Thos.—*continued.*
Vertalingen en Navolgingen in Poezy. 1834, 8vo.

ODES OF ANACREON, translated into English Verse, with Notes by Thos. Moore. Lond. 1800, 4to. pp. 220, with three plates, 15s. — Second Edition. Lond. Carpenter, 1802, 12mo. 2 vols. 2 plates. 10s. LARGE PAPER. Dent, pt. 1. 40, morocco, 1l. 2s.— Fourth Edition, 1804. — Sixth, 1806. — Seventh, 1810.—Eighth, 1813.—Ninth, 1815.
See ANACREON.

EPISTLES, ODES, and other POEMS. Lond. 1806, 4to. Streetmill, 1850, morocco, 2l. 6s.—Fifteenth Edition. Lond. Carpenter, 1817, fcap. 8vo. 2 vols. front. and vignette.

Corruption and Intolerance. Two Poems, with Notes, addressed to an Englishman by an Irishman. Lond. Carpenter, 1808, fcap. 8vo.

M. P., or the Blue Stocking; a comic Opera. Lond. Power, 1811, 8vo.

INTERCEPTED LETTERS; or the Two-Penny Post Bag. By Thomas Brown, jun. Lond. 1812, fcap. 8vo.—Eighth edition, Lond. 1813, 12mo. 6s. Seventeen editions have appeared.

The World at Westminster; a periodical Periodication, by Tho. Brown, the younger. Lond. 1816, 12mo.

ALCIPHRON, a Poem (in five Letters). Lond. Macrone, 1839. This was first published at the end of the Epicurean of this date; but was also sold with a separate title.

The FUDGE FAMILY IN PARIS. Lond. 1818, 12mo. 7s. 6d.

The FUDGES IN ENGLAND; being a Sequel to the 'Fudge Family in Paris.' By Thomas Brown, the younger. Second edition. Lond. 1835, 12mo.

TOM CRIB'S MEMORIAL to CONGRESS. With a Preface, Notes, and an Appendix. By one of the Fancy. Lond. 1819, fcap. 8vo. 4s. 6d.

FABLES for the HOLY ALLIANCE, Rhymes on the Road, &c. &c. By Thomas Brown, the younger. Lond. 1823, 12mo.

The LOVES of the ANGELS, a Poem. Lond. Longman and Co. (January 1) 1823, 8vo. 9s. (five editions in one year, and none since.) — Paris, 1823, 8vo. pp. iv. 134. ON VELLUM, two copies struck off.

ODES upon CASH, CORN, and CATHOLICS; and other Matters. Selected from the columns of the Times Journal. Lond. 1828, 12mo.

SONGS, BALLADS, and SACRED SONGS, with Notes, &c. Lond. Longman and Co., 1858, post 8vo. (or sq. 16mo.) vignette title by Doyle, 5s.—New edition, *printed in Ruby Type*; with the Notes and a Vignette from a Design by T. Creswick, R.A. Lond. Longman, 1849, 32mo. 2s. 6d.— Again, 1856, 32mo. 2s. 6d.

Musical Editions of the Irish Melodies, National Airs, Sacred Songs, &c.

A SELECTION OF IRISH MELODIES, with Symphonies and Accompaniments by Sir J. A. Stevenson. Lond. J. Power, 1807-34, folio, 10 parts, pub. 16s. each. This was the first edition of both words and music. Each part contains 12 melodies and 4 harmonised airs. The first and second appeared in 1807; the third in 1810; the fourth November, 1811; the fifth, December, 1813, dated 1814; the sixth, March, 1815; the seventh, October 1, 1818; the eighth, May, 1821; the ninth, 1822; the tenth and last, June, 1834, with Supplements at 5s. additional.

Irish Melodies, *the Music with the Words*, the Symphonies and Accompaniments by Sir John Stevenson, Mus. Doc. Complete in 1 vol. small music size, imp. 8vo. 21s. 6d. Lond. Addison, and Longman and Co. 1857.—Reissued, 1858, in twelve 1s. parts, sm. 4to. or in cloth, 12s.

Irish Melodies (A Selection of the)— THE HARMONISED AIRS, with the original Symphonies and Accompaniments by Sir John Stevenson and Sir Henry Bishop. *For two, three, or four Voices.* Lond. Addison and Longman and Co., 1856, imp. 8vo. pp. 190, 16s.

With Symphonies and Accompaniments by Sir J. Stevenson and Sir Hen. Bishop. Lond. Longman and Addison, 1859, 4to. pp. 320, published in 12 parts at 1s. each.

A Set of Glees, written and composed by Thos. Moore (Seven Glees, one of which is 'Flip, hip, hurrah.') Lond. J. Power (1827).

In the following non-copyright editions of the Irish Melodies those originally published since 1818 are necessarily omitted.

Irish Melodies; with new Symphonies and Accompaniments for the Pianoforte by M. W. Balfe. Lond. Novello, 1859, fol. pp. 240, 25s.

Irish Melodies; with Symphonies and Accompaniments by Sir John Stevenson. —Edited by J. W. Glover. New edition. Dublin, Hall, 1859, 4to. pp. 340, 12s. 6d.

Irish Melodies; with Symphonies and Pianoforte Accompaniments, complete. Lond. (Musical Bouquet Office), 1859, folio, 3 vols. in 1, 15s.

Irish Melodies; with Symphonies and Accompaniments for the Pianoforte, including the most popular and those most esteemed by the Author. Lond. (Musical Bouquet Office), 1859, 4to. 4s.

POPULAR NATIONAL AIRS, A Selection of, with Symphonies and Accompani-

MOORE, Thos.—*continued*.
ments by H. R. Bishop, the Words by
Thomas Moore, Esq. 6 parts, folio. at 12s.

Each part contains 12 airs, four of them
harmonized. The 1st number was published in 1819; the 2nd, 1820; the 3rd
1821; the 4th, December, 1822; the 5th
May, 1826; the 6th Feb. 1828.

MOORE'S SELECTION OF NATIONAL AIRS,
and other Songs, now first collected; with
Symphonies and Accompaniments by H.
E. Bishop; the music printed with the
Words: to which are appended (arranged
as single Songs), a few Airs and Glees
which the Author is known to have regarded with especial favour, and was himself accustomed to sing as solos. Lond.
Longman, 1858, imp. 8vo. pp. 321, ll.
11s. 6d.

The same, *People's Edition*, edited by
C. W. Glover. Lond. Longman and Co.,
Addison and Co. 1860, sm. 4to. 12s.

SACRED SONGS, DUETTS AND TRIOS, the
words by Thomas Moore, *the Music* composed and selected by Sir John Stevenson
and Mr. Moore. Lond. J. Power, 1816,
folio. 2 parts, 1l. 1s. each.

SACRED SONGS; with Symphonies and
Accompaniments by Sir John Stevenson.
To which are added, six Songs from
Scripture, arranged by John Goss; the
words by Thomas Moore. Lond. Longman and Addison, 1859, sm. folio. pp. 222,
16s.

EVENINGS IN GREECE; with *Music* by
Bishop. Lond. Power, n.d. [1825?] sm.
folio, 2 parts, at 15s. each.

LEGENDARY BALLADS; *with Music* arranged by H. R. Bishop. Lond. J. Power,
n. d. [1830?] sm. folio, 1l. 1s.

The Summer Fete; a Poem, with Songs.
The *Music* by M. R. Bishop. Lond. 1831,
sm. folio. 8s.

Vocal Miscellany by Thos. Moore, the
Music by Henry P. Bishop. Lond. J.
Power, 1828, sm. folio. Part 1 (all published), 8s.

MOORE'S PROSE WRITINGS.

A Candid Appeal to Public Confidence,
or Considerations on the actual and imaginary Dangers of the present Crisis,
1803, 8vo. 1s.

A Letter to the Roman Catholics of
Dublin. Dubl. 1810, 8vo. 1l. 1s.

MEMOIRS of CAPTAIN ROCK, the celebrated Irish Chieftain; with some Account
of his Ancestors, written by himself.
Second edition. Lond. Longman, 1824,
fcap. 8vo, 9s. An agreeable and witty little
work.—Fourth edition, 1824.

MEMOIRS of the Rt. Hon. R. D. SHERIDAN. Lond. 1825, 4to. Hibbert, 5609, 16s.
—8vo. 2 vols. Lond. 1825.—Lond. 1827,
8vo. 2 vols. An Account of Sheridan, in

which many of Moore's doubts and inaccuracies are cleared up, will be found in
Blackwood's Edinb. Mag. xix. 118-30, xx,
23-41, and 201-14.

For Mr. Moore's edition of Sheridan's
Works, pub. 1818, see SHERIDAN.

Life of Lord Byron. *See* BYRON.

THE EPICUREAN, a Tale. Lond. Longman and Co. (June) 1827, 12mo.

Epicurean, new edition, with Notes: to
which is added, Alciphron, a Poem. Lond.
Macrone, 1839, fcap. 8vo. with 4 plates by
Goodall, after J. M. W. Turner; published at 10s. 6d. Mr. Macrone made a bargain with Mr. Moore for an illustrated
edition, of which he printed 12,000, and
soon afterwards failed. Of these, 6,000
came into the hands of Mr. Bohn, who
reduced the price to 8s. and soon sold
them all.

Epicurean, new edition, with the Notes
from the collective edition of Moore's
Poetical Works; and a Vignette, engraved
on Wood, from an original Design by D.
Maclise, R.A. Lond. Longman, 1858,
post 8vo, 5s.

Translated into French by A. A. Renouard. Paris, 1827, 12mo.—Into Italian.
Milan, 1836, 24mo.—Venice, 1835.—Into
German. Inspruc, 1828.—Into Dutch, by
H. van Logbem. Deventer, 1829.

LIFE AND DEATH OF LORD EDWARD FITZGERALD. Lond. (July) 1831, post 8vo. 2 vols.
portrait. 1l. 1s.

TRAVELS OF AN IRISH GENTLEMAN IN
SEARCH OF A RELIGION. Lond. Longman,
1833, 12mo. 2 vols.—With Notes and Illustrations, and a Biog. and Lit. Introduction by J. Burke. Lond. Dolman, 1853,
12mo. 5s.

HISTORY OF IRELAND from the earliest
Kings of that Realm down to the last
Chief (1648). Lond. (Lardner's Cab. Cy.)
1839-46, 12mo. 4 vols. 1l. 4s.

Translated into German by C. Ackers.
Baden, 1846, 8vo. 2 vols.

Notes from the Letters of Thos. Moore
to his Music Publisher, James Power (the
publication of which was suppressed in
London). With an Introductory Letter
from T. Crofton Croker, Esq. New York,
Redfield, n. d. (but on the engraved title,
Lond. Rosworth, 1853), post 8vo. with two
portraits, one by Haines, the other by N.
Bate, after Slater, and four plates and
vignette title.

In his preface the editor says (following
the Literary Gazette of July 8, 1853):
'From copies of above twelve hundred
letters, forwarded at Mrs. Moore's request
for Lord John Russell's information, fifty-seven only were selected and published by
his Lordship. The original letters having
passed into the hands of Messrs. Puttick
and Simpson for public sale, they pointed

MOORE, Thos.—*continued.*
ont the circumstance, and many of the
letters were purchased for the American
publisher of the present volume.'

MEMOIRS, JOURNAL, AND CORRESPON-
DENCE of THOMAS MOORE. Edited by
the Right Hon. Lord John Russell, M.P.
With Portraits, &c. Lond. Longman, 1852-6,
post 8vo. 8 vols. 4l. 4s.—People's edition,
in 1 vol. 8vo. 1860, 12s. 6d.
Correspondence between the Rt. Hon.
J. N. Croker and the Rt. Hon. Lord John
Russell, on some Passages of Moore's
Diary. Lond. Murray, 1854, 8vo. 35 pages.
Thomas Moore, his Life, Writings, and
Contemporaries, by H. R. Montgomery.
Lond. Newby, 1860, 2s. 6d.

Engraved Illustrations of Moore's Poems.

POETRY and Pictures from Tho. Moore;
being Selections, with original Designs
(80) by Cope, Corbauld, Birket Foster, &c.
Lond. Longman, 1858, fcap. 4to. pp. 396,
1l. 1s.
The Beauties of Moore; a Series of
Portraits of his principal Characters, engraved by, or under the superintendence
of, E. Finden; with descriptive letter-
press. Lond. Chapman and Hall, 1846,
imp. 4to. 48 plates.—Again, 1849, imp. 4to.
2l. 8s. LARGE PAPER, 5l. 5l.
New edition, with Memoir. Lond.
Edinb. and New York, (1853), folio.
Moore's Poems, Illustrations of; from
Designs by G. Jones, portrait and 19
plates. Lond. 4to.
Moore's Poems, Illustrations to, by R.
Westall, 6 plates. Lond. 1825, 12mo.
Moore's Poems, Illustrations to, by Stot-
hard; portrait and 6 plates. 4to.
A Portrait of Thomas Moore, by John
Durnet after M. A. Shee, PRINTS, 1l. 1s.
PROOFS, 1l. 11s. 6d.
Seven Illustrations by Smirke.
Westall's Illustrations (six), engraved
by Charles Heath. Lond. 1817, INDIA
PROOFS, 18s.
Stothard's Illustrations; front. and 14
very small plates, 3s. 6d.
Illustrations, from Designs by Corbould
and Stephanoff, 13 plates, 4to. 6s.
A Series of six Illustrations for Moore's
Lalla Rookh, from Designs by Corbould.
roy. 8vo.
Pearls from the East, or Beauties from
Lalla Rookh; designed and Drawn by
Fanny and Louisa Corbaux. Lond. Tilt,
n. d. (1837), imp. 4to. 18 plates.
Scenes from the Fire-worshippers, illus-
trated by O. S. T. D. 1837, 4to.
Lebende Bilder bei dem Festspiel Lalla
Rookh, nach der natur gezeichnet van W.
Hensel. Berl. 1823, fol. plates.

A Series of Illustrations for Moore's
Loves of the Angels, engraved by C.
Heath, from Designs by R. Westall, R.A.
5s. PROOFS in 4to. 10s. On INDIA PAPER,
15s. On INDIA PAPER before the letters,
1l.

Six Engravings in Illustration of
Moore's Melodies, after Stothard's Designs. 4to. PROOFS, 6s.
Illustrations of Moore's Irish Melodies;
consisting of seven Plates, with a vignette
title-page, from Designs by Westall. 5s.
PROOFS, 7s. 6d.
Landscape Illustrations of the Irish
Melodies, with Comments. Lond. 1836,
sm. 4to. Parts 1 and 2, each containing
4 plates, all published.

Miscellanea.

An Epistle to Thomas Moore, Esq., in
Imitation of the thirteenth Satire of Ju-
venal. Lond. 1819, 8vo. Privately print-
ed (50 copies only). Reprinted in Lit.
Gaz., Sept. 4, 1819.
Captain Rock detected. By a Munster
Farmer. Lond. 1824, 12mo. "By — O'
Sullivan. Tolerably abusive."—*Moore.*
A Letter to T. Moore, Esq. on the Sub-
ject of [his Criticism upon] Sheridan's
School for Scandal. By the Author of an
Essay on Light Reading. [? Edw. Mangin.]
Bath, 1826, 8vo.

MOORE, Sir W. the younger. The
True Crucifixe for true Catholickes,
or the Way for true Catholicks to
have the true Crucifixe. Edinb.
Writtoun, 1629, 12mo.
Heber, pt. iv. 18s. Geo. Chalmers, da-
maged, 10s. 6d. Jolly, 1843, 2l. 8s.
The Cry of Blood and of a broken Co-
venant, written out at first upon the sad
Relation of our Soveraignes most treach-
erous and inhumane murther. Edinb.
1650, 4to. In verse. Dedicated to Chas. II.
Bright, cut close, 1l. 1s.
The History and Descent of the House
of Rowallane. Printed from the original
MS. Glasg. 1825, post 8vo. *See* MURE.

MORABIN, James. The History
of Cicero's Banishment. Translated from the French. Lond.
1725, 8vo.
Roxburghe, 7766, 2s.

MORAES, Fr. de. *See* PALMERIN
of England.

MORANT, Philip, M.A. The History and Antiquities of the County
of Essex. Lond. 1768, folio, 2 vols.

Marquis of Townshend, 2440, 18l. 16s. North, pt. II. 1253, 8l. 6s., Gardner, 9l. 15s. Utterson, russia, 9l. 5s. LARGE PAPER, in royal folio. Dent, pt. II. 780, 15l. 5s. Hibbert, 5649, 17l. 5s. (Leath, 4528, russia, 22l. Willett, 1659, 31l. 10s. (Some of the plates in the L.P., especially those which fold, are shorter than the book.) *Collation.*—Vol. I. Title, contents, and dedication to Lord Dacre, 8 leaves; preface, two pages (dated 1768); introduction, xxviii pages; title-page 'The History—of Colchester, one leaf; dedication to Terrick, Bp. of London, 2 pages; names of the subscribers, 2 pages; historical part, 196 pages; appendix. 28 pages; addenda, pages 25-9 repeated; the Continuation of the History of Essex, including index, errata and *directions for placing the prints in each volumes*, pp. 1—570. (The list of plates does not mention *Audley House*, commonly called Audley End, engraved by Austin, which should face page 550 in vol. 2). Pages 231 and 232 are repeated. Vol. II. title-page, contents and dedication to Lord Maynard, 3 leaves; preface, 2 pages; (this preface being superseded by that subsequently given for the first volume, is usually cancelled, according to the direction given at the foot of title page); the History, including index and errata, 646 pages. Pages 243 and 244 are omitted. Pages 671 and 672, 585 and 596, are repeated. Some copies have a title-page, dated 1768, after the table of contents 'The History and Antiquities of the County of Essex.'

[A new edition, without date and without the plates, was printed in numbers at Chelmsford in 1817, folio, 2 vols. A shabby and worthless book.]

History and Antiquities of Colchester. Lond. 1748. Folio. Afterwards much enlarged by the author, and incorporated in his History of Essex. A copy, with Morant's MS. notes, is in the library of the Royal Institution.

The Cruelties and Persecutions of the Romish Church displayed. Lond. 1728.

MORAVIANS.—The History of the Moravians from their first Settlement in Herrnhaag, in the County of Budingen, down to the present Time. Translated from the German. Lond. 1754, 8vo. 2s. 6d.

Eleven Tracts relating to the Moravians. Lond. 1753-5, 8vo. 2 vols. Hollis, 961, 17s. *See* Monthly Review, vols. viii. ix. x. xi. xii. xvi. and xvii.

Periodical Accounts relating to the Missions of the United Brethren among the Heathen, 1790-1830, 8vo. 9 vols.

Select Narratives from the ancient History of the United Brethren, 1806, 8vo.

An Account of the Moravian Brethren. In four parts:—I. An Account of John Huss. II. Historical Account of the Commencement of the Ancient Church of the Brethren. III. A Sketch of the Ritual and Ecclesiastical Discipline of the United Fratrum, in Bohemian Moravia and Poland. IV. The Address of J. A. Comenius to the faithful Remnant on their Dispersion. Bradford, 1822, 12mo.

Asspb; or the Harrnhutters, being a Rhythmical Sketch of the principal Events, and most remarkable Institutions in the modern History of the Church of the United Fratrum, commonly called Moravians. Lond. Ogle and Co. 1827, 12mo.

See CRANTZ, David. HOLMES, John. LATROBE, T. RIMIUS, Henry.

MORAVIUS, T., Scotus. Motaphrasis poetica Naupactiados (sive Lepantiados) Regis. Lond. 1604, 4to.
Bindley, pt. III. 580, 18s. Bright, 3913, 1l. 16s.

MORAY.—A Survey of the Province of Moray; historical, geographical and political. Aberdeen, 1798, 8vo. *See* SHAW, Rev. L.

MORDANT, John. The complete Steward. Lond. 1761. 8vo. 2 vols. 8s.

MORDAUNT, Elizabeth, Viscountess. Anecdotes, &c. commencing 1656. Lond. 1810, 12mo.

— Mr., second Son of John Earl of Peterborough. Trial of, at the pretended high Court of Justice at Westminster Hall, June 1 and 2, 1658. Lond. 1661, folio, portrait (which is rare).

See PETERBOROUGH, Earl of.

MORDECAI, Benjamin Ben. *See* TAYLOR, Henry.

MORDEN, Rob. A Book of the Prospects of the remarkable Places in and about the City of London. By Rob. Morden and Phil. Lee.
Thirty plates, size 7½ inches long by 2½ inches wide. Printed about 1700.

MORE, Alexander. Fides publica, contra Calumnias Johann. Miltoni. Hag. 1654, 12mo.

Poemata. Paris, 1669, 4to. With portrait. Hibbert, 5615, 1l. 5s. Bright 2s. 6d.

MORE, Cresacre. The Life of Sir Thomas More by his great Grandson, Cresacre More, with a biographical Preface, Notes and other Illustrations by the Rev. Joseph Hunter, F.S.A. Lond. 1828, 8vo. 14s. Portrait.

Two editions of this life have before appeared (see MORE, Sir Thomas, p. 1608), in both of which it is assigned to a member of the family of More who could not have been the writer of it. In the preface of the edition it is restored to the true author Cresacre More, and some account is given of several members of the family of Sir Thomas More who are connected with our literature. LARGE PAPER, twelve copies printed, at 5l. 5s.

— Edward. A lytle and bryefe Treatyse called The Defence of Women, an especially of Englishe Women, made agaynste The Schole-Howse of Women. Lond. by John Kynge, 1560, 4to.

A production more deserving of notice from the object it had in view, than for its poetical merit. It is reprinted (from a mutilated copy) in the second volume of Utterson's Pieces of popular Poetry.

MORE, or MURE, Elizabeth. See GORDON of Buthlaw, p. 915. ROBERT II., King of Scotland. SCOTIA Rediviva.

— Sir George, Knt. A true Discourse concerning the certain Possession and Dispossession of seven Persons of one Familie in Lancashire. Lond. 1600, 8vo.

Boswell, 1805, 1l. 2s. Bindley, pt. II. 1805, 17s. 6d. Nassau, pt. 1. 2207, 1l. 2s. Heber, pt. II. 11s. See DARRELL, John.
A Demonstration of God in his Workes. Lond. J. R. for Th. Charde, 1597, 4to. Heber, pt. II. 11s. Collation.—A to X in fours; epistle. 5 pages; preface. 19 pages; table. 4 pages; faults. 2 page. Bindley, pt. III. 617, 11s. Ulles, 14s.—1598, 4to. —1624, 4to.

— George. Principles for young Princes, collected out of sundry Authours. Lond. 1611, 18mo.

Gordonstoun, 1531, 14s. Heber, pt. VII. 1s.—1629, 4to. Gordonstoun, 1532, 6s.

— Gertrude. The spiritval Exercises of D. Gertrvde More of the holy Order of S. Benet, and English Congregation of our Ladie of Comfort in Cambray. Paris, 1658, 12mo. 6s.

Pp. 512, including the title. Prefixed is a portrait of Gertrude More by K. Lochom. The authoress was the granddaughter of Sir Thomas More.

MORE, Hannah. Works, including Bible Rhymes. Lond. T. Cadell, 1818-21, crown 8vo. 19 vols. pub. at 6l. 15s.—Second edition, with Additions and Corrections. Lond. Cadell and Davis, 1830, post 8vo. 11 vols. 5l.

New edition, complete, with Memoir and Notes. Lond. H. G. Bohn, 1853, fcap. 8vo. portrait and vignette title-pages, 11 vols. 1l. 18s. 6d. or 3s. 6d. per volume.

Contents of this edition:

VOL.	VOL.
1. Stories for Persons in the Middle Ranks. Tales for the Common People.	5. Tragedies & Poems.
	6. Poems, Sacred Dramas, and Essays.
2. Tales for the Common People. Rellgion of the fashionable World. Thoughts on the Manners of the Great. Remarks on the Speech of M. Dupont.	7. Cœlebs in Search of a Wife.
	8. Practical Piety.
	9. Christian Morals.
	10. On the Character and Writings of St. Paul. The Spirit of Prayer.
3. Strictures on modern Female Education.	11. Moral Sketches. Tracts written during the Riots of 1817. Poetical Works, Ballads, &c. General Index.
4. Hints towards forming the Character of a young Princess.	

'How many have thanked God for the hour that first made them acquainted with the writings of Hannah More. She did perhaps as much real good in her generation as any woman that ever held the pen. It would be idle for us to dwell here on works so well known. They have established her name as a great moral writer, possessing a masterly command over the resources of our language, and devoting a keen wit and a lively fancy to the best and noblest of purposes.'— *Quarterly Review.*

Horace Walpole declared that Hannah More was not only one of the cleverest of women, but one of the best. Her writings, said he, promote virtue, and their repeated editions prove their worth and utility.

SEARCH AFTER HAPPINESS; a Pastoral Drama. First edition, 1773. Composed in her 17th year.—Eleventh edition, with additions. Lond. 1796. 8vo.—New edition, to which are added, Ballads, Tales, Hymns, and Epitaphs. Lond. Cadell, 1818, 8vmo. 2s. 6d.; reduced, Bohn, 1s. 6d.

MORE, Hannah—*continued.*
Sacred Dramas; chiefly intended for young Persons. The subjects taken from the Bible. To which is added, Sensibility, a Poem. Lond. 1782, 8vo. 4s.—Sixteenth edition. Lond. Cadell and Davies, 1810, post 8vo.—Twenty-third edition. Lond. Cadell, 1845, 32mo. 2s. 6d.—Twenty-fourth edition, with additions. Lond. Bohn, 1850, 32mo. 2s. portrait.

Thoughts on the Importance of the Manners of the Great to general Society. Lond. 1788, 8vo.—Seventh edition. Lond. 1799.—Eighth edition. Lond. 1792, 12mo. Seven large editions were sold in a few months; the second, in little more than a week; the third, in *four hours.*

Essays on various Subjects, principally designed for Young Ladies. Lond. 1778, crown 8vo.—Sixth edition. Lond. Cadell, 1796. Afterwards incorporated in her other writings.

An Estimate of the Religion of the fashionable World. Lond. 1790, 12mo. 6s.—Fifth edition. Lond. 1793.

Village Politics, by Will Chip. 1793, 12mo. price twopence.

Remarks on the Speech of M. Dupont in the National Convention, on Religion and public Education. Lond. 1793, 2s. 6d.—Second edition, 1794, 8vo.

Strictures on the modern System of Female Education, with a View of the Principles and Conduct prevalent among Women of Rank and Fortune. Lond. 1799, crown 8vo. 2 vols. 10s.—The thirteenth Edition. Lond. 1829, post 8vo. 2 vols.—Lond. 1830, post 8vo. 2 vols.

Hints towards forming the Character of a young Princess. Lond. 1805, crown 8vo. 2 vols.—Fifth edition. Lond. 1819, post 8vo. 2 vols. pub. 10s. 6d.

Cœlebs in Search of a Wife; comprehending observations on domestic Habits and Manners, Religion and Morals. Lond. 1809, post 8vo. 2 vols.—Sixteenth edition. Lond. Cadell and Davies, 1826.—And again, 1830, post 8vo. 2 vols. This work passed through ten editions in the space of one year. Lond. Bohn, 1860, fcap. 8vo. vignette title, 8s. 6d. There are besides several small editions, from 5s. to 1s. 6d.

Practical Piety; or, the Influence of the Religion of the Heart on the Life and Manners. Lond. 1811, 12mo. 2 vols.—The fourteenth Edition. Lond. 1828, post 8vo. 2 vols. 10s. 6d.—Seventeenth edition. Lond. 1834, 12mo. port. 5s.—Eighteenth edition. Lond. Bohn, 1848, 12mo. frontispiece, 5s. — Nineteenth edition. Lond. Bohn, 1850, 32mo. portrait, 2s. 6d.

Christian Morals. Fifth edition. Lond. Cadell and Davies, 1813, 8vo. 2 vols. 12s. —The eighth Edition. Lond. 1829, post 8vo.—Ninth edition. Lond. Cadell, 1836, post 8vo. pub. 10s. 6d. reduced, Bohn, 5s. 6d.

An Essay on the Character and practical Writings of St. Paul. Lond. 1815, 8vo. 2 vols. 12s.—The fifth Edition. Lond. 1819, 8vo. 2 vols. — Seventh edition. Lond. Cadell, 1837, post 8vo. 10s. 6d. reduced, Bohn. 6s.

Moral Sketches of prevailing Opinions and Manners, foreign and domestic, with Reflections on Prayer. Lond. 1819, 8vo. 9s.—The ninth Edition. Lond. 1821, 8vo. The first edition was sold on the day of publication.—Tenth edition. Lond. Cadell, 1830, post 8vo. pub. at 9s. reduced, Bohn, 5s. 6d.

The Spirit of Prayer. Lond. 1825, 12mo. 6s.—Seventh Edition. Lond. 1828, 12mo. —Eleventh edition. Lond. Cadell, 1843, fcap. 8vo. portrait, 6s.—Twelfth edition. Lond. Bohn, 1849, fcap. 8vo. port. 5s. 6d.

Stories for the middle Ranks of Society. Lond. Cadell, 1818, post 8vo. 6s. Lond. Tegg, 1839, 32mo. 3s. 6d.

Tales for the common People. Lond. Cadell, 1818, post 8vo. 6s.—Lond. Tegg, 1839, 32mo. 3s. 6d.

Bible Rhymes on the Names of all the Books of the Old and New Testament. Lond. 1821, 12mo.

Poetical Works. A new Edition. Lond. Cadell, 1829, post 8vo. 7s.

The Inflexible Captive. A Tragedy. 1774. A free translation of Metastasio's Attilio Regolo.

The Fatal Falsehood. A Tragedy. Lond. 1779, 8vo. Originally called the Bridal Day.

Percy. A Tragedy. 1777.—Lond. 1783, 8vo. — Fifth edition. Lond. 1812, 8vo. Nearly 4000 copies were sold in the first fortnight. It has been translated into French and German.

Tragedies (viz. Percy, the Fatal Falsehood, and the Inflexible Captive). Lond. 1818, post 8vo. 7s.

Cheap Repository Tracts. Published in Nos. 1795-8.— New edition. Lond. Rivington, 1837, 12mo. 3 vols. 15s.—New edition. Lond. Houlston, 1860, 12mo. 5 vols. 10s. 6d. This popular series of religious tales in tracts was translated into French and Russian.

The Feast of Freedom, or the Abolition of domestic Slavery in Ceylon: a Poem, by Hannah More; the vocal Parts adapted to Music by Charles Wesley. To which are added, several unpublished little Pieces. Lond. 1827, 8vo.

Life of Hannah More, by Sir Archibald Mac Sarcasm, Bart. (Satirical.) Bristol, 1802.

Life, with a critical review of her writings. By W. Shaw, Lond. 1802, 8vo.

MORE, Hannah—continued.
Memoirs of the Life and Correspondence of Mrs. Hannah More. By W. Roberts. Lond. 1834.—Second edition, 1835, post 8vo. 4 vols. — Abridged (Seeley's Fam. L.), 1838, fcap. 8vo. 5s.—1856, 3s. 6d.
The Life of Hannah More; with Notices of her Sisters. By the Rev. Henry Thompson. Lond. Cadell, 1838, post 8vo. printed uniformly with her Works, and forming an additional volume, portrait, and numerous wood engravings, 12s. reduced, Bohn, 6s.
'This may be called the official edition of Hannah More's Life. It brings so much new and interesting matter into the field respecting her, that it will receive a hearty welcome from the public. Among the rest, the particulars of most of her publications will reward the curiosity of literary readers.'—*Literary Gazette.*
Life, by Mrs. E. Smith. Lond. 1844, 8vo. 9s.

MORE, Henry, D.D. Theological Works. Lond. 1708, folio, 12s. Portrait by Loggan.
This volume contains, 1. An Explanation of the grand Mystery of Godliness. 2. An Enquiry into the Mystery of Iniquity. 3. A prophetical Exposition of the seven Epistles of the seven Churches in Asia. 4. A Discourse of the Grounds of Faith in Points of Religion. 5. An Antidote against Idolatry, with an Appendix. 6. Some divine Hymns.
ΨΥΧΩΔΙΑ Platonica; or, a Platonical Song of the Soul. In four several Poems. Cambridge, 1642, 12mo. First edition. Cambridge, 1645, 12mo. Heber, pt. iv. 4s. Nassau, pt. l. 2308, 5s.
Philosophical Poems. Cambridge, 1647, 8vo. Boswell, 1907, 6s. Nassau, pt. i. 2310, 11s. Bibl. Anglo-Poet. 413, 2l. 12s. 6d. Bindley, pt. ii. 1570, 7s. Stegg, with portrait, 18s. Two editions printed same year. *Collation.* — A 4 leaves, B—Hh, in eights, the last leaf containing an errata. A notice will be found in the Retrospective Review, v. 223—38.
Opera theologica, ex Anglico Latine reddita. Londini, 1675, folio, with portrait of More, æt. 61, sitting under a tree, by W. Faithorne.
Opera philosophica, latine reddita. Lond. 1679, folio, 3 vols. with portrait of More, æt. 65, and of John Cockshutt, his disciple, both by Loggan, Heath, 1868, 18s.
The philosophical Writings of Henry More, D.D. viz. 1. Antidote against Atheism, with an Appendix. 2. Enthusiasmus triumphatus. 3. Letters to Des Cartes, &c. 4. Immortality of the Soul. 5. Conjectura Cabbalistica. The fourth Edition, corrected and much enlarged. Lond. 1712, folio, 10s. 6d.—Lond. 1662, folio.
Divine Dialogues; containing disquisitions concerning the attributes and providence of God. Glasg. Foulis, 1743, 12mo.
Discourses on several texts of Scripture. Lond. 1691, 12mo.
Enchiridion ethicum, præcipua moralis philosophiæ rudimenta complectens. Amst. 1668, 1695, 12mo.
Translated by Edw. Southwell. Lond. 1690.
Enchiridion metaphysicum. Lond. 1671, 4to.
Life of Henry More, D.D. by R. Ward Lond. 1710, 8vo. with portrait of More, by Loggan, 5s. Williams, 1858, morocco, 1l. 7s.

MORE, Henricus. Historia Provinciæ Anglicanæ Societatis Jesu. Audomari, 1660, folio. Frontispiece, 5l. 5s.
A copy is in the British Museum.
Heber, pt. l; pt. ii. 4l. 5s. Bright, 4l. 13s.
Narratio gloriosæ mortis quam per religiosos catholicos P. Hen. Morus, &c. fortiter oppetiit. Londini, 1 Feb. 1645. Gandav. 1645, 4to. 2l. 12s. 6d.

— John. A Table from the Beginning of the World to this Day. Cambridge, Legat, 1593, 12mo.
Bindley, pt. ii. 1944, 2s. Gordonstoun, 1693, 2s. Townley, pt. ii. 750, 2s. 6d.
Three Sermons, &c. Camb. 1594, 4to.
A lively Anatomie of Death, occasioned by the Death of Mr. South. Lond. 1596, 18mo.

— Richard. A true Relation of the Murders committed in the Parish of Clunne, in the County of Salop, by Enoch ap Evan, upon the Bodies of his Mother and Brother, with the Causes moving him thereunto. Lond. 1641, 12mo.
Printed by order of the House of Commons. Heed, 5251, 7s. *See* STUDLEY, Peter.

— Sir Thomas. Omnia Latina Opera, quorum aliqua nunc primum in lucem prodeunt. Lovanii, 1565 et 1566, folio. Portraits of Sir T. More and Bishop Fisher. (The Utopia is omitted in this edition.)

MORE, Sir Thos.—*continued.*
Heber, pt. i. Thuanus's copy, 1l. 11s.
First edition. Basiliæ, 1563, 8vo. The
best edition is Franc. 1689, folio.

Utopia, authore Thoma Moro. Cara
Petri Ægidii Antuerpiensis. (Lovanii,
1516), 4to. First edition. Fifty-four leaves
including twelve of introductory matter.
The last page is filled with the device of
Theodore Martin. Bright, 19s.—Pettick
in 1855, 2l. 2s.—Ant. 1516, 4to.—Heber, pt.
ix. 15s.—Paris, Gourmont (1516-17), 12mo.
Bright, 13s.—Basil, 1517-1518, 4to. Heber,
pt. ix. 15s. This edition, printed by Froben,
also contains the epigrams of More and
Erasmus, preceded by Erasmi Querela Pacis undique gentium, et alia opuscula. The
engraved and typographical ornaments
were probably designed by Hans Holbein.
—Viennæ Pannoniæ,1519, 4to. This edition
also contains the epigrams of Sir Thomas
More and of Erasmus. On the last leaf is a
print with the inscriptions, ' Si Laxas ere-
pit,' and ' Si Stringas, erumpit.'—Basil.
1520, 4to. with border round title designed
by Holbein. Heber, pt. vi 4s. 6d. Hibbert,
1514, with Germani Brizii Anti-Morus.
Paris, 1519, 4l. 8s.—Lovanii, 1548, 12mo.
Probably a reprint of Froben's edition. In
the Grenville Collection—Colonia, 1555,
12mo. 5s. — Basil, 1563. Subjoined is a
Latin epistle by Nucerinus ' De Morte D.
Thomæ Mori et Episcopi Roffensis.'—Wi-
tebergæ, 1591, 8vo. An accurate edition.
—Francof. 1601, 12mo. An accurate edition ' cura Eberradi Van Weiha.'—Colon
Agrip. 1629, 32mo. This diminutive edition contains an additional epistle by J.
Palindanus of Cassel to Peter Giles, com-
plimenting the English.—Hanoviæ, 1613,
12mo. 2s. 6d.—Amst. 1631, 32mo. A diminutive edition ' a mendis vindicata.'—
Oxonii, 1663, 32mo. A neat and correct
edition. — Glasg.' Foulis, 1750, 12mo.
Gough, 2411, 6s. Williams, 1217, morocco,
9s.

Progymnasmata Tho. Mori, et Gul. Lilii
Sodalium. Das. 1518, 4to. See Knight's
Life of Colet, p. 135.

Thomas Mori Epistola ad Germanum
Brixium; qui quum Morus in Libellum
eius, quo contumeliosis Mendaciis incos-
serat Angliam. Lond. in Ædibus Pyn-
sonii, 1520, 4to. Contains sig. f 6. A copy
is in the British Museum. Bright, 4l. 6s.
Heber, pt. vii. 5l. 2s. 6d. This piece was
called in at the request of Erasmus, and
it is said that only seven copies escaped.
It was intended as a reply to the piece by
Germain de Brie, or Germanus Brixius
entitled ' Antiesiodorensis and Morus,'
Paris. 1519, 4to. which was an answer to
the ridicule cast upon him by Sir Tho.
More in some of his Epigrams. A copy
of this sold, Heber, pt. vii. for 1l. 17s. pt
viii. 10s.

Epigrammata Thomæ Mori ad emenda-
tum Exemplar ipsius Autoris excusa.
Basil. 1520, 4to. 1l. 1s. Printed by Froben.
—Lond. 1638, 32mo. In the title is a portrait by Marshall. White Knights, 2s50,
1l. 8s. Nassau, pt. i. 2306, 12s.—1678.
Drury, 4627, 8s.

A translation of some of More's Epigrams will be found in Tho. Pecke's Par-
nassi Puerperium.

Poemata Latina. Printed in Cayley's
Life, vol. 2.

Lucubrationes, 8vo. Basil. 1563. An
accurate edition, containing the Utopia
and the minor Latin works of Sir Thomas
More.

Epistola ad Academ. Oxon. cum Epiced.
R. Cottoni et T. Allent. Oxon. 1633, 4to.
Bindley, pt. iii. 579, 10s. 6d.

— The Workes of Sir Thomas
More, Knyght, sometyme Lorde
Chancellour of England, wrytten
by him in the English Tonge.
Lond. at the Costes and Charges
of Iohn Cawood, Iohn Waly and
Richarde Tottell, 1557, folio.

BLACK LETTER. Bindley, pt. ii. 847,
4l. 16s. Townsley, pt. ii. 1018, russia,
5l. 7s. 6d. Boswell, 1719, 7l. 7s. Hibbert,
5650, 5l. 2s. 6d. Sir M. M. Sykes, pt. ii.
412, russia, 12l. Williams, 1421, morocco,
15l. Heber, pt. i. 6l. 16s. 6d. pt. v. morocco,
8l. 12s. Bright, 10l. Gardner, 9l. 10s.
Crawford, mor. 14l. 5s. Singer in 1860,
8l. 12s. *Collation.*—The volume consists
of 1458 pages, besides title, dedication to
Q. Mary by Wylliam Rastell, two tables,
9 leaves, also More's youthful Poems, 8
unpaged leaves, sometimes wanting. Between pp. 1138-9, is a leaf containing a
letter of Sir Tho. More's ' to the Christian
Reader' respecting the printer's faults—
which leaf is frequently wanting. See
Oldy's British Librarian, 194-7.

The Sergeant and Frere. Lond. by
Julyan Notary. n. d. The first effusion
of More's youthful muse.

The Supplycacyon of Soulys against the
Supplycacyon of Beggars, (Lond. by W.
Rastell), n. d. follo. Inglis, 1015, 3l. 15s.
Sir M. M. Sykes, pt. ii. 413, with Morn's
Dialogue of Images and Reliques, 1530,
4l. 16s. Bright, both pieces, 2l. 4s. This
volume contains xlliii leaves. At the end,
' Cum priuilegio' and 'The fawtes es-
caped in the prynting.' The last page is
blank. A copy is in the Lambeth Library.

A Dyaloge of Syr Thomas More
Knyghte; wherin be treatyd divers Mat-
ters, as of the Veneration & Worshyp of
Ymagys & Relyques, prayyng to Sayntys,

MORE, Sir Thos.—*continued.*

nd goyng on Pylgrymage, wyth many there thyngys touchyng the pestylent sect of Luther and Tyndale, by the tome bygone in Saxony, and by the tother laboryd to be brought into England. Lond. (by John Rastell), 1529, fol. The volume contains fo. C*xxvi. Inglis. 1016, morocco, 2l. 18s. Kerr, 8l.—1830, folio. Marquis of Townshend, 3441, 2l. 2s. Heber, pt. vi. 1l. 10s. Bright, 2l. 4s. Inglis, 1017, 8l. This edition, printed in long lines, contains 154 leaves, besides a table, which commences on the back of the title page. On the last leaf are 'The fautes escaped in the pryntyge.' A copy is in the Lambeth Library.—Lond. (W. Rastell), 1831, folio. Puttick, June 10, 1858, 1l. 14s.

The Confutacyon of Tyndales Answere. Lond. by Wyllyam Rastell, 1533, folio. Sir M. M. Sykes, pt. II. 414, 4l. 6s. Heber, pt. vi. 1l. 10s. This work is paged in numerals, and contains ccxxvi folios, also a preface, consisting of 37 pages, and a leaf at the end with 'The fautes escaped in the pryntynge' amended.

The second Parte of the Confutacion of Tyndals Answere, in which is also confuted the Chyrche that Tyndale deuyseth and the Chyrche also that Frere Barns deuyseth, made by Syr Thomas More Knyght. Lond. by Wyllyam Rastell, 1533, folio. This second part contains from book the fourth to book the ninth inclusive. In the folio edition of his Works, 1557, it is stated that the ninth book is there finished for the *first* time. A copy is in the British Museum.

The Debellacyon of Salem and Bizance. Printed by W. Rastell, 1533, 8vo. Roxburghe, 584, 1l. 2s. Inglis, 1043, 2l. 9s. Heber, pt. II. 1l. 16s. Another, one, 2l. Sotheby, 1851, mor. 3l. 8s. The work, preceded by a preface, begins on fol. viii., and is divided into two parts. The first has xiiii chapters, and ends on fol. clii.; the second begins with the fifteenth chapter and a fresh set of signatures and numerals, and concludes the xxi chapter on fol. clxxiii. 'The fautes escaped in pryntynge' occupy two leaves. A copy is in the Lambeth Library.

The Apologye of Syr Thomas More Knyght, made by him Anno 1533, after he had gouen ouer Thoffice of Lord Chancellour of Englande. Prynted by W. Rastell, 1533, 18mo. This volume contains 390 leaves, and consists of 50 chapters. In the former 10 he apologises for his writings against Tindall, Barns, &c., and the last 40 are pointed against a Treatise entitled the Pacifier of the Division between the Spirituality & the Temporalty. Gardner, mor. 8l. 5s.

A Letter impugnynge the erroneous wrytyng of John Fryth, against the blessed Sacrament of the Aultare. Lond. W. Rastell, 1533, 12mo. Gardner, 1854, 4l.

The answer to the first Part of the poysoned Booke whyche a namelesse heretike (John Frith) hath named the Supper of the Lord. By Syr Thomas More Knight. Anno 1533, after he had giuen ouer the Offyce of Lorde Chauncellour of Englande. By W. Rastell, 1534, 8vo. Contains folio cclxxiii, besides the preface and a table of 'The fautes escaped in the pryntynge of thys booke.' Inglis, 1044, 6s. Sotheby's in 1824, 16s.

UTOPIA, written in Latine by Syr Thomas More Knyght, and translated into Englyshe by Raphe Robynson, Citizein and Goldsmythe of London, at the Procurement, and earnest Request of George Tadlowe, Citezein and Haberdassher of the same Citie. Lond., by Abraham Vele, 1551. FIRST EDITION, 12mo. BLACK LETTER, A—8 iv. Heber, pt. v. 1l. G. Chalmers, 1l. 8s. Saunders' in 1818, russia, 3l. 3s. Bindley, pt. II. 1970, 1l. 1s. Towneley, pt. I. 485, 3l. 5s.—Second edition newly perused and corrected. Lond. Vele, n.d. 12mo.—1556, A. Vele, 16mo. A—8, in eights. Nassau, pt. I. 2204, 11s. Reed, 2537, 12s. Hindley, pt. II. 1970, 1l. 1s. Caldecott, 10s. Heber, pt. II. 8s. Saunders' in 1818, 2l. 10s. Gardner, 1l. 10s. Bright, 1l. 1s. Third edition, 1597, sm. 4to. Contains sign. T.—1634, 4to. BLACK LETTER. Dedicated to Cresacre More of More Place, in North Mimms. Bindley, pt. II. 859, 5l.—1639, 12mo. A very erroneous edition. In the title-page is a portrait of More by Marshall. Hibbert, 5629, 2s. 6d. Bright, 6s. 6d.

Utopia, translated into English by Dr. Gilbert Burnet, afterwards Bishop of Sallisbury. Lond. 1684, 8vo. First edition.—1685, 8vo. Heber, pt. II. 6s. 6d.—Dublin, 1737, 12mo. with short account of his life and trial.—Glasg. Foulis, 1743, sm. 8vo. port. Prefixed are Testimonys.—Oxford, 1751, 12mo. To this edition is added a short account of Sir Thomas More's life and trial, and a prayer made by him when he was a prisoner in the Tower.—Glasg. Foulis, 1763, 12mo.—Lond. Jones and Bamford, 1808, 12mo. A neat edition, to which is prefixed a life of the author (extracted from Macdiarmid's Lives of British Statesmen.)

A new Edition (Rolinson's translation of 1551), with copious Notes, and a biographical and literary introduction by the Rev. T. F. Dibdin, D.D. Lond. 1808, crown 8vo. 2 vols. with a portrait of More. Bright, 10s. 6d. LARGE PAPER, in 1 vol. 4to. 250 copies printed, with an extra plate of the family of More, in outline. 2l. 2s.—Goldsmid, 542, 2l. 5s. Hibbert, 5610, russia, 1l. 17s. Roscoe, 1675, morocco, 2l. 11s. Sir M. M. Sykes, pt. II. 528, 1l. 7s. In this edition the

MORE, Sir Thos.—*continued*.
portraits (41) of More are critically discussed.

Utopia, a Philosophical Romance. To which is added, the New Atlantis, by Lord Bacon, with a Preliminary Discourse, and Notes, by J. A. St. John. Lond. 1838, 12mo. 4s.—New edition. Lond. Bohn, 1845, 3s. 6d.

Another Translation will be found in Cayley's Life of Sir T. More.

La description de l'Utopie, traduite par J. le Blond. Paris, 1550, 12mo. woodcuts. Heber, pt. i. mor. 1*l*. 4s.

L'Utopie, traduit par Gueudeville. Leyde, 1715, and Amst. 1730, 12mo.

A Dyalogue of Comfort against Tribulacion. Lond, by Richarde Tottel, 1553, 4to. X 4, in eights.—Now newly set forthe, with many Places restored and corrected by Conference of sundrie Copies. Antwerp, 1573, 16mo. Dedicated by the printer, John Fouler, to the 'Ladie Jane, Duchesse of Feria.' In this edition will be found a woodcut portrait of More, unknown to Granger or Bromley. Bindley, pt. ii. 1817, 1*l*. 1s. Lloyd, 375, 10s. 6d. Bright, 1*l*. 7s. Inglis, 1047, 17s.—Heber, pt. vi. 12s. Bright, 1*l*. 7s.—Ant. 1574. Lloyd, 676, 18s.—Ant. 1578. Towneley, pt. i. 496, with a portrait of More, 2*l*. 12s. 6d.—New edition. Lond. Dolman (English Cath. Lib.), 1847, post 8vo. 5s.

A Treatise to resume the blessed Body of our Lord sacramentally and virtually bothe. With certain devout and vertuous Instructions, Meditacions and Prayers. Lovaine, by John Fouler, 1573, 4to.

The Historie of the pitiful Life and unfortunate Death of King Edward V. and the Duke of York, his Brother; with the Troublesome and Tyrannical Government of the Usurpation of Richard III, and his miserable end. Edited by W. Sheares. Lond. Thomas Payne, 1641, 16mo. An elegant history. The volume consists of 481 pages, with two portraits, dedicated to Sir John Leuthall, Knt. There are two title-pages, the first 'The Historie &c. of Edward the V.' The other, 'The tragicall Historie, &c. of Richard the III.' Roxburghe, 6284, 2*l*. 2s. Towneley, pt. i. 487, 2*l*. 5s. Graves, 239, 12s. Dent, pt. i. 1449, russia, 1*l*. 1s. More's Life of Edward and Richard, with a continuation from Hall and Holinshed's Chronicles, will be found in the first volume of Kennett's History of England; and his Richard III. in Cayley's Life of Sir Thos. More.

The History of Richard III. Edited by S. W. Singer, Esq. Chiswick, 1821, with portrait, post 8vo. 10s. LARGE PAPER, demy 8vo. Twenty-five copies printed, pub. at 1*l*. 4s. Hibbert, 5555, 1*l*. 4s. Sir M. M.

Sykes, pt. ii. 455, 1*l*. 8s. Fonthill, 3576, 2*l*. 1s.

The Boke of the fayre Gentlewoman, Lady Fortune. Lond. Rob. Wyer, n. d. 12mo. In the Lambeth library.

Expositio fidelis de Morte Thomæ Mori et quorundam aliorum insignium Virorum in Anglia. Lut. Par. 1535, 4to. Heber, pt. vi. 15s. Aniv. 1536, 8vo. Bibl. Crofts, no. 7283. Bibl. Paris, no. 573. Lord Guildford, 5*l*.

Philomorus; a brief examination of the Latin poems of Sir Thomas More. Lond. 1842, post 8vo. Bright, 2*l*.

Vita di Tomaso More, Grand Cancellario, d'Ingbilterra, 1675, 8vo—Bologna, 1681, with portrait, Bindley, 7s. 6d.

Thomas Morus, Lord Chancellor du Royaume d'Angleterre au xvi eme siecle. Paris, Gosselin, 1833, 8vo. 2 vols. port.

The Household of Sir Thomas More. Lond. Hall, 1851, post 8vo. 7s. 6d.—Second edition, 1853.

The Life and Death of Sir Thomas More, Lord High Chancellor of England, written by M. T. M. and dedicated to the Queen's most gracious Majestie. (Paris, 1626), 4to. Towneley, pt. i. 501, 2*l*. 12s. 6d. Sir M. M. Sykes, pt. ii. 523, russia, 1*l*. 15s. Horner, 2*l*. 12s. Heber, pt. ii. 1*l*. 11s. 6d. Nassau, pt. ii. 160, with plate of the family of More and portrait of Sir Thomas inserted, 2*l*. This volume consists of 452 pages exclusive of the dedication.—Lond. 1726, 8vo. with part of More by Vertue, after Holbein. Drury, 2725, 9s. Bindley, pt. ii. 1573, 12s. Reed, 4501, 9s. 6d. LARGE PAPER. Dent, pt. i. 1448, 1*l*. 4s. Hibbert, 5534, morocco, 18s. Lloyd, 153, 1*l*. 11s. 6d. Brockett, 3144, 1*l*. 6s. Williams, 1216, with portrait of More by Valdor inserted, morocco, 4*l*. 10s.

This Life is attributed to Cresacre More. See MORE, Cresacre.

Life of Sir T. More, by the Rt. Hon. Sir James Mackintosh. Lond. Longman, 1844, 12mo. (Printed separately from the Lives of British Statesmen in Lardner's Cyclopædia, vol. 21. Lond. 1831).

Memoir of Sir T. More (by Emily Taylor.) Lond. Houlston, 1834, 12mo. port.

Life, by Walter. Lond. Dolman, 18 ., 12mo. 5s.

Life of, in Wordsworth's Ecclesiastical Biography.

Sir Thomas More. A Play. See SHAKSPEARE SOCIETY, App.

See BRIXIUS, Germanus. CATLEY, Arthur. FAITH, John. HARRIES, Fernando de. HEYWOOD, Ellis. HODDESDON, John. MACDIARMID, John. MORE, Cresacre. NICHOLS, John. PICUS, Earl of Mirandula. ROPER, William. STAPLETON, Thomas. WARNER, Ferd.

MORE, Thomas, de Eschallers de la. The English Catholick Christian, or the Saint's Utopia. Lond, 1649, 4to.
Evidently the production of an enthusiastic madman. It is dedicated to K. Charles I.

MOREAU, Cæsar. Tables.
East India Company's Records, founded on official Documents; showing the British Possessions in India, their Revenues, Expenditure, &c. Lond. Treuttel, 1825, fol. 16s.
Past and Present Statistical State of Ireland, exhibited in series of Tables. Lond. Treuttel, 1827, fol.
Chronological Record of British Finance. Lond. Treuttel, 19 , folio. 16s.
State of the Trade of Great Britain. Lond. Treuttel, [1822], fol. 10s. 6d. Also in French.
British and Irish Manufactures exported from Great Britain from 1696 to 1824. Lond. 1825, folio.
Rise and Progress of the Silk Trade. Lond. 1826, folio.
The past and present State of the Navigation between Great Britain and all Parts of the World. In 3 views. Lond. 1827, folio.
Chronological Records of the British Royal and Commercial Navy, from A.D. 827 to 1827. Lond. Treuttel, 1827, folio.—From A.D. 66 to the present Time. Lond. 1828, folio.
— Simeon. A Tour to the Royal Spa at Cheltenham : or Gloucestershire displayed. Bath, 1797, 12mo. Pp. 208, and three plates. The first edition appeared in 1783.

MOREHEAD, William. Lachrymæ, sive Valedictio Scotiæ sub Discessum D. Georgii Monachi in Angliæ revocati. Lond. 1660, 4to.
In Latin and English, consisting of eight sheets and a half.

MOREIRA, Jac Rodrigues. Kehi'ath Jahacob; being a Vocabulary of Words in the Hebrew Language, found in the Holy Bible and divers Eminent and Rabinnical writers, done into English and Spanish. Lond. A. Alexander, A.M., 5533, 4to. 5s.

MOREL, William. Verborvm Latinorum cum Græcis Anglicisqve conjunctorum locupletissimi Commentarii ; ad elaboratum Guilielmi Morelli archetypum excusi, &c. Lond. 1583, folio.
The volume consists of 1153 pages, printed in double columns. It is dedicated to the Earl of Leicester, after which are a preface, a list of authors, and some Latin verses, addressed to the studious youth, by Abr. Flaming. Parry, pt. l. 1802, 3l. 7s. 6d.

MORELL, Thomas. Lexicon Græco-prosodiacum, olim vulgatum Typis denuo mandavit, permultis in Locis correxit, Exemplis a se allatis, et Animadversionibus illustravit, Verbis a Th. Morello omissis, quamplurimis auxit ; et Græcis Vocibus suxit, et Græcis Vocibus Latinam Versionem subjecit Edv. Maltby. Cantab. 1815, royal 4to.
An elaborate and accurate edition, which entirely superseded the original (mentioned below). Hibbert, 5611, russia, 2l.— Editio altera. Lond. 1824, demy 4to. pub. 3l. 3s. Reduced 1l. 1s.
An English abridgment of this learned work was edited for the use of schools, under the following title: — 'Maltby's Greek Gradus, or Poetical Lexicon of the Greek Language, with a Latin and English Translation, an English-Greek Vocabulary, and a Treatise on Quantity, and on Greek Metres.' Lond. 1830, 8vo.
Thesaurus Græcæ Poeseos, sive Lexicon Græco-prosodiacum. Etonæ, 1762, 4to. with a portrait of the author by Basire after W. Hogarth. Dent, pt. ii. 741, russia, 19s. Townsley, pt. l. 679, 1l. 10s. White Knights, 2946, russia, 2l. Heath, 50, 5l. 15s.
Notes and Annotations on Locke on the Human Understanding. Lond. 1794, 8vo.
— Thomas. The Elements of the History of Philosophy and Science, from the earliest authentic Records to the commencement of the Eighteenth century. Lond. 1827, 8vo. pp. 560.
Studies in History. St. Neots, 1815, 8vo.

MORER, Thomas. A short Account of Scotland, with an Appendix on the difference of the Scotch and English Liturgy. Lond. 1702, 8vo.
Reed, 5368, morocco, 8s. Reuuld, Heber, pt. ix. 1l. 1s. Some copies have a different title-page, dated 1706 or 1715. Steevens, 1793, 15s. 6d. Gardner, in 1854, 4s.

MOBERI, L. Dictionary. *See*
COLLIER, Jeremy.

MORES, Edward Rowe. A Dissertation upon English Typographical Founders and Foundries. With an Appendix. Lond. 1778, 8vo.
Of this curious and valuable work (in which will be found the Narrative of Ged) only 100 copies were printed; and of the Appendix by Nichols (pp. 4) only 60. Sir M. M. Sykes, pt. ii. 457, 16s. Baker, 578, 16s. Brockett, 21s, 16s. Bindley, pt. ii. 1873, 19s.
Nomina et Insignia Gentilitia Nobilium, Equitumque sub Edvardo primo Rege militantium: accedunt Classes exercitus Edvardi tertii Regis Caletum obsidentia. Oxon. 1749, 4to. This tract was printed for private distribution. Bindley, pt. iii. 568, 2l. 15s. Sir M. M. Sykes, pt. ii. 615, mor. 1l. 7s. Nassau, pt. ii. 978, 1l. 14s. Gough, 2991, with MS. notes, 1l. 16s. Heber, pt. ii. 7s.
De Ælfrico Derobernensi Archiepiscopo, Commentarius: Edidit et præfatus est Grimus Johannes Thorkelin, LL.D. Lond. 1789, 4to. 7s. 6d.
See CADMON Monachus. Nichols' Bibl Top. Brit. nos. i. viii. and xvi.

MORESINUS, Tho. M.D. Papatus, seu, depravatæ Religionis Origo et Incrementum. Edinb. Waldegrave, 1594, 12mo.
Dedicated to K. James VI. of Scotland, Roxburghe, 419, 9s. Constable, 653, 1l. 10s.

MORESON, John. *See* HOLY LAND.

MORETON, Andrew. An Essay on the History and Reality of Apparitions. Lond. 1727, 8vo.
Roxburghe, 1983, 8s.—1729, 8vo. Steevens, 1514, 9s. Fonthill, 1219, 1l. 5s. Heath, 1495, 18s.—1735, 8vo.—1738, 8vo. Dent, pt. ii. 14s. 6d. Dowdeswell, 509, 6s. This and the following work are attributed to DANIEL DEFOE.
Parochial Tyranny, or the Housekeeper's Complaint against the Assessments of Select Vestries. Lond. 8vo.

MORGAGNI, John Baptist. The Seats and Causes of Diseases investigated by Anatomy; in five Books, containing a great Variety of Dissections, with Remarks. To which are added, very accurate and copious Indexes of the principal Things and Names therein contained. Translated by Benjamin Alexander, M.D. Lond. 1769, 4to. 3 vols.
A much-esteemed work. Willett, 1634, 2l. 12s. 6d.—Abridged and elucidated with copious Notes by W. Cooke. Lond. 1822, 8vo. 2 vols. 16s.

MORGAN, Sir Henry. Voyage to Panama, 1670. Lond. 1683, 12mo.

— J. Phœnix Britannicus: being a miscellaneous Collection of scarce and curious Tracts. Lond. 1732, 4to.
Of this work only six numbers appeared. Nassau, pt. ii. 163, 9s. Bindley, pt. iii. 304, 14s. Gough, 2687, 12s. Dowdeswell, 592, 18s. 6d. Heath, 4479, 1l. 6s. Bright, 10s. 6d.
History of Algiers; to which is prefixed, an Epitome of the general History of Barbary, from the earliest Times. Lond. 1728, 4to.—1731, 4to. Heath, 3719, 4s. Willett, 1635, 11s. 6d. LARGE PAPER.

— John. A short Analysis of St. James's Epist. ch. 2. v. 14, &c. Lond. 1588, 16mo.

— John. Essays upon the Law of Evidence, new Trials, special Verdicts, Trials at Bar, and Repleaders. Lond. 1789, 8vo. 3 vols.
The Attorney's Vade-mecum and Client's Instructor. Lond. 1787, 8vo. 3 vols.

— Lieut. J. C. The Emigrant's Note Book and Guide; with Recollections of Upper and Lower Canada, during the War. Lond. 1824, 12mo.
'A partial, though at the same time a useful work.'—*Quart. Review.*

— Mrs. Mary. A Tour to Milford Haven in 1791. Lond. 1795, 8vo.
Dent, pt. i. 1451, 7s. 6d. Fonthill, 2150, 17s.

— Nic. of Crolane, Kent. The Perfection of Horsemanship, drawne from Nature, Arte, and Practise. Lond. 1609, 4to.

Contains separate dedications to King James; Prince Henry; Edward, Earl of Worcester, Lord Herbert of Royland, and the Gentlemen of England, 2 leaves; and 1 leaf of verses by the author, in commendation of that worthy and renowned rider, Robert Alexander, Knt. deceased.

MORGAN, Sylvanus. The Sphere of Gentry, deduced from the Principles of Nature: an historical and genealogical Work of Arms and Blazon, in four Books. Lond. 1661, folio.

This work, though written in a pedantic style, contains much curious matter. Towneley, pt. ii. 1014, russia, 4l. 14s. 6d. Some copies contain a GENEALOGICAL TREE of the HOWARD FAMILY at page 82 of Book IV.; also, between pages 82 and 83, two engraved leaves referring to the same, with an engraving on each. Bindley, pt. ii. 846, 5l. 5s. LARGE PAPER. Dent, pt. ii. 761, morocco, 8l. 12s. Nassau, pt. ii. 205, morocco, 10l. Bernal, 15l. *Collation.*—Two titles, one engraved, the other printed, the former by R. Gaywood, containing a portrait of the author; To the King, one leaf; To the reader, two leaves; an acrostick, &c. two leaves; the words of art and the names of the constellations, two leaves; the first book, pp. 120, after which is a leaf containing a portrait of Camden. This book likewise contains five plates at pp. 9, 19, 27, 47, 59, independent of those on the letterpress. The second book, pp. 118. The third book, pp. 120 [and 2 leaves unpaged, consisting of title, and dedication to Earl of Clarendon]. The fourth book, pp. 116, also pp. (33) to (40), and a leaf containing 'the Atchievement of a Baron,' a duplicate plate. The table, 10 leaves. Copies vary as regards the cuts on the letterpress.

A Treatise of Honor and honorable Men. 1612, 4to. pp. 168. A MS. consisting of 168 pages. See BRYDGES' Censura Literaria.

London, King Charles his Augusta, or City Royal; Of the Founders Names, and oldest Honours of that City, an historical and antiquarian Work, in Verse, with Annotations. 1648, 4to.

Horologiographia Optica, Dialling universal and particular. Lond. 1652, 4to.

Armilogia, sive Ars Chromocritica: the Language of Arms by the Colours and Metals. Lond. 1666, 4to. Dedicated to Edward, Earl of Manchester, whose arms are on the back of the title-page. Introduced by the author as a supplement to his Sphere of Gentry. Lloyd, 809, 1l. 11s. LARGE PAPER. Nassau, pt. ii. 182, morocco, 1l. 4s. In the Grenville Collection.

MORGAN, T. The Welchmens Irbilee to the Honour of St. David. Lond. (1641), 4to.

Nassau, pt. ii. 184, 8s.

— Sir Thomas. A Relation of Major-General Sir Thomas Morgan's Progress in France and Flanders, with the six thousand English, in the Years 1657 and 1658, at the Taking of Dunkirk, and other important Places; as it was delivered by the General himself. Lond. 1699, 4to.

Pp. 16. This curious piece of history is reprinted in Morgan's Phœnix Britannicus; in the 3rd volume of the Harleian Miscellany; and in the 7th volume of the Somers Collection.—Glasg. 1752, 12mo. 4s.

— Thomas, Dr. The Moral Philosopher, in a Dialogue between Philalethes, a Christian Deist, and Theophanes, a Christian Jew, &c. Second edition, corrected. Lond. 1738, 8vo. 3 vols. 15s.

In this work revelation was attacked with the greatest virulence. It was most ably and satisfactorily answered by Drs. John Chandler, John Leland, and other celebrated divines.

A Defence of the Moral Philosopher, against a Pamphlet intitled The Immorality of the Moral Philosopher. By the Author. Lond. 1737, 8vo. pp. 40.

A Vindication of the Moral Philosopher, against the false Accusations, Insults, and personal Abuses of Samuel Chandler. Lond. 1741, 8vo. pp. 70.

A brief Examination of the Rev. Mr. Warburton's Divine Legation of Moses, in which the Mosaic Theocracy, the Nature and Character of the sacred Writings, the antiquity of Hero-Gods, and a future, separate State of animal Life, and Action for Souls after Death; with other Principles and Positions of that learned Writer, are occasionally considered and discussed. By a Society of Gentlemen. Lond. 1742, 8vo.

The running title of this work is Sacerdotism Displayed.

— Sir Thomas Charles, M.D. Sketches of the Philosophy of Life. Lond. 1818, 8vo.

Morgan was a disciple of the school of Bichat, and a fellow-labourer with Mr. William Lawrence, the eminent surgeon,

1612   MOR   MOR

In advocating those doctrines of physiological structure which have since been strenuously repelled by Mr. Bennell and other able writers.
Sketches of the Philosophy of Morals. Lond. 1822, 8vo. Intended as a continuation to the Philosophy of Life.
The Book without a Name, by Sir T. Charles and Lady Morgan. Lond. 1841, post 8vo. 2 vols. 1l. 1s.

MORGAN, William. Principles and Doctrine of Assurances, Annuities on Lives, and contingent Reversions. Lond. 1828, 8vo. 12s.
Useful. This gentleman, who was actuary of the Equitable Assurance Office, published other works on finance, &c. and contributed papers to the Philosophical Transactions, Monthly Magazine, &c.
See PRICE, Dr. R.
— Lady Sydney. Italy. Lond. 1821, 4to. 2 vols.
'Quoted, with respect, by Byron.' Sir M. M. Sykes, pt. ii. 527, 15s.—Lond. Colburn, 1821, 8vo. 3 vols. Drury, 2756, 1l. 5s.
Letter to the Reviewers of 'Italy,' including an Answer to a Pamphlet entitled Observations on the Calumnies and Misrepresentations in Lady Morgan's Italy. Lond. 1821, 4to.
Le Morganiche : ossia Lettere scritte da un Italiano a Miledi Morgan sopra varii articoli relativi a Milano ed al Regno d'Italia, che si trovano nel tomo primo della sua Italia. Edinb, Tait, 1824, 8vo. pp. 82.
Poems. 1797, 12mo. Published in her 14th year.
Lay of an Irish Harp, or Metrical Fragments. 1795.—Lond. 1807, post 8vo. This volume appears to have been preceded by 'Twelve of the most pathetic Irish Melodies, arranged to English Words,' which is said to have suggested Moore's Irish Melodies.
St. Clair, or the Heiress of Desmond. By Miss Owenson. Lond. 1810, post 8vo. 2 vols.—Third edition, corrected and much enlarged, with a portrait of the author. Lond. Stockdale, 1812, post 8vo. 2 vols.
The Novice of St. Dominick. By Miss Owenson, Lond. R. Phillips, 1806, post 8vo. 4 vols.
The Wild Irish Girl; a national Tale. By Miss Owenson. Lond. 1801, post 8vo. 3 vols.—Lond. R. Phillips, 1806, post 8vo. 3 vols.—New edition. Lond. Bryce, 1854, 12mo. 2s. This work passed through seven editions within two years.
Patriotic Sketches of Ireland, Lond. 1807. 12mo. 2 vols.
Woman: or, Ida of Athens. By Miss Owenson, Lond. Longman and Co. 1809, post 8vo. 4 vols.

The Missionary: an Indian Tale. By Miss Owenson. With a portrait of the author. Lond. Stockdale, 1811, post 8vo. 3 vols.
O'Donnell; a national Tale. By Lady Morgan (late Miss Owenson). Lond. Colburn, 1814, post 8vo. 3 vols.—New edition. Lond. Bryce, 1856, 12mo. 2s.
France, in 1816. By Lady Morgan. Lond. 1817, 4to.—Paris, 1817, 8vo.—Fourth edition, with additional notes. Lond. 1818, 8vo. 2 vols.
Observations sur l'Ouvrage intitulé La France, par Lady Morgan. Paris, 1817, 8vo.
France, as it is. *Not* Lady Morgan's France, (by W. Playfair). Lond. 1820, 8vo. 2 vols.
Florence Macarthy; an Irish Tale. Lond. 1818, post 8vo. 4 vols.—New edition. Lond. (Colburn's Novels) 1839, post 8vo.—New edition. Lond. Bryce, 1856, 12mo. 2s.—Lond. Lea, 1859, 12mo. 2s.
The Life and Times of Salvator Rosa. Lond. 1824, 8vo. 2 vols. portrait, 12s.—New edition. Lond. Bryce, 1855, 12mo. 3s. 6d.
The O'Briens and the O'Flahertys. Lond. 1827, post 8vo. 4 vols. 1l. 4s.
Dramatic Scenes from real Life. Lond. Saunders, 1833, post 8vo. 2 vols. 1l. 1s.
Absenteeism. Lond.1825. post 8vo.2s.6d.
The Book of the Boudoir. Lond. 1829, post 8vo. 2 vols.
France in 1829-30. Lond. 1830, 8vo. 2 vols. 1l. 11s. 6d.
The Princess; or the Beguine. Lond. 1825, post 8vo. 3 vols. A story founded on the revolution in the Netherlands.
Woman and her Master. Lond. 1840, post 8vo. 2 vols. 1l. 1s.— New edition. Lond. Bryce, 1855, post 8vo. 2 vols. 7s. 6d.
'A philosophical history of woman down to the fall of the Roman empire.'
Luxima, the Prophetess; a Tale of India. Lond. Westerton, 1859, post 8vo. 10s. 6d. A rifacimento of the Missionary.
Passages from my Autobiography. Lond. Bentley, 1859, 8vo. 14s. Published only a few months before her death.
The Friends, Foes, and Adventures of Lady Morgan. By W. J. Fitzpatrick. Dublin, 1859, 8vo. 4s.
Before her marriage (in 1811), this lady's works bear her maiden name, Sydney Owenson. For "The Book without a Name," published in conjunction with her husband, *see* MORGAN, Sir T. C.

MORGANN, Maurice. An Essay on the dramatic Character of Sir John Falstaff. Lond. 1777, 8vo.
'This essay (published anonymously) forms a more honourable monument to the memory of Shakspeare than any which has been reared to him by the

united labours of his commentators.'—*Dr. Symmons.* Bindley, pt. III, 1l. 10d, 14s. Roxburghe, 8884, 14s. 6d. Marq. of Townshend, 2912, 7l. LARGE PAPER.—Lond. 1825, 8vo. 5s.

MORIER, James. A Journey through Persia, Armenia, and Asia Minor to Constantinople in 1808-9. In which is included some Account of his Majesty's Mission under Sir H. Jones to the Court of the King of Persia. Lond. 1812, 4to. plates and maps, 2l. 12s. 6d.

A SECOND JOURNEY THROUGH PERSIA to Constantinople between the Years 1810-16; with a Journal of the Voyage by the Brazils and Bombay to the Persian Gulf; together with an account of the Proceedings of his Majesty's Embassy under Sir Gore Ouseley, Bart. Lond. 1818, 4to. plates and maps, 2l. 12s. 6d.

The two Journeys. Lond. 1812-18, 4to. 2 vols.—with plates on INDIA PAPER. Hibbert, 5618, 6l.

Morier's Journeys are justly regarded as works of authority on the civil, political, domestic, and commercial circumstances of the Persians.

The Adventures of Hajji Baba of Ispahan. Lond. 1824, fcap. 8vo. 3 vols.—In one vol. Lond. Bentley, 1849, post 8vo. 2s. 6d.

The Adventures of Hajji Baba of Ispahan, in England. Lond. Murray, 1828, fcap. 8vo. 2 vols.—In 1 vol. Lond. Bentley's Stand. Nov., 1849, post 8vo. 3s. 6d.—Lond. Ward and Lock, 1856, 12mo. 1s. 6d.

Ayesha, the Maid of Kars. Lond. 1834, post 8vo. 3 vols. 1l. 11s. 6d.—In 1 vol. Lond. Bentley's Stand. Nov., 1846, post 8vo. 3s. 6d.—Lond. Ward and Lock, 1856, post 8vo. 1s. 6d.

Zohrab, the Hostage. Lond. Bentley, 1832, post 8vo. 3 vols. 1l. 11s. 6d.—In 1 vol. Lond. Bentley's Stand. Nov., 1849, post 8vo. 3s. 6d.

Abel Allnutt; a Novel. Lond. Bentley, 1837, 8vo. 3 vols. 1l. 11s. 6d.

The Banished; a Swabian historical Tale. Lond. Colburn, 1839, post 8vo. 3 vols. 1l. 11s. 6d.

The Mirza. Lond. Bentley, 1841, post 8vo. 3 vols. 1l. 11s. 6d.

Martin Toutrond: a Frenchman in London in 1841. New edition. Lond. Bentley, 1849, post 8vo. 12s.—1852, 12mo. 1s.

MORIN, John. Antiquitates Ecclesiæ Orientalis. Cum Vita I. Morini. Lond. 1682, 12mo. 5s.

Bishop Warburton styles this writer's 'Exercitationes' a master-piece of criticism.

MORINDOS.—The famous and renowned History of Morindos, a King of Spain, who maryed with Miracola, a Witch. Lond. 1609, 4to.

MORISINE, R. *See* MORISON, Sir Richard.

MORISON, Rev. John. An Exposition of the Book of Psalms, explanatory, critical, and devotional. Lond. 1828, 8vo. 2 vols.

This publication, written by a dissenting minister, is commended by Mr. Horne in his Introduction to the Study of the Scriptures.

—— Mauritius. Threnodia Hiberno-Catholica, sive Planctus universalis totius cleri et populi Hiberniæ de transcendenti crudelitate Anglorum adversus Catholicos in Hibernia. Œniponti, 1659, 8vo.

A curious and rare piece, detailing some of the cruelties inflicted on the Irish by Cromwell.

Sotheby's (Bishop Daly), June 25, 1858, 41. 4s. Heber, pt. viii. 4l. 16s. A copy is in the Grenville Collection.

——, or MORYSIN, Sir Richard, Kt. An Invective aysenste Treason, wherein the secrete Practises and traiterous Workinges of theym that suffrid of late are disclosed. Lond. Berthelet, 1539, 16mo.

F 4, in eights, besides six of prefatory matter. Roxburghe, 8426, 2l. 4s. Copies are in the British Museum and Lambeth Libraries.

Apomaxis Calumniarum J. Cochlaei contra Hen. VIII. Lond. Berthelet, 1537, 4to. Dedicated to Thomas Cromwell, secretary of state. Copies are in the Lambeth, Trinity Coll., Cambridge, and British Museum Libraries. *See* COCHLÆUS.

An Exhortation to styrre vp all Englyshemen to the Defence of their Country. Lond. 1539, 8vo. A copy is in the Bodleian Library.

Comfortable Consolation for the Birth of Prince Edward, rather than Sorrow for the Death of Queen Jane. 1534, 4to. *See* Wood's Athen. Oxon.

Introduction to Wisdome, Banket of Sapience, Precepts of Agapetus. Lond. T. Powell, 1563, 12mo. Heber, pt. v. in a vol. 4l. 14s. 6d. *See* AGAPETUS. FROISSART'S. VIVES.

MORISON, Robert, M.D. Plantarum Historia universalis Oxoniensis Pars II. et III. Oxon. 1680, 99, seu 1715, folio, 2 vols. 2l. 2s.

A valuable work. Part I. never appeared, but the Plantæ Umbelliferæ, published in 1672, is usually substituted. LARGE PAPER, 3l. 3s. Hibbert, 5854, with Plantar. umb. Distributio, the plates colored, and the arms emblazoned, mor. 5l. 7s. 6d. *Collectio.*—Pars secunda. Oxon. 1680. Half-title and title, 2 leaves; preface, 4 pages; pars secunda, sect. i.—v. 617 pages; index, &c. 3 pages. The volume contains 126 plates, worked on 65 leaves, divided into five sections. Subjoined to each plate is a different dedication. Pars tertia. Oxon. 1699. Half-title, title, and dedication. 5 leaves; life of Dr. Morison, 6 pages; præfacæ, 5 pages; botanologiæ summarium, 4 pages; errata, 2 pages; pt. iii. sect. vi.—xv. 657 pages, and index, 9 pages. The volume contains 166 plates worked on 87 leaves, sect. vi. to xv. A portrait of Morison by White, after Sonman, faces the volume.

Plantarum umbelliferarum Distributio nova, per Tabulas Cognationis et Affinitatis ex Libro Naturæ observata et detecta. Oxonii, 1672, folio. This portion frequently forms the first part of the Plantarum Historia, though it is sometimes found at the end of the work. LARGE PAPER. *Collation.*—Title and two dedications, 3 leaves; præfacæ, 8 pages; plants umbelliferæ, 91 pages; explanation of the plates, 3 pages. The volume contains nine general tables, one of which is folded, and ten botanical plates, beginning with Tab. 2, having the explanations printed on the reverse.

Hortus Regius Blesensis auctus. Lond. 1669, 12mo.

MORITZ, Chas. P. Travels, chiefly on Foot, through several Parts of England, in 1782, described in Letters to a Friend. Translated from the German, by a Lady. Lond. 1795, 12mo. 3s. 6d.

Remarks on this entertaining pedestrian tour will be found in the Quart. Rev. xv. 542-4. It is reprinted in the second volume of Pinkerton's Collection of Voyages and Travels.

MORLAND, George. Authentic Memoirs of the late George Morland; together with Specimens of his Sketches, &c. By Francis Wm. Blagdon. Lond. 1806, oblong folio. 2l. 2s.

Sketches from the Works of; taken from Nature. Lond. J. Harris, 1792, 6 pts. oblong folio.

Memoirs of George Morland, including an Account of his works, by W. Collins. Lond. 1806, 5s.

The Life of George Morland, with Remarks on his Works, by G. Dawe. Lond. 1807. 8vo.

MORLAND, Sir S. The History of the Evangelical Churches in the Valleys of Piedmont. Lond. 1658, folio, fine portrait by Lombart, after Lely, map, and curious plates.

Dedicated to Oliver Cromwell.

A minute account of an unparalleled scene of religious butchery, in 1655, drawn up at the request of Archbishop Usher. Bindley, pt. ii. 1051, 2l. 10s. Hollis, 1129. 3l. 12s. resold Hibbert, 5855, 4l. 7s. There are copies on FINE or LARGE PAPER. Thurloe's copy in old blue mor. sold for 6l.

Morland, who was master of mechanics to K. Charles II., and a man of considerable celebrity in his day, published other works, chiefly mathematical.

Account of the Life, Writings, and Inventions of Sir Sam. Morland, [by J. O. Halliwell, Esq.] Cantab. 1838, 8vo. 1s.

— Sir Scrope D. Description of the Shields of Arms in the Hall of Wotton House, Bucks. Lond. 1823, imp. 8vo.

An anonymous work, privately printed. It was not completed, on account of the house being burnt down.

MORLEY, Geo., Bp. of Winchester. Several Treatises, written upon several Occasions, both before and since the King's Restoration, wherein his Judgement is fully made known concerning the Church of Rome, and most of the Doctrines which are controverted betwixt her and the Church of England. 1683, 4to. 3s. 6d.

— Henry Parker, Lord. Declaration of the Psalm 94, Deus ultionum. Lond. 1539, 8vo.

Sotheby's in 1852, 2l. 5s. An account of this nobleman will be found in Dr. Bliss's edition of Wood's Athen. Oxon.

See Boccacio de Præclaris Mulieribus; PETRARCH's Triumphs.

— Earl of. Catalogue of the Pictures, Casts, and Busts belonging to the Earl of Morley. Plymouth, 1819.

Privately printed.

MORLEY, Thos. A plaine and easie Introduction to practicall Musicke, set downe in Form of a Dialogue; deuided into three Partes. Lond. 1597, folio, 1*l.* 1*s.*

An ample and luminous general treatise.—1608, folio. Inglis, 1208, morocco, 1*l.* 2*s.* Bright, 1*l.* Lond. 1771, 4to. This edition contains an Appendix, in which the several compositions printed in separate parts in the body of the work are given in score. *See* HAWKINS and BURNEY.

Canzonets, or little short Songs to three Voyces. Lond. T. Est, 1593, 4to. 3 parts. Dindley, pt. iv. 600, 15*s.*—Newly imprinted, with some songs added by the author. Lond. T. Este, 1606, 4to. Bright, 1*l.* 19*s.*—Lond. W. Stansby, 1631, 4to.

Madrigalles to foure Voyces, the first Booke. Lond. by Thomas Este, 1594, 4to. Twenty songs. 4 parts. White Knights, 2*l.* 50, with Madrigals, 1600, 4*l.* 10*s.*

Madrigals to foure Voices. Newly imprinted, with Songs added by the Author. Lond. by T. Este, 1600, 4to. Twenty-two songs. 4 parts. Skegg, 3*l.* 17*s.*

The first Booke of Ballets to five Voyces. Lond. by Thomas Este, 1595, 4to. 5 parts. Sotheby, 1849, 13*l.*—Lond. by T. Este, 1600, 4to. Not mentioned by Wood. Reprinted in score for the Musical Antiquarian Society. *See* APPENDIX.

Il primo libro delle Ballette a cinque voci. Londra, Tomaso Este, 1595, 4to.

The First Booke of Canzonets to two Voyces. Lond. by Thos. Est, 1595, 4to. 2 parts. (Cantus and tenor.)

Canzonets, or little short Songs to fowr Voyces: selected ovt of the best and approved Italian Authors. Lond. by Peter Short, 1597, 4to. 4 parts. Midgely, 4*l.*

Canzonets, or little short Aers to five and sixe Voyces. Lond. by Peter Short, 1597, 4to. 6 parts. In the Ashmolean and British Museums. Streitloll, 1854, 2*l.* 18*s.* Saunders in 1818, 4*l.* Wood mentions an edition dated 1595.

Madrigals to fine Voyces, selected out of the best approved Italian Authors. Lond. by T. Este, 1598, 4to. 5 parts. Heber, pt. viii. in lot 1589, 4*l.* 8*s.* Bright, in lot 3985, with other collections, 5 vols. 18*l.* Wood mentions an edition dated 1596.

Madrigales: the Triumphes of Oriana, to five and six Voyces; composed by divers severall Auctors. Lond. by T. Este, 1600, 4to. 6 parts.

(Twenty-five songs, set by the best musicians of the age, to commemorate the beauty and virginity of Queen Elizabeth, then in her sixty-eighth year. This collection, according to T. Warton, was made at the expense of the Earl of Nottingham, Lord High Admiral; with a view to soothe the queen's despair for the recent execution of Lord Essex. Bright in lot 3985. Heber, date 1601, pt. iii. 5*l.*)

The same. In score. Edited by Wm. Hawes. Lond. [1814] folio. Heber, pt. viii. 1*l.* LARGE PAPER, only 25 printed.

The same. In separate parts. Edited by William Shore. Forming Book 1 of Novello's Choral Hand-Book. Lond. 8vo.

First Book of Ayres; or little short Songs to sing and play to the Lute, with the Base-viol. Lond. 1600, folio.

The Canzonets and Madrigals for three and four Voices, of Thomas Morley, Mus. Bac. Oxon. 1588. Arranged in score, and collated with a Manuscript in the Bodleian Library, by W. W. Holland and W. Cooke. Lond. [? 1808], oblong folio.

The First Books of Consort Lessons, made by diuers exquisite Authors, for sixe Instruments to play together: viz. the Treble Lute, the Pandora, the Citterne, the Base-Violl, the Flute, and the Treble-Violl. Collected by Thomas Morley. Gentleman, and now newly corrected and inlarged. Lond. by Thomas Snodham, 1611, 4to. LARGE PAPER.

A Burial Service by Morley is printed in Boyce's Cathedral Music, vol. i.

MORMON, the Book of; an account written by the hand of Mormon upon plates taken from the plates of Nephi, translated by Joseph Smith, Junr. Palmyra, 1830. 12mo. pp. 588.

Third edition, carefully revised by the translator. Nauvoo, 1840, 12mo.

First European from the second American edition. Printed by J. Tompkins, Liverpool, England: for Brigham Young, Heber C. Kimball, and Parley P. Pratt. By order of Translator. 1841, 16mo. pp. 643.

Llyfr Mormon (translated into Welsh) gan J. Davis. Merthyr-Tydfil, 1852, 8vo.

This work, the Bible of the Mormonites, was, there is good reason to believe, written about 1812, by a clergyman named Solomon Spaulding, as a religious romance. It fell into the hands of Rigdon and Smith, who determined to palm it off as a new Revelation, and accordingly established a church at Kirtland, Ohio. The sect now numbers sufficient adherents to form a large settlement.

The History of the Saints; or an exposure of Joe Smith and Mormonism, by John C. Bennet, Boston, 1842, 12mo. 5*s.*

Mormonism: its Rise, Progress, &c., with Biography of its Founder, by Prof. J. B. Turner. York, 1842, 12mo. pp. 304.

Times and Seasons; ed. by Jos. Smith; a periodical extending to 766 pages, print-

MORMON—*continued.*
ed fortnightly prior to April 15, 1842. Nauvoo, 8vo.
Book of Covenants and Revelations. Kirtland, 1835, 18mo. pp. 250.
Trial of Joseph Smith, for High Treason and other crimes, Feb. 15, 1841. Several editions.
The Prophet of the 19th Century; or the History of the Mormon, with Analysis of the Book of Mormon, by Henry Caswall. Lond. 1843, 12mo., 7s. 6d.
Female Life among the Mormons: a Narrative of many years' personal experience, by the Wife of a Mormon Elder, recently from Utah. New York, 1855, crown 8vo., pp. 450. 6s.
Utah and the Mormons: The History, Government, Doctrines, Customs, and Prospects of the Latter-Day Saints; from personal observation during a six months' Residence at Great Salt Lake City, by Benjamin G. Ferris, late Secretary of Utah Territory. With numerous illustrations. N. York, 12mo. 6s.
The Mormons at Home: or a residence at the Great Salt Lake City, by Mrs. Ferris, Wife of the late U. States Secretary for Utah. N. York, 1856. 12mo. 5s.
Mormon Wives; a Narrative of Facts stranger than Fiction, by Metta Victoria Fuller. New York, 1857, post 8vo. 6s.
Fifteen Years among the Mormons; being the Narrative of Mrs. Mary E. F. Smith, late of Great Salt Lake City, a Sister of one of the Mormon High Priests, by N. W. Green. N. York, 1858. 12mo. 7s. 6d.
The Mormons, or Latter-Day Saints in the Valley of the Great Salt Lake; a History of their Rise, Progress, Doctrines, Present Condition, and Prospects, derived from personal observation, during a residence among them, by Lieut. T. W. Gunnison. Philadelphia, 1852, 5s. 6d.
Mormonism and the Mormons; an Historical View of the Rise and Progress of the Sect self-styled Latter-Day Saints, by D. T. Kidder. New York, 12mo. 2s. 6d.
The Mormons, or Latter-Day Saints; with Memoirs of the Life and Death of Joseph Smith, 'The American Mahomet,' with 40 engravings. 2s. 6d.
The Prophets, or Mormonism Unveiled. With Illustrations. Philad. 1856. 12mo. 5d.
Expedition to the Valley of the Great Salt Lake of Utah; including a Description of its Geography, natural History, and Minerals, and an Analysis of its Water; with an authentic Account of the Mormon Settlement, by Howard Stansbury, Captain of the Corps of Topographical Engineers, U.S. Army. Numerous Illustrations of the Country, natural History, &c. and a separate Volume of Maps. Philadelphia, 1852, royal 8vo., 1l. 5s.
Spiritual Delusions; being a Key to the Mysteries of Mormonism; exposing the Particulars of that astounding Heresy, the Spiritual-Wife System, as practised by Brigham Young of Utah. By Increase van Dunsen and Maria his Wife, Seceders from that singular Sect, with Illustrations. New York, 8vo. pp. 64. 1s. 6d.
Mormonism Examined. A few kind Words to a Mormon. Birm. [? 1855], 8vo.
The Book of Mormon examined; and its Claim to be a Revelation from God proved to be false. By J. Haynes. 1853. 12mo.
Divine Authenticity of the Book of Mormon. By O. Pratt. [1851] 8vo.
The Mormon Imposture; or an Exposure of the fraudulent Origin of the Book of Mormon. Second edition. Lond. Newbury, [1851] 8vo.
Reply to a Pamphlet entitled 'Remarks on Mormonism.' By O. Pratt, 1849, 8vo.
Mormonism. [By W. J. Conybeare.] Reprinted from the Edinburgh Review, No. 202, for April, 1854. Lond. (Longman's Trav. Lib. vol. 25), 1854.
Friendly Warnings on the Subject of Mormonism. By a Country Clergyman. Lond. 1850, 12mo.
Mormonism or the Bible? By a Cambridge Clergyman. 2d ed. Lond, 1852, 12mo.
The Mormons, or Latter-Day Saints. By Charles Mackay, LL.D. Lond. Ingram and Cooke, 1851, fcp. 8vo. Fourth edit. 1856.
Brief History of the Church of Christ of Latter-Day Saints, by J. Cerrill. 8vo.
Mormonism Pourtrayed; its Errors and Absurdities exposed, by W. Harris. 8vo.
An Appeal to the American People, being an Account of the Persecutions of the Church of the Latter-Day Saints, and of the Barbarities inflicted upon them by the State of Missouri. Cincinnati, 18mo. pp. 84.
Mormonismen och Swedenborgianismen. Upsala, 1854, 8vo.

MORNAY, Philip of, Lord of Plessis and Mornay. A Worke concerning the Trueness of Christian Religion, translated into English by Syr Philip Sidney, Knight, and Arthur Golding. The third Time published. Lond. 1604, 4to.
Best edition of this esteemed work.— 1587, 4to. Inglis, 987, 16s. Heber, pt. ix. 17s. Bright, 13s.—1592, 4to. Bindley, pt. iii. 324, 1l. 6d.—1617, 4to.
A notable Treatise of the Church, translated by J. Fielde. Lond. 1570, 8vo. Bright, 12s. — Lond. 1579, 8vo. Inglis, 1048, 5s. 6d.—1580.—1581, 16mo. Heber, pt. v. 5s.—16mo. 1606.
Christian Meditations on the 6, 25, and 32 Psalmes. A Meditation on the 127 Psalme, by P. Plissoon P. Both translated by John Field. Lond. 16mo.
The Defence of Death, done into English by E(dward) A(ggas). Lond. 1577 16mo. H. 6, in eights, dedicated to Mar,

MORNAY, Philip of—*continued.* garet Countess of Darby. In the Lambeth Library.
A Christian and Godly View of Death and Life, as also of human Actions, translated by A. W. Lond. 1593, 8vo.
A Discourse of Life and Death, done into English by the Countess of Pembroke. Lond. 1600, 16mo. G 2, in eights, F only 4 leaves. Heber, pt. v. half the title MS. 1*l*. 7s. Caldecott, 12s.—1592, 4to. —Lond. 1607, 17mo. Bliss, 11s. *See* GARNIER, Robt.—Another translation, falsely ascribed to Sir John Fenwick, Bart. Lond. 1597, 4to. pp. 31. Reprinted in the first volume of the Harleian Miscellany.—Another, by A. W. Lond. 1693, 8vo.—Another, by E(dward) Aggen). Lond. 1676, 8vo.
Fowre Bookes of the Institutions, Vse, and Doctrine of the Holy Sacrament of the Eucharist in the old Church; as likewise how, when, and by what Degrees the Masse is brought in, in Place thereof. Translated by R. S. Lond. 1600, folio.
The Mysterie of Iniquitie; or, the Historie of the Papacie, englished by Samson Lennard. Lond. 1612, folio, 5s.
His Teares for the Death of his Sonne, englished by J. Healey. Lond. 1609, 12mo Bright, 9s.
Several other pieces written by this illustrious French protestant, who was privy counsellor to Henry the Great, have been translated into English.

MORNING EXERCISES at Cripplegate, Saint Giles's in the Fields, and in Southwark. Lond. 1660-90, 4to. 6 vols. 4*l*. 4s.
By Owen, Manton, Baxter, Bates, Jenkyns, Alsop, Vincent, Burgess, Tillotson, &c. &c. Williams, 1032, 11*l*. 15s. fine set.—Fifth edition, carefully collated and corrected, with notes and translations by James Nichols. Lond. Tegg, 1841. Large 8vo. 6 vols. 3*l*. 12s.
The Morning Exercise Methodiz'd. Lond. 1680, 4to. 14s. Published by Thos. Case.—1676, 4to.
The Morning Exercise at Cripplegate; or, several Cases of Conscience practically resolved by sundry Ministers. Lond. 1661, 4to. 15s. Published by Samuel Annesley. —1677, 4to.
A Supplement to the Morning Exercise at Cripplegate. Lond. 1674-76, 4to. 15s. Published by Annesley.
The Morning Exercise against Popery. Lond. 1675, 4to. 18s. Published by Nath. Vincent.—1679, 4to.
Continuation. Lond. 1683, 4to. 18s.
Casuistical Morning Exercises. The fourth volume. By several Ministers in and about London, preached in October

1689. (With a Preface by Samuel Annesley.) Lond. 1690, 4to. 16s.

MORRAY, William. A short Treatise of Death, together with the ænigmatick Description of old Age and Death, &c. in English-Meeter, Edinb. 1631, 12mo.
Gordonstown, 1501, 1*l*. 11s. 6d.—Again. Edinb. 1633.

MORRELL, William. New England; or, Enarration of the Ayre, Earth, Water, Fish, and Fowles of that Country, and of the Natives. Lond. 1625, 4to.
In Latin and English. A copy is in the British Museum. Heber, pt. iv. 1*l*. 5s.

— William. The notorious Impostor, or the Life of W. Morrell, alias Bowyer, sometime of Banbury. Two Parts. Lond. 1692, 4to.
Nassau, pt. II. 186, 7s.
The Compleat Memoirs of the Life of that notorious Impostor W. Morrell, alias Bowyer, alias Wickham, &c. Lond. 1694, 12mo.

MORRENNUS, John. Reverendi Episcopi Wyntoniensis Doctoris Gardineri Angliæ Cancellarii Epitaphium. Lond. 1555, 4to.
Reprinted in Hearne's Collection of Discourses.

MORRICE, Thomas. An Apology for Schoolmasters. Lond. 1619, 12mo.

MORRIS, Corbyn. Essay towards fixing the true Standards of Wit, Humour, Raillery, &c. Lond. 1744. 8vo. 5s.
An ingenious work.
Observations on the past Growth, and present State of the City of London. Lond. 1751, folio. A curious pamphlet. Dent, pt. II. 619, 8s. 6d.

— Richard, F.L.S. Essays on Landscape Gardening, and on uniting picturesque Effect with rural Scenery. Lond. 1827, 4to. 1*l*. 11s. 6d. six plates.

— Captain. A Collection of Songs by the inimitable Captain Morris. Lond. 1786, 8vo. 2 pts.
Said to contain more humour than genius, and more obscenity than humour.
The Festival of Anacreon, containing a Collection of modern Songs written for

MORRIS, Capt.—*continued.*
the Anacreontic Society, the Beef Steak, and Humbug Clubs, by Capt. Morris, Mr. Brownlow, Mr. Howardine, Sir John Moore, Capt. Thompson, and other lyric writers. With some account of the above convivial Societies, Part I. (104 pp.) Lond. 1753, 8vo. port. of Capt. Morris.—Sixth edition, 1789. The second Part, with Col. Ironside's Election Canzonetta. (80 pp.) Lond. 1789, 8vo. port. of W. Hewardine. Part 3. (80 pp.)

The Bee, a Collection of Songs. Lond. 1790, portrait by Van Assen.

Songs, political and convivial. Lond. 1797, 12mo. port.—1802.

Miscellanies in Prose and Verse. Lond. 1791, 8vo.

Quashy; or, the coal-black Maid. A Tale relative to the Slave Trade. Lond. 1796, 8vo.

Lyra Urbanica, or social Effusions. Lond. Bentley, 1844, post 8vo. 2 vols, 1l. 1s. part. by Greatbatch. (Contains 'The Bee,' first published in 1790.)

Capt. Morris is said to have been a principal contributor to 'Hilaria, or the Festive Board.' *See* **SWANDING**.

Two of his compositions are to be found in the Festival of Love, Lond. 1789, 18mo.

MORRISON, Robert, D.D. A Dictionary of the Chinese Language, in three Parts, viz. Chinese-English, arranged according to the Radicals (3 vols.) — Alphabetical Arrangement (2 vols.) — English and Chinese (1 vol.) Macao, 1815-23, royal 4to. 6 vols, 14l. 14s.

This dictionary 'may be considered as the most important work in Chinese literature that has yet (1816) reached Europe.'—*Quart Rev.* Dr. Morrison has taken as his ground-work the 'Imperial Dictionary of Kang-he,' but has made many important alterations and improvements.

A Parallel between the two intended Chinese Dictionaries, by the Rev. R. Morrison and Ant. Montucci; together with the Horæ Sinicæ. Lond. 1817, 4to.

Horæ Sinicæ; Translations from the popular Literature of the Chinese. Lond. 1812, 8vo. 7s. 6d. A valuable and interesting work.

A Grammar of the Chinese Language. Serampore, 1815, 4to. 1l. A valuable work, short and comprehensive.

Translations from the original Chinese, with Notes. Canton, 1815. 8vo.

Dialogues and detached Sentences in the Chinese Language, with a free and verbal Translation in English. By the Rev. R. Morrison and others. Macao, 1816, royal 8vo. 10s.

A View of China, for philological purposes; designed for the use of Persons who study the Chinese Language. Macao, 1817, 4to, 1l.

Chinese Miscellanies, or Extracts from Chinese Authors, in the native Character, with Translations, &c. Lond. 1825, 4to.

Memoirs of the Rev. W. Milne. Malacca, 1824, 8vo.

Memoirs of his Life and Labours, by Mrs. Morrison; with critical Notices of his Chinese Works by S. Kidd. Lond. 1639, 8vo. 2 vols. port. 9s.

Vocabulary of the Canton Dialect; English and Chinese. Macao, 1828, 8vo.

Grammar of the English Language, for the Use of the Anglo-Chinese College. English and Chinese. Macao, 1823, 8vo.

A Parting Memorial; consisting of Miscellaneous Discourses, written and preached in China, at Singapore, on board Ship at Sea, in the Indian Ocean, at the Cape of Good Hope, and in England: with Remarks on Missions, Lond. W. Simpkin and R. Marshall, 1625, 8vo. 5s.

Dr. Morrison translated the Morning and Evening Prayers of the Church of England into Chinese, in 1817. He also co-operated largely in the translation of the Bible and Testament into that language.

—— William Maxwell. The Decisions of the Court of Session, from its Institution until the Separation of the Court into two Divisions in 1808, digested under proper Heads in the form of a Dictionary. Edinb. 1811-23, 4to. 21 vols.

The Decisions of the Court of Session, from its Institution to the present Time. Edinb. 1801-7, 4to. 68 parts, or 19 vols.

Supplemental Volume, containing omitted Cases, Indexes, &c. Edinb. 1815, 4to.

General Synopsis of the Decisions of the Court of Session until Nov. 1827, by M. P. Brown. Edinb. 1829, 4to. 4 vols.

A Supplement to Morrison's Dictionary of Decisions. By M. P. Brown. Edinb. 1823-4, 4to. 5 vols.

Index to the Decisions of the Court of Session, contained in all the original Collections, and in Morrison's Dictionary of Decisions, by William Tait. Edinb. 1823. 4to. 3l. 3s.

See **ELCHIE**, Lord. **HALKERSTON**, Peter.

MORRITT, J. B. S. A Vindication of Homer and of the ancient Poets and Historians who have recorded the Fall and Siege of Troy. York, 1798, 4to. 12s.

Written in answer to Jacob Bryant's publications on that subject.
Additional Remarks on the Topography of Troy. Lond. 1800, 4to.
Miscellaneous Translations and Imitations of the minor Greek Poets. Lond. 1802, crown 8vo. 4s.

MORS, Roderyck. The Complaynt of, sometyme a gray Fryre, unto the Parliament Howse of Ingland, his naturall Country, for the Redresse of certen wicked lawes, evel customs, and cruel decroys. Imprinted at Savoy, per Franciscoum de Turona, n. d. (1536) 16mo.

FIRST EDITION. In the Grenville Collection. Inglis, 1049, 8l. 6s. White Knights, 2363, russia, 5l. 7s. 6d. Utias, 2l. 10s. Bright, 5l. 5s. Sotheby, 1852, 4l. 10s. Heber, 2l. 5s. See Brydges' British Bibliographer, ii. 178-81. — Geneve in Savoye, by Myghell Boys, 16mo. n. d. (circa 1586). Two editions, one containing it, in eights, the other O. in fours. Sotheby's, 1854, 3l. 6s. Both editions are in the British Museum, and the second is in Lambeth Library. [*Vide* BALE.]

The Lamentation of a Christian against the Citie of London, made by Roderigo Mors. Printed in Jericho in the Land of Promise, 1542, 12mo. Horner, 1854, 2l. 8s. — Another edition, Nurenbergh, 1545, 18mo. — Another edition, no place, 1548, 18mo. Contains F, in eights. A copy is in Lambeth. Library.

The real name of this author was R. Brinklow.

MORTALITY. — A Collection of the yearly Bills of Mortality, from 1657 to 1758 inclusive. Together with several other Bills of an earlier Date. Lond. 1759, 4to.

To which are subjoined — I. Natural and political Observations on the Bills of Mortality, by Capt. John Graunt, F.R.S. reprinted from the sixth edition in 1676. II. Another Essay on political Arithmetic, concerning the Growth of the City of London; with the Measures, Periods, Causes, and Consequences thereof. By Sir William Petty, Knt., F.R.S., reprinted from the edition printed at London in 1683. III. Observations on the past Growth and present State of the City of London; reprinted from the edition printed at London in 1751; with a Continuation of the Tables to the end of the Year 1757. By Corbyn Morris, Esq., F.R.S. IV. A comparative View of the Diseases and Ages, and a Table of the Probabilities of Life, for the last Thirty Years. By J. P., Esq.,

F.R.S. Willett, 2658, 6s. Collection. — Title, one leaf; preface, 16 pages; the bills of mortality, 210 pages; a folded table of diseases, &c. between the bills for 1629-1630; the various tracts, 151 pages, and six folding tables.

MORTE D'ARTHURE The most ancient and famous History of the renowned Prince Arthur, King of Britaine. (*Anon.*, but by Sir Thomas Malory.) Lond. 1634, 4to.

New edition. Lond. 1816, 18mo. 2 vols.
La Morte d'Arthure. The History of King Arthur and the Knights of the Round Table, edited from the Text of the edition of 1634, with Introduction and Notes by Thomas Wright. Lond. 1858, post 8vo. 3 vols.

See ARTHUR, pp. 174-5. CAXTON, p. 397. ROXBURGHE CLUB, Appendix.

MORTIMER, Lieut. George. Observations and Remarks made during a Voyage to the Islands of Teneriffe, Amsterdam, Maria's Islands near Van Diemen's Land, Otaheite, Sandwich Islands, the Fox Islands on the north-west Coast of America, Tinian, and from thence to Canton. Lond. 1791, 4to.

A hasty voyage of ten months and one day, containing but little information.

— Thomas. Commercial Dictionary. A new Edition, revised to the present Time by W. Dikinson, Esq. Lond. 1823, 8vo. 5s.
Superseded by Waterston and Macculloch.

MORTIMER. — The Fall of Mortimer, an historical Play (by — Hatchett). Lond. 1731, 8vo. 4s.

The play was pronounced by the Grand Jury for the County of Middlesex, July 7, 1731, 'a false, infamous, scandalous, seditious, and treasonable libel.' — 1763, 8vo. Prefixed to this edition is a dedication by John Wilkes to the Earl of Bute, couched in language the most insulting and sarcastic.

The History of Mortimer, being a Vindication of the Fall of Mortimer. Lond. 1731, 8vo.

MORTON, Ann, Countess of. Devotions. Fourteenth Edition. Lond. 1689, 24mo.

It is from this manual that Hor. Walpole quotes the remarkable expression of

'Lord, wilt thou hunt after a flea?' The Imprimatur to the volume is dated 1685.

MORTON, Jas., B.D. The Monastic Annals of Teviotdale, or the History and Antiquities of the Abbeys of Jedburgh, Kelso, Melros, and Dryburgh. Edinb. 1832, 4to. plates. (pub. 2l. 2s.) 16s. LARGE PAPER, proofs, royal 4to. (pub. 3l. 12s.) 1l. 5s.

— John. *See* BUDDEN, John.

— John, M.A. The Natural History of Northamptonshire; with some account of the Antiquities; to which is annexed, a transcript of Doomsday-Book, as far as it relates to that County. Lond. 1712, folio.

'A work of very considerable industry, written on Dr. Plot's method, and on Dr. Woodward's hypothesis.'—*Nicolson*. Dowdeswell, 616, 1l. 17s. Bindley, pt. II. 648, 2l. 8s. Willett, 1685, 2l. 12s. 6d. Marquis of Townshend, 2445, russia, 3l. 5s. LARGE PAPER, Dent, pt. II. 782, 4l. 4s. Heath, 4678, russia, 6l. Nassau, pt. II. 408, russia, 5l. 5s. *Collation.*—Title and dedication to Q. Anne, 2 leaves; preface and errata, 4 pages; the history, 651 pages; Doomsday-Book, pp. 1—x. Plates: 1. Eight fossils, &c. p. 170. 2. Twelve fossils, p. l. 184. 3. Thirteen shells, p. 192. 4. Thirteen shells, p. 202. 5. Sixteen shells, p. 208. 6. Twenty-five shells, p. 212. 7. Thirty-two shells, p. 220. 8. Ten ammonites, p. 224. 9. Eleven ammonites, p. 228. 10. Thirty fossils, &c. p. 246. 11. Fossils and celestial phænomena, p. 556. 12. Specimens of veins on trees, &c. p. 504. 13. Birds, &c. p. 452. 14. Fragment of a Roman pavement, discovered in 1699, p. 532. Prefixed to the volume is a sheet map of the county by John Harris. A copy in the British Museum contains MS. notes by the author.

MORTON, Joshua. Sermons on various interesting Subjects. Lond. 1788, 8vo. 2 vols.

In considerable estimation.—1805, 8vo. 2 vols. Williams, 1316, 1l. 9s.

— J. H. Etchings, 50 historical Subjects. Lond. 1780, fol. 16s.

— Nathaniel. New England's Memoriall; being the History of the Plymouth Colony to 1668. Lond. 1669, 4to.

Nassau, pt. II. 187, 11s.—Second edition, with Supplement by Colton. Boston, 1721, 12mo. Heber, pt. II. 5s. 6d.—Third edition. Newport, 1722, 12mo.—Fourth edition, Plymouth, Mass. 1826.—Fifth edition, re-written by Judge Davis. Boston, U.S. 1826, 8vo. with a map.

— Thomas, successively Bishop of Chester, Lichfield, and Durham. Life and funeral Sermon, from 2 Tim. iv. 7, 8. By John Barwick. Lond. 1660, 4to. 12s.

Prefixed is a portrait of the bishop (by Faithorne). Bishop of Ely, 202, 14s. The writings of this prelate, which were principally directed against the Romanists and Nonconformists, are now of little value.

A Discharge of Five Imputations of Misallegations, falsely charged upon the (now) Bishop of Durham, an English Baron, 1633, 12mo. Bright, 10s.

An Answer unto the scandalous exceptions which Theoph. Higgins has lately objected. Lond. 1604. Bright, 8s.

The Life of Dr.Thomas Morton, Bishop of Duresme, by R. B. and J. N. York, 1669, 12mo. with wood-cut portrait of the bishop. Brockett, 1591, 8s. 6d. Nassau, pt. I. 125, 8s. Heber, pt. viii. 2s.

— Thomas, of Clifford's Inn. New English Canaan, or New Canaan. Containing an Abstract of New England in three Books, written upon tenne Yeares Knowledge and Experiment of the Country. Amst. 1637, 4to.

A number of poetical pieces are interspersed through this curious work; among others, one entitled "Of the Bacanall Triumphs of the nine Worthies of New Canaan," by Ben Jonson, which is not included in any edition of his Works. White Knights, 2963, 1l. 2s. Gordonstoun, 1634, 1l. 16s. Caldecott, date cut off, 1l. 3s. Bindley, pt. III. 629, 13s. North, pt. II. 600, date 1634, 14s.

MORTON, Rev. Wm., Missionary. A Dictionary of the Bengali Language, with Bengali Synonymes, and an English Interpretation, compiled from Native and other authorities. Bishop's College (Calcutta), 1828, 8vo. 1l. 5s.

MORUS, *Anglicè* MORE.

MORVINE. The most Famous and Renowned Historie of that Woorthie and Illustrious Knight, Morvine, son to Oger the Dane. Translated by J. Markham. Lond. 1612, 4to.

Heber, pt. v. 3l. 13s. 6d

MORWYNG, Peter. *See* EVONI-
MUS.
MORYSIN. *See* MORISON, R.
MORYSON, Fynes. An Itinerary,
containing his Ten Yeeres Travel
through Germany, Bohmerland,
Switzerland, Netherland, Denmark,
Poland, Italy, Turkey, France, England, Scotland, and Ireland; in
three Parts. Lond. 1617, folio.

A valuable and much esteemed work.
Bindley, pt. ll. 843, 2l. 19s. Marquis of
Townshend, 2446, 5d. 5s. Jadis, 815, 3l. 6s.
North, pt. ll. 885, 4l. 10s. Hibbert, 5656,
russia, 6l. 6s. 6d. Willett, 1686, 8l. 15s.
Heber, pt. x. #l. 14s. Craufurd, russia,
fine, 5l. 12s. 6d. Singer, fine, in original
binding, 8l. A notice of the Itinerary will
be found in the Retrospective Review, xi.
308-42. The leaf opposite the Title, containing the words 'An Itinerary,' is occasionally wanting.

The History of Ireland, from the Year
1599 to 1603; giving an Account of the
Rebellion of the Earl of Tyrone, with a
short Narration of the State of that Kingdom, from 1169 to which is added, a
Description of Ireland. Dublin, 1735, 8vo.
2 vols. These volumes are extracted from
his Itinerary. North, pt. ll. 901, 1l. 11s.

MOSCHUS. *See* ANACREON. BION.
MUSÆUS. STANLEY, Thomas. THEOCRITUS.

MOSCOVY, or MUSCOVY. *See* Russia.

MOSCOW. — The Reports of a
bloody and terrible Massacre in
Mosco; with the fearful End of
Demetrius, the last Duke. Lond.
1607, 4to.
A copy is in the British Museum. Caldecott, 1l. 2s.

An historical Sketch of Moscow, with
12 coloured imitations of drawings. Lond.
1813, imp. 4to. 1l. 1s.
See LYALL, Rob. BROWN, Count.

MOSELEY, Benjamin, M.D. A
Treatise on Sugar, with miscellaneous medical Observations. Lond.
1799, 8vo. 5s.
Second edition, with considerable additions. Lond. 1800.

A Treatise concerning the Properties
and Effects of Coffee. 1785, 8vo.— Fifth
edition, with considerable Additions.
Lond. 1792, 8vo.

— Walter Michael. An Essay
on Archery, describing the Practice of that Art in all Ages and
Nations. Lond. 1792, 8vo. 7s.
A work of considerable learning and
taste. Bindley, pt. ll. 1553, 10s.

— William. Reports of Cases
determined in the Court of Chancery during the Time of Lord Chancellor King. Dubl. 1744, folio,
15s.
Reprinted, Dublin, 1793, 8vo.

MOSER, Justus. Harlequin: or a
Defence of grotesque comic Performances. Translated from the
German by J. A. F. Warneoke.
Lond. 1766, small 8vo.
Garrick, 1660, morocco, 7s.

MOSER, Joseph. Turkish Tales.
Lond. 1794, 12mo. 2 vols.

Adventures of Timothy Twig, Esq.;
in a Series of poetical Epistles. Lond.
1794, 12mo. 2 vols.

Tales and Romances of Ancient and
Modern Times. 1800, 12mo. 5 vols.
This author, who was a justice of the
peace, wrote several other works of fiction, dramas, pamphlets, &c. He also
contributed to the European Magazine
and other periodicals.

MOSES. *See* Exodus. Genesis.
Pentateuch.

A Relation of the finding out of Moses
his Tombe, near Mount Nebo. Lond.
1657, 12mo.

— Chorenensis. Historiæ Armeniacæ, et Epitome Geographiæ,
Armen. et Lat. cum Notis Gul. et
Geo. Gul. Whistoni. Lond. 1736,
4to. 3l. 3s.

— Henry. Picturesque Views
of Ramsgate, with Descriptions.
To which is prefixed, an historical
Account of Ramsgate. Lond. 1817,
imperial 8vo.

Duke of York, 8402, 6s. 6d. *Collation.*
—Pp. 8, with a plan and 25 plates, to each
of which is an explanatory letter-press.

A Collection of antique Vases, Altars,
Pateræ, Tripods, Candelabra, Sarcophagi,
&c. from various Museums and Collections, engraved (in Outline) on 170 Plates,
several of which are coloured, with historical Essays (by Thomas Hope, Esq.)
Lond. 1814, sm. 4to. 2l. 2s. Reduced,

Bohn, 1l. 5s. LARGE PAPER. Hibbert, 5621, morocco, 3l. 7s.

See CANOVA, ANT. ENGLEFIELD, Sir H. C. Bart.

MOSHEIM, John Lawrence, D.D. An Ecclesiastical History, ancient and modern, from the Birth of Christ to the Beginning of the 18th Century. Translated from the original Latin, with Notes and chronological Tables, by Archibald Maclaine, D.D. New edition, with a Continuation by Charles Coote, LL.D. Lond. 1811, 8vo. 6 vols.

Drury, 2759, 2l. 8s. Williams, 1220, in pig-skin, 5l. 2s. 6d. A work indispensable in the department of Church history. 'Mosheim's compendium is excellent, the method admirable. In short the only one deserving of the name of an ecclesiastical history.'—*Bishop Warburton.*—First Edition of Maclaine's Translation, with a Supplement. Lond. 1765-8, 4to. 2 vols. Willett, 1753, 1l. 14s. Roscoe, 537, 1l. 17s. —1768, 8vo. 5 vols. Gough, 2413, 1l. 17s. —1774, 8vo. 5 vols. Dent, pt. II. 12, 18s. —1782, 8vo. 6 vols. Hindley, pt. II. 1528, 1l. 14s. Earl of Kerry, 835, 2l. 18s.—1790, 8vo. 5 vols.—1806, 8vo. 6 vols.—With a Dissertation on the State of the primitive Church, by George Gleig, Bishop of Stirling, 1826, 8vo. 6 vols.

A New and Literal translation from the original Latin, with copious additional Notes, original and selected, by James Murdock, D.D. Edited with Additions, by the Rev. Henry Soames, M.A. Lond. 1841, 8vo. 4 vols.—Lond. Longman, 1845, and again, 1850, 8vo. 4 vols. 2l. 8s.

An Abridgment of Mosheim's Ecclesiastical History, by J. Parkinson, 1797, 8vo. 2 vols.—Lond. Tegg, 1842, 8vo. 2 vols.

A Summary of Mosheim's Ecclesiastical History, with a Continuation to the Year 1819, by C. T. Collins. Lond. Dublin, 1824, 8vo. 2 vols. 1l. 1s.

Memoirs of the Christian Church, translated from the German. Lond. 1780, 8vo.

Commentaries on the Affairs of the Christians before the Time of Constantine the Great. Translated from the Latin of Dr. Mosheim, by R. S. Vidal, Esq. Lond. 1813—1835, 8vo. 2 vols. 1l. 11s. 6d. This translation only reaches to the end of the 7th section of the third century.—Reprinted, with the translation completed by James Murdock, D.D. New York, 1851, 8vo. in 2 vols. A valuable companion to the Ecclesiastical History, supplying many important particulars, which the author could not treat at length in his general history.

MOSLEY, Sir Oswald, D.C.L. History of the Town and Castle of Tutbury, in the co. of Stafford. Derby and Lond. 1832, 8vo. plates.

MOSS, J. W. A Manual of classical Bibliography. Lond. 1825, 8vo. 2 vols.

Drury, 2750, 17s. Williams, 1231, 1l. 11s. 6d.—With additions (by H. G. Bohn). Lond. 1837, 8vo. 2 vols. 12s.

— Robert, D.D. Sermons and Discourses on practical Subjects. Lond. 1732-8, 8vo. 8 vols.

With portrait of Moss by Vertue. Bp. of Ely, 524, 1l. 1s.

— Thomas, B.A., of Trentham, co. Stafford. Poems. Wolverhampton, 1769, 4to. published anonymously.

In this volume will be found the much-admired Beggar's Petition, commencing 'Pity the Sorrows of a Poor Old Man.' The author also wrote 'The Vanity of Human Wishes,' in blank verse. Lond. 1768, 4to.

— W. G. History and Antiquities of the parochial Church of St. Saviour, Southwark; Descriptions, historical and biographical, by the Rev. J. Nightingale, 17 Plates. Lond. 1818, 4to. 12s. Proofs, 1l. 1s. INDIA PROOFS and Etchings, 2l. 2s.

The History and Antiquities of the Town and Port of Hastings, Sussex. Lond. 1824, 8vo. 20 plates, 7s. LARGE PAPER, royal 8vo. proofs, 10s. 6d.; India proofs, 1l. 1s.

History and Antiquities of the Rape of Hastings, Sussex. Lond, 1828, 4to. Part I, containing the Hundred of Baseie: all published, pp. 40, and 4 plates, 10s. 6d. Proofs on India paper, 1l. 1s.

MOSSE, Miles. The Arraignment and Conviction of Vsurie in sixe Sermons vpon Pro. 28 : 8. By Miles Mosse. Lond. 1595, 4to.

Inglis, 988, 7s. 6d. Heber, pt. v. 2s. 6d.

MOSSOM, R., D.D. Minister of St. Pet. P. W. (St. Peter's, Paul's Wharf.) A Plant of Paradise, being a Sermon preached at St. Martin's in the Fields, at the Funeral of John Goodhand Holt, the youngest son, only child, and hopeful heir of Thomas Holt, Esq. of Grislehurst, in the County of Lancaster, Esq. 19 March, 1669. Lond. 1660, 4to. Portrait of J. G. Holt, by Loggan.

A Narrative panegyrical of the Life, Sickness, and Death, of George (Wilde), Lord Bishop of Derry, in Ireland. As it was delivered at his Funeral in the Cathedral Church of the Holy Trinity, commonly called Christ Church in Dublin, on Friday, the 13 of January, Anno Domini 1665-6. Lond. 1665-6, 4to. Ten leaves.

MOTE, Humphrey. The Primrose of London, with her valiant Adventure on the Spanish Coast, bearing of the Burthen of 150 Tunne. Lond. for Tho. Nelson, 1585, 4to.

Four leaves. A copy is in the British Museum.

MOTHE LE VAYER, Francis de la. Of Liberty and Servitude, translated from the French by John Evelyn, 12mo. Lond. 1649, 12mo.

Evelyn's first production.

MOTHERBY, George, M.D. A new Medical Dictionary. Lond. 1801, folio, 2 vols.

The first edition of this popular work appeared in 1776.

MOTHERWELL, William. Minstrelsy; ancient and modern, with an historical Introduction and Notes. Glasgow, 1827, 4to. 18s.

Pp. cv, 390 and xxiv, besides title, dedication, contents, and errata, 5 leaves; likewise engraved title, two etchings, and nine plates of music. Singer, 9s. 6d.

Essay on the Poets of Renfrewshire. (Prefixed to the Harp of Renfrewshire.) Paisley, 1819, 12mo.

Poems, Narrative and Lyrical. Glasg. 1832, 12mo. Some copies on LARGE PAPER, 4to.

Poetical Works, enlarged; with Memoir by Dr. J. M'Conechy. Third edition. Lond. 1849, 12mo. 4s. 6d.—With Supplement. 1849, 12mo. 7s. (Supp. sep. 2s. 6d.)

MOTIVES, humble, for Association to maintaine Religion established; an Antidote against the pestilent Treatises of secular Priests. 1601, 4to.

Privately printed. Wrangham, 2l. 8s.

MOTRAYE, Aubry de la. Travels through Europe, Asia, and into Part of Africa. Lond. 1723, 2 vols.—Travels in Prussia, Russia, and Poland (forming vol. 3), 1732. Together 3 vols. folio.

With maps and cuts, several of which are by Hogarth, and sometimes cut out. Veracity and exactness, particularly so far as regards the copying of inscriptions, characterise these travels. They are also valuable for information respecting the mines of the north of Europe. (The 3rd volume is occasionally found at the end of the 2nd, but is oftener deficient.) Roxburghe, 7l. 8s., 2 vols. 1l. 4s. Willett, 1607, 1l. 13s. Heath, 2581, 2 vols. 2l. 6s. North, pt. ii. 1256, 2l. 4s. LARGE PAPER.? Steevens, 1918, 2 vols. 1l. 2s. Reed, 8158, 2 vols. 1l. 2s. Caillard, 57 francs.

MOTTE, Countess de la. The Life of Jean de St. Remy de Valois, containing a compleat Justification of her Conduct, and an Explanation of the Intrigues and Artifices used against her by her Enemies relative to the Diamond Necklace. Written by herself. Lond. 1791, 8vo. 2 vols. 9s.

MOTTEUX, Peter, wrote about 14 Plays (see Biographia Dramatica), and translated Montaigne's Essays, Bayle's Dictionary, Cervantes' Don Quixote, &c. &c. and several other works.

MOTTEVILLE, F. B. de. Memoirs of Anne of Austria. Lond. 1726, 12mo. 5 vols.

Roxburghe, 8086, 6s. 6d. LARGE PAPER, 1l. 10s.

MOTTLEY, John. History of Peter I., Emperor of Russia. Lond. 1739, 8vo. 3 vols.

Roxburghe, 7810, 16s. 6d. LARGE PAPER, 1l. 10s.

History of the Life and Reign of the Empress Catharine of Russia. Lond. 1744, 8vo. 2 vols.

See MILLER, Jos. SEYMOUR, Robert.

MOTTOS, The, of the English Nobility in the Year 1800, freely translated into Verse. 1822, 8vo. 5s.

Privately printed.

MOUETTE, The Sieur. Travels in Fez and Morocco. Lond. 1710, 4to. map by Moll. *See* Voyages and Travels.

MOUFET. *See* MUFFET.

MOULE, Thos. Bibliotheca Heraldica Magnæ Britanniæ. An analytical Catalogue of Books on Genealogy, Heraldry, Nobility, Knighthood, and Ceremonies. Lond. 1822, roy. 8vo. portrait of W. Camden, 1*l.* 5*s.*

An accurate and valuable work, consisting of pp. xxiii and 668. LARGE PAPER in 4to. Hibbert, 5672, 1*l.* 18*s.* 6*d.*

Antiquities of Westminster Abbey, Illustrated by twelve Plates, from Drawings by G. P. Harding. By T. Moule. 4to.

The Heraldry of Fish, with Notices of the principal Families bearing Fish in their Arms. Lond. 1842, 8vo. cuts, 1*l.* 1*s.* LARGE PAPER, 2*l.* 2*s.*

An Essay on the Roman Villas of the Augustan Age, their Architectural Disposition and Enrichments, and on the Remains of Roman domestic Edifices discovered in Great Britain. Lond. 1833, 8vo. plates, 14*s.* LARGE PAPER.

English Counties delineated; or a Topographical Description of England. Illustrated by a Map of London and a complete Series of County Maps. Lond. Virtue, 1837, 4to. 2 vols. maps—New title, 1839, 2*l.* 2*s.* or maps coloured, 3*l.* 3*s.*

MOULIN, Lewis du. Rerum nuper in Regno Scotiæ gestarum Historia, per Irenæum Philalethem. Dantisci, 1641, 12mo.

Gordonstoun, 1821, 3*s.* 6*d.*

Epistola de Episcopatu Anglicano contra Jo. Hall. Lond. 1641, Heber, pt. vi. 7*s.*

The first work sometimes attributed to Lud. Mollanæus, or Du Molin, was written by William Spang, minister at Camprere in Holland, chiefly from communications sent him by Robert Baillie. *See* LAING's edition of Principal Baillie's Letters and Journals, vol. i. p. cxli.

L. du Moulin published many other works which were printed at London, 1641-61. *See* Wood's Fasti. *See* BURNET, p. 800, col. 2. Theatrum Tragicum.

— Peter du, D.D., Pastor of the Reformed Church at Paris. The Papal Tyranny as it was exercised over England for some Ages, represented. Now set forth by his Son, P. du Moulin, Chaplain to King Charles IInd. Lond. 1674, 4to.

The Accomplishment of the Prophecies, or the third Book in Defense of the catholicks Faith. Translated by I. Heath (the Epigrammatist). Oxford, 1618, 12mo. Towneley, pt. ii. 362, 3*s.* 6*d.*

This celebrated French protestant minister published many other works. *See* PATERSON, Matthew.

— Peter du, Prebendary of Canterbury. Regii Sanguinis Clamor ad Coelum adversus Parricidas Anglicanos. Hag. Com. 1652, 12mo. 5*s.*

Published anonymously; by some attributed to Alex. More. It was answered by Milton, in his 'Defensio secunda pro Populo Anglicano.'

A Treatise on Peace of Soul and Content of Mind, translated into English, with additional Notes, by John Scrope, D.D. Lond. 1875, 8vo. 2 vols. 7*s.*

MOULTON, Thomas. The Myrrour or Glass of Healthe. Lond. by Thomas Colwel. 16mo. 6*s.*

A work shewing 'how the planettes do raygne in every houre of the daye and nyghte, with the natures and exposicions of the xii synges.' Herbert notices several other editions.—An edition. Lond. by Richard Kele, 16mo. White Knights, 1877, morocco, 1*l.* 5*s.*—Lond. Hugh Jackson, n.d.—Lond. W. Myddleton, n.d. Heber, pt. vi. 3*s.*

MOUNTAGU. *See* MONTAGU.

MOUNTAIN, Didymus. The Gardeners Labyrinth. Lond. 1577, 4to. 2 pts. in 1 vol. BLACK LETTER.

'Gathered out of the best approved writers of gardening, husbandry, and physicke.' White Knights, 1348, mor. 16*s.* Heber, pt. ix. 10*s.*—1586, perfected by H. Dethicke. Heber, pt. i. 8*s.* 6*d.* —1594, 4to. A copy in the Grenville Library.—1608, 4to.—Newly corrected and enlarged. Lond. 1652, small 4to.

— James. The History of Selby, ancient and modern. York, 1800, 12mo.

Title, one leaf; table of contents, preface, and Introduction, 12 pages; the history of Cawood, 40 pages, not including the title, the Selby directory, list of its principal inhabitants, and subscribers, 25 pages. The volume also contains a folded plan of Selby, and a N.W. view of the church of St. Germain's.

MOUNTEBANK.—The merry Mountebank; or the Humorous Quack Doctor; being a certane Cure for Hypochondriac-Melancholy, by Timothy Tulip of Cuckoldshire,

Esq. Lond. W. Pearson, 1782, 8vo. pp. 132. *See* SONGS.

MOUNTEBANKS.—Harrangues and Orations of several famous Mountebanks. Lond. 12mo. *See* JESTS.

MOUNTENOY, B. Selections from the Journals of Travellers in Brazil. 1825, 8vo. 7s.

MOUNTFORT, William. Six Plays, with Memoir. Lond. 1720, 12mo. 2 vols.

Roxburghe, 5923, 7s. 6d. Reed, 5597, 6s. 6d. Heath, 1947, 14s. 6d.
All printed separately, in 4to. between 1699 and 1697.

MOUNTMORRES, Rt. Hon. H. R. Morres, Lord. The History of the principal Transactions of the Irish Parliament, 1634-66. To which is prefixed, a preliminary Discourse on the ancient Parliaments of that Kingdom. Lond. 1792, 8vo. 2 vols.

Marquis of Townshend, 2129, 7s. 6d. Bindley, pt. ii. 1564, 8s. 6d.

MOUNTNORRIS, F. Annesley, Baron. A true Copie of the Sentence of Warre, pronounced against him in the Castle Chamber at Dublin, the 12th Dec. 1635, &c. Lond. for J. B. 1641, 4to.

Nine leaves.

MOURT, G. Proceedings of the English Plantation at Plimouth in New England. Lond. 1622, 4to.

MOXON, Joseph. Mechanical Exercises; or the Doctrine of Handyworks. Lond. 1677-96. Published in separate Nos. or Parts. The second volume dated 1683, pp. 394, is wholly 'applied to the Art of Printing,' has for a frontispiece 'the true Effigies of Laurens Iano Koster.' 4to. 3 vols.

Willett, 1754, Mechanick Exercises and Powers, 1593-6, 2 vols. russia, 1l. 14s.
Discourse of a Passage by the North Pole to Japan, China, &c. Lond. 1674, 4to. —1697, 4to.

Moxon published many other mathematical works.

MOYER, Lady. Sermons in Defence of the Divinity of Christ, preached at the Lecture founded by her Ladyship.

1719-20. By Dan. Waterland. Camb. 1720, 8vo. 5s.
1720-1. By James Knight. Lond. 1721, 8vo. 3s. 6d.
1723-4. By William Berriman. Lond. 1725, 8vo. 3s. 6d.
1734-5. By Thomas Bishop. Lond. 1725, 8vo. 3s.
1728-9. By Henry Felton. Oxf. 1732, 8vo. 3s. 6d.
1739-30. By Joseph Trapp. 8vo. 3s. 6d.
1730-2. By John Browne. Lond. 1732, 8vo. 3s. 6d.
1732-3. By Jeremiah Seed. 8vo. 2 vols. 12s.
1734-5. By Charles Wheatley. 8vo. 3s. 6d.
1737-8. By John Berriman. Lond. 1741, 8vo. 4s.
1738-9. By Edward Twells. 8vo. 2 vols. 7s.
1739-40. By Arthur Bedford. Lond. 1741, 8vo. 4s.
1740-1. By Gloucester Ridley. Lond. 1742, 8vo. 6s.
1757. By William Clements. Lond. 1767, 8vo. 4s.
1764-5. By Benjamin Dawson. Lond. 1765, 8vo. 4s.
1765-6. 1766-7. 1767-8. 1768-9. 1769-70. 1770-1. 1771-2. 1772-3. Unknown.
1774. By Thomas Morell, D.D. Lond. 1774, 4to.

The Lectures terminated about this time.

MOYLE, Walter. Works, with some Account of his Life and Writings, by Anth. Hammond, Esq. Lond. 1726-7, 8vo. 3 vols. 7s. 6d.

With portrait by Vertue. The third volume consists of Works not published by himself, with a Dedication signed E. C. (Edmund Curll.) This author is styled by Dryden 'a most ingenious young gentleman, conversant in all the studies of humanity much above his years.'

MOYSANT ET LEVIZAC. Bibliothèque portative des Ecrivains Français, ou Choix des meilleurs Morceaux extraits de leurs Ouvrages. Lond. 1803, royal 8vo. 8 vols.

Duke of York, 3717, 1l. 10s.—1200, roy 8vo. 8 vols. An abridgment for Schools was published in 12mo.

MOYSES, David. Memoirs of the Affairs of Scotland, 1577-1603. Together with a Discourse of the Conspiracy of Gowry. Edinb. 1755, 12mo.
The author was a domestic servant to James VI, to whom he dedicates his work. 1 labor, pt. ix. 8s.—New edition, 1830. See BANNATYNE CLUB, Appendix.

MOYSEY, Chas. Abel, D.D. Lectures on the Gospel according to St. John. Oxford, 1821, 8vo.

MOZART. See BOMBET, L. A. C. (a pseudonym of Henri Beyle).
An Account of Mozart as an Infant musician is contained in Daines Barrington's Miscellanies. Lond. 1781, 4to.
Life of Mozart. By Edward Holmes. Lond. 1845, post 8vo. 9s.

MOZEEN, Thomas. Miscellaneous Essays. Lond. 1762, 8vo.
Roxburghe, 3951, 6s.
The Lyrick Pacquet, containing most of the favourite Songs, performed for three seasons past at Sadler's Wells, likewise all them composed for the service of the said place this present season. Lond. 1764, 8vo.
Fables in Verse. Lond. 1768, 12mo. 2 vols. 5s.

MUCEDORUS.—A most pleasant Comedy of Mucedorus, the Kings Sonne of Valencia, and Amadine the Kings Daughter of Arragon. With the merry Conceits of Mouse, &c. Lond. 1598, 4to.
This droll or farce is in some old catalogues attributed to Shakspeare; also to Robert Greene. Other editions.—1610, 4to.—1613, 4to. Halliwell, in 1858, 1l. 7s. Rhodes, 263, 1l. 4s. Bright, 1l. 19s. A copy in the Grenville Collection.—1615, 4to.—1626, 4to. Boswell, 1618, 1l. 1s.—1634, 4to. Roxburghe, 4722, 1l. 6s.—1639, 4to. Roxburghe, 4723, 18s.—1668, 4to. Rhodes, 289, 13s. In the Malone Collection.—Amplified with new Additions, as it was acted before the Kings Majesty at Whitehall, on Shrove-sunday Night. Lond. for Francis Coles (1668) 4to. A-F 3 in fours, a list of Romances sold by Coles occupying F 1v.

MUDFORD, William. An historical Account of the Battle of Waterloo; comprehending a circumstantial Narrative of the whole Events of the War of 1815. Lond. 1817, imp. 4to.

Published in parts, with twenty-seven coloured plates. Duke of York, 5403, mor. 7l. 10s.

MUDGE, Thomas. A Description of the late T. Mudge's Timekeeper. Lond. 1799, 4to.
Roxburghe, 1577, 6s. 6d. Suppl. 631, 10s.
Narrative of Facts relating to Mudge's Timekeeper. Lond. 1792, 8vo.
Reply to Dr. Maskelyne's Answer to a Narrative of Facts, &c. with some Remarks of the Count de Brubl. Lond. 1792, 8vo.
See MASKELYNE, Nevil.

— W. An Account of the Operations carried on for accomplishing a Trigonometrical Survey of England and Wales. By William Mudge, Isaac Dalby and Thomas Colby. Lond. 1799, 1800, 1811, 4to. 3 vols. 29 plates, 3l. 3s.
See ORDNANCE SURVEY.

— Zach. An Essay towards a new English Version of the Book of Psalms, from the original Hebrew. Lond. 1744, 8vo.
A learned work. How highly Mr. Mudge was esteemed by Dr. Johnson may be seen in the character of him drawn by the latter in Boswell's Life of Johnson.

MUDIE, Alexander. Scotiæ Indiculum: or, the present State of Scotland; together with divers Reflections upon the ancient State thereof. Lond. 1682, 12mo. 4s.
Lloyd, 660, 5s.

— J. An Account of a grand Series of National Medals, during the reign of K. George III. Lond. 1820, 4to. With engravings of the entire series.
Brockett, 2272, 10s. 6d. Combe, 1413, 10s. 6d. Duke of York, 5404, mor. 19s.

— Robert. British Birds; or History of the Feathered Tribes of the British Islands. Lond. 1835, post 8vo. 2 vols. plates in colours.
Fifth edition, revised by W. C. L. Martin, Esq. Lond. Bohn's Illustrated Lib. 1854, post 8vo. 2 vols. with 52 figures of Birds, and 7 additional plates of Eggs, 10s.; or coloured, 15s.
First Lines of Zoology; in seven Parts. Lond. 1831.

MUDIE, J.—continued.
First Lines of Natural Philosophy.
Lond. 1832.
A popular Guide to the Observation of Nature. Lond. 1832, 12mo. front.—1841, 8s. 6d. (Vol. 77 of Constable's Miscellany.)
The Heavens. Lond. 1835, 12mo. coloured front. and vignette.—Second edit. Lond. 1847 12mo. 3s. 6d.
The Earth. Lond. 1837, 12mo. coloured front. and vignette.—Second edit. Lond. 1847, 12mo, 3s. 6d.
The Air. Lond. 1635, 12mo. coloured front. and vignette.—Second edit. Lond. 1847, 12mo. 3s. 6d.
The Sea. Lond. 1835, 12mo.—Second edit. Lond. 1847, 12mo. 3s. 6d.
Spring. Lond. 1837, 12mo. coloured front. and vignette.—New edit. Lond. 1847, 12mo. 3s. 6d.
Summer. Lond. 1837, 12mo.—New edit. Lond. 1847, 12mo. 3s. 6d.
Autumn. Lond. 1837, 12mo.—New edit. Lond. 1847, 12mo 3s. 6d.
Winter. Lond. 1837, 12mo.—New edit. Lond. 1847, 12mo. 3s. 6d.
Mental Philosophy ; a popular View of the Human Mind. Lond. 1838, 12mo. 7s.
Man, in his physical Structure and Adaptations. Lond. 1838, 12mo. coloured front. and vignette, 5s.
Man, in his intellectual Faculties and Adaptations. Lond. 1839, 12mo. coloured front. and vignette, 5s.
Man, in his Relations to Society. Lond. 1840, 12mo. coloured front. and vignette, 5s.
Man, as a moral and accountable Being. Lond. 1840, 12mo. 5s.
The World, familiarly but philosophically described. Being a Companion to Gilbert's Illustrated Map of the World. Lond. 1840, 12mo.
The Isle of Wight; its past and present Condition, and future Prospects. Lond. (1840), royal 8vo. 23 illustrations, 10s. 6d.; imp. 8vo. 1l. 1s.
Historical and Topographical Description of the Channel Islands. Lond. (1840), royal 8vo. 22 illustrations, 10s. 6d.; imp. 8vo. 1l. 1s.
China and its Resources, and Peculiarities; with a View of the Opium Question, and a Notice of Assam. Lond. 1840, fcap. 8vo. 3s. 6d.; with map coloured, 4s.
Lessons in Astronomy. Second edition. Lond. 1842, 12mo. front. 4s. 6d.
Domesticated Animals. Lond. Orr, (Rural Library), 1839, fcap. 8vo. 5s.
Gleanings from Nature. Lond. 1838. imp. 8vo. 1ds.
History of Hampshire. Lond. 1840, roy. 8vo. 2 vols, 2l. 4s., imp. 8vo. 4l. 4s.

Surveyor, Engineer, and Architect. Lond. Weale, 1841-2, 4to. 2 vols. 1l. 7s.
Winchester Arithmetic. Lond. 1841, 12mo, 4s. 6d.
All these works, which are of a popular character, are said to have been written to Robert Mudie's dictation.

MUFFET, Peter. A Commentarie vpon the Prouerbs of Salomon. Lond. 1596, 8vo.
Best edition.—Lond. 1592. Dedicated to 'Edward Earle of Bedford.' Heber, pt. 1s. 2076, 13s.

— Thomas, M.D. Insectorum, sive minimorum Animalium Theatrum. Lond. 1634, folio.
A work of some merit, consisting of 326 pages, with numerous wood cuts, wretchedly executed, published by Sir Theod. de Mayerne.—In English, by J. R. M.D. Lond. 1658, folio.
Silk Wormes and their Flies, lively described in Verse. Lond. V. S., for Nich. Ling. 1599, 4to. Caldecott, 16s. See M. T. P. 1431.
Health's Improvement, or Rules, comprising and discovering the Nature, Methods, and Manner of preparing all sorts of Food, used in this nation. Corrected and enlarged by Christopher Bennett, M.D. Lond. 1655, 4to. p. 296. Caldecott, 2l.
An account of Moufet or Muffet, will be found in Wood's Athen. Oxon.

MUGGLETON, Lodowick. The Acts of the Witnesses of the Spirit. Lond. 1699, 4to. 7s. 6d.
With portrait. Muggleton, who styles himself 'one of the two witnesses and true prophets of the only high, immortal, glorious God, Christ Jesus,' published other works.
A True Representation of the absurd and mischievous principles of the Sect commonly known by the name of Muggletonians. Lond. 1694, 4to. By J. Williams, D.D., Bp. of Chichester.

MUIR, William, D.D. Discourses explanatory and practical, on the Epistle of St. Jude. Glasg. 1822, 8vo.
Practical Sermons on the Character and Work of the Holy Spirit. Edinb. 1842, post 8vo. 6s.

MULART, Philip. Commissarius Generalis Pape Leonis X. in Anglia Dispensatio, etc. Lond. impressum per me, Richardum Pynson Regium Impressorem (1520). 4to.
A single broadside.

1628 MUL   MUL

Forma Absolutionem in Peccata varia.
Lond. Richardum Pynson Impress (circa.
1520), 4to. Heber, 1l. 16s.

MULBERRY.—Instruction for the
Increasing of Mulberrie Trees, and
the Breeding of Silke-wormes.
Lond. 1609, 4to.
A copy is in the British Museum.

MULCASTER, Richard. The first
Part of the Elementarie which entreateth chefelie of the right Writing of our English Tung. Lond.
1582, 4to. 10s. 6d.
'A work of considerable merit and utility, containing many pertinent observations on the structure of the language.'—
Dr. Drake. No second part is known to
have been printed. Reed, 807, 3l. 3s.
Bright, 6s. Geo. Chalmers, &c.
Positions wherein those primitive Circumstances be examined, which are necessarie for the Training up of Children,
either for Skil in their Bookes, or Health
in their Bodie. Lond. 1581, 4to. 10s. 6d.
Reed, 208, 1l. Caldecott, 9L. Bright, 19s.
Heber, pt. ix. 19s.—1591, 4to.
Catechismus Paulinus, in Usum Scholæ
Paulinæ conscriptus. Lond. 1599, 8vo.
Reprinted 1601, &c.
Poemata. Lond. 1599, 12mo.
In Mortem R. Elizabethæ Nænia consolans, Lond. 1603. Attached is an English translation. Lond. 1603, forming 1
vol. of 12 leaves 4to. A Copy of both
parts is in the British Museum.
This vol. contains an early specimen of
English blank verse. The author is supposed to be the Holofernes of Love's Labour Lost.

MULEY HAMET.—A true historical Discourse of Muley Hamets
Rising to three Kingdomes of Moruecos, Fes, and Sus. The Disvnion of the three Kingdomes, by
ciuill Warre. The Religion and
Policy of the More or Barbarian.
The Aduentures of Sir Anthony
Sherley. With other Nouelties.
Lond. 1609, sm. 4to. Black letter.
A copy is in the British Museum.

MULGRAVE, Lord. *See* PHIPPS,
Constantine John.

MULLALA, James. View of Irish
Affairs, 1688 to 1795. Dublin,
1795, 8vo. 2 vols.

MULLARD, Edward. The lamentable Ruines of the Towne of Shuffnall, alias Idsall, in Shropshire, by
Fire. Lond. 1591, 4to.

MULL'D Sack, or the Apologie of
Hic Mulier, 1620, portrait on Title.
In the Chimney Scuffle, 1662, 4to., is
the following curious allusion to this singular character, whose portrait has produced upwards of 40l.
'That old Mull'd Sack, who to such
fortunes crept,
And from a chimney to a Mannor
lept.'
A note stating that he changed his
name on payment of a sum of money by
his fellow chimney-sweepers. *See* HOLLAND'S BAZILIOLOGIA, and MAN-WOMAN,
p. 1469.
White Knights, 6l. 16s. 6d.

MULLER, John. Works on Fortification, &c. 8vo. 8 vols.
Formerly in high estimation. Roxburghe, 1699, 2l. 2s.
A Treatise concerning the elementary
Part of Fortification. Lond. 1746, 8vo.
Willett, 1741, 7s.—1756, 8vo. Lond. 1782,
8vo.
The Attack and Defence of fortified
Places, in three Parts. Lond. 1747, 8vo.
Enlarged by J. Landmann, Lond. 1791, 8vo.
A Treatise concerning the Practical
Part of Fortification, in four Parts. Lond.
1755, 8vo. Willett, 1745, 1l. 1s.
A Treatise of Artillery. With an Appendix or Supplement. Lond. 1757, 8vo.
Willett, 1743, 12s. With Supplement,
Lond. 1780-2, 8vo. 2 vols.
The Field Engineer, from the French
of M. Clairac, with Observations, &c.
Lond. 1759, 8vo.
Elements of Mathematics, Lond. 1748,
8vo. 3 vols. (in 1.)—Third edition, improved. Lond. 1765, 8vo. Plates. Willett,
3s. 6d.
A new System of Mathematics. Lond.
1769, 8vo. Willett, 1745, 6s. 6d.
Mathematical Treatise on Conic Sections. Lond. 1736, 4to.

MULLER, John von. A universal
History, in twenty-four Books.
Lond. 1818, 8vo. 3 vols. 16s.

— Karl Ottfried, Professor in
University of Göttingen. The
History and Antiquities of the
Doric Race. Translated by Henry
Tufnell and (Sir) George Cornewall
Lewis. Oxf. 1830, 8vo. 2 vols.

MUL MUN 1629

Second edition, Lond. 1859, 8vo. 2 vols. 1L. 6s.

History of the Literature of Ancient Greece, (translated by George Cornewall Lewis). Lond. Baldwin, printed for the Society of Useful Knowledge, 1840, 8vo. vol. I. (Vol. II. part I, being the continuation to p.128, all published, 369 pages) 7s.—New edition, completed from the manuscripts of Prof. Müller, the concluding portion translated by J. W. Donaldson, D.D. Lond., J. W. Parker & Son, 1858, 8vo. 3 vols. 1l. 16s.

Introduction to a Scientific System of Mythology. Translated by John Leitch. Lond. Longman, 1844, 8vo. 12s.

Ancient Art and its Remains, or a Manual of the Archæology of Art. New edition, with numerous additions. Translated by John Leitch. Lond. Bohn, 1852, 8vo. pp. 630, 12s.

"Like the author's 'Dorians,' and 'Mythology,' it has taken its place among the best classical interpretations produced by the modern German school of inquiry...... We have nothing approaching it for accuracy of research and subtlety of appreciation..."—*Athenæum.*

Dissertations on the Eumenides of Æschylus. Translated from the German. Lond. 1836, 8vo.—Second edition, revised. Lond. 1853, 8vo. 6s. 6d.

— Philip De Cometa Anni 1618 et brevis Descriptio Partus monstrosi ex Irlandia adducti. Lips. 1619, 12mo.

A copy is in the British Museum.

— S. Voyages from Asia to America, for compleating the Discoveries of the North-West Coast of America. To which is prefixed a Summary of the Voyages made by the Russians on the Frozen Sea, in Search of a North-East Passage. Translated from the High Dutch, with the Addition of three new Maps, by Thomas Jefferys. Lond. 1761, 4to. 6s.

— William. The Elements of the Science of War; containing the modern, established, and approved Principles of the Theory and Practice of the Military Sciences. Lond. Longman & Co., 1811, 8vo. 3 vols. 75 plates, pub. 3l. 3s. reduced 1l. 1s.

MULLINER, John. A Testimony against Periwigs and Periwig-making, and Playing on Instruments of Music among Christians, or any other in the Days of the Gospel, being several Reasons against these Things. 1677, 4to.
Hindley, pt. III. 596, 11s. Heber, pt. II. 6d.

MUMCHANCE, Mihil. *See* DYCE-PLAY. GREENE, R., p. 938.

MUN, Thomas. England's Treasure by forreign Trade. Lond. 1664, 8vo.

A valuable work containing some curious and interesting documents relative to the trade with East India.—1664.—1698. Roxburghe, 9340,3s.—1700.—1713.—Glasg. 1755.

MUNCHHAUSEN, Baron. Gulliver revived; or, the singular Travels, Campaigns, Voyages, and Adventures of Baron Munikhousen, commonly called Munchhausen. Third Edition, considerably enlarged and ornamented with a number of Views, engraven from the original Designs. Lond. 1786, 12mo.

—Oxford, 1786, 12mo. Fonthill, 2383, 17s.—1792, 12mo. with front. and eight plates.—Eighth edition, ornamented with twenty explanatory engravings, from original designs. Lond. Kearsley, 1799, 12mo., with plates by Rowlandson, (sometimes coloured).—Lond. T. Tegg. 1809, 12mo. Bliss, 9s.—Again, 1811.

Sequel to the Adventures of Baron Munchausen; humbly dedicated to Mr. Bruce, the traveller. Lond. Symonds, 1792, 12mo., with 20 plates, including the Baron's portrait.

The Surprising Travels, &c., (complete, with sequel, in 1 vol.) Lond. for the Booksellers, n. d. post 8vo., with portrait, and 28 plates from the original coppers.—New edition, (sequel abridged). Edinb. Black, 1858, 12mo. pp. 176, woodcuts, 1s.6d.—Illustrated by A. Crowquill. Lond. Trübner, 1859, post 8vo. pp. 200, woodcuts and coloured plates, 7s. 6d. Again, 1859.

The authorship of this Work has never been settled. It is attributed by Mr. West (Fifty Years' Recollections of an Old Bookseller,) to Mr. St. John, of Oxford; by Sir Charles Lyell (Principles of Geology, 1850, p. 44,) to Rudolph Eric Raspe, the editor of Leibnitz, and author of De Novis a mari natis insulis, &c. and various English works mentioned under his name. The book was intended as a satire on the Memoirs of Baron de Tott. The Sequel, as will be seen, is 'humbly addressed to Mr. Bruce, the Abyssinian traveller.'

MUNDA, Constantia. *See* SWETNAM, Joseph.

MUNDAY, Anthony. Works.

Notices of this writer will be found in Warton's History of English Poetry, Baker's Biographia Dramatica, and Ritson's Bibliographia Poetica.

The Mirrour of Mutabilitie; or principal Part of the Mirrour of Magistrates. Selected out of the Sacred Scriptures. Imprinted by J. Alde, 1579, 4to. In verse. A copy in the library of the Earl of Bute. Boswell, 1821, title wanting, 7l. Heber, pt. iv. 5l. 7s. 6d. G. Chalmers, ii. 620, 5l. 10s. Bright, wanting title and dedication, 1l. 2s.

The Fountaine of Fame erected in an Orcharde of amorous Adventures. Lond. 1580, 4to.

The Paine of Pleasure, profitable to be perused of the Wise, and necessary to be by the Wanton. Lond. for Henrie Car, 1580, 4to. In Verse. A copy in the Pepysian Library, Cambridge.

A breefe Discourse of the taking Edm. Campion, and divers other Papists in Barkeshire, &c. Lond. 1581, 8vo.

A Discoverie of Edmund Campion and his Confederates, their most horrible and traiterous Practises against her Majesties most royal Person and the Realm. Whereunto is added, the Execution of Edmund Campion, Ralph Sherwin, and Alexander Brian, executed at Tiborne, the 1st of December. Published by A. M. Lond. 1582, 16mo. Fifty-five leaves. Hibbert, 5555, morocco, 2l. 5s. Heber, pt. ix. 1l. 15s. *See* CAMPION, Ed.

A breefe and true Reporte of the Execution of certaine Traytours at Tiborne, the xxviij and xxx Dayes of May, 1582. Gathered by A. M. who was there present. Lond. 1582, 4to. BLACK LETTER. Ten leaves.—Lond. Charlewood, 4to. Sotheby, 1858, mor. 4l. 12s. 6d. Horner, 2l. 10s. Bright, 1l. 18s.—Reprinted, 1859, at the end of 'John a Kent' and 'John a Comber'—see SHAKESPEARE SOCIETY, in Appendix—where is also his 'View of sundry Examples reporting many strange Murthers.'

A breefe Answer made unto two seditious Pamphlets; [a Defence of Edmund Campion and his Accomplices, with Verses.] Lond. 1582, 18mo. 15s. pp. 76. Hibbert, 5554, 1l. 18s. Hindley, pt. ii. 1787, 5l. Bibl. Anglo-Poet. 941, 6l. 6s.

The English Romayne Life; discovering the Lives of Englishmen at Roome, the Orders of the English Seminarie, the Dissention betweene the Englishmen and the Welshmen, &c. &c. Lond. J. Charlewood, 1582, 4to. woodcuts. BLACK LETTER. Pp. 76, without dedication. Heber, pt. vi. 3l. 9s. Bindley, pt. ii. 1183, 4l. 8s.—1590, 4to. pp. 73. Inglis, 989, 1l. 6s. Heber, pt. vi. wanting a cut, 19s. This edition is reprinted in the seventh volume of the Harleian Miscellany.

A Watch-woord to Englande, to beware of Traytors and treicherous Practises, which haue beene the Ouerthrows of many famous Kingdomes and Commonweales. Lond. 1584, 4to. Forty-seven leaves. This volume contains some curious particulars relating to the history of Q. Elizabeth's imprisonment in the Tower during the reign of her sister Q. Mary. Steevens, 1711, 8s. Reed, 6177, 18s. Sir M. M. Sykes, pt. ii. 633, 4l. 8s. Inglis, 1615, 2l. 4s. Horner, 1l. 19s. Caldecott, 18s. Heber, pt. v. 1l. 8s. Gardner, in 1854, 1l. 5s. Bright, 1l. 12s.

Godly Exercise for Christian Families, containing an Order of Praiers for Morning and Evening, with a little Catechism betweene the Man and his Wife. Lond. 1586, 8vo. From Munsell's Catalogue, p. 66.

A Banqvet of Daintie Conceits; furnished with verie delicate and choyse Inventions to delight their Mindes who take Pleasure in Musique; and there-withall to sing sweete Ditties, either to the Lute, Bandora, Virginalles, or anie other Instrument. Lond. 1588, 4to. Contains sign. J iii. Bibl. Anglo-Poet. 457, 50l. Reprinted in the ninth volume of the Harleian Miscellany.

Archaioplutos: or the Riches of elder Ages. 1592, 4to. *See* THELIA, W.

The Masqve of the League and the Spanyard discouvered. Faythfully translated out of the French Copie printed at Tovrres by Iamel Mattayer. Lond. for Richard Smyth, 1592, 4to. Twenty-two leaves. At the end I. M. Published with a new title in 1605.

The Defence of Contraries. Paradoxes against common Opinion, debated in Forme of Declamations in Place of public Censure; calls to exercise yong Wittes in difficult Matters. Translated out of French by A. M. Lond. 1593, 4to. pp. 99. Perry, pt. ii. 867, 6s. Reed, 3484, 11s. 8s. Attributed by Mr. Halliwell to Thomas Lodge. *See* p. 1383.

The Life of Sir John Oldcastle. 1600. 4to. *See* SHAKESPEARE, William.

The Strangest Adventure that ever happened; containing a Discourse of the King of Portugall, Dom Sebastian. By Munday and Chettle, 1601, 4to. See SEBASTIAN, Bibl. Farmer, No. 8478. Heber, pt. vi. 17s.

The Downfall of Robert Earl of Huntington, afterwards called Robin Hood, &c. Lond. 1601, 4to. ascribed by Kirkman to Tho. Heywood. Rhodes, 1759, (3 leaves MS.) 2l. 11s. Inglis' Old Plays, 77, 9l. 12s. Roxburgh, 5070, 1ll. Evans, very fine Jan. 1825, 2l. 2s. Hibbert, 5677, 3l. 3s.

The Death of Robert Earle of Huntington. Lond. 1601, 4to. This is also ascribed by Kirkman to Heywood, but by Malone to Munday and Chettle. Rhodes, 1761, Pt. 6s. Inglis' Old Plays, 78, 12l. 15s. Roxburghe, 5071, 3l. 8s. Hibbert, 5624, 8l. 1s. North, 5l. 5s. Dright, 3l. 4s. Heber, pt. ii. 4l. Gardner, 1854, 5l. A very copious analysis of the two plays, the Downfal and Death, will be found in the first volume of Ritson's, and in Gutch's Robin Hood. Both were reprinted in 1828, cr. 8vo. by Mr. J. Payne Collier, who ascribes the latter to A. Munday and Henry Chettle.

The Triumphs of Reunited Britannia, performed in Honour of Sir Leonard Holliday, Knight, to solemnise his Entrance as Lorde Maior of the City of London, on Tuesday the 29 of October, 1605. Lond. Jaggard, 1605, 4to. A copy is in the Bodleian Library. Roxburghe, 5537, 2l. 14s. Heber. pt. ii. 3l. 3s. Reprinted in Nichols' Progresses of K. James I.

Falsehood in Friendship; Union's Vizard; or Wolves in Lambskins. Lond. 1605, 4to. Heber. pt. ii. 3l. 5s.

A briefe Chronicle of the Successes of Times from the Creation of the World to this Instant. Lond. 1611, 8vo. Bindley, pt. ii. 1730, 12s. Nassau, pt. i. 2217, 15s. Towneley, pt. ii. 748, 18s. See Dr. Dibdin's Library Companion, 182-3.

Chryso-thriambos: the Triumphes of Golde. At the Inauguration of Sir James Pemberton, Knt, in the Dignity of Lord Maior of London, on Tuesday the 29th of October, 1611, Lond. 1611, 4to. Bindley, pt. i. 2204, 7L.

Triumphs of Old Drapery; or the rich Clothing of England. At the Installation of Sir Thomas Hayes. Lond. 1614, 4to. No copy can be traced.

Metropolis coronata, the Triumphes of Ancient Drapery; or, rich Cloathing of England; in the second Yeares Performance. In Honour of the Advancement of Sir John Jolles, Knight, to the Office of Lord Maior of London, on the 30 Day of October, 1615. Lond. G. Purslue, 1615, 4to. Bindley, pt. iv. 512, 7L. 17s. 6d. Jolley, pt. vii. 895, 3l. Reprinted in Nichol's Progresses of King James I. In Gough's Collection, Bodleian Library.

Chrysanaleia, the golden Fishing: or, Honour of Fishmongers; applauding the Advancement of Mr. John Leman to the Dignity of Lord Mayor of London. Lond. G. Purslue, 1616, 4to. In the Marquis of Bath's Collection. Bindley, pt. iv. 513, 7L. 7s. Jolley, pt. vii. 897, 1l. 15s. Reprinted in Nichols' Progresses of King James I. vol. iii. pp. 196-207.

John a Kent, and John a Cumber. A Play. See Shakespeare Society, App. PALMERIN; SILVAYN, Alex.; STOW, John, &c.

MUNDAY, Major. Life and Correspondence of Admiral Lord Rodney. Lond. 1830, 8vo. 2 vols. portrait.

MUNDORUM EXPLICATIO, or hieroglyphical Figure of the World, a Poem by S. P. (Samuel Pordage). Lond. 1662, 8vo.

Nassau, pt. i. 2216, 1l. 2s. Roxburghe, 3403, 1l. 14s.

MUNDUS alter et idem. See HALL, Joseph.

MUNDUS et Infans. An Interlude. See ROXBURGHE CLUB, App.

MUNDUS muliebris or Ladies' Dressing-Room unlock'd. See EVELYN, John.

MUNDUS FOPPENSIS, or the Fop displayed; being the Ladies' Vindication, in Answer to Mundus Muliebris (in Verse). Lond. 1691, 4to.

Bliss, 3s. 6d.

MUNDY, John, Gent., Batchelor of Music, and one of the Organists of her Majesties (Queen Elizabeth) Free Chapel of Windsor. Songs and Psalmes composed into 3, 4, and 5 Parts, for the Vse and Delight of all such as either loue or learne Musicke. Lond. T. Este, 1594, 4to.

Dedicated to the Earl of Essex. See Burney's History of Music. A copy in the British Museum. Heber, pt. i. 4911, 1l. 9s.

MUNOZ, Don Juan Baptista. The History of the New World, translated from the Spanish, with Notes by the Translator, an engraved Portrait of Columbus, and a Map of Espanola. Lond. 1797, 8vo. vol. 1.

All printed. Hibbert, 5559, 4s. 6d.

MUNRO, Innes. A Narrative of the military Operations on the Coromandel Coast, 1780-4. Lond. 1789, 4to.
Pp. 392, with 12 plates. Foothill, 227, 12s.
The Defence of Innes Munro, Esq., Captain in the late Seventy-third, or Lord Macleod's Regiment of Highlanders, against a Charge of Plagiarism from the Works of Dr. William Thompson; with the original Papers on both Sides. Lond. 1790, 8vo.

— Gen. Sir Thomas. Life of Major-General Sir Thomas Munro, Bart. and K.C.B., late Governor of Madras. With extracts from his Correspondence and private papers. By the Rev. G. R. Gleig, M.A. Lond. 1830. 8vo. 3 vols. portrait.
Originally in 2 vols., vol. 3 being supplementary.

MUNSTER, Sebastian. A treatyse of the newe India, with other newes founde landes and Ilandes as well eastwarde as westwarde. Translated into English by Rycharde Eden. Lond. by Edward Sutton (1553), 16mo.
A copy is in the British Museum. The treatise contains M 6, in eights, besides title, dedication to the Duke of Northumberlande, a preface, and a table. Caldecott, 4l. 14s. 6d.
It appeared again, under the title of 'A briefe Collection and compendious Extract of straunge and memorable Thinges, gathered out of the Cosmographye of Sebastian Munster.' Lond. 1574, 16mo. A copy is in the British Museum. Heber, pt. vi. imperfect, 2l. The volume contains fol. 101, besides an address 'To the Reader.'
An Abridgement of Sebastian Munster's Chronicle. Lond. for Will. Marshall, 1542, 16mo.

MUNTER, D. A faithful Narrative of the Conversion and Death of Count Struensee, late Prime Minister of Denmark. To which is added, the History of Count Enevold Brandt, from the Time of his Imprisonment to his Death. The whole translated from the original German. Lond. 1773, 8vo. 4s. portrait.

An excellent work.—Lond. 1824, republished by the learned Mr. Rannell of Kensington.

MUNTZ, J. H. Encaustic: or Count Caylus's Method of Painting in the Manner of the Antients. To which is added, a sure and easy Method of fixing of Crayons. Lond. 1760, 8vo.
Edwards, 394, 5s. 6d. Baker, 86, morocco, 1l. 3s.

MURALT, M. Lettres sur les Anglois et les François et sur les Voiages. Col. 1725, 8vo. 2s.
Letters describing the characters and customs of the English and French nations, with an Essay on Travelling. Lond. 1726, 8vo.

MURALTO, Onuphrio. *See* WALPOLE, Horace.

MURATORI, L. A. A Relation of the Missions of Paraguay, now done into English from the French Translation. Lond. 1759, 8vo. 3s. 6d.
An entertaining work, describing the wonderful zeal and merit of the Jesuits in converting and civilizing the Indians.

MURCOT, John. Several Works, with his Life. Lond. 1657, 4to. portrait by Faithorne.
Grave, 394, 7s. 6d. Sotheby's in 1821, 2l. 9s. According to Wood, 'our author Murcot was a forward, prating, and pragmatical precisian.'

MURDER.—A brief Discourse of two of the most cruell and bloudie Murders, committed both in Worcestershire. Lond. 1583, 16mo.
A copy is in the British Museum.
A View of sundry Examples, reporting many strange Murders from that of M. Saunders by George Browne, and of Abel Bourn. Lond. W. Wright (1580), 4to. A copy is in the Lambeth Library.
Newes out of Germanie, of a cruel Murderer who had killed nine hundred three score and odd Persons. Ipswich, George Ive, 1584, sm. 8vo.
Sundry strange Murders lately committed, one on Master Page of Plymouth. Lond. Thos. Scarlet, 1591, 4to.
Parricide Papist, or cut-throat Catholike, a tragical Account of a Murder committed at Padstow, in the Counties of Cornwall, by a Papist killing his own Fa-

ther and then himself. 1606, 4to. BLACK LETTER, with woodcuts. King and Lochée's in April 1810, 9s.

Two horrible and inhuman Murders done in Lincolnshire by two Husbands upon their Wives, 1607, 4to. with a frontispiece. Nassau, pt. II. 19l.

Report of a Murder at Meaco. Lond. 1607, 4to. Caldecott, 1l. 2s.

True Report of the horrible Murther which was committed in the house of Sir Jerome Bowes, 1607, 4to. Nassau, pt. II. 163. 2l. 1ls. 6d.

True Relation of the most inhumane and bloody Murther of Master James, Preacher at Rockland in Norfolk, by his Curate, one Lowe, and consented to by his wife. 1609, 4to. Reed, 6047. Nassau, pt. II. 194, 2l. 1s. Heber, pt. vi. 12s.

Murder of Sir J. Tindall, Master in Chancery, by Bartram, 1616, 4to. with wood-cuts.

Relation of the horrible Murther of Sir T. Tyndal, 1616, 4to. Nassau, pt. II. 195, with the former tract, 3l. 5s.

Confession of the two Murderers, John de Paris and J. de la Vigne, of the Murder of Mr. Wely, Merchant Jeweller, 1616, 4to. with frontispiece. Bindley, pt. I. 2021, 1l. 3s.

Murther, Murther, or a bloody Relation howe Anne Hamton dwelling in Westminster, by Poyson, murthered her deare Husband, Sept. 1641, being assisted and counselled thereunto by Margaret Harwood, 1641, 4to. Nassau, pt. II. 351, 9s.

The Bloody Husband and cruell Neighbour, Historie of two Murthers, 1653, 4to. Bindley, pt. I. 1101, 4s.

Two horrid Murthers, one on Henry the IVth of France, the other on Charles the 1st, his Son in Law, 1661, 4to. with portrait of Charles by Mollar. King and Lochée's in March 1810, 16s. 6d.

An exact Narrative of the bloody Murder and Robbery committed by Stephen Eaton, Sarah Swift, George Rhodes, and Henry Richard, upon the Person of John Talbot, 1669, 4to. Nassau, pt. II. 354, 8s.

Bloody News from Clerkenwell, or a full Relation of a most horrid Murder committed by a Journey-Man Cooper, who killed his wife in a most cruel Manner. Lond. 1670, 4to.

Relation of the three inhumane Murders committed by William Bliss, alias Watts, upon the Bodies of W. Johnson his near kinsman, and Robert Porter. Also the Manner how he killed, and stripped a Drover's Boy, with his Sentence and Execution, 1672, 4to. Nassau, pt. II. 355, 7s.

The murderous mid wife with her roasted Punishment: being a true and full Relation of a Midwife that was put into an Iron Cage with sixteen wild Cats, and so roasted to Death, by hanging over a Fire,

for having found in her House of Office no less than sixty-two Children, at Paris, 1673, 4to. Nassau, pt. II. 357, 10s.

The penitent Murtheress, or an unnatural Crime miraculously discovered by Providence; being a Relation of an inhuman Murther committed by Margaret Bidley on her own Child, which she buried in a Cellar, at her Master's House in Wapping, &c., 1673, 4to. Nassau, pt. II. 358, 4s.

The penitent Murderer, a true Relation taken from the Mouth of Mr. W. Ivy, concerning the Murder by him committed upon the Body of William Pew, Servant to Sir Robert Leay, with the Reasons inducing him to that horrid Crime, his Resolution likewise to have killed the Maid: his taking away seven hundred pound in Bags, and his Manner of disposing of them, 1673, 4to. Nassau, pt. II. 360, 10s.

A true relation of a Robbery and Murder committed by five notorious Highwaymen near Colbrook. Lond. 1674, 4to.

A true Relation of the horrible bloody Murther and Robbery committed in Holborn, in the House of Esq. Bluck, one of the six Clarks, on the Body of Widdow Brown, an ancient Retainer to that Family, 1674, 4to. Nassau, pt. II. 363, 10s.

Murther will out; or a true and faithful relation of an horrible Murther committed thirty-three Years ago, by an unnatural Mother upon the Body of her own Child, 1675, 4to.

Three inhuman Mothers committed by one bloody Person, upon his Father, his Mother, and his Wife, at Cank in Staffordshire, and the Manner how he acted this bloody Tragedy. Together with his Examination, Confession, Condemnation, Execution, 1675, 4to. Nassau, pt. II. 364, 6s.

Full and true Relation of a most barbarous and cruel Robbery and Murder committed by six Men and one Woman near Wakefield in Yorkshire, on the Body of Anthony Wilson, 1677, 4to. Nassau, pt. II. 366. 9s.

Miraculous Revenge against Murder, 1677, 4to. Bindley, pt. III. 390.

Strange but true Relation of the Discovery of a most horrid and bloody Murder committed on the Body of a Traveller thirty Years ago in the West of England, and also how the Skull of the said murdered Person was taken up with a linnen Cap, thereon, &c., 1678, 4to. Nassau, pt. II. 368, 10s.

True Relation of the late most horrid and barbarous Murder, committed by eleven Phanaticks, upon the Person of James, late Lord Archbishop of St. Andrews; as likewise an Account of the Burning of New Prison in Clerkenwell, 1679, 4to. Nassau, pt. II. 370, 8s.

A true Relation of a horrid Murder committed upon the Person of Thomas Kidderminster, of Tapsley in Hereford, at the White Horse Inn in Chalmsford, 1654, with a true Account of the Discovery of the same, nine Years after, for which Moses Drayne, an Hostler in the said Inn, was executed, 1692, 4to. Reed, 2901. Lloyd, 1049, 5s. 6d. Nassau, pt. ii. 371, 15s.

A hellish Murder committed by a French Midwife on the Body of her Husband, January 27, 1687-8, for which she was burnt. Lond. 1688, 4to. with a frontispiece. Nassau, pt. ii. 372, 2l. 5s.

Examples of the Interposition of Providence in the Detection of a Murderer, 1752. Nassau, pt. i. 1079, 10s.

MURDOCH, John. The Dictionary of Distinctions, in three Alphabets. Lond. 1811, 8vo. 10s. 6d.

Containing, 1. Words the same in Sound, but of different Spelling and Signification. 2. Words that vary in Pronunciation and Meaning, as accentuated or unaccented. 3. The Changes in Sound and Sense, produced by the addition of the Letter E. Hollis, 963, 7s.

MURE, And. The Discoverie of St. Peter's Well at Peterhead. Edinb. 1636, 12mo.

A copy is in the British Museum.

— (or MOORE, which see). Sir William, of Rowallan. Caledons Complaint against infamous Libells, 1641, 4to.

Four leaves. Reprinted in 'Various Pieces of fugitive Scottish Poetry' edited by Mr. Laing.

True Crucifixe for true Catholickes. Edinb. 1629, 8vo.

The Cry of Blood and of a broken Covenant, Edinb. 1650, 4to. pp. 23. A poem on the death of K. Charles I.

The Historie and Descent of the Honse of Rowallane, by Sir W. Mure, Knight, of Rowallane, written in or prior to 1657. Glasgow, 1825, 12mo. 4s. LARGE PAPER, 8s.

MUNFORD, Nicholas. Fragmenta Poetica; or Miscellanies of Poetical Musings, Moral, and Divine. Lond. H. Moseley, 1850, 12mo.

With a portrait of the author. Bindley, pt. ii. 1960, 20l. Resold, Heber, pt. iv. 8l.

MURILLO, Bartolomé B. The Life of, compiled from the Writings of various Authors. Translated by Captain Edward Davies. Lond. 1819, post 8vo.

Hibbert, 5560, 5s. 6d. Nassau, pt. i. 2818, 10s.

MURMELLIUS, J. De Verborum Compositione. Lond. per Wm. de Worde, 1529, 4to.

Bindley, pt. iv. 1025, with eight Grammatical treatises by Whittinton, 3l. 13s.

MURMERER, A. (Lond.), printed by Robert Roworth, and are to be sold by John Wright, 1667, 8vo. 50 leaves. An anonymous production.

A copy at Bridgewater House.

MURPHY, Arthur. (Dramatic) Works. Lond. 1786, 8vo. 7 vols. Portrait by Cook, after Dance.

Now in little estimation. Roxburghe, 8964, 1l. 13s. Heber, pt. iv. 16s. Drury, 2763, with Murphy's Life, &c. of Garrick, and Essay on Dr. Johnson, 3l. 4s. Reed, 8799, 2l.

The Spouter, or the triple Revenge, a Farce, 1756, 8vo. Not in the collective edition of Murphy's works. Rhodes, 1784, 11s. Field, 543, 13s.

Memoirs of the Life and Writings of Miss Ann Elliot, Lond. 1769, 12mo. Field, 1176, 7s.

The Life of David Garrick, Esq. containing Anecdotes of his Contemporaries, a History of the Stage, Letters, Characters, Pieces of Poetry, Prologues, Epilogues, &c. Lond. 1801, 8vo. 2 vols. Portrait of Garrick. Reed, 5251, 7s. 6d. Roxburghe, 9307, 1l. 1s.

The Life of Arthur Murphy, Esq. by James Foot, Esq. his Executor. Lond. 1811, 4to. Portrait.

— Edmund. The present State and Condition of Ireland, but more especially the Province of Ulster, Lond. 1681. folio.

Bright, 5s. 6d.

— James Cavanah. Plans, Elevations, Sections, and Views of the Church of Batalha, in the Province of Estremadura in Portugal. To which is prefixed an introductory Discourse on the Principles of Gothic Architecture. Lond. 1795, imp. folio, pub. in 5 parts, with 27 plates, 2l. 8s.

Marquis of Townshend, 2449, 9l. 17s. Gosgh, 2500, 2l. 12s. 6d. Hibbert, 5681, 1l. 11s. New title, 1836.

Travels in Portugal; through the Provinces of Entre Douro e Minho, Beira, Estremadura, and Alem-tajo, in the Years 1789 and 1790. Consisting of Observations on the Manners, Customs, Trade, Public Buildings, Arts, Antiquities, &c. of that Kingdom. Lond. 1795, 4to. pp. 311, with 24 plates. Of the Sanskrit Inscription at p. 274, a translation is given p. 274-287, by the learned Orientalist Sir Charles Wilkins. Gough, 2609, 12s. Duke of York, 8407, 1l. 1s. LARGE PAPER. Garrick, 1570, 12s. 6d.

A general View of the State of Portugal; containing a Topographical Description thereof, in which are included an Account of the physical and moral State of the Kingdom; together with Observations on the animal, vegetable, and mineral Productions of its Colonies. The whole compiled from the best Portuguese Writers, and from Notices obtained in the Country. Lond. 1798, 4to. pp. 278, with 16 plates. Duke of York, 3408, 18s.

MURPHY, James Cavanah. The Arabian Antiquities of Spain; representing in 100 very highly finished line engravings by Le Keux, Finden, Landseer, G. Cooke, &c., the most remarkable Remains of the Architecture, Sculpture, Paintings, and Mosaics, of the Spanish Arabs, now existing in the Peninsula, including the Alhambra; the Mosque and Bridge at Cordova; the Royal Villa of Generaliffe; and the Casa de Carbon: accompanied by letter-press descriptions. Lond. 1816, atlas fol.

A SPLENDID WORK, with one hundred engravings, chiefly by Fittler and Landseer, from drawings made on the spot. Published at forty guineas, but of late years re-issued by Mr. H. G. Bohn, with 4 additional plates, at 8l. 8s. Drury, 3044, with the 4to. volume, (History of the Mahomedan Empire), rusus, 35l. 14s. Hibbert, 5662, with the 4to. volume, 18l.

The History of the Mahomedan Empire in Spain. Lond. 1816, 4to. map, 16s.

This volume, designed as an Introduction to the previous splendid volume of the Arabian Antiquities, was compiled by John Shakespear, Thos. Hartwell Horne, and William Milford, for the publishers.

MURRAY. James, Earl of. The Deploratioun of the cruel Murther of James, Erle of Murray, umquhile Regent of Scotland. 1570.

A broadside. In 26 eight-line stanzas, printed by Lekpreuik.

— Lady Charlotte. The British Garden; a descriptive Catalogue of hardy Plants, indigenous or cultivated in the Climate of Great Britain. Lond. 1799, 8vo. 2 vols.

— Lady Mary, of Stanhope. Memoirs of the lives and characters of the Rt. Hon. George Baillie of Jerviswood and of Lady Grissel Baillie. Edited by T. Thomson, Esq. Edinb. 1822, 8vo.

Privately printed.

Another edition reprinted for sale. Edinb. 1824, post 8vo.

— Alexander, D.D. History of the European Languages; or, Researches into the Affinities of the Teutonic, Greek, Celtic, Sclavonic, and Indian Nations. With a Life of the Author. Edinb. 1823, 8vo. 2 vols. 1l. 8s.

— Sir David, of Gorthy. Poems, containing the tragicall Death of Sophonisba, 1611.—Cœlia, or certaine Sonets.—Paraphrase of the CIV Psalme, 1615. Edinb. 1823. 4to.

Privately printed for the members of the Bannatyne Club, by Thomas Kinnear, Esq. See APPENDIX.

The Tragicall Death of Sophonisba. Cœlia, containing certaine Sonnets (with a separate title). Lond. 1611, 8vo. or sm. 4to. Bindley, pt. II. 1859, 33l. 12s.: resold Heber, pt. IV. 92. 9s. A copy is in the Bridgewater Collection.

Paraphrase of the CIV Psalme. 1615. 4to.

— George. Sermons and Treatises. Edinb. 1823, 8vo.

This work discovers very considerable learning, research, and originality.

— Hugh. ENCYCLOPÆDIA OF GEOGRAPHY, comprising a complete Description of the Earth, physical, statistical, civil, and political, exhibiting its Relation to the heavenly Bodies, its physical Structure, the natural History of each Country, and the Industry, Commerce, political Institutions, and civil and social State of all Nations. Lond. 1834, 8vo. 82 maps drawn by Sidney Hall, and 1000 other engravings, 3l.—Second edition. Lond. 1840, 8vo. 3l.—Third edition, with Supplement, 1844, 8l. Supplement separately, 1s.

Historical Account of Discoveries and Travels in Africa, from the earliest Ages to the present Time. Edinb. 8vo. 2 vols.—Second edition, enlarged. Edinb. 1818, 8vo. 2 vols.

Historical Account of Discoveries and Travels in Asia, from the earliest Periods to the present Time. Edinb. 1820, 8vo. 3 vols. 2l. 2s.

Historical Account of Discoveries and Travels in North America; with Observations on Emigration. Lond. 1829, 8vo. 2 vols. 1l. 7s.

History of British India. Edinb. Cab. Lib. 1832, 3 vols.—New edition. Edinb. 1849, 12mo. 5s.—Continued to 1854, Edinb. 1855, cr. 4to. 6s. 6d.

Inquiries respecting the Characters of Nations. Lond. 1808, 8vo.

Narrative of Discovery and Adventure in Africa. Third edition. (Edinb. Cab. Lib. vol. I.) 1842, 12mo. 2s. 6d.

Narrative, &c., in the Polar Seas and Regions, (Edinb. Cab. Lib. vol. II.)

British America. New edition, (Edinb. Cab. Lib. vol. xxv-xxvii.) 1843, 12mo. 3 vols. 7s. 6d.

The United States of America, from the earliest period. New edition, (Edinb. Cab. Lib. vol. xxxv-xxxvii.) 1844, 12mo. 3 vols. 7s. 6d.

MURRAY, Rev. James. History of Religion. Lond. 1764, 8vo. 4 vols.—Second edition. Lond. 1765, 8vo. 4 vols.

Select Discourses. 1765, 8vo. Brockett, 2151, 7s.

Essay on Redemption. 1768, 8vo. Brockett, 1252, 10s. 6d.

Sermons to Arses. 1768, 12mo. 2s. Brockett, 2153, 8s. 6d.

New Sermons to Asses. 1773, 12mo. 2s. Brockett, 2155, 15s.

Sermons to Doctors in Divinity. Being the second volume of Sermons to Asses. 177—, 12mo. 3s.

Sermons to Ministers of State. Lond. 1781, 12mo. Brockett, 2149, 7s.

Sermons to Asses, to Doctors in Divinity, to Lords spiritual, and to Ministers of State, with portrait of the author. Lond. W. Hone, 1819, 8vo. 5s.

History of the Churches of England and Scotland, from the Reformation to this Time. Newcastle, 1771, 8vo. 3 vols. Brockett, 2154, 1l. 1s.

Travels of the Imagination. Lond. 1778, 12mo. Brockett, 3156, 8s.

Lectures on Lords Spiritual; or Advice to the Bishops, concerning religious Articles, Tythes, and Church Power; with a Discourse on Ridicule. Lond. 1774, 8vo. 5s. Brockett, 2157, 6s. 6d.—1781, 8vo.

Lectures on the Lives of the Patriarchs, and the most remarkable Characters and Transactions recorded in the Book of Genesis. Newcastle, 1777, 8vo. 3 vols. Brockett, 2158, 8s.—Quoted as Lectures on Genesis.

Sermons on the Revelations. Lond. 1778, 8vo. Brockett, 2159, 6s. 6d.

History of the American War. Lond. 8vo. 4 vols.

—— John, late Secretary to the Young Pretender. Genuine Memoirs of. Lond. 1747, 8vo. 4s. Lloyd, 551, 7s. 6d.

—— Joseph. Reports of Cases tried in the Jury Court. Edinb. 1818-28, 8vo. 3 vols.

—— J. P. De Coloniis Scandicis in Insulis Britanicis et Maxime Hibernia Commentatio. Gott. 1771, 4to. 5s.

—— Lindley. Memoirs of his Life and Writings in a Series of Letters, written by himself, with a Preface and Continuation of the Memoirs, by Elizabeth Frank. York, 1826, 8vo. 9s. — Second edition. York, 1827, 8vo.

With a portrait and facsimile of an autograph letter.

ENGLISH GRAMMAR.

The first edition of this work appeared at York, 1795, in 1 vol. 12mo. It was followed, in 1797, by the Exercises (with Key). In the same year the Author published (price 1s.) a small Abridgment of the two Works conjoined. In 1808, he collected in a library edition (York, 2 vols. 8vo.) his previous labours on the subject, with large additions. All of these works were kept in print and constantly revised until his death in 1826.

ENGLISH GRAMMAR, adapted to the different classes of learners, with an Appendix containing rules for assisting the more advanced students to write with perspicuity and accuracy. York, 1795, 12mo.—Second edition, 1796, 12mo.—Fifth edition, improved, with an Appendix containing Exercises. York, 1799, 12mo.—Seventh edition, improved. York, 1801, 12mo.—

MURRAY, Lindley—continued.
Eighth edition, with considerable improvements. York, 1802, 12mo.—Ninth edition, with corrections and additions. York, 1804. 12mo. — Thirteenth edition, improved. York, 1806, 12mo.—Sixteenth edition, improved. York, 1807, 12mo.— Twentieth edition. York, 1810.—Sixtieth edition. Lond. Longmans, 1858, 12mo. 3s. 6d.

English Grammar...with an appendix. New York, 1818, 12mo.

Enlarged by the Rev. John Davis, A.M. Belfast, 1830, 12mo.

Key to ditto. Belfast, 1830, 12mo.

Murray's System of English Grammar, improved and adapted to the present mode of instruction in this branch of science. By E. Pond. Third edition. Worcester, (U.S.) 1830, 12mo.—Larger arrangement, by E. Pond. Sixth edition. Worcester, (U.S.) 1835, 12mo.

Murray's Grammar of the English Language, altered and abridged. Printed at the New England Institution, for the education of the blind. [Edited by S. G. H.] [Boston, U.S.] 1835, 4to.

Murray's Grammar simplified, by A. Flak. Hallowell, 1840, 8vo.

Pinnock's Improved edition of Murray's English Grammar, with the Exercises, for the first time incorporated, accompanied with Questions for Examination, and Explanatory notes. Lond. 18—, 12mo. 5s.

Murray's abridged English Grammar and Exercises. York, 1797.—One hundred and thirty-first edition. Lond. Longmans, 1859, 1s.

An Abridgment of Murray's English Grammar, by the Rev. J. Ellis, Junr. Lond. 1837, 16mo.

An Enlarged edition of Lindley Murray's abridged English Grammar, by the Rev Dr. Giles. Lond. 1829, 18mo. 1s. 6d. —New edition. Lond. Longman, 1859, 18mo. 1s. 6d.

(Questions on Lindley Murray's English Grammar, [adapted to the editions published at York, by Wilson and Sons, and in London by Longman & Co.] 12mo. 1820, and since.)

An Abridgment of Murray's English Grammar, improved with an enlarged appendix. By J. Harvey. Lond. 1841, 12mo.

Pinnock's Improved edition of Murray's Abridged English Grammar, with numerous Exercises; accompanied with Questions for examination, and explanatory notes. Lond. Holdsworth, 1830, 1s. 6d. —New edition. Lond. Piper, 1856, 18mo, pp. 208, 1s. 6d.—Again, 1858.

Alger's Abridgment of Murray's English Grammar, with an Appendix, &c. Boston, [U.S.] and Philadelphia, 1842, 12mo.

An Abridgment of Murray's English Grammar, in questions and answers, with explanatory notes, &c. By L. Ellis. Lond. [1853], 8vo.

Murray's English Grammar—designed for the younger classes of learners. A new edition, with copious Parsing questions. Edinb. Mackenzie, [1854] 12mo.

Murray's Grammar and Exercises abridged; comprising the substance of his large Grammar and Exercises, with additional Notes and Illustrations by G. Gartly. New edition. Lond. Tegg, 1859, 18mo. pp. 232, 1s. 6d.

Abridgment of Murray's English Grammar, with an Appendix.. A new edition, by the Rev. W. B. Smith. Lond. Tegg, 1860, 12mo. 1s.

FIRST LESSONS; an Introduction to English Grammar.

ENGLISH GRAMMAR (the large, or 'library'), comprehending the principles and rules of the language; illustrated by appropriate Exercises, and a Key. York, 1808, 8vo. 2 vols.—York, 1816, 8vo. 2 vols. —Fifth edition, York, 1824, 8vo. 2 vols. —Eighth edition, York, (Lond. Longman & Co.) 1853, 8vo. 2 vols. 1l. 1s.

English Exercises adapted to the Grammar. York, 1797, 12mo. — York, 1806, 12mo.—New edition, Lond. Longman & Co. 1860, 12mo. 2s.

Key to English Exercises. York, 1797, 12mo.—New edition, Lond. Longman & Co. 2s.

Key to the Exercises, adapted to Murray's English Grammar, &c. New York, 1819, 12mo.

The English Teacher, containing a new arrangement of Murray's Exercises and Key, &c. By J. Alger, Junr. Boston, (U.S.), 1834, 12mo.

Murray's English Exercises, revised by J. Alger. Boston, (U.S.), 1839, 12mo.

The Pupils' Assistant; consisting of Grammatical Questions taken from Murray's English Grammar. By F. I. C. Trenton. Dorchest. 1819, 12mo.

The first part of the Progressive Parsing Lessons, or an Introduction to Murray's Grammar. Maldon, 1833, 8vo.— Second part, Maldon, 1834, 8vo.

The Etymology and Syntax of Murray's English Grammar, systematically arranged, and containing additional matter, with Exercises and directions for Parsing. By C. Keunion. Lond. 1842, 12mo.

Lindley Murray examined; or, an address to ... teachers in which several... grammatical errors in Mr. Murray's Grammar are pointed out. By a Member of the University of Oxford. Lond. [1807] 8vo.

MURRAY, Lindley—*continued*.
Mr. Murray also published—

ENGLISH READER, or Pieces in Prose and Verse, selected from the best writers. York, 1799, 12mo. — Sixteenth edition, York, 1821, 12mo.—Twenty-sixth edition, Lond. Longman, 1858, 3s. 6d.

Sequel to the English Reader, or elegant Selections in Prose and Poetry. York, 1800, 12mo. — York, 1815, 8vo.— Eighth edition, Lond. Longman, 1843, 4s. 6d.

Introduction to the English Reader. York, 1801, 12mo.—New edition, Lond. Longman & Co., 1858, 2s. 6d.

The Pronouncing English Reader. The English Reader, by Lindley Murray, to which, by the aid of a Key, is scrupulously applied Mr. Walker's pronunciation of the classical proper Names, &c. By J. Alger, Junr. Boston, (U.S.) 1836, 12mo.

ENGLISH SPELLING BOOK; with Reading Lessons adapted to the capacities of Children. York, 1804, 12mo.—Tenth edition, York, 1810, 12mo.—Twenty-ninth edition, York, 1821, 12mo.—Fifty-third edition, Lond. Longman & Co., 1860, 1s. 6d.

First Book for Children. York, 1804, 12mo. Seventeenth edition, York, 1825, 12mo.—Twenty-fifth edition, Lond. (Longman & Co.) 1855, 6d.

Introduction au Lecteur Français, on recueil de pieces en prose et vers tirées des meilleurs écrivains. York, 1802, 12mo.—Second edition, York, 1800, 12mo.—Sixth edition, York, 1832, 3s. 6d.

THE POWER OF RELIGION ON THE MIND in Retirement, Affliction, and at the approach of Death, exemplified in the testimonies and experience of Persons distinguished by their Greatness, Learning, or Virtue. Second edition, York, 1787, 12mo.—Again, Birmingham, 1788, 12mo.—Sixth edition, enlarged, 1793, 12mo. — Eighth edition, corrected, Lond. 1795, 12mo.—Ninth edition, improved, York, 1795, 12mo.—Tenth edition, York, 1801, 12mo. — Eleventh edition, York, 1802, 12mo. — Thirteenth edition, enlarged and improved. York, 1807, 12mo. — Fifteenth edition, York, 1810, 8vo.—Sixteenth edition, York, 1812, 12mo.—Nineteenth edition, York, 1833, 5s.

Selections from Bp. Horne's Commentary on the Psalms. 1812, 12mo.

A Biographical Sketch of H. Tuke. York, 1815, 12mo.

A compendium of Religious Faith and Practice, designed for young persons of the Society of Friends. York, 1815, 12mo. — Second edition, (with an appendix of interrogatories, &c.) York, 1821, 12mo.— Third edition, York, 1832, 12mo.

The Duty and Benefit of a Daily Perusal of the Holy Scriptures in Families. York, 1817, 8vo. — Second edition improved, York, 1819, 8vo.

Sentiments of Pious and Eminent Persons on the pernicious tendency of Dramatic Entertainments, and other vain Amusements; with a few Reflections on the same subject subjoined. New edition, Lond. 1823, 12mo. [being No. 18 of Tracts published by the Tract Association of the Society of Friends]. New edition, Lond. 1835, 12mo.

A Memorial of the York Monthly Meeting of Friends respecting Lindley Murray. York, 1826, 12mo.

— Mungo. A Treatise on Ship-Building and Navigation. With an Appendix and Supplement. Lond. 1754, 4to.

A plain, ingenious, and perspicuous treatise. Willet, 1756, 11s. 6d.

— Rev. Richard. An Introduction to the Study of the Apocalypse. To which is added a brief Outline of prophetic History, from the Babylonian Captivity to the Commencement of the 19th Century. Dublin, 1826, 8vo.

— Sir Robert. *See* MANLEY, R.

— Thomas. The Literary History of Galloway; with Notices of the Civil History of Galloway till the end of the 13th Century. Edinb. 1822, 8vo. 10s. 6d.

A valuable literary history.

— Thomas. *See* MORAVIUS

— William. A short Treatise of Death, in nine Chapters; together with the enigmatick Description of old Age and Death, &c. in English-Meeter. Edinb. 1631, 12mo. In verse.

Gordonstoun, 1501, 11. 11s. 6d. Edinb. 1633.

— Hon. Mrs. of Aust. A Companion and useful Guide to the Beauties of Scotland, &c. Lond. 1799-1803, 8vo. 2 vols. 12s.—Third edition. Lond. 18—, 8vo. 2 vols.

MURRELL, John. New Booke of Cookerie, with the newest Art of Carving or Serving (1630) 12mo.

BLACK LETTER. Bright, 6s. 6d.—1638, Chalmers, 12s.

Two Bookes of Cookery and Carving. Lond. 1641, 12mo. BLACK LETTER. Bliss, 9s. *See* COOKERY.

MURTADI, —. The Egypt of Murtadi, the son of Gaphiphs; or a Treatise on or concerning the Pyramids and the Banks of the Nile. Translated from the French of Vattier by John Davies. Lond. 1672, 8vo.

A curious work of the middle ages, from an Arabic MS.

MUSÆ.—Musarum Deliciæ; containing more than a Century of royal Latine Anagrams, published by Arthur Pyne. Lond. 1635, 4to. *See also* FAGSTLE, and MENNIS, Sir John.

Heber, pt. iv. 1s.
Musarum Anglicanarum Analecta. Oxon. 1692-9, 8vo. 2 vols. 10s. 6d. LARGE PAPER. Williams, 1228, date 1699, morocco, 1l. 9s.
Editio secunda, priore multo emendatior. Oxon. 1699, 8vo. 2 vols. Edited by Joseph Addison. LARGE PAPER.
Editio tertia, priore multo emendatior. Lond. 1714, 12mo. 2 vols.—Vol. III. 1717.
Editio quarta, prioribus auctior. Lond. 1721, 12mo. 2 vols.
Editio quinta. Lond. 1741, 12mo. 3 vols. —Editio sexta, 1761, 12mo. 3 vols. Edited by Vincent Bourne. Drury. 2765, 7s. 6d.
Musæ Juveniles. (By W. Cooke). 1732. Heber, pt. II. 1l. LARGE PAPER. Drury, 2769, russia, 19s.
Examen Poeticum Duplex; sive Musarum Anglicanarum Delectus alter. Lond. 1698, 8vo.
Musæ Britannicæ e Poematis varii argumenti. Lond. 1711, 12mo. Heber, pt. vii. 2s.
Musæ Anglo-Rhetoricæ, sive Eclogæ quatuor, una cum Ode ab Alexandro Pope Anglice conscripta, a Rhetoribus Collegii Anglicani Bregis Latine redditæ. Anno, 1763.
Musæ Seatonianæ. Cambridge Prize Poems (English). Lond. 1772, 8vo. 8s. 6d. Edited by Isaac Reed.—1793, LARGE PAPER; twelve copies printed. Steevens, 1016, 5s. — New edition (to 1806). Cambridge, 1817, or. 8vo. 2 vols.
Musæ Etonenses (edente J. Prinsep). Lond. 1755, roy. 8vo. 2 vols. Bishop of Ely, 610, 1l. 6s. Bindley, pt. II. 1610, 1l. 2s. White Knights, 2276, 1l. Garrick, 1664, 1l. 18s. Drury, 2765, russia, 18s.
Musæ Berkhamstadienses; or Poetical Prelusions by some young Gentlemen of Berkhampstead School. Eng. and Lat. Berk. 1794, 8vo.
Musæ Etonenses; seu Carminum Delectus nunc primum in lucem editus (a Gul. Herbert). Eton. 1795, roy. 8vo. 2 vols. This is a second series, not a reprint of the former work. White Knights, 2579, 1l. 1s. Drury, 2763, 2l. 8s. LARGE PAPER, Sir M. M. Sykes, pt. II. 472, 1l. 10s. Bindley, pt. II. 1611, 1l. 9s. — Editio altera aucta; opera et cura Gul. Herbert. Etonæ, 1817, 8vo. 2 vols. in 2. Drury, 2767, russia, 2l.

Musæ Etonenses; Series Nova fasciculus I. edidit R. Okes, 1866. 8vo. 5s.

Musæ Cantabrigienses; seu Carmina quædam Numismate aureo Cantabrigiæ ornata. Lond. in æd. Valp. 1810, 8vo. pp. 232, 10s. 6d. Edited by Bishop Blomfield, and The. Rennell.

Musæ Hydesmæ. Hyde Abbey Prize Poems, Winton, 1828, 12mo.

MUSÆUS.—Musæi, Moschi et Bionis quæ extant omnia, quibus accessere quædam selectiora Theocriti Eidyllia, Gr. et Lat. Autore Davide Whitfordo. Lond. 1655, 4to.

With two fine plates by Faithorne. Heath, 3410, 10s. 6d. LARGE PAPER. Nassau, pt. II. 574, 5s.—With new title only, 1659, 4to. with the two plates. White Knights, 2984, morocco, 1l. 6s.
Musæ amatoriæ, sive Musæi Poema de Herone et Leandro, e Græca in Latinam Linguam translatum, Authore C(arolo) B(lake). 1694, 4to. 8s. 6d.
The divine Poem of Musæus (Hero and Leander). First of all Bookes; translated according to the Originall by George Chapman. Lond. Isaac Jaggard. 1616.
An exceedingly rare and diminutive volume, its size being only two inches in height by one broad. Dedicated to Inigo Jones. A copy is in the Bodleian Library, probably unique. It is reprinted in Mr. Hooper's recent edition of Chapman's Classical Translations. See MARLOWE, Christ.
The second Part of the Loves of Hero and Leander, by Hen. Petowe. 1598, 4to.
Musæus, or the Loves of Hero and Leander. With Annotations upon the Originall. By Sir Robert Stapylton, Knight. Lond. 1647, 12mo. pp. 142, with a frontispiece by Marshall. A close and laboured translation. Nassau, pt. I. 2321, 6s. Bibl. Anglo-Poet. 721, 1l. 10s. Heber, pt. iv. 7s. —Oxford, 1645, 4to.
Hero and Leander, paraphrased into English heroick Verse, by Alex. Stopford Catcott. Oxford, 1715, 8vo. Dedicated to Lady M. W. Montagum.
The Loves of Hero and Leander, by Mr. James Sterling; with new Translations from Greek Authors by another Hand. Lond. 1728, 12mo. front.

MUSÆUS—*continued*
Hero and Leander, translated from the
Greek by G. Baily. Cambridge, 1747,
4to.
Hero and Leander, translated by the
Rev. Lawrence Eusden. Glasgow, 1750.
Originally published in Dryden's Miscellany Poems, 1716, vol. vi.
The Loves of Hero and Leander; a poetical Translation from the Greek of Musæus, by J. Stade. Lond. 1753, 4to. 2s. 6d.
An indifferent translation.
Hero and Leander; a Poem from the
Greek of Musæus (by E. B. Greene). Lond.
1774, 4to. 2s.
Musæus, the Loves of Hero and Leander
(in English verse, with the Greek text).
Lond. 1797, 4to. pp. 53, with two titlepages. Privately printed for G. C. Bedford, the translator. Bindley, pt. III. 573,
10s. Reed, 6994, 6s— ON VELLUM.
Hero and Leander, a Tale. Translated
from the Greek of the ancient Poet Musæus. With other Poems. By Francis
Adam, Surgeon. Lond. 1822, 8vo. pp. 50.
See ANACREON. BION et MOSCHUS. Poetæ Græci minores. Translations of Musæus will be found in Mrs Behn's Miscellany, 1685; by Lewis Theobald in "The
Grove," 1721, 8vo.; in the Poetical Works
of James Sterling, Dublin, 1734; in a Miscellany by M. Lock, 1728; by — Hussell
in Fenton's Oxford and Cambridge Miscellany; in Merritt's Miscellaneous Translations, 1802, &c. &c.

MUSCIPULA. *See* HOLDSWORTH,
Ed.

MUSCULUS, Wolfgangus. Common Places of Christian Religion,
with two other Treatises, one of
Othos, and an other of Vauryo.
Lond. 1563, folio.
Dedicated to Archbishop Parker, by
the translator, John Man.— Lond. R.
Wolfe, 1563. Pnttick, June 10, 1858,
2l. 10s.—Lond. Byneman, 1578, 4to. Dedicated to Sir Chr. Hatton by R. D.
Of the lawful and the unlawful Usuris
amongest Christians. Lond. n.d. 18mo.
Heber, pt. vi. 6s. 6d.
The Temporisour, that is to say, the
Observer of Tyme, translated into Jagilelse by R. P. 1555. Imprinted Anno
Domini 1555, 16mo. Heber, pt. v. 13s.
11 7, in eights.—Edinb. 1584, 16mo.
An Exposition of the fifty-first Psalme,
translated by John Stockwood. Lond.
1586, 16mo.
A Treatise of Matrimony and Burial of
the Dead, translated by Richard Nyce.
16mo. White Knights, 2851, russia, 17s.
See HERMAN of Cologne.

MUSES (the) Cabinet (a Collection of Poems). Lond. for F. Coles
(circa 1666), 8vo.
The Muse of New-market; or, three
Farces acted before the King. Lond. 1680,
4to.
The Muses Farewell to Popery and
Slavery. Lond. 1689, Bibl. Anglo-Poet.
480, 15s. 6d.—Second edition, with large
additions, most of them never before
printed. Lond. 1690, 8vo. pp. 256. Bibl.
Anglo-Poet. 481, 10s. 6d. Heber, pt. iv.
8s.
Muses Mercury, or Monthly Miscellany
for 1707. 4to. Nassau, pt. ii. 275, 8s.
Reed, 2486. 6s. 6d. Bindley, pt. iii. 682,
7s. In the number for June will be found
a republication of the Nut Brown Maid.
Muses Library. *See* COOPER, E.
Muse in Masquerade; or, a Collection
of Riddles, serious and comic. Lond. 1745,
8vo. Nassau, pt. i. 2323, 9s.; 2334, 16s.
The Muse in Good Humour; a Collection
of Poems and Comic Tales by the most
eminent Poets. Lond. 1745, 12mo. 2 vols.
plates.—1751, 12mo, 2 vols. ll. 1s. (*Some
of the Tales are very free.*)
The Muses Vagaries, or the Merry
Mortal's Companion, by Solomon Grundy
and Margery Merry-pin. Lond. 1745, two
parts.
Muses Choice, or the Merry Fellow
and Winter Evening's Companion, being
a Collection of Wit and Humour. 1754.
Hibbert, 5565, 13s. 6d.
The Muse in a Moral Humour; being a
Collection of agreeable and instructive
Tales, Fables, Pastorals, &c. by several
Hands. Lond. 1757-8, 12mo, 2 vols. 6s.
Vol. i, pp. iv. and 252. Vol. 2, pp. iv. and
242.
The Muses Mirror; being a Collection
of Poems by Gray, Churchill, Colman,
&c. &c. &c. Lond. 1778, sm. 8vo. 2 vols.
Nassau, pt. i. 2401, 5s. Bindley, pt. ii.
1603, 19s.
See JESTS. SONGS.

MUSEUM.—The Museum, or literary historical Register. Lond.
Dodsley, 1746-7, 8vo. 3 vols.
A valuable collection of Essays, &c. by
Lowth, Warton, Spence, Horace Walpole,
&c. Reed, 2587, 6s. Bindley, pt. i. 1582,
10s. 6d. Heath, 1712, 11s.

MUSEUM CRITICUM, or Cambridge Classical Researches. Camb.
1814-25, 8vo. 8 parts, or 2 vols.
Drury, 2770, 1l. 10s. With new title,
Camb. 1826, 8vo. 2 vols. 15s.
For Continuation, *see* PHILOLOGICAL MUSEUM.

MUSEUM MINERVÆ. *See* GER-
BIER, Sir B., p. 880. KINASTON,
Sir F., p. 1269.
Corona Minervæ, or a Masque, presented before Prince Charles, his Highnesse the Duke of Yorke his Brother, and the Lady Mary his Sister, the 27th of February, at the Colledge of the Musæum Minervæ. Lond. 1635, 4to. Gordonstoun, 6*l*. 4*l*. 10*s*. Rhodes, 86, with the Const. of the Mus. Min. 1636, 2*l*. 6*s*. Bindley, pt. ii. 156, with the Const. of the Mus. Min. 1636, 5*l*. 5*s*.

MUSEUM of Painting and Sculpture, or Collections of the Principal Pictures, Statues, and Bas-Reliefs in the Public and Private Galleries of Europe; containing 1150 outline plates by Réveil, with descriptions in French and English by Duchesne, 17 vols. cr. 8vo. Paris and Lond. 1829-1833, 6*l*. 6*s*.

MUSEUM BRITANNICUM. *See* BRITISH MUSEUM.

MUSGRAVE, Sir Richard. Memoirs of the different Rebellions in Ireland. Dublin, third edition, 1802, 8vo. 2 vols.
A party work, abounding in misrepresentations. Drury, 2777, 18*s*.— Dublin, 1801, 4to. pp. 638 and 210. Roxburghe, 4830, 14*s*. 6*d*. THICK PAPER. Duke of York, 8409, 19*s*. Sotheby's, 1657, 2*l*. 9*s*.— Dublin, 1801, 8vo. 2 vols. Fonthill, 3069, 12*s*.

— Samuel, M.D. Two Dissertations. 1. On the Grecian Mythology. 2. An Examination of Sir Isaac Newton's Objections to the Chronology of the Olympiads. Lond. 1782, 8vo. 6*s*. 6*d*.
Published after the author's death by Th. Tyrwhitt. LARGE PAPER. Willett, 1749, &c.

— William, M.D. Antiquitates Britanno-Belgicæ, præcipue Romanæ, Figuris illustratæ. Iscæ Dunm. 1711, 16, 19, 20, 8vo. 4 vols.
Heath, 6557, 1*l*. 1*s*. Dent, pt. ii. 17, 10*s*.
Each of the volumes is apparently independent. The titles are respectively as follows:—
Julii Vitalis Epitaphium cum Notis criticis Explicationesque V. C. Hen. Dodwelli et Commentario Guil. Musgrave. Quibus accedit illius ad Cl. Graevium de Puteolana et Italana Inscriptionibus Epistola. Iscæ Dunm. MDCCXI, with Index and plates.
Gulihelmi Musgrave Regiæ Societatis Utriusque Sociii Geta Britannicus. Accedit Domus Severianæ Synopsis Chronologica et de Icunculâ quondam M. Regis Alfredi Dissertatio. Iscæ Dunm. MDCCXVI, plates.
Antiquitates Britanno-Belgicæ, præcipue Romanæ, figuris illustratæ, tribus voll. comprehensæ; quorum i. de Belgio Britannico. ii. De Geta Britannico. iii. De Julii Vitalis epitaphio: Quibus accedit Appendix. Auctore Guilh. Musgrave, Belga, &c. Iscæ Dunm. MDCCXIX. port. and plates.
Antiquitatum Britanno-Belgicarum Volumen quartum (quod tribus ante editis est Appendix.) Auctore Guilh. Musgrave, M. B. U. S. Iscæ Dunm. MDCCXX. port. and plates.

— William, Esq. A brief and true History of Sir Robert Walpole and his Family, from their Original to the present Time. Lond. 1738, 8*s*. portrait.
Pp. viii. and 78, published by Carll.— 1745, 8vo.

MUSH, Job. Declaratio Motuum ac Turbitationum inter Jesuitas et Sacerdotes Seminariorum in Anglia. Rothom. 1601, 4to.

MUSIC.—The Praise of Music, 1586. *See* CASE, John.
A shorte Introduction to the Science of Musick. Lond. John Day, 1570, sm. 8vo.
A new Booke of Tabliture, containing sundrie easie and familiar Instructions, shewing howe to attaine to the Knowledge to guide and dispose thy Hand to play on sundry Instruments, as the Lute, Orpharion, and Bandore: together with divers new Lessons to each of these Instruments. Whereunto is added, an Introduction to Pricksonge, and certaine familiar Rules of Descant. Collected out of the best Authors professing the practise of these Instruments. Lond. 1588, oblong 4to.
Musica Sacræ. 1608.
Musick (Gospel). Certaine Reasons, by way of Confutation, of singing Psalmes in the Letter. Lond. 1644, 4to. 80 pages.
Musick (Gospel), or the singing of David's Psalmes, &c. vindicated [against the previous Pamphlet] by N. H., D.D. Unto which is added, The Judgments of our worthy Brethren of New England, teaching singing of Psalmes, as it is

Music—*continued.*
learned by and gravely set forth in their Preface &c. to the singing Psalms set forth by them. Lond. 1644, 4to.
Select Musical Ayres and Dialogues. Lond. 1652. fol.—A second edition, much enlarged, in 1653, fol. Bindley, pt. II. 1056, 4l. 14s. 6d.—A third edition in 1659, fol.—The last edition was put forth in 1663, without any alteration beyond the title, as the first Book of the Treasury of Musick.
Musick's Recreation on the Lyra Viol; being a choice Collection of new and excellent Lessons for the Lyra Viol, both easie and delightfull for all young Practitioners. To which is added, some few plain Directions as a Guide for Beginners; Lond. 1650, oblong small 4to.
A Musick Lector, or the Art of Musick discours'd of. Lond. 1667, 4to. Sotheby's, in Feb. 1821, 10s.
A philosophical Essay of Musick. 1677, *See* NORTH, Hon. Roger.
The Treasury of Musick, containing Ayres and Dialogues. Composed by Mr. Henry Lawes and other excellent Masters. In three books. Lond. 1669, small fol.
Choice Ayres, Songs, and Dialogues, composed by several Gentlemen of his Majestie's Musick and others. Five books. Lond. 1676-84, small folio.
The Theater of Musick, or choice Collection of the best Songs. In four Books. Lond. 1685-7, folio, 2l. 2s.
Cantus; Songs and Fancies. *See* FORBES, John, pp. 615-16.
Comes Amoris, or the Companion of Love; being a choice Collection of the newest Songs now in use. Four books. Lond. 1687, small folio.
Harmonia Sacra, or Divine Hymns and Dialogues; composed by the best Masters of the last and present Age. The Words by several learned and pious Persons First book. Lond. 1688, small folio. Second book, 1693.—Second edition of the first book, —Third edition, very much enlarged and corrected, 1714.—Second edition of the second book, very much enlarged and corrected. 1714.
Banquet of Musick, a Collection of the newest and best Songs sung at Court and Publick Theatres. Six books. 1688-92, folio.
Thesaurus Musicus: being a Collection of the newest Songs. Five books. Lond. 1693-6, small folio.
Deliciæ Musicæ; being a Collection of the newest and best Songs sung at Court and the publick Theatres. Five books. Lond. 1695-6, small folio.
Mercurius Musicus, or the monthly Collection of new teaching Songs, compos'd for the Theatres and other occa-

sions. Lond. 1699, oblong 4to.—Lond. 1700-2, small folio.
MONTHLY MASKS of VOCAL MUSIC, containing all the choicest Songs by the best Masters, made for the Play-houses, publick Consorts, and other Occasions, with a Thorough Bass to each Song, and most of them within the compass of the Flute. Lond. J. Walsh, folio. Published monthly in sixpenny parts, from 1703 to 1709, each part containing 4 pages of music and an engraved title-page. The whole forming 3 vols. with general title-pages. Dr. Kitchiner's copy, the only one he had ever seen, contained only the years 1707-9.
The Merry Musician; or a Cure for the Spleen. Lond. 1716, 12mo. vol. 1, 536 pp.; vol. 2, no date, 180 pp.; vol. 8, 1730. This collection of songs, with the music, was completed (according to Sir John Hawkins) by Lewis Hamondon, a singer in the Anglo-Italian operas of the period.
The Divine Companion, or David's Harp New Tun'd; being a choice Collection of new and easy Psalms, Hymns, and Anthems, compos'd by the best Masters. Fourth edition. Lond. 1722, 8vo.
Musical Miscellany. Lond. 1729-31, 8vo. 6 vols. with fronts. Hibbert, 5568, 12s. Nassau, pt. I. 294, 14s. Inglis, 1050, 1l. 1s. Bindley, pt. II. 1591, H. 18s. Goldsmid, 513*, 3l. 8s.
The Modern Music Master, or the Universal Musician. Lond. 1780, 8vo.
The Merry Mountebank, or the Humerous Quack Doctor; being a certain Cure for Hypochondriac Melancholy, a choice Collection of old Songs, compiled with great Judgment, *Secundum Artem*, by Timothy Tulip of Fidler's Hall, revised by several knowing Musicians, Poetasters, and Ballad Mongers. Lond. 1733, 8vo.
The Musical Entertainer, engraved by George Bickham, jun. [A Collection of Songs by various Composers, edited by John Frederick Lampe, and engraved on copper-plates, with a vignette on every page. Copies are frequently mutilated by print-collectors.] Lond. 1737-8. 2 vols. fol.
Songs in the Opera of Flora, with the humorous Scenes of Hob, design'd by ye celebrated Mr. Gravelot, and engrav'd by G. Bickham, jun. Lond. 1737, 8vo.
Amaryllis, consisting of such Songs as are most esteemed for Composition and Delicacy, and sung at the public Theatres and Gardens. All chosen from the Works of the best Authors, with Engravings on every page. Lond. n. d. 4to.
A Miscellany of Lyric Poems, the greatest part written for and performed in the Academy of Music [held in the Apollo.] Lond. 1740, 8vo.—Another impression in the same year, with the words between brackets omitted from the title-page.

MUSIC—continued.

Thesaurus Musicus; a Collection of two, three, and four part Songs. Lond. n. d. [circa 1748], 2 vols. folio. Contains a copy, one of the earliest printed, of 'God, save the King,' which is described as 'a Loyal Song, sung at the Theatres Royal.'

Universal Harmony, or the Gentleman and Lady's Social Companion; consisting of a great variety of the best and most favourite English and Scots Songs, Cantatas, &c. With a curious design, by way of head-piece, expressive of the sense of each particular song, all neatly engraved on 4to. copperplates. Lond. 1746, 4to.

A short Explication of such Words or Terms as are made use of in Vocal and Instrumental Music. (Circa 1748), 8vo. Title and 17 leaves wholly engraved.

An Antidote against Melancholy; being a Collection of fourscore Merry Songs, the Music of all of them entirely new. Lond. 1749, small 8vo.

The Cathedral Magazine, or Divine Harmony; being a Collection of the most valuable and useful Anthems in score. Lond. n. d. 3 vols. 4to.

Harmonia Sacra, or Divine and Moral Songs, with Hymns and Anthems by several eminent Masters, and an easy Introduction to Singing. Lond. n. d. small 4to.

Flores Musicæ, or the Scots Musician; a Collection of the most celebrated Scots Tunes. Edinb. 1773, folio.

An Essay upon Tune, being an Attempt to free the Scale of Music and the Tune of Instruments from Imperfection. [By John Maxwell.] Lond. 1781, 8vo. plates.

Observations on the present State of Music in London, by W. Jackson of Exeter. 1791, 8vo. pp. 33. See BURNEY, Dr. C. HAWKINS, Sir John. CLIO. ESTE, Mich. MULLINAR, John.

MUSICIANS.—A Musical Directory for the Year 1794, containing the Names and Addresses of most of the Professors of Music, with the Parts they respectively perform, &c. and an historical Sketch of the Academy of Ancient Music. Lond. 1794, 8vo.

An Essay or Instruction for learning the Church Plain Chant; to which are added, various Hymns, Anthems, Litanies, Motists, &c. Lond. 1709, 12mo.

Vocal Anthology, or the Flowers of Song; being a Selection from the Vocal Music of Italy, Germany, France, Switzerland, and England, the whole adapted to English words; also, twelve original vocal Compositions. Lond. 1824, 4to.

A Dictionary of Musicians from the earliest Ages to the present Time. Lond. 1824, 8vo. 2 vols.

Musical Biography, or Lives of eminent Composers, &c. by the Rev. W. Dingley. Lond. , 8vo. 2 vols.

The British Musical Miscellany, or the delightful Grove; being a Collection of celebrated English and Scotch Songs, by the best Masters, set for the Violin, German Flute, the common Flute, and Harpsichord. 8vo. 4 vols. In 2, 1l. 11s. 6d. The text and music both engraved.

Popular Music of the Olden Time; a Collection of ancient Songs, Ballads, and Dance Tunes, illustrative of the National Music of England, with short Introductions to the different Reigns, and Notices of the Airs from Writers of the sixteenth and seventeenth Centuries; also a short Account of the Minstrels, by W. Chappell, Esq., F.S.A.; the whole of the Airs harmonized by G. A. Macfarren. Lond. n. d. imp. 8vo. This edition contains about 400 airs.—A previous edition, under the title of National English Airs, 2 vols. imp. 8vo. contains only 245 airs.

Musical Reminiscences of an old Amateur, chiefly respecting the Italian Opera in England for fifty Years from 1773. Lond. 1827, 12mo. 6s. Written by the Earl of Mount Edgcumbe. The first edition was privately circulated among the friends of the noble author.—Fourth edition, continued to the present time, and including the Festival in Westminster Abbey. Lond. 1834, 12mo.

Concert-Room and Orchestra Anecdotes. Lond. 1825, 12mo. 2 vols. Compiled by Dr. Busby.

A Ramble among the Musicians of Germany, with Remarks upon Church Music [by Edward Holmes]. Lond. 1828, post 8vo.

MUSICAL LIBRARY: a Selection of the best Vocal and Instrumental Music, both English and Foreign, edited by W. Ayrton (of the Opera House), comprising upwards of 400 pieces of Music by the most eminent Composers. Lond. C. Knight, 1843, folio. 8 vols. 4l. 4s. Reduced, Bohn, 1l. 10s.

MUSICAL CABINET AND HARMONIST: a Collection of Classical and Popular Vocal and Instrumental Music; comprising Selections from the best productions of all the great Masters; English, Scotch, and Irish Melodies; with many of the National Airs of other Countries; the whole adapted either for the Voice, the Pianoforte, the Harp, or the Organ, with Pieces occasionally for the Flute and Guitar. 4 vols. small folio. Lond. C. Knight, 1845, 2l. 2s. Reduced, Bohn, 16s.

MUSICAL CLASSICS, published by Chas. Knight, 1843, folio, only four parts published, viz.:

GLEES: a Selection of forty-four Compositions by Arnold, Atterbury, Baildon,

1644 MYD MYV

MUSIC—*continued.*
Battishill, Boyce, Callcott, Cooke, Danby, Fitzherbert, Hayes, Horsley, Lock, Mornington, Mouchelos, Nares, Paxton, Spofforth, Smith, Stevens, and Webbe; arranged for Soprano, as well as other Voices. Pianoforte Accompaniment, 2 parts, 15s.

MADRIGALIAN FEAST, a Collection of twenty Madrigals, for Soprano and other Voices, selected chiefly from the Works of the great Masters of the sixteenth and seventeenth Centuries, viz. Bennett, Cavendish, Croce, Converai, Dowland, Ford, Gastoldi, Orlando Gibbons, Morley, Palestrina, Ward, Weelkes, and Wilbye. Pianoforte Accompaniment. Folio, 1848, 7s. 6d.

HAYDN'S TWELVE CANZONETS, together with 'O Tuneful Voice,' the Spirit Song, and four German Songs, with English Words, folio, 1848, 5s.

The three preceding articles are included in the Musical Library, printed from the same stereotype plates.

MUSICAL GEM; a Collection of nearly three hundred modern and favourite Songs, Duets, Glees, &c. by the most celebrated Composers of the present day, adapted for the Voice, Flute, or Violin, edited by John Parry. Lond. 1845, 8vo. title, and Illuminated front. 10s. 6d.

Musical Antiquarian Society.—Handel Society.—Motett Society. *See* APPENDIX.

See GLEES, SONGS.

MUSKET and Pike. *See* MILITARY.

MUSTAPHA, by Sir F. Greville. *See* BROOKE.

MUSŒUS, Marcus. M. Musuri Carmen in Platonem. Isaaci Casauboni in Josephum Scaligerum Ode. Accedunt Poemata et Exercitationes utriusque Linguæ. Auctore S. Butler. Appendicis Loco subjiciuntur Hymnus Cleanthis Stoici, Clementis Alexandrini Hymni duo, Henrici Stephani Adhortatio ad Lectionem novi Fœderis. Conscripsit atque edidit Sam. Butler. Cantabrigiæ, 1797, 8vo.

Drury, 634, 4s. The Poem of Musæus will also be found in Foster's Essay on Accent and Quantity.

MYDDELMORE, Henry. A Translation of a Letter by a Frenche Gentilwoman, upon the Death of Lady Elenor of Roye, Princesse of Conde. Lond. John Daye, 1564, 16mo.
BLACK LETTER. In the Grenville Collection.

MYLES, William. A chronological History of the Methodists, from their Rise in 1727. Lond. 1813, 8vo. 8s.

The first edition was published at Liverpool in 1799, 12mo.

MYLN, Alexander. Vitæ Dunkeldiensis Ecclesiæ Episcoporum, a prima Sedis Fundatione ad Annum 1515, ab Alexandry Myln ejusdem Ecclesiæ Canonico conscripta. Edinb. 1823, 4to.

With arms and facsimile letter emblazoned. Seventy-five copies printed, at the expense of the Bannatyne Club, under the superintendence of Thomas Thomson, Esq. An Appendix was printed in 1831. *See* BANNATYNE CLUB.

MYNSHULL, Geffray, of Grayes-Inne, Gent. Essayes and Characters of a Prison and Prisoners. Lond. 1618, 4to. woodcut on title.

Pp. 48, with title, dedication, &c. 8 more. Steevens, 986, 5s. 6d. Gordonstoun, 1585, 1l. 9s. Roxburghe, 6682, 13s.—With some new Additions, Lond. 1638, 4to. A to H—2, in fours; title containing a woodcut. Reed, 2537, 15s. Nassau, pt. ii. 376, 1l. 1s. Brand, 2l. 10s.—Edinb. 1831, post 8vo. 4s. with cut by Bewick. Dibd. 6s.

MYRROUR. *See* MIRROR.

MYSTERIES, The, of Love and Eloquence. *See* PHILLIPS, Edw.

Mysteries and other Latin Poems of the XIIIth and XIVth Centuries, edited by Tho. Wright. Lond. Nichols, 1838, 8vo. 9s.

A Collection of English Miracle Plays or Mysteries, edited by W. Marriott. Basel, 1838, 8vo.

See Abbotsford Club. CHESTER Mysteries. COVENTRY Mysteries. DIGBY Mysteries. HONE, William. Roxburghe Club, and Shakespeare Papers, Appendix. SHARPE, Tho. Surtees Society. TOWNELI Mysteries. YORK Mysteries.

MYTHOMYSTES, a Survey of true Poesy; with Narcissus, a poetic Tale. Lond. 1843, 4to.
Bindley, pt. III. 537, 2l. 12s.

MYVYRIAN ARCHAIOLOGY of Wales. *See under* WALES.

N.

A.—NIXON, Anthony.
N. A. — See NEWMAN, Arth.
N. B. The inverted initials of Nicholas BRETON.
N. C. NABY, Cornelius. NEB, C.

N. E. Caesar's Dialogue, or a familiar Communication containing the first Institution of a Subject in allegiance to his Soveraigne. Lond. T. Purfoot, 1601. 12mo.
Heber, presentation copy to Q. Elizabeth, with portrait on back of title, 1l. 1s. Bright, 5s.

N. F. B. i. e. Francis NERO. See NIGER, F. Bossentinus.

N. G. A Geographicall Description of the Kingdom of Ireland, according to the five Provinces and thirty-two Counties, &c. Lond. for Geo. Emerson, 1642, 4to.

N. H. See NICHOLAS, Henry.

N. I. A perfect Catalogue of all the Knights of the most noble Order of the Garter. Whereunto is prefixed a short Discourse touching the Institution of the Order, &c. by I. N. Lond. 1661, 4to.
Twenty leaves.

N. K. The History of Miss Katty N——, containing her amorous Adventures and various turns of Fortune in England. Lond. n. d. 8vo.

N. M. See NEDHAM, March. These letters were also employed as a signature by William CAMDEN, being his *Anals*.

N. N. America; or, an exact Description of the West Indies. By N. N. Lond. 1666, 12mo.
With a map. Jadis, 109, with portrait of Columbus inserted, 14s. Nassau, pt. I. 81, 9s. Caldecott, 9s.—1657, 12mo.

N. N. Romes Follies, or the amorous Fryars, a Comedy. Lond. 1681, 4to.
Roxburghe, 1776, 5s.

N. N. See WARNER, Lady.

N. N. An Epistle of a Catholike young Gentleman, being imprisoned, to his Father, a Protestant, who commanded him to set down in Writing what were the Motives that induced him to become a Catholike. Doway, 1629, 12mo.

N. N. The Progenis of Catholicks and Protestants. Rouen, 1638, 12mo.
Supposed to have been written by Jas. Anderton, who also assumed the name of Brerely. See p. 222. Sotheby, July 1855, 1l. 10s.

N. N. The English Nunne, being a Treatise wherein (by way of Dialogue) the Author endeavoureth to draw young and unmarried Catholike Gentlewomen to embrace a votary religious Life. 1642, 12mo.
Heber, pt. vii. 6s. 6d.

N. N. Treatise of the Nature of Catholick Faith and Heresie. Rouen, 1657, sm. 8vo. 1s.

N. N. Sylvester Jenks made use of this signature. See Dod's Ch. History. Peter Talbot, Archbp. of Dublin, and Nicholas French, Bp. of Ferns, also used the same.

N. R. See NICOLS, Richard.

N. S. The Loyal Garland. Lond. 1671, 12mo.
Black letter, pp. 128. Bibl. Anglo-Poet. 431, russia, 6l. 6s.

1046 NAB

N. S. Aula Lucis, or the House of Light. Lond. 12mo.
Heber, pt. ix. 8s. 6d.

N. T. Analecta. See ROOTH, David.

N. T. See NEVILLE, Thomas.

N. T. G. See NEWTON, Thomas, Gentleman.

N. W. A Perswasion to godlie Purposes. By W. N. Lond. 1583, 16mo.
D 4, in eights.

N. W. Barley-breake, or a Warning for Wantons. Written by W. N., Gent. Lond. Simon Stafford, 1607, 4to.
Pp. 32. In verse. Dedicated to 'Mistresse Ella. C.' This work is attributed to Nicholas Breton. Bibl. Anglo-Poet. 41, 10l. 10s. resold Saunders' in 1818, 2l. 8s.; again, Bright, 1l. 1s. Bindley, pt. iv. 169, 7l. 7s. Perry, pt. l. 619, 5l. Nassau, pt. ii. 381, 6l. 2s. 6d. Heber, pt. iv. 2l. 16s.

N. W. See NEADE, W.

NABBES, Thos. Plays and Poems. Reed, a collection of, in one vol. 4to. &10, 1l. 7s. Roxburghe, 6905, 2l. 2s. Bindley, pt. iii. 778, 3l. 8s. North, pt. iii. 513, 3l. 10s.
Microcosmos, a morall Masque. Lond. 1637, 4to. 'A very poetic rhapsody.'—W. Gifford. Hibbert, 5789, 11s. Roxburghe, 5549, 10s. Rhodes, 1772, 13s. Heber, pt. ii. 5s. 6d. Reprinted in the new edition of Dodsley's Old Plays.
Hannibal and Scipio, a Tragedie. Lond. 1637, 4to. Boswell, 1966, 4s. 6d. Roxburghe, 5548, 10s. Rhodes, 1771, 18s. Inglis' Old Plays, 97, 11s. Heber, pt. ii. 10s. 6d.
Covent Garden, a pleasant Comedie. Lond. 1638, 4to. Steevens, 1256, 6s. Heber, pt. ii. 13s. Rhodes, 1768, 2l.—1620, 4to. Inglis' Old Plays, 51, 14s. Roxburghe, 5547, 10s. 6d. Heber, pt. ii. 3s. 6d.
The Spring's Glorie, a Masque. Lond. 1638, 4to. Roxburghe, 5550, 13s. Inglis' Old Plays, 80, 1l. 13s. Caldecott, 16s. Bindley, pt. iii. 779, 1l. 10s—Together with Sundry Poems, Epigrams, Elegies, and Epithalamiums. Lond. 1639, 4to. Lloyd, 931, 14. 12s. Strettell, 1421, 13s. Hibbert, 5790, 19s. Rhodes, 1778, 1l. 19s. Heber, pt. ii. 1l. 10s.
Presentation on the Prince's Birth Day. Lond. 1638, 4to.
Tottenham Court, a Comedie. Lond. 1638, 4to. Roxburghe, 5551, 10s. 6d. Rhodes, 1769, 2l. 2s. Heber, pt. ii. 12s.—1639, 4to.—1718, 12mo.
Entertainment on the Prince's Birth Day, a Masque. Lond. 1639, 4to.

NAL

The Unfortunate Mother, a Tragedie never acted, but set down according to the intention of the Author. Lond. 1640. Roxburghe, 5552, 9s. Rhodes, 1775, 18s. Heber, pt. ii. 4s.
The Bride, a Comedie. Lond. 1640, 4to. Roxburghe, 5546, 6s. 6d. Rhodes, 1774, 10s. Heber, pt. ii. 3s. 6d.

NADIR CHA.—A genuine History of Nadir-Cha, formerly call'd Thamas Kouli-Khan, done into English (from the Persian). Lond. 1741, 8vo.—Lond. 1746, 12mo.
Prefixed is an introduction, containing a description of Persia and India.
See FRASER, James. JONES, Sir Wm.

NAILE, Robert. A Relation of the royal Entertainment given to Queen Anne, in June 1613, at the Citie of Bristol. Lond. 1613, 4to.
Reprinted in Nichols' Progresses of K. James I. from a copy in the Bodleian Library.

NALSON, John, LL.D. An impartial Collection of the great Affairs of State, from the Beginning of the Scotch Rebellion in 1639 to the Murder of K. Charles I. Taken from authentick Records, and methodically digested. Lond. 1682-3, folio, 2 vols. frontispieces by White, 2l. 2s.
In the historical part Nalson is an partial in his narrative on the side of the King, as Rushworth is on the side of the Parliament; and they are both to be consulted with great allowance for their party. 'Nalson is worth turning over, being full of vastly curious and valuable authentic pieces.'—By. H'arburton. Willett, 1675, 1l. 8s. Heath, 4434, 1l. 16s. Heber, pt. x. 1l. 3s. Collation,—Vol. i. Title and dedication to the King, 8 leaves; the introduction, lxxix pp.; the table, 15 pp.; the work, 817 pp. with a frontispiece by White, and the mind of the frontispiece (a poem of 97 lines).—Vol. ii. Title, epistle dedicatory to K. Charles II. 8 leaves; the introduction, xll pp.; the work, 920 pp.; a table, 22 pp.; also a frontispiece, M. W. sculp. and the meaning of the frontispiece (a poem of 34 lines).
A true copy of the Journal of the High Court of Justice for the trial of K. Charles I., with an introduction. Lond. 1684, folio. With an allegorical caricature frontispiece. Bindley, pt. ii. 1495, 7s. 6d. Sir M. M. Sykes, pt. ii. 540, 10s.
The Common Interest of King and People. Lond. 1678, 8vo.

Foxes and Firebrands, or a Specimen of the Danger and Harmony of Popery and Separation. [The first part written by Mr. N., the second by Robert Ware.] Dub. 1682, 8vo.

NALUS, Carmen Sanscritum, è Mahabharato edidit, Latine vertit, et Adnotationibus illustravit Franciscus Bopp. Lond. 1819, royal 8vo. 1l. 1s.

Nala and Damayanti, and other Poems, translated from the Sanscrit into English verse, with critical and mythological Notes by the Rev. H. H. Milman, M.A. Oxford, 1835, imp. 8vo.

NANI, Battista. The History of the Affairs of Europe in this present Age, but more particularly of the Republic of Venice, englished from the Italian, by Sir Robert Honywood, Knight. Lond. 1673, folio.

Pp. 574, besides dedication to Sir Walter Vane, Knight, and title. Roxburghe, 1825, 17s. 6d.

NANTES.—The History of the famous Edict of Nantes, translated into English (by — Cooke). Lond. John Dunton, 1694, 4to. 2 vols.

Marquis of Townshend, 1250, 1l. 2s. For this work the publisher obtained a license from Queen Mary, dated 30 June, 1693. The only book for which she ever granted a license. See Dunton's Memoirs, vol. I. page 153.

NANTWICH.—An historical Account of Nantwich; with a particular Relation of the remarkable Siege it sustained in the grand Rebellion in 1643. Shrewsbury, 1774, 8vo.

Pp. 88, and errata, one page. Lloyd, 14l. 14s.

NAOGEORGUS, Thomas. The Popish Kingdome, or Reigne of Antichrist. Written in Latine Verse by Thomas Naogeorgus, and englyshed by Barnabe Googe. Lond. 1670, 4to.

Two editions same year; one with name of H. Denham only, the other H. Denham for Richarde Watkins. Bibl. Anglo-Poet. 310, imperfect, 4l. 4s. resold at Saunders' in 1818, 1l. 16s. Heber, pt. viii. 8l. 1s. Perry, pt. I. 2348, 2l. 17s. North, 4l. 14s. Brand, 4l. 15s. Heber, pt. iv. 3l. 5s. A notice of the work will be found in Brydges' Censura Literaria.

See GOOGE, Barnaby.

NAPIER, Archibald, Lord. Memoirs of Archibald, first Lord Napier, (written by himself). Edinb. 1793, 4to.

Privately printed. Roxburghe, 23NF 6s. 6d.

— John, of Merchiston. WORKS. A plaine discovery of the whole Revelation of St. John, set downe in two Treatises; whereunto are annexed certaine Oracles of Sibylla, agreeing with the Revelation, and other Places of Scripture. Edinb. Waldegrave, 1593, 4to. This curious and learned work, which produced a great sensation when first published, has been translated into the French, Dutch, and German languages. Bindley, pt. iii. 793, 13s. Inglis, 990, 15s.—Lond. for J. Norton, 1594, 4to. A corrected edition. Bliss, 11s.—Edinb. A. Hart, 1611, 4to.—Lond. [Edinb.] 1611. Gordonstoun, 1846, 1l. 1s. Gardner, in 1854, 10s. 6d.—Edinb. 1645, 4to.

Napier's Narration, or an Epitome of his Book on the Revelation. Lond. 1641, 4to.

Mirifici Logarithmorum Canonis Descriptio. Edinb. Hart, 1614, 4to. The first treatise on Logarithms. White Knights, 8130, russia, 1l. 5s. Roxburghe, 1619, 5s. Constable, 773, 15s. Geo. Chalmers, 9s.

Copies of this volume are occasionally met with, dated in 1619, containing his posthumous work, Mirifici Logarithmorum Canonis Constructio. Edinb. 1619, 4to.

De Arte Logistica. See BANNATYNE CLUB, Appendix.

Rabdologiæ, seu Numerationis per Virgulas, Libri duo. Edinb. 1617, 12mo. Constable, 671, 14s. Hibbert, 5693, 5s. Roxburghe, 1530, 17s. Inglis, 1055, morocco, 11s.

Arcanum Suppot. Arithmet. Lugd. 1658, 8vo. Roxburghe, 1531, 1l. 5s.

See BARCOS, Henry.

Life of John Napier (Inventor of Logarithms) by Lord Buchan and Dr. Minto. 1778, 4to. portrait.

Memoirs of John Napier of Merchistan, his Lineage, Life, and Times; with a History of the Invention of Logarithms. By Mark Napier. Edinb. 1834, 4to. ports. and plates, pub. at 8l. 8s.

NAPIER, Macvey. Remarks illustrative of the Scope and Influence of the philosophical Writings of Lord Bacon. Edinb. 1818, 4to.

Not printed for sale. (From the Royal Society of Edinburgh's Transactions.)

Lord Bacon and Sir Walter Raleigh. Camb. 1853, post 8vo.

Professor Napier was editor of the Supplement to the fourth, fifth, and sixth editions of the Encyclopædia Britannica, 1824, 6 vols, 4to.; and also of the seventh edition, in which the Supplement was incorporated. See ENCYCLOPÆDIA.

— Lieut.-Col. William F. P. History of the War in the Peninsula and in the South of France, from the year 1807 to 1814. Lond. 1828-40, 8vo. 6 vols. plates, 6l.

Second edition, (with additions, consisting of the controversial pamphlets, placed at beginning or end of the volumes) Lond. 1834-40, 8vo. 6 vols, 6l. (Of this demy 8vo. edition, a fourth was published of vol. 1, a third of vols. 2 and 3, a second of vol. 4, and only one edition of vols. 5 and 6.)

New edition, revised by the author. Lond. 1851, and again 1853, post 8vo, 6 vols. 3l. Re-issued in 12 shilling parts, 1856.

Observations on some Passages in Lieut.-Col. Napier's History of the Peninsular War. By Percy, Viscount Strangford. Lond. 1828, 8vo. pp. 85.

Reply to Lord Strangford's Observations. By Lt.-Col. W. Napier. Lond. 1828, 8vo.

Further Observations by Percy, Viscount Strangford. Lond. 1828, 8vo.

Notes on the Campaign of 1808-9, in reference to Lieut.-Col. Napier's History. By Lieut.-Col. T. S. Sorell. 1828, 8vo.

Beresford's Letter to Long, 8vo. 2s.

Long's Letter in reply to do. 8vo. 3s.

Strictures on certain passages of Col. Napier's History, which relate to the military opinions and conduct of Gen.Lord Viscount Beresford. Lond. 1831, 8vo.

Further Strictures, &c., to which is added a Report of the Operations during the Campaign of 1811. By M. General Sir Benjamin D'Urban. Lond. 1832, 8vo. map.

A Reply to various Opponents, together with Observations Illustrating Sir John Moore's Campaigns. By W. F. P. Napier, C.B., Colonel, &c. Lond. 1832, 8vo. 2s.

A Justification of the third volume of the History of the Peninsular War, forming a Sequel to his Reply to various Opponents. 1833, 8vo. pp. 51, 1s. 6d.

Beresford's Refutation of Col. Napier's Justification of his 3rd vol. 1834. 8vo. 6s.

Napier's Letter to Beresford, 1834. 8vo. 1s. 6d.

Long's reply to Beresford's Second Letter. 1835, 8vo. 2s.

Counter Remarks to Mr. D. M. Percival's remarks by Col. Napier, 1835. 8vo. 1s. 6d.

Percival's Remarks with Postscript, in reply to the above. 1835, 8vo. 2s. 6d.

Observations on the Corn Law, 1841, 8vo.

The Conquest of Scinde, with some Introductory passages in the Life of Major General Sir Charles J. Napier. Lond. Boone, 1845, 8vo. 1l.—Second edit., Lond. Westerton, 1857, 8vo. 12s.

The History of General Sir Charles Napier's Administration of Scinde, and Campaign in the Cutchee Hills. With Maps and Illustrations. Lond. Chapman and Hall, 1851, 8vo. 16s. Second edition, Lond. Westerton, 1853, 8vo. 12s.—Third edition. 1857, 8vo. 12s.

The Scinde Policy; a few comments on Major General Napier's Defence of Lord Ellenborough's government. Lond. 1845, 8vo.

English Battles and Sieges in the Peninsula. Lond. Westerton, 1853, post 8vo. 10s.—Second edition. Lond. Murray, 1856, crown 8vo. 10s. 6d.

NAPOLEON I. Mémoires pour servir à l'Histoire de France, écrits à Sainte-Hélène sous la Dictée de l'Empereur Napoléon, par les Généraux qui ont partagé sa Captivité et publiés sur les MSS. entièrement corrigés de sa Main. Lond. 1823-4, 8vo. 7 vols. 2l. 8s.

This work is divided into two parts, the first entitled 'Mémoires' dictated to Generals Gourgaud and Montholon, consists of 4 vols., the second is entitled 'Notes et Mélanges' and consists of 3 vols. containing Napoleon's remarks on the principal works, &c. relating to him published during his life. A fifth volume of the Memoires, called the 3rd of Montholon, was published in 1829; but being chiefly on the Politique du Directoire, had little sale, and is seldom found with the set. It was not comprised in the English translation.

Memoirs of the History of France during the Reign of Napoleon, dictated by the Emperor at St. Helena to the Generals who shared his captivity, and published from the original Manuscripts corrected by himself. Vols. 1 and 2 dictated to General Gourgaud; vols. 3 and 4 dictated to the Count de Montholon. Forming 4 vols.—Historical Miscellanies dictated to the Count de Montholon, 3 vols. Lond. Colburn, 1823-4, 8vo.—Together 7 vols. maps and plans.

Memorial de Sainte-Helene: Journal de la Vie Privée et des Conversations de l'Empereur Napoléon a Sainte Hélène par le Comte De Las Cases. Lond. Colburn, 1823, 8vo. 8 parts or vols. generally bound in 4.

Journal of the Private Life and Conversations of the Emperor Napoleon at St. Helena, by the Count De Las Cases. Lond. 1823, 8vo. 4 vols. in 8 parts.

The Life of Napoleon Bonaparte, by M. de Bourrienne, his private Secretary. With Notes, now first added, from the Dictation of Napoleon, at St. Helena, from the Memoirs of the Duke of Rovigo, of General Rapp, of Constant, and nu-

NAPOLEON I.—*continued.*
merous other authentic Sources. Lond. Colburn, 1820, 8vo. 4 vols. pub. at 2l. 12s. —Third edition. Lond. Colburn, 1831, post 8vo. 3 vols. port. and illustrations, 15s.
Translated by Mesars. Lond. Whittaker, 1831, (Constable's Miscellany), 4 vols. 18mo. 14s.—New edition, compressed into one volume. Lond. Bohn, 1852, 12mo. port. and front. 5s. 6d.
History of Napoleon, by George Moir Bussey, illustrated by Horace Vernet. Lond. Thomas, 1840, roy. 8vo. 2 vols. with 468 woodcuts, pub. 2l. 2s., reduced 1l. 4s.
History of Napoleon, edited by R. H. Horne, illustrated by Raffet and Horace Vernet. Lond. Tyas (for Vizitelly), 1841, roy. 8vo. 2 vols. with 501 woodcuts, pub. 2l. 2s. reduced 1l. 1s.
History of Napoleon, from the French of Lanrent de l'Ardeche, with 419 illustrations by Horace Vernet. Lond. Willoughby, n. d. 8vo. 10s. 6d.
The Life of Napoleon Buonaparte, by William Hazlitt. Lond. Templeman, 1836, 5vo. 4 vols. 2l. 10s. Second edition, revised by his Son. Lond. 1852, post 8vo. 4 vols. portraits and vignette title-pages, 14s.
Memoirs of Napoleon, his Court and Family, by the Duchess d'Abrantes, [Madame Junot]. Lond. Bentley, 1831, 8vo. Reissued, 1836, 8vo. 2 vols. 16 portraits and plates, 1l. 1s.
Napoleon Gallery, or Illustrations of the Life and Times of the Emperor, in a Series of 69 etchings engraved on steel by Revell, from the most celebrated pictures produced in France during the last forty years. Lond. 1837, post 8vo. 1l. 1s. —New edition, same plates. Lond. Bohn, 1846, post 8vo. 10s. 6d.
Memoirs of the Private Life, Return, and Reign of Napoleon in 1815, by Fleury de Chambonlon. Lond. 1820, 8vo. 2 vols.
The Last Days of Napoleon: Memoirs of the last two Years of Napoleon's Exile, by F. Antommarchi. Lond. 1825, 8vo. 2 vols.
The Life of Napoleon, a Hudibrastic Poem in fifteen Cantos, by Doctor Syntax, with 30 coloured engravings by George Cruikshank. Lond. 1815, roy. 8vo.
Copies of original Letters from the Army of General Bonaparte in Egypt, intercepted by the Fleet under the command of Admiral Lord Nelson, with an English Translation. Lond. 1798, 8vo.
Bonaparte's Campaign in Italy in 1796-7, by a General Officer; translated by T. E. Ritchie, with a Narrative of the French Army on the Rhine, &c. Edinb. 1799, 8vo.
Bonaparte's Promises and Performances detailed, for the information of those Irishmen who favour the French Cause. Dublin, 1803, 8vo.
An Appeal to the People of the United Kingdoms, against the insatiable ambition of Bonaparte, &c. Lond. 1803, 8vo.
Bonaparte, and the French People under his Consulate; from the German. Lond. 1804, 8vo.
Plunder and Partition, as practised on the continental Neighbours of France by Napoleon I., &c. Lond. 1804, 8vo.
The Nativity of N. Bonaparte, Emperor of all the French, calculated by a Professor. High Wycombe, 1805, 4to.
Bonaparte compared with Philip of Macedon; or a comparative View of the similar Schemes employed by Philip to subvert the Liberty of Greece, and by Bonaparte to enslave Europe; to which are added, Observations on the critical Situation of Ireland, and the Emancipation of the Irish Catholics. Bath, 1805, 8vo.
The Exposé; or N. Buonaparte unmasked. Lond. 1809, 8vo.
The Secret History of the Cabinet of Bonaparte, including his Private Life and Character, by Lewis Goldsmith. Lond. 1810, 8vo. 15s.
Recueil de Décrets, Ordonnances, Traités de Paix, Manifestes, Proclamations, Discours, &c. de Napoléon Bonaparte depuis Nov. 1799, jusqu'en 1815, par L. Goldsmith. Lond. 1813-16. 8vo. 7 vols. 2l. 5s.
History of the Secret Societies of the Army, and of the military Conspiracies which aimed at the Destruction of his Government. Lond. 1815, 8vo.
Critical Situation of Bonaparte in his Retreat out of Russia. Lond. 1815, 8vo.
Eighteen original Journals [each by a General Officer] of the eighteen Campaigns of the Emperor Napoleon, in which he personally commanded in chief. Translated from the French. Lond. 1816, roy. 8vo. 2 vols.
French Account of the last Campaign of Bonaparte, written by an Eye-witness. Translated by Captain Thornton. Lond. 1816, 8vo.
The Bonaparteid; a serio-comic Sketch of the Life and Adventures of N. Bonaparte, in verse. Lond. 1816, 8vo.
Manuscrit venu de St. Hélène d'une manière inconnue. Lond. 1817, 8vo.
Anecdotes of the Court and Family of Bonaparte, translated from the French. Lond. 1818, 8vo.
Napoléon peint par lui-même; extraits du véritable Manuscrit de N. Bonaparte par un Américain. Lond. 1818, 8vo.
The same, in English. Lond. 1818, 8vo.
Bonaparte in Britain every man's Friend; or Briton's Monitor. Part I. An historical Narrative of the Invasions of England from Julius Cæsar down to the

NAPOLEON I.—*continued.*
French landing in Wales. Part II. A Catalogue of French Cruelties, &c. Lond. n. d. 8vo.
Observations on Lord Bathurst's Speech in the House of Peers, on March 18, 1817, sent sealed to Sir Hudson Lowe. Lond. 1818, 8vo.
The Historical and unrevealed Memoirs of the political and private Life, &c. of Bonaparte. Lond. 1819, 8vo.
Letters from the Count de Las Cases, consisting of a second Letter to Prince Lucien Bonaparte on his removal from St. Helena, and a Letter to Sir Hudson Lowe, on his oppressive Conduct towards Napoleon, with an Appendix. Lond. 1819, 8vo.
Historic Doubts relative to Napoleon Bonaparte. [By Abp. Whately.] Lond. 1819, 8vo.
Ode on the Death of Napoleon, Lines on the Neapolitan Revolution, and other Poems. Lond. 1871, 8vo.
Napoleon Anecdotes, edited by H. Ireland. Lond. 1822-3, 8vo. 6 vols.
Extrait des Memoires de M. le Duc de Rovigo concernant la Catastrophe du Duc d'Enghien. Lond. 1823, 8vo.
Memoirs of General Count Rapp, first Aid-de-camp to Napoleon. Lond. 1823, 8vo.
Napoleon in the other World. Lond. 1827, 8vo.
Life of Napoleon, by J.G. Lockhart. Lond, 1829 (Murray's Fam. Library), 2 vols. 10s.—Reissued, Tegg. 1848, 7s.
The Court and Camp of Bonaparte. Lond. Murray (Family Library), 1831, 17mo. port. of Talleyrand, &c. Tegg. 3s. 6d.
Memoirs of the Invasion of France by the Allied Armies, and of the last six Months of the Reign of Napoleon, by Baron Fain. Lond. 1834, 8vo.
The Bonaparte Letters and Despatches, secret, confidential, and official; from the Originals in his private Cabinet. Lond. 1846, 8vo. 2 vols. 1l. 8s.
Life of Napoleon Bonaparte by Viensleux. Lond. C. Knight, 1846, 18mo. 2 vols. 3s.
Political Aphorisms, Moral and Philosophical Thoughts of the Emperor Napoleon, collected by G. de Liancourt, edited by J. A. Manning; in *French and English.* Lond. 1848, post 8vo.
History of the Captivity of Napoleon at St. Helena, from the Letters and Journals of Sir Hudson Lowe, and official Documents not before made public, by W. Forsyth. Lond. 1853, 8vo. 3 vols. 2l. 5s.
See LASKEY, J. O'MEARA. PELTIER, J. SCOTT, Sir Walter. THIERS.

NAPS upon Parnassus, 1658. *See* AUSTIN, Samuel.

NAPHTALI, or the Wrestlings of the Church of Scotland. *See* SCOTLAND, and in Howie's Scots Worthies, vol. 2.

NABBOROUGH, Sir John. *See* Voyages.
Narrative of the Burning in the Port of Tripoli four Men of War by Sir John Narborough, 1676, folio. Plate by Hollar. King and Lochée's in 1814, 1l. 12s.

NARES, Edward, D.D. Memoirs of the Life and Administration of William Cecil, Lord Burghley. Lond. 1828-31, 4to. 3 vols. port. &c., pub. 9l. 9s. red. 2l. 12s. 6d.
Remarks on the Version of the New Testament edited by the Unitarians. Second Edition enlarged. Lond. 1814, 8vo. An able and valuable discussion of the merits of this 'improved version' of the Socinians.—Lond. 1810, 8vo.
Elements of General History, ancient and modern; being a Continuation of Professor Tytler's work, 8vo. *See* TYTLER.
Thinks I to myself: a Novel. 1811, 12mo. 2 vols.
Heraldic Anomalies. Lond. 1824, 12mo. 2 vols. An entertaining work, presenting much curious information.

— Robert, Archdeacon. A Glossary; or, a Collection of Words, Phrases, Names and Allusions to Customs, Proverbs, &c. which have been thought to require Illustration in the Works of English Authors. Lond. 1822, 4to.
An excellent work. Hibbert, 5791, 2l. 2s. Drury, 3188, russia, 3l. 16s. FINE PAPER. Sir M. M. Sykes, pt. ii. 616, 4l. 4s.
Reprinted, Stralsund, 1825, 8vo. 18s.
New Edition, edited by James O. Halliwell, Esq., and T. Wright, Esq. Lond. 1859, 8vo. 2 vols. 1l. 8s.
Elements of Orthöepy. Lond. 1784, or 1792, 8vo. A systematic, perspicuous, and most useful work. Bindley, pt. ii. 2183, 6s. 6d. Edwards, 11, 5s. Also, with another title, 'Elements of the English Language.'
Discourses preached before the honorable Society of Lincoln's Inn. Lond. 1794, 8vo. 6s.
Essays and other occasional Compositions. Lond. 1810, post 8vo. 2 vols.
A connected and chronological View of the Prophecies relating to the Christian Church; in twelve Sermons, preached in Lincoln's Inn Chapel from the year 1800 to 1804, at the Lecture founded by the

Right Rev. William Warburton, Lord Dp. of Gloucester. Lond. 1805, 8vo. 7s.
The Veracity of the Evangelists demonstrated, by a comparative View of their Histories. Lond. 1816, 8vo. 8s. An accurate and well-written production.—1818, 12mo.
Archdeacon Nares was the projector of the British Critic, and for years its principal contributor.

NARRIEN, John. Historical Account of the Origin and Progress of Astronomy. Lond. 1833, 8vo. 12s.
Elements of Geometry, consisting of Books I.—IV. and VI. of Euclid, for the use of Sandhurst College. Lon. 1842. 8vo. 10s. 6d.
Practical Astronomy and Geodesy. Lond. 1845, 8vo. 14s.
Analytical Astronomy, with the Properties of Conic Sections. Lond. 1846, 8vo. 8s. 6d.

NARY, Cornelius. A new History of the World. Dub., 1720, fol.

NASH, Frederick. Picturesque Views of the City of Paris and its Environs, with Descriptions written in English, by J. Scott, translated into French by M. de la Brossiere. Lond. 1823, roy. 4to. 2 vols.
Published at 8l. 8s. Pinors, 16l. 15s. India proofs and etchings, 31l. 10s. Hibbert. 5658. India, morocco, 10l. 15s.
A Series of Views of the exterior and interior of the collegiate Chapel of St. George at Windsor. Lond. 1805, fol. pub. at 4l. 4s., reduced, 1l. 1s.
Twelve Views of the Antiquities of London; for the Illustration of Lysons, Pennant, &c. Lond. 1805-10, 4to. 6s.
Views of the Pavilion at Brighton. Lond. 1826, imp. folio. 28 Plates, mounted and coloured as drawings. The title ornamented, 10l. 10s.
The original drawings (said to have cost 1150l.) were in Thorpe's Cat. 1838, for 84l.

— Richard, commonly called Beau. His Life, extracted from his own papers. Edited by Dr. Goldsmith. Lond. 1762, 8vo. portraits.
Other Memoirs of this celebrated character, M. C. at Bath, have been printed, but they are of little repute. *See Jvars.*

— Thomas, of St. John's Coll. Cambridge. Works, Poetical and Satirical.
Of this writer, Mr. Gifford observes 'Nash had an inexhaustible vein of caustic raillery, never yet surpassed.' In 1599 it was ordered 'That all Nashe's bookes and Dr. Harvey's bookes be taken wheresoever they may be found, and that none of the same bookes be ever printed hereafter.'

Pialue Pervavell the Peace-maker of England, 4to. n.d. Eighteen leaves. Bindley, pt. III. 4l. 4s. Midgley, 4l. 10s. Utterson, 1852, mor. 4l. 16s. Gardner in 1854, 6l. *See Brydges' Censura Literaria.* 'Attributed to Nash, but in fact a last gasp of the Puritans.'—*Haslell.*
Martin's Months Minde, 1589. A Counterouffe given to Martin Junior, 1589. Mar Martin, n. d. Antimartinus, Lond. 1589. An Almond for a Parrat, n. d. These tracts are usually attributed to Thomas Nash. *See* MARTIN MARPRELATE.
Pappe with an Hatchet (1549.) *See* LILLY, John. MARTIN MARPRELATE.
The Returne of the renowned Cavaliere Pasquill of England, from the other side of the Seas, and his Meeting with Marforious at London upon the Royall Exchange, where they encounter with a little household Talke of Martin and Martinisme, discovering the Scabbs that is bredde in England; and conferring together about the speedie Dispersing of the Golden Legends of the Lives of the Saints, 1589, 4to. 16 leaves. Hibbert, 6791, 2l. 15s. Heed, 2439, 8l. 1s. Bright, 2l. 12s. 6d. Gardner in 1854, 1l. 16s. Utterson, 1852, 8l. 5s. Heber, pt. viii. 1l. 1s.
Addresse to the two Universities, 1589.
The Anatomie of Absurditie, contayning a breefe Confutation of the slender imputed Prayses to feminine Perfection, with a short Description of the severall Practises of Youth and sundry Follies of our licentious Times. Lond. Charlewood, 1589, 4to. Reed, 2438, 6l. 6s. Hibbert, 5795, 7l. Heber, pt. iv. 5l. 5s.—1890, 4to. Heber, pt. viii. 1l. 6s.

The first Parte of Pasqualls Apologie. Wherein he renders a Reason to his Friendes of his long Silence; and gallops the Fielde with the Treatise of Reformation lately written by a Fugitive John Penrie. Anno Dom. 1590, 4to. E 1, in fours, without prefix or appendage. Heber, pt. viii. 1l. 6s.
'Somewhat to reade for them that list,' is printed with the Astrophel and Stella of Sir Philip Sidney. Lond. 1591, 4to.
A wonderful, strange, and miscellaneous Astrological Prognostication for 1591, 4to. Reed, 2443, 6l. 16s. 6d.
Pierce Penilesse his Supplication to the Divell. Describing the Overspreading of Vice, and Suppression of Vertue. Pleasantly interlaced with variable Delights; and pathetically intermixed with conceipted Reproofe. Lond. 1592. 4to. There are two editions with this date, I. for Rd. Jones, Heber, pt. iv. 1l. 8s., last leaf MS. II. By Abel Jeffes, for John B(usbie), in the Malone Collection. Reprinted by the SHAKESPEARE Society. *See Appendix.* Extracts from this severe satire on the

NASH, Thomas—*continued*,
reigning views of the age will be found in
Drydges' Censura Literaria. It was the
most popular of all Nash's publications,
and which, to use the author's own phrase
in 'Have with you to Saffron Walden,'
1596, 'passed through the pikes of at least
six impressions.'—Lond. 1593, 4to. to sign.
I not paged. Reed, 1l. 11s. 6d.—Lond. N.
Ling. 1595, 4to. J, in foam. Reed, 2l.4l,
1l. 6s. North, pt. III. 763, 1l. 7s. Perry,
pt. iv. 392, 9l. 15s. Nassau, pt. ii. 567,
russia, 4l. 4s. Bindley, pt. III. 770, 4l. 14s. 6d.

Strange Newes of the intercepting certaine Letters, and Convoy of Verses, as
they were going privilie to victuall the
Low Countries. Lond. no printer's name,
1592. This confutation of Gabriel Harvey's four letters is inscribed to 'Maister
Apis lapis' by Tho: Nashe, after which is
an address 'To the Gentlemen Readers.'
The volume contains O 2, in fours. Nassau, pt. ii. 580, 16l. Heber, pt. iv. 7l. 7s.
Bright, 9l. 6s.—Lond. Thos. Danter, 1599.
4to. Bindley, pt. III. 425, 3l. 3s. Reed, 244l.
1l. 11s. 6d.

Apologie of Pierce Pennilesse: or,
Strange Newes of the Intercepting certaine
Letters and Verses. Lond. 1592. There
are three editions with this date E. for
Rd. Jones. Heber, pt. iv. 1l. 3s. II, by
Abel Jeffes, for John B——, in the Malone
Collection. 1ll. by Abel Jeffes, for John
Busble. Reprinted by the Shakespeare
Society. *See* Appendix.

New Letter of notable Contents, with a
strange Sonet, intituled the Gorgon, 1593,
4to. Bindley, pt. III. 762, with Gabriel
Harvey's Pierce's Supererogation, 1593,
17l. 5s. Reprinted in the Archaica.

Christ's Teares over Jerusalem. Whereunto is annexed a comparative Admonition to London. Lond. 1593, 4to. Heber,
pt. viii, uncut but damaged, 4l. 2s. 6d.
Printed for A. Wise, 1594. Heber, pt. iv. 4l.
With prefatory Epistle in Reply to Gabriel
Harvey, not given to the edition of 1613.
Lond. T. Thorpe, 1613, 4to. 90 leaves, Rewold,
Gardner in 1854, M. 9s. Sotheby's in 1821,
1l. 10s. Reed, 9443, 7l. 17s. 6d. Heber, pt.
iv. 19s. Reprinted in the first volume of
the Archaica.

Dido, Queen of Carthage, 1594. *See*
MARLOW, E. p. 1479.

The Unfortunate Traveller: or, the Life
of Jacke Wilton. Lond. printed by T.
Scarlett, 1594, 4to. A copy is in the library
of King George III. now in the British
Museum. Heber, pt. iv. 8l. 5s.

The Terrors of the Night, or, a Discourse
of Apparitions. Lond. by John Danter,
1594, 4to. 31 leaves. Copies are in the
Malone collections, the Bodleian Library,
and at Bridgwater House. Boswell, 1820,
5l. 16s. 6d. Resold, Heber, pt. iv. 5l. 13s.
Another, part of leaf MS. 2l. 5s.

Have with you to Saffron Waldron, of
Gabriel Harvey's Hunt is up. Lond. J.
Danter, 1596, 4to. This pamphlet contains
an inexhaustible stock of Humour, full of
the most amusing temporary allusions;
seems to have closed the wordy conflict between Nash and Harvey. Reed, 2442, 5l.
12s. 6d. Strettell, 1420, 7l. 7s. Hibbert,
5793, 3l. 13s. 6d. Bindley, pt. III. 767, 2l. 9s.
Perry, pt. ii. 1193, MS. title, 1l. 1s. Gough,
3339, 3l. 13s. 6d. Saunders in 1818, 2l.
Heber, pt. 4l. Resold, Gardnar, 4l. 14s.
Utterson, 4l. 16s.

Royal Exchange to such worshipful
Gentlemen as resorts there, 1597, 4to.
Bindley, pt. III. 1634, 3l. 4s.

Nashe's Lenten Stuffe; containing the
Description and first Procreation and Increase of the Towne of Great Yarmouth,
Norfolke: with a new Play, never played
before, of the Praise of the Red Herring.
Fitte of all Clearks of NoblemensKitchens
to be read; and not unnecessary by all
Serving-men, that have short Board-Wages, to be remembered. Lond. N. L.
for C. B., 1599, 4to. pp. 63, including the
title, epistle dedicatory and address. Copies are in the British Museum and Bodleian. Hibbert, 5797, 3l. Nassau, pt. ii.
226, 5l. 5s. Inglis, 802, 4l. 14s. 6d. Bindley, pt. iv. 571, 6l. Midgley, 6l. 6s. Jolly,
1853, 2l. 4s. Utterson, 1652, 4l. 4s. Heber, pt. iv. 2l. 2s. Gardner, 3l. It is reprinted in the sixth volume of the Harleian Miscellany.

A pleasant Comedie called Summers last
Will and Testament. Lond. 1600, B.
Stafford, 4to. Rhodes, 1776, 5l. Boswell,
2397, 4l. 8s. Roxburghe, 5553, 4l. 4s.
Sotheby's in Nov. 1826, 3l. 6s. Bright,
5l. 10s. resold Halliwell, May, 1856, 7l.
18s. Heber, pt. ii. 5l. 5s. Reprinted in
the new edition of Dodsley's Collection of
Old Plays.

The Returne of the Knight of the Poste
from Hell, with the Divels Answere to
the Supplication of Pierce Pennilesse.
Lond. Windet, 1606, 4to. Attributed, but
probably erroneously, to Tho. Nash. Gordonstoun, 1658, 5l. Reed, 2447, 5l. 15s. 6d.

Tom Nash his Ghost. Appearing to the
Anabaptist, the Libertine and the Brownist. Lond. 1642, 4to. 5s.

See LICHFIELD, Rich. HARVEY, Gabriel.

NASH, Thomas, of the Middle
Temple. Qvaternio, or a sovrefold
Way to a happie Life, set forth in
a Dialogue betweene a Countryman
and a Citizen, a Divine and a
Lawyer. Lond. 1633, 4to.

A store-house of translation from various languages. Bindley, pt. III. 774,
13s. pt. iv. 188, 8s. — 1636, 4to. Bindley,
pt. II. 820, 4s. Bliss, 8s. — 1639, 4to.

NASH, Treadway, D.D. Collections for the History of Worcestershire. Lond. 1781-2. With a Supplement. Lond. 1799, folio, 2 vols.
The materials of this work were collected by William Habington, or Abingdon (see Abingdon, p. 4, one) of Hindlip, author of the History of Edward IVth, &c.; they were transcribed by his son, the priest, author of Castara, &c. Beckford in 1817, 17l. uncut, 7l. 7s. Nassau, pt. ii. 408, russia, 7l. 7s. North, pt. ii. 1428, russia, 7l. 17l. 6d. Bindley, pt. ii. 1486, russia, 10l. 5s. Heath, 4630, russia. 10l. 10s. Marquis of Townshend, 2453, russia, 11l. 11s. Willet, 1674, 13l. 13s. LARGE PAPER. Dent, pt. ii. 765, russia, 11l. Hibbert, 5634, without the supplement, russia, 6l. 6s. The absence of the supplement, which separately is scarce, reduced the value full 2l.2s. Collation.—Vol. i. Lond. 1781, pp. xcii. and 610, not including the title and dedication. Vol. ii. 1782, pp. 484, not including the title and dedication; Appendix, pp. i.—clxviii.; two engraved dedications; thirteen fac-simile pages from Domesday; observations on Domesday, pp. 1-59; index, &c. 10 pages. SUPPLEMENT, 1799, pp. 104, not including the title; published separately at one guinea. The directions for placing the plates will be found at the end of each volume; Upcott adds Portrait of John Hooper, Bishop of Worcester, (Dyer pinx. J. Faber, sc. page clxiii. of Appendix.) But this portrait was not published with the work, and does not belong to it. The View of "Kyre Houses," mentioned in the list to vol. ii. as being at page 70, will be found engraved on the same leaf as "Hallow Park," given with vol. i. at p. 472. To some copies a new title-page was affixed bearing the date of 1799. To these an oval portrait of Nash is prefixed.

NASMYTH, Arthur. Divine Poems in three Parts, viz., Poeticall Applications, Job's Adversity, Poeticall Prayers, with Man's Looking-Glasse. Edinb. 1666, sm. 12mo.
Bindley, pt. iii. 53, 3l. Heber, pt. iv. 1l. 2s.

— James, D.D. Catalogus Librorum MSS. quos Collegio Corporis Christi in Academia Cantabrigiensi legavit Matthæus Parker, Arch. Cantuar. Cantab. 1777, 4to.
An excellent catalogue. Towneley, pt. ii. 1280, 10s. Bindley, pt. iii. 803, 10s. 6d. Itineraria Symonis Simeonis et Willielmi de Worcestre. Cantab. 1778, 8vo.
Hibbert, 7117, 8s. 6d. LARGE PAPER. Willett, 1838, 1l. 6s.

NATHAN, Rabbi. Tractatus de Patribus, in Ling. Lat. transl. cum Notis per Franc. Tailerum. Lond. 1654, 4to.

NATTER, Laur. A Treatise on the ancient Method of Engraving on precious Stones, compared with the modern. Lond. 1754, folio.
(Two editions, one in English, the other in French), 1l. 1s.
Catalogue des Pierres gravées du Mylord Comte de Bessborough. Lond. 1761, 4to. 5s. Privately printed.

NATTES, John Claude. Bath Illustrated by a Series of Views, from his Drawings; with Descriptions to each Plate. Lond. 1806, super royal folio. 18s.
The volume consists of thirty coloured plates, with half title, 2 leaves, preface and list of plates, 4 pages, and descriptive letter-press, 56 pages.
Views of Versailles, Paris, and St. Denis, 40 coloured plates, with descriptive letter-press in French. Lond. 1809, roy. folio, 1l. 1s.
Scotia Depicta. See FITTLER, JAMES.

NATURA BREVIUM. Emprinted by Richarde Pynson, folio, 1l. 1s.
This work served as a model for Fitzherbert in the framing of his own. Several other editions appeared in the sixteenth century, printed by Pynson, Middleton, Rastell, Redman, Tottell, Powell, H. Smith, &c.

NATURE, and NATURAL HISTORY. A Philosophical Survey of Nature. Lond. 1763, small 8vo.
Hollis, 1269, morocco, 6s.
Nature displayed. See Spectacle de la Nature. LA PLUCHE, Abbé.
The Naturalist's Pocket Magazine. 1790, 12mo. 9 vols. 1l. 4s.
A New System of the Natural History of Quadrupeds, Birds, Fishes, and Insects. Edinb. 1791, 8vo. 5 vols. plates.
Recreations in Natural History, or popular Sketches of British Quadrupeds. 8vo. With 74 engravings by John Scott. Published at 2l. 8s. LARGE PAPER, roy. 8vo. at 3l. 12s.
The Naturalist's Guide for collecting and preserving all Subjects of Natural History and Botany, intended for the use of Students and Travellers. Lond. 1822, 12mo. with plates.

1654 NAU NAY

The Naturalist's Companion. 1824, 8vo. with plates, plain, 12s. coloured, 1l. 1s. See GRAVES.

Naturalist's Library. See Sir W. JARDINE.

Nature's Cruel Step Dames; or matchless monsters of the female sex, Eliz. Harries and Anne Willis, who were executed at Tyburne, 1637, woodcuts, 4to. &c. Sotheby, 1856, 1l.

NAUDEUS, Gabriel. Instructions concerning erecting a Library, translated by John Evelyn. Lond. 1661, sm. 8vo.

An excellent little work Willet, 1839, 11s. 6d. Heber, pt. v. 6s.

News from France; or, a description of the Library of Cardinal Mazarine, before it was bitterly ruined. Sent in a Letter from Monsieur G. Naudeus, Keeper of the Public Library. Lond. 1652, 4to. six pages. Reprinted in the third volume of the Harleian Miscellany.

The History of Magic by way of Apology, &c. Translated by John Davies. Lond. 1657, 8vo. 4s.

NAUNTON, Sir Robert. The Court of Queen Elizabeth, with considerable biographical Additions by James Caulfield. Lond. 1814, 4to. 21 portraits.

Pp. 114, not including title and dedication to the Princess Charlotte of Wales. 15s. LARGE PAPER in folio, 1l. 10s. Four copies were struck off with the portraits on satin, 3l. 5s.—Original edition, 1641, 4to. pp. 49. Gordonstoun, 1866, 6s.—1642. — 1650, with portrait of Q. Elizabeth. Nassau, pt. i. 2412, 10s. White Knights, 2798, morocco, 17s.—Edited by P. W. Dodd. Lond. 1824, post 8vo. with 9 portraits engraved by Cooper, 12s. 6d. LARGE PAPER, 12 1s. PROOFS on INDIA PAPER, demy 8vo. Only fifteen copies printed.

Fragmenta Regalia, or Observations on the late Queen Elizabeth, her times and favourites, 4to. n. p. 1641.—4to. n. p. 1642.— Lond. 1653, 8vo.—With explanatory observations. Edinb. 1808, 8vo.

The Fragmenta Regalia were reprinted in the first volume of the Phenix, in the second volume of the Harleian Miscellany, and at the end of the Memoirs of Robert Cary, Earl of Monmouth. Lond. 1808, 8vo. See Retrosp. Review, v. 303-14.

Memoirs of Sir Robert Naunton [by J. Caulfield]. Lond. 1814, 4to. with portrait. LARGE PAPER, in folio. Nassau, pt. i. 2596, 6s.

NAUSE, Fred. Bithop of Vienna. Of all blasing Starrs in generall, translated by Abr. Fleming. Lond. 577, 16mo. 10s. 6d.

E. in eights, dedicated to Sir William Cordell, Knight.

NAUTICAL ALMANACK, The, and astronomical Ephemeris, from the Commencement in 1767 to 1864. Lond. 1766-1860, 8vo. 98 vols. 10l.

A work most useful to the practical astronomer, and absolutely essential to nautical men. It is published annually by order of the Admiralty, generally three years in advance. The price was 5s. until July, 1851, when it was reduced to 2s. 6d. It was edited at first by Dr. Maskelyne; from 1772 to 1820, by Mr. Hitchins of St. Hilary, Cornwall; subsequently by Dr. Young; Mr. W. S. Stratford; and since the 1857 volume inclusive by Mr. J. R. Hind.

Tables requisite to be used with the Nautical Almanac, in Order to find the Latitude and Longitude at Sea. 8vo. 1767, 1781, &c.

NAVARRETE, R. F. F. Dominick Fernandez. An Account of China, with a Supplement.

In the first and sixth volumes of the Churchill Collection of Voyages and Travels.

NAVY. —The Naval Chronicle, from its Commencement in January 1799 to Dec. 1818 inclusive. Lond. royal 8vo. 40 vols.

With portraits and other plates. Projected by the Rev. J. S. Clarke. Fonthill, 870, 15l. Reed, 2568, 07 nos. 6l. 15s.

A Collection of Papers on naval Architecture. Lond. 1791-1800, 8vo. 2 vols.

Naval Biography; or Lives of distinguished Characters in the British Navy. Lond. 1805, 8vo. 2 vols.

The Naval Sketch Book (by Captain Glascock). Lond. 1826, post 8vo. 2 vols.— Second series, post 8vo.

Naval Affairs, 1850 to 1858. A most extraordinary Series of Printed Papers, MSS. and Autographs, in 47 vols. folio, the property of Sir George Duckett, Hart. Sold at Sotheby's, June 23, 1852, for 70l. The description extends over 8 pages.

NAYLER, Sir George, Garter Principal King of Arms. The Coronation of K. George IV. solemnised in the Collegiate Church of

St. Peter Westminster upon the 19th Day of July, 1821. Lond. 1824, atlas folio. Pub. by subscription. Parts 1 and 2, at 12*l.* 12s. each. Parts 3 and 4, completed by H. G. Bohn, who republished the whole at 12*l.* 12s.
See Coronation of George IV., p. 526.

A Collection of the Coats of Arms borne by the Nobility and Gentry of Gloucestershire, 4to. with 372 Coats of Arms, on 62 plates, LARGE PAPER. Published anonymously in 1792.

NAYLIER, John. The new made Colonel: or, Ireland's jugling pretended Reliever. Lond. 1649, 4to.
King and Lochée's in March, 1819, 1*l.* 13s.

NAYLOR, Francis Hare. History of the Helvetic Republics, containing the Rise and Progress of the federative Republics, to the Middle of the fifteenth Century. Lond. 1801, 8vo. 2 vols. 8s.
Second edition, enlarged and continued to a recent period, including the troubles in the Pays de Vaud. Lond. 1809, 8vo. 4 vols.
The Civil and Military History of Germany, from the Landing of Gustavus to the Conclusion of the Treaty of Westphalia. Lond. 1816, 8vo. 3 vols. 15s.

NAYLOR, James, the Quaker's Apostle. Memoir of his Life, Ministry, Tryal and Sufferings. Lond. 1710, 8vo.
In the British Museum are many tracts by and relating to this singular enthusiast, 1653-76.

NAZARENUS, Abra. A Reproofe spoken and geeuen forth by Abra Nazarenus against all false Christians, &c. Translated out of Nether-Saxon, 1579, 8vo.
Eight leaves, in defence of H. N. and the Family of Love.
See TOLAND, J.

NEADE, William. The double-armed Man, by the new Inuention; briefly showing some famous Exploits atchieued by our British Bowmen; with seuerall Portraitures proper for the Pike and Bow. Lond. 1625, 4to. frontispiece.

Twenty leaves with wood-cuts, dedicated to K. Charles I. Heber, pt. vi. 1*l.* 4s. Gordonstoun, 1653, 8*l.* 13s. 6d. Gough, 2675, 2*l.* 15s. Inglis, 923, 1*l.* 16s. Nassau, pt. II. 391, 18s. Sotheby, 1656, 1*l.* 16s.— 1628, 4to. King and Lochée's in 1814, 2*l.* 8s.—n. d. 4to. Hindley, pt. iv. 159, 10s. 6d. The author's copy of this impression is in the Grenville collection.

NEAL, Daniel, M.A. The History of the Puritans, or Protestant Non-Conformists: from the Reformation to the Death of Queen Elizabeth; with an Account of their Principles; their Attempts for a farther Reformation in the Church; their Sufferings; and the Lives and Characters of their most considerable Divines. A new Edition, revised, corrected, and enlarged, by Joshua Toulmin, A. M. Bath, 1793-7. 8vo. 5 vols.

Best edition. Hollis, 977, 5*l.* Williams, 1235, 5*l.* 'The most dishonest book in our language, Dod's Roman Catholic Church History not excepted.—*Quart. Review.* Mr. Warburton says, 'I took home (Neal's History) to my house, and, at breakfast-time, filled the margins quite through; which I think to be a full confutation of all his false facts and partial representations.'—Lond. 1732—8, 8vo. 4 vols. Sir P. Thompson, 607, 2*l.* 3s. Bishop of Ely, 647, 2*l.* Marquis of Townshend, 2244, 2*l.* 2s. Hindley, pt. II. 2007, 3*l.* 6s.—Lond. 1754, 4to. 2 vols. with portrait of Neal by Havenet after Woolaston. Heath, 569, 2*l.* 12s. 6d. Willett, 1760, 3*l.* 13s. 6d. North, pt. II. 1036, russia, 4*l.* 4s. Hollis, 1057, 2*l.* 6s. Roxburghe, 7862, 2*l.* 12s. 6d.—Dublin, 1736, 8vo. 4 vols.—Lond. Baynes, 1872, 8vo. 5 vols.—Lond. Tegg, 1822, 8vo. 5 vols. with Life.—Again, revised and corrected. Lond. 1837, 8vo. 3 vols.

Neal's History of the Puritans, abridged by Edward Parsons. Lond. 1811, 8vo. 2 vols.

An expostulatory Letter to Mr. Daniel Neal, upon occasion of his publishing the History of the Puritans (by A. B.) Lond. 1733, 8vo. pp. 30, including title and half-title.

A Vindication of the Government, Doctrine and Worship of the Church of England established in the Reign of Queen Elizabeth, against the injurious Reflections of Mr. Neal in the late History of the Puritans. By Isaac Madox, Bishop of Worcester. Lond. 1783, 8vo. 6s.

NEAL, Daniel, M.A.—*continued.*
A Review of the principal Facts objected to the first volume of the History of the Puritans (by Bishop Madox). By Daniel Neal, M.A. Lond. 1734, 8vo. pp. 82, including title.

An Illustration of Mr. Daniel Neal's History of the Puritans, in the Article of Peter Smart, M.A., July 27, 1628, prosecuted for preaching a vile sermon at Durham. With Remarks. By Christopher Hunter. Durham, 1736, 8vo.

An Impartial Examination, &c. of Neal's History of the Puritans. By Zach. Grey, LL.D. and Isaac Madox, Bp. of Worcester. Lond. 1736, &c. 8vo. Bishop of Ely, £14. 4 vols. 3l. 5s. Williams, 804, 4 vols. 2l. 7s. *See* GREY, Z.

Schismatics delineated from authentic Vouchers, in reply to Neal; with Downing's Journal, &c. by Philalethes Cantabrigiensis (Zach. Grey, LL.D.) Lond. 1739, 8vo.

A Letter to Mr. Su—l, occasioned by some injurious Reflections in the fourth volume of Mr. Neal's History of the Puritans. By a Protestant Dissenter. Lond. 1739, 8vo. pp. 28, not including title and half-title.

A Review of Mr. Daniel Neal's History of the Puritans, with a Postscript, in which the Exceptions of that Author to the Bishop of Worcester's Vindication of the Church of England are impartially considered. In a Letter to Mr. David Jennings. By Zachary Grey, LL.D. Cambridge, 1744, 8vo. pp. 82, not including title.

History of New England; containing an Account of the civil and ecclesiastical Affairs of the Country to the Year 1700. To which is added, an Appendix containing their Character, their ecclesiastical Discipline and their municipal Laws. Lond. 1720, 8vo. 2 vols. Bindley, pt. II. 200s, 14s. Willett, 1841, 1l. 5s.—1747, 8vo. 2 vols. Bishop of Ely, 649, 15s.

NEALE, Adam, M.D. Letters from Portugal and Spain; comprising an Account of the Operations of the Armies under Sir A. Wellesley and Sir J. Moore, from the Landing of the Troops in Mondego Bay to the Battle of Corunna. Lond. 1809. 4to.
An interesting and excellent work. Foothill, 422, 1l.

Travels through some parts of Germany, Poland, Moldavia and Turkey. Edinb. 1818, 4to. plates.

— J. Good News from Heaven. Lond. W. Gilbertson, 1664. 12mo.
BLACK LETTER. Hibbs, cut into, 2s. 6d.

— John Preston. Views of the Seats of Noblemen and Gentlemen in England, Wales, Scotland and Ireland. *First Series,* Lond. 1818-1823, 6 vols. 432 plates.
Second Series, Lond. 1824-1829, 5 vols. royal 8vo. (all published) 360 plates, together, 11 vols. published at 26l. 8s. reduced 10l. 10s. LARGE PAPER, India proofs, 4to. 11 vols. pub. at 52l. 10s. reduced 21l.
Each volume consists of 12 nos., each number containing 6 views, with appropriate descriptions, published at 4s. LARGE PAPER, in royal 4to. with proofs on India paper, pub. at 8s.

The History and Antiquities of the Abbey Church of St. Peter, Westminster; including Notices and biographical Memoirs of the Abbots and Deans of that Foundation by Edward Wedlake Brayley. Lond. 1818, royal 4to. 2 vols. Published in 12 numbers, the first in 1818, the last no., 13, in 1823, 10l. 10s. LARGE PAPER, in imp. 4to. with proofs on India paper. Fifty copies printed. Hibbert, 5567, morocco, 10l. 15s. PROOFS and ETCHINGS, pub. at 31l. 10s. Brockett, 2337, 12 parts, 13l. 6s. LARGEST PAPER, in imperial folio. India proofs. Twenty-five copies printed, to match the large paper Dugdale's Monasticon, pub. at 31l. 10s. reduced 10l. 10s.
Portraits of the Deans of Westminster. 8 pls. complete. PROOFS. Drockett, 2338, 19s.

Neale and Le Keux's Views of the most interesting collegiate and parochial Churches in Great Britain, including Screens, Fonts, Monuments, &c. &c. With historical and architectural Descriptions. Lond. 1824-5, royal 8vo. 2 vols. Published at 5l. LARGE PAPER, PROOFS on India paper, in 4to. 10l.

Six Views of Blenheim, by J. F. Neale, with an historical Description of that Edifice, royal 8vo. 6s. LARGE PAPER, in royal 4to. with Proofs on India paper, 10s.

Graphical Illustrations of Fonthill Abbey, the Seat of John Farquhar, Esq.; with an historical Description and Notices of Works of Art formerly preserved there. Lond. 1834, 8vo. PROOFS, 4to.

— Sir Thomas. Treatise of Direction how to travell safely and profitably into forraign Countries. Lond. 1664. 8vo.
This book should have a portrait of the Author by W. Marshall. Nassau, pt. I.

9116, 1l. 15s. Dowdeswell, 514, 2l. 8s. Heber, pt. vi. 13s. Hibs, no portrait, 17s.

NEALE, W. H. The Mohammedan System of Theology; or, a Survey of the History and Doctrines of Islamism contrasted with Christianity. Lond. 1828. 8vo.

NEARCHUS. The Voyage of Nearchus. See Geographiæ veteris Scriptores. VINCENT, William.

NECTARIUS, Patriarcha Hierosol. Confutatio Imperii Papæ in Ecclesiam, Latine, per P. Allix. Lond. 1702. 8vo.

NEDHAM, or NEEDHAM, Marchamont. The Excellencie of a free State. Lond. 1767. 8vo. 4s.
Edited by Richard Baron. Hollis, 490, morocco, 7s.—Lond. 1656, 8vo. Hollis, 480, 8s. 6d.
The Levellers levell'd, or the Independents Conspiracie to root out Monarchie, an Interlude. By Mercurius Pragmaticus. Lond. 1647, 4to. Rhodes, 1777, 15s.
Digitus Dei; or, God's Justice upon Treachery and Treason, exemplified in the Life and Death of the late James Duke of Hamilton. Lond. 1649, 4to. Bliss, 1s.
The Case of the Commonwealth of England stated. Lond. 1650, 4to. Hollis, 1049, morocco, 10s. 6d. A former edition appeared in 1649.
News from Brussels. In a Letter from a near attendant on his Majesties Person to a Person of Honour here; which casually became thus publique. Printed in the year 1660, 4to. Reprinted with the answer in Evelyn's miscellaneous Works.
A short History of the English Rebellion completed in Verse. Lond. 1661, 4to. Hindley, pt. iv. 597, 2s.—1680, 4to. Reprinted in the second number of Morgan's Phœnix Britannicus, and also in the second volume of the Harleian Miscellany.
A Rope for Pol, or Hue and Cry after Marchmont Needham, the late seurrilous News-writer. Lond. 4to. 1660. Bliss, 3s.
An account of this noted writer of weekly news in the civil wars, with a list of his publications, will be found in Wood's Athen. Oxon.

NEEDLE.—A Schole House for the Needle. 1624. oblong 4to.
White Knights, 3127, russia, 3l. 15s.

NEEDLER (Henry). Works. Lond. 1724. 12mo. 4s. — Lond. 1728. 12mo. 4s.

NEELE, Henry. Lectures on English Poetry, from the Reign of Edward III. to the Time of Burns and Cowper, with miscellaneous Tales and Poems, being the Literary Remains, &c. Lond. 1829, portrait.
—Second edition, 1830, post 8vo. 12s.
See Romance of History.

NEILD, James. State of the Prisons in England, Scotland, and Wales. Lond. 1812. 4to.

NEILL, Patrick. A Tour through some of the Islands of Orkney and Shetland. Edinb. 1806. 5s.
On Scottish Gardens and Orchards. 8vo. Not printed for sale.
Journal of a Horticultural Tour through some parts of Flanders, Holland, and the North of France, in 1817, by a deputation of the Caledonian Horticultural Society. Edinb. 1823, 8vo.

NELME, L. D. An Essay towards an Investigation of the Origin and Elements of Language and Letters, that is, Sounds and Symbols. Lond. 1772, 4to.
Gosset, 3925, 7s.

NELSON, Horatio, Lord. The Letters of Lord Nelson to Lady Hamilton; with a Supplement of interesting Letters, by distinguished Personages. Lond. 1814. 8vo. 2 vols.
A scandalous publication, tending to lower the reputation of one of the greatest heroes that ever lived.
Order to be observed in the public funeral Procession of Horatio Viscount Nelson. Lond. (1806) folio. Seven leaves.
The Ceremonial of the public Funeral of the late Vice Admiral Horatio Viscount Nelson, K.B. &c. &c. &c. on Wednesday, Jan. 9, 1806. Lond. 1806, folio, with four prints, in aquatinta, from drawings by C. A. Pugin.
Orme's graphic History of the Life, Exploits, and Death of Horatio Nelson, Viscount and Baron Nelson of the Nile, &c. &c. &c.; containing 15 Engravings; and intended as an Accompaniment to the three celebrated whole-sheet Plates of his Lordship's splendid Victories, viz. the Battles of St. Vincent's, the Nile, and Trafalgar, which are explained by References and Keys. The Memoirs by Francis Wm. Blagdon. Lond. 1806, folio. 2l. 2s.

1658 NEL NEM

The Naval Keepsake, containing the Life of Nelson, by the Old Sailor (M. H. Barker). Lond. 1839, 12mo. plates, 5s.

Nelson's Letters and Despatches, edited by Sir Harris Nicolas, 7 thick vols. 8vo. Lond. Colburn, 1845–46, pub. at 5l. 10s. Reduced, Bohn, 1l. 11s. 6d.

See CHARNOCK, John. CHURCHILL, T. O. CLARKE, James Stanier. HARRISON, Jas. PETTIGREW, T. J. SOUTHEY, Robert.

NELSON, John. The History, Topography, and Antiquities of the Parish of St. Mary Islington, in the County of Middlesex; including biographical Sketches of the most eminent and remarkable Persons who have been born, or have resided there. Lond. 1811, 4to.

Pp. 416, with title, preface, and list of subscribers, four leaves; also 17 engravings on 13 plates. Nassau, pt. ii. 863, 17s. Towneley, pt. ii. 1275, 16s. Bindley, pt. iii. 765, 16s. 6d.—Second edition. Lond. 1829, 4to.

—— Robert. A Companion for the Festivals and Fasts of the Church of England, with Collects and Prayers for each solemnity. Lond. 1704, 8vo.

According to Dr. Johnson, 'a most valuable help to devotion, and which has, I understand, the greatest sale of any book ever printed in England, except the Bible.' —1708, 8vo. 6s. LARGE PAPER, Williams, 1216, 2l. 14s.

Sixteenth edition. Lond. 1736, 1748, 1761, 8vo.—New edition. Lond. Togg, 1843, 8vo. 8s.—Lond. Soc. Prom. C. K. 1849, 8vo. 6s., 12mo. 4s.—Lond. Rivington, 18—, 8vo. 8s., 12mo. 5s.

Companion for the Festivals and Fasts, abridged. Lond. 1739, 12mo.

Fasts and Festivals, abridged by Elizabeth Nelson. Lond. 1810, 8vo.

Fasts and Festivals abridged, with Notes by John Poynder. Lond. 1842, fcap. 8vo. 7s.

The Practice of True Devotion in relation to the end as well as the means of Religion, with an office for the Holy Communion. Lond. 1708, 8vo.—1715, 12mo.—Seventh edition. To which is added the character of the author. Lond. 1726, 12mo. —New edition, Lond. Soc. Prom. C. K 1849, 8vo. 2s. 8d.; 12mo. 1s. 10d.

The Great Duty of frequenting the Christian Sacrifice, and the nature of the preparation required, with suitable devotions, partly collected from the ancient Liturgies. Fifth edition, to which is prefixed Instruction for Confirmation.

Lond. 1714, 12mo.—New edition, Lond. Burns, 1841, 12mo. 5s.

The Whole Duty of a Christian, by way of Question and Answer, exactly pursuant to the method of the Whole Duty of Man, and designed for the Use of Charity Schools. Ninth edition, corrected, pp. 96. Lond. 1737, 12mo.

Instructions for them that Come to be Confirmed; by way of Question and Answer. With Prayers for them to use before and after their Confirmation. Forty-fifth edition, pp. 15. Lond. 1827, 12mo.

Thomas à Kempis.—The Christian's Exercise; or, rules to live above the World while we are in it, with Meditations, Hymns, and Soliloquies, suited to the several stages of Christian Life, with an Appendix of Letters, Dialogues, &c., addressed to all true Lovers of Devotion, by Robert Nelson, Esq. Lond. 1715, 8vo. From the Latin of Th. à Kempis.

Life of Bishop Bull. Lond. 1714, 8vo.— Lond. J. H. Parker, 1840, 16mo. 3s. 6d.

See BULL, George; KETTLEWELL, J.

—— Thomas. A short Discours, expressing the Substance of all the late pretended Treasons against the Queenes Majestie and Estates of this Realme by sundry Traytors, who were executed for the same, 1586: with a godly Prayer for the safetie of her Highnesses Person. Lond. G. Robinson for T. Nelson, 1586, 4to.

Bright, 5l. Heber, pt. iv. 8/. 13s. 6d.

—— William. Reports of special Cases in Chancery in the Reigns of Charles I. and II., and William III. Savoy, 1717, 8vo. 3s. 6d.

Nelson published other law books, now obsolete.

NELUS, Thomas. Collegiorum Scholarumque Publicarum Academiæ Oxoniensis Topographica delineatio.

Printed in 'Dodwell de Parma,' edited by Tho. Hearne. The work is dedicated to Queen Elizabeth, and has cuts of the Colleges.

NEMESIANUS, M. Aur. Olympius. Cynegeticon. *See* GRATIUS, Faliscus.

NEMESIUS, Episcopus Emesenus. De Natura Hominis Liber, Gr. et Lat. in integrum restitutus. Oxon. 1671, 8vo. 5s.

The best edition. FINE PAPER, 10s. 6d. Williams. 1827, morocco, 19s.
The Nature of Man, englished and divided into Sections, with briefs of their principall Contents, by Geo. Wither. Lond. 1636, 12mo. pp. 642, besides a preface to the reader, and a dedication to John Selden, Esq. Lloyd, 887, 8s. Inglis, 1054, 5s. Bibl. Anglo-Poet. 798, 1l. 1s. Bright, 7s. 6d.
The Character of Man; now made Englhsh. Lond. 1657, 24mo. Bliss, 8s. 6d.

NENNA, Sir John Baptist, of Bari. Nennio, or a Treatise of Nobility. Done into English (from the Italian) by Wm. Jones. Lond. 1595, 4to.
Prefixed are commendatory verses by Spenser, Chapman, Day, &c. Bindley, pt. iii. 790, 1l. 11s. 6d. Bright, 1l. 17s. Bliss, 2l. 9s. — 1600, 4to. Bright, 1l. 6s.

NENNIUS, Bancherensis. Nennii Historia Britonum de Prima inhabitatione Britanniæ insulæ accurante Tho. Gale, notisque et Indice, auxit Car. Bertramus. Hauniæ, 1758, 8vo. 7s. 6d.
A few copies printed separately from Bertrami Scriptores tres, see p. 155. The work is also in Gale's Script. Hist. Brit.
Historia Britonum, ad fidem Codicum MSS. recensuit Joseph Stevenson. Lond. 1838, 8vo. Printed for the English Historical Society; those for Members, on LARGE PAPER in royal 8vo.
Historia Britonum, with an English Version and Notes, by the Rev. W. Gunn. Lond. 1819, roy. 8vo. with facsimile plate.
History of the Britons, translated from the Text of Stevenson, by the Rev. J. A. Giles, LL.D. Lond. 1840, 8vo. In Bohn's Antiquarian Library, included among the 'six old English Chronicles.' Lond. post 8vo. 5s.
The work of 'a credulous compiler, though, from the antiquity of his materials, valuable to an inquisitive historian.'—Athæ.

NEOT, Saint. The Life of St. Neot, the eldest Brother of King Alfred. By the Rev. John Whitaker, B.D. Lond. 1809, 8vo. 10s. 6d.
See NEWMAN, J. H. Lives of the Saints.

NEOTS, St., in Cornwall. Some Account of the Church and Windows of St. Neots in Cornwall. Lond. 1786, 4to.

By the Rev. Benjamin Foster, Rector of Boconnoc. Pp. 26, ending with 'Cornu-British,' two titles, list of subscribers, 4 plates, and two folded plates of the windows.
Parochial History of St. Neots, with the Life and Miracles of St. Neot, and the Ballad of Tregeagle. By James Michell. Bodmin, 1833, 12mo.

NEOTS, St., in Huntingdonshire. History and Antiquities of. See GORHAM, G. C.

NEPER. See NAPIER.

NEPOS, Cornelius. Excellentium Imperatorum Vitæ.
Corn. Nepotis excellentium Imperatorum Vitæ, accessit Aristonenis Mesenii Vita, ex Pausania, Gr. et Lat. Oxon. 1697, 8vo. A correct edition. LARGE PAPER. Hindley, pt. i. 1547, 13s. 6d. Williams, 1236, morocco, 1l. 4s. Drury, 1021, morocco, by Roger Payne, 1l. 6s. Willett, 628, morocco, 1l. 16s. Bishop Randolph, 301, 19s. LARGEST PAPER. Dent, pt. i 552, date 1696, morocco, by Roger Payne, 3l. — Oxon. 1675, 12mo. 2s.
Cornelii Nepotis excellentium Imperatorum Vitæ, edidit Michael Maittaire. Lond. 1715, 12mo. A correct edition, with a valuable index. LARGE PAPER, sm. 8vo. Drury, 7s. Heath, 10s. 6d. Edwards, 1l. 7s.
Cornelius Nepos de Viris excellentibus Imperatorum, Interpretatione et Notis in Usum sarem. Delphini. 8vo. Lond. 1691, 1720, 1729, 1786, &c. Frequently reprinted for the use of schools.
Cornelius Nepos. Lond. typis Brindley, 1774, 24mo. 8s.
Cornelius Nepos. Glasg. 1749, 24mo. — 1761. A correct and beautiful book. Williams, 1829, morocco, by Roger Payne, 7s. 6d. — 1777. LARGE PAPER. Duke of Grafton, 951, morocco, 6s.
Cornelii Nepotis Vitæ, cum Fragmentis, variis Lectionibus, et Indice locupletissimo. 1816, 12mo. 4s. 6d.
Cornelius Nepos et Pomponius Mela. Lond. 1819, 18mo. 8s. Regent's edition.
Cornelii Nepotis Vitæ, cum Fragmentis, variis Lectionibus, et Indice locupletissimo. Oxon. 1819, 12mo. 4s. LARGE PAPER, 6s.
The Life and Death of Pomponius Atticus; (with observations by Sir Matthew Hale.) Lond. 1677, 8vo.
The Lives of Illustrious Men, done into English by several Gentlemen of the University of Oxford. Oxford, 1684, sm. 8vo. 2s. 6d. Reprinted, Lond. 1685, 1712, 1713, 1723, 1728, 12mo.
Cornelius Nepos, with a literal English

Translation by John Clarke. Lond. 1712,
8vo. 4s. 6d. Frequently reprinted.
Cornelius Nepotis Vitæ, with an English
Translation by — Arrol. Edinb. 1744,
12mo. 8s.
Cornelii Nepotis Vitæ, with a literal
Translation, &c. by John Stirling, D.D.
Lond. 1767, 8vo. 5s. An excellent school
edition.
Cornelii Nepotis Vitæ excellentium Imperatorum, castigatæ, notis illustratæ,
&c. Studio Alex. Stewart. Sixteenth
edition. Edinb. 1843, 12mo. 8s.
Cornelii Nepotis Vitæ, with English
Notes and Questions by Bradley. New
edition, by the Rev. T. White. Lond.
Longman, 1856, 12mo. 3s. 6d.
Cornelius Nepos, with English Notes,
in 'Usum Scholæ Etonensis.' Eton, 1844,
12mo. 3s. 6d.
On the Hamiltonian System. Lond.
12mo. 6s. 6d.
Cornelius Nepos; literally translated
with Notes, by the Rev. J. S. Watson,
(with Justin and Eutropius). Lond. 1853,
(Bohn's Classical Library), post 8vo. 5s.

NERI, Antonio. The Art of
Glass; wherein are shewn the Wayes
to make and colour Glass, Pastes,
Enamels, Lakes, and other Curiosities. Translated from the Italian
by Christ. Merrett, M.D. Lond.
1662, 8vo. portrait.
Dent, pt. ii. 19, 7s. 6d.

NERITA, Philip, Founder of the
Congregation of the Oratory, &c.
The holy Life of. Paris, 1659, 8vo.

NERO, Claudius Tiberius. The
Stately Tragedie of Claudius Tibe-
rius Nero, out of the rarest records
of those times. Lond. 1607, 4to.
Anonymous. Roxburghe, 4076, 19s. re-
sold Rhodes, 731, 1l. 1s.; again, Heber, pt.
ii. 7s. 6d. Utterson, 4s. 6d.
The Tragedy of Nero, newly written.
Lond. 1624, 4to.
Also Anonymous. Reed, 8211, 6s. Rox-
burghe, 4277, 6s. 6d. resold Heber, pt. ii.
7s. 6d.—Lond. 1633, 4to. Reed, 7504, 8s.
Rhodes, 974, 8s.
The Tragedy of Nero, Emperor of Rome,
acted at the Theatre Royal [by Nathaniel
Lee]. Lond. 1675, 4to.—Altered to 'Piso's
Conspiracy.' Lond. 1676, 4to. Roxburghe,
4249, 4s.—Included in the third volume of
Lee's Plays, 12mo.
See GWYNNE, Matthew, p. 962.

NERO CÆSAR. See BOLTON, Edmund.

NERO, Fr. See NIGER, Franc.
NESBIT, P. Abridgment of Ecclesiastical History. Edinb. 1776,
8vo.
Williams, 1344, 10s. 6d.

NESS, Christopher. History and
Mystery of the Old and New Testaments logically discussed and
theologically improved. Lond.
1690-6, folio, 4 vols. 8l. 3s.
This work, by a celebrated nonconformist, is said to have been of great use
to Matthew Henry in his Exposition.
Peace Offerings and Lamentations, 1666,
4to. Bliss, 2s. 6d.

NETHERLANDS.—The Netherland
Historian. A true and exact Re-
lation of what passed in the late
Wars, from 1671 to 1674. Amst.
1675, 12mo.
With 60 sculptures. Gordonstoun, 1689,
6s. 6d. Nassau, pt. i. 9416, 7s. Bliss,
7s. 6d.
An accurate Description of the United
Netherlands, written by an English Gen-
tleman. Lond. 1691, 8vo.
Journal of a Tour through the Nether-
lands in 1821. Lond. 1822, 12mo. Pp. 171.
By Lady Blennington.

NETHERSOLE, Sir Francis. Memoriæ sacræ Henrici Wallisæ Principis &c. Laudatio funebris. Cantab. 1617, 4to.
Bliss, 6d. Reprinted by Bates in his
Vitæ selectorum aliquot Virorum. Lond.
1704, 4to.
Oratio id Obitum Henrici Principis
Walliæ. Cantab. 1612, 4to.

NETTLETON, Thomas, M.D. A
Treatise on Virtue and Happiness.
The seventh edition. Edinb. 1774,
12mo.
An esteemed work.—Glasg. 1751, 3s.
LARGE PAPER. Williams, 1045, morocco,
12s.

NEUBRIGENSIS, Gul. Historia
sive Chronica Rerum Anglicarum,
seu de Rebus Anglicis, Libris V.
Ant. 1567, 12mo.
This chronicle begins at the Norman
conquest and ends with the year 1197.
Gordonstoun, 1667, 6s. 6d.—Paris, 1610,
8vo. Heber, pt. vi. Sir R. Twysden's
copy; collated with the Lambeth MS.
8l. 8s. De Thou's copy is in the Grenville Collection.

See HEARNE, Thomas. William of Newbury will likewise be found in Gale's and Fell's collection of English historians, and in the Historical Society's Publications. (App.)

NEUMAN, Henry. A new Dictionary of the Spanish and English Languages. Lond. 1806, 8vo. 2 vols.
Second edition. 1809, 8vo. 2 vols. Drury, 3364, 10s. 6d.—Third edition, incorporating Baretti. Lond. 1817, 2 vols.—Fourth edition, Lond. 1823, 8vo. 3 vols.—Fifth edition, revised and greatly enlarged by D. Vicente Salva and Prof. Seoané. Lond. 1831, 8vo. 2 vols. 1l. 10s.—Sixth edition, revised by M. Seoané, M.D. Lond. 1841, 8vo. 2 vols.—Tenth edition, further revised. Lond. 1854 (stereotyped), 8vo. 2 vols.—Eleventh edition, 1858, 1l. 6s.
A pocket abridgment of this Dictionary, printed in pearl type, has gone through numerous editions; the last is, Lond. 1858 (stereotyped), 18mo. roan, 6s.

NEUMANN, Caspar, M.D. The chemical Works, abridged and methodized, with large Additions, by William Lewis. Lond. 1759, 4to.

NEUMAYR VON RAMSSLA, Johann Wilhelm. Des durchlauchtigen Fürsten Johann Ernst des Jüngern, Hertzog zu Sachssen, Reise in Franckreich, Engelland, und Niederland. Leipzig, 1620, 4to.
Second edition, with Life and Notes by M. J. H. Pagendarm. Jena, 1734, 8vo. pp. 431.
An interesting account of the Travels of John Ernest, Duke of Saxe-Weimar, in England, in 1613. The author describes the pictures in the several Royal Palaces. (See BECKMANN'S Litteratur der älteren Reisebeschreibungen, i. 535–534.)

NEVE, Philip. Cursory Remarks on some of the ancient English Poets, particularly Milton. Lond. 1789, 8vo.
Two hundred copies of this volume, consisting of 146 pages, were printed for presents, without the author's name being affixed. White Knights, 2296, 14s. Steevens, 980, 11s. 6d. Field, 1663, 18s. 6d. Fonthill, 1591, 15s. Sir M. M. Sykes, pt. II. 491, 11s. Bindley, pt. II. 2169, 8s. 6d.
Narrative of the Disinterment of Milton's Coffin. With a Postscript. Lond. 1790, 8vo. This narrative was immediately and ably answered in the St. James' Chronicle. Bindley, pt. iv. 960, G. Steevens's copy, with MS. notes, clearly proving it was not Milton's coffin, 1l. resold Heber, pt. II. 11. 12s.

— Robert. The merry Companions, or Delights for the Ingenious. Lond. 1721, 12mo.
Prefixed is a woodcut portrait of the author.

NEVELL, ——. The Generous Usurer, Mr. Nevell in Thames Street, who alloweth his Maid, usually a black pudding to dinner, and made lamentable Mowne that his Maid had rob'd him; because shee gave her Sweet-heart a Piece of Bread and Cheese. Lond. 1641, 4to.
Nassau, pt. I. 1700, 1l. 9s.; pt. II. 1556, 1l. 1s. Reprinted in facsimile, 1816, 4to. Bindley, pt. iv. 103, 2s.

NEVILLE, Francis de. The Pope's Missionary, &c. The Conversion of, wherein many Secrets of the Romish Clergy are revealed; with a Narration of the Author's Life. Lond. 1644, 4to. portrait.

NEVIL, William, son of Lord Latimer. The Castell of Pleasure, a Poem. Emprynted in Paules Church yarde by me Hary Pepwell, 1518, 4to.
BLACK LETTER. 18 leaves. Caldecott, 221, 10s. Now in the Grenville Collection.

NEVILE, Henry. Shuffling, Cutting, and Dealing, in a Game at Picquet: being acted from the Year 1653 to 1658, by O. P. and others, with great Applause. Printed in the Year 1659, 4to.
Ten pages. Rhodes, 1779, 5s. Roxburghe, 5555, 1l. 1s. Reprinted in the fifth volume of the Harleian Miscellany.
Plato Redivivus; or a Dialogue concerning Government. Lond. 1681, 8vo. —1763. Hollis, 960, morocco, 6s. Bindley, pt. II. 2177, 5s.
See LADIES, SLOETTON, H. C. Van.

— Robert. The Poor Scholar, a Comedy. Lond. 1622, 4to.
Rhodes, 1781. 2l. Bindley, pt. III. 782, with Nanston's Fragmenta Regalia, 1641, 1l. Heber, pt. II. 3s. Caldecott, 7s. 6d.

— Thomas. Imitations of Horace and of Juvenal and Persius. Lond. 1758, 69, small 8vo. 3s. 6d.

NEVILLE, Alexander. De Furoribus Norfolciensium Ketto duce, liber vnus. Ejusdem Norvicus. Ex officina Henrici Bynneman, 1575, 4to.

According to Hearne, there are two editions of this date of 1575; the first, without the passage displeasing to the Watchmen, dedicated only to Archb. Parker; the other, with two dedications; viz. that to Archb. Parker, and a new one to Archb. Grindall. The offensive passage is at p. 132, 'Sed enim Kettiani rall,' &c. to 'Nam præterquam quod,' &c. p. 133. Roxburghe, 8439, 6s. Bishop of Ely, 1244, 4s. 6d. *Collation.*—Title, one leaf, on the reverse of which are the arms of Archb. Parker; Latin verses, 6 pages; dedication to Abp. Grindal, 5 pages; epistle to Abp. Parker, and 'De Furoribus,' &c. pp. 1-86. Norvicen, pp. 207, besides title 1 leaf; Ad Lectorem, 5 pages; Latin verses, 8 pages; errata, 1 page; and 'Nomina Prætorum,' &c. 12 pages. Prefixed is a map of the descent of the British and Saxon kings.—Another edition was published in 1569, 16mo. without the map or Archb. Parker's arms, at the end of Ocland's Anglorum Prælia.

Norfolk Furies and their Foyle, under Kett, their accursed Captaine. With a Description of the famous Citie of Norwich, &c. Englished by Rich. Woods. Lond. 1623, 4to. Dent, pt. II, 750, 12s. Nassau, pt. II. 567, with a plan of Norwich inserted, 2l. 15s. *Collation.*—Pp. 110, not including title and dedication to Sir Thomas Hirsn, Knight, Mayor of Norwich, signed R. W(oods), 2 leaves; and To the Christian Reader, 4 pages. Geo. Chalmers, 10s.—1815, 4to. Gordonstoun, 1863, 11. 17s. Bliss, stained, 5s. 9d.

Ad Wallise præsens Apologia. Ex Off. filius Hauriei Bynanaaei. 1576, 4to. 10s. 6d. Nine leaves.

See OCLANDUS, Chr. SENECA. SIDNEY, Sir Philip.

NEVILLE FAMILY. *See* ROWLAND, D.

NEVIS.—Acts of Assembly passed in the Island of Nevis, from 1664 to 1739. Lond. 1740, folio. *See* SMITH, Wm., M.D.

NEVILLUS. *See* NEVILLE.

NEW ALBION.—A Description of the Province of New Albion, with a Letter from R. Evelin, that lived there for many Years. Lond. 1648, 4to.

Nassau, 1007, 1l. 12s.

NEWBERY, Francis. 'Donum Amicis.' Verses on various Occasions. Lond. 1815, crown 8vo.

An unpublished volume. Bindley, pt. II, 2187, 14s., resold Dillon, 7s. Heber, pt. IV. 2s.

— Thomas. Dives Pragmaticus. A Booke on English Metre called Dives Pragmaticus, or the great Marchantmen—very prettie for Children to rede. 1563, 4to.

Roxburghe, 5312, russia, 30l. This volume, supposed unique, is now in the Earl Spencer's collection.

NEW BRITAIN.—The Discovery of New Brittaine, began August 27, Anno Dom. 1650, by Edw. Bland, Merchant, Abraham Woode, Captaine, Sackford Brewster, and Elias Pennaut, Gentlemen. Lond. 1651, 4to. 1l. 5s.

NEWBURGH PEERAGE CASE. A Disquisition concerning the Law of Alienage and Naturalization according to the Statutes in force between the 10th June, 1816, and 25th March, 1818. Illustrated in an elaborate opinion of Counsel, written upon the claim of Prince Guistiniani to the Earldom of Newburgh. Paris, 1818, 8vo.

NEWCASTLE, John, Duke of, Lord Privy Seal. The whole Life and noble Character of, who died at Welbeck, 15 July 1711, with an Account how he has disposed of his Estate, and who is to marry his Daughter, the greatest Heiress in England; as also an Elegy on his death. Lond. n. d. 8vo.

— Margaret Cavendish, Duchess of. Letters and Poems in Honour of the incomparable Princess Margaret, Dutchess of Newcastle. Written by several Persons of Honour and Learning. In the Savoy, 1676, folio.

A gross and fulsome panegyric on the Duke and Duchess of Newcastle, but especially on her Grace. Bindley, pt. ii. 812, date 1678, 8s. Dillon (Farmer's copy), 2l. 8s. In Ballard's Memoirs will be found a copious memoir of the Duchess. Philosophical Fancies. Lond. 1653, 12mo. Nassau, pt. i. 2426, 7s. Sir M. M. Sykes, pt. II. 526, russia, 2l. 1s.

Poems and Fancies. Lond. 1653, folio, with portrait by P. V. Schuppen after V. Diepenbeke, 3l. 8s. Prince, 16s. In the British Museum is a copy with MS. notes in the Duchess's own hand.—Lond. 1664, fol. Bindley, pt. II. 1492, 1l. 18s. Dillon (Walpole's copy), 1l. 6s. Heber, pt. IV. 12s.

Some copies have a portrait of the Duchess sitting in a chair.—The third edition. Lond. 1664, folio, pp. 391. Bibl. Anglo Poet. 490, illustrated with several portraits of the Duchess, 7l. 7s. Singer, pt. iii. 336, 2l. 15s.

Philosophical and physical Opinions. Lond. 1655, folio, 7s. Bliss, 16s. Hindley, pt. ii. 1490, with Nature's Pictures, &c. 1656, 17s.—1663, folio. Sir M. M. Sykes, pt. ii. 344, 14s.

The World's Olio. Nature's Pictures drawn by Fancie's Pencil to the Life. Lond. 1655, folio. In the British Museum is a copy with MS. notes by the Duchess.—Lond. 1656, folio, also with notes (Grenville Coll.) Hindley, pt. ii. 1490, with her Ladyship's Opinions, 1655, 17s. Inserted in some copies is a print, Diepenbeek del. P. Clouret, sc. half sheet, containing portraits of William Cavendish, Marquis of Newcastle, his Marchioness, and their family, a proof impression of which, sold at the sale of Sir M. M. Sykes' prints, for 5l. 1s. Constable, 608, 5l. 12s. 6d.

Plays (21 and 6). Lond. 1762-8, folio, 2 vols. Vol. 1 is always smaller than vol. 2.— besides being dedicated to her husband, it is prefaced by no less than ten other addresses to her noble readers. Prefixed is a frontispiece by Van Schuppen, with full length portrait of the Duchess, after Diepenbeke. Roxburghe, 3915, 4l. 4s. Rhodes, 2069, 5l. 15s. 6d. Constable, 667, 3l. 13s. 6d. Prince, both plates, 4l. 19s.

Orations of divers Sorts, accommodated to divers Places. Lond. 1662, folio. Roxburghe, 2537, date 1663, 11s. Heber, pt. ix. 1l. 16s. Gardner, 9s.

Philosophical Letters, or modest Reflections upon some Opinions in natural Philosophy. Lond. 1664, folio. Bindley, pt. ii. 1491, 10s. 6d. Bliss, pt. i. 16s.

CCXI sociable Letters. Lond. 1664, folio. Letters CXXIII and CLXII are respecting Shakespeare. Heber, pt. x. 17s. Bliss, stained, 15s. Gardner, 5s.

Observations upon experimental Philosophy; to which is added, the Description of a new World. Lond. 1666, folio. Heber, pt. x. 13s.—Second edition, with a Description of a new World, called The Blazing World. (Separate title.) Lond. 1668, folio.

The Life of William Cavendish, Duke, Marquess, and Earl of Newcastle. Lond. 1667, folio. Prince, 6s. Nassau, pt. ii. 409, date 1669? 11s. Hindley, pt. ii. 1488, 14s. Bliss, 8s.—Lond. 1675, 4to. 7s. 6d.—Latine, Lond. 1668, folio. Bindley, pt. iii. 1032, 5s. Heber, pt. ii. 1s. A copy is in the British Museum with MS. notes by the authoress.

Grounds of natural Philosophy. Lond. 1668, folio.

Select Poems of the Duchess of Newcastle, edited by Sir Egerton Brydges, Bart. Kent, 1813, 8vo. Twenty-five copies printed as a specimen of the Lee Priory Press, and the first work printed there. Utterson, 16s. Bliss, morocco, 1l. 15s.

A true Relation of the Birth, &c. of Margaret Cavendish, Duchess of Newcastle. Written by herself. With a critical preface, &c. by Sir Egerton Brydges. Kent, 1814, royal 8vo. Printed at the private press of Lee Priory, with a portrait, B. Harding, del. W. N. Gardiner, sculp. It is extracted from her Ladyship's Nature's Pictures drawn to the Life. Hibbert, 5691, 17s.

NEWCASTLE, William Cavendish, Duke of. La Methode et Invention nouvelle de dresser les chevaux. Anvers, chez Jacques van Meurs, 1657, folio.

First and most esteemed edition, very rarely found complete. (The printed title is sometimes altered by hand to 1658.) Willett, 1676, russia, 3l. Bindley, pt. ii. 1707. 3l. 2s. 6d. LARGE PAPER. MacCarthy, 301 fr. resold Lond. 1815, 14l. 14s. The vol. should contain two title-pages, one printed the other engraved, also 42 fine plates. Among them is a print of the Cavendish Family by Diepenbeke, of the Duke's (then Marquis of Newcastle) sons, Charles, Viscount Mansfield and Mr. Henry Cavendish, on horseback; the Marquis and Marchioness, their three Daughters, and their Husbands; the Earl of Bridgewater, the Earl of Bollingbrooke, and Mr. Cheyne are under a colonnade as spectators. A very fine and perfect copy is in the Grenville Collection.

Second edition. Lond. 1737, folio, handsomely printed. 3l. 3s. LARGE PAPER, 6l. 6s. The plates in this London edition are from the original coppers, but the impressions are less brilliant.

A general System of Horsemanship in all its Branches. Lond. 1743 or 1748, roy. folio, 2 vols. Sir M. M. Sykes, pt. ii. 545. 2l. 17s. LARGE PAPER. Roxburghe, 1707, 6l. 16s. 6d. Inglis, 1206, russia, 4l. 5s. The first volume contains the translation of the Duke's treatise, with 43 plates; the second volume has eight and twelve plates, several of which are coloured.

Several other editions with additional plates have been published at Paris and Nuremberg.

A new Method and extraordinary Invention to dress Horses, and work them according to Nature; as also to perfect Nature by the Subtlety of Art. Lond. 1667, folio. Bindley, pt. ii. 1494, 16s. LARGE PAPER, 1l. 1s. The Duke informs his readers that 'this is neither a translation of the former, nor an absolute necessary addition to it; and may be of use without the other, as the other has been hitherto,

NEWCASTLE, W. C.—*continued.*
and still is, without this; but both together will questionless do best.'
A new Method and extraordinary Invention to Dress Horses. Lond. 1677, fol. without plates, 1l. 5s.
Methode nouvelle et Invention extraordinaire de dresser les Chevaux. Nouvellement traduit en François. Lond. 1671, folio. 1l. 5s.
This work on the *Management* of Horses, both the English original and the French translation, is quite distinct from the previous one on *Horsemanship*.
The Country Captaine and the Varietie. Two Comedies. At the Hague, 1649, 12mo. Heed, 5302, 5s. 6d. Hanburghe, 7916, 9s. 6d. Rhodes, 731, 2l. 3s. Lond. 1l. Moseley, 1649, 12mo. Fisher, pt. iv. 5s. Dilly, 1l. 1s. According to Wood, Shirley assisted his patron in the composure of certain plays.
The humorous Lovers. A Comedy. Lond. 1677, 4to. Roxburghe, 5557, 1l. 7s.
The triumphant Widow, or the Medley of Humours. A Comedy. Lond. 1677, 4to. Hanburghe, 5558, 1l. 1s.

NEWCASTLE UPON TYNE.—Hints on the Propriety of establishing a Typographical Society in Newcastle upon Tyne. Newcastle, 1818. 8vo. 2s. 6d.
Only 200 copies printed. A short time after the printing of these Hints, the author of them, and several other literary gentlemen, belonging to Newcastle and its neighbourhood, formed themselves into a society; and they agreed that the same should be denominated 'The Typographical Society of Newcastle upon Tyne,' and that their number of members should not exceed thirty.
See ALLAN, George. Newcastle Society Tracts, APPENDIX.
Chorographia. 1649. *See* GREY, William.
An Impartial History of Newcastle upon Tyne. 1801. *See* BAILEY, Rev. ——, BRAND, John, M.A.; COLLIER, John; GARDNER, Ralph.
The Picture of Newcastle upon Tyne. Newcastle upon Tyne, 1812, 12mo. Pp. 310. with a map and plan, one sheet, by Lambert. There are 19 wood-cuts on the letterpress.

NEWCOME, Rev. Peter. The History of the ancient and royal Foundation, called the Abbey of St. Alban, in the County of Hertford; from the Foundation thereof in 793 to its Dissolution in 1539; exhibiting the Life of each Abbot, and the principal Events relating to the Monastery during his Rule and Government. Lond. 1795, 4to.
Bindley, pt. iii. 752, 7s. 6d. Roscoe, 452, 8s. 6d. Towneley, pt. ii. 1277, russia, 17s. Drury, 8189, 19s. Dent, pt. ii. 751, 6s. Edwards, 642, 9s. *Collation.*—Title, errata and names of the abbots, 2 leaves; p. iii – xiii.; the history, two parts, with appendixes, 1—547, also a map by F. Vivares, and three plates at pp. 1, 235, and 342.

— Rev. R. Memoirs of Dr. Gabriel Goodman, Dean of Westminster, and of Godfrey Goodman, Bishop of Gloucester. Ruthin, 4to. 1825, portraits.
See GOODMAN, Godfrey.

— William, successively Bishop of Ossory and Waterford, and Archbishop of Armagh. An Harmony of the Gospels. Dublin, 1778, folio.
'Many other Harmonies of the Gospels have been published, but none preferable to this.'—*Bishop Watson.* Duke of Grafton, 94, 1l. 2s. Heath, 617, 1l. 12s.—1873, 8vo.
The Duration of our Lord's Ministry particularly considered; in Reply to a Letter from Dr. Priestley on that Subject, prefixed to his English Harmony of the Evangelists. Dublin, 1780, 12mo. 2s. 6d.
Observations on our Lord's Conduct as a divine Instructor, and on the Excellence of his moral Character. Lond. 1782, 4to. Gosset, 3928, 11s. 6d. Williams, 1163, 1l. 10s.—The second Edition corrected. 1795, 8vo. Edwards, 765, 6s. 6d.—Third edition, Lond. Priestley, 1820, 8vo. 10s.6d. —Oxford, 1852, 8vo. 6s.
A Review of the Chief Difficulties in the Gospel History, relating to our Lord's Resurrection: intended to retract some Errors contained in the Author's Greek Harmony, and to show that Dr. Benson's Hypothesis is satisfactory. 1791, 4to. This pamphlet is necessary to complete the Harmony.
An historical View of the English Biblical Translations; the Expediency of revising by Authority our present Translation: and the Means of executing such a Revision. With a list of the various editions of the Bible, and parts thereof, in English, from the year 1526 to 1776. Dublin, 1792, 8vo. 9s. An important work. Bindley, pt. ii. 2164, 1l. Gosset, 3716, 7s.
An Attempt towards revising our English Translation of the Greek Scriptures, or the new Covenant of Jesus Christ, and towards illustrating the Sense of Philological and explanatory Notes. Dublin, 1796, 8vo. 2 vols. A valuable accession to

the means of Interpreting the Scriptures. Gospel, 3717, 1l. 11s. 6d. Gough, 2529, 1l. 10s.

An English Harmony of the Four Evangelists, generally disposed after the Manner of the Greek of William Newcome, Archbishop of Armagh. Lond. 1802, 6s. —1827, 8vo.

See EZEKIEL. PROPHETS, The XII minor. TESTAMENT, The new.

NEWCOURT, Ric. Repertorium Ecclesiasticum Parochiale Londinense: an ecclesiastical parochial History of the Diocese of London. Lond. 1708-10. folio. 2 vols.

Marquis of Townshend, 2450, 3l. 15s. Edwards, 616, russia, 6l. 6s. Hindley, pt. ii. 1488, 5l. 10s. Dowdeswell, 621, 2l. 5s. Heber, pt. ix. 3l. 10s. LARGE PAPER, Heath, 4838, bl. 6s. Sir M. M. Sykes, pt. ii. 545, russia, 10l. North, pt. ii. 1429, bf. Towneley, pt. ii. 1174, russia, 9l. 19s. 6d. Nassau, pt. ii. 410, 21.9s. Dent, pt. ii. 780,9l. *Collation.*—Vol. I. Comprising all London and Middlesex, with the Parts of Hertfordshire and Buckinghamshire to the said Diocese belonging. Pp. 924, not including half-title, title and dedication to Henry Compton, Bishop of London, 8 leaves; preface, 7 pages; and errata, one page. Pages 67, 69 and 871—80 are omitted; pp. 71, 72 are repeated; pp. 764, 765, 764, 769, 772, 773 follow page 761; and after p. 773 are pages 776, &c. The paging is erroneous in many places. *Plates.*—1. Portrait of the Author, J. Sturt, sc. 2. View of old St. Paul's Cathedral, p. 1. 3. The west End of old St. Paul's Cathedral, p. 2. 4. South View of the present Cathedral, p. 4. 5. Views of St. Peter's Church, Westminster, &c. p. 709. Vol. II. 1'p. 692, including appendix; also halftitle and title, 2 leaves; list of subscribers, 4 pages; index, 51 pages, and a folded map of the diocese of London.

NEW CUSTOME. An Interlude. 1577. 4to.

Black letter. Roxburghe, 4279, 11l.0s.6d.

NEWELL, Rev. R. H. Letters on the Scenery of Wales. 1821. royal 8vo.

With plates. Hibbert, 5892, 13s.

NEW ENGLAND.—A briefe Relation of the Discovery and Plantation of New England. 1607 to 1622. Lond. 1622. 4to.

Gordonstoun, 2031, 7s. 6d. North, pt. iii. 398, 10s. 6d.

A Relation; or Journall of the Beginnings and Proceedings of the English Plantation settled at Plymouth, in New England, by certaine English Adventurers, &c. Lond. 1622, 4to. Gordonstoun, 2030, 12s. Jadis, 297, 1l. 8s.

A True Relation of the late Battell in New England, between the English and the l'equot Salvages. Lond. 1637, 4to.— 1638, 4to. Heber, pt. v. 1l. 10s. Caldecott, 1l. 4s.

An Abstract of the Lawes of New England, by John Cotton. Lond. 1641, 4to.— 1655, 4to. Sotheby's, Feb. 1860, 8l. 5s.

A brief Narration of some Church Courses held in opinion and practice in the Churches lately erected in New England. By W. R. Lond. 1644, 4to. Sothebys, in 1860, 3l. 8s.

Certaine Queres propounded to such as affect the Congregational way and specially Samuel Eaton and Timothy Taylor. By Richard Hollinworth, 1646. Sothebys, Feb. 1860, 19s.

Further Queries upon the present state of the New English Affaires. By H. E. 1659, 4to. Sothebys, Feb. 1860, 4l. 6s.

A Brief Relation of the State of New England to this present year. Lond. for Richard Baldwin, 1689. Puttick, May, 1858, 2l. 2s.

New England's first Fruits; in Respect of the Conversion, &c. of the Indians. Second of the Progress of Learning in the College of Cambridge, &c. Lond. 1643, 4to. Puttick, May, 1859, 3l. 10s.

Ill News from New England. 1652, 4to. by — Clare.

Simplicities Defence against a seven-headed Church Government in New England. Lond. 1646, 4to. Hibbert, 7516, 7s. 6d.

The Glorious Progress of the Gospel among the Indians in New England. Manifested by three Letters under the hand of Mr. John Eliot, and another from Mr. Thomas Mayhew. Published by Edward Winslow, Lond. for Hannah Allen, 1648, 4to.

A History of New England from the English Planting in 1628 until the Years 1652. Lond. 1654, 4to. By — Johnson of N. E. but sometimes stated to be by Sir F. Gorges.

Sad and Deplorable News from New England, poetically related by an Inhabitant there. Lond. 1675, 4to.

A brief and true narration of the late Wars arisen in New England. Lond. 1675-6, 4to. Two parts.

Now England's Tears for her present Miseries. Lond. 1676, 4to.

A Narrative of the Troubles with the Indians in New England from the first Planting thereof in the Year 1607 to this present Year 1677. By W. Hubbard. Boston, 1677, 4to. Nowcoe, 1856, 14s.

A Confession of Faith, owned and consented to by the Elders, and at Boston in New England, May 12, 1680. Boston, 1680, 12mo.

A Memorial of the present deplorable state of New England under the Maladministration of Joseph Dudley, the Governor, and his son Paul. Boston, 1707, 4to.
Witchcraft in New England. See MATHER, COTTON AND INCREASE, pp. 1512, 1513; WITCHCRAFT. HUBBARD, p. 1152.
Many tracts, &c. relating to New England, 1622—1761, are in the British Museum. See Kennett's Bibliotheca Americana; Rich's Bibliotheca Americana; Granville Catalogue; H. Stevens' American Nugget.

NEWENHAM, Thomas. A View of the natural, political, and commercial Circumstances of Ireland. Lond. 1809. 4to. 15s.
A valuable mass of historical and statistical information. Newenham has published other tracts, &c. relative to Ireland.

NEW-EXCHANGE.—A Narration of the late Accident in the New-Exchange, on the 21st and 22d of November 1653. Written by Don Pantaleon Sa, extraordinary Legate in England. Lond. 1653. 4to.
Pp. 14. Nassau, pt. II. 353, 14s. It is printed in the third volume of the Harleian Miscellany.
See LADIES.

NEWFOUNDLAND.—A short Discourse containing Reasons and Inducements for planting that Country. Dublin, 1633. 4to. 10s. 6d.
His Majesty's (K. Charles I.) Commission for the Well-governing of Newfoundland is in the second volume of the Oxford Collection of Voyages and Travels.

NEWGATE.—Discouery of a London Monster, called The Black Dog of Newgate: profitable for all Readers to take Heed by. Lond. 1612. 4to.
Black letter. Pp. 48, with a frontispiece. Written by Luke Hutton. Reed, 1770, 7l. 12s. Bibl. Anglo-Poet. 224, 25l. resold Saunders' in 1818, 11l. 11s.—1838, 4to. Bindley, pt. iv. 123, 1l. 17s. Roxburghe, 6072, 3l. 13s. 6d. Jolley, 94. 2s. 6d.—Lond. by G. Simson and W. White, 4to. 29 leaves, a poetical BLACK LETTER tract with a wood-cut on title-page. A—F 2, in fours. A 1 blank. On sign. D 2 commences 'A dialogue (in prose) betwixt the author and one Zawny, who was a prisoner in Newgate, and perfectly acquainted with matters touching the discoueris of the superlative degree of cunni-catching.'

The Newgate Calendar. 1700.—1760. By Robert Sanders. Lond. 1764, 8vo. 6 vols.
The Newgate Calendar, or Malefactor's Bloody Register, with the last dying Speeches of the most notorious Criminals, from 1700—1772. Lond. J. Cooke [1775]. 8vo. 5 vols. plates.
Annals of Newgate, or Malefactor's Register. By the Rev. Mr. Villette. Lond. J. Wenman, 1776. 8vo. 4 vols. 1l. 16s.
The Malefactor's Register; or, the Newgate and Tyburn Calendar. Lond. Hogg. [1778—80]. 8vo. 5 vols. with many neat plates, mostly designed by Dodd, vl. 11s. 6d.
Old Bailey Chronicle. Edited by J. Mountague. Lond. Randall, 1783. (Reissued 1788.) 8vo. 4 vols. 40 plates by Valois, 1l. 8s.
Criminal Chronology; or, the New Newgate Calendar (containing Trials from the year 1700 till 1811). By Andrew Knapp and William Baldwyn, Attorneys-at-Law. Lond. Nuttall, &c. 1811, 8vo. 4 vols. plates.
The same (with Continuation to 1812, 5 vols. and a Supplementary, or 6th vol. to 1825). (This edition was issued as complete in five volumes about 1820; the sixth volume, which contains Trials from 1813 to 1825, with a general Index, was published about 1826.) Lond. Robins and Co. n.d. 8vo. 6 vols. plates, 2l. 12s. 6d.—In double columns, 1824—5, 8vo. 2 vols.
The New and Complete Newgate Calendar. By William Jackson, Esq. Barrister. Lond. Hogg, 1800—1808, 8vo. 7 vols. pub. in 112 monthly Nos., plates. New edition (continued to 1818). Lond. Hogg, 1818, 8vo. 8 vols. (forming 6 vols. the 6th volume being in two parts), plates, 2l. 2s.
See CRIMINALS, TRIALS, TYBURN. VILLETTE, Rev. J.

NEW GUINEA.—Discoveries of the French in 1768 and 1769, to the South-East of New Guinea, with the subsequent Visits to the same Lands by English Navigators, who gave them new Names: to which is prefixed, an historical Abridgement of the Voyages and Discoveries of the Spaniards in the same Seas. Translated from the French. Lond. 1791, 4to.
Pp. xxiv and 323, with 12 plates. Willet, 715, 11s. Drury, 1858, russia, 10s. LARGE PAPER.

NEW HAMPSHIRE. See LITHOBOLIA.

NEW HOLLAND.—The History of New Holland, from its first Discovery in 1616 to the present Time. Lond. 1787, 8vo. 6s.

NEW JERSEY. The Grants, Concessions, and Original Constitutions of the Province of New Jersey, before the surrender thereof to Queen Anne and Philadelphia. W. Bradford, fol. n. d. p. 763.
Puttick, May 1859, 3l. 13s. 6d.

A further Account of New Jersey in Letters from thence, by Richard Hartshorn and others of the first Settlers. 1676, 4to. Puttick, May, 1859, 1l. 12s.

NEW YORK. Laws of the State of Albany, 1825, 8vo. 2 vols. *See* HISTORICAL SOCIETY COLLECTIONS, Appendix.

NEWLIN, Tho. Sermons on several Occasions. Oxford, 1720, 8vo. 2 vols.
Williams, 1248, 2l.

NEWMAN, Arthur. The Bible-Bearer, by A. N. of Trinity College, Oxford. Lond. 1607, 4to.

Black letter, consisting of 23 leaves. Bindley, pt. 1. 892, 9s. Heber, pt. II. 5s. 6d. Williams, 231, morocco, 3l. 5s. It is a 'shrewd satire upon all hypocritical, puritanical, and sanctified sinners, all trimmers, time-servers, and holy cameleons, or conformists to any preachers, parties, or fashionable principles, who are only politically pious for profit or preferment.'

— Pleasures Vision with Desert's Complaint; and a short Dialogue of a Woman's Properties between an old Man and a young. Lond. 1619, 16mo.

Pp. 62. Perry, pt. iv. 305, M 8. title, 3l. 4s. Steevens, 990, 2l. 5s. Bibl. Anglo-Poet. 501, 20l. Hibbert, 5697, 4l. 8s. Bindley, pt. II. 2018, 21l. 10s. 6d. resold, Heber, 2l. 15s. Sir M. M. Sykes, pt. II. 680, 4l. 8s. Midgeley, 12l. 10s. resold, Jolly (title MS.), 2l. 10s.—Reprinted for Mr. Utterson, 1840, 18mo. by E. Hartnall, Ryde, Isle of Wight. Bliss, 10s.

NEWMAN, John Henry, B.D. The Arians of the Fourth Century, their Doctrine, Temper, and Conduct; chiefly as exhibited in the councils of the Church between A.D. 325 and A.D. 381. Lond. Rivingtons, 1833, 8vo.

This edition was at one time worth 2l. 2s. In consequence of the author's objection to have it republished, but it was surreptitiously reprinted under the original date, which reduced the price.—Reviewed in Edinb. Rev. lxiii. 44.

Reprinted. Lond. Lumley, 1834, 10s. 6d.

The Restoration of Suffragan Bishops recommended, as a means of affecting a more equal distribution of episcopal duties, as contemplated by his Majesty's recent Ecclesiastical Commission, 1.—1v. pp. 52. Lond. 1835, 8vo. 1s. 6d.

Parochial Sermons. Lond. Rivington and Parker, Oxf. 1834–42, 8vo. 6 vols. 3l. 8s. (Some of the volumes having undergone several editions, we give the date of the first and last. Vol. 1, 1834, fifth edition, 1844; vol. 2, 1835, fifth edition, 1851; vol. 3, 1836, fourth edition 1844; vol. 4, 1839, third edition 1842; fourth edition, materially altered according to Roman Catholic views, Lond. Burns, 1850; vol. 5, 1840, second edition 1842; third edition, Lond. Rivingtons, 1857; vol. 6, 1842, second edition 1845.)

Sermons selected from vols. 1—4 of Parochial Sermons. Lond. Rivingtons, 1841, 12mo. 7s. 6d.

Lectures on the Prophetical Office of the Church, viewed relatively to Romanism and popular Protestantism. Lond. Rivingtons, 1837, 8vo.—Second edition, Lond. 1838, 8vo. 10s. 6d. (This volume was withdrawn from sale in 1845, when the author became Romanist, and consequently rose to more than double its published price.)

A Letter to the Rev. Godfrey Faussett, D.D., Margaret Professor of Divinity, on certain points of Faith and Practice. Pp. 99. Lond. Rivingtons. Oxf. Parker, 1838. 8vo. 2s.

Lectures on Justification. Lond. Rivingtons, 1838, 8vo. 10s. 6d.—Second edit. ib. 1840, 8vo. 10s. 6d. Reviewed in Brit. Critic, 24, 82.

A Letter addressed to the Rev. R. W. Jelf, D.D., Canon of Christ Church, in explanation of No. 90, in the series called 'The Tracts for the Times.' By the author. Second edition, Pp. 31. Oxf. 1841, 8vo. 1s.

A Letter to the Bishop of Oxford, on occasion of No. xc. in the series called 'The Tracts for the Times.' Oxf. 1841, 8vo. 1s. 6d.

The Church of the Fathers. [Anonymous.] Lond. Rivingtons, 1842, 8vo.—Second edition. Lond. Rivingtons, 1842, sm. 8vo. 7s.—Third edition, revised. Dubl. Duffy, 1858, 4s.

Sermons bearing on subjects of the day. Lond. Rivingtons, 1843, 8vo. 12s.—Second edition. Lond. ib. 1844, 8vo. 12s.

Sermons, chiefly on the Theory of religious belief, preached before the University of Oxford. Lond. Rivingtons, 1843,

NEWMAN, J. H.—*continued.*
8vo. 9s. 6d.—Second edition. Lond. Rivingtons, 1844, 8vo. 9s. 6d.

An Essay on the Miracles recorded in the Ecclesiastical History of the early ages. Oxf. Parker. Lond. Rivingtons, 1843, 8vo. 6s. Also in Fleury's Ecclesiastical History, translated by Newman, vol. 1.

An Essay on the Development of Christian Doctrine. Lond. Toovey, 1845, 8vo. —Second edition. Lond. Toovey, 1846, 8vo. 12s.—Reviewed by the Rev. H. H. Milman, in Quart. Review, lxxvii. 404.

Remarks on Mr. Newman's Doctrine of Purgatory. By a Country Clergyman. Oxf. 1841, 8vo.

A Review of his Essay on the Development of Christian Doctrine. By an English Churchman. Lond. 1846, 8vo.

A few words addressed to the author of 'An Essay on the Development of Christian Doctrine.' By an Anglican Priest. Lond. 1846, 8vo.

Mithridates; or, Mr. Newman's Essay on Development its own confutation. By a quondam disciple. Lond. 1846, 8vo.

Dissertatiunculæ quædam critico-theologicæ. Romæ. (Lond. Toovey), 1847, 8vo. 4s. 6d.

Loss and Gain; or, the Story of a Convert. [Anon.] Lond. Burns, 1848, 12mo. 6s.—Fourth edition, ib. 1859, 4s.

Discourses addressed to mixed Congregations. Lond. Longmans, 1849, 8vo. 12s. —Second edition. Lond. Longmans, 1850, 8vo. 12s.

Lectures on Certain Difficulties felt by Anglicans in submitting to the Catholic Church. Lond. Burns, 1850, 8vo.—Second edition, ib. 1850, 8vo. 12s.—Third edition, ib. 1857, 8vo. 7s.

Lectures on the Present Position of Catholics in England; addressed to the brothers of the Oratory. Lond. Burns, 1851, 8vo. 12s.—Third edition, ib. 1857, post 8vo. 7s.

Callista, a Sketch of the third century. Lond. Burns, 1852, 8s. 6d.—Fourth edition, 1859, 9s. 6d.

Lectures on the History of the Turks as to Christianity. Dublin, Duffy, (Lond. Dolman), 1853, 1s.

Office and Work of Universities. Lond. Longmans, 1856, 12mo. 6s.

Sermons preached on various occasions. Lond. Burns, 1857, cr. 8vo. pp. 236, 6s.— Second edition, 1858, fcap. 8vo. 5s.

Letters on Sir Robert Peel's Speech at Tamworth. Lond. Mortimer, n. d. (1829?) 8vo.

Lectures and Essays on University Subjects. Lond. Longmans, 1859, 12mo. pp. 390, 6s.

The Scope and Nature of University Education. Second edition. Lond. Longmans, 1859, post 8vo. pp. 350, 6s.

Lives of the English Saints, by the Rev. J. H. Newman and others, comprising upwards of Thirty Biographies of the most eminent Ecclesiastics and pious Women of the early English Church. Lond. Toovey, 1844, 12mo. 14 vols. frontispieces, pub. 2l. 8s. Reduced, Bohn, 1l. 1s. Containing—

Part 1.—St. Stephen, Abbot and Founder of the Cistercian Order, 4s.

2.—St. Richard the Saxon; St. Willibald; St. Walburge; and St. Winibald, 3s.

3 & 13.—St. Augustine of Canterbury, Apostle of the English, and his Companions St. Mellitus, St. Lawrence, St. Peter, St. Justus, and St. Honorius; together with some account of the early British Church, 2 vols. 6s.

4.—The Hermit Saints; being the Histories of St. Gundleus, St. Haller, St. Herbert, St. Edelwald, St. Bettelin, St. Neot, and St. Bartholomew, 3s.

5.—St. Wulstan, Bishop of Worcester; and St. William, Archbishop of York, 3s.

6.—St. Paulinus, Archbishop of York, and companion of St. Augustine; St. Edwin, King, and St. Ethelburga, Queen; St. Oswald and St. Oswin, Kings and Martyrs; St. Ebba and St. Bega, Virgins and Abbesses; and St. Adamnan, Monk of Coldingham, 4s.

7.—St. Gilbert, Prior of Sempringham, 3s.

8.—St. Wilfred, Bishop of York, 4s.

9 & 11.—St. German, Bishop of Auxerre, in Normandy, 2 vols. 7s.

10.—Stephen Langton, Archbishop of Canterbury, 3s.

12.—St. Aelred, Abbot of Rievaux; and St. Ninian, 4s.

14.—St. Edmund, Archbishop of Canterbury; St. Richard, Bishop of Chichester; St. Waltheof, and St. Robert, of Newminster, 4s.

Dr. Newman made his debut in the Tracts for the Times, (which see). He contributed vol. 5 of the 'Plain Sermons,' by the authors of Tracts for the Times. (Lond. Rivingtons, 1840-48, 10 vols. 6s. 6d. each.) Some Poems in the 'Lyra Apostolica,' (Lond. 1836, 8th edition 1848.) He also contributed to the Manual of Greek and Roman Philosophy and Science, republished from the Encyclopædia Metropolitana. Lond. Griffin, 1859, post 8vo. 4s.

His works and new editions since 1845, are presumed to bear evidence of his accession to the Church of Rome. The previous works, chiefly published by Rivington and Co., are English High Church.

NEWMAN, Selig. A Grammar of the Hebrew Language, with Points; together with a short Sketch of the Chaldee Grammar. Lond. 1827, 8vo.

NEWMARKET FAYRE: or, a Parliament Outcry: or State Commodoties set to Sale; a Tragi-comedy. Lond. 1649, 4to.

A copy of this dramatic satire is in the British Museum.

The second Part of the Tragi-Comedy called New-Market Fayre, or Mrs. Parliaments new Figaryes, written by the Man in the Moon. 1649, 4to. Sotheby's in April 1821, 13s. 6d.

The Muse of New-market, or Mirth and Drollery, in three Farces. Lond. 1680, 4to.

New-market; or an Essay on the Turf. Lond. 1771, small 8vo. 2 vols.

NEWSHAM, John. His Nightcrowe, a Bird that breedeth Brawles in many Families and Householdes. Lond. 1590, 4to.

This tract, consisting of pp. 50, dedicated to Thomas Owen, Esq. Sergeant at Law, is divided into two parts; the first is concerning fathers, and the second part upon stepmothers. Nassau, pt. II. 551, russia, 3l. 5s. Heber, pt. iv. 4l. 6s. Bindley, pt. III. 776, 5l. Roxburghe, 6673, 4l. 18s. Brand, 4l. 18s. Bright, mor. 3l. 5s. Jolly, 6l.

NEWS OUT OF HELL: a Dialogue betweene Charon and Zebul, a Deuil. Lond. by John Byddell, 1636, 8vo.

In it (says Ames) mention is made of Harry VIII. and Cromwel, Hunne and Bulney; Rastall their advocate, 1536, a waterman belong to Temple bridge, and dwelling in Chancery-lane.

Newes come from Hell; of Love to Usurers. See USURY.

News Newes, contayning a short Rehearsall of Stukley and Mac Morice's Rebellion. Charlewood, 1579, 8vo. BLACK LETTER. Geo. Chalmers, pt. III. 1196, but could not be found at time of sale.

Newes from the North, or a Conference between Simon Certain and Pierce Plowman. Lond. Allde. 1579, 4to. BLACK LETTER. Roxburghe, 5321, 12l. 12s. In the Malone Collection.—An edition, 1585. BLACK LETTER. Coll. 44 leaves. Supposed to have been written by Francis Thynne. See F. T. p. 77.

Newes out of Germanie. 1584. See MURDERS.

Wonderfull and strange Newes out of Suffolk and Essex, where it rayned Wheat,

the space of 6 or 7 miles, on Feb. 1, 1583, 12mo.

Newes from Spayne and Holland. Anno 1588, 8vo. See Ames' Typog. Antiq. by Herbert, vol. III. 1724-5.

Newes from Rome concerning the blasphemous Sacrifice of the Papisticall Masse, transl. by Randall Hurleston. Canterbury, by J. Michell, for E. Campion. Inglis, 1057, 16s.

Newes from Rome, Venice, and Vienna, touching the Turkes. Lond. John Danter, for Tho. Gosson, 1595, 4to.

Newes out of Cheshire of the new found Well. 1600, with a frontispiece. Bindley, pt. III. 783, 2l. 11s.

Newes from Graves-end, sent to Nobody. Lond. by T. C. for Thomas Archer. 1604, 4to. A Poetical Tract, very much in the style of Thomas Nash. Sotheby in 1821, 1l. 8s. Heber, pt. iv. 2l. 9s.

News from Lough-Foyle in Ireland, of the Rebellion of Sir Carey Adougherty and Filly-me-Read Mac Davy. 1608, 4to. King and Lochée's in March 1810, 14s. 6d.

Newes from the Sea of two notorious Pyrats, Ward and Daenscker. 1609, 4to. With cuts. Bindley, pt. III. 794, 2l. 3s. Sotheby, June, 1838, 2l. 6s.

Newes from Spain. Lond. for Nathaniel Butter, 1611, 4to. 12 pages.

Newes out of Germany. 1612, 4to.

Wofull Newes from the west Parts of England of the lamentable burning of Teverton. 1612, 4to. with frontispiece. Bindley, pt. iv. 958, 12s.

Strange Newes of a prodigious Monster born at Adlington. 1613, 4to. with frontispiece. Nassau, pt. II. 178.

Newes from Spain. Lond. 1618, 4to. Foothill, 3646. 1l. 11s.

Newes from Italy. 1618, 4to.

Newes from Mamora. 1614, 4to.

Good Newes from Florence. 1614, 4to.

Newes from Guliok and Cleve. 1615, 4to.

Newes from Perin in Cornwall of a Murther committed by a Father on his owne Sonne (lately returned from the Indyes). Anno 1618, 4to. BLACK LETTER. From this pamphlet Lillo took his tragedy entitled 'The Fatal Curiosity.' Bindley, pt. III. 780, 4l. 4s.

Newes from Spayne. 1620, 4to. with plates.

Good Newes to Christendome sent to a Venetian in Ligorne, from a Merchant in Alexandria. 1620, 4to. with woodcut. Bindley, pt. iv. 146.

The certain Newes of this present week. Published by Nathaniel Butter, who was proprietor of several of the Intelligencers, from 1622 to about 1640.

Strange Newes out of divers Countries, never discovered till of late Years, by a strange Pilgrim. Lond. 1622, 4to.

A Couranto of Newes from the East
India: a True Relation of the taking of
Quanlers and Palurouse, in the Ports of
Ilanda in the East Indies, by the Holland-
ers. Lond. 1622, 4to. 6 pages.

A second Courante of Newes from the
East India, in two Letters, the one written
by Master Patricke Coplande, then
Preacher to the English in the East India,
to Master Adrian Jacobson Hulembus,
Preacher to the Dutch: the other, written
by Master Thomas Knowles, Factor, &c.
Printed the 18 Februarie, 1622, still noove.
4to. 6 leaves.

Newes from Parnassus. Printed at He-
licon, 1622, 4to. Reed, 2450, 7s. Bright,
2s. 6d.

Weekly News and Affairs of Europe.
1622-5, 8 vols. King and Lochée's in
March, 1810, 2l. 2s.

Newes and strange Newes from St.
Christophers of a tempestuous Spirit,
which is called by the Indians a Hurry-
cano or Whirlwind: wherennto is added,
the true and last Relations (in Verse) of
the dreadful Accident which happened at
Witticombe in Devonshire, 21 Octobre,
1638. Lond. 1638, 12mo. with a wood-cut.
Gordonstoun, 1675, 1l. 18s. Inglis, 1297,
1l. 8s.

Newes from the North, or Dialogue betwixt David Dammeslash, a Souldier, and
Walter Wheeler, a rich Northerne Farmer, 1641, 4to. with front. King and Lochée's in March 1810, 1l. 5s.

Sad News from the Seas, being a true
Relation of the Losse of that good Ship
called the Merchant Royall, which was
sent away ten Leagues from the Land's
End, on Thursday Night, being the 23 of
September last, 1641; having in her a
World of Treasure, as this Story following
doth truly relate. Printed in the Yeare
1641, 4to. Two leaves.

Old Newes newly revived, or the Discovery of all Occurrences happened since
the Beginning of the Parliament. 1641, 4to.
White Knights, 8152, 1l. 5s.

Newes from Home, with an Elegiacal
Confabulation betweene Death and Ho-
nour. A Poem. Lond. 1641, 4to. wood-cut.
Heber, pt. viii. 6s.

News from the narrow Seas, of the
fearful Fight between the Danes and Van
Trump. 1642, 4to. Jadis, 304*, 5s.

News from the narrow Sea. Being a
Relation of a mighty Fight upon the Coast
of Friezland. Lond. 1642. 4to.

Lamentable and sad News from the
North. Lond. 1642, 4to.

Newes, true Newes, laudable Newes,
Citie Newes, Court Newes, Countrey
Newes: the World is mad, or it is a mad
World my Masters, especially now when
in the Antipodes these Things are come to
passe. 1642, 4to. Nassau, pt. II. 310, 10s.

Newes from Sally; or a strange Deli-
very of foure English Captives fr. m the
Slavery of the Turkes. 1642, 4to.

Happy Newes to England, sent from
Oxford. 1642, 4to. with a wood-cut. King
and Lochée's in March 1810, 12s. 6d.

News from the King's Bath, Bristoll.
1645, 4to. G. Chalmers, pt. III. 978, 2l.
See Paucket, B.

Strange Newes from Campania. 4to.
Attalla, 1047. Sotheby's in 1821, 1l. 2s.

Newes from Smith the Oxford Jaylor.
1645, 4to. with a frontispiece. King and
Lochée's in March 1810, 13s.

News out of the West; or, the Character
of a Mountebank. 1647, 4to. Lloyd, 906,
10s. Heber, pt. viii. 6s. 6d.

Strange News from Scotland, or a
strange Relation of a terrible and prodigious Monster, borne to the Amusement
of all Spectators, in a Village neere Eden-
borough, called Hadensworth, Sept. 14,
1647, and the Words the said Monster
spake at its Birth. 4to. with a wood-cut.
Inglis, 1348, 6s. Marquis of Townshend,
2332, 7s. 6d.

Newes from the New Exchange. 1650.
See Ladies.

Newes from the Dead. 1651. See Greene,
Anne.

News from Newcastle, a Poem. 1651, 4to.
Townley, pt. I. 720°, 10s. 6d. Hindley,
pt. III. 787, 1l. 2s. Brand, II. 11a. 6d. Heber, pt. II. 1l. 9s.

Strange News from the West, being an
Account of several miraculous Sights seen
in the Air, westward, by divers Persons
of Credit, standing upon London Bridge.
Two Great Armies marching forth of two
Clouds and encountering each after, but
after a sharp Dispute they suddenly va-
nished, &c. 1661, 4to. Nassau, pt. II. 1158,
5s.

Newes published for the Satisfaction of
the People. 1664, 4to. Bindley, pt. III.
764, 9s.

Bloody News from Shrewsbury, a true
Relation of a horrible Villain, by name
Thomas Reynolds, who before he was
eighteen, murdered Alice Stephens and
her Daughter Martha, and set their House
on fire. He likewise set on fire one Goodman Merick's House, and twice attempted
to murder one Miss Corfields. 1673, 4to.
Nassau, pt. II. 858, 9s.

Newes from Puddle Docke, or a Narrative of Apparitions and Transactions in
the House of Mr. E. Pitts at Puddle Dock.
1674, 4to. Nassau, pt. II. 899, 12s.

Newes from Kensington: being a Relation how a Maid there is supposed to have
been carried away by an Evil Spirit. 1674,
4to. Nassau, pt. II. 400, 5s.

Strange and terrible News from Shoreditch of a Woman that hath sold herself

to the Devil, living in Badger Alley. 1674. 4to. Nassau, pt. II. 1160, 7s.
Strange and terrible News from Oakingham, in Berks, of a Thunder Clap, &c. 1675.
News from Snanes; or, the barbarous Robber strangely convicted. 1676, 4to. Nassau, pt. II. 401, 5s.
News from St. John Street of a Monster brought forth by a Sow. 1676, 4to. Towneley, pt. I. 719, 3/. 7s.
News from Buckinghamshire, or a perfect Relation how a young Maid hath been for twelve Years and upwards possest with the Devil. 1677, 4to. Nassau, pt. II. 402, 13s.
Horrid News from St.Martin's In a Relation of a Girl not 16 poysoning her Mother, a Servant Maid, and two Gentlewomen. 1677, 4to.
Lamentable and bloody News from St. Albans, an Account of the late great Robbery and barbarous Murder committed there by Highwaymen. 1677, 4to. Nassau, pt. II. 385, 6s.
Strange News from the Deep, with an Account of a large prodigious Whale. 1677, 4to. with a woodcut. Nassau, pt. I, 1497.
Strange and Wonderful News from Bridewell of a converted Whore. 1677, 4to. Nassau, pt. II. 1161, 4s.
News from Bartholomew-Fair. (1678), 4to. with a woodcut. Lloyd, 594, 13s. 6d.
Bloody News from Angel Alley, being a true Account of the cruel murdering of one Dorothy Jewars, who was barbarously robbed and killed by two of her Lodgers. 1678, 4to. Nassau, pt. II. 387, 9s.
News from Maidstone, a Narrative of the Tryals and Condemnations of four notorious House-breakers, &c. 1678, 4to. Nassau, pt. II. 404, 8s.
News from Wicklow, a Relation how Dr. Moore was taken invisibly by his Friends. 1678, 4to. Nassau, pt. II. 405, 5s.
News from Dullidy Wells of a barbarous Father who kill'd his own Son. 1678, 4to. Bindley, pt. III. 752, 18s.
Strange and wonderful News from Glasgow, being a full and true Account of a terrible Earthquake that happened there. 1679, 4to. Lloyd, 995, 4s. 8d. Nassau, pt. I, 1709, 5s.
News from Pannier Alley, or a true Relation of some Pranks the Devil hath lately played with a plaster Pot there. 1677, 4to. Nassau, pt. II. 406*, 12s.
Strange News from Arpington, near Bexley in Kent, a true Relation of a young Maid who was possest with several Devils or Evil Spirits, &c. 1679, 4to. North, pt. III. 701, date 1679, 7s. Nassau, pt. II. 403, 12s.
Newes from Ipswich. 4to. with a woodcut. King and Lochée's in March, 1810. 15s.

Newes from Ipswich, on the Practises of Lordly Prelates. 4to. with a woodcut. King and Lochée's in March, 1810, 16s.
Newes newly revived. 4to. with a woodcut. King and Lochée's in March, 1810, 1l. 6s.
Strange and fearfull Newes from Plaisto, in the Parish of West Ham, of one Paul Fox, a Silk Weaver, where is dayly to be seene throwing of Stones, Brickbats, &c. 4to. Gough, 5849, 11s.
Strange News from Sattou in Cornwall; or true Relation of a cruel bloody Murther committed by one J. R. upon his own Father for Lucre of enjoying his Estate, written by W. Maddish. 4to. Nassau, pt. II. 573, 5s.
More strange Newes: of wonderfull Accidents hapning by the late Overflowing of Waters, in Summersetshire, Glocestershire, Norfolke, and other Places of England. 4to. BLACK LETTER. Lloyd, 800, 1l. 14s.
An excellent Account of 'Newes Pamphlets,' of which Burton, in 1614, complained, as being, along with Play Books, almost the exclusive reading, will be found in Mr. George Chalmers' Life of Thomas Ruddiman.

NEWSTEAD, Christopher. An Apology for Women, or the Woman's Defence. Lond. 1620, 12mo. Gordonstoun, 18s.

NEWTE, Thomas. Prospects and Observations on a Tour in England and Scotland: natural, œconomical, and literary. Lond. 1791, 4to. With a map of Scotland and plates. Nassau, pt. II. 552, 10s. Fonthill, 745, 1l. 8s. Heber, pt. VIII. 5s. 6d.
A Tour in England and Scotland in 1785. By an English Gentleman. Lond. 1788, 8vo. with six views by Heath. 4s.

NEWTON, Henry. Epistolæ, Orationes et Carmina. Lucæ, 1710, 4to.
Prefixed is a portrait of the author, who was the friend of Lord Somers, and Envoy extraordinary to the Court of Tuscany. Heber, pt. x. morocco, 10s.

— Sir Isaac. Opera, quæ extant omnia, Commentariis illustrabat Samuel Horsley, Episc. Roffensis. Lond. 1779-85, 4to. 5 vols. 10l. 10s.
Duke of Grafton, 172, 7l. 10s. Bishop Randolph, 1149, 7l. 14s. 6d. Heath, 1316, 8l. Willett, 1783, 8l. 7s. 6d. Hibbert,

1672 NEW NEW

NEWTON, Sir Isaac—*continued.*
6503, 9l. Nassau, pl. 1l. 503, russia, 12l.
Williams, 1165, in pig-skin. 13l. 13s. An
edition of Newton's philosophical Works,
prepared with learning and ability, is still
a desideratum.
OPUSCULATA MATHEMATICA, Philosophica, etc. collegit Jo. Castillioneus. Lausannæ, 1744, 4to. 3 vols. 1l. 1s.
PHILOSOPHIÆ NATURALIS PRINCIPIA MATHEMATICA. Lond. 1687, 4to. Roxburghe, 1633, 4s. 6d.—Cantab. 1713, 4to. Published with a preface by Roger Cotes, at the desire of Dr. Bentley. Roxburghe, 1534, 5s. 6d.—Amst. 1714, 4to. 8s.—Amst. 1723, 4to. 8s.—Lond. 1726, 4to. 10s. 6d. Best edition, published by Dr. Pemberton, with portrait of Newton. LARGE PAPER. Roxburghe, 1535, morocco, 2l. 12s. 6d. LARGEST PAPER, in folio, printed for presents only. Constable, 687, 6l. 10s. 6d. Gardner in 1854, 2l. 17s.—Illustrata a Geo. Pet. Domchlo. Lond. 1730, 8vo. 3 vols. 10s. 6d.
Philosophiæ Naturalis Principia Mathematica, perpetuis Commentariis illustrata, communi Studio T. L. Seur et Fr. Jacquier. Genev. 1739-42, 4to. 4 pts. in 3 vols. 2l. 2s, Willett, 1764, 6l.—Col. Alloh. editio nova, 1760, 4to. 4 pts. in 3 vols. 2l. 2s. Hibbert, 5804, 3l.—Glasg. 1822, royal 8vo. 4 vols. 1l. 8s, Drury, 4023, russia, 2l. 4s.
Excerpta quædam e Newtoni Principiis Philosophiæ Naturalis, cum Notis variorum. (Ed. Jebb.) Lond. 1765, 4to. 7s. 6d.
Excerpta ex Principiis Naturalis Philosophiæ, cum Annotationibus T. Le Seur et F. Jacquier. (Sect. 1, 2, 3, 6, 7, 8.) Oxon. 1831, 8vo. 6 folding plates. 10s. 6d. reduced 5s. 6d.
Principia, 3 first sections and part of the 7th, with preface on a geometrical course, and on the atomic constitution of matter, and the laws of motion, by Cooke. Oxf. Parker, 1850, 8vo. 6s.
Mathematical Principles of Natural Philosophy, translated by Andrew Motte. With the Laws of the Moon's Motion according to Gravity, by J. Machin. Lond. 1729, 8vo. 2 vols. Hibbert, 5696, 8s.—With Additions by W. Davis. Lond. 1803, 8vo. 3 vols. 1l. 7s.—Lond. 1819, 8vo. 3 vols. portrait and 52 plates, 1l. 7s. — New edition, to which is added Newton's System of the World; with Life by Chittenden. New York, 1850, roy. 8vo. 1l. 1s.
Mathematical Principles of Natural Philosophy, by Sir Isaac Newton, Knight, translated into English, and illustrated with a Commentary, by Robert Thorp, A.M. Lond. 1777, 4to. vol. 1. (all published)—Second edition, (new title only), 1802, 4to. 15s.
Principes mathematiques de la Philosophie naturelle, trad. par Mme. la Marquise du Chastelet. Paris, 1759, 4to. 2 vols. 15s.

This translation is accompanied by a commentary of Mme. du Chastelet, illustrations by Clairaut, and an historical preface by Voltaire.
The first three Sections of Newton's Principia (in English), with copious Tables, Illustrations, and Problems, by the Rev. John Carr, M.A. Second Edition. Lond. 1829, 8vo. 10s. 6d.
Principia (in English), Book I. Sections 1, 2, 3. Edited by W. Whewell. Lond. Parker & Son, 1846, 2s. 6d. Sections 1, 2, 3, with notes and examples by Percival Frost. Cambridge, Macmillan, 1854, crown 8vo. 10s. 6d. Lond. Bell, 18 —, post 8vo. 10s. 6d. —By Wright. Lond. Whittaker & Co., 18—, 8vo. 10s. 6d.—First three Sections with 9 & 11, by J. Evans. Fourth edition. Lond. Bell, 1865, 8vo. 6s.
A short Comment on Sir Isaac Newton's Principia. Lond. 1770, 8vo. 8s. By William Emerson.
Examination of the third and fourth Definitions of the first Book of Sir I. Newton's Principia, and of the three Axioms or Laws of Motion, by Robert Young. Lond. 1787, 4to.
A Commentary on Newton's Principia, with a supplementary Volume, designed for the use of Students at the Universities, by J. M. F. Wright. Lond. 1828, 8vo. 2 vols. with plates, 1l. 8s. reduced 14s.
Commentaries on Newton's Principia. Lond. Whittaker, 1846, roy. 8vo. 4s.
Rigaud. — Historical Essay on the first publication of Sir Is. Newton's Principia. Oxford, 1838, 8vo. 5s.
A Demonstration of some of the principal Sections of Sir Isaac Newton's Principles of natural Philosophy, by John Clarke, D.D. Lond. 1730, 8vo. 2s.
A general Treatise on the Laws of Nature and Motion, with their Application to Mechanics; also the Doctrine of centripetal Forces and Velocities of Bodies, describing any of the conick Sections, being a Part of the great Mr. Newton's Principles. By Humphrey Ditton. Lond. 1705, 8vo.
Prælectiones physico - mathematicæ; sive Philosophia Newtoni mathematica illustrata, a W. Whiston. Cantab. 1710, 8vo. Afterwards translated and published in English.
Sir Isaac Newton's mathematick Philosophy more easily demonstrated, with Dr. Halley's Account of Comets illustrated, by W. Whiston. Lond. 1716, 8vo.
Lectures on Sir Isaac Newton's mathematic Philosophy, and on Dr. Halley's Account of Comets, by W. Whiston. Lond. 1716, 8vo.
Remarks upon the Newtonian Philosophy; wherein it is proved to be false and absurd, by George Gordon. Lond. 1719, 12mo.

NEWTON, Sir Isaac—*continued.*

Recueil de plusieurs Pieces de Physique, où l'on fait principalement voir l'Invalidité du Système de Mr. Newton, par Nich. Hartsoeker. Utrecht, 1722, 12mo.

A View of Sir Isaac Newton's Method for comparing the Resistance of Solids, by Christopher Robinson. Lond. 1734, 8vo. 2s. 6d.

Elements of Sir I. Newton's Philosophy, by M. de Voltaire, translated by J. Hanna. Lond. 1738, 8vo.

Response à toutes les Objections principales fait en France contre la Philosophie de Neuton, par M. de Voltaire. Amst. 1739, 8vo.

An Introduction to the Newtonian Philosophy, by Benj. Martin. Lond. 1765. 8vo. 8s.

Philosophia Britannica; or, a complete System of the Newtonian Philosophy, by Benjamin Martin. Lond. 1759, 8vo. 2 vols. 7s. 6d.

Examination of the Newtonian Argument for the Emptiness of Space, by George Martin. Lond. 1740, 8vo.

Vrai Système de Physique générale de Newton, par L. B. Castel. 1743, 4to.

View of Sir Isaac Newton's Philosophy, by Henry Pemberton, M.D. Lond. 1728, 4to. 7s. 6d. LARGE PAPER, 10s. 6d.

An Account of Sir Isaac Newton's philosophical Discoveries, by Colin Maclaurin. Lond. 1748, 4to. 4s.—1750, 8vo. 6s.

Réflections sur la Physique moderne, ou la Philosophie Newtonienne comparée avec celle de Descartes, par l'Abbé D***. Paris, 1751, 8vo.

The Theology and Philosophy in Cicero's Somnium Scipionis explained; or a brief Attempt to demonstrate that the Newtonian System is perfected agreeable to the Notions of the wisest Ancients, &c. Lond. 1751, 8vo.

Panegyrics of the Newtonian Philosophy, by Benj. Martin. 1754, 2s. 6d.

An Explanation of the principal Proposition of Sir Isaac Newton's Philosophy, 1766. In Nic. Saunderson's Method of Fluxions, 8vo.

A Treaty of Peace between Descartes and Newton; to which is prefixed, an Account of the Lives of these eminent Philosophers. In French, by A. H. Paulian. Avignon, 1764, 12mo. 3 vols.

Observations philosophiques sur le Systeme de Newton, le Mouvement de la Terre, et la Pluralité des Mondes, par F. X. de Feller. 1771.

An Examination of Sir Isaac Newton's Philosophy. 1779. In Lord Monboddo's Ancient Metaphysics. 4to.

An Essay on Sir Isaac Newton's second Law of Motion, by the Rev. William Ludlam. Lond. 1780, 8vo.

An Illustration of Sir Isaac Newton's Method of Reasoning, by prime and ultimate Ratios, comprehending the first Section of his Principia, and as much of the second and third as is necessary to explain the Motions of the heavenly Bodies, by Thomas Newton, M.A. Lond. 1805.

Il Newtonianismo per le Dame, de Franc. Algarotti. Napoli, 1737. 12mo.—Translated from the Italian (by Eliz. Carter). Lond. 1739, 12mo. 2 vols.—1742, 12mo. 2 vols.

OPTICKS: or, a Treatise of the Reflections, Refractions, Inflections, and Colours of Light: also two Treatises of the Species and Magnitude of curvilinear Figures. Lond. 1704, 4to. Roxburghe, 1877, 4s. 6d.—1730, 8vo. 3s. 6d.—Lond. 1740, 4to. 10s. 6d.

Optice sive de Reflexionibus, Refractionibus, Inflexionibus, et Coloribus Lucis, Libri III. Latine reddidit a Sam. Clarke, necnon ejusdem Tractatus duo de Speciebus et Magnitudine Figurarum curvilinearum. Lond.1706 vel 1719, 4to. 5s.—Genev. 1740, 4to. 10s. 6d. Sir Is. Newton gave Clarke 500l. for this Translation.

A French translation by P. Coste. Paris, 1722, 4to. 6s. Another, by Marat, published by Nich. Beauzée. Paris, 1787, 8vo. 2 vols. 6s.

Optical Lectures read in the publick Schools of the University of Cambridge. Lond. 1729, 8vo. 3s.

Lectiones Opticæ in Scholis publicis habitæ, 1669-71. Lond. 1729, 4to. 6s.

Critical Remarks on Sir Isaac Newton's Opinions on Colours, &c. in experimental Outlines for a new Theory of Colours, Light and Vision, by Joseph Reade, M.D. Dublin, 1816, 8vo. Some papers respecting Newton by Dr. Reade will be found in the Philosophical Magazine, and in Thomson's Annals of Philosophy.

Theory of Light and Colours. Lond. 1742, 12mo. 2 vols. Roxburghe, 1859, 4s. 6d.

The Observation of Newton concerning the Inflections of Light; accompanied by other Observations differing from his; and appearing to lead to a Change of his Theory of Light and Colours. Lond. 1799, 8vo. 4s. pp. 184, with nine plates.

The Reviewers reviewed: being a Reply to the Animadversions of the Monthly Review on a late Pamphlet, entitled Sir Isaac Newton's Æther realized. By R. Lovett. Lond. 1760, 8vo. 2s.

Dissertation on the Æther of Sir I. Newton, by Brian Robinson, M.D. Dublin, 1743, 8vo.

Account of the Aether, with some Additions by Way of Appendix, by B. B(ohines). M.D. Dublin, 1745, 8vo.

An Account of Sir Isaac Newton's Op-

NEWTON, Sir Isaac—*continued.*
tion, part 1, forms no. 56 of the Library of
Useful Knowledge, published in 181–.
Original Papers between Sir Isaac Newton and Dr. James Gregory relating to
reflecting Telescopes. In David Gregory's
Elements of Catoptrics and Dioptrics.

NEWTON'S QUADRATURE OF CURVES,
edited by P. R. de Montmort, 1700.
Two Treatises of the Quadrature of
Curves, and Analysis by Equations of an
infinite Number of Terms explained; containing the Treatises themselves translated into English from the Original of
Sir Isaac Newton; with a large Commentary, by John Stewart, A.M. Lond. 1745,
4to. 5s.
Tractatus de Quadratura Curvarum,
cum Explanationibus Danielis Melander.
Upsaliæ, 1762, 4to. 5s.
LINEÆ TERTII ORDINIS NEOTONIANÆ a
Jac Stirling. Oxon. 1717, 8vo.
Enumeratio Linearum tartii Ordinis
sequitur Illustratio ejusdem Tractatus,
auc. Jac. Stirling. Paris, 1797, 8vo. 6s.
Newtoni Genesis Curvarum per Um-
bras; seu Perspectivæ universalis Elementa, Exemplis Coni Sectionum et Linearum tertii Ordinis Illustrata, a Patr.
Murdoch, D.D. Lond. 1746, 8vo.
Sir Isaac Newton's Enumeration of
Lines of the Third Order; Generation of
Curves by Shadows; Organic Description
of Curves, and Construction of Equations
by Curves. Translated from the Latin,
with Notes and Examples, by C. R. M. Talbot, M.D., F.R.S. Lond. IL. G. Bohn, 1860,
8vo. folding plates.
ANALYSIS per QUANTITATUM SERIES,
Fluxiones, ac Differentias, cum Enume-
ratione Linearum tertii Ordinis, edidit
Will. Jones. Lond. 1711, 4to. 10s. LARGE
PAPER, 15s.—Amst. 1723, 4to.
Analysis per Equationes numero termi-
norum infinitas. Lond. 1711, 4to.
Translated by Stewart. Lond. 1745, 4to.

THE METHOD OF FLUXIONS and INFINITE
SERIES, with its Application to the Geometry of curve Lines; to which is subjoined, a perpetual Comment upon the
whole Work. Translated from the original Latin of Sir Isaac Newton by the
Rev. John Colson. Lond. 1736, 4to. 10s. 6d.
LARGE PAPER, 1l. 1s. Second edition, Lond.
1737, 8vo.
Methode des Fluxions, trad. (par Buf-
fon). Paris, 1740, 4to.
A Discourse concerning the Nature and
Certainty of Sir Isaac Newton's Method
of Fluxions, and of prime and ultimate
Ratios, by Benj. Robins. 1735. 8vo.

Letters of Sir Isaac Newton, relating to
his Dispute with Leibnitz upon his Right
to the Invention of Fluxions, are printed
in the Commercium Epistolicum D. Johannis Collinsei aliorum de Analysi promota, 1712.
Responce aux Auteurs des Remarques
sur la Difference entre M. de Leibnitz et
M. Newton, par J. Keill, 1713, 8vo.
Epistola J. Keilli ad Joannem Bernoulli-
um, in qua Isaacum Newtonum ei ipsum
contra Criminationes in Actis Lip-
siensibus a Crusio quodam publicatas
defendit. Lond. 1720, 4to. This relates
to the contest between Leibnitz and Keill
respecting the Invention of Fluxions.
ARITHMETICA UNIVERSALIS, seu de Compositione et Resolutione Arithmetica Liber. Cantab. 1707, 8vo. Printed under the
Inspection of Whiston without the author's
consent.—Lond. 1722, 8vo. Roxburghe,
15s8, 8s.—Lugd. Bat. 1732, 4to.—Commentariis illustrata et aucta a J. A. Lecchi.
Milan, 1752, 8vo. 3 vols.—Cum Commentariis Joh. Castillionei. Amst. 1761, 4to.
2 vols. Hibbert, 5606, 16s.
Universal Arithmetick, (by Sir Isaac
Newton); to which is added Dr. Halley's
Method of finding the Roots of Æquations
arithmetically. Translated from the Latin
by Raphson and revised and corrected by
Cunn. Lond. 1720, 8vo.—1728, 8vo.
Universal Arithmetic, to which is added
a Treatise upon the Measures of Ratios,
by James Maguire, A.M. The whole illustrated and explained in a Series of
Notes, by the Rev. Theaker Wilder, D.D.
Lond. 1769, 8vo. 2 vols. 10s. 6d. New
edition, 1 vol. Lond. Whittaker, 18—, 8s.
Arithmétique universelle trad. du Latin,
avec des Notes par Noel Beaudeux. Paris,
1802, 4to. 2 vols.

DE MUNDI SYSTEMATE. Lond. 1728, 4to.
This is a popular account of the truths
contained in Book 3 of the Principia.
Treatise of the System of the World in
a popular Way. Lond. 1728, 8vo. 5s.
De Methodo differentiali Newtoniana
Canonotechnia. In the Opera miscellanea
of Roger Cotes. 1722, 4to.
Méchanisme de la Nature; ou Systeme
du Monde, fondé sur les Forces de Feu;
procédé d'un Examen du Systeme de
Newton. Par l'Abbé Jadelot. Lond. 1787,
8vo.
Newton refuted: a geographical, nautical, mechanical and mathematical View
of the Universe, by W. Parkes. Lond.
1804, 8vo. 3s.

CHRONOLOGY of ancient Kingdoms
amended; to which is prefixed a short
Chronicle from the first Memory of Things
in Europe to the Conquest of Persia by
Alexander the Great. Lond. 1728, 4to.
Bishop of Ely, 1235. 5s. LARGE PAPER.
Willett, 1705, 17. 3s. Williams, 1164, 1l. 16s.

NEWTON, Sir Isaac—continued.
—Lond. 1770, 4to. 10s. 6d. Heath, 2141, morsin, 1l. 12s.
A French Translation by the Abbé Grasset. Paris, 1728, 4to. Refuted by Freret in his 'Defence de la Chronologie.' Paris, 1755, 4to.
Strictures on Sir Is. Newton's Chronology, in the Rev. Rob. Walker's work on Historical Time, 1799.
Animadversions upon Sir I. Newton's Chronology, by Arthur Bedford. Lond. 1728, 8vo. 2s.
Reponse anx Observations sur la Chronologie de Mr. Newton. Lond. 1728, 8vo.
Apologie du Santiment de Monsieur le Chevalier Newton, sur l' ancienne Chronologie des Grecs, contenant des Reponses à present. Par Mons. le Chevalier B——L. Francfort sur le Mein, 1757, 4to. By Sir James D. Stewart, Bart. This defence of Sir Isaac Newton's Chronology will be found in the sixth volume of the works of Sir James D. Stewart.
An Examination of Sir Isaac Newton's Objections to the Chronology of the Olympiads. 1781. See MUSGRAVE, Samuel.

OBSERVATIONS UPON THE PROPHECIES of DANIEL, and the Apocalypse of St. John. By Sir Isaac Newton. Lond. 1733, 4to. All subsequent commentators in this field are largely indebted to the labours of Sir Isaac Newton. Roxburghe, 12s, 7s. 6d. Bishop of Ely, 1236, 12s. Heath, 751, 7s. LARGE PAPER in royal 4to. 15s.—Dublin, 1733, 8vo. 6s. Edited by —— Borthwick. Lond. Nisbet, 18—, 10s. A Latin version of this elaborate work was published by M. Sudemann, at Amsterdam, 1737, 4to.
An Examination of the 14th Chapter of Sir Isaac Newton's Observations upon the Prophecies of Daniel, by Zachary Grey, LL.D. Lond. 1736, 8vo. 3s.
Two Letters of Sir Isaac Newton to Mr. Le Clerc, late Divinity Professor of the Remonstrants in Holland (on the Reading of the Greek Text, 1 John v. 7, and on Timothy iii. 16). Lond. 1754, 8vo. 3s. 6d. Williams, 1248, 3s. 6d. New edit. 12mo. 3s.
Four Letters from Sir Isaac Newton to Dr. Bentley, containing some Arguments in Proof of a Deity. Lond. 1756, 8vo. These Letters, published without any preface or introduction, are answers to some Letters written by Dr. Bentley to Sir Isaac, in relation to the system of the universe. A review of Sir Isaac Newton's arguments in proof of a deity, by Dr. Johnson was published in the Literary Mag.
Letters in Answer to some Queries sent to the Author, concerning the genuine reading of the Greek Text, 1 Tim. iii. 16, now first printed on occasion of Sir Isaac Newton's two Letters to Mr. Le Clerc lately published. York, 1759, 8vo.

Geometry no Friend to Infidelity; or, a Defence of Sir Isaac Newton and the British Mathematicians, in a Letter to (Geo. Berkeley, Bishop of Cloyne) the Author of the Analyst, by Philalethes Cantabrigiensis (James Jurin, M.D.) Lond. 1734, 8vo. A second letter, entitled 'The minute Mathematician; or the Free-thinker no just Reasoner,' appeared in 1735, 8vo.
TABLES for renewing and purchasing of Leases of Cathedral Churches and Colleges. Lond. 1722, 12mo.—Lond. 1731, 12mo. Generally attributed to Sir Isaac Newton, but not included in Bishop Horsley's edition of his works.
His Tables of Assays will be found in Arbuthnot's Tables.
Recueil de diverses Pieces par Mess. Leibnitz, Clarke, Newton et autres Auteurs célèbrés. Par Des Maizeaux. Amst. 1720
The LIFE of SIR ISAAC NEWTON; with an Account of his Writings, by B. de Fontenelle. Lond. 1728, 4to.—1729, 8vo. 2s.
Eloge de M. le Chevalier Newton, par Barnard de Fontenelle. Paris, 1728, 4to.
A memoir of Sir Isaac Newton forms No. 50 of the Library of Useful Knowledge.
Life of, by Sir David Brewster, (vol. 24 of Murray's Family Library), 3s. 6d.
Memoirs of the Life, Writings, and Discoveries, of Sir Isaac Newton, drawn up from Family Papers; by Sir David Brewster. Edinb. 1855, 8vo. 2 vols. portraits, 1l. 4s. An enlarged edition of the volume in Murray's Family Library, 12mo. but essentially different as regards the Biography or Personal History; while that part of the book relative to his Chemical, Alchemical, and Theological pursuits, is entirely new.
Correspondence of Sir Isaac Newton and Professor Cotes, including Letters of other eminent men, from the originals at Cambridge. With Notes by J. Edleston, M.A. Lond. 1850, 8vo. portrait.
Thirteen Letters from Sir Isaac Newton, representative in Parliament of the University of Cambridge, to Dr. John Covell, Vice Chancellor. Norwich, 1848, royal 8vo. pp. 30, with facsimile holograph. Privately printed for Mr. Dawson Turner, from original MSS. 10s. 6d.
Memoirs of Sir Isaac Newton, from the original MSS. In the Possession of the Earl of Portsmouth, will be found in the History of Grantham by Edmund Turner.
Many articles respecting Sir Is. Newton's philosophy, &c. will be found in the Philosophical Transactions.
Catalogue of the Library of the late Mrs. Anne Newton, containing chiefly the Collection of the great Sir Isaac Newton. Lond. 1813, 8vo.

NEWTON, James, M.D. Herbal.
Lond. 1752, 8vo. plates.
With a portrait of the author, æt. 78, in a cap. Hibbert, 5696, 5s. Heber, russia, 1l.

— James William. A new and easy Introduction to the Hebrew Language. Lond. 1806, 12mo.

— John, D.D. Astronomia et Trigonometria. Lond. 1656-8, folio. 2 vols.

An account of John Newton and his works will be found in Wood's Athen. Oxon.

The English Academy; or a Brief Introduction to the Seven Liberal Arts; Grammar, Arithmetick, Geometrie, Musick, Astronomie, Rhetorick, and Logick, 8vo. Lond. 1677.

— John. Works of the Rev. John Newton, Rector of St. Mary Woolnoth, edited by Richard Cecil. Lond. 1816, 8vo. 6 vols. 2l. 12s.

With a portrait of the author.—Lond. 1821, 12mo. 12 vols. portrait, 1l. 16s.— Works, new edition, with a Life of the Author by the Rev. Richard Cecil, and an Introduction by the Rev. T. Cunningham, M.A. Lond. 1839, complete in one volume imperial 8vo. portrait, ll. 5s. Re-issued, Lond. H. G. Bohn, 1854, 15s.

Messiah. Fifty Expository Discourses on the series of Scriptural Passages which form the subject of the celebrated oratorio of Handel. Preached in the year 1784 and 1785, in the Parish Church of St. Mary Woolnoth, Lombard Street, 2 vols. 8vo. Lond. 1786.

Cardiphonia, or Utterance of the Heart, in the course of a real Correspondence. Lond. 1781, 12mo. 2 vols. 7s. frequently reprinted in cheaper editions.

— Richard, D.D. University Education, or Explanation of the Statute prohibiting young Men going from one College to another. Lond. 1726, 8vo.

Reprinted, Lond. 1733, 8vo. Remarks on this work by Nicholas Amhurst will be found at the end of his Terræ Filius.

Rules and Statutes for the Government of Hertford College. Lond. 1747, 8vo. pp. 167, including the preface. Bent, pt. II. 2l. 2s. 6d.

Sermons preached before the University of Oxford, by Richard Newton, D.D. Founder and Principal of Hertford College. Published by his Grandson, E. Adams, LL.B. To which are added, Four Sermons, published by the Author, and placed here by particular request. Oxf. 1784, 8vo. 6s. LARGE PAPER? Williams, 1849, 14s.

— Thomas. A notable Historye of the Saracens, drawn out of Augustine Curio, and sundry other good Authours. Lond. 1575, 4to.

Fol. 144, without preface, &c. Dedicated to 'Lordes Charles Howardes, Baron of Effyngham,' &c. Bindley, pt. III. 786, 1l. 1s. Inglis, 995, 1l. 15s. Caldecott, 10s.

Approved Medicines and cordial Receipts. Lond. 1580. 16mo.

The Old Man's Dictorie, 8vo. BLACK LETTER, 1586.

Herbal for the Bible. Lond. 1587, 16mo. Steevens, 1513, 5s. Inglis, 1053, 6s. 6d.

Illustrium aliquot Anglorum Encomia. Lond. 1589, 4to. At the end of Jo. Leland's Encomia Trophæa, &c. and reprinted by Hearne at the end of Leland's Collectanea.

Atropion Delion, or the Death of Delia: with the Teares of her Funerall. A poetical excursive Discourse of our late Eliza. Lond. 1603, very small 4to. Reprinted in the third volume of Nichols' Progresses of Queen Elizabeth.

A pleasant new History; or, a fragrant Posie made of three Flowers; Rose, Rosalynd, and Rosemary. Lond. 1604, 4to.

Thos. Newton translated many works. See LEMNIUS, Levinus. Notices of him will be found in Wood's Athen. Oxon., Warton's History of English Poetry, and Ritson's Bibliographia Poetica.

— Thomas, Bishop of Bristol. The Works, with some Account of his Life, and Anecdotes of several of his Friends. Lond. 1782, 4to. 3 vols. portrait by J. Collier, after Sir Joshua Reynolds.

Heath, 861, 2l. 19s. Nassau, pt. II. 554, 3l. 1s. Bindley, pt. III. 757, 1l. 16s. LARGE PAPER? Williams, 1126, russia, 3l. 15s.— Second edition, Lond. 1787, 8vo. 6 vols. 1l. 4s.

Dissertations on the Prophecies, which have remarkably been fulfilled, and at this Time are fulfilling in the World. Lond. 1754-8, 8vo. 3 vols. A well-known and much-esteemed work. Gough, 2539, 19s. 6d.—Second edition. Lond. 1759-60, 8vo. 3 vols.—Lond. 1766, 8vo. 3 vols. Mon-burghe, 139, 10s.—Ninth edition. Perth, 1790, 8vo. 2 vols.—Lond. 1792, 8vo. 2 vols. Tenth Edition.—1804, 8vo. 2 vols.—1617, 8vo. 2 vols.—In one vol. Lond. 1831, 10s. 6d.—Lond. Tegg, 1843 and since, &c.

Analysis of Bp. Newton on the Prophecies, Butler's Analogy and Graves on the Pentateuch, by J. E. Smith. Lond. 1836, 12mo.

NEWTON, Rev. William. The History and Antiquities of Maidstone, the County-Town of Kent. Lond. 1741, 8vo.

Lloyd, 628, 9s. Nassau, pt. I. 2498, 5s. Towneley, 825, 9s. 6d. LARGE OR THICK PAPER. Nassau, pt. II. 8, russia, 19s. Nassau, pt. I. 2429, 14s. Heath, 4657, 10s. Dent, pt. II. 20, russia, 1l. 5s. *Collation*—Pp. xvii (not including list of books, 2 pages, and errata, one page) and 162. The view of Maidstone never appeared.

NEW YEAR'S GIFT. — A new Year's Gift, dedicated to the Pope's Holiness. *See* GARTER, Bernard, p. 665, col. 2.

— A; or a Heavenly Act of Parliament. Lond. 1569, 12mo.

NEW YORK.—Acts of Assembly from 1691 to 1725. New York, 1726, folio.

Another, from 1691 to 1718. Lond. 1719, folio.

NEY, Marshal. Memoirs of Marshal Ney, published by his Family. Illustrated with Portrait, Maps, and Plans. Lond. 1833, 8vo. 2 vols. 12s.

Military Studies, Written for the use of his officers; accompanied with diagrams. Edited by Major James. Lond. 18—, 8vo. 5s.

NICANDER NUCIUS. Travels in England. *See* CAMDEN SOCIETY, APPENDIX.

NICCHOLES, Alex., B.A. A Discourse of Marriage and Wiving, and of the greatest Mystery therein contained: How to chuse a good Wife from a bad. Lond. 1615, 4to.

FIRST EDITION. Pp. 61, including the dedication and preface. Jieber, pt. viii. 81, Bright, 2l. 6s. Gardner, in 1854 5l.,— 1620, 4to. Reed, 2461, 1l. 6s. Gordonstoun, 1360, 1l. 18s. 6d. Bright, 2l. 8s. Gardner, 3l. The edition of 1615 is reprinted in the second volume of the Harleian Miscellany.

NICCOLS, J. *See* NICOLS, John.

— Richard, the elder. A Treatise setting forth the Mystery of our Salvation. A Day Starre for darke wandering Soules. Lond. 1613, 8vo.

A copy is in the Bodleian Library.

— Richard. Poetical Works.

Niccols was 'a poet of great elegance and imagination, and one of the ornaments of the reign of Elizabeth.'—*Headley*. *See* Warton's History of English Poetry and Wood's Athen. Oxon.

The Cvckow. Lond. (1607), 4to. Pp. 56, inscribed to Master Thomas Wroth. Bibl. Anglo-Poet, 491, 8l. 8s. Resold, Midgeley, 5l. 12s. 6d. Caldecott, title wanting, 1l. 3s. Holland, 6l. Jolley, 6l. *See* Brydges' Restituta, 1l. 1—8.

England's Eliza and a Winter Nights Vision. 1610. Affixed to Niccols' edition of the Mirror of Magistrates.

The Twynnes Tragedye. Entered on the Stationers' books in 1611.

The Three Sisters Tears, shed at the late solemne Funerals of Henry Prince of Wales. Lond. 1613, 4to. sig. F 2. pp. 40, dedicated to Lady Hay. The three sisters are Angela (England), Albana (Scotland), and Cambera (Wales). Lloyd, 747, 2l. Birettall, 1423, 2l. 5s. Resold, Dillon, 2l. 19s. Bibl. Anglo-Poet, 492, 7l. 7s. Resold, Midgeley, 4l. Gs. Bright, 2l. 5s.

The Furies: with Vertues Encomium, or the Image of Honour. In two Bookes of Epigrammes, satyricall and encomiastick. Lond. 1614, 8vo. pp. 76. Bibl. Anglo-Poet, 483. Hindley (with his Monodia, or Waltham's Complaint) 2l. 5s.

Virtue's Encomium; or, the Image of Honour. Lond. 1614, sm. 8vo. The second piece of the previous volume separate. Eleven leaves. Reprinted in the tenth volume of the Harleian Miscellany.

Monodia; or, Waltham's Complaint upon the Death of the Lady Honor Hay. Lond. 1615, small 8vo. Two sheets. Bibl. Anglo-Poet. 483, with 'the Furies,' and 'Vertue's Encomium,' in one volume, 20l., resold Heber, Lot 1672, pt. iv. 4l. A copy in the Bodleian. Reprinted in the tenth volume of the Harleian Miscellany.

London's Artillery, briefly containing the noble Practise of that wo(r)thie Societie, &c. Lond. 1616, 4to. Pp. 104, without introduction. It is dedicated to Sir John Jollre, Knt. Lord Major, &c., two introductory sonnets, a preface to the rea-

1078 NIC NIC

NICCOLS, Richard—*continued.*
der, afterwards London's Artillerie, with
an induction in rhime, and illustrative
notes attached. The poem is divided into
ten cantos with illustrations. Bibl. Anglo-Poet. 494, 10*l.* 10*s.* resold Midgeley,
3*l.* 10*s.* Nassau, pt. ii. 555, 2*l.* 2*s.* Bindley,
pt. iii. 777, 7*l.* Jolley, 4*l.* 4*s.* Heber, pt. iv.
1*l.* 2*s.* pt. viii. 1*l.* 11*s.* *See* Brydges'
British Bibliog. i. 863-70.

Sir Thomas Overberries Vision: with
the Ghoasts of Weston, Mrs. Turner, the
late Liefteneant of the Tower, and Franklin. By R. N. Oxon. Printed for D. M.
and T. I. 1616, 4to. woodcuts, pp. 58, or
29 leaves. Nassau, pt. ii. 556, 1*l.* 16*s.*
Strettell, 1422, russia, 2*l.* 6*s.* Perry, pt. iv.
635, 2*l.* 10*s.* North, pt. iii. 789, russia,
2*l.* 19*s.* Bibl. Anglo-Poet. 842, 6*l.* 6*s.*
resold Midgeley, 3*l.* 13*s.* 6d. Heber, pt. iv.
11. 2*s.* Jolley, 2*l.* 6*s.* It is reprinted in the
7th volume of the Harleian Miscellany.

The Beggar's Ape, n.d. *See* DROOAB,
page 146.

NICE.—An historical and picturesque Description of the Country
of Nice. Lond. 1792, imp. folio,
2*l.* 2*s.* [by Beaumont, Albanis.]
Containing twelve etchings finished in
water-colours.

NICETAS, Heracleæ Metropolitæ.
Catena Græcorum Patrum in Job,
Gr. et Lat. cum Notis Pat. Junii.
Lond. 1637, fol. 10*s.* 6d.

NICHOLAS, Henry or Harry. Comœdia, a Worke in Ryme, contayning an Enterlude of Myndes : wit-
nessing the Man's Fall from God
and Christ. Translated out of Base-
Almayne into English, 16mo.

BLACK LETTER. A to D in eights, 52
leaves. This play, printed in a foreign
and antiquated type, without date (1574,
according to Baker's Biog. Dram.), is
divided into four pauses or acts, and seventeen chapters or scænes, with a collo-
quial prologue. A copy is in the British
Museum. Inglis, 1064, with ten other
pieces, written by Nicholas, 7*l.* 17*s.* 6d.
Rhodes, 1787, 18*l.* Jolley, 7*l.* *See* Brydges'
Restituta, iv. 140-6. The works of Nicholas were by royal proclamation, 13 of
October, 22nd Elizabeth, ordered to be
burnt, and all persons declared punish-
able for having them in their possession
without the ordinarie's permission.

The Prophetie of the Spirit of Love.
Set foorth by H. N : and by him perused
a-new, and more distinctlie declared.
Translated out of Base-almayne into English. Anno 1574, 8vo. Forty leaves.

A Publishing of the Peace vpon Earth,
and of the gratious Tyme and acceptable
Yeare of the Lorde, which is now in the
last Tyme ; out of the Peace of Jean Christ,
and out of his holie Spirit of Loue; published by H. N. on the Earth. Translated
out of Base-almayne into English. Anno
1574, 8vo. eight leaves.

Terra Pacis. Set foorth by H. N. and
by him newly perused and more playnly
declared. Translated out of Base-almayne,
8vo. Contains 82 leaves, including title
and preface.

Eevelatio Dei. Set foorth by H. N.
and by him perused and more distinctlie
declared. Translated out of Base-almayne,
8vo. 10*s.* Contains 55 leaves, including
title and preface.

Evangelium Regni. Set foorth by H.
N. and by him perused a-new and more
distinctlie declared. Translated out of
Base-almayne, 8vo. 10*s.* Contains 100
leaves, including title and preface.

Proverbia. Translated out of Base-
almayne. 8vo. On 40 leaves, including
the title. Bindley, pt. ii. 2379, 19*s.* Heber, pt. v. 4*s.*

Dicta. Translated out of Base-almayne.
8vo. On 47 leaves, the last page blank.

Documental Sentences, euen as those
same were spoken foorth and written up
out of the words of his mouth. Translated
out of the base-Almayne. Lond. n.d.
BLACK LETTER, 2*l.* 2*s.*

Epistolæ. Translated out of Base-
almaine. 8vo. Twenty epistles paged
progressively to p. 418, exclusive of the
preface and table of contents prefixed.
Probably several, if not all, of these epistles, have been published separate.

Introdvction to the holy Vnderstanding
of the Glasse of Righteousness. 8vo. The
first division, containing chapters 1—7,
has 40 leaves, the last blank ; the second,
ch. 8—13, has 40 leaves, the last also
blank ; the third, ch. 14—17, on 26 leaves ;
the fourth, ch. 18—21, on 18 leaves ; the
last, ch. 22—5, on 20 leaves. BLACK LET-
TER. At the commencement and conclusion of the volume are separate leaves,
containing copper-plate engravings.

A Figure of the true and spiritual Tabernacle, according to the inward Temple,
or House of God in the Spirit. Whereunto is added, the eight Vertues of God-
lynesses. —Printed 1655, 8vo. plates.
Bright, 9*s.*

Fidelitas. Set foorth by Fidelitas, a
Fellowe-elder with H. N. in the Familie
of the Loue. Translated out of Base-
almayne, 8vo. C, in eights.

A good and fruitfull Exhortation vnto
the Familie of Loue, &c. Testified and

NICHOLAS, Henry—*continued*,
set fourth by Elidad, a Fellow-elder with
the elder H. N., to the Famelia of Love
of Iesu Christ. Translated out of Base-
almayne, 8vo. A, in eights.

Mirabilia Opera Dei. Published by
Tobias, a Fellow Elder with H. N. in the
Household of Love. Translated out of
Hans Almain, 4to. BLACK LETTER. Con-
tains 137 pages, exclusive of the preface.
Reed, 676, 7s. Heber, pt. ii. 4s. 6d.

The first Exhortation of H. N. to his
Children, and to the Family of Love. By
him newly perused, and more distinctly
declared. Likewise H. N. upon the Beatitudes, and the seven deadly Sins. Translated out of Base-almayne into English.
Reprinted 1656.

An Apology for the Service of Love,
and the People that own it, commonly
called the Family of Love, &c. Reprinted
1656.

Certen of the Songs of H. N.

Joyful Message of the Kingdom.

Epistle sent unto two Daughters of
Warwick from H. N. the oldest Father of
the Family of Love. Amst. 1608, 4to.
Constable, 779, 3s.

A second Exhortation of H. N.—A
Dialogue between the Father and Son.—
The Declaration of the Mass.—The new
and heavenly Jerusalem.—The Glass of
Righteousness.—The Holy Lamb. Men-
tioned in 'The Displaying the Family of
Love, by L. R. (John Rogers.)' Heber, 10
tracts, printed about 1574, 1l. 16s.

Many of this author's pieces were
reprinted about 1648-60. The tenets
of the turbulent and mischievous sect
called the Family of Love, may be found
in Blount. See also Neal's History of the
Puritans, Strype's Annals, and Ames'
Typogr. Antiq. by Herbert. For Confutation of his Heresies, see KNEWSTUB,
John.

NICHOLAS, J. L. Voyage to
New Zealand in 1814-15. Lond.
1817, 8vo. 2 vols. map.

— Thomas. *See* CHINA. LOPEZ
DE GOMARA, F. ZARATE, Aug.

— and SACHARLES, John de.
The Reformed Spaniard. Lond.
1621, 4to.

Eighteen leaves.—Latino. Lond. 1621,
12mo.

NICHOLAY, Nicholas. The Na-
uigations, Peregrinations, & Voyages made into Turkie by Nicholas
Nicholay Daulphinois, &c. Translated out of the French by T. Washington the Younger. Lond. T.
Dawson, 1585, 4to.

One hundred and sixty leaves, including
three leaves of a table. The volume is dedicated to Sir Henry and to Sir Philip Sidney, Knights, by John Stell, and is adorned
with cuts said to be after Titian. Nassau,
pt. II. 537, russ. 1l. 6s. Heath, 2576, 1l. 17s.
Dodsworth, 504, russ. 2l. 10s. Roxburghe,
7251, 3l. 8s. Gordonstoun, 1673, 2l. 13s. 6d.
North, pt. iii. 668, mor. 4l. Towneley, pt. i.
714, 6l. Nicholay's Navigations, &c. will
be found in the first volume of the Oxford
Collection of Voyages and Travels.

NICHOLL, John. An Houre-
glasse of Indian Newes; or, a Discourse shewing Miseries, and distressed Calamities indured by 67
Englishmen, which were sent for a
Supply to the Planting in Guiana,
in the Yeare 1605. Lond. 1607,
4to.

A copy is in the Library of K. George
III. now in the British Museum.

NICHOLLS, John. Recollections
and Reflections during the Reign of
George III. Lond. 1822, 8vo. 2
vols.

Duke of York, 5779, 1l. 8s.

— Sutton. Prospects of the
most considerable Buildings in and
about London. Lond. by John
Bowles, 1724, folio (or oblong 4to.)

Containing 24 plates, 8½ in. by 6¼.
A copy is in the British Museum. *See*
Upcott's Account of Works relating to
English Topography, II. 680-1.

— W. *See* NICHOLS, William.

NICHOLS, Francis. *See* Compendium.

— Francis, M.D. Fran. Ni-
cholsii, M.D. Georgii II. Medici,
Vita; cum Conjecturis ejusdem de
Natura et Usu Partium humani
Corporis similarium. Lond. 1780,
4to. port. by Hall.

This classical piece of biography, written by Dr. Lawrence, the friend of Dr.
Johnson, was never published. Gough,
£25, 4s.

De Anima medica Prætectio, et Lumieli
et Caldwalli Instituto, in Theatro Coll.
Reg. Medic. Lond. habita Dec. 16, 1748,
cum Notis. Cui accessit, Disquisitio de
Motu Cordis et Sanguinis in Homine nato
et non nato, Tabulis aeneis illustrata. Lond.
1773. 4to.

NICHOLS, James. Calvinism and Arminianism compared in their Principles and Tendency. Lond. 1824, 8vo.

This highly valuable work 'ought to have a place in every historical, and in every ecclesiastical library.'—*Quart. Rev.*

— John. *See* NICOLS, John.

PARSONS, Robert.

— John. Bibliotheca Topographica Britannica. 8 vols. Lond. 1780-90. Supplement called "Miscellaneous Antiquities, in continuation of the Bibliotheca Topographica Britannica." 2 vols. (containing 8 Nos.) Lond. 1791-1800. Together, 10 vols. 4to.

North, pt. ii. 1033, 8 vols. russ. 44*l.* 2*s.* Heath, 4545, 8 vols. 47*l.* 5*s.* Heber, pt. vii, 8 vols. 16*l.* 10*s.* Sir M. M. Sykes, pt. ii. 621, 10 vols. russia, 84*l.* Lloyd, 437, 25 vols. 1788-97, 51*l.* Towneley, pt. ii. 371, 9 vols. 60*l.* Nassau, pt. ii. 568, 10 vols. 64*l.* la. Bindley, pt. i. 725, 8 vols. uncut, 42*l.* Beckford in 1817, 10 vols. 72*l.* 10*s.* Dent, pt. ii. 755, nos. 8 and 9 of Supplement wanting, 43*l.* Mr. Grenville's uncut copy, now in the British Museum, has the second edition of the second Appendix to the History of Croyland, 1815, added to it, making 11 vols. The two supplementary volumes are worth more than the previous eight, a large part of the edition having been destroyed in Mr. Nichols' fire, Feb. 8th, 1808.

Collation.—VOL. I. General title, advertisement, general contents of the eight volumes, particular contents, a second title-page 'Antiquities in Kent and Sussex,' &c. general contents of the first volume, pp. i—xi. The general title-pages, &c. to the eight volumes were delivered with no. LII.

No. I. containing, 1. Queries for the better illustrating the Antiquities and natural History of Great Britain and Ireland. 2. The History and Antiquities of Tunstall in Kent. By Edward Rowe Mores. Lond. 1780. Title and half-title, two leaves; advertisement, &c. pp. i—xxvi (facing p. xvii is a folding pedigree of E. R. Mores); preface, pp. iii—vi; the history, &c. pp. 1—154. Page 74 is repeated with an asterisk, and the number contains all plates. The copy formerly belonging to E. George III. as far as page 118, is on thick paper.

No. VI. Parts I. and II. containing Mr. Thorpe's illustration of several Antiquities in Kent, which have hitherto remained undescribed. To which is added, a Letter from Dr. Plott, intended for the Royal Society. Lond. 1782-3. Title and half-title, 2 leaves; Antiquities, pp. 1—64. After p. 28 is the title-page to part ii. and the two parts contain 13 plates.

No. XVII. The History and Antiquities of Reculver and Herne, in the County of Kent. By John Duncombe, M.A. Lond. 1784. Half-title, title, and advertisement, 6 leaves; Antiquities in Kent, pp. 65—162, with eight plates.

No. XLV. containing an Appendix to the Histories of Reculver and Herne; and Observations by Mr. Boone on the archiepiscopal Palace of Mayfield in Sussex. Lond. 1787. Pp. 163—212, not including the title, one leaf, and plates ix. to xvi.

No. XXX. The History and Antiquities of the three archiepiscopal Hospitals at, and near Canterbury; viz. St. Nicolas, at Harbledon; St. John's, Northgate; and St. Thomas, of Eastbridge; with some Account of the Priory of St. Gregory, the Nunnery of St. Sepulchre, the Hospitals of St James and St. Lawrence, and Maynard's Spittle. By John Duncombe, M.A. and Nicholas Battely, M.A. Lond. 1785. Two titles and dedication, 3 leaves; Harbaldown, &c. pp. 173—452, with 10 plates. Pages 201 to 204 are repeated with asterisks.

No. XLIX. containing, I. The History and Antiquities of Saint Radigund's, or Bradsole Abbey, near Dover. II. A Collection of Tradesmen's Tokens issued in the Isle of Thanet, and in such of the Cinque Ports as are within Kent. III. A Description of the Moat, near Canterbury. IV. Sketch of Hawkhurst Church. V. Original Letter from Mr. Eaves, on Canterbury Cathedral. VI. Dissertation on the Urbs Rutupiæ of Ptolemy, by Mr. Douglas. VII. Memoirs of William Lambarde. Lond. 1787. Title, one leaf; History, &c. pp. 453—532, not including the title-page, with eight, not six, plates, and a pedigree of Poynings. Pages 473 and 474 are repeated with asterisks, and pp. 489—492 are on one page. Pp. *473, *474, and two plates of Highborough Castle, were delivered with No. LII.

No. XXXIII. Two Dissertations on the Celts, and other Arms of the Antients, found in this Island. By the Rev. James Douglas. Lond. 1785, pp. 32, including two title-pages, with two plates in aquatints. Brockett, 1045, 9*s.* Reed, 2776, 11*s.* 6*d.*

No. XLV. An historical Account of the Textus Roffensis; including Memoirs of Mr. William Elstob and his Sister. By Samuel Pegge, M.A. To which are added, biographical Anecdotes of Mr. Johnson, Vicar of Cranbrooke; and Extracts from

NICHOLS, John—*continued.*
the Registers of that Parish. Lond. 1784, pp. 47, not including two title-pages.
VOL. II. Title, 'Antiquities in Middlesex and Surrey,' and general contents, iv. pages.
No. v. containing the History of St. Katharine, near the Tower of London, from its Foundation in the Year 1273 to the present Time (by Dr. Ducarel). Lond. 1782, pp. viii and 46; appendix, pp. 128; pages 74 and 75 of the appendix are repeated with asterisks, and the number contains 19, not 17, plates. Plates all and xiii are on one leaf, plate xvii is on p. 40, and plates xviii and xix. also a portion of the appendix, pp. 113—26, were given in No. LII. Towneley, pt. II. 810, 1l. 5s.
No. IX. containing Sketches of the History and Antiquities of the Parish of Stoke Newington, in the County of Middlesex (by James Brown). 1769, pp. 53, not including title and half-title, with two views of Newington Church at p. 18, a trader's token of John Hall, on p. 19, and a pedigree of Fleetwood, folded, at p. 29.
No. xiv. containing Additions to the History of Stoke Newington (by James Brown). 1783, pp. 55—70, not including the title, with the expanses of the funeral of John Dudlie, Esquier, 1580. 8 pages. This latter was delivered with No. LII.
No. XLIX. The History and Antiquities of Canonbury House at Islington, &c. By John Nichols. Lond. 1788, pp. 76, not including title and half-title, with five plates.
No. XXVII. The History and Antiquities of the archiepiscopal Palace of Lambeth. By Dr. Ducarel. Lond. 1785, pp. x and 132; appendix, 72 pages, also 10 plates. Towneley, pt. II. 1289, 1l. 11s. *See* vol. X. no. V.
No. XXXIX. The History and Antiquities of the Parish of Lambeth, in the County of Surrey (by John Nichols). Lond. 1786, pp. vii and 128 (pages 15 and 16 are repeated with asterisks, and pp. 19—23 are on one page); appendix, pp. 164. The number contains twenty plates.
No. XLI. Some Account of Croydon. By Dr. Ducarel. Lond. 1783, pp. 80, not including two titles, advertisement, and contents, 4 leaves; appendix, pp. 156. In the appendix, pages 25—28 are repeated with asterisks, and pages 153—156 are likewise repeated. The number contains 10 plates, one of which, no. 7, containing 4 tokens, was cancelled, and another, containing 6 tokens, delivered with no. LII.
No. XLVI. The Case of the Inhabitants of Croydon, 1673: with an Appendix to the History of that Town. A List of the

manorial Houses which formerly belonged to the See of Canterbury. A Description of Trinity Hospital, Guildford; and of Albury House, with brief Notes on Battersea, Chelsham, Nutfield, and Tatsfield, in the County of Surrey. Lond. 1787, pp. 159—238, not including two titles, and 6, not 4, plates. An additional leaf to Surrey, pp. 237-8, with two plates. Weston House at Sutton, and a portrait of John Aubrey, were delivered with no. LII.
VOL. III. Title, 'Antiquities in Lincolnshire,' and general contents, 2 leaves.
No. XL. An Account of the Gentlemen's Society at Spalding. Being an Introduction to the Reliquiæ Galeanæ. Lond. 1784, pp. vi; l—xxlvi l—lxi (pp. xxxv, xxxvi, xli, xliii in the latter are repeated with asterisks), and pp. 116.
No. II. Parts I. II. III. containing Reliquæ Galeanæ; or miscellaneous Pieces by Roger and Samuel Gale. Lond. 1781-2. No. II. Part I. 1781. Title, half-title, general preface and contents, 6 leaves; preface, pp. 1—xvi; a Tour, &c. pp. 1—48, with two plates and folded pedigree of Gale: Mr. S. Gale's Account, &c. pp. 49* to 98*; Queries proposed to the Nobility, &c. pp. 49—68. No. II. Part II. 1781. Additions, &c. pp. [49] and [50]; pp. 49 to 220, not including title, and 6 plates. No. II. Part III. 1782, pp. 221 to 266, not including title; pp. 221 to 480, pp. 253 to 256 are repeated with asterisks, pp. 463 to 500. This part contains two plates.
No. XI. The History and Antiquities of Croyland Abbey (by Richard Gough). Lond. 1783, pp. xvi and 112, pp. 76, 77 are repeated with asterisks; appendix, pp. 162; pp. 83 to 96, and 131 to 142 are repeated with asterisks. This number contains 7 plates, besides one containing an Inscription 'A I O,' &c. at p. xvi and a plan of Croyland Abbey Church at p. 83, and facing pp. 25 and 28 of the appendix are two leaves containing extracts from Domesday.
No. XXII. containing Mr. Essex's Observations on Croyland Abbey and Bridge, and other Additions to the History of that Abbey. Lond. 1784, pp. 163 to 204, not including the title, and a folded sheet containing two plans. For second appendix, *see* vol. X.
VOL. IV. Title, 'Antiquities in Bedfordshire, Berkshire, Derbyshire, Northamptonshire, Staffordshire, and Warwickshire,' and general contents, iv pages.
No. XIII. Some Account of the Parish of Great Coxwell, in the County of Berks. Lond. 1783, pp. v. and 26, with 6 plates, and two pedigrees, viz. of Mores of Great Coxwell, and of Pleydell and Pratt. Page 6 is repeated with an asterisk.
No. XVI. Collections towards a parochial

NICHOLS, John—*continued.*
History of Berkshire. Being the Answers returned to Mr. More's circular Letters and Queries for the Parishes of Bisham, Chadlesworth, Coleshill, Commer, East-Garston, Shaw, Shifford, Sparsholt, Speen, Stanford, Suthamsteda, and Yattendon. To which are added, a few Particulars collected by the Editor for those of Aldworth, Shottesbrook, and White Waltham. Lond. 1783, pp. vii (including index) and 164, and 8 plates, one at p. 43*. Pages 54, 48 to 45, 68 to 78, 78 to 84, and 81 to 84 are repeated with asterisks.

No. VIII. Collections towards the History and Antiquities of Bedfordshire, viz. Puddington, Luton, and Dunstaple. Lond. 1783, Title, one leaf; pp. 1—v, 1—14, 11—166, 169—208, 217—234, then a single leaf, containing errata. Pages 49 to 55, 57*—62* (these latter delivered with Nos. XXVI. and XXIX.) are repeated with asterisks, and the number contains 8 plates.

No. XXVI. containing Collections towards the History and Antiquities of Bedfordshire: being Additions to Luton and Dunstaple. Lond. 1784, pp. 235 to 252, not including the title. With this part were delivered pp. 57* to *62, as also a plate described in no. VIII. p. 169.

No. XXIX. An historical Account of the Parish of Wimmington, in the County of Bedford. By Oliver St. John Cooper. Lond. 1785, pp. 96, not including the two title-pages. With this number were delivered 4 pages, viz. pp. *63 to *68 Luton Hoo.

No. XLIV. An historical Account of the Parish of Odell, in the County of Bedford. By Oliver St. John Cooper. Lond. 1787, pp. 51—61, not including the two title-pages, and genealogies of Wahut and Chetwode.

No. XL. The History and Antiquities of Fotheringay, in the County of Northampton. With several Particulars of the Execution and Funeral of Mary, Queen of Scots. Lond. 1787, pp. xiii and 118, with three plates. Pages 79 to 89 are repeated with asterisks. Pp. 113—18 were delivered with no. LII. Page 118 contains a list of the fifty-two numbers of the Bibl. Topog. Brit.

No. XVII. Extracts from the black Book of Warwick. To which are added, Mr. Pegge's Memoir of Guy of Warwick, and Sir Thomas More's Narrative of a religious Frenzy at Coventry. Lond. 1783, pp. viii and 43, with a plate of Guy, Earl of Warwick.

No. XXI. The History and Antiquities of Ecclesial Manor and Castle; and of Lichfield House in London. By Samuel Pegge. Lond. 1784, pp. 30, including the titles, &c.

No. XXXII. Sketch of the History of Bolsover and Peak Castles, in the County of Derby. By the Rev. Samuel Pegge. Illustrated with various Drawings by Hayman Rooke. Lond. 1785, pp. 30, not including the two title-pages and seven plates.

No. XXIV. The Roman Roads, Ikenild-street and Bath-way discovered and investigated through the Country of the Coritani, or the County of Derby. To which is added, a Dissertation on the Coritani. By Samuel Pegge, M.A. Lond. 1784, pp. 56, including the title-pages.

VOL. V. Title 'Antiquities in Cambridgeshire, Suffolk, Scotland and Wales,' and contents, iv pages.

No. XXXVIII. The History and Antiquities of Barnwell Abbey and Sturbridge Fair. Lond. 1786, pp. 1—84, 1—101, and 1—32, with two plates.

No. XXIII. The History and Antiquities of Hawsted, in the County of Suffolk. By the Rev. Sir John Cullum, Bart. Lond. 1784, pp. vii and 247, with four plates, also the pedigrees of the Cloptons, the Drurys (which consists of four parts), and the Cullums. Reprinted with additions in 1813. See CULLUM, Sir John, page 567.

No. LII. Collections towards the History and Antiquities of Elmeswell and Campsey Ash, in the County of Suffolk. Lond. 1790, pp. 32, not including two title-pages, with one plate. With this, the last number, was delivered title-pages, plates, &c. a list of which will be found on the back of the first title-page.

No. III. containing a Description of the Chancery in Old Aberdeen, in the Years 1724 and 1725. By William Orem, Town-Clerk of Aberdeen. Lond. 1782, pp. xlviii and 192, with title and half-title, also a map by G. and W. Paterson, 1746. Pages XXXVI., XXXVIII. of the preface are omitted.

No. XLVII. The History and Antiquities of St. Rule's Chapel, in the Monastery of St. Andrews, in Scotland. By Mr. George Martin, of Clermont; with Remarks by Mr. Professor Brown. To which are added, the Hiding of the Parliament of Scotland in 1606 and 1681, and the Ceremonials observed in 1685; the Statutes and Fees of the Order of the Thistle, &c. The Suspension of Lyon King of Arms; and a particular Description of the Regalia of Scotland. Lond. 1787, pp. 163—240, not including two title-pages, with three plates.

No. XXXVI. Remarks on the Progress of the Roman Army in Scotland during the sixth Campaign of Agricola; with a Plan and Description of the Camp at Raedykes (by the Earl of Buchan). Also an Account of the Roman Camps of Battle Dykes and Haerfauds, with the Via militaris extending between them, in the County of Forfar, by the Rev. Mr. Jameson (of Forfar).

NICHOLS, John—*continued*.
Lond. 1786, pp. 66, not including two title-pages, with six plates.
No. XXXVII. An historical Description of the Zetland Islands. By Thomas Gifford, Esq. Lond. 1786, pp. 86, pp. xviii (not xvi) and 104, with a map.
No. X. Containing a short Account of Holyhead, in the Isle of Anglesea (by the Rev. John Price, Keeper of the Bodleian Library, Oxford). Lond. 1783, pp. iv and 36 with two plates. Pp. 85 and 86 were delivered with No. LII.

VOL. VI. Title 'Antiquities biographical and miscellaneous' and general contents, iv pages.
No. IV. Memoirs of Sir John Hawkwood. Lond. 1762, pp. 86, not including title and half-title, with one plate.
No. XIX. Containing Additions to the Memoirs of Sir John Hawkwood, 1784, pp. 37—47, not including the half-title, with a plate.
No. XV. Extracts from the MS. Journal of Sir Simonds D'Ewes, with several Letters to and from Sir Simonds and his Friends. From the Originals in the British Museum. Lond. 1783, pp. xi and 82, not including two title-pages.
No. XXXI. A short genealogical View of the Family of Oliver Cromwell. To which is prefixed a copious Pedigree. Lond. 1785, 4to. pp. xviii and 64, with two pedigrees. The preface is signed R[ichard] G[ough].
No. XXXV. Archbishop Sharp's Observations on the Coinage of England. With his Letter to Mr. Thoresby, 1695. Lond. 1785, pp. viii and 69, with one plate. Page 69 is a folded strip, containing an account of the 'gold and silver coined for each reign from July 23, 1660, to June 24, 1754 inclusive.'
No. XXXIV. Biographical Anecdotes of the Rev. John Hutchins, M.A., Author of the History of Dorset, &c. By the Rev. Geo. Bingham, B.D. Lond. 1785, pp. 5—19, not including two title-pages and an advertisement.—Second edition. Lond. 1813, 4to. Title and pp. 3 to 15, portrait. Some copies printed in *Folio* to bind with History of Dorset.
No. XXVIII. Some Account of suffragan Bishops in England (by the Rev. John Lewis, of Margate, and the Rev. Sam. Pegge). Lond. 1785, pp. 52, not including two title-pages and an advertisement.
No. XLI. A Sylloge of the remaining authentic Inscriptions relative to the Erection of our English Churches; embellished with a Number of Copper Plates, exhibiting Facsimiles of some of the most material. By the Rev. Samuel Pegge. Lond. 1787, pp. v—xvi, and 1—130, not including two title-pages, and a dedication to Richard Gough, Esq. with 29 plates,

not including one of inscriptions, at p. 130, engraved by Basire, and delivered with No. LII.
No. XLVIII. Fragments of English and Irish History in the ninth and tenth Century. In two Parts. Translated from the original Icelandic, and illustrated with some Notes by Grimr Johnson Thorkelin, LL.D. Lond. 1788, pp. xii, 39 and [95] with a map.

VOL. VII. Title 'Antiquities in Leicestershire' and general contents, iv pages. Prefixed is a portrait of John Nichols, after Towne, by Cook.
No. VII. Containing the History and Antiquities of Hinckley, in the County of Leicester; including the Hamlets of Stoke, Dadlington, Wykin, and the Hyde. With a large Appendix. (By John Nichols). Lond. 1782, pp. vi and 240, with 13 plates. Pages 55 and 56 are repeated with asterisks, and at page 134 is the genealogy of Cleveland.
No. XLIII. The History and Antiquities of Aston Flamville and Burbach, including the Hamlets of Sketchley and Smockington, and the Granges of Leicester and Horeston, in the Counties of Leicester and Warwick. With an Appendix to the History of Hinckley; and genealogical and biographical Collections for the County at large. By John Nichols. Lond. 1787, pp. vi and 241—420, also pages *421—*428. In this number are 16 plates, and five folded genealogical tables, viz. of the families of Turville, De Verraro, Onsby, Wrights, and Chapman. Pages 253, 254, also 341 to 800, are repeated with asterisks.
No. L. Collections towards the History and Antiquities of the Town and County of Leicester. Published by John Nichols. Lond. 1790, pp. 421—714, not including two title-pages, and four pages of queries, which latter are sometimes placed at the conclusion of vol. viii. Pages 426, 427, 436, 437, 450, 451, 452 to 456, 461 to 466, 465 to 470, 4a3 to 518, 539, 540, 545, 546, are repeated with asterisks and pp. 439—440 are on one page. Contains 19 plates.

VOL. VIII. Title 'Antiquities in Leicestershire' and general contents, two leaves.
No. LI. Additional Collections towards the History and Antiquities of the Town and County of Leicester. Published by John Nichols. Lond. 1790, pp. x and 715—1508, misprinted 1068. Pages 1175, 1176, 1233 to 1245, 1307 to 1312, 1317, 1318, 1465, 1466, are repeated with asterisks, and the number contains forty plates.

VOL. IX. Half title 'Miscellaneous Antiquities, (in Continuation of the Bibliotheca Topographica Britannica).' No. I. Manduessedum Romanorum: being the History and Antiquities of the Parish of

5 P

NICHOLS, John—*continued.*
Manceter, (including the Hamlets of Hartshill, Oldbury and Atherstone), and also the adjacent Parish of Ansley, in the County of Warwick. By the late Benjamin Bartlett, Esq. Lond. 1791, pp. v-viii, not including title, 1—118, 119°—°124, 121—129, 121—136, 137°—°167, 187—142, *143—*146, 143—162. On p. viii will be found directions for placing the 24 plates, &c. A chronological chart faces p. 35.

No. II. Hawkhurst. A Sketch of its History and Antiquities, upon the Plan suggested in the Gentleman's Magazine, for procuring parochial Histories throughout England. Lond. 1792, pp. 24, not including the two titles, with two plates.

No. III. An History of the Manor and Manor-house of South Winfield, in Derbyshire. By Tho. Blore. Lond. 1793, pp. 100, not including two title-pages, and a leaf containing the errata, and directions for the (7) plates. Reprinted in 1816 with additions.

No. IV. The History and Antiquities of Shenstone in the County of Stafford, illustrated. Together with the Pedigrees of all the Families and Gentry, both antient and modern, of that Parish. By the Rev. Henry Sanders. Lond. 1794, pp. IV and 366, with a 'view of Shenston.'

VOL. X. No. V. Historical Particulars of Lambeth Parish and Lambeth Palace; in addition to the Histories by Dr. Ducarel in the Bibliotheca Topographica Britannica. By the Rev. Samuel Denne. Lond. 1795, pp. i—iv and 165—468. *See* vol. II. No. XXVII.

No. VI. The History and Antiquities of Twickenham. By Edward Ironside, Esq. Lond. 1797, pp. 106, not including the two title-pages, with 8 plates.

A second Appendix to the History of Croyland; illustrated with ten Plates of the legendary History of St. Guthlac (by Richard Gough). Lond. 1797, pp. 205—98, not including the title, with ten folded plates. Reprinted 1815, with an additional engraving of Croyland abbey, by J. Carter, engraved by Basire.

A Comment upon part of the fifth Journey of Antoninus through Britain. To which is added, a Dissertation on an Image of Jupiter found at Castor. By the Rev. Kennet Gibson. Enlarged with the History of Castor, an Account of Marham, &c. (by Richard Gough). Lond. 1800, pp. iv and 304, with 18 plates. Reprinted 1819, royal 4to. with additions and four additional plates. LARGE PAPER, in Imperial 4to. Thirty copies printed.

A List of the Members of the Society of Antiquaries of London from their Revival in 1717, to June 19, 1796. Arranged in chronological and alphabetical order. Lond. 1798, pp. 53, not including the half-title and title. Pp. 1—6 occupy five leaves.

NICHOLS, John. The History and Antiquities of the County of Leicester. Lond. 1795—1815, folio, 4 vols. in 8, 60*l*. LARGE PAPER, 80*l*.

North, pt. II. 629, russia, 52*l*. 10s. LARGE PAPER in royal folio. Marquis of Townshend, 3488, vol. I. II. and III. and part I. of vol. IV. 25*l*. 14s. Sir M. M. Sykes, 647, russia, 105*l*. Baker, 568, 87*l*. 15s. Beckford in 1817, No. 94, uncut, 66*l*. 2s. Dent, pt. ii. 921, vol. iii. pt. ii. on small paper, russia, 60*l*. *Collation.*—Vol. I. Part I. Containing Introduction and History of the Town OF LEICESTER. Title, dedication to George the Third, &c. pp. i—xlv; half-title, dedication of the introduction to the Rev. Sir Chas. Cave, Bart. 2 leaves; Leicestershire, extracted from Domesday Book, pp. I—XXX; a dissertation on Domesday Book, pp. xxxiii—liv; comes acne, &c. tab. I—xxiii, 24 pages; essay on the mint &c. pp. xli—xlviii; Testa de Nevill, &c. pp. xlvii—clxxii, a catalogue, &c. pp. clxxvii—ccvii; returns made to parliament, pp. 1—164; half-title and dedication to the Earl of Leicester, two leaves; history, pp. 250; appendix and index, 51 pages. Pages xxxi, xxxii, clxxiii to clxxvi, are omitted, pp. xlvii, xlviii, also 4 and 5 of the history, are repeated with asterisks; pp. clxxix, clxxx, also 19 and 20 are repeated. Vol. I. Part II. Containing a Continuation of the History of the Town OF LEICESTER, 1815. Title, prefatory advertisement, brief memoirs of the author, contents and list of plates, eight pages; the history and a brief index, pp. 261—678 (p. 468 repeated with an asterisk, the reverse blank); appendix, pp. 65—158; abstract of answers, &c. pp. 1—10; indexes, pp. 1—28, 1—113, 1—90, and 1—28. Vol. II. Part I. Containing FRAMLAND HUNDRED, 1795. Title and dedication to the Duke of Rutland, two leaves; the history, 424 pages; appendix, 140 pages, ending with the catch-word 'appendix;' index, pp. 425—6. Pages 17—30, 232-3 383-4, and 417—8 are repeated with asterisks; pp. 259 and 262 are twice repeated with one and two asterisks; p. 231 is twice repeated with two and three asterisks, and p. 353 is omitted. Vol. II. Part II. Containing GARTREE HUNDRED, 1798. Title and dedication to Joseph Cradock, Esq. two leaves; the history continued, pp. 431—896; appendix, 141—8; a brief index, with the list of plates, pp. 149-50. Pp. 445-6, 471-4, 531-2, 635-6, and 693-4 are repeated with asterisks, and pp. 813—6 are mis-

NICHOLS, John—*continued.*
printed 918—6. Vol. III. Part I. Containing EAST GOSCOTE HUNDRED, 1800. Title, dedication to Viscount Tamworth and advertisement, pp. i—xxii; the continuation of the history, with additions and corrections, pp. 1—500; appendix, brief indices and list of plates, 16 pages. Pages 5, 6, 61 to 60, 167 to 170, and 513 to 516 are repeated with asterisks. Pp. 115 and 116 (sign. III 8) are also repeated. Vol. III. Part II. containing WEST GOSCOTE HUNDRED, 1804. [*This portion of the work is the scarcest, as many copies perished in the fire of Feb. 8, 1808.*] Title and dedication to the Earl of Moira, 2 leaves; the history continued, also additions and corrections, pp. 561—1150: continuation of the appendix in vol. III. pt. i. brief index and directions to the binder, pp. 17—72. Pages 637 to 640, 687 to 664, 715 to 720, 731 to 734, 783-4, 791-2, 859-60, 873 to 876, 889 to 896, 979 to 990, 1011-12, 1047 to 1050, 1095-6, and 1125-6, are reprinted with asterisks. Pp. 721—2 and 1007—10 have asterisks. Vol. IV. Part I. Containing GUTHLAXTON HUNDRED, 1807. Pp. 1—424, not including title and dedication to Baron Fielding, 2 leaves, and a leaf of errata, pp 421-2, not in the reprint of 1810, being corrected therein, and therefore not required. At page 293 and 294 are pedigrees. *The second Edition,* with a few Corrections, &c. 1810. Title and dedication to Baron Fielding, two leaves; the history of the county continued, with additions and corrections, brief index and a list of plates, pp. 1—620. Pages 294—5, containing the pedigree of Fielding, are repeated with asterisks. *The original edition was destroyed by fire, and not reprinted on Larger Paper, which is accordingly very rare.* Vol. IV. Part II. Containing SPARKENHOE HUNDRED, 1811. Title, dedication to Baron Wentworth, preface, list of subscribers and two indexes, pp. i—xiv; the history of the county continued, with additions and corrections, a pedigree of Shirley, brief index, directions to the binder, list of plates in the volume, and for vol. I. part II. pp. 425—1054. Pages 451-2, 519 to 524, 629-30, 633-4, 725, 807-8, 845 to 856, 883-4, 889 to 892, 915-16, 903-4, and 979 to 984, are repeated with asterisks. Pages 525-6, 841 to 844 have asterisks; pp. 856-8, are on one page; and a separate leaf, the continuation of the pedigree of Clarke Jervoise, faces p. 602. For the list of plates and directions to the binder, *see* vol. I. part I. pp. xii—xiv. vol. i. part II. page viii, i.e. the page preceding p. 231, also pp. 115, 116, of the appendix, and again p. 26, the last page in the volume. vol. II. part II. p. 150. vol. III. part I. p. 16, the last in the volume. vol. III. part II. p. 1128 and p. 72, the last in the volume. vol. iv. pt. I. edition 1807. p. 424. vol. iv. p. l. edition 1810. p. 420, and vol. iv. pt. II. p. 1053-4.

A Collection of royal and noble Wills, now known to be extant, of the Kings and Queens of England, Princes and Princesses of Wales, and every branch of the Blood-Royal, from the Reign of William the Conqueror to that of Henry VII. inclusive; with explanatory Notes, and a Glossary. Lond. 1780, 4to. Bindley, pt. III. 760, 7s. Edwards, 664, 10s. 6d. Roxburghe, 1147, 7s.

A select Collection of Poems, with Notes biographical and historical. Lond. 1780-2, small 8vo. 6 vols. with portraits. Heath, 1861, 8 vols. 1l. 18s. Hibbert, 5597, 17s.

Biographical Memoirs of William Ged; including a particular Account of his Progress in the Art of Block-printing. Lond. 1781. 8vo. 3s. 6d.—Newcastle, with additions, 1819, crown 8vo. One hundred and sixty copies printed. LARGE PAPER, 8vo. Thirty copies printed.

Biographical Anecdotes of William Hogarth: and a Catalogue of his Works, chronologically arranged; with occasional Remarks. Lond. 1781—1782, 8vo. 6s. 6d. Bindley, pt. II. 2178, 9s. 6d.—1785, 8vo. best edition, with knife and fork in title page. Bindley, pt. II. 2011, 3s. 6d. Field, 1492, 10s. 6d. Lloyd, 589, 11s.—New and considerably enlarged edition. Lond. J. Nichols, 1833. *See* HOGARTH, p. 1052.

The PROGRESSES AND PUBLIC PROCESSIONS OF QUEEN ELIZABETH. Lond. 1788-1807. 4to. 3 vols. Hibbert, 5807, 6l. Constable, 778, 10l. 5s. Dent, pt. II. 754, russia, 10l. 13s. 6d. Baker, 512, 11l. 0s. 6d. Nassau, pt. II. 569, 15l. 10s. Sir M. M. Sykes, pt. II. 672, russia, 25l. 4s. Bindley, pt. III. 761, 26l. 5s. Gough, 2686, 28l. 10s. North, pt. II. 1032, 28l. 7s. Fonthill, 4583, morocco, 31l. 10s. Steevens, 1712, vol. I. and II. 2l. Willett, 1769, vol. I. and II. 3l. 9s. White Knights, vol. I. and II. 17l. 17s. Many copies of vol. III. were destroyed by fire in 1808.—Lond. 1823, 4to. 3 vols. Second edition, chronologically arranged, with valuable additions and some necessary indexes. It also has several additional plates, but some Latin complimentary poems are omitted. Published at 9l. 9s. reduced, Hobn, to 4l. 14s. 6d. Rhodes, 2778, 6l. 6s. Drury, 3191, 11l.

PROGRESSES, PROCESSIONS AND MAGNIFICENT FESTIVITIES OF K. JAMES THE FIRST, his royal Consort, Family, and Court. Lond. 1828, 4to. 4 vols. Published at 10l. 10s. but since reduced (Bohn) to 5l. 5s.

At the end of the fourth volume is a list of 31 additional engravings advertised at 1l. 1s. They are merely impressions from old plates in Mr. Nichols' possession, and are of no import.

NICHOLS, John—*continued.*
ILLUSTRATIONS OF THE MANNERS AND EXPENCES of ancient Times in England, in the 15th, 16th, and 17th Centuries, deduced from the Accompts of Churchwardens, and other authentic Documents, collected from various parts of the Kingdom; with explanatory Notes. Lond. 1797, 4to. Roxburghe, 8589, 3l. 5s. Dent, pt. ii. 755, 5l.

Biographical and Literary Anecdotes of William Bowyer, Printer, F.S.A. and of many of his learned Friends; containing an incidental View of the Progress and Advancement of Literature in this Kingdom, from the Beginning of the present Century to the End of the Year 1777. Lond. 1782, 4to. with portrait of Bowyer by Basire. Bindley, pt. iii. 759, 19s. Willett, 1786, 11.8s. Steevens, 1811, 11.17s. FIRST EDITION, 1778, 8vo. Fifty-two copies printed. Brockett, 2163, 4s. 6d.

The following work is an amplification and completion of the single quarto volume published in 1782.

LITERARY ANECDOTES of the 18th Century, comprising Biographical Memoirs of William Bowyer, Printer, and many of his learned Friends, an incidental View of the Progress and Advancement of Literature in this Kingdom during the last Century, and Biographical Anecdotes of a considerable Number of eminent Writers and ingenious Artists, with general indexes, 9 vols. Lond. 1812-1815. (Vol. 7 is in two parts, the first, published in 1813, contains an Index to the first seven volumes, the second part, published in 1816, contains index to vols. viii. and ix.)—ILLUSTRATIONS of the literary History of the eighteenth Century; consisting of authentic Memoirs and original Letters of eminent Persons, and intended as a Sequel to the Literary Anecdotes. *With a general index*, 8 vols. Lond. 1817—1858, 8vo. Together 17 vols. North, pt. ii. 942, vols. i. to ix. 10l. 5s. Duke of York, 8778, 9 vols. and Illustrations, vols. i.—iii. 11l. Brockett, 2181, 10 vols. 12l. 12s. Hibbert, 5632, 15 vols. 1812-29, 15l. 14s.—Sotheby's, in 1860, 17 vols. calf, 19l.

The above 'Illustrations of Literary History,' 6 vols. pub. at 8l. 8s., now sells separately for about 6l. 6s.

HISTORY AND ANTIQUITIES OF HINCKLEY, in the County of Leicester: including the Hamlets of Dadlington, Stoke, Wykin and the Hyde. The second edition, embellished with twenty-two plates. To which is added, the History of Witherley, in the same county, and a large Extract *of the Manduessedum Romanorum*: being the History and Antiquities of Mancster (including the Hamlets of Hartshill, Oldbury and Atherstone), and also of the adjacent Parish of Ansley, in the county of Warwick: by the late Benjamin Bartlett,

Esq., with Additions. By John Nichols. Illustrated by seventeen Plates. 1813, folio. Fifty copies, printed separately from the History of the County. *Collation.*— Title and dedication, two leaves; the history of Hinckley, &c. pp. 669—758. The history of Witherley, &c. 1007—44; Index, &c. one page.

(The first edition was printed in the Bibliotheca Topographica, vol. vii.)

Brief Memoirs of John Nichols. 1804, 8vo. Twelve copies printed. Reed, 8139, with Anecdotes of W. Bowyer, 1778, 8vo. 2l. 12s.

Memoir of John Nichols, Esq. F.S.A. by A(lexander) C(halmers). Extracted from the Gentleman's Magazine for December, 1826, 4to. 17 pages. Printed for private distribution.

This industrious man was either author or editor of upwards of 60 different works, a list of which may be seen in the Gentleman's Magazine for December, 1826, of which valuable periodical he was the editor and proprietor for many years.

NICHOLS, John Bowyer. Account of the royal Hospital and collegiate Church of Saint Katherine, near the Tower of London. Lond. 1824, 4to.

Pp. iv. and 62, with six plates.

A brief Account of the Guildhall of the City of London. Lond. 1819, 8vo. pp. iv. and 64, with two plates.

London Pageants: Accounts of Sixty royal Processions and Entertainments in the City of London, from Henry II. to present Time; with a bibliographical List of Lord Mayors' Pageants. Lond. 8vo. 1831, 4s. LARGE PAPER, royal 8vo. 6s.

Collectanea Topographica et Genealogica. Lond. 1834-43, 8vo. 8 vols. Contains indexes in each volume, and at end of vol. 8 an Index of additions to Dugdale and a Synopsis of contents of the 8 vols. Published at 1l. per volume.

This work is continued by the 'Topographer and Genealogist,' edited by John Gough Nichols. Lond. 1846-8, royal 8vo. 2 vols. 2l. 2s.

Historical Notices of Fonthill and its Abbey, by J. B. Nichols. Lond. 18—, 8vo. plates, 15s. LARGE PAPER, 1l. 1s.

Mr. Nichols was likewise editor of the third and fourth volume of the second enlarged edition of Hutchins' Dorset, and of the new edition of Duston's Memoirs.

— John Gough. Autographs of royal, noble, learned and remarkable Personages, conspicuous in English History, from the Reign of Richard II. to that of Charles II. including some illustrious Foreigners; containing many Passages from important Letters. Engraved under

the direction of C. J. Smith, accompanied by concise biographical Memoirs and interesting Extracts from the original Documents by J. G. Nichols. Lond. 1820, imp. 4to.
In eleven parts, published at 5s. each, or 7s. 6d. tinted.
Examples of Inlaid and Encaustic Tiles. Lond. 1842-47, 4to. 1l. 1s.

NICHOLS (Josias). Plea of the Innocent, wherein is averred that the Ministers and people falselie termed Puritanes, are injuriously slandered for enemies or troublers to the State, against all sycophantising Papistes, statising Priests, &c. 12mo. 1602, 1l. 4s.
Recently printed. The author was of Eastwell, in Kent.

— Samuel. Acolastus his After-Witte, a Poem. Lond. Daylie, 1600, 4to.
Remarkable as containing some parallel passages to Shakspeare. Steevens, 891, 1l. 3s. resold Hibbert, 5600, 4l. 4s. Bindley, pt. III. 775, 8l. 15s. Bright, 8l. 10s. Jolley, 10l. 10s.

— William, D.D. A Commentary on the Book of Common Prayer. Lond. 1710, folio.
With portrait of the author by Vander Gucht. Bindley, pt. II. 1489, 18s. An Appendix appeared in 1711.—Second edition. Lond. 1712, fol. with portrait, 1l. 1s.
A Paraphrase on the Common Prayer and Psalms of David. Lond. 1707. 8vo. 4s.
A Conference with a Theist; containing an Answer to all the most usual Objections of the Infidels against the Christian Religion. Third edition. Lond. 1723, 8vo. 2 vols. 6s.
Nicholls published other works.

NICHOLSON, John. Operative Mechanic and British Machinist, being a practical Display of the Manufactories and Mechanical Arts of the United Kingdom. Lond. 1825, 8vo.
Third edition. Lond. Sherwood, 1849, 8vo. 1l. 11s. 6d.—Fourth edition, with a Supplement relating to British Public Works and National Improvements; and a further Supplement, continuing the work to the present time, especially in regard to the Steam Engine, Navigation, and Railroads, Machinery and Manufactures, Strength of Materials, &c. &c. by G. Fluden Warr. Lond. Bohn, 1855, 8vo plates, 15s.

— Peter. Architectural Dictionary, containing a correct Nomenclature and Derivations of the Terms employed by Architects, Builders, and Workmen, exhibiting the Theory and Practice of the various Branches of Architecture, with the Lives of the principal Architects. Lond. 1811-19, 4to. 2 vols. numerous engravings, pub. at 10l. 10s. in bds. reduced 4l. 4s. LARGE PAPER, 6l. 6s.
Second edition, edited by Lomax and Gwayne. Lond. Jackson, 1853, 4to. 2 vols. plates, 4l. 4s.
Principles and Practice of Architecture, containing the fundamental Rules of the Art, in Geometry, Arithmetic, and Mensuration, with the Application of those Rules to Practice. The true Method of drawing the Ichnography and Orthography of Objects; including Treatises on Arches, Mouldings, spiral Lines, and Foliage, and geometrical Rules for Shadows; also the Five Orders of Architecture, with a great variety of beautiful Examples selected from the Antique, and many useful and elegant Ornaments, with Rules for projecting them. Lond. 1795-9, 8vo. 3 vols. with 213 plates by Lowry. pub. at 3l. 8s.—Fifth edit. Lond. Bohn, 1841, 8vo 3 vols.—Sixth edit. revised and enlarged by Joseph Gwilt, Esq., complete in one large vol. royal 8vo. with 213 fine plates by Lowry. Lond. H. G. Bohn, 1848, 1l. 11s. 6d.
One of the most useful guides to the architectural student. Mr. Goldscott, an eminent architect, declared it to be 'not only the most useful book of the kind ever published, but absolutely indispensable to the student;' adding, that 'he always kept a copy on his own table, as well as another in the office for the use of his pupils.'
Student's Instructor in Drawing and Working the Five Orders of Architecture. 1837, 8vo. 41 plates, 10s. This work is incorporated in Nicholson's Principles of Architecture.
Builder's and Workman's New Director. Edinb. Fullarton, 1843, 4to. 141 plates, 2l. 12s. 6d.
The Carpenter's New Guide; or, the Book of Lines for Carpenters geometrically explained: comprising all the elementary Principles essential for acquiring a Knowledge of the Theory and Practice of Carpentry. Lond. 1792, 4to.—Lond. Taylor, 1797, 4to. 78 plates, 1l. 1s.—New edition, founded on that of the late Peter Nicholson's standard Work, revised by Arthur Ashpitel; with practical Rules on Drawing, by Geo. Pyne. Lond. Weale, 1857, 4to. 1l. 1s.

NICHOLSON, Peter—*continued*.
Practical Treatise on the Art of Masonry and Stone-cutting. Lond. 1823.—
Third edition. Lond. Maynard, 1835, roy. 8vo. 43 plates.—New edition. Lond. Taylor, 1828, roy. 8vo. 12s.
Practical Builder. Lond. Kelly, 1847, 4to. 3 vols. plates, 5l. 5s.
The Guide to Railway Masonry, containing a complete Treatise on the Oblique Arch; in four parts, with an Appendix. By Peter Nicholson.—Third edition. Lond. Groombridge, 1846, 8vo. 12s. 6d.—Revised and corrected throughout by R. Cowen. Lond. 8pon, 1860, cr. 8vo. *ib.*
Treatise on Projection; together with a complete System of Isometrical Drawing. Lond. Groombridge, 1840, 8vo. 10s.
On the Construction of Staircases and Hand-Rails. Lond. 1820, 4to.—New edition. Lond. Taylor, 1847, 4to. 12s.
Practical System of Algebra, by Nicholson and Rowbotham. Lond. 1824.—Fifth edition. Lond. Baldwin, 1844, 12mo. 5s.—Seventh edition. Lond. Simpkin, 1855, 12mo. 5s.—New edition, 1856, 3s. 6d.—Key, 3s.
Essay on the Combinatorial Analysis. Lond. 1818, 8vo. 10s.
Essays on Involution and Evolution; with an Appendix shewing the Use of figurate Numbers and arithmetical Equivalents in the Extraction of Roots. Lond. 1820.
The Rudiments of practical Perspective. Lond. Lumley, 1822, 8vo. 7s. 6d.
Cabinetmaker and Upholsterer's Guide. Lond. P. Jackson, 16—, 4to. 2l.
Carpenter, Joiner, and Builder's Companion. Lond. P. Jackson, 1846, 8vo. 1l. 1s.
Carpentry, Joining, and Building. Lond. Weale, 1851, 4to. 2 vols. 2l. 16s.
Elements of Mathematics. Lond. Whittaker, 18—, 8vo. 1l. 1s.—Key, 7s. 6d.
Mechanical Exercises, or the Elements and Practice of Carpentry, Joining, &c. Lond. 1811, 8vo. 18s.—Lond. M. Taylor, 1819, 8vo. 18s.
Tables of Logarithms. Lond. Whittaker, 18—, 8vo. 5s.
Treatise on Dialling. Lond. Weale, 1836, 8vo. 4s.
Carpenter's and Joiner's Assistant. 1798, 4to. 1l. 1s.
An Introduction to the Method of Increments, expressed by a new Form of Notation; shewing more intimately its Relation to the Fluxional Analysis. 1817, 8vo. 6s.

NICHOLSON, William, Bp. of Gloucester. Davids Harp strung and tun'd; or, an easie Analysis of the whole Book of Psalms. With a devout Meditation or Prayer at the End of each Psalm. Lond. 1662, folio, 9s.
William, 1423, 1l. 1s. The work, though written in a quaint and scholastic style, may nevertheless be consulted with advantage. Dr. Adam Clarke has inserted Bishop Nicholson's analyses in his commentary on the Psalms, omitting the Prayers.
Exposition of the Catechism of the Church of England. Lond. 1662, 8vo. Bliss, 1s. 6d.—Oxford, 1842, 8vo.

— William. A Journal of Natural Philosophy, Chemistry, and the Arts. Lond. 1792-1802, 5 vols. 4to. Continuation, 8vo. 36 vols.—1802-12, together 41 vols. 8l. 3s.
Introduction to Natural Philosophy. Lond. 1782, 8vo. 2 vols.—1787, 8vo. 2 vols.—1790, 8vo. 2 vols. Edwards, 845, 5s.
Dictionary of Chemistry. Lond. 1795, 4to. 2 vols. Hibbert, 5810, 6s.
The British Encyclopaedia, or Dictionary of Arts and Sciences. Lond. 1809, 8vo. 6 vols. plates, published at 6l. 6s. and once very popular, now 1l. 1s.

NICHOLLS, J. Original Letters and Letters of State found amongst Milton's Papers. *See* MILTON, John.

NICOBAR ISLANDS.—Letters on the Nicobar Islands. Lond. 1813, 8vo.
An interesting little work, 64 pages, published by the Moravians.

NICODEMUS.—Nicodemus's Gospel; containing an Account of our blessed Saviour's Trial and Accusation, &c. By Joseph Wilson. Lond. 1767, 8vo. 2s. 6d.
A poor translation from the Latin of a forged gospel, never heard of till the fourth century. The original, with a translation and a full account of it, will be found in Jones' Method of settling the Canon of the New Testament. *See also* in vol. iv. of Horne's Introduction to the Scriptures by Dr. Tregelles. An Anglo-Saxon version, from the Cambridge Manuscript, is printed with Heptateuchos ed. Thwaites.
Nicodamus his Gospel. Lond. by Jolyan Notary, 1507, 4to. A doubtful edition.
Nychodemus Gospell. Lond. by W. de Worde, 1509, 4to. Twenty-three leaves, including the title-page, with cuts. A copy is in the public library at Cambridge.—1511, 4to. Horne Tooke, 489, 9l. As resold White Knights, 8147, morocco, 7l. 11s. 6d. resold Hibbert, 5849, 12l. 15s.

—1512, 4to.—1518, 4to. A copy is in the British Museum.—1532. 4to. This edition contains F 6, the former signatures all quartos, with cuts.
Nychodemus Gospell. Lond. by John Skot, 1529, 4to.—n. d. 4to. woodcuts. Herbert, pt. 1s. 2l. 5s. The signature A has six, B, C, D, E, F have each four leaves.
Nichodemus his Gospel, (Rouen), by John Cousturier, small 8vo. A copy is in the British Museum. Ingils, 10C0, 6s.
Nichodemus his Gospel. 16td, 12mo. Heber, pt. viii. 6s. 6d.
The Gospel of Nicodemus, with other false Gospels, is contained in Hone's Apocryphal New Testament, which see, at p. 1103.

NICOL, James. An Essay on the Nature and Design of Scripture Sacrifices. Lond. 1823, 8vo. 7s. 6d.
The production of a minister of the Church of Scotland, in support of Unitarian doctrines.

— John. The Life and Adventures of John Nicol, Mariner. Edinb. 1822, 12mo. 5s. 6d.
An interesting volume of autobiography, consisting of 215 pages, with port.

NICOLAI, Frederic. The Life and Opinions of Sebaldus Nothanker, translated from the German by Thomas Dutton. Lond. 1796-8. 12mo. 3 vols. 10s. 6d.

NICOLAS, Nicholas Harris, Knt. History of the Battle of Agincourt, and of the Expedition of Henry V. into France, with the Roll of the Men at Arms in the English Army. Second edition. Lond. 1831, 8vo.
A former edition appeared in 1827, cr. 8vo. LARGE PAPER.—Third edition, revised and improved. Lond. 1833, 8vo. 1l. 1s.

Life of William Davison, Secretary of State and Privy Counsellor to Queen Elizabeth. Lond. 1823, 8vo. with Facsimiles of Writing (pub. at 12s.) reduced 4s. 6d.
"A minute investigation of the question as to Elizabeth's privity and consent to the death of her sister, Mary Queen of Scots."—Gentleman's Magazine.

Catalogue of the Heralds' Visitations, with References to many other valuable genealogical and topographical MSS. in the British Museum. Second edition. Lond. 1825, 8vo. 5s. LARGE PAPER, 9s.

Notitia Historica; containing Tables, Calendars, and miscellaneous Information for the Use of Historians, Antiquaries, and the Legal Profession. Lond. 1824, crown 8vo. Bliss, 3s. 6d.—An improved edition, under title of the Chronology of History, is printed in Lardner's Cyclopaedia. Lond. 1833, 12mo. 6s. red. 8s. 6d.

A Synopsis of the Peerage of England, exhibiting, under alphabetical Arrangement, the Date of Creation, Descent, and present State of every Title of Peerage which has existed in this Country since the Conquest. Lond. 1825, 18mo. 2 vols. 15s. New edition, (under the title of Historic Peerage of England). Revised and continued to the present time, by W. Courthope. Lond. 1857, roy. 8vo. 1l. 10s.

Testamenta Vetusta, being Illustrations from Wills, of ancient Manners, Customs, Dresses, &c. as well as of the Descents and Possessions of many distinguished Families, from the Reign of Henry II. to the Accession of Queen Elizabeth. Lond. 1826, royal 8vo. 2 vols. 2l. 5s.

History of the Town and School of Rugby, in the County of Warwick. Coventry, 1827, 4to. pts. I. II. III. 6s. each.

Proofs of Barons sitting in Parliament, as occur in the Rolls of Parliament; with Observations. (Extracted from the Synopsis of the Peerage.) Lond. n. d. sm. 8vo.

Alphabetical List of the Knights of the Garter, Knights of the Bath, and the Grand Crosses, from 1725. Lond. n. d. 12mo.

Memoir of Augustine Vincent, Windsor Herald, temp. James the First, with Addenda. Lond. 1827, crown 8vo. 5s.

A Roll of Arms of Peers and Knights in the Reign of Edward the Second, from a contemporary MS. in the British Museum. With a Preface. Lond. 1828, 8vo. 10s. 6d. LARGE PAPER in 4to. Fifty copies printed, 1l. 1s.

The Statutes of the Order of the Guelphs, translated from the original German, with introductory Remarks. 1828, 4to. One hundred and fifty copies printed for the use of the English members of the order. (Afterwards included in his History of the Orders of Knighthood.)

The Statutes of the Order of the Thistle, to which are added, a History of the Order, and a Catalogue of the Knights since its revival by James the Second in 1687. Lond. 1828, 4to. Fifty copies printed.

A Journal by one of the Suite of Thos. Beckington, afterwards Bishop of Bath and Wells, during an Embassy to negotiate a Marriage between Henry VI. and a daughter of the Count of Armagnac, A.D. MCCCCXLII. With Notes and Illustrations. Lond. 1828, 8vo. 10s. 6d. LARGE PAPER. only 12 printed, 1l. 4s.

Rolls of Arms of the Reigns of Henry III. and Edward III.; edited by N. H. Nicolas, Esq. Lond. 1829, 8vo. 10s. 6d.

NICOLAS, Sir N. H.—*continued.*
LARGE PAPER in 4to. Fifty copies printed,
1l. 1s.
Report of Proceedings on the Claim to
the Barony of L'Isle. In the House of
Lords, with Notes and an Appendix containing the Cases of Abergavenny, Botetourt, and Berkeley, accompanied by Observations on Baronies by Tenure, by
N. H. Nicolas. Lond. 1829, 8vo, 1l. 1s.

A Letter in Defence of the Statement
relative to the Barony of Chandos, in the
Synopsis of the Peerage. Lond. 1841,
12mo. pp. 14. This is a reply to a note
of Sir Egerton Brydges relative to the
Barony not being extinct, first printed in
1823.
Letter to the Duke of Wellington on
the Propriety and Legality of Creating
Peers for Life, with Precedents. Second
edition, 1830, 8vo. 2s. 6d.
Report of Proceedings on the Claim to
the Earldom of Devon, with Notes and
Appendix. Lond. 1832, 8vo. 12s.
Observations on the State of Historical
Literature, and on the Society of Antiquaries, and other Institutions for the
Advancement in England; with Remarks
on the Record Offices, and on the Proceedings of the Record Commission. With
additional Facts, and a Refutation of Mr.
Palgrave's 'Remarks in Reply to this
Work.' Lond. 1831, 8vo. 12s. 6d.
Treatise on Adulterine Bastardy, with
a Report of the Banbury Case, and of all
other Cases bearing on that subject. Lond.
1836, 8vo. — Second edition, corrected.
Lond. 1838, 8vo. 1l. 1s.
Lives of Isaak Walton and Charles
Cotton, from an edition of the Complete
Angler. Lond. 1837, imp. 8vo. Bliss, 10s.
See WALTON, ISAAC.
Letter to the Lord Chancellor on the
Record Commission. 1832, 8vo. swd. 6s.
Proceedings and Ordinances of the
Privy Council of England, from 10 Rich.
II. to 33 Hen. VIII. with Indexes. 1834-7,
royal 8vo. 7 vols. 2l. 12s.
History of the Orders of Knighthood
of the British Empire; of the Order of the
Guelphs of Hanover; and of the Medals,
Crosses and Clasps, conferred for Naval and
Military Service. Lond. 1842, impl. 4to.
4 vols. numerous coloured plates, reduced
to 3l. 13s. 6d. or, with the plates illuminated, and with full-length portraits of
Queen Victoria, Prince Albert, the King
of Hanover, and the Dukes of Cambridge
and Sussex, (pub. at 14l. 14s.) reduced
to 5l. 15s. 6d. The copies last issued have
a continuation to 1841.
"The first comprehensive History of
the British Orders of Knighthood; and
one of the most elaborate and splendid
works that ever issued from the press.

The Author appears to have neglected no
source of information." — *Quarterly Review.*
History of the Earldoms of Strathern,
Menteith, and Airth. Lond. 1842, 8vo. 12s.
Life and Times of Sir Christopher Hatton. Knt. Lond. 1847, 8vo. port. 15s.
On the Library and Catalogue of the
British Museum. Lond. 1846, 8vo.
History of the Royal Navy of England,
from the earliest times to the Wars of the
French Revolution. Lond. 1847, 8vo. 2
vols. 1l. 8s. (All printed, extending only
to the reign of Henry V. 1422.)
See Carlaverock. CHAUCER, Geff. DAVISON, Francis. DIGBY, Sir Kenelm. FANSHAW, Lady. GREY, Lady Jane. HENRY
VIII. King of England. LONDON, Chronicle of. MARVELL, Andrew. NELSON
Dispatches. PALGRAVE, F. SCROPE and
Grosvenor Controversy. YORK, Ellis. of.
Sir H. Nicolas was one of the editors
of the second series of the Retrospective
Review, and a member of the third Record Commission. He contributed many
papers to the Archæologia.

NICOLL, Alexander. Notitia Codicis Samaritano-Arabici Pentateuchi in Bibl. Bodleiana, complectentia. Oxonii, 1818, roy. 8vo.
LARGE PAPER, 10 printed. Bliss, 2s.
Sermons. Oxford, 18—, 8vo. Published posthumously. *See* Bodleian Library, p. 227.

NICOLLES, Philip. Here begynneth a godly newe Story of XII Men
that Moyses sent to spye out the
Land of Canaan. Lond. William
Hill, 1548, 12mo.
Fifty-one leaves. Hibbert, 7671, mor.
10s. Sotheby, 1855, 1l. 12s. Geo. Chalmers, pt. 1.1040, in a volume. Jolley, 1l. 10s.
The Copie of a Letter sente to one
Maister Chrisnyme, Chanon of Exeter, for
that he denied the Scripture to be the
Touchstone or Trial of al other Doctrines, &c. Written 7 Nov. 1547. Lond.
John Daye and Wm. Seres, n. d. 12mo.
Containing P 10, in eights, C having but
7. Heber, pt. v. in a volume. A copy is
in Lambeth Library.

NICOLS, John. A Declaration of
the Recantation of John Nichols,
for the Space of two Years the
Pope's Scholar at the English Seminarie at Rome, which desireth to
be reconciled and received as a
Member into the true Church of
Christ in England. Lond. 1581,
16mo.

NICOLS, John—*continued.*
N l, in eights, with dedication and preface to Odoenus Ilopton, and preface. A notice of this work will be found in the Crypt, new series, no. viii. Inglis, 1058, 2s. 6d. Sir M. M. Sykes, pt. —, 839, 11s.
Pilgrimage, wherein is displaied the Liues of the proude Popes, ambitious Cardinals, lecherous Bishops, fat bellied Monkes, and hypocritical Iesuites (with Poetry). Lond. 1581, 16mo. Dedicated to Q. Elisabeth, after which are two addresses to the reader. R, in eights. Inglis, 1060, 10s. Sotheby, June 1816, 2l. Heber, pt. viii. 19s. A work replete with the most virulent abuse of the Catholic clergy, and scandalous representations of their licentiousness and vices. *See* Helot's Anecdotes, vi. 163-5.
The Oration and Sermon made at Rome, vpon the Faine of Death. Lond. 1581. 16mo. Inglis. 1062, 11s.
A true lieport of the late Apprehension and Imprisonment of John Nicols, Minister at Roan, and his Confession, &c. Rhemes, 1583, 16mo. Thirty-four leaves, not including a preface and an admonition to the reader.
See FENNER, Dudley. PARSONS, Robt. An account of John Nicols will be found in Wood's Athen. Oxon.

NICOLS, William. De Literis inventis Libri VI. Lond. 1711, 8vo. 3s. 6d.
Written in hexameter and pentameter verse, with valuable notes.

NICOLSON, Joseph. The History and Antiquities of the Counties of Westmorland and Cumberland. By Joseph Nicolson, Esq., and Richard Burn, LL.D. Lond. 1777, 4to. 2 vols.
Drury, 8193, 2l. 3s. Dent, pt. II. 757, with additional plates, russia, 5l. 7s. 6d. Heath, 4572, 1l. 19s. Marquis of Townshend, 2403, 1l. 14s. Brockett, 7283, 4l. Nassau, pt. II. 581, 2l. 7s. Willett, 1769, 4l. *Collation.*—Vol. I. Pp. cxxxiv and 630, not including the title with a folded map of Westmorland by Tho. Kitchin. Vol. II. Pp. 624, not including the title, with a folded map of Cumberland by Thomas Kitchin.

— William, successively Bishop of Carlisle and Derry; afterwards Archbishop of Cashel. The English, Scotch, and Irish historical Libraries. To which is added, a Letter to White Kennet, D.D., in Defence of the English historical Library, &c. A new (third) edition corrected. Lond. 1776, 4to. 2l. 2s.
A valuable work, indispensable to the study of English history. Bindley, pt. III. 756, 2l. 2s. Dowdeswell, 595, 2l. 12s. 6d. Edwards, 576, 2l. 6s. Heath, 4367, russ. 3l. Brockett, 2282, 2l. — Second edition. Lond. 1736, fol. Hollis, 1130, 1l. 17s. LARGE PAPER? Willett, 1677, 2l.
The first edition of this work was published in three divisions, at Intervals, viz. English Historical Library. Lond. 1696-9, 8vo. 3 pts. in 2 vols. &c.—Second edition, 1714, folio.—Scottish Historical Library. Lond. 1702, 8vo. Bliss, 3s. 6d.—Irish Historical Library. Dublin, 1724, 8vo. 7s.
A Letter to Dr. White Kennett, in Defence of the English Historical Library against the unmannerly and slanderous attack of Dr. Atterbury in his Rights, powers, &c. of an English Convocation. By W. Nicolson. Lond. 1709, 4to. pp. 84.
To the Bishop of Carlisle on his Scotch Library (by T. Rymer). Letter I. Lond. 1702, 8vo. pp. 62.
To the Bishop of Carlisle, containing an historical Deduction of the Alliances between France and Scotland (by T. Rymer). Letter II. Lond. n. d. 8vo. pp. 101.
Answer to the second Letter to the Bishop of Carlisle, occasioned by some passages in his Scotch Library. (By Sir Robert Sibbald.) Edinb. 1704, 8vo.
Leges Marchiarum: or Border laws. With a Preface and an Appendix. Lond. 1705, 8vo. Roxburghe, 981, 3s. Bindley, pt. III. 25, 3s. 6d. Heed. 5271, 1s. 6d. *Collation.*—Pp. 888, besides half-title and title, two leaves; dedication, 4 pages, and preface, 56 pages.—Lond. 1747, 8vo. Dent, pt. II. 23, 4s. 6d.
Letters on various Subjects, literary, political, and ecclesiastical. Lond. 1809, 8vo. 2 vols. Edited by John Nichols. Bindley, pt. II. 2180, 8s. Hibbert, 6703, 8s. Bishop of Ely, 854, 8s. 6d.

NIEBUHR, Barthold Georg. The HISTORY of ROME, translated by F. A. Walter. Lond. 1827, 8vo. 2 vols.
A translation from the first edition of the original, now of no value.
A new translation by Julius C. Hare and Connop Thirlwall. Camb. 1828-32, 8vo. 2 vols. 1l. 12s. Of this there is a second edition of vol. 1, incorporating the additions contained in the third edition of the original. Camb. 1831, 8vo.; and a third edition, 1837, with map.
Vol. 3, translated by W. Smith and Leonard Schmitz (with general index). Lond. 1842, 8vo. 18s. 6d.

NIEBUHR, B. G.—*continued.*
New edition of the three volumes. Lond.
1847-51, 8vo. 8 vols. 1l. 16s.—Again, Lond.
1855. 8vo. 8 vols. 1l. 16s.—Lond. 1859, 8vo. 3
vols. 1l. 16s.

Lectures on the History of Rome from
the earliest Times to the Commencement
of the first Punic War. Edited by M.
Isler. Translated, with many additions
from MSS. by L. Schmitz. Lond. 1847,
8vo. 12s. This volume embraces the same
period as the 3 vols. of Roman History.
The following two volumes are in continuation of both, forming either the 2d and
3d of the Lectures, or the 4th and 5th of
the original unabridged work.

Lectures on the History of Rome from
the first Punic War to the Death of Constantine; including an introductory Course
on the Sources and Study of Roman History. Edited by L. Schmitz. Lond. 1844,
8vo. 2 vols. port. of author, 1l. 6s.
(Form vols. 4 and 5 of the History, and
have an additional title-page. 'The History of Rome from the first Punic War,'
&c.)

Lectures, both Series. Second edition.
Lond. Taylor, W. and M. 1849-50, 8vo. 3
vols. 1l. 4s.—Third edition. Lond. 1853,
8vo. 3 vols. port. 1l. 4s.

Lectures on Roman History. Translated by H. L. M. Chapmell and F. C. F.
Demmler. Edinb. Fullarton, 1848-50, fcp.
8vo. 3 vols. front. 16s.—New edition. Lond.
Bohn, 1855, fcap. 8vo. 3 vols. 10s. 6d.

Niebuhr's History of Rome, epitomised
from the larger work, and adapted to the
use of Schools and Colleges, by Travers
Twiss, D.C.L. With Chronological Tables
and an Appendix. Oxf. Talboys, 1836-7,
8vo. 2 vols. 1l. 1s. The 2 vols in 1, reduced, Lond. H. G. Bohn, 1845, 8vo. 6d.

Lectures on Ancient History, from the
earliest Times to the taking of Alexandria by Octavianus. Comprising the History of the Asiatic Nations, the Egyp-
tians, Greeks, Macedonians, and Cartha-
ginians. Translated by Dr. Leonhard
Schmitz, with additions and corrections.
Lond. 1852, 8vo. 3 vols. front.

Lectures on Ancient Ethnography and
Geography, comprising Greece and her
Colonies, Epirus, Macedonia, Illyricum,
Italy, Gaul, Spain, Britain, the North of
Africa, &c. Translated from the German
edition of Dr. Isler, by Dr. Leonhard
Schmitz, with additions and corrections.
Lond. 1853, 8vo. 2 vols. 1l. 1s.

According to the Quarterly Reviewers,
'Niebuhr has thrown new light upon our
knowledge of Roman affairs, to a degree,
of which those who are unacquainted
with it, can scarcely form an adequate
idea.'

A Dissertation on the Geography of
Herodotus, Researches into the History
of the Scythians, Getæ, and Sarmatians.
Translated from the German. Oxford,
1830, 8vo. map, 5s.

On the Age of the Coast-describer,
Scylax of Caryanda. Translated from
the German by J. C. H(are). Lond. n. d.
8vo.

Dissertation on the Metre of Homer,
by T. S. Brandreth. Lond. Pickering,
1844, 8vo.

Stories from Greek History, in a Series of Tales related to his Son. Translated from the German. Lond. Nutt,
1843, 8vo. 2s.

Stories of the Gods and Heroes of
Greece, told to his Son. Translated from
the German by Sarah Austin. Lond. J.
W. Parker, 1843, 12mo. 2s.

Heroic Tales of Ancient Greece; related to his Son, Marcus. Translated from
the German. Edited, with notes and references to ancient Sculpture, &c. in the
British Museum, by F. Summerly. Lond.
Chapman and Hall, 1843, 16mo. with four
coloured illustrations by H. J. Town-
hend, 4s. 6d.—Again, 1849.

Heroengeschichte. — Tales of Greek
Heroes (the German Text); with grammatical and explanatory Notes, Questions
for Conversation, and a complete Vocabulary. By Dr. A. Bucheim. Lond. Williams and Norgate, 1858, 12mo. 2s. 6d.

Reminiscences of an Intercourse with
B. G. Niebuhr, the Historian of Rome. By
Francis Lieber. Lond. 1835, post 8vo. port.

The Life and Letters of Barthold George
Niebuhr [founded upon and translated
from the Lebensnachrichten, &c. edited
by Madam Hensler]. With Essays on
his Character and Influence, by the Chevalier Bunsen and Professors Brandis and
Loebell Lond. Chapman and Hall, 1852,
8vo. 2 vols. 1l. 12s.—Second edition, with
selections from his minor writings, edited
and translated by Susannah Winkworth,
1852, 8vo. 3 vols. 1l. 2s.

NIEBUHR, Carsten. Travels
through Arabia, and other Countries
in the East, translated into English
by Robert Heron, with Notes by the
Translator. Lond. 1792, 8vo. 2
vols. 9s.

This English translation, besides omitting the most valuable and scientific parts,
is, in other respects, totally unworthy of
the original. Niebuhr's Travels in Arabia will be found in the tenth volume of
Pinkerton's Collection of Voyages and
Travels.

NIEUHOFF, John. An Embassy
from the East India Company of
the United Provinces to China, by

Mr. John Nievhoff. Also an Epistle of Father John Adams concerning the whole Negotiation, with an Appendix of Several Remarks out of Father Athanasius Kircher. Englished and set forth with their several Sculptures by John Ogilby, Esq. Lond. 1669, folio.

Nieuhoff's Voyages and Travels into Brasil, 1640-9, and into the East Indies, 1653-78, will be found in the second volume of Churchill's Collection of Voyages and Travels, and in the fourteenth volume of Pinkerton's Collection, and his Travels in China are in the seventh volume of the latter collection.

NIEUWENTYT, Bernard. The religious Philosopher, translated from the Dutch by John Chamberlayne. Lond. 1730, 8vo. 3 vols.

A work formerly in much estimation. Paley, in his Evidences of the Christian Religion, was much indebted to it. Willich, 1846, 7s. 6d.—1718-19, 8vo. 3 vols.—1724, 4to. 3 vols.—1745, 8vo. 3 vols.

NIGER, Franc. B(assanicusis). A certayne Tragedy wryten fyrst in Italian, entituled Freewyl, and translated into Englishe by Henry Cheeke, n. d. (1589?) 4to. BLACK LETTER.

One of the old moralities, shewing the 'devylish devise of the Popish religion.' White Knights, 8141, 12l. 5s. Garrick, 509, title wanting, 4l. 15s. Roxburghe, 4469, 5l. 15s. 6d. Bindley, 5l. 15s. 6d. Heber, 1l. 2s. It consists of 211 pages, besides dedication, preface, and an errata.

Fr. Niger de Acuentu. See WHITTINTON, Robert.

— Fr. Petr. Fr. Petreü Nigri Britannicarum Nuptiarum Libri tres. Mediol. 1559, 4to.

With wood-cut portraits of Philip and Mary. See Bibl. Crofts, no. 7285. Heber, pt. viii. 18s.

NIGHTINGALE, Rev. Joseph. British Atlas; comprising a set of County Maps of England and Wales, with a General Map of Navigable Rivers and Canals, and Plans of Cities and principal Towns. Lond. 1810, royal 4to.

Printed to accompany the Beauties of England and Wales, for which work this writer compiled several of the counties.

Reissued, with new Title. English Topography; or a Series of historical and statistical Descriptions of the several Counties of England and Wales; accompanied by a Map of each County. Lond. 1816, 4to.

A Portraiture of Methodism. Lond. 1807, 8vo.

Report of the Trial Nightingale v. Stockdale, in an Action for a Libel contained in a Review of the Portraiture of Methodism. Lond. 1809, 8vo. pp. 99.

A Portraiture of Catholicism. Lond. 1812, 8vo.

The Religions and religious Ceremonies of all Nations, accurately and impartially described; including Christians, Mahomedans, Jews, Brahmins, and Pagans, of all Sects and Denominations. Lond. 1821, 12mo.

NILE.—A short Relation of the River Nile. Written by an Eyewitness, who lived many Years in the chief Kingdoms of the Abyssine Empire. Lond. 1669, 12mo.

This relation was written by Father Jeronymo, and translated by Sir P. Wyche. Bruce has evidently been greatly indebted to it. Jadis, 107, 5s. Heber, pt. ix. 3s. 6d. White Knights, 2302, 6s.—1678, 12mo. Nassau, pt. ii. 1439, 14s.—With a new Preface. Lond. Lackington, 1791, 8vo. 2s.

NILUS, Archb. of Thessalonica. A Treatise conteyning a Declaration of the Popes usurped Primacie: written in Greeke aboue seuen hundred Yeres since. Translated by Thomas Gressop. Lond. 1560, 8vo.

Sotheby, 1834, 1l. 10s.

NIM. A satirical Puppy. See MAY, Thomas.

NIMMO, Rev. William. A General History of Stirlingshire, second Edition, with a Continuation by the Rev. W. M'Gregor Stirling. Stirling, 1817, 8vo. 2 vols. Map and 5 Engravings, 12s.

The former edition was published at Edinb. 1777, 8vo. Nassau, pt. i. 2433, 4s.

NIMROD; a Discourse on certain Passages of History and Fable. See HERBERT, Hon. Algernon.

NISBET, Alexander. A brief Exposition of the first and second Epistles general of Peter. Edinb. 1658, 8vo.

A very judicious work.—Orme.

An Exposition, with practical Observations upon the Book of Ecclesiastes. Edinb. 1694, 4to.

NISBET, Alexander. A System of Heraldry, speculative and practical, with the true Art of Blazon. Edinb. 1722-42, fol. 2 vols. plates of Arms.

An able work, of great utility as regards Scotch families. Dent, pt. ii. 824, 4l. 4s. Hexburghe, 8803, 4l. 12s. Willet, 1679, Cl. 8s. 6d. Nassau, pt. ii. 411, 3l. 10s. Marq. of Townshend, 2460, russia, 7l. 10s. Heber, pt. ii. 4l. 6s.—New edition. Edinb. 1804, or Lond. 1816, folio, 2 vols. 4l. 4s.

An Essay on additional Figures and Marks of Cadency. Edinb. 1702, 12mo. This essay was printed at the author's own expense. Nassau, pt. i. 2434, 6s. Roxburghe, 8301, 3s. Heber, pt. i. 2s. 6d.

An Essay on the ancient and modern Use of Armories. Edinb. 1718, 4to. Marquis of Townshend, 5457, 15s. Drockett, 2284, 9s. Towneley, pt. ii. 1267, 6s. Bindley, pt. iii. 796, 9s. Roxburghe, 8302, 5s.

— John. Epicedium nob. Rob. Devereux, Comitis Essexiæ. Lond. 1648, folio.

NITHSDALE, Winifred, Countess of. Letter relating the particulars of the Escape of the Earl of Nithsdale from the Tower of London, 23 Feb. 1716. Lond. 1827, 8vo.

Privately printed by S. Grace, Esq. and occasionally attached to his History of the Family of Grace, royal 8vo.

NIVERNOIS, Duke of. Fables, translated into English Verse. Lond. 1799, small 8vo. 4s.
Roxburghe, 3717, 11s.

NIXON, Anthony. The Blacke Year. Lond. 1606, 4to.

Sign. E iiij. Heber, pt. vi. 1l. 2s. A notice of this satirical work will be found in Brydges' British Bibliographer, ii. 555-7.

The Christian Navy, wherein is playnely described the perfect Course to sayle to the Haven of Happinesse. Lond. 1602, 4to. Dedicated to Arch. Whitgift. G. Chalmers, 104, 16s.

Elizas's Memoriall. King James, his arrival, and Rome's downfall. Lond. 1603, 4to. Skegg, 5l. 18s.

The Ground and Original of the Wars of Swetheland. Lond. 1609, 4to.

The Dignitie of Man. Lond. 1612, 4to. Nassau, pt. ii. 562, 5s. Heber, pt. iv. 6s.

London's Dove; or, the Mirrour of Merchant Taylors: a Memorial of the Life and Death of Mr. Robert Dove. Lond. 1612, 4to. Bindley, 1l. 4s. Bright, 1l. 14s.

A strange Foot-Post, with a Packet full of Strange Petitions. Lond. 1613, 4to. Wood cut head. A copy is in the British Museum. Heber, pt. iv. 8l. 18s. Caldecott, 2l. 4s.

The Scovrge of Corruption, or a crafty Knave needs no Broker. Lond. 1615, 4to. pp. 40, BLACK LETTER. Roxburghe, 6681, no dedication, 2l. 6s. Reaold, Heber, pt. ix. 4l. 16s. Bibl. Anglo-Poet. 497, 4l. Heber, pl. iv. dedication wanting, 3l. 18s.

Cheshire Prophecy. Lond. 1719, 8vo. 2s. A chap book, frequently reprinted.

Oxford's Triumph, in the Royall Entertainment of his moste Excellent Majestie, the Queene, and the Prince, the 27 of August last, 1605. Lond. (1605) 4to. Not contained in Nichols' Progresses of James I. Marked in a recent catalogue, 10l. 10s.

— John, Secretary to the Beefsteak Club, &c. Sketches from Nature. Lond. 1795, 4to. A series of Engravings of Characters.
Bindley, pt. iii. 2002, 1l. 1s.

NOBBES, Robert. The complete Troller; or, the Art of Trolling. Lond. 1682, 12mo.

Two editions appeared in 1682, and it was reprinted in fac-simile, 1790. Strettell, 969, 4s. Bindley, pt. ii. 1240, 7s. Towneley, pt. i. 726*, 7s. 6d. Haworth, 667, 15s. Stanley, 59*, 18s.—Third edition, prefixed to the Angler's Pocket-Book. Norwich, n.d. 8vo.—Fourth edition, appended to another edition of the Angler's Pocket-Book. Lond. 1805, 8vo. Nobbes' Art of Trolling, new edition. Lond. 1814, 8vo. Frequently reprinted.

NOBILITY.—A Treatise of the Nobilitie of the Realme. Lond. 1642, 12mo.

Bird's Magazine of Honour with a new title-page. Nassau, pt. ii. 734, 6s. Bright, 3s. 6d.

An Historical and Critical Essay on the true Rise of Nobility, political and civil. Lond. C. Rivington, 1716, 8vo.—1720, 8vo. 2 vols. 7s. By Maurice Shelton, Esq. of Barningham Hall, co. Norfolk; but sometimes found with titles attributing the authorship to the Rev. John Randall, of Guilford. LARGE PAPER. Hollis, 400, 14s. 6d.

NOBLE, James. An Arabic Vocabulary and Index for Richardson's Arabic Grammar. Edinb. 1820, 4to. 10s. 6d.

NOBLE, Mark. Memoirs of the protectoral House of Cromwell. Lond. 1787, 8vo. 2 vols.
Best edition of a 'work of little repute.' Noble is 'one of the most laborious and accurate and useful of the pioneer class.'— *Quart. Review.* Bindley, pt. II. 2002, 14s. Dent, pt. II. 25, 19s. LARGE PAPER. Bindley, pt. II. 2002, 2l. Fonthill, 3375, 2l. 11s.—Birm. 1764, 8vo. 2 vols. Edwards, 45, 10s. 6d. Bindley, pt. II. 2157, 9s. Willett, 1847, 15s.
A Review of the Memoirs of the protectoral House of Cromwell. By William Richards, M.A. Lynn, 1788, 8vo. 3s. 6d. pp. 82. A severe, but at the same time a just review.
Two Dissertations upon the Mint and Coins of the episcopal Palatines of Durham. Birmingham, 1780, 4to. with plates. Dent, pt. II. 854, 17s. Brockett, 2296, 11s. Hollis, 1028, 9s. 6d. Combe, 1429, 5s.
A Genealogical History of the present Royal Families of Europe. Lond. 1781, 12mo. pp. 252, with a plate of arms and crowns.
An Historical Genealogy of the Royal House of Stuart. Lond. 1795, 4to. Duke of York, 8250, 9s.
Memoirs of the House of Medici, from 1428 to 1787. Illustrated with several genealogical Tables. Lond. 1797, 8vo. Bindley, pt. II. 2003, 5s. Roxburghe, 6274, 6s. Duke of York, 5789, 10s. 6d. Fonthill, 1574, 12s.
Lives of the English Regicides and other Commissioners of the pretended High Court of Justice appointed to sit in Judgment upon their Sovereign (Charles I.) Lond. 1798, 8vo. 2 vols. Duke of York, 5790, 10s. Bindley, pt. II. 2158, 9s. Reed, 5273, 11s.
A History of the College of Arms, and the Lives of all the Kings, Heralds, and Pursuivants, from the reign of Richard III. Founder of the College, until the present Time; with a preliminary Dissertation relative to the different Orders in England, particularly the Gentry, since the Norman Conquest. Lond. 1804, 4to. Dent, pt. II. 855, 5s. Towneley, pt. II. 1296, 7s. LARGE PAPER. Duke of York, 3531, 1l. 3s. Nassau, pt. II. 483, 1l. 15s. Sir M. M. Sykes, pt. II. 629, 19s. *Collation.*—Pp. 1—449, not including half-title, title, and dedication to K. George III. three leaves; preface, four pages; authorities, two pages; list of subscribers, four pages; appendix pp. i—ixii, and directions for placing the (four) plates, one page.
Continuation of Granger's biographical History of England, from the Revolution to the end of the Reign of George I. Lond. 1906, 8vo. 3 vols. 16s. LARGE PAPER, in royal 8vo. 1l. 7s.

— Thomas. Practical Perspective exemplified on Landscapes. Lond. 1805, 4to.

— T. Blackheath: a Poem in five Cantos. Lumens; or, the ancient British Battle: and various other Poems; including a Translation of the first Book of the Argonautics of C. Valerius Flaccus. Lond. 1808, 4to.

NOBLENESS.—The Boke of Nobleness. *See* LARKE, John.
The Porteous of Nobleness, translatit out Ffrenche in Scottis be Maister Andro Cadiou. Edinburgh be Walter Chepman and Andrew Myler, 1508, 4to. The only copy known is in the Advocates' Library at Edinburgh.—Reprinted in 1827, with Golagrus and Gawane. *See* p. 908.

NOBODY and Somebody. With the true chronicall History of Elydure, who was fortunately three several Times crowned King of England. Printed by John Trundle, (circa 1600) 4to.
Collation. Title, with wood-cut (A 2) to J in 4 B, last leaf has wood-cut of Part of Somebody on one side only. A copy is in the Garrick collection in the British Museum. Sotheby's in Nov. 1826, morocco, 5l. 7s. 6d. Evans, Jan. 1823. Sotheby's in 1623, 13l. Bright, 7l. 5s. Halliwell, 1856, 13l. 13s. Jolley, 7l. 10s.

— is my Name, (a Treatise entitled). E. Waldegrave, n. d. sm. 8vo.

— A Letter from Nobody in the City to Nobody in the Country. Printed for Somebody, 1679, 4to. Bliss, 4s. 6d.

NOCTURNAL OCCURRENCES, or Deeds of Darknesse; committed by the Cavaliers in their Rendezvous; whereunto is conjoined the several Postures used with their Whores and Pimpes, &c. Lond. 1642, 4to.
Gordonstoun, 1687, 1l. 11s. 6d.

— Revels; or Secret History of King's Place. Lond. 1779, 12mo. 2 vols.
Heber, pt. vii. 1s.

NOE, ———. Travels of Noe into Europe, containing the first Inhabitants and Peopling thereof, done into English by Rich. Lynche. Lond. 1601, 4to.
Steevens, 1874, 1l. 5s.

NOEHDEN, Dr. G. H. A Selection of Ancient Greek Coins, chiefly of Magna Græcia and Sicily, from the Cabinet of the Rt. Hon. the Lord Northwick, drawn by Del Frates and engraved by Henry Moses. The Descriptions by Dr. Noehden. Lond. 1824-6, folio. In four parts, pub. at 4l. 10s.

Bright, 1l. 5s. Two hundred and fifty copies printed. A few have proof impressions of the plates on India paper. Sotheby's, 1868, 5l. 5s.

German and English Dictionary (founded on Rabenhorst's). Lond. 1814, square 12mo. Frequently reprinted; fourth edition (stereotyped), Lond. 1847, 12mo. 7s.—Again, Lond. 1857, 12mo. 5s. 6d.

A Grammar of the German Language for the Use of Englishmen. Lond. 1800, 12mo. — Second edition, corrected and improved. Lond. 1807, 12mo. — Third edition, revised. Lond. 1816, 12mo.—Seventh edition (revised and enlarged). Lond. 1826, 12mo.—Ninth edition. Lond. 1843, 12mo. 7s. 6d.

Elements of German Grammar, intended for Beginners (extracted from the Grammar). Lond. 1807, 12mo — Fifth edition, with Reading Lessons and a Vocabulary. Lond. 1842, 12mo, 5s. — New edition. Lond. Maynard, 1854, 12mo. 5s.

Exercises for writing German according to the Rules of Grammar. Lond. 1800, 12mo.—Fourth edition. Lond. 1826, 12mo.—Seventh edition, corrected and revised by C. H. F. Bialloblotzky. Lond. 1842, 12mo. 6s.

Key to Dr. Noehden's Exercises for Writing German. By John R. Schultz. Lond. 1817, 12mo.—New edition. Lond. 1854, 12mo. 5s. 6d.

NOELLUS, *Anglice* NOWELL.

NOLAN, Rev. Frederick, LL.D. An Inquiry into the Integrity of the Greek Vulgate, or received Text of the New Testament; in which the Greek MSS. are newly classed; the Integrity of the authorised Text vindicated; and the various Readings traced to their Origin. Lond. 1815, 8vo. 18s.

This learned work, with that of Dr. Lawrence, has done a good deal to shake the fabric of Griesbach's system of classification.

A Polyglott Grammar, in ten Languages. 1819, 2s. 6d. each.

An Introduction to Hebrew Grammar. Lond. 1821, 12mo.

An Introduction to the Syriac Language. Lond. 1821, 12mo.

An Introduction to the Chaldee Grammar. Lond. 1821, 12mo.

Harmonical Grammar of the principal ancient and modern Languages. 1822, 2 vols. 1l. 5s.

— Michael. A Treatise of the Laws for the Relief and Settlement of the Poor. Lond. 1825, 8vo. 3 vols. 1l. 16s.

Fourth edition, with considerable additions.—1805, 8vo. 2 vols. —1808, 8vo. 2 vols.—1814, 8vo. 3 vols.

Reports of Cases relative to the Duty and Office of a Justice of the Peace, from Michaelmas Term 1791, to Trinity Term 1792. Lond. 1792-3, royal 8vo. 2 pts. 9s.

NOLI ME TANGERE; or a Thinge to be thought on, or Vox Carnis sacræ clamantis ab Altari ad Aquilam Sacrilegam Noli me tangere ne te perdam. 1642, 4to.

With two titles, one engraved by Marshall, the other, a wood-cut. Strettell, 1419, 3s. Nassau, pt. II. 554. 5s. Bindley, pt. III. 785, 11s. Heber, pt. 12. 7s.

NOLLIUS, Henr. Hermetical Physic, translated by H. Vaughan. Lond. 1665, 12mo.

NONABUM INQUISITIONES in Curia Scaccarii. Tempore Regis Edwardi III. Lond. 1807, folio, 2l. 2s.

Printed by authority of the commissioners of the Public Records. The inquisitions taken by the assessors and venditors in twenty-seven counties, pursuant to the third commission, dated January 26, 1341, to levy the ninth lamb, the ninth fleece, and the ninth sheaf, granted to the King by stat. 14 Edward III.

See RECORDS, Public.

NONCONFORMIST REMAINS; being Original Sermons, by Oliver Heywood, Thomas Jollie, Henry Newcome, and Henry Pendlebury; selected from MSS. with Memoirs, by Richard Slate. Bury, 1814, 8vo.

NONCONFORMISTS.—Farewell Sermons of some of the most eminent of the Nonconformist Ministers, delivered at the Period of their Ejectment by the Act of Uniformity in the Year 1662; to which is prefixed a historical and biographical Preface, 8vo. 11s.

First edition, 1662, 8vo.—Second, 1663, 4to.

Cabala: the Mysteries of Conventicles Unvail'd. In an Historical Account of the Principles and Practices of the Nonconformists against Church and State, from the first Reformation under K. Edward VI. Anno 1558, to this present Year, 1664; with an Appendix of an cxx. Plots against the present Government that have been defeated. Lond. T. Holmwood, Anno 1664, with a front. Written under the name of Oliver Foulis, but the production of David Lloyd.

Apologia pro ministris Nonconformistis Anno 1662 ejectis. Lond. 1684, 8vo.

An Humble Apology for Nonconformists, &c. Lond. 1669, 8vo.

See BAXTER, Richard. CALAMY, Ed. PALMER, Sam.

The true Nonconformist; an Answer to the modest and free Conference betwixt a Conformist and a Nonconformist about the present Distempers of Scotland, by a Lover of Truth. Printed in the Year 1671. 8vo.

See DELAUNE, p. 623. Delaune was answered by T. Hart in 'The Bulwark Stormed,' with a letter in vindication of the primitive Church from the corruptions which T. Delaune has cast upon it, by T. Bray, D.D. Lond. 1707, 8vo.

NONCONFORMITY, History of, as it was argued and stated by Commissioners on both Sides, in 1611. Lond. 1704, 8vo.

This volume consists of Ten Papers on the Reformation of the Liturgy (as settled at the Savoy conference), and the Discipline of the Church, with a Preface relating to occasional conformity.

NONJURORS.—History of Passive Obedience. Two parts, with an Appendix by Abraham Seller. Amst. 1689-90, 8vo.

See LATHBURY, Rev. Tho.

NONPAREIL, The; or, the Quintessence of Wit and Humour. To which is added, an Index to Mankind. Lond. 1757, 12mo.

A selection from the Midwife; or, the Old Woman's Magazine. Hibbert, 5710, 4s. 6d.

NOODT. See VANDER NOODT.

NOORTHOUCK, John. A new History of London, including Westminster and Southwark. Lond. 1773, 4to.

Towneley, pt. II. 1268, russia, 1l. 2s. Collation.—Pp. 902, besides title and dedication, two leaves; preface, 8 pages; table of contents, 4 pages; index, 40 pages; errata and list of (42) plates, two pages.

An historical and classical Dictionary; containing the Lives and Characters of the most eminent and learned Persons, in every Age and Nation, from the earliest Period to the present Time. By John Noorthouck. Lond. 1776, 8vo. 2 vols. Drury, 2284, 6s.

NORDEN, Fred. Lewis. Travels in Egypt and Nubia, by Frederick Lewis Norden, translated from the Original, and enlarged with Observations from ancient and modern Authors, that have written on the Antiquities of Egypt, by Dr. Peter Templeman. Lond. 1757, atlas fol. 2 vols.

Norden is the first writer who published a picturesque description of Egypt: every subsequent traveller has borne evidence to the accuracy and fidelity of his researches and descriptions. Original Edition. Heath, 2682, 9l. North, pt. II. 1430, 2l. 17s. Gough, 2507, 4l. 6d. Duke of York, 3233, russia, 4l. 6s. LARGE PAPER. Nassau, pt. II. 412, 4l. Garrick, 1889, 1l. 5s. Willett, 1681, 10l.—Jeffery's Edition. Lond. 1757 (1792), folio, 2 vols. Hibbert, 5684, russia, 4l. 5s. Edwards, 618, 2l. 6s.—Lond. 1757, 8vo. abridged text, and no folio plates. Reed, 5374, 11s. 6d. Fonthill, 2709, 15s.

Drawings of some Ruins and colossal Statues at Thebes, engraved by M. Tuscher. Lond. 1741, 4to.

— John, Surveyor and Topographer. Preparatius to his Speculum Britanniæ. (1596), 4to. 24 pages. Dedicated to Sir William Cecill, Knt. [Reprinted with the third article below.]

Speculum Britanniæ. The first Parte. An historicall and chorographicall Discription of MIDDLESEX. Anno 1593, small 4to. Dedicated to Queene Elizabeth, with an Address to Lord Burleigh. Marquis

NORDEN, John,—*continued.*
of Townshend, 2406, 1*l*. 1*s*. Nassau, pt.
ii. 565, 2*l*. 8*s*. Lloyd, 1001, 1*l*. 1*s*. Bindley,
pt. iii. 791, 1*l*. 6*s*. Jadis, 132*, russ. 2*l*. 2*s*.
H. Thomas, Dec. 1852. Bright, *no map of
the county*, 1*l*. 11*s*. *Collation.*—A—H 2, in
fours, 80 leaves; also three maps, viz.
Myddlesex, London, and Westminster.
There are 21 shields of arms on the letter-
press. The Harleian, vol. 570, contains
the first draught of this work, to which a
description of Surrey was to have been
added. In two or three places it has
corrections in the hand-writing of Lord
Burleigh.

Speculum Britanniæ Pars. The Description of HARTFORDSHIRE. 1598, 4to.
Bright, 1*l*. 8*s*. The presentation copy to
Queen Elizabeth, wanting part of the map.
Heber, pt. viii. 54, *Collation.*—Pp. 51, with
a map; also three leaves, viz. an engraved
title-page, dedication 'D. Edwardo Seamor
militi, Baroni Beauchamp, Comiti Hart-
fordiæ,' 'To Gentlemen well affected to
this travaile,' 'Thinges to be considered
in the vse of this booke and Mappe,' and
Corrections. The original Hartfordshire,
with dedication to Lord Burleigh, in *English*, dated 1597, is in the Lambeth Library. Many copies of the Middlesex and
Hartfordshire were bound together at an
early period.

Speculum Britanniæ: an historical and
chorographical Description of MIDDLESEX
and HARTFORDSHIRE. To which is added,
a Preparative to this Work, 1596.—Lond.
1637, 4to. This (the second) impression
consists of the three previous articles bound
together.—The third edition. Lond. 1723,
4to. Marquis of Townshend, 2407, 1*l*.
Baker, 483, 1*l*. 3*s*. Towneley, pt. ii. 1271,
19*s*.; 1272, 1*l*. 2*s*. Bindley, pt. iii. 792, 13*s*.
Hibbert, 5820, morocco, 1*l*. 3*s*. Dent, pt.
ii. 656, morocco, 1*l*. LARGE PAPER, Heath,
4524, 1*l*. 4*s*. *Collation.*—Two title-pages
and a leaf commencing 'To the right worshipful M. William Waade, Esquire,'
Preparative A—C, 12 leaves;—Middlesex,
A—H 1, 29 leaves; another leaf containing commendatory verses, signed Robert
Nicolson and H. C.; also 5 maps, copied
by Senex; woodcuts of the Arms of the
principal persons interred in the county
of Middlesex.—Hartfordshire, A—D, 32
pages, and 5 leaves, containing an engraved title, dedication, &c. also a map of
Hartford Shire.

Speculi Britanniæ Pars altera: or a
Delineation of NORTHAMPTONSHIRE, in the
Year M.DC.X. Lond. 1720, 8vo. 3*s*. 6*d*.
LARGE PAPER. Bindley, pt. iii. 9*s*. Reed,
5276, 10*s*. Marquis of Townshend, 2263,
13*s*. Towneley, pt. ii. 983, 10*s*. 6*d*. *Collation.*—Pp. 54, not including the title, a
dedication to Sir Wm. Halton, Knt. and
'Things to be considered in the Use of
this Booke, and the Mappe thereunto belonging.' 4 leaves. The map and plans
referred to were never engraved.

Speculi Britanniæ Pars: a topographical and historical Description of CORN-
WALL. Lond. 1728, 4to. The larger part
of this survey is a mere transcript from
Carew. Heath, 4710, 1*l*. 6*s*. Willett,
1771, 2*l*. 15*s*. Bright, 9*s*. 6*d*. LARGE
PAPER. Towneley, pt. ii. 1273, 1*l*. 15*s*.
Nassau, pt. ii. 566, 1*l*. 9*s*. ON VELLUM.
Four copies printed. Dent, pt. ii. 859,
morocco, 20*l*. 9*s*. 6*d*. The Harleian copy
is in the British Museum, and Dr. Rawlinson's is in the Bodleian. According to
Osborne's catalogue for 1754–5, no. 2055,
'There are more cuts in this book than in
any printed upon paper.' *Collation.*—Pp.
104, not including two titles, one engraved,
the other printed; and engraved dedication to Edward, Earl of Oxford, signed
Christopher Bateman, a table of Cornwall, dedication to King James, rules of
direction, the principal matters, a table,
and some account of the author, together
19 leaves. Maps, 1. Cornwall, p. 1. 2.
Penwithe Hundred, p. 34. 3. Kirrier
Hundred, p. 43. 4. Powder Hundred, p. 53.
5. Pyder Hundred, p. 65. 6. Trig Hundred, p. 71. 7. Lesnewith Hundred, p. 77;
8. Stratton Hundred, p. 83. 9. West
Hundred, p. 86. 10. East Hundred, p. 90.
11. West Prospect of the Conventual
Church of St. Germans, p. 93. There are
also several engravings on the letter-
press. The MS. presented to King James
is in the Harleian Collection, Brit. Mus.
no. 6252, accompanied with the original
drawings, but not the maps, the printed
ones being inserted.

Speculi Britanniæ Pars, an historical
and chorographical Description of ESSEX
in 1594, with a Map (1594), never before
printed. From a MS. in the Burleigh
Collection at Hatfield, edited by Sir H.
Ellis. Lond. 1840, 10*s*. 6*d*. *See* CAMDEN
CLUB Books, Appendix. An original and
very curious manuscript survey of this
county is in the Grenville Library, British Museum.

See Gough's British Topography, i. 44,
who assures us, the survey of KENT was in
MS.; and Rawlinson [Eng. Topog. p. 228]
says, a survey of Surrey was drawn up
by John Norden, which fell into the hands
of a curious Hollander. The maps of
Hampshire, Hertford, Kent, Middlesex,
Surrey, and Sussex appear upon a large
scale, with his name, in the sixth edition
of Camden's Britannia, Lond. 1607, folio;
also in Speed, 1611, with the exception of
Kent; but one of Cornwall is added in his

NORDEN, John—*continued*.
Theatre of the Empire of Great Britain, 1611.

Surveyors Dialogue divided into five Books. Lond. 1607, 4to. pp. 244. Bindley, pt. II. 2510. Bright, 1s. 6d. Gardner, 4s. 6d.—1610, with a sixt booke newly added, 4to.—1618, dedicated to Sir R. Smith, surveyor of London to Prince Charles, 4to. Bright, 3s.—Fourth edition. Lond. 1738, 8vo.

England. An intended Guyde for English Travailers. Shewing in generall how far one Citie and many Shire-Townes in England are distant from each other. Together, with the Shires in particular; and the cheife Townes in euery of them. With a generall Table of the most of the principall Townes in Wales. Inuented and collected by Iohn Norden. Lond. 1625, 4to. A copy is in the British Musænm. Dent, pt. II. 837, 1l. 6s. *Collation.*—Title and dedication, two leaves; tables of the Counties, 34 in number,—at the bottom is 'Heare with defectes, the vse is necessary.' The volume concludes with three folding sheets, viz. 1. 'A Table shewing the distances betweene all the Cities and Shire Townes of England, that are comprehended in the same.' 2. 'Yorke Shire.' 3. 'A Table shewing the distances of the most of the chiefe townes in Wales.' *See* LONDON, under date 1893, page 1893. Maps and plans.

Another impression, sold by John Garrett, at the South Entrance of the Royal Exchange, n. d. The Tables, which are triangular ones, continued to be used until the publication of the Magna Britannia. 1720, 4to. 6 vols.

Norden's Map of London, engraved by Peter Van den Keere, 1623, entituled 'A Guide for Countrymen in the famous Citiey of London,' by the help of which plate they shall be able to know how far it is to any street, as also to go vnto the same without furder trouble. A.D. 1612. *See* LONDON BARON, page 1891.

The Survey of Windsor Forest, and of the Little Park, as taken in 1607, are copied in facsimile in Mr. R. R. Tighe's Letter to the Earl of Lincoln on the Parks and Thoroughfares of Windsor. Imp. fol. 1845. Privately printed.

The father and son obtained a patent from King James I., in 1607, as joint-officers of his Majesty's Crown Lands.

NORDEN, John, of Hart Hall, Oxford. A sinful Man's Solace. Lond. 1585, 8vo. 1*l*. 11s. 6d.

Pp. 163, with dedication to Sir Edmund Anderson, twelve pages. This work is partly in verse and partly in prose.

A Pensiue Mans Practise. Newly corrected and enlarged. Lond. 1585, 4to.—1561, 24mo.—Fortieth edition. Lond. 1629, 12mo.

A Mirror for the Multitude, wherein may be seen the Violence, the Error, the Weakness, and the rash Consent of the Multitude. Lond. 1586, 18mo. Pp. 116, dedicated to the Queen, after which is an address to the Christian reader. Bliss, 12s.

Antithesis or Contrarietie betweene the Wicked and the Godlie. Set forth in form of a paire of Gloues fit for every Man to wear. Lond. 1587.

A Christian familiar Comfort and Incouragement vnto all English Subiects not to dismaie at the Spanish Threats. Lond. 1596, 4to. White Knights, 3l.3s. 6s. Heber, pt. I. 6s. 6d.

A Reforming Glass. Lond. 1806, 16mo.

A Progresse of Pietie, or the Harberer of Heavenly harts Ease, to recreate the afflicted Soules of all such as are shut vp to truye inward or outward Affliction. Lond. 1596, 24mo. One hundred leaves, dedicated to Queene Elizabeth.—Another edition, 'whose Iames lead into the Harborough of heavenly Hearts-ease to recreate the afflicted Souls of all such as,' &c. Lond. 12mo. n. d. Reprinted by the PARKER SOCIETY, which *see*.

The Mirror of Honour, wherein every Professor of Armes, from the General to the inferior Soldier may see the Necessity of the Fear and Service of God. Lond. 1597, 4to. Pp. 93, dedicated to Robert Earle of Essex, after which is an address 'To the Reader.' Inglis, 951, 4s. Marq. of Townshend, 2408, 13s. Lloyd, 1000, 16s. Bliss, 16s.

Vicissitudo Rerum, an elegiacall Poeme of the Interchangeable Courses and Varietie of Things in this World. The first Part. Lond. 1600, 4to. Twenty-three leaves. Sotheby's in 1821, 3*l*. 15s. Heber, pt. iv. 1*l*. 6s. Bibl. Anglo-Poet. 496, 19*l*. 12s. Bright, 1*l*. 14s. This Poem, inscribed to Sir Wm. Howard, Knt. the Lord Howard of Effingham, had a new title in 1603, when it was called 'The Storehouse of Varieties.' *See* Brydges' Restituta, iii. 127-30.

A Pensive Soules Delight. Lond. 1603, 4to.—Lond. 1615, 12mo.

The Labyrinth of Mans Life, or Vertues Delyght and Envies Opposite. Lond. 1614, 4to. pp. 94. A poem, dedicated, in a style of the most fulsome panegyric, to Sir Robert Carr, Knt. Sir M. M. Sykes, pt. II. 631, 3*l*. 13s. 6d. Bibl. Anglo-Poet. 496, poor copy, 7*l*. 7s. resold Utterson; again, Bliss, 1*l*. 4s. Bindley, pt. III. 766, 9*l*. 12s. Heber, pt. iv. 1*l*. Midgley, 2*l*. *See* Baker's Anecdotes, II. 103-6.

5 Q

NORDEN, John—*continued.*
Loadstone to a spiritual Life. Lond.
1614, 16mo.
— An Eye to Heaven in Earth: a necessary Watch for the Time of Death, consisting in Meditations and Prayers fit for that Purpose. With the Husband's Christian Counsel to his Wife and Children left poor after his Death. Lond. 1619, 12mo.
— Poor Mans Rest; founded upon Motives, Meditations, and Prayers, &c. Eighth Edition. Lond. 1620, 12mo.—Fifteenth edition, 1641, 12mo.
— Imitation of David, his Godly and constant Resolution (by way of Meditation and Prayers). Lond. 1624, 18mo. printed within borders. Constable, 676, 64. Bliss, 7s.
— Pathway to Patience in all Manner of Afflictions, &c. Lond. 1626, 8vo.

NORFOLK, Charles, tenth Duke of. *See* HOWARD, Charles.

— Henry Howard, Earl of, afterwards Duke of Norfolk. Journey to Constantinople. 1671. *See* BURBURY, John.

— A Letter from a Gentleman of Lord Howard's Retinue, dated at Fez, Nov. 1, 1669, giving a full Relation of their Voyage thither, and of the present State of the Countries under the Emperour of Morocco, with Account of the merchandizing Commodities of Africa, as also of the Manners and Customs of the People. Lond. 1670, 4to. 7s. 6d.
Fonthill, 194, 9s. Inglis, 916, 19s.

— Thomas Howard, Duke of Norfolks. 1554-72. *See* MARY, Queen of Scots.

— Thomas Howard, Duke of, 1604-48. Embassy. 1637.
See CROWNE, William. MANDELSLO, J. A. de.

— Thomas Howard, Duke of. The Arraignment of Thomas Howard, Duke of Norfolk, before the Earl of Shrewsbury, Lord High Steward of England. Also a brief Derivation of the most honourable Family of the Howards. With an Account of what Families they are related to by Marriage. Transcribed out of ancient Manuscripts, never before published. Lond. 1685, 4to.
Reprinted in the fourth volume of the Harleian Miscellany.
See HOWARD FAMILY.

NORFOLK. — History and Antiquities of the County of Norfolk. Norwich, 1781, 8vo. 10 vols.
Originally published in weekly numbers at 6d. each. Marquis of Townshend. 2284, 3l. 5s. Dent, pt. I. 723, russia, 3l. 10s. *Collation.*—Title, dedication to the Duke of Norfolk, and preface, pp. 1—xx; description of Norfolk, with an index villaris, and directions for placing the plates, pp. 21—204; The Hundred of Blofield, 60 pages; of Brothercross, 28 pages; Hundred and Half of Clackclose, 205 pages. Prefixed to the volume is a map of Norfolk. 8. Pyle, &c. Vol. II. The Hundred of Clavering, 96 pages; of Depwade, 197 pages, with one plate; of Diss, 193 pages, with two plates; of Earsham, 98 pages, with two plates. Vol. III. The Hundred of North Erpingham, 120 pages, with six plates; of South Erpingham, 326 pages, with five plates; of Eynesford, 143 pages, with one plate. Vol. IV. The Hundred of East Flegg, 228 pages, with two plates; of West Flegg, 59 pages; of Forehoe, 214 pages, with three plates. Vol. V. Frewbridge Hundred and Half, 870 pages (pp. 57—96 are repeated with asterisks), with six plates; Hundred of Gallow. 145 pages, with two plates. Vol. VI. The Hundred of N. Greenhoe, 113 pages, with five plates, one of which, Stiffkey Hall, at p. 68, is not in the printed list; of S. Grimeshoe, 144 pages, with two plates; of Grimeshoe, 139 pages; of Giltcross, 153 pages. Vol. VII. The Hundred of Happing. 74 pages; of Henstead, 118 pages, with 3 plates; of Holt, 131 pages, with 1 plate; of Humble-yard, 123 pages; of Loddon, 102 pages, with a View of Langley House, p. 61, not in the printed list. Vol. VIII. The Hundred of Launditch, 196 pages, with one plate; the Hundred and Half of Mitford, 102 pages, with 3 plates; the Hundred of Shropham, 208 pages, with 3 plates. Vol. IX. The Hundred of Smithdon, 120 pages, with 3 plates; of Taverham, 96 pages; of Tunstead, 116 pages, with 3 plates; of Walsham, 52 pages, and of Wayland, 115 pages. Vol. X. Title and half-title, two leaves; Introduction, pp. III—III; the History of the City of Norwich, 499 pages, with 8 plates.
A General History of the County of Norfolk, with Biographical Notices. Norwich, 1829, post 8vo. 2 vols. 1l. 11s. 6d.
Biographies of Eminent Persons of the Counties of Essex, Suffolk, and Norfolk.

NORFOLK—*continued*.
Lond. small 8vo. with heads at the top of
each leaf, 10s. 6d. LARGE PAPER PROOFS,
demy 8vo. 1l. 1s.; and on INDIA PAPER,
royal 8vo. 1l. 11s. 6d. Printed to accompany the Excursions through those Counties. *See* EXCURSIONS.
The most lamentable and dreadful
Thunder and Lightning in the County of
Norfolk, and the City of Norwich, on July
20. Lond. 1656, 4to. pp. 5, with a wood-
cut. Reprinted in the second volume of
the Harleian Miscellany.
Norfolk Poetical Miscellany. 1744, 8vo.
2 vols. By A. Cowper.
The History of the Rebellion in Norfolk, in the year 1549, which was conducted by Rob. Kett, a Tanner by Trade
at Wymondham: their final Overthrow,
on the 27th of August, by the Conduct
and valiant Behaviour of the noble Earl of
Warwick. Norwich, 1751, 8vo. 40 pp.
See NEVILLE, ALEX.
A new and complete History of Norfolk.
Lynn, 1778, 8vo. vols. I. and II. Published
in weekly numbers at 6d. each, by W.
Smith.
The Norfolk Tour; or Traveller's Pocket
Companion :—The sixth edition, greatly
enlarged and improved. Norwich, 1808,
12mo. pp. 899, with a map by Neele. First
printed in 1772.
Norfolk Anthology, being Poems, Ballads, Songs, and rare Tracts relating to
the County of Norfolk. 4to. 80 copies privately printed (by Orchard Halliwell). It
contains the Norfolk Drollery, &c.
Views of Norfolk Churches, from Drawings by R. Ladbroke. Norwich, 1823, 4to.
Woodward's [Sam.] The Norfolk Topographer's Manual; being a Catalogue
of Books and Engravings hitherto published in Relation to the County. The
whole revised and augmented by W. C.
Ewing. To which are appended, a Catalogue of the Drawings, Prints, and Deeds
collected for the Illustration of the County History by Dawson Turner; and also
Lists of the Norfolk Chartularies now
known to be in existence; and of the Manuscripts and Drawings relating to Norfolk in the British Museum. Lond. 1842,
8vo. 1l. 1s.
Architectural Notes of the Churches,
Chapels, and other Buildings in the City
of Norwich and Neighbourhood, by J. H.
Parker and Goddard Johnson, Esq. 1847,
4to.
See BLOMEFIELD. COTMAN, J. Sell. NE-
VILLE, ALEX. STARK, JAMES. STEVENSON,
Matthew.

NORIE, J. The complete North
Sea and Baltic Pilot, including the
Cattegat, Sound and Gulf of Fin-
land; exhibiting the whole Naviga-
tion from London to St. Petersburg,
in a Set of Charts. A new Edition.
Lond. 1814, atlas folio.
A valuable work.
Nautical Tables. Lond. 1803, 8vo.—
New edition. Lond. 1818, 12s.
Epitome of practical Navigation. Lond.
1805, 8vo.—New edition. Lond. 1832, 15s.
A set of lunar Tables for correcting the
apparent Distance of the Moon from the
Sun, or a fixed Star from the Effect of
Refraction; whereby Lyon's Method of
finding the true Distance is rendered one
of the Easiest that have been proposed:
to which are added, Tables for Parallax
and Rules for computing the true Distance.
Lond. 1815.— New edition. Lond. 1822,
15s.
Other Nautical Works were published
by this map and chartseller.

NORMAN, Robert. The new At-
tractive, containing a short Discourse of the Magnet or Loadstone,
now first found out. Lond. 1581,
4to.
Inglis, 1117, 6s. This celebrated hy-
drographer was the first who discovered
the 'dip.'—Lond. 1585, 4to. Bright, 3s.
—Hereunto are annexed certaine necessarie Rules for the Art of Navigating.
Newly corrected and amended by M. W.
B(orough), 1596. Lond. 1563, 4to.—Lond.
1596, 4to.
The Safegard of Saylers, or great Rutter.
Translated out of Dutch into English.
Lond. 1587, 4to.—1590, 4to. Nassau, pt. II.
568, russia, 11 5s.—1612, 4to. Inglis, 1118,
8s.—1619, 4to. Nassau, pt. II. 906, 6s.—
1633, 4to.—1640, 4to.

NORMANDY.— A Tour through
Normandy. Lond. 1754, 4to.
2s. 6d.
This tract (by Dr. C. Ducarel) chiefly
relates to the monumental remains of
Normandy.
Historiæ Normannorum Scriptores, *See*
DUCHESNE, A.
Excursions in Normandy, illustrative
of the Character, Manners, Customs, and
Traditions of the People; edited from the
Journal of a recent Traveller by F. Sho-
berl. 1841, post 8vo. 2 vols. 10s. 6d.
See COTMAN, J. Sell. PICCARD, C.
STOTHARD, Mrs. Chas. TURNER, Dawson.

NORNELL, Robert. *See* NORVELL.

NORRIS, Charles. Etchings of
Tenby; including many ancient
Edifices which have been destroyed,
and tending to illustrate the most

striking Peculiarities in early Flemish Architecture. With a short Account of that Town and the principal Buildings in the Neighbourhood. Lond. 1818, 4to.

A faithful and accurate work, consisting of 40 plates. Towneley, pt. II. 1276, 1l. 3s.

The Architectural Antiquities of Wales. Lond. 1810-11, 4to. nos. I. II. and III. published at 1l. 1s. each. Proofs on INDIA PAPER, published at 3l. 3s. each.

Saint David's, in a Series of Engravings, illustrating the different Edifices of that ancient city. Lond. 1811, oblong folio, published at 3l. 7s. but now 1l. 1s.

NORRIS, Sir John. Ephemeris Expeditionis Norreysi et Draki in Lusitaniam. Lond. T. Woodcock, 1589, 4to.

Prefixed is an epistle, 'Michaeli Ahiscolt Amersforti O. H. S. D. P.' 24 pages. Towneley, pt. II. 638, 2l. 4s.

Newes sent out of Britayne and other places on the third of June, 1591, concerning the Exploits of Sir John Norris. Lond. J. Wolfe. 1591, 4to. Heber, pt. v. 10s.

A Journall of the late service in Britaigne by the Prince de Dombes, assisted with her Majesties forces at this present there under the command of Sir John Norris. Lond. J. Wolfe, 1591, 4to. See CHURCHYARD, Thomas, p. 454.

Newes from Brast, or a Diurnal of Sir John Norris, &c. Lond. 1604, 4to.

See BLANDY, Wm. DRAKE, Sir Francis. PEELE, George.

— John, M.A. of Bemerton. Collection of Miscellanies, consisting of Poems, Essays, Discourses, and Letters. Oxford, 1687, 8vo.— Lond. 1692, 8vo.— Lond. 1717, 8vo.—Ninth edition. Lond. 1730, 8vo. 5s.

Dent, date 1717, mor. by Roger Payne, 1l. This celebrated Platonist, who was accounted one of the most eminent of the Idealists, published many other volumes.

Practical Discourses on the Beatitudes. Lond. 1690, 8vo. 4 vols.—Lond. 1713, 8vo. 4 vols.—Tenth edition, entitled Christian Blessedness. Lond. 1724, 8vo. 4 vols. 18s.

Theory of an Ideal World. Lond. 1691-1701, 8vo.—Second edition. Lond. 1701-1704, 8vo. 2 vols. 7s. This philosophical work was designed to support the System of Malebranche. Mr. Hallam says, 'Norris is a writer of fine genius, and a noble elevation of moral sentiments.' It was satirised in Gabriel John's Theory of the Intelligible World. *See* page 1214.

In Sir E. Waring's Quid ait Amor? will be found an account of Norris's Life, and titles of 21 pieces written by him.

NORRIS, Robert. Memoirs of the Reign of Bossa Ahádee, King of Dahomy, an inland Country of Guiney; to which are added, the Author's Journey to Abomey, the Capital; and a short Account of the African Slave Trade. Lond. 1789, 8vo.

Prefixed is a map. The work was edited by Edw. Long, author of the History of Jamaica. Willett, 1849, 3s. 6d. Fonthill, 2655, 19s.

— Silvester. The Antidote, or Treatise of Thirty Controversies, with a large Discourse of the Church. [Douay], 1662, 4to. 3 parts, and an Appendix.

The last part is frequently wanting.

NORTH, Francis Dudley, third Lord. A Forest promiscuous of several Season's Productions. Lond. 1659, folio.

Second edition, with an additional part. Hibbert, 5667 12s. Bindley, pt. II. 1700, 19s. Bright, 15s. Bliss, 12s.

A Forest of Varieties. 8 pts. Lond. 1645, folio. FIRST EDITION. Nassau, pt. II. 414, 2l. Gardner, 1l. 8s. White Knights, 2994, 1l. 1s. Bindley, pt. II. 1680, 3l. 3s. Bliss, 1l. 11s. The author's copy is in the Grenville Collection. *See* Walpole's Royal and Noble Authors, by Park, and Brydges' British Bibliographer.

— Francis Dudley, fourth Lord. Observations and Advices Œconomical. Lond. 1669, 12mo.

Reed, 2715, 3s. 6d. Hibbert, 5713, 16s. Bliss. 4s. 6d.

A Narrative of some Passages in, or relating to, the Long Parliament. By a person of Honour. Lond. 1670, 18mo. Bright, 3s. Bliss. 6s. 6d. Reprinted in the sixth volume of the Somers Collection of Tracts.

Light in the Way to Paradise, with other Occasionals. 1682. 8vo. Bliss. 3s.

— Francis, Lord. A philosophical Essay of Musick, directed to a Friend. Lond. 1677, 4to.

Pp. 35. 'An ingenious tract written by the Lord Keeper North, but published anonymously. Though some of the philosophy of this essay has been since found to be false, and the rest has been more clearly illustrated and explained, yet considering the small progress which had been made in so obscure and subtle a subject as the propagation of sound when this book was written, the experiments and conjectures must be allowed to have considerable merit.'—*Burney*.

NORTH, Sir Dudley. Discourses upon Trade. Lond. 1691.—Edinb. 1822, 4to. 80 copies reprinted.

— George. The Description of Swedland, Gotland and Finland. Lond. by John Awdeley, 1561, 4to.
On 28 leaves At the end is the Lord's Prayer in the Swedish language. Sotheby's in 1825, 2l. 2s.
A Stage of Popish Toyes, collected out of M. Stephanus in his Apologies upon Herodotus. Lond. H. Binneman, 1581, 4to. Heber, pt. v. 12s.

— Roger. Lives of the Right Hon. Francis North, Baron of Guildford; Sir Dudley North, and the Hon. and Rev. Dr. John North. Lond. 1742-4, 4to. 2 vols.
(These two volumes were published separately, as described in the next article.) Bishop of Ely, 1234, 5l. 5s. Nassau, 569, 8l. Brockett, 2l. 7s. Bindley, 3l. 3s.—Third edition, with Notes and Illustrations (by Henry Roscoe), Lond. 1826, 8vo. 8 vols. with portraits, 1l. 11s. 6d.
The Life of the Hon. Sir Dudley North, Knt. and of the Hon. and Rev. Dr. John North. Lond. 1744, 4to. With portrait of Sir Dudley by Vertue. Townsley, pt. II. 1278, 2l. 4s. Reed, 6191, 2l. See Retrosp. Review, v. 136-68.
The Life of the Rt. Hon. Francis North, Baron of Guildford, Lord Keeper of the Great Seal under K. Charles II. and K. James II. Lond. 1742, 4to. with portrait of Lord Guildford. Lloyd, 1008, 1l. 4s. Reed, 6190, 3l.—New edition, 1808, 8vo. 2 vols. Hibbert, 5714, 13s. *See* Retrospective Review, ii. 238—56.
Examen; or, an Enquiry into the Credit and Veracity of a pretended compleat History of England (by White Kennet). Lond. 1740, 4to. With portrait of H. North by Vertue. Hibbert, 5872, 7s. Bp. of Ely, 1233, 1l. 1s. Heath, 4387, 17s. LARGE PAPER. Sir M. M. Sykes, pt. ii. 832, 1l. 6s. Gardner, in 1854, 1l. 15s. *See* Retrosp. Review, vii. 169—217, viii. 1—30. Like the other works of the same author, the Examen is valuable for the many original anecdotes it contains, and the view it presents of party politics, but as an impartial authority it cannot be relied on.

A Discourse of Fish and Fish Ponds. By a Person of Honour. Lond. 1713. Published anonymously. Nothingbe, 1788, 5s. Haworth, 523, 1l. 2s.—The second edition, Lond. 1715, 12mo. pp. 94, with title, introduction and contents, 4 leaves. Nassau, pt. II. 4, 9s. — 1794, 4to. *See* ALBIN, Elezar.
A Discourse on the Study of the Laws, now first printed from the original MS. in the Hargrave Collection, with Notes and Illustrations by a Member of the Inner Temple. Lond. 1824, 8vo. pp. xv. and 105, 3s.
Memoirs of Musick. Edited by Dr. Rimbault. Lond. 1846, sm. 4to.

— Sir Thomas. A voluminous Translator. *See* DONI. PLUTARCH.

NORTHALL, John. Travels through Italy. Lond. 1766, 8vo. 4s.
With a map and several plates, published by Roll.

NORTH-ALLERTON, History of, [by Miss Crossfield]. North-Allerton, 1791, 8vo.

NORTHAMPTON, Henry Howard, Earl of. A Defensative against the Poyson of supposed Prophecies. Lond. 1583, 4to.
Reed, 2189, 2l. 2s. *See* Oldys' British Librarian, 331-43. — 1620, folio. Gordonstoun, 1110, 7s. 6d. Bindley, pt. I. 2066, 5s. 6d. Heber, pt. v. 5s. 6d. — Another, with autograph of Oliver Cromwell, 2l. Gardner, in 1854, 5s. *See* Brydges' Censura Literaria. In a MS. note in Edm. Malone's copy this Earl is entitled "one of the basest men of the age in which he lived."

NORTHAMPTON.—The History of Northampton and its Vicinity. Northampton, 1815, 12mo.
Pp. 151, and 2 pages of table of contents, with a view of Queen Eleanor's Cross, by J. Smith.
The State of Northampton, from the beginning of the Fire, Sept. 20, 1675, to Nov. 5. Lond. 1675, 4to.
See BAKER, George. BRIDGES, John. MORTON, John.

NORTH-BRITAIN. *See* Scotland.

NORTH-BRITON. The North Briton, 46 Nos. complete, by John Wilkes, Esq., C. Churchill, and others. Illustrated with Notes, &c. &c. Lond. 1772, 12mo. 4 vols. 15s.
With portraits of Wilkes, Churchill, Lord Camden, and Serjeant Glynn. This

1704 NOB

seditious publication was the source of Wilkes' celebrity and misfortunes, as well as the cause of his ultimate independence.—First edition, 1763, folio, 3 vols. In this edition, No. 45, containing the celebrated attack on the King, is often deficient, as it was strictly suppressed.—1769, folio, 4 vols. White Knights, 2£2, 1l.

NORTHBROOKE, John. A Treatise wherein Dicing, Daunceing, vaine Playes or Enterludes with other idle Pastimes, &c. commonly vsed on the Sabbath day, are reproued by the Authoritie of the Word of God and auntient Writers. Lond. by H. Bynneman for George Byshop, 4to.

BLACK LETTER. *Collation.*—Pp. 148, besides title, dedication to Sir John Yong, Knt. and to the reader 7 leaves.—1577, 4to. —1579, T. Dawson, 4to. Dedicated to Sir John Yong. To the Reader. An Admonition, in verse, 72 leaves. Heber, pt. i. 2l. 5s., pt. ii. 3l. 18s. Gardner, in 1854, mor. 1l. 10s. Brand, 1l. 12s. Southgate, 1818, 3l. Reprinted by the Shakespeare Society. *See* Appendix.

A Homme of the Christian Faith. Lond. 1571, 4to.—15?2, 12mo. Bright, 1l. 11s.

The poor Man's Garden. Lond. 1600. 16mo. 5s.— Lond. by John Charlewood, 8vo.—Lond. by W. Williamson, 8vo.

NORTHCOTE, James, R.A. Memoirs of Sir Joshua Reynolds ; a brief Analysis of his Discourses, and Varieties on Art. With a Supplement. Lond. 1813-15, 4to.

Brockett, 2294, 14s. Sir M. M. Sykes, pt. ii. 633, 12s.—1818, 8vo. 2 vols. Drury, 2397, 1l. 6s.

One hundred Fables, original and selected (first series). Lond. 1828, post 8vo. 1l. 1s. Pp. 274, with 280 engravings on wood, chiefly after William Harvey, by Thompson, &c. Royal 8vo. with India proofs, 1l. 11s. 6d. A few copies printed entirely on INDIA PAPER.—A second edition, with a portrait of Northcote, appeared in 1830. LARGE PAPER, royal 8vo. the cuts were also printed off separately on India paper. 1l. 11s. 6d.

A Second Series of the same set of Fables. Lond. 1833, post 8vo. with 280 woodcuts, after W. Harvey, by Thompson, T. Williams, &c. 1l. 1s. LARGE PAPER, roy. 8vo. India proofs, 1l. 11s. 6d. A few copies were printed entirely on INDIA PAPER. This volume was re-issued in 1845, with new title, as 'The Artist's Book of Fables,' 7s.

NOB

Life of Titian, with Anecdotes of distinguished persons of his Time. Lond. 8vo. 2 vols. portrait. Meally compiled by W. Hazlitt.

Several papers by Mr. Northcote are contained in THE ARTIST, edited by Prince Hoare, 4to. 2 vols. *See* HAZLITT, W.

NORTH-EAST PASSAGE.—Of the Circumference of the Earth, or a Treatise of the North-east Passage. Lond. 1612, 12mo.

Heber, pt. vii. 1l. 11s. Bright, 1l. 10s. A copy is in the British Museum.

NORTHERN BARDS, &c.—Rhymes of Northern Bards ; being a Collection of old and new Songs and Poems peculiar to the Counties of Northumberland and Durham. Newark, Bell, 18—, 12mo. 6s.

New Voyage into the Northern Countries, with description of the Manners of the Norwegians, Laponians, Kilops, Borandians, Zemblans, &s. 1874, 8vo. Nassau, pt. i. 2423, 1l. 1s.

History of the Feuds of the Northern Clans. Glasg. 1764, 12mo. Nassau, pt. i. 1614, 10s. Reprinted in the MISCELLANEA SCOTICA. *See* SCOTLAND.

Popular Tales and Romances of the Northern Nations. Translated by W. H. Leeds. 1823, 3 vols. Drury, 3356, 1l. 3s.

NORTHINGTON, Robert Henley, Earl of, and Chancellor of England. Life, by Lord Henley. Lond. 1831, post 8vo. portrait.

Reports from Lord Northington's Papers. *See* EDEN, R. H., p. 713.

NORTHLEIGH, John. Topographical Descriptions in two Voyages through most Parts of Europe. Lond. 1702, 8vo.

Bliss, 1s. Northleigh's travels will be found in the second volume of Harris' Collection.

NORTHMORE, Thomas. Washington ; or Liberty restored : a Poem in ten Books. Lond. 1809. 8vo.

A notice of this poem will be found in the Quarterly Review, ll. 366-75.

NORTH of England and Scotland in MDCCIV. Edinb. 1818. 12mo. 5s.

One hundred copies 'now first published from the original MS. formerly in the possession of the late Col. Johnes of Hafod.'

NORTHUMBERLAND, Elizabeth,
Countess of. Meditations and
Prayers. Lond. 1709, 12mo.
Brockett, 1889, 3s. 6d. Constable, 676,
7s. 6d. Bliss, 4s.

— C. F. Duchess of. The
Castles of Alnwick and Warkworth.
With 39 Etchings by the Duchess.
Lond. 1823, 4to. (250 copies printed.)

— Henry Algernon Percy, Earl
of. The Regulations and Establishment of the Household of
Henry Algernon Percy, the fifth
Earl of Northumberland, at his
Castles of Wresill and Lekinfield
in Yorkshire, begun Anno Domini
1512. Lond. 1770, 8vo.

Not printed for sale. There are title pages dated 1768 and 1770. The earlier dated copies appear to be printed upon finer paper, no other difference is discernible. Hollis, 990, russia, 4l. 14s. 6d. Hindley, pt. II. 2159, 4l. 14s. 6d. Stevens, 1710, 6l. Nassau, pt. I. 2441, mor. 5l. 18s. Howell, 2073, russia, 5l. 18s. Roxburghe, 6588, 6l. Towneley, pt. II. 862, russia, 6l. 6s. Sir M. M. Sykes, pt. II. 562, morocco, 8l. 15s. Brockett, 2186, 10l. 10s. Fonthill, 3297, 20l. 1s. 6d. Sotheby, 15 Dec. 1857, 5l. 17s. 6d. Mitns, 1l. 11s. Skegg, 1l. 11s. 6d. Collation. — Title, half-title, and preface by Thomas Percy, Bishop of Dromore, pp. i—xxvi, (the preface is often deficient, and destroys the value of the book), advertisement, 2 pages; the kalendar, pp. 1—x; household book, 464 pages; extract from Leland's Itinerary, index and errata, 4 pages not numbered. — Second edition. Lond. Pickering, 1827, 8vo. 1l. 1s. LARGE PAPER, six copies printed. It is also reprinted entire, preface and all, in the fourth volume of Grose's Antiquarian Repertory, 1808, 4to.

— Henry Percy, Earl of. A
true and summarie Reporte of the
Declaration of some Part of the
Earl of Northumberland's Treasons,
with the Examinations and Depositions of sundrie Persons concerning the manner of his Murder in
the Tower of London, &c. 1585.
In Ædibus C. Barker. 4to.

Pp. 22, not including the preface. Gordonstoun, 855, 15s. Bindley, pt. IV. 533, 2l. 12s. 6d. Heber, pt. VI. 10s. Bliss, 1l. 10s. Bright, 10s.

PERCY, James. The Petition and
Claims of James Percey to the
Earldom of Northumberland. 1670-
94. Lond. folio.

— John Dudley, Duke of. The
Saying of John, late Duke of Northumberland, vpon the Scaffolde,
at the Tyme of his Execution, the
22 August. Lond. 1553, 8vo.

Oratio (ad Populum Loudinensem) quum ad Supplicium producitus esset. Coloniæ, 1554, 12mo.—Humm F. Marutius, 1570, 4to. Consisting of only 4 leaves. Heber, pt. VII. 3l. 15s. Guildford, in 1828, L bp. Butler, in 1840, 16l. Of this rare tract only two or three copies are known. It is, however, reprinted in 'the Case Oxxorse nel regno d'Inghilterra,' 1558.

An Italian translation of the preceding work appeared under the title of: La Confessione di Giov. Duca di Northumberlando sopra il Palco, 4to. See also Rosso, Giulio Roviglio, i Successi d'Inghilterra, 1560.

Instructions to his Son, Algernon Percy, touching the Management of his Estates and affairs. 1609-10. Written during his confinement in the Tower. See Archæologia, vol. xxvII. p. 306.

— Istoria delle Cose occorse nel
Regno d'Inghilterra in Materia del
Duca di Notomberlan dopo la
Morte di Odoardo vi. Venet. 1558,
8vo. 10l. 10s.

See INGHILTERRA; MANOLESSO, Maria.

— Robert Dudley, Duke of.
Del Arcano del Mare di Roberto
Dudleo, Duca di Nortumbria e
Conte di Warwick, libri VI. Firenze,
1630-46, 47, royal folio, 3 vols.

A work full of schemes, charts, plans, &c. chiefly valuable for the author's projects towards the improvement of navigation and the extending of commerce. Earl of Guildford, 30l. 9s.—Second edition. Firenze, 1661, complete in 2 vols. atlas folio, 5l. 5s.

The Duke of Northumberland's Voyage to the Isle of Trinidada and Coast of Paria, 1594, 5, will be found in Hakluyt's Collection.

Laws and Ordnances of Warre established by the Duke of Northumberland, for the better conduct of the service in the Northern parts. Lond. 1640, 4to.

NORTHUMBERLAND. — A historical and descriptive View of the
County of Northumberland, and of

the Town and County of Newcastle upon Tyne, with Berwick upon Tweed, and other celebrated Places on the Scottish Border. Newcastle upon Tyne, 1811, 8vo. 2 vols.

Collation.—Vol. I. pp. xx. and 780, not including contents and directions for the binder, 4 pages, also 5 plates. Vol. ii. pp. l—vi, and 8—812, not including errata, one page, also six plates.

Northumberland Garland. 1793. *See* Ritson, Jos.

An Account of the great Floods in the Rivers Tyne, Tees, Wear, Eden, &c. in 1771 and 1815, with the Names of the principal Sufferers in Northumberland, the Amount of their Estimates, and of the Damage done in each Township; also an Account of the Subscriptions made for their Relief, in 1771. To which is added an Account of the Irruption of Solway Firth. Newc. 1818, 12mo, 3s.

The Marriage of the Coquet and the Alwine, two noble Rivers in the County of Northumberland; a Poem, with two wood cuts by Bewick. Newc. 1817, 12mo.

See Hutchinson; Hodgson, William.

NORTH-WEST PASSAGE. — The Impracticability of a North-west Passage for Ships impartially considered. By Scrutator. Lond. 1824, 8vo.

This pamphlet, written by a British Naval Officer, is in opposition to an article which appeared in the Quarterly Review.

See Franklin, Sir John. Hearne, Sam. Parry. Phipps. Ross, Sir John.

NORTON, Robert. A Mathematical Appendix, containing many propositions and Conclusions Mathematical. Lond. 1604, 8vo.

— Thomas. Ferrex and Porrex, or the Tragedie of Gorboduc. *See* Buckhurst, Lord.

A Serpent of Division, (by Jno. Lydgate), whereunto is annexed the Tragedie of Gorboduc. Lond. 1590, 4to.

An Answere to the Proclamation of the Rebels in the North (in Verse). Lond. by Wyllyam Seres, 1569, 12mo. pp. 22. Bibl. Anglo-Poet. 11, 21l.

'To the Queenes Majesties poor deceived Subjectes of the north Countrey, drawen into Rebellion by the Earles of Northumberland and Westmerland. Imprinted by Hen. Bynneman, 1569, 12mo. D 4, in eights, twenty-eight leaves. Inglis, 1s. Hibbert, mor. 13s. Gordonstoun, Mor. 6d. Heber, 10s. Hibra, 1l. 19s.

A Warning agaynst the dangerous Practises of Papistes, and specially the Partners of the late Rebellion. Lond. by John Daye, 12mo. Heber, pt. vi, 1s.4d. Bliss, 17s. O, in fours, half sheets 53 leaves. Caldecott, 9s. Hibra, 15s. Another, no name of printer. Hibra, 15s.

A Bull graunted by the Pope to Doctor Harding and others, by Reconcilement and assoyling of English Papistes, to undermine Faith and Allegeaunce to the Queenes. With a true Declaration of the Intention and Fruites thereof, and a Warning of Perils thereby imminent not to be neglected. Lond. John Day,12mo.10 leaves. Inglis,10s.

A Disclosing of the great Bull, and certein Calues that he hath gotten, and specially the Monster Bull that roared at my Lord Byshops Gate. Imprinted over Aldersgate by John Daye, 16mo. n. d. 10 leaves. Bindley, 18s. 6d. Bliss, 1l. Reprinted in vol. 7 of the Harleian Misc.

An Addition declaratorie of the Bulles, with a Searching of the Maze. Imprinted ouer Aldergate (by John Daye), 16mo. Eight leaves.

A Collection of these pieces with this general title, 'All such Treatises as haue lately been published by Thomas Norton, the titles whereof appeare in the next side,' which list named the last five pieces (all with separate titles), and Ferrex and Porrex, 29 leaves, the last blank, n. d. which proves they were sold together. No other known. Sotheby, Aug. 1800, 54l.

A series of the same five pieces without the Ferrex and Porrex, sold at Sir M. Sykes' in 1824, for 12l. 12s. resold Bright, in 1845, 3l. 10s.

A notice of Thos. Norton and his works will be found in Wood's Athen. Oxon.

NORTON, Hon. Mrs. The Undying One, and other Poems. Lond. Colburn and Bentley, 1830, post 8vo. 7s. 6d.—1853, 12mo. 2s. 6d.

The Dandies' Rout.

The Sorrows of Rosalie. Lond. Ebers, 1829, post 8vo. 8s. 6d.

The Coquette. Lond. Churton, 1834, post 8vo. 2 vols. 1l. 1s. — Republished in 1850, under the title of Tales and Sketches in Prose and Verse. 1s. 6d. These are a collection of early contributions to the Lady's Magazine, published later as a whole, without consent of the author, who endeavoured to restrain the publication by injunction in the Court of Chancery. The Coquette is merely the name of the first story.

The Wife, and Woman's Reward. Lond. Saunders and Otley, 1835, post 8vo. 3 vols. 1l. 11s. 6d.

The Dream, and other Poems. Second edition. Lond. Colburn, 1841, post 8vo. 10s. 6d. Reprinted, New York, 1845, 12mo. This poem called forth the following remark from the Quarterly Review: 'This

NORTON, Hon. Mrs.—*continued.*
Lady is the Byron of our modern poetesses. She has very much of that intense personal passion by which Byron's poetry is distinguished from the larger grasp and deeper communion with man and nature of Wordsworth. She has also his beautiful intervals of tenderness, strong practical thought, and forcible expression. It is no mere artificial imitation, but a natural parallel.'

The Child of the Islands. Lond. Chapman and Hall, 1845, royal 8vo. 12s.—Second edition, ib. 1846, crown 8vo. 6s.

Aunt Cary's Ballads. [Juvenile Poems.] Lond. Grant and Griffith, 1847, cr. 8vo. 6s. plain; 10s. 6d. cold.—Second edit. 1848.

Stuart of Dunleath; a Novel. Lond. Colburn, 1851, post 8vo. 3 vols. 1l. 11s. 6d. —Cheap edition, 1853, 12mo. 1s. 6d.

Tales and Sketches in Prose and Verse. Lond. Churton, 1850, 12mo. 1s. 6d.

Letters to the Mob [Chartists], by Libertas.

Letter to the Queen on Lord Chancellor Cranworth's Marriage and Divorce Bill. Lond. Longman, 1855, 8vo. 2s. 6d.

English Laws (of Custom and Marriage) for Women of the 19th Century. 1854, 8vo.

Mrs. Norton has also contributed to Colburn's New Monthly and most of the Annuals; and edited the Lady's Magazine for several years, the Keepsake one year, Fisher's Drawing-Room Scrap-Book for three years.

She is now engaged in writing a Life of her grandfather, Richard Brinsley Sheridan.

NORTON, Thomas. The several Confessions of Thomas Norton, and Christopher Norton, two of the Northern Rebels, who suffered at Tyburn, and were drawn, hanged, and quartered, for Treason, May 27, 1570. Lond. by William How, for Richard Johnes, 16mo.

Reprinted in the fifth number of Morgan's Phoenix Britannicus.

These so-called Northern Rebels (ancestors of the Hon. Mr. Norton) were Roman Catholics, and suffered for their religion. The brother who recanted, and the sister who survived, are the subject of Wordsworth's poem, the 'White Doe of Rylstone.'

NORVELL, Robert. The Meroure of an Christian, composed and drawn forthe of Holye Scriptures. By Robert Noruell, man of armis, during the tyme of his captiuetie at Paris, in the Bastillie, for the testimonie of our Sauiour Jesus Christ. (In Verse, containing godlie Ballades, and other Poems.) Edinb. by Rob. Lekpreuik, 1561, 4to. 62 leaves.

Geo. Chalmers, pt. III. 871, 40l. The only copy known. In Chalmers' sale catalogue the name is by mistake printed Nowell; Ames, vol. III. p. 1486, and Maunsell, p. 71, have it Norwell. Pinkerton, in his list of Scottish Poets, p. 120, thinks it is probably Norval, or Norval.

NORWICH.—The History of the City and County of Norwich, from the earliest Accounts to the present Time. In 2 pts. Norwich, 1768, 8vo.

Originally published in Numbers. Heath, 4821*, 19s. Dent, pt. I. 1080, 1l. 6s. Heber, 8v. Skegg, 17s. *Collation.*—Pp. 1—874, 876—648, not including title and dedication to Thomas Starling, Esq. two leaves; index, 4 pages, and 7 plates, at pp. 1, 342, 577, 579, 409, 446, 489 and 494.

Relation of the Mutiny at Norwich. Lond. 1648. 4to. Townshend, 2112, 1l.

A true Description of the City of Norwich, in its ancient and modern State; collected out of the choicest MSS. and anthentick Authors. Norwich, 1706, 4to.

A short History of the City of Norwich, 1708, 8vo.

A complete History of the City of Norwich, from the earliest Accounts to this present Year 1768, with an Appendix. Lond. 1768, 8vo. Pp. 28, with a new map, John Hoyle, &c. Appendix, pp. 41 to 62, and pp. 1—19. Reed, 7s. 6d. Lloyd, 7s. 6d.

An Essay on the Antiquity of the Castel of Norwich, its Founders and Governors, from the Kings of the East Angles. Norwich, 1728, 8vo.—Reprinted 1834, 8vo, but not published.

History of the Religious Orders and Communities, and of the Hospitals and Castles of Norwich, written [by John Kirkpatrick] about the year 1725, edited by Dawson Turner, Esq. Yarmouth, 1845, 8vo. VELLUM, a single copy taken off.

A Description of the Diocese of Norwich. By a Gentleman of the Inner Temple and Native of the Diocese of Norwich. Lond. 1735, 8vo. Pp. 68, including the title-page and preface. Attributed to Thornhaugh Gordon, Esq.

The Records of Norwich: In two Parts. Lond. 1726-8, 12mo.

Twenty Etchings of remarkable Churches and other Picturesque Buildings in and near Norwich, drawn and etched by R. Dixon. Norwich, 1810, 4to. LARGE PAPER, folio, only one copy printed.

Views of the Churches, Chapels, and Buildings in the City of Norwich, by J. Sillett and others. 1828, oblong 4to.

See TAYLOR, Richard.

NORWOOD, Cornelius. Divine Eloquence; or an Essay upon the Tropes and Figures contained in the holy Scriptures. Lond. 1694, 12mo.

NOSEGAY, (A Civil), wherein is contained the offyce and dewty of all Magistrates and Judges, &c. gathered out of Latin, and translated by J. G. Lond. 8vo. R.Wyer, for J. Goodall, n. d. 12mo.
Collation.—E iv in eights. Sotheby, 1832, 1l. 19s. A copy is in Lambeth Library.

—— The ; a Poem. [By Thomas Grady, Esq.] Dublin, 1816, royal 8vo. A second edition with plates, Dublin, 1816, royal 8vo. 1l. 4s. Dedicated to Tho. Moore, the Poet.

A most violent satire, and the most malignant piece of invective that the history of literature can furnish. Geo. Evans Bruce, Esq. against whom it was directed, recovered 600l. damages, at the Limerick assizes in 1818, against the author, who retired to the continent, and died unpitied there.

NOSTOCK, J. The Confusion of the Muhamed Sect. Lond. 1652, 12mo.

NOSTRADAMUS, Mich. de. The true Prophecies or Prognostications, translated by Theoph. de Garencieres. Lond. 1672, folio.

With frontispiece, containing portraits of Theophilus de Garencieres, M.D. the translator, and Nathaniel Parker, of Gray's Inn. Roxburghe, 866, 9s. 6d. Gardner, 64,—1835, folio, with front. Nassau, pt. II. 415, 2l.

An excellent Treatise, showing such perilious and contagious Infirmities, as shall issue 1559 and 1560, with the Signes, Causes, Accidents and Cure tion for the Health of such as inhabit G. n 7, 8, and 9 Climate. Compiled by Maister Michael Nostradamus, Doctor in Phisicke, and translated into English. at the Desire of Lawrentius Philotus Tyl. Lond. by John Daye, 1559, 16mo.

Mich. Nostradamus his Prognostication for the Year 1559. With the Predictions and Presages of every Moneth. Antwerpie, 16mo.

Prophecies concerning the Fate of all the Kings and Queens of Great Britain since the Reformation. Lond. 1715, 8vo.

NOTITI ANGLICANA (by Andrew Johnston). Lond. 1724, 8vo. 2 vols. 12s.

The second volume consists entirely of 'Arms of the Nobility on 190 plates, engraved by the ingenious Mr. Gardner and other eminent artists.'

NOTT, G. F., D.D. Sermons preached at the Bampton Lecture. Lond. 1803, 8vo.

This Dr. Nott was Prebend of Winchester and tutor to Princess Charlotte. He translated CATULLUS, some of the Sonnets of PETRARCH, and JOANNES SECUNDUS; and edited SURREY and WYATT'S Poems; which are.

NOTT, John, M.D. On the Bristol Waters and their Influence. Bristol, 1803, 8vo.

He edited OVULA' Hornbook. See DECKER, T., page 609.

NOTTINGHAM, Charles, Earl of. The royal Entertainment of the Earls of Nottingham, sent Ambassador to the King of Spaine. Lond. 1605, 4to.

Lloyd, 1305, 12s. Bindley, pt. III. 1641, 19s. Towneley, p. l. 742, 4l. 7s.

NOUE, Lord de la. The politicke and militarie Discourses of the Lord de la Nove, translated out of French, by E. A. Lond. 1587, 4to.

Pp. 456, dedicated by the translator To 'George, Earle of Cumberland,' &c. and by the author ' To the King of Navarre.' —Lausanne, 1 April 1587.

The Declaration of the Lord de la Noue, upon his taking Armes for the just Defence of the Townes of Sedan and Jametz; Frontiers of the Realme of Fraunce, and under the Protection of his Majesty, truely translated, according to the French Copie, printed at Verdun, by A.M. Lond. by John Wocife, 1589, 4to. twelve leaves.

Profit of Imprisonment, a Paradox against Libertie, by Odet de la Noue, Lord of Teligny, being Prisoner in the Castle of Tournay, translated by Joshua Sylvester. Lond. 1594, 4to. A poem not noticed by Ames or Herbert. Constable, 832, 4l. 14s. 6d.

NOVA BRITANNIA, offering most excellent Fruites by Planting in Virginia. Lond. 1609, 4to. See VIRGINIA.

NOVA FRANCIA; or, the Description of that Part of New France, which is one Continent with Virginia, translated from the French. Lond. 1609, 4to.

Nova Francia. Three lasts Voyages of De Monts, Du Pont, and De Poutrincourt into L'Acadie, 4to. Jadis, 234, 6s.

NOVÆ NARRATIONES. The Booke called Articuli ad Novas Narrationes and the Booke of Diversitees of Courtes. Lond. R. Tottel, 1561, 16mo.
Bright, 4s. 6d. Several editions in BLACK LETTER.

NOVA SCOTIA.—Perpetual Acts relating to Nova Scotia. Halifax, 1767, folio.
The present State of Nova Scotia: With a brief Account of Canada, and the British Islands on the Coast of North America. The second Edition, corrected and enlarged, and Illustrated with a Map. Edinb. 1787, 8vo. 4s.
Memorials of the English and French Commissioners concerning the Laws of Nova Scotia. Lond. 1755, 4to. 2 vols. Puttick, May 1859, 1l. 10s.
Numerous Pamphlets relating to Nova Scotia, and other Parts of British America, are in the British Museum.
See HALIBURTON, p. 976. MARTIN, Montg.

NOVATIANUS.—Opera quæ supersunt omnia, a Joan. Jackson. Lond. 1728, 8vo.
The best edition. Heath. 646, 3s. 6d.
Novatiani Opera quæ extant omnia, Notis Illustrata ab Edvardo Welchman. Oxon. 1721, 8vo. An accurate edition. Williams, 1854, 5s. 6d.

NOVELISTS.—The British Novelists, with an Essay and Prefaces, biographical and critical, by Mrs. Barbauld. Lond. 1810, roy. 18mo. 50 vols.
This selection contains Clarissa Harlowe, Sir C. Grandison, Robinson Crusoe, Joseph Andrews, Tom Jones, Old English Baron, Castle of Otranto, Pompey the Little, Vicar of Wakefield, Female Quixote, Rasselas, Almoran and Hamet, Julia Mandeville, Nature and Art, Simple Story, Man of Feeling, Julia de Roubigné, Humphrey Clinker, Spiritual Quixote, Zeluco, Old Manor House, Evelina, Cecilia, Romances of the Forest, Mysteries of Udolpho, Man as he is not, Belinda, and Grimelda. Dent, pt. I. 257, 7l. 10s. Duke of York, 620, 6l. 6s.—Second edition. Lond. 1820, roy. 18mo. 50 vols. Fonthill, 3329, 12l. 12s.
Choice Novels and Amorous Tales, by the refined Wits of Italy. Lond. 1654, small 8vo. 7s. 6d.
A select Collection of Novels. *See* CROXALL, S.
Novelist's Magazine. Lond. 1780-6, 8vo 23 vols. Published by Harrison, with plates by Stothard and others. Sotheby's in 1821, 8l. 15s.; in 1827, 6l. 6s.; in 1836, 3l. 15s. 6d. Saunders' in 1818, 14l.
New Novelist's Magazine. Lond. 1786, 8vo. 2 vols. Sir M. M. Sykes, pt. II. 354, 9s.
Ballantyne's Novellist's Library. Edinb. 1821-5, royal 8vo. 10 vols. complete, published at 14l. reduced to 5l. 5s. The prefatory memoirs were written by Sir Walter Scott, Bart. CONTENTS:—Vol. I. Joseph Andrews. Tom Jones. Amelia. Jonathan Wild.—Vol. II. Roderick Random. Peregrine Pickle. Humphrey Clinker.—Vol. III. Count Fathom. Launcelot Greaves. Don Quixote.—Vol. IV. Gil Blas. Devil on Two Sticks. Vanillo Gonzales. Adventures of a Guinea.—Vol V. Tristram Shandy. Sentimental Journey. Vicar of Wakefield. Rasselas. Man of Feeling. Man of the World. Julia de Roubigné. Castle of Otranto. Old English Baron.—Vols. VI. and VII. Pamela. Clarissa Harlowe.—Vol. VIII. Sir Charles Grandison.—Vol. IX. Gulliver's Travels. Mount Henneth. Barham Downs. James Wallace. Henry.—Vol. X. Sicilian Romance. Romance of the Forest. Mysteries of Udolpho. Italian. Castles of Athlin and Dunbayne.
British Novelists, with a biographical Sketch of the Authors, and a critical Preface to each Work, by W. Mudford. Lond. 1810-16, 8vo. 5 vols.

NOVELLE.—Novello Otto; stampate a spese de i Signori Giacomo Conte di Clanbrassil, Tomaso Stanley, e Wogan Browne. Lond. 1790, 8vo.
Of this work twenty-five copies were printed. Roxburghe, 6323, 8l. 18s. 6d. Sotheby's in May 1823, morocco, 5l. 10s. Dent, pt. II. 862, morocco, 3l. 10s. White Knights, 8146, morocco, 5l. 10s. Baker, 455, 6l. 16s.- Steevens, 611, blue turkey, 9l. 5s. Hibbert, 5832, morocco, 3l. 6s. On VELLUM. Four copies printed. *Contents.*—1. Lacrimoso Novella. Venetia, 1461. 2. Historia Dilettevole. a. l. et a. 3. La Giulietta. Venetia, 1539. 4. Opera Dilettevole et Nuova di Gratitudine et Liberalita. a. l. et a. 6, 7. Amorose Novelle. a. l. et a. 8. Cosa Notabile. Venezia. a. a.
Novelle scelte rarissime. Lond. 1814. 8vo. Only fifty copies printed. Edited by S. W. Singer, Esq. Goldsmid, 520, 2l. 5s. Sotheby's in 1823, 1l. 11s. 6d. White Knights, 2910, 1l. 1s. Hindley, pt. II. 2106, 1l. 19s. Hibbert, 5727, 8s. A copy on VELLUM, in 2 vols. 12mo. is in the Grenville Library.

NOVEMBRIS MONSTRUM, or Rome brought to Bed in England, with

the Whore's Miscarrying, a Poem. 1641.—2 parts, 8vo.

With a frontispiece. Bindley, pt. III. 32, 2l. 19s. Nassau, pt. I. 2444, 6s. Heber, pt. I. 7s. 6d.

NOTERER, ——. The Works of Monsieur Noverra, translated from the French. Lond. 1785, 8vo. 3 vols.

NOWELL, Alex, D.D. Catechismus, sive prima Institutio Disciplinaeque Pietatis Christianae, Latino explicatè, &c. Lond. Reg. Wolfio. 1570, 4to.

FIRST EDITION OF THE LARGER CATECHISM, 170 pages. Sotheby's in July, 1821, 2l. 12s. 6d. Hillas, mended, 9181, 1l. 1s. There were two different editions in the same year, one dated June 16, the other July 18, the latter containing some additional matter about Confirmation. The earliest is easily distinguished by having a list of eight typographical errata at the end—SECOND EDITION. Lond. R. Wolfe, 1571, 4to. pp. 100. There are two editions of this also, under the same date, one bearing only the year, the other having in addition iii. Calend. Jun.— THIRD EDITION. Lond. R. Wolfe, 1572, 4to. pp. 160. — FOURTH EDITION. R. Wolfe, 1573, 8vo. pp. 170, the appendix unpaged. CATECHISMVS, GRÆCE et LATINE (a Gul. Whittaker). Lond. apud Reginaldum Wolfium, 1573, 8vo. 668 pages, besides the prefaces. This edition containing the Greek translation appeared for the first time simultaneously with the fourth edition of the original Latin. We have not had an opportunity of comparing them, but presume they are one and the same, with the addition of the Greek. Heber, pt. II. 1083, 1l. 6s.; pt. VII. 4068, 1l. 1s. Hibbs, pt. I. 8029, 2l. 2s.—FIFTH EDITION (Latin). Lond. J. Daye, 1574, 4to.—SIXTH EDITION (Latin). Lond. J. Daye, 1575, 4to.—Gr. et Lat. Lond. J. Daye, 1577, 12mo. This would appear to be the seventh edition, but it is probably only the sixth edition, with the addition of the Greek version and a new title. Heber, 2l. 3s.—SEVENTH EDITION. Lond. J. Daye, 1580, 4to. pp. 159.—Other editions, 1590, 8vo.—1603, 8vo.

Catechismus, &c. (Latin) accedit J. G. Vossii Disputatio theologica de Sacramentorum VI et Efficaciâ, adente Guilielmo Cleaver. Oxon. 1795, 8vo. 7s.—Gr. et Lat. Lond. 1816, 12mo. 4s.—New edition. Lond. Simpkin and Marshall, 1851, 5s. 6d. Nowell's Latin Catechism will be found in Bishop Randolph's Enchiridion Theologicum.

Editio nova, cura Jacobson. Oxford, 1835, 8vo. This edition was printed from the original manuscript, and contains an English preface by the editor.—Second edition, enlarged. Oxford, 1844, 5s. 6d.

A Catechisme, or first Instruction and Learning of Christian Religion. Translated out of Latine into ENGLISH (by T. Norton). Lond. by John Daye, 1570, 4to. The Catechism contains, besides the dedication by T. Norton to the Archbishops and Bishops, and a table at the end, in all 79 leaves. At the end are Day's device of the resurrection, and colophon.—Again, 1571, 4to. — 1573, 4to. — Lond. by John Daye, 1575, 4to.—New edition, with fac-simile, edited by Professor Corrie. Camb. 1853, 8vo. See Parker Society, APPENDIX. Nowell's English Catechism is reprinted in the eighth volume of The Fathers of the English Church.

Christianæ Pietatis prima Institutio, ad Vsum Scholarum Latine scripta. Lond. 1570, 4to. FIRST EDITION OF THE MIDDLE CATECHISM.—1577, 8vo. — Græce et Latine (Whittaker). In Ædibus Ioan. Dayi, 1578, 16mo.—Latino. Cantab. 1633, 12mo.

A Catechism or Institution of Christian Religion, to bee learned of all Youth next after the little Catechisme appointed in the Booke of Common Prayer. Lond. by John Daye, 1579, 12mo. First edition of Norton's translation of the Middle Catechism. H 10, in eights.—1577, 4to.

Nowell wrote three catechisms; this is the middle sort, and is an abridgment of the largest.

CATECHISMVS PARVVS Pueris primum Latinè qui ediscatur proponendus in Scholis. Lond. apud Ioh. Dayum, 1573, 12mo. FIRST EDITION OF THE SMALLER CATECHISM. Contains B in eights, dedicated to the Archbishops, Bishops, &c.

The Little Catechism. Lond. Richard Day, 1582, 12mo. Dean Nowell's smallest catechism, but larger than what was printed with the Book of Common Prayer.

All these Catechisms are extremely rare, and some of them not satisfactorily identified. See Churton's Life of Dean Nowell, and Jacobson's Preface, 1844.

A Reproofe of a Booke Intituled, A Proofe of certayne Articles in Religiou denied by M. Iuell, set forth by Tho. Dorman, B.D. Lond. by Henry Wykes, 1565, 4to. J1, in fours. Heswell. 1634, 11s. Heber, pt. I. 10s., pt. II. 1l. 8s.

The Reproofe of M. Dorman his Proufe of certaine Articles in Religion, &c. continued. With a Defence of the chief Authoritie and Gouernment of Christian Princes as well in Causes ecclesiasticall as ciuill within their own Dominions, by M. Dorman maliciouslie oppugned. Lond. by Henry Wykes, 1566, 4to. Pre-

fixed are 'An admonition to the Reader,' and 'The faultes mended,' 239 leaves. Boswell, 1573, 10s.
A Confutation as wel of M. Dorman's Boke entituled A Disproufe, &c. as also of D. Sander his Causes of Transubstantiation. Lond. 1567, 4to. It is introduced with a copious preface, and contains besides, 4 M leaves, including Dorman's treatise as also part of Dr. Sander's book of The Supper of our Lord.
The Life of Alexander Nowell. *See* CHURTON, Ralph.

NOY, Sir William. Reports and Cases taken in the Time of Q. Elizabeth, K. James and K. Charles. Lond. 1656, folio, 7s.
A collection of scraps of cases made by Serjeant Sizer from Noy's loose papers.— 1669, folio.
The compleat Lawyer. Lond. 1651, 8vo. Frequently reprinted. — 1665, 8vo. with portrait (by Faithorne). — 1670, 8vo. with portrait. Nassau, pt. i. 2448, 3s.
The Grounds and Maxims of the English Law. 1641, 4to.—1757, 12mo.—1791, 12mo. 3s. 6d. — 1808, 12mo. — 1817, 12mo. 7s.—Ninth Edition, by W. M. Bythewood, with a Sketch of the Author's Life, Corrections of the Translations of the Maxims, Notes and References: to which is added, a Treatise of Estates, ascribed to Sir John Doddridge. Lond. 1821, 12mo. 10s.

NUBILA Jubila Britannico-Stuartica. Franckf. 1662, 12mo.
In German, with numerous English portraits and historical prints. Heber, pt. vii. 1s.

NUCIUS. *See* NICANDER.

NUGÆ derelictæ. *See* MAIDMENT, James.

NUGÆ Venales, sive Thesaurus Ridendi et Jocandi. Lond. 1741, 12mo.
Steevens, 580, 5s.

NUGENT, Hon. Geo. Grenville, afterwards Lord Nugent. An Essay on Duelling. Buckingham, 1807, 4to.
Privately printed. The Chancellor's prize was adjudged to this Essay—but withheld in consequence of his Lordship not being of the proper standing to compete for it. Bliss, pt. ii. 12s.
Portugal: a Poem. Lond. 1812, 4to.
Some Memorials of John Hampden, his Party and his Times. Lond. 1832, 8vo. 2 vols. port.—Second edition. Lond. 1832, 8vo. 2 vols. port. and 6 plates, 1l. 10s.— Fourth edition, in one volume, with a Memoir of the author and a general Index. Lond. Bohn, 1860, post 8vo. 12 portraits, 5s.
A Letter to John Murray, Esq. touching an Article in the Quarterly Review on the Memorials. Lond. 1832, 8vo. This produced a Reply, entitled a Letter to John Murray, Esq. in reply to a letter from his Lordship by the writer of the Article in the Quarterly. Lond. 1833, 8vo.
Legends of the Library at Lilies. Lond. 1832, post 8vo. 2 vols. 1l. 1s.
The Ballot discussed, in a Letter to the Earl of Durham. Second edition. Lond. Ridgway, 1836, 8vo. pp. 63, 1s. 6d.
Lands, Classical and Sacred. Lond. 1845, post 8vo. 2 vols. 18s.—1846, 18mo. 2 vols. 3s.
— Robert Craggs, Lord. Odes and Epistles. Lond. 1739, 8vo.
— Richard. Cynthia, containing Direfull Sonnets, Madrigalls and passionate intercourses. Lond. H. Tomes, 1604, 4to.
Roxburghe, to lot 3342, unique, resold, Heber, pt. iv. 6l. 8s. 6d.
— Thomas, LL.D. The History of Vandalia, containing the ancient and present State of the County of Mecklenburg; its Revolutions under the Vandals, the Venedi, and the Saxons; with the Succession and memorable Actions of its Sovereigns. Lond. 1766, 9, 73, 4to. 3 vols.
The Grand Tour; or, a Journal through the Netherlands, Germany, Italy and France. By Mr. Nugent. The second edition, corrected, &c. To which is now added, the European Itinerary. Lond. 1756, 12mo. 4 vols. Willett, 1830, 9s.
Travels through Germany, with a particular Account of the Courts of Mecklenburg. Lond. 1768, 8vo. 2 vols Willett, 1831, 5s. Reed, 5283, 10s. Fonthill, 2030, 1l. 11s.
Nugent likewise translated MONTESQUIEU'S Spirit of Laws, the Life of Benvenuto CELLINI, and other works; and published a Pocket French and English Dictionary, which has been frequently reprinted.

NUMERUS INFAUSTUS: the unfortunate Reigns of William II., Henry II., Edward II., Richard II., Charles II., and James II. Lond. 1689, 12mo.
A small piece, by Charles Cæsar, printed anonymously. Reprinted in Lodge's Life of Sir Julius Cæsar.

NUMISMATIC CHRONICLE. See Appendix.

NUN, Thomas. A Comfort against the Spaniard. Lond. 1596, 4to.
Eleven leaves, dedicated to the Bishop of Norwich. Inglis, 1118, 2s.

NUN.—A Nunne's Prophecy, or the Downefall of Friers. Lond. 1623, 8vo.
With a wood-cut. Gordonstoun, 1642, 14s.—1615, 4to. Nassau, pt. ii. 190, in a lot.

The English Nunne, being a Dialogue, wherein the Author endeavoureth to draw young and unmarried Catholike Gentlewomen to embrace a Votary and Religious Life. 1642, 12mo. Heber, pt. vii. 4020, 6s. 6d.

The Nunns Complaint against the Fryars: the Charge by the Nunns of St. Katharine near Provins, against the Fathers Cordeliers their Confessours, translated from the French into English. Lond. 1676, sm. 8vo. with a frontispiece, 5s.

NUNEHAM COURTENEY. — Description of Nuneham Courtoney in the County of Oxford (the Seat of the Earl of Harcourt). 1806, 12mo.
Pp. 68. Privately printed. Originally printed in 1783, and a second time in 1797. See VETUSTA MONUMENTA.

NUT-CRACKER, The. See JESTS, page 1204.

NUTTALL, Thomas. A Journal of Travels into the Arkansas Territory during the Year 1819. Philadelphia, 1821, 8vo. map and plates.
Reprinted, Boston, 1834, 12mo.
Introduction to Systematic and Physiological Botany. Boston, U.S. 1827, 8vo.
Manual of the Ornithology of the United States and of Canada: Land Birds and Water Birds. Camb. Mass. 1832, 12mo. 2 vols.—1853, 12mo. 2 vols.
The Genera of North American Plants, and a Catalogue of the Species to the Year 1817. Philadelp. 1818. 18mo. 2 vols.
See MICHAUX's North American Sylva.

NYCOLLS, Phillyp. See NICOLLES, Philip.

NYE, Nathaniel. The Art of Gunnery, 1644. With portrait æt. 20, by W. Hollar. Lond. 1647, 8vo.
1648, with port. by Hollar. Townelay, pt. ii. 1545, 11s.—1670. Bliss, 13s.

— Stephen. A Discourse concerning natural and revealed Religion. Glasg. 1752, 12mo.
Williams, 1254, morocco, 15s.—Lond. 1696. 8vo. Nye published several other works.

NYM. See MAY, Thomas, p. 1244.

NYMPHA LIBETHRIS. See BARKSDALE, Clement.

NYNDGE, Ed. M.A. Narration of his Brother Alexander Nyndge's being most horribly tormented with the Devill. Lond. 1615, 4to.
Nassau, pt. ii. 571, 16s. Heber, pt. vi. 2566, 10s.

NYXON. See NIXON, Ant.

O.

Chr. The Fountain and Wellspring of all Variance, Sedition, and deadlie Hate. Wherein is declared at large, the Opinion of Hiperius, &c; that Rome in Italie is signified and noted by the Name of Babylon, in the 14, 17, and 18 Chapters of Reuelation of S. Iohn. Lond. 1589. 4to.

Pp. 39, dedicated to the Earls of Huntington and Warwicke, by Chr. O.

O. I. The Lamentation of Troy for the Death of Hector. Whereunto is annexed, an olde Woman's Tale in hir solitarie Cell. Lond. P. Short for W. Matts, 1594, 4to.

In verse. Thirty-two leaves, inscribed to Sir Peregrine Bertie, Knt., Lord Willoughby of Eresby, by I. O. Gordenstoun, 1814, title and two leaves wanting, 7s. 6d. Bibl. Anglo-Poet. 424, part of last leaf wanting, 25l. resold Saunders in 1818, 3l. 13s. 6d. resold Heber, pt. iv. 1l. 15s. Caldecott, 4l. 6s. See Beloe's Anecdotes of Literature, and Brydges' Censura literaria. On sign. D 2 are some lines in praise of Spenser.

O. I. Venus' Looking-Glass, or a rich Store-house of choice Drollery. Lond. n. d. 8vo.

O. J. See OLDE, John.

O. J. M. See MONTROSE.

O. L. See OWEN, Lewis or Luke.

O. N. A Dialogue between two Priests named Watkin and Jeffry. Attributed to William Roy.

O. R. Mans Mortalitie, or a Treatise wherein 'tis proved that whole Man is a Compound wholy mortall. Amsterdam, printed by John Canne, 1643, 4to.

A—O. in fours, besides title to the reader, and verses, signed S. C. and S. B. two leaves.—Amst. 1644, 4to. with a frontispiece. Hibbert, 5843, 2s. Hollis, 1096, 2l. 2s. resold Heber, 1l. 2s.

OAKLEY, Benjamin. Selections from Shakspeare. Lond. 1828, post 8vo. 7s.

Letters on Miscellaneous Subjects. Lond. 1823, royal 8vo. lithographic portraits, 15s. Only 50 copies printed.

OATES, Titus. The Memoirs of Titus Oates. Lond. 1685, 4to.

With a frontispiece. Sir M. M. Sykes, pt. ii. 497. 16s. Reprinted in the ninth volume of the Somers' Collection of Tracts.

Εικων βασιλικη; or the Picture of the late King James, drawn to the Life. In which is made manifest that the whole course of his Life hath to this Day been a continued Conspiracy against the Protestant Religion, Laws, and Liberties of the three Kingdoms. Third edition. Lond. 1696, 4to. 4 pts.

Numerous other tracts by and relative to Titus Oates were published 1679—1705.

OATHS.—The Book of Oaths, and the several Forms, ancient and modern. Lond. 1649, 12mo.

Nassau, pt. i. 234, 8s. Bright, 6s.—1689, 8vo.—1715. 8vo.

A briefe Treatise of Oathes exacted by Ordinaries and ecclesiastical ludges, to answere generallie to all such Articles or Interrogatories as pleaseth them to propound. And of their forced or constrained Oathes ex Officio, wherein it is proued that the same are vnlawfull. 4to. pp. 58, circa 1588. Privately printed. Bright, 1s. 6d. Heber, pt. vi. in lot 2568.

Oaths, their Origin, Nature, and History. By J. Endell Tyler, D.D. Second edition. Lond. 1835, post 8vo. 9s.

The Oaths of Allegiance, Supremacy, Simony, Canonical Obedience, and Residence, are in Sparrow's Collection.

OAT-MEALE, Oliver. A Quest of Enquirie by Women to know whether the Tripe-wife were trimmed by Doll yea or no; gathered by

Oliver Oat-meale. Lond. by I. G.
1595, 4to.
A poetical tract. Bindley, pt. iv. 527,
10l. 10s. Perry, 7l. 10s. Jolley, 13l. 5s.

OBADIAH. Abdias the Prophet
interpreted by T(homas) B(ras-
bridge), Fellow of Magdalene College in Oxforde. Lond. by Henry
Binneman for Geo. Bishop, 1574,
16mo.
A.—G, in eights, dedicated to the Earle
of Huntingdon, and one leaf containing
errata. Williams, 8, morocco, 1l. 1s.

OBEDIENCE.—History of Passive
Obedience. *See* SELLER, Abednego.

OBEDIENCE, The, of a Chrysten
Man. *See* TYNDALE, William.

O'BEIRNE, Thomas Lewis, Bp. of
Meath. Sermons on important
Subjects. Lond. 1795-1821, 8vo.
3 vols. 9s.

O BRAZILE, or the inchanted
Island; being a Relation of a late
Discovery of the Dis-inchantment
of an Island in the North of Ire-
land. Lond. 1675, 4to.
Usually ascribed to Richard Head.
Lloyd, 1006, 1l. 6s. Heber, pt. vii. 4s.
O Brasael, the western Wonder, with
a Description of a Place called Montaca-
pernia. Lond. 1674, 4to.

O'BRIEN, Henry. The Round
Towers of Ireland; or the Mysteries of Free Masonry, of Sabaism,
and of Budhism for the first time
unveiled. Prize Essay of the Royal
Irish Academy, enlarged. Lond.
1834, 8vo. plates, 1l. 10s.
Ellis, 12s.
Phœnician Ireland; translated from the
Spanish of J. L. Villanueva, and illustrated with Notes. Lond. 1833, 8vo. 12s.

— J. Focaloir Gaoidhilge-Sax-
Bhéarla; or, an Irish-English Dic-
tionary. Paris, 1768, 4to. 3l. 3s.
—Second edition, revised and cor-
rected by the Rev. Robert Daly.
Dublin, 1832, 8vo. 18s.
In this edition each language is printed
in its proper characters, not, as before, all
in roman. For English-Irish part, see
M'CURTIN, H. p. 1421.

— Rev. Paul. A practical Grammar of the Irish Language. Dublin, 1809, 8vo. 15s.

— Lusorium; a Collection of
Convivial Songs. 1782, 16mo. cu-
rious plates.
Heber, pt. vii. 8s.

OBSEQUENS, Julius. De Prodi-
giis. Oxon. 1703, 8vo.
A good edition, subjoined to Hearne's
edition of Eutropius.

OBSERVATOR, The, by Sir Roger
L'Estrange. folio.
This periodical paper, written to vindi-
cate the measures of the court and the
character of the king, from the charge of
being popishly affected, commenced April
13, 1681, and was continued for some years.
Heber, pt. II. (3 vols, 1681 to 1685), 6s. 6d.
and vols. 2 and 3, 1687, 1s.
The Observator, with a Summary of Intelligence. This paper, the first number of
which appeared Oct. 24-31, 1654, was continued for several years.
The Observator, for 1702, 1703, and 1704,
folio. By John Tutchin. Field, 971, 10s.
This paper commenced April 1, 1702, and
was published every Wednesday, at one
penny. It excited much attention, and
was extremely obnoxious to the Tories.
It expired in 1712.

OBSERVER, The, A Collection of
moral, literary, and familiar Essays.
(By Richard Cumberland.) Lond.
1785-90, post 8vo. 5 vols.
Second edition, Lond. 1791, post 8vo.
5 vols.—1798, 6 vols.—Third edition, 1803,
post 8vo. 3 vols. An esteemed work,
since reprinted in the British Essayists.

OCCASIONAL PAPERS.—A Collec-
tion of the Occasional Papers.
Lond. 1716-19, 8vo. 3 vols.
The authors of the Occasional Papers
were 'the Rev. Joshua Barnes, Benjamin
Avery, Ll.D., Benj. Grosvenor, D.D.,
Sam. Wright, D.D., John Evans, D.D.,
Mr. Eames, and the Rev. Moses Lowman;
the initials of their names forming the
word Bagwsel.'—*MS. note by Dr. Henley.*
Hollis, 286, 7s. 6d. Gosset, 3776, 7s. Vol. I.
1716, Nos. 1. to xii. Vol. II. 1717-8, Nos.
I. to XII. with a preface and a table of
contents to both volumes. Vol. III. 1718-19,
Nos. I. to xii. Heber, pt. vii. 7s.

The Occasional Paper, in ten Numbers.
Lond. 1697-8, 4to. An anonymous publication by Richard Willis, Bishop of Winchester.

OCCAM, or OCKAM, William of.
Disputatio inter Clericum et Militem
super potestate Prelatis ecclesiæ
atque Principibus terrarum com-
missa in forma dialogi; et Compendium de Vita Antichristi. Colon.
1475, 4to.—Paris, 1498, 4to. and
other editions.

A Dialogue between a Knyght and a
Clerke concerninge the Power spiritual
and temporal, by William Occham, the
great Philosopher, in English and Latin.
Lond. Tho. Berthelet, s. a. 12mo.—Again,
1540. This notable little tract was written
in 1305, to silence the clergy, and answer
their unreasonable expectations that the
Pope might exercise jurisdiction over
the temporalities of Princes, and the
Church be exempted from contributing to
the relief of the poor or the security of
the nation. *See* Oldys' B. Libr. 8–10. Fox's
Martyrs, vol. 1. 510. Caldecott, 1*l*. 12s.

Dialogorum libri septem adversus hæreticos; et Tractatus de dogmatibus Johannis XXII. s. l. [Paris, Stoll], 1476, fol.
FIRST EDITION.—Lugd. 1495 and 1496, fol.

Opus nonaginta dierum et dialogi, compendium errorum contra Jobannem XXII.
Lovan. 1481, fol.—Lugd. 1495 and 1496, fol.

Compendium Errorum Johannis Papæ
XXII. Lugd. 1496, fol.

Scriptum in primum librum sententiarum, in quo theologica simul et arcium
atque philosophiæ dogmata utque ad principia resolvuntur stilo clarissimo facili et
apto. 1483, (s. l.) folio. A copy is in the
Lambeth Library.

Quodlibeta septem. Paris, 1487, 4to.—
Idem, cum Tract. de sacramento altaris.
Argent. 1491, fol.

De sacramento altaris. Paris, 1513, 8vo.
—Venet. 1514, fol.

Tractatus Logicæ divisus in tres partes.
Paris, 1488, fol.

Centiloquium Theologicum. Lugd. 1494,
5, 6, fol.

Summa totius logicæ. Bon. 1499, fol.—
Ven. 1508, 4to.—Ven. 1552, fol.—Oxon.
1675, 8vo.

Summulæ in libros physicorum. Bon.
1494, fol.—Ven. 1500, 4to.

Quæstiones et Decisiones in quatuor
libros Sententiarum. Lugd. 1495, 6, 7, fol.

Expositio aurea super totam artem Ve-
terem, continens hosce tractatus. I. Super
Porphyrii Prædicabilia, II. in Aristotelis
Prædicamenta, III. in libros duos *περι ερμηνειας*; una cum Quæstionibus Alberti
Parvi da Saxonia; studio Marci de Bene-
vento Cœlestini. Bon. 1496, fol.

Super potestate Pontificis octo quæstio-
num Decisiones. Lugd. 1496, fol.

Occam was the only schoolman whose
writings Luther studied or kept in his
library. Several other of his works are
named in *Jöcher's Gelehrten Lexicon*, but
without particulars.

OCCLEVE. *See* HOCCLEVE.

OCELLUS LUCANUS. De universi
Orbis Natura. Cantab. 1670, 8vo.
In Opuscula Mythologica Tho. Gale.
A translation will be found in the Euro-
pean Magazine for 1762.
On the Nature of the Universe, &c.
translated by Thomas Taylor. Lond. 1831,
12mo.

OCHINUS, Bernard, of Siena. A
Tragedie or Dialoge of the uniuste
vsurped Primacie of the Bishop of
Rome, and of the iust Abolishyng
of the same, translated out of La-
tine into Englishe by John Ponet,
D.D. (Lond. W. Lynne.) Anno
Do. 1549, 4to. BLACK LETTER.

Gordonstoun, 1681, last leaf wanting,
1*l*. 15s. White Knights, 3148, 2*l*. 16s. Inglis, 1120, 1*l*. Williams, 1167, morocco,
3*l*. 3s. Heber, pt. ix. 1*l*. 10s. Caldecott,
two leaves MS. 10s. Gardner, in 1854, 2*l*.

Fine Sermons, translated out of Italian
into Englishe, Anno Do. MDXLVIII. Lond.
by R. C. (probably Robert Crowley) for
William Reddell, sm. 8vo.

Sermons, (6) translated by Richard Ar-
gentine. Ippeswych, by Anthony Scoloker, 1548, sm. 8vo. The six sermons on
48 pages. Dedicated to Edward, Duke of
Somerset, by 'Rychard Argentyne.' Heber, pt. vi. 6s.

Certayne Sermons, faythfully translated
into Englyshe. Lond. by Jhon Day,
n.d. sm. 8vo. This volume, A—N 7, in
eights, contains 25 sermons, 6 of them
being those given in the preceding volume.

Certaine Sermons, translated by Wm.
Phiston. Lond. 1580, 4to. This volume
is divided into 38 sermons, or rather sections, 19 on Faith, 8 on Hope, and 11 on
Charity, and consists of 100 leaves, besides the dedication to the Archb. of Canterbury, to the reader, and the table, four
leaves. Sotheby's, May 1854, 6s.

Fouretene Sermons, concerning the Pre-
destinacion and Election of God: very
expedient to the settynge forth of hys
Glarye among his Creatures. Translated
out of the Italian into oure natyue
Tounge by A(nna) C(ook), (one of the
daughters of Sir Anthony Cook, afterwards wife of Sir Nich. Bacon, and mother of the great Sir F. Bacon). Lond. by
John Day, sm. 8vo. The whole contains
11 7 in eights, Dedicated by A. C. to her
Mother, the Lady F. Ullas, 16s.

A Dialogue of Polygamy and another of
Divorce, rendered into English by a Person of Quality. Lond. 1657, 12mo. Bright,

5 E

3s. 6d. Bliss, 8s. To this translation, dedicated to the author of 'Advice to a Son' (Francis Osborne), Madan in his Thelyphthora was under great obligation.

Two Dialogues on Polygamy and Divorces, with some Memoirs and Testimonies of the Life and Writings of Bernardino Ochin, will be found in 'Select and curious Cases of Polygamy, Concubinage, Adultery, Divorce, &c. seriously and learnedly discussed.' Lond. 1736, 12mo.

OCKLEY, Simon. History of the Saracens, containing the Lives of Mahomet and his immediate Successors, an Account of their most remarkable Battles and Sieges, and of the Religion, Rites, Customs, &c. of that warlike People. Third edition, with additions by Dr. Long; and a Plan of the Temple of Mecca, &c. Lond. 1757, 8vo. 2 vols.

A curious and very entertaining work. Heath, 2672, 1l. 10s. Nassau, pt. i. 9449, 1l. Hibbert, 5756, 1l. 7s. Williams, 1263, blue morocco, 4l. 10s.—First edition, 1708, 8vo. 1 vol. Roxburghe, 6845, 9s. 6d. Vol. II. appeared in 1718.—Second edition, 1718, 8vo. 2 vols. Willett, 1852, 17s. LARGE PAPER. Dindley, pt. II. 2037, 1l. 8s.—Fourth edition, in one volume, with Notes from the Works of later Writers, a Memoir of the Author, Synoptical View of the later Saracenic History, Index, &c. edited by Henry G. Bohn. Lond. (Bohn's Standard Library) 1847, post 8vo. port. 3s. 6d.—Fifth edition, 1848.—Sixth edition, 1857.

Introductio ad Linguas Orientales. Cantab. 1706, 8vo. Hibbert, 5756, 2s. 6d.

History of the present Jews. With Faber Simon's Account of the Samaritans and the Sect of the Carraites. Lond. 1707, 12mo. Read, 5390, 6s.

An Account of the Authority of the Arabick Manuscripts in the Bodleian Library, controverted between Dr. Grabe and Mr. Whiston. Lond. 1712, 8vo.

An Account of south-west Barbary. Lond. 1713, sm. 8vo. Nassau, pt. i. 2451, 2s. Roxburghe, 7323, 3s. 6d.

See ALI, JAAFAR, ABI.

OCLANDUS, Christoph. Anglorum Prælia, 1327—1558, Carmine perstricta. Item, Eironarchia, sive de pacatissimo Angliæ Statu, imperante Elizabetha Narratio. Lond. excudebat R. Neuberie, 1580, 4to.

Editio altera. Hijs Alexandri Nevelli Kettum adjunximus. Lond. Nubary, 1582, 12mo. 2 parts.

Each of the pieces has a title-page so as to sell separately. The work was appointed by Q. Elizabeth and her privy council to be received and taught in every grammar and free-school within the kingdom, 'for the renewing of such lascivious poets as are commonly reade and taught in the said grammar schooles.' Dent, pl. ii. 39, 4s. 6d. Bliss, 2s. Nassau, pt. i. 2452, 9s.—Lond. 1580, 4to. Hibbert, 5846, morocco, 1l. 11s. 6d.—1582, 4to.

ElPHNAPXIA, sive Elizabetha; De Pacatissimo Angliæ statu. Lond. Barker, 1582, 4to.

The same, done into English Verse, by John Sharrock. Lond. Rob. Waldegrave, 1585, 4to. Heber, pt. iv. 1913, 6l. 6s. now in the Grenville Collection. Dedicated in verse to the Lady Myldred, wife to Lord Burghley. Unknown to Ames, Herbert, or Ritson.

Elizabetheis, sive de Angliæ Statu sub Elizabethæ Imperio. Liber secundus in quo præter cætera, Hispania profligatio explicatur. Lond. T. Orwin, 1589, 4to. Bright, 19s.

O'CLERY, Michael. Lexicon Hibernicum præsertim pro Vocabulis antiquioribus et obscuris. Lovanii, 1643, 8vo.

In this work many of the obsolete words in the Irish language are explained by modern words in common use. Gen. Vallancey, 6l. 6s. Sotheby (Bp. Daly), June 25, 1858, 18l. 5s. A transcript sold at Mason's sale in 1857, for 7l.

Speculum vitæ, vel Desiderina. Lovan. 1616, 6vo. Printed in the Irish character. Sotheby (Bp. Daly), June 25, 1858, 3l. 3s. In the Grenville Collection.

O'CONNOR, The. Chronicles of Eri; being the History of the Gaal Sciot Iber, or the Irish People. Translated from the original Manuscripts in the Phœnician Dialect of the Scythian Language. Lond. 1822, 8vo. 2 vols. portrait of the author, 10s. LARGE PAPER, 15s.

— Arthur. The State of Ireland. (Lond. 1798, 8vo. Not published.) Translated into French. Paris, 1804, 8vo. *See* BEAUTIES of the PRESS, 1800, page 140.

— Roderic. Works; with an Abstract of Irish History, and of the Monarchs of the Belgian Dynasty. Cork, n. d. 8vo. 2 vols.

A scarce work.

O'CONOR, Charles. Dissertations on the History of Ireland. Dublin, 1766, 8vo.

An elegant and valuable work. Garrick, 1694, 7s. Gosset, 8780, 9s. 6d. Boswell, 2042, 15s. Towneley, pt. ii. 685, 19s.—Dublin, 1753, 8vo. a, b, c, B—E r, in fours. At page 43 a folding leaf of ' The Scottish Feadha or Letters,' at p. 171 a map of 'Scotia antiqua,' or Ireland. Lloyd, 400, 6s.—1704, new title only.—Dublin, 1812, 8vo.

An Account of the Nature and Conditions of a Charter to be granted for the working and manufacturing Mines and Minerals in Ireland. 1754.

See O'FLAHERTY, R.

— Charles, D.D., Member of the Academy of Cortona. Memoirs of the Life and Writings of the late Charles O'Conor, of Belanagare, Esq. M.R.I.A. Vol. I. (all printed.) Dublin, 1796, 8vo. portrait.

This biographical and genealogical work is of great rarity, a few copies only having been printed for circulation amongst the friends of the author. By some it is said to have been suppressed. Sir M. M. Sykes, pt. il. 569, morocco, 14l. resold Heber, pt. iv. 6l. No second volume appeared.

Columbanus ad Hibernos, or, seven Letters on the present Mode of appointing Catholic Bishops in Ireland, &c. Buckingham, 1810-16, 8vo. 1l. 11s. 6d. 'A singular work, abounds with information.'—C. Butler. Answered by Dr. F. Plowden.

Rerum Hibernicarum Scriptores. 1814-25-26, 4to. 4 vols. *See* IRELAND.

A Narrative of the most interesting Events in modern Irish History. 1812, 8vo. 7s.

Appeal to the Pope. Lond. 1622, 8vo.

Bibliotheca MS. Stowensis; a descriptive Catalogue of the Manuscripts in the Stowe Library, by the Rev. Charles O'Conor, D.D. Buck. 1818-9, 2 vols. and an Appendix, 4to. Eyton, in 1848, russia, 15l. 15s. Of this elaborate and valuable catalogue 200 copies were printed at the expense of the Duke of Buckingham and Chandos. [The MSS. are now in the possession of the Earl of Ashburnham, who purchased them in 1849 for 6000l. after they had been catalogued for public sale by Messrs. Sotheby and Wilkinson. His Lordship, at the same time, obtained nearly the whole impression of the auction catalogue, of which some copies were on LARGE PAPER, sm. 4to.]

— E. A Grammar of the Gaelic Language. By E. O'C. Dublin, 1818, 12mo. 4s.

— et Daly. La vie e le martyre du Rev. P. Frere Corneille O'Conor et du Frere Eugene Dalil, Religieux de l'ordre de Saincte Trinité et redemption des captifs au pays d'Hybernie, par F. J. de Vilette. Paris, 1645, 8vo.

Sotheby (Bp. Daly), June 25, 1858, 5l. 7s. 6d.

OCTAVYAN. Here begynneth Octavyan the Emperoure of Rome. Lond. (probably by Copland), 4to. with a wood-cut on the title.

Heber, pt. iv. Imperfect at the end, 2l. 11s.

OCTAVIAN, Emperor of Rome, a Romance. Oxford, 1809, post 8vo.

Fifty copies of this elegant translated abridgment, from a French MS. in the Bodleian Library, were printed for private distribution by the Rev. J. J. Conybeare. Bindley, pt. iii. 268, 16s. Inglis, 1070, 1l. Boswell, 2472, 1l. 4s. Bishop Randolph, 631, 1l. 2s. Bright, 9s.

Another version, from MSS. at Lincoln and Cambridge. *See* PERCY SOCIETY, Appendix.

Octavian Imperator. An ancient English metrical romance printed in the third volume of Weber's Collection. It is remarkable for the singularity of its stanzas, and its giving a curious specimen of the Hampshire dialect, nearly as it is now spoken.

OCTOBER CLUB. History of the Lond. 1711, 8vo.

O'DALY, Dom. de Rosario. Initium, Incrementa et Exitus Familiæ Geraldinorum Desmoniæ Comitum, Palatinorum Kyerriæ in Hibernia, ac Persecutionis Hereticorum descriptio, ex nonnullis Fragmentis collecta, ac Latinitate donata. Ulyssip. 1655, 8vo.

Collation. Pp. 1-408; title and prefatory matter, 41 leaves; index, &c. 9 leaves. Bindley, pt. ii. 2165, 21l. resold Heber, pt. iv. 12l. Sotheby (Bp. Daly), June 25, 1858, 15l.

ODDITIES.—Book of Oddities, or wonderful Story-teller, by Jacky Strange. Lond. Cooke, n. d. 12mo.

Nassau, pt. i. 255, 12s.

ODDY, J. Jepson, European Commerce. Lond. 1805, 4to.
Pp. 651, with a canal and river map of Europe. Goldsmid, 657, 10s.

ODELL, J. M. A. An Essay on the Elements, Accents, and Prosody of the English Language. Lond. 1806, 12mo. 3s. 6d.
Intended to have been printed as an introduction to Mr. Boucher's Supplement to Dr. Johnson's Dictionary.

— Thomas. A brief and short Treatise called the Christian's Fatherland. Amst. 1635, 4to.
A living author boasts that he was the first to introduce the word 'Fatherland' into the English language; but it will be seen that Thomas Odell anticipated him nearly two centuries.

O'DRISCOL, John. The History of Ireland. Lond. 1827, 8vo. 2 vols. 7s.
An excellent, clear, concise, and manly work. See Quarterly Review, xlvi. 43—70.

Moral, Political, and Religious Views of Ireland. Lond. 1823, 8vo. 2 vols. 7s.
An eloquent work, highly praised by Moore in his Memoirs of Capt. Rock.

OECOLAMPADIUS, John. A Sermon of Jhon Oecolampadius to yong Men and Maydens, translated by John Foxe. Lond. hy me Humfrey Powell—sould by Hugh Syngleton, &c. 16mo.
Contains C 7, in eights. Inglis, 1071, 6s.
John Oecolampadius his Epistle, that there ought to be no Respect of Personages of the Poore, but all to be holpe and comforted in their Necessities. Ipswich by John Oswen, 1548, 16mo. From Maunsell's Catalogue, p. 76.

OFFICES.—Office for Penitents, or a Form of Prayer fit to be used in sinful and distracted Times. 1691, 8vo. 9s.
Privately printed. Prefixed is a portrait of John Ashton.

Office of Christian Parents. Camb. 1616. 4to. 6s.

The Office of the Holy Week. Paris, by the widow Chrestien, 1670, 8vo. with plates by Hollar. Blim, 6s. Sir M. M. Sykes, pt. II. 569, 1l. 2s. Bindley, pt. II. 2030, 1s. 6d. White Knights, 3149, 1l. 11s. Nassau, pt. I. 2454, morocco, 14. 15s. Townley, pt. —. 567, 5l. 2s. 6d.

The compleat Office of the Holy Week, with Notes and Explications out of Latin and French (by Walter Kirkham Blount). Lond. 1687, 8vo. With plates by Hollar.

Office of the B. V. Mary. Antwerp, 1604 and 1615, sm. 8vo.—Rouen, 1632.—St. Omers, 1651.—Antwerp. (Lat. and Eng.) 1652.—Lond. by Henry Hills, 1687, 8vo. Hawtrey, pt. II. 14. 2s. The Roman Catholic form of prayer published by order of King James II. Garrick, 1704, 2s.
.*Modern editions of all the Roman Catholic Service Books are kept in print.

OFFICIA S. S. Patricii, Columbæ, Brigidæ et aliorum quorandam Hiberniæ Sanctorum. Parisiis, Blagaert, 1620, 8vo.
This collection was edited by Thomas Messingham, author of the Florilegium Sanctorum. Heber, pt. iv, 1241, 5l. 1s.

OFFICIUM beatæ Mariæ Virginis, in Usum Ecclesiæ Sarum. Paris, per T. Kerver, 1510, 8vo.—1531, 8vo.
See Bibl. Harleians, 8vo. vol. i. p. 90, where a copy of this date is described as being on VELLUM, and other impressions of this Roman Catholic Service are noted.
—In English, 1531, 8vo.—Latin, 1534, 8vo.—Latin and Eng. 1535, 8vo—Latin and Eng. Lond. 1536, 8vo.—Rothomagi, Lat. and Eng. 1538, 8vo.—Rothomagi, Lat. and Eng. 1556.—Lat. and Eng. Lond. 1557, 8vo. Also three other editions in 8vo and 4to. printed at London without date.

O'FLAHERTY, Roderic. Ogygia, sive Rerum Hibernicarum Chronologia. Lond. 1685, 4to.
A great fund of knowledge and information relating to Irish transactions and eras. Hibbert, 5847, 14. 6s. Heber, pt. I. fine, morocco, 2l. 12s. 6d. The volume consists of pages 44 and 700, not including title, epistola dedicatoria Jacobo Duci Eboracensi et Albaniensi, approbatio Dom. Dudlei Loftus D. Richardi Belling literæ, seven leaves.

Ogygia; or, a chronological Account of Irish Events, translated by the Rev. James Heley, A.D. Dublin, 1793, 8vo. 2 vols. Sotheby's in 1825, 14. 5s. Collation—Vol. I. pp. lxxxiii. and 262, also a list of subscribers and errata, 8 pages. Vol. II. pp. 418, with title and contents, two leaves.

Ogygia vindicated against the Objections of Sir George Mackenzie, by C. O'Conor. Dublin, 1775, 8vo. Garrick, 1703. 11s. 6d.

O'GALLAGHER, Felix. An Essay on the Investigation of the first Principles of Nature; together with the Application thereof to solve the Phænomena of the physical System. Lond. 1785-6, 8vo. 2 pts.

OSBORNE, Elizabeth. The History of Essex from the earliest Period to the present Time. Lond. 1814, 4to. vol 1. plates, 7s.
Published at 15s.; no more has appeared. LARGE PAPER, with proof plates. Published at 5l. 5s. Mr. Strutt, the antiquary, was related to Mrs. Ogborne, and assisted largely in this work.

OGDEN, Samuel, D.D. Sermons to which is prefixed, an Account of the Author's Life, together with a Vindication of his Writings against some late Objections. Camb. 1780, small 8vo. 2 vols.
Published by Dr. Hallifax. Heath, 1111, 11s. 6d. Bp. of Ely, 680, 17s.—Second edition. Lond. 1786, 2 vols. Bindley, pt. ll. 2027, 11s. 6d.—Fourth edition. Lond. 1788, 2 vols. Willett, 1264, 1l. 10s.—Fifth edit. Lond. 1805, 12s.
Gilbert Wakefield observed: 'These sermons display that perfect propriety and purity of English diction, that chastised terseness of composition, which have scarcely been equalled by any writer. Like Cicero, he wants nothing to complete his meaning; like Demosthenes, he can suffer no deduction without essential injury to the sentence.' Dr. Johnson said, 'he fought the infidels with their own weapons.'

OGILBY, John. Relatione de Incarceratione et Martyrii P. Joannis Ogilbei nationis Scoti e Soc. Jesu Presbyteri. Duaci, 1615, 8vo.
Bright, 17s.

— John (Cosmographer). Works.
Towneley, pt. ll. 1191, 5 vols. viz. China, Asia, America, and England, 8l. 5s. North, pt. ll. 1434, 7 vols. 7l. 12s. 6d. Nassau, pt. ll. 416, 7 vols. viz. Britannia, 2 vols. in 1; China, 2 vols.; Japan, Asia, and Africa. 11l. 11s.
The Relation of his Majesties (King Chas. II.) Entertainment passing through the City of London to his Coronation, with a Description of the triumphal Arches and Solemnity. Lond. 1661, folio, pp. 40. This may be considered only as a rough sketch of the ceremonial, published in 1662. Rhodes, 2290, with John Tatham's Aqua-triumph, 1662, 2l. 15s.—Edinb. 1661, 4to. Rhodes, 1606, 1l. 2s.— New edition, by Wm. Morgan. Lond. Wilkinson, 1686, folio, 29 pages, 10s. 6d.

The Entertainment of his most Excellent Majestie Charles II. in his Passage through the City of London to his Coronation. Lond. 1662, folio, pp. 192, with plates by Hollar, &c. A splendid volume, published at the King's command. It has proved of infinite service in succeeding coronations. Bindley, pt. II. 1717, 2l. 10s. Dent, pt. II. 627, 5l. 5s. Hibbert, 5881, 2l. 14s. Willett, 1788, 9l. 19s. 6d. Sharp, 5l. 5s.

Africa, being an accurate Description of the Regions of Ægypt, Barbary, Lybia, and Billedulgarid, &c. &c. Lond. 1670, folio, 1l. 1s. pp. 768. and 8 leaves, including frontispiece, title, dedication to King Charles II. &c. with maps and sculptures. Page 763 contains directions for placing the maps and sculptures. Ogilby's Africa is little more than an English version of Dapper's work.

America; being the latest and most accurate Description of the New World. Lond. 1671, folio, 2l. 2s. pp. 675, beside frontispiece, title, catalogue of the authors, and contents, 8 leaves, with maps and sculptures. Page 675 contains directions for placing the whole-sheet prints. LARGE PAPER.

Atlas Japannensis; being remarkable Addresses, by Way of Embassy, from the East India Company of the United Provinces to the Emperor of Japan. Lond. 1670, folio, 1l. 1s. North, pt. II. 1435, with Embassy to China, 1673, 2l. 2s.

Atlas Chinensis; being a Relation of remarkable Passages in two Embassies from the East India Company of the United Provinces. From the Original of A. Montanus. Lond. 1671-3, folio, 2 vols. 1l. 11s. 6d.—Second edition (only one volume). Lond. 1673, folio.

Asia, in two Parts. The first Part, being an accurate Description of Persia, the Empire of the Great Mogul, and other Parts of India. Part II. containing an Embassy from the East India Company of the United Provinces to the Emperor of China. (This part 2 is not in the volume, and refers to the China published in the same year.) Lond. 1673, fol. 1l. 5s.

Britannia, Volume the first; or, an Illustration of the Kingdom of England and Dominion of Wales, by a geographical and historical Description of the principal Roads thereof, printed on 100 copper plates. Lond. 1675, folio, 1l. 1s. Marquis of Townshend, 2462, 1l. 5s. Brockett, 2347, russia, 5l. 5s. — Second edition, revised, and apparently abridged. Lond. 1698, fol. New edition, improved by John Owen and E. Bowen. Lond. 1731 (engraved throughout), sm. 4to. 10s. 6d. See OWEN.

Explanation of the large Map of London, by J. Ogilby and W. Morgan. Lond. 1677, 4to.

Ogilby likewise published splendid translations of *Æsop*, *Homer*, and *Virgil*, also a fine edition of the BIBLE; which see.

OGILVIE, Sir George, Bart. A true Account of the Preservation of the Regalia of Scotland, viz. Crown, Sword, and Sceptre, from falling into the Hands of the English Usurpers, by Sir George Ogilvie of Barras, Knight and Baronet ; with the Blazon of that Family. Edinb. 1701, 4to.

A curious and authentic narrative, reprinted in the eleventh vol. of the Somers Collection of Tracts; also in the Bannatyne Club volume, Regalia of Scotland *See* APPENDIX.

OGILVIE, John. A true Relation of the Proceedings against John Ogilvie, a Jesuit, executed at Glasgow, the last of Februarie, Anno 1615. Edinb. 1615, 4to.

A copy is in the British Museum, Gordonstoun, 1971, 1l. 11s. 6d.

— John, D.D. Poems on several Subjects. Lond. 1769, 8vo. 2 vols. 9s.

Dr. Johnson observed of these poems, 'he could find no thinking in them.' A former edition, 1762, 4to.

Sermons (6) on several Subjects. Edinb. 1767, 12mo.

Philosophical and critical Observations on the Nature, Characters, and various Species of Composition. Lond. 1774, 8vo. 2 vols. 6s.

Rona, a Poem, in seven Books, illustrated with a correct Map of the Hebrides and elegant Engravings. Lond. 1777, 4to. 5s.

An Inquiry into the Causes of the Infidelity and Scepticism of the Times; with occasional Observations on the Writings of Herbart, Shaftesbury, Bolingbroke, Hume, Gibbon, Toulmin, &c. Lond. 1783, 8vo. 6s.

The Theology of Plato compared with the Principles of the Oriental and Grecian Philosophers. Lond. 1793, 8vo. Cosset, 5793, 5s.

Britannia, a national epic Poem, in twenty Books; to which is prefixed, a critical Dissertation on epic Machinery. Aberdeen, 1801, 4to.

OGLE, George. Antiquities explained ; or, a Collection of figured Gems. Illustrated by Descriptions taken from the Classics. Lond. 1737, 4to. vol. 1, (all published), 100 plates.

Bright, 6s. 6d. Combe, 1437, 7s. Heber, pt. 1s. 15s.

OGSTON, William. Oratio funebris in Obitum maximi Virorum Georgii (Keith) Marischalli Comitis, Academiæ Marischallanæ, Aberdoniæ, Fundatoris et Mæcenatis munificentissimi. Aberdoniæ, 1623, 4to. 10 leaves.

O'HALLORAN, Sylvester. An Introduction to, and a History of Ireland. Dublin, 1803, 8vo. 3 vols. 18s.

Best edition of these excellent works, which are here printed together.

An Introduction to the Study of the History and Antiquities of Ireland; in which the Assertions of Hume and other Writers are occasionally considered. Illustrated with copperplates. Also two Appendixes; containing, 1. Animadversions on 'an Introduction to the History of Great Britain and Ireland, by J. Macpherson, Esq. 2. Observations on the Memoirs of Great Britain and Ireland, by Sir John Dalrymple. Dublin, 1772, 4to. 7s. 6d. pp. 384, besides title, contents, account of the (four) plates, and subscribers' names, 6 leaves ; also a preliminary discourse, xx pages.

A general History of Ireland, from the earliest Accounts to the close of the twelfth Century, collected from the most authentic Records. In which new and interesting Lights are thrown on the remote Histories of other Nations, as well as both Britains. Lond. 1778, 4to. 2 vols. 18s.

O'HEYN, Joannes. Epilogus Chronologicus, exponens succincte Conventus et Fundationes Sacri Ordinis Prædicatorum in Regno Hyberniæ. Lovanii, 1706, 4to.

O'KEARNAIGH, Joh. Alphabetum Hibernicum. s. l. 1571, 8vo.

A copy is in the Bodleian Library.

O'KEEFFE, John. Dramatic Works. Lond. 1798, 8vo. 4 vols.

Roxburghe, 3876, 2l. 12s. 6d. Duke of York, 3838, 1l. 19s.

Recollections of the Life of John O'Keeffe. Written by himself. Lond. 1828, 8vo. 2 vols. 1l. 8s. With portrait.

Legacy to his Daughters, being his Poetical Works. Lond. 1834, 18mo. 7s. 6d.

OKELEY, Francis. Memoirs of the Life, Death, Burial, and wonderful Writings of Jacob Behmen. Northampton, 1780, 8vo.
— William. Ebenezer, or, a small Monument of great Mercy in his, and four others Deliverance from Slavery at Algiers. Lond. 1674, 8vo.

Jadis, 1s. 9d. 2s. Nassau, pt. 1. 2458, date 1675, with frontispiece, 6s. Heber, pt. 1. 5s., Bliss, 6s.

O'KELLY de Aghrim (William). Descriptio bipartita antiquissimi et Inclyti Regni Hiberniæ, seu majoris Scotiæ Sanctorum Insulæ Vol. I. Viennæ, Austriæ, 1703, 8vo.

Sir Wm. O'Kelly resided at Vienna, where he wrote this History of Ireland, partly in Latin verse and partly in prose. It is supposed that death intervened, as no more was printed. It has been translated into French, and printed at Brussels, 1837, 8vo. with genealogical Table.

OKELY, William, M.D. Pyrology; or, the Connexion between natural and moral Philosophy: with a short Disquisition on the Origin of Christianity. Lond. 1797, 8vo. 4s.

In the Missionary Magazine this author published a renunciation of the opinions expressed in this work.

OLD BAILEY CHRONICLE. *See* NEWGATE CALENDAR.

OLDCASTLE, Hugh. Work on Bookkeeping. Lond. 1543.

Mentioned by John Mellis in 'A briefe Instruction.' 1588.

— Sir John. The Mirror of Martyrs, or the Life and Death of that thrice-valiant Captaine and most godly Martyr, Sir John Oldcastle, Knt. [Lord Cobham.] Lond. V. S. for William Wood, 1601.

In verse. A copy in the Pepysian Collection, Cambridge.

Life and Times of Sir John Oldcastle. Lond. 18—, 8vo. 2 vols. 1l. 1s.

See BALE, John, p. 108. GILPIN, Wm. SHAKESPEARE, W. WEEVER, John.

OLDE, John. The Acquital or Purgation of Edward the VI. Kyng of Englande, &c. and of the Churche of Englande refourmed and gouerned vnder hym, agaynst al suche as blasphemously and traiterously infame hym or the sayd Church, of Heresie or Sedicion. (By John Bale.) 16mo.

F, in eights, neatly printed in BLACK LETTER, with the quotations in Italics, and the following colophon in Roman:—
'Emprinted at Waterford the 7 Daye of Nouembre, 1555,' (supposed to be the second book printed in Ireland), but certainly with the types of the Confession by Trudial in Southwark. Roxburghe, 8429, 1l. 6s. George Chalmers, pt. iii. 2l. 2s. Sir M. M. Sykes, pt. ii. 570, with John Story's Epistle, 1555, 17s. 6d. 6d. Heber, pt. II. with the Confession, 1556, and the Societie of the Rosarie, 1500, 6l. 16s. Heber, pt. vi. corner of leaf wanting, 2l. Sotheby's, H. Thomas, Dec. 1853, 6l.

A Confession of the most auncient and true Christen Catholike olde Beliefe, according to the Ordre of the xij Articles of our common Crede, set furthe in Englishe by J. O. Southwarke by Christopher Truthal. 1556, 16mo. BLACK LETTER. Contains E in eights. Heber, pt. II. 18s. russold Bliss, 2l. 2s. Herber, 1834, mor. 1l. 10s.

A shorte Description of Antichriste, with a warnyng not to be desceaved by the hypocrisie and craftie conveyance of the Clergie. Southwark, C. Truthal, n. d. 12mo. BLACK LETTER, 43 leaves, and one blank. Heber, pt. II. 2l. 10s.

See GOALTAM, Rodolph. RIDLEY, N.

OLDFIELD, Mrs. Anne. Authentick Memoirs of Mrs. Oldfield. Lond. 1730, 4to.

Reed, 8632, 2s. 6d. Hibbert, 5530, 4s See EGERTON, W. The Lover's Miscellany, p. 1402. With a small head on the title, should be found attached to Betterton's History of the Stage, published by E. Curll, Lond. 1741, 8vo.

— H. G. Anecdotes of Archery. Lond. 1791, 12mo. 2s.

A short collection of historical passages, tracing the practice of archery from the earliest notices among almost all nations. History and Antiquities of Tottenham High Cross. *See* DYSON, R. H.

— Thomas Hinton Burley. The representative History of Great Britain and Ireland, being a History of the House of Commons, and of the Counties, Cities, Bo-

1722 OLD OLD

roughs, &c. Lond. 1816, 8vo. 6 vols. 1l. 1s.
Best edition. The earlier ones were in 8 and 4 vols. 8vo.

OLDHAM, John. The Compositions in Prose and Verse of Mr. John Oldham. To which are added Memoirs of his Life, and explanatory Notes by Edward Thompson. Lond. 1770, 12mo. 3 vols.
Best edition. Garrick, 1708, 6s. Nassau, pt. I. 2460, 6s. Bibl. Anglo-Poet. 507, 15s. — 1710, 8vo. 2s. Bibl. Anglo-Poet. 600, 12s. — 1722, 12mo. 3 vols. Hibbert, 5764, 2s. 6d.

OLDISWORTH, G. The Holy Royalist. Lond. 1660, 4to. Dedicated to King Charles II.
Heber, pt. viii. the dedication copy, 1l. 11s.

OLD MAID, The, a periodical Paper. A new Edition revised and corrected by the Editor, Mary Singleton, Spinster. Lond. 1764, 12mo.
By Mrs. Frances Brooke.—Nos. 1 to 57 1755-6, folio. Bright, 4s.

OLDMAYNE, Timothy. Life's Brevitie and Deathes Debility, a funeral Sermon on 'Edward Lewkenor, Esquire, in whose Death is ended the Name of that renowned Family in Suffolke. 1636, 4to.
Inglis, 1122, 7s.

OLDMIXON, John. History of England. Lond. 1730, 5, 9, folio, 3 vols. 3l. 3s.
A violent party history, written in opposition to the Stuart family. According to the Edinburgh Reviewers, Oldmixon is 'an historical writer of moderate talent, whose works are not without useful information.' Hollis, 1192, with Reply to Bp. Atterbury, 1732, 5l. 16s. 6d. Heber, pt. xi. 1l. 13s. Contents. — Vol. I. The Reigns of Henry VIII. Edward VI. Mary and Elizabeth, 1739. Gough, 2714, 1l. Vol. II. The Reign of the Stuarts. 1730. Gough, 2713, 1l. 16s. Marquis of Townshend, 2463, 1l. 2s. Vol. III. The Reigns of William and Mary, Anne, and George I. 1735. The volumes often occur separately.
Remarks on Oldmixon's History of the Stuarts. Lond. 1731, 8vo.
Letter to the Subscribers to the History of the Stuarts. 8vo. 8s.

Reply to Bishop Atterbury's Vindication of Smalridge, Aldrich and himself. Lond. 1732, folio.
Memoirs of North Britain; wherein it is proved that the Scots Nation have always been zealous in the Defence of the Protestant Religion and Liberty. Lond. 1715, 8vo. 5s. Like several other of his works, this is anonymous.
Memoirs of Ireland from the Restoration to the present Time. Lond. 1716, 8vo. 5s. Bishop of Ely, 639, 6s.
A Defence of our ancient and modern Historians against the frivolous Cavils of a late Pretender to critical History, by Zachary Grey, LL.D. Lond. 1725, 8vo. Reed, 4099, 12s. — With an Appendix. Lond. 1730, 8vo.
A Review of Dr. Zach. Grey's Defence of our ancient and modern Historians, by J. Oldmixon. Lond. 1725, 8vo.
Critical History of England, ecclesiastical and civil. Lond. 1728, 8vo. 2 vols. Hollis, 555, 2s. Gough, 1736, 2s. 6d. — 1728, 2 vols. Marquis of Townshend, 918, 4s.
British Empire in America, containing the History, Discovery, Settlement, Progress, &c. of the British Colonies in America. Lond. 1708, 8vo. 2 vols.
Clarendon and Whitlock compared. Lond. 1727, 8vo. Bindley, pt. i. 1054, 5s. 3d.
Memoirs of the Press, historical and political, from 1710 to 1740. Lond. 1742, 8vo. Hollis, 995, 6s.
Poems in Imitation of Anacreon. Lond. 1696, 8vo. pp. 148. 3s. Bibl. Anglo-Poet. 843, 15s. LARGE PAPER. Skegg, 1l. 2s.
Dramatic Pieces, viz. Amyntas, the Grove; or, Love's Paradise, and the Governor of Cyprus. Lond. 1698, 1700, 1703, 4to. Roxburghe, 3230, 13s.
Muses Mercury: or, the Monthly Miscellany, consisting of Poems, Prologues, &c. never before printed, to which is added an Account of the Stage. Lond. 1707, 4to. Field, 972. 10s. 6d.
Amores Britannici, or heroic Epistles in Imitation of Ovid's. Lond. 1703, 8vo. Oldmixon published other Poems. Pope has assigned him a place in his Dunciad, among the devotees of Dulness.
Poems and Translations by several Hands; to which is added, the Hospital of Fools, by the late William Walsh, Esq. Lond. 1714, 8vo. pp. (20) and 122. This volume contains The Salisbury Ballad, with curious learned and critical notes by Dr. Walter Pope, 1713, being a delicate satire on Dutch commentators.
Court Tales; or, a History of the Amours of the present Nobility. To which is added, a compleat Key. Lond. Roberts, 1717, 8vo. front.—Second edition (with dedication to Sir W. Temple). Lond. Curll, 1720, 8vo. front. [ANONYMOUS.]

OLDNALL, W. R. Practice of the Court of Great Sessions on the Carmarthen Circuit, much of which is common to all the Courts of Great Sessions in Wales. Lond. 1814, 8vo. 1*l*. 10s.

Formerly an esteemed work, but now obsolete.

OLDYS, William. The British Librarian; exhibiting a compendious Review or Abstract of our most scarce, useful and valuable Books in all Sciences as well in Manuscript as in Print: with many Characters, historical and critical, of the Authors, their Antagonists, &c. Lond. 1738, 8vo.

An esteemed work. Pp. 402, with introduction and contents. Some copies have separate titles to the six numbers. No. 1 was published Jan. 1737, No. 6, June, 1737. Reed, 2720, 15s. Strettell, 1047, 15s. Gough, 649, 16s. Bindley, pt. II. 2023, 1*l*. 5s. Towneley, pt. I. 384, uncut, 1*l*. 9s. Williams, 1363, 1*l*. 10s. Sir F. Thompson, 615, 1*l*. 11s. 6d. Jadis, 57, portrait inserted, 1*l*. 11s. 6d. resold Bliss, 8v. 6d. LARGE PAPER! Dowdeswell, 529, russia, 1*l*. 1s.

The Life of Sir Walter Raleigh. 1735, folio. With portrait. Gough, 2716, 5s. 6d.— 1760, 8vo. Gough, 2574, 5s. 6d.

This writer, Oldys, to whom the lovers of biography and literary history are much indebted, edited many valuable works, particularly the Harleian Miscellany, Biographia Britannica, &c. His MS. Notes on Langbaine's Account of the English Dramatic Poets are frequently quoted by Steevens, Malone, &c. &c. See LANGBAINE, Gerard. PAMPHLETS. RALEIGH, Sir W.

OLEARIUS, Adam. The Voyages and Travels of the Ambassadors from the Duke of Holstein to the great Duke of Muscovy and King of Persia; began in the year 1639 and finished in 1646. Translated by John Davies. Lond. 1662, folio.

In this volume will also be found The Travels of Joh. Albert de Mandelslo from Persia into the East Indies, and from thence through England into Germany; began in the year 1633, and finished 1660. Willett, 1796, 13s. Marquis of Townshend, 2464, 13s. Nassau, pt. II. 4171, 1*l*. 8s. Drury, 8226, 1*l*. 4s.—1669, folio. Gordonstoun, 1707, 7s.

O'LEARY, Rev. Arthur. Miscellaneous Tracts. Dublin, 1781, 8vo.

Roxburghe, 6984, 2s. Marquis of Townshend, 2274, 8s. 6d. O'Leary published other volumes.

The Life of the Rev. Arthur O'Leary, by T. R. England. 1822, 8vo. 6s. With portrait of O'Leary.

OLERON.—The Laws of Oleron or Auleron.

These laws, instituted by King Richard I. on his return from the Holy Land, anno 1194, were received by the nations of Europe, as the basis of their marine constitution. They will be found in The Rutter of the Sea, printed by W. Copland, The Sea Laws, in Malyne's Lex mercatoria, in Godolphin's Jurisdiction of the Admiralty, &c.

OLEVIAN, Gasper. An Exposition of the Symbols of the Apostles, or rather of the Articles of Faith, gathered out of the catechising Sermons of Gasper Olenian Treuir, and translated by John Fielde. Lond. 1581, 8vo.

Pp. 253, with two dedications, one to 'Ambrose Earl of Warwicke,' by L F., the other to 'Frederike, Counts Palatine of the Rhene,' by G. O. Inglis, 1075, 6s.— 1582, 8vo.

Gasp. Olenian on the Creede, Commandements, Lords Praier, and Sacraments, translated by Rich. Saintbarbe. Lond. 1581. From Maunsell's Catalogue, p. 31.

OLIVE LEAF, The, or universal A.B.C. 1603.

Mentioned in Ritson's Bibliog. Poet. p. 171, note.*

OLIVER and ROSE. A Dialogue of Familiar Talk between two Neighbours, concerning the chiefest Ceremonies, that were by the mighty Power of God's most holy Word suppressed in England, and now for our Vnworthinees set vp again by the Bishops. Interlocut. Olyuer, Professor of the Gospel, and Nicholas Rose, led in blynd Superstition. Roan, by Michael Woode, 20 February, 1564, 16mo.

— Rev. George, D.D. of Exeter. Historic Collections relating to the

Monasteries in Devon. Exeter, 1820, 8vo.
Privately printed. Hibbert, 5771, 15s.
Monasticon Dioecesis Exoniensis; being a Collection of Records and Instruments Illustrating the ancient conventual, collegiate, and eleemosynary Foundations in the Counties of Cornwall and Devon. With a SUPPLEMENT, comprising a List of the Dedications of Churches in the Diocess. Exeter, 1846, folio, pp. 488, besides title, dedication, contents, a list of subscribers, all leaves; 2 plates of Illuminated letters from an ancient Psalter belonging to the Dean and Chapter, and three of engraved seals. The book pub. at 4l.; the Suppl. at 12s. 6d.
Collections towards illustrating the Biography of the English, Scotch, and Irish members of the Society of Jesus. Exeter, 1838, 8vo.—Lond. Dolman, 1845, 8vo. pp. 282, only 250 printed.
Ecclesiastical Antiquities in Devon, being Observations on several Churches in Devonshire, &c. Lond. Nichols, 1844, 8vo. 2 vols. 3 plates. 1l.
Visit to Exeter. Exeter, 1821, 8vo. Hibbert, 5772, 6s.
History of Exeter. Exeter, 1821, 8vo. Drury, 2009, 8s. 6d.
Collections Illustrating the History of the Catholic Religion in the Counties of Cornwall, Devon, Dorset, Somerset, Wilts, and Gloucester, (in two parts) Historical and Biographical; with Notices of the Dominican, Benedictine, and Franciscan Orders in England. Lond. Dolman, 1857, 8vo. pp. 576, 12s.

OLIVER, Rev. George, D.D. History and Antiquities of the Town and Minster of Beverley, in the County of York. Beverley, 1829, 4to. 2 vols. (generally bound in 1), numerous plates, 2l. 2s. LARGE PAPER, 3l. 3s.
An historical and descriptive Account of the collegiate Church of Wolverhampton. Wolv. 1836, 8vo. plates, 7s.
The existing Remains of the ancient Britons, within a small District lying between Lincoln and Sleaford; in a Letter to Sir E. F. Bromhead. Lond. 1847, 12mo. 1s. 6d.
An historical Account of the Religious Houses formerly situated on the eastern Side of the River Witham (Lincolnshire). Lond. 1846, 12mo. 4s.
The Monumental Antiquities of Grimsby. Hull, 1825, 8vo. 10s. 6d.
An Account of the Corpus Pageants, Miracle Plays, Religious Mysteries, &c. which were practised at Sleaford in the fifteenth Century; with an Appendix, containing the Traditions of Lincoln Heath. 1836, 8vo. 5s.
The History and Antiquities of St. James's Church, Grimsby. 18—, 8vo. 1s. 6d.

Masonic Works.

The Antiquities of Freemasonry; comprising Illustrations of the five grand Periods of Masonry, from the Creation of the World to the Dedication of Solomon's Temple. Lond. 1823, 8vo. four maps, 12s.—New edition, improved. Lond. 1843, 8vo. 10s. 6d. LARGE PAPER, roy. 8vo. 16s. reduced 12s.
The Star in the East, shewing the Analogy which exists between the Lectures of Freemasonry. The Mechanician of Initiation into its Mysteries, and the Christian Religion. Lond. 1825, fcap. 8vo. 5s. 6d.—New edition, revised and enlarged. Lond. 1842, fcap. 8vo. 5s. 6d.
Signs and Symbols, illustrated and explained in a Course of twelve Lectures on Freemasonry. (Vol. I.) Grimsby, 1826, 8vo. 9s.—Second edition. Lond. 1837, 8vo. 9s.—New edition. Lond. 1857, 12mo. 7s.
Signs and Symbols, Vol. II.; or the History of Initiation, in twelve Lectures; comprising a detailed Account of the Rites, Ceremonies, &c. of all the Secret Institutions of the ancient World. Lond. 1829, 8vo. 7s. 6d.—New edition. Lond. 1841, 8vo. 10s. 6d. LARGE PAPER, 16s.; reduced, 12s.
Illustrations of Masonry. By W. Preston. Fourteenth edition, with copious Notes, and bringing the History of Freemasonry down to the Year 1829, by the Rev. G. Oliver, D.D. Lond. 1829, 12mo. 8s.—Fifteenth edition, 1840, 9s.—Sixteenth edition, 1849, 9s.
The Theocratic Philosophy of Freemasonry, in XII Lectures. Lond. 1840, 8vo. 10s. 6d.—New edition, with additional notes and Illustrations. Lond. 1856, 12mo. 7s.
Brief History of the Witham Lodge, Lincoln. Lond. 1841, 8vo. 1s. 6d.
History of Freemasonry from 1829 to 1841. Lond. 1841, 12mo. 4s.
The Historical Land Marks, and other Evidences of Freemasonry explained in a series of Practical Lectures, with copious Notes, Portrait, and Illustrations. Lond. 1844-6, 8vo. 2 vols. 2l. LARGE PAPER, roy. 8vo. 3l. 6s.
Jacob's Ladder; the Ascent to Heaven plainly pointed out in a Series of practical Sermons. Lond. 1845, 12mo. 4s. red. 2s. 6d.
An Apology for the Freemasons. Lond. 1846, 8vo. 1s.
Some Account of the Schism during the last Century amongst the free and accepted Masons in England, &c.; in a Letter to Dr. R. T. Crucifix. Lond. 1847, 8vo. 2s. 6d.

OLIVER, Rev. Geo.—*continued.*
The Origin of the Royal Arch Degree; the Insignia of the Royal Arch Degree illustrated and explained. Lond. 1847. 8vo. woodcuts and plate, 5s. 6d.
A Mirror for the Johannite Masons. In a Series of Letters. Lond. 1848, fcap. 8vo. 5s.
Institutes of Masonic Jurisprudence; being an Exemplification of the English Book of Constitutions. Lond. 1849, 12mo. —Again, 1859, 12mo. 9s.
Book of the Lodge, or Officers Manual. Lond. 1849, 17mo. 4s.—New edition, to which is added A Century of Aphorisms, 1856, 12mo. 5s.
The Symbol of Glory, showing the Object and End of Masonry. In thirteen Lectures. Lond. 1860, 8vo. front. 10s. 6d.
The Revelations of a Square, exhibiting a graphic Display of the Sayings and Doings of Masons. Lond. 1855, 12mo. with curious engravings, 9s. 6d.
Portrait of the Rev. Dr. Oliver in Masonic Costume, engraved on steel, 9 by 5 inches, 1s. India paper, 1s. 6d.
The Golden Remains of the early Masonic Writers. For this, and other books on Freemasonry edited by Dr. Oliver, see FREEMASON, p. 822.

OLIVER, Peter, LL.D. The Scripture Lexicon: or, a Dictionary of above 4000 proper names of Persons and Places mentioned in the old and new Testament; divided into Syllables with their proper Accents. Oxford, 1810, 8vo. 6s.
A useful work. With an Appendix. Birmingham, 1784-5, 8vo. 4s.—1792, 8vo. Williams, 12s7, 12s.—Oxford, 1818, 8vo. 8s.—Lond. Washbourne, 1843, 18mo. 8s. 6d. —Edited, with an explanation of obsolete words, by the Rev. H. C. Cotton. Oxford, 1832, 12mo. 6s.

—— Thomas. The new Handling of the Planisphere. By Thomas Olyver. 1601.

—— William, M.D. A practical Dissertation on Bath Waters. Lond. 1707, 8vo.
'A full and finished practical discourse.' —*Nicholson.*

OLIVER of Castile. The Historye of Olyuer of Castylle and the fayre Helayne. Lond. by W. de Worde, 1518, 4to.
Heber, pt. vi. 6l. 16s. wanting title-page. It ends on the reverse of the fourth leaf after sign. Q IIIJ. The signatures run in fours and eights alternately.

Olivares of Castille and Arthur of Dalgarve. 1586. Goldsmid, 529, 15s.

OLIVET, Joseph. Josephi Oliveti Delectus Commentariorum in M. T. Ciceronis Opera omnia. Oxonii, Talboys, 1821, 4to. pub. at 5l. 5s.
Printed (250 copies only) to complete the Clarendon Press edition of Olivet's Cicero. —Lond. R. Priestley, 1819, 8vo. 3 vols. 1l. 10s. This edition was printed as a sequel to Priestley's edition of Ernesti's Cicero, 8 vols. 1819. See p. 457.

OLIVIER, G. A. Travels in the Ottoman Empire, Egypt and Persia. Lond. 1801, 4to. 2 vols. with atlas (generally bound in one).
An esteemed work. Hibbert. 6017, 5s. 6d. —1801, 8vo. 2 vols. with atlas in 4to. Gough, 2702, 17s.

OLLA PODRIDA.—The Olla Podrida, complete in forty-four Numbers. Lond. 1788, 8vo. 6s.
A weekly publication edited by the Rev. Tho. Monro, containing Papers by Bishop Horne, the Rev. Mr. Kett, &c. Fonthill, 59, 14s.—1890, 2 vols. Hibbert, 5775, 5s. See MARRYAT.

OLOR ISCANUS. See VAUGHAN, Henry.

OMBRE.—The royal Game of the Ombre. Lond. 1665, 12mo. 5s.

O'MEARA, Barry E. Napoleon in Exile. Lond. 1822 (three editions in one year), 8vo. 2 vols. with three portraits of Napoleon.
New editions (from stereotype plates). Lond. Virtue and Co., 8vo. 2 vols. 1l. 8s.
Copious notices of this work appeared in the Edinb. Review, xxxvii. 164-204, Quart. Rev. xxviii. 219-64. See also Edinb. Review, xxxiii. 148-70.

—— Dermot. See MEARA, Dermitius.

OMNIBUS et Singulis. See SCOTT, Patrick.

O'MOLLOY, Francis. Grammatica Latino-Hibernica. Rome, 1677, 12mo.
An abstract of this work will be found in E. Lluyd's Archæologia Britannica. Heber, pt. viii. 1l. 8s. pt. x. 16s.
Lucerna Fidelium, or the Lamp of the Faithful. Roma, Propaganda fide, 1676 12mo. 7s. 6d. *Printed in the Irish character.*

A Catechism in Irish. Rome, 1677. Also printed in the Irish character, and sometimes attached to the former volume, 7s. 6d. *See also* MOLLOY.

O NEAL, Philom. Petition of Sir Philom O Neal, Generall of Ireland, to the Parliament of England. 1641, 4to.
Townley, pt. 1. 729, 5s.

O'NEIL, ——. Six Etchings by William Crouch, from Sketches by Mr. O'Neill, of the Ruins of the late Fire at Christ Church, Oxford (March 3, 1809). To which is prefixed some Account of the Fire and the Buildings injured by it. Oxford, 1809, folio.
These etchings are accompanied by a ground plan of the building, a page of reference, and 4 pages of descriptive letter press. Proofs on India Paper.

—— (A.) Dictionary of Spanish Painters, with an Account of the present localities of their pictures, &c. Lond. 1833, roy. 8vo. 2 vols. Pub. at 2l. 12s. red. 1l. 1s.

ONESIMUS, (*i. e.* P. L. Courtier). The Pulpit; or a biographical and literary Account of eminent popular Preachers; interspersed with occasional clerical Criticism. Lond. 1809-14, 8vo. 3 vols. 18s.
This work occasioned some controversy.

ONOSANDER. Onosandro Platonico, of the generall Captaine and of his Office, translated by Peter Whytehorne. Lond. 1563, 12mo. 1l. 1s.
BLACK LETTER. Dedicated to Thomas, Duke of Norfolk. 136 pages, besides 8 leaves of preface, 3 of table, and 1 of imprint.

OPENSHAW, Robert. Short Questions and Answeares, containing the Summe of Christian Religion, newly enlarged with the Testimonies of Scripture. Lond. 1590, 16mo.
E 7, in eights. The dedication is dated 28 Jan. 1584.
The Testimonies of Scripture quoted in Page's Catechisme. Lond. 1592, 16mo.
Meditations on eternal Judgment. Lond. 1597, 12mo.

O'PHELAN, John. Epitaphs on the Tombs in the Cathedral Church of St. Canice, Kilkenny, with a Preface, and Observations on the Round Towers of Ireland. Dublin, 1813, folio, 9s.

OPIE, John, R.A. Lectures on Painting, delivered at the Royal Academy of Arts; with a Letter on the Proposals for a public Memorial to the naval Glory of Great Britain. To which are prefixed, a Memoir of his Life, by Mrs. Opie, and other Accounts of his Life and Character. Lond. 1809, 4to. portrait, 10s. 6d.
Dent, pt. ii. 684, 6s.
Reprinted in conjunction with the Lectures of Barry and Fuseli, under the title of 'Lectures on Painting by the Royal Academicians.' Lond. 1848, in Bohn's Standard Library, post 8vo. 5s.

—— Mrs. Amelia. Poems. Lond. 1802-8, 12mo. 7s. 6d.
Frequently reprinted. This lady published a variety of novels and tales, still in much estimation.
Illustrations of Lying in all its Branches, Lond. 1827, 12mo. 2 vols.
Memorials of the Life of Mrs. A. Opie, by C. L. Brightwell. Norwich, 1854, 8vo. portrait.

OPPIAN'S Halieuticks; of the Nature of Fishes and Fishing of the Ancients, in five Books. Translated from the Greek; with an Account of Oppian's Life and Writings, and a Catalogue of his Fishes. Oxford, 1722, royal 8vo. 7s. 6d.
The translators of this celebrated work were Messrs. Diaper and Jones, M.A. both of Balliol College, Oxford. Nassau, pt. i. 2466, 6s. Hibbert, 5785, 8s. 6d. Stanley, 189, morocco, 1l. 5s. Dent, pt. ii. 45, morocco, 1l. 15s.
The first Book of Oppian's Cynegeticon: or Poem of Hunting; trans. into English Verse; with a Dissertation and Oppian's Life prefixed, by John Mawer, A.M. York, T. Gent, 1736, 8vo. 6s.—New title, Lond. 1736, 8vo.

OPUSCULA MYTHOLOGICA, Ethica et Physica, Gr. et Lat. a Tho. Gale. Cantab. 1671, 8vo. 2s. 6d.
A much-improved edition of this work appeared at Amsterdam, 1688, in 8vo. Contents.—Palæphatus, Heraclitus & Ano-

nymns de Incredibilibus; Phornutus de Natura Deorum; Sallustius de Diis; Ocellus Locanus; Timæus Locrus de Anima Mundi; Demophili, Democriti et Secundi Philosophorum Sententiæ; Joannis Pedrasimi Desiderium de Muliere bona et mala; Sesti Pythagorei Sententiæ; Theophrasti Characteres; Pythagoreorum Fragmenta, et Heliodori Larissæi Capita Opticorum. The latter is not included in the Amsterdam edition of 1688, which in all other respects is the best.

Opusculum de universali Mundi Machina. Lond. R. Pynson, n. d. 4to. In a volume. Heber, pt. iv. 2820, 6£.

ORANGE, House of. Lives of the Princes of the illustrious House of Orange. Lond. 1734, 8vo. 6s. with portraits.

Williams, 1192, morocco, 1l. 1s. Copies on FINE PAPER. See MAURIER, Baron.

A Declaration and Publication of the Prince of Orange, contayning the Cause of the necessary Defence against the Duke of Alba. Lond. by John Day, 16mo. Eleven leaves, dated 'Geven the 20 of July, 1568.' Inglis, 1074, 5s.

Supplication to the King of Spayne made by the Prince of Orange, &c. Translated by W. T. Lond. 1573, 16mo. 5s.

A Justification or Clearing of the Prince of Orendge against the false Slaunders wherwith his lillwillers goe about to charge him wrongfully. Lond. Day, 1575, 16mo. This was the famous justification by the Prince on the throwing off the allegiance of Spain. It consists of ninety-four leaves. Reed, 4506, 7s. Heber, pt. v. 2941, 2s. 6d.

The Prince of Orange's Supplication to the King of Spain. Lond. 1576, 4to.

The Apologie or Defence of Prince William of Orange, &c. against the Proclamations and Edict, published by the King of Spaine. Delft, 1581, 4to. Bright, 2s. Reprinted in the Phœnix.

A true Discourse of the Assault committed upon the Person of the Prince of Orange. Lond. 1582, 16mo. Gordonstoun, 807, 3s.

The Prince of Orange's royall Entertainment of the Queen of England. Lond. 1641, 4to.

An Ordinance of the Prince of Orange in Behalf of the Queen of England, forbidding Delinquents to come within ten miles of her Majesty's Court. Whereunto is added the Manner of setting her Majesties Court at the Hague. Lond. 1641, 4to.

See PORTON, W. MEARES, W. WILLIAM III. King of England.

ORARIUM, seu Libellus Precationum. Lond. Grafton, 1546, 16mo.

Inglis, 1075, 1l. 6s. Sotheby, Apl. 1837, 1l. 10s.—Lond. 1547, 12mo. In University Library, Cambridge. — Lond. Gul. Seres, 1560, 12mo. This appears to be the first Latin Prayer Book printed in Q. Elizabeth's Reign. Seres was suspended printing during the reign of Mary I., but regained his privileges after her death. 16mo. L 6, in eights. Heber, wormed, pt. v. in lot 5192.—Lond. Petyt, n. d. 4to. In King's Coll. Cambridge.

ORATIO Dominica, plus centum Linguis, Versionibus, et Characteribus reddita et expressa. Lond. 1700, 4to. 7s. 6d.

Nasman, pt. II. 575, 16s.

Oratio Dominica in diversas omnium fere gentium linguas versa, et propriis cujusque linguæ characteribus expressa; una cum dissertationibus nonnullis de linguarum origine, &c. ; editore Jo. Chamberlayno, (sive potius D. Wilkins). Amst. 1715, 4to. 15s. A few copies were printed on LARGE PAPER, one of which, at Caillard's sale, sold for 240 francs.

ORATIONES ex Poetis Latinis excerptæ. Oxon. 1711, 8vo. vol. 1.

See BENTHAM, Edward.

ORATORES ATTICI, Gr. ex recensione Immanuelis Bekkeri cum Indicibus a Tho. Mitchell. Oxon. 1822-28, 8vo. 10 vols.

In 1823, four leaves of addenda and corrigenda were published. Fifty copies of these 10 vols. were printed on LARGE PAPER, at 16l. 10s. Contents.— Vol. I. 1822, Antiphon, Andocides, and Lysias, 6s. 6d. Vol. II. 1822, Isocrates, 6s. 6d. Vol. III. 1823, Isæus, Æschines, Lycurgus, Dinarchus, 6s. 6d. Vol. IV. (in 4 parts) 1823, Demosthenes, Bekkeri.

To these so-called 4 vols. which are in reality 7, are to be added the following 3 vols. of INDICES, which make up the 1st vols. enumerated in our leading title:—

Indices Græcitatis in Oratores Atticos a T. Mitchell. Oxf. 1828, 8vo. 2 vols. 13s.

Indices Græcitatis Isocraticæ a T. Mitchell. Oxf. 1828, 8vo. 6s. 6d.

Nearly twenty years after the publication of these 10 vols. Bekker's Demosthenes having become out of print, Dindorf was employed to re-edit it, and in doing so added Annotations and Scholia, and subsequently Scholia to Æschines. The vols. are thus stated in the Oxford Catalogue :

DEMOSTHENES, ex recensione G. Dindorfi. Tomi IV. 1846, 8vo. 2l.

— Tomi V. VI. VII. Annotationum Interpretum (in Demosthenem), 1849, 1l. 14s. 6d.

DEMOSTHENES, Tom! VIII. et IX. Scholia (in Demosth.) 1851, 14s.

Scholia Græca in Æschinem et Socratem ex codd. aucta et emendata. Ed. Gul. Dindorfius. Oxf. 1852, 8vo. (a very thin volume) 5s. 6d.

It will be seen that, with Dindorf's additions, the *Oxford Oratores Attici* now form 16 vols. 6l. 11s. No LARGE PAPER copies of Dindorf's volumes have been printed.

ORATORES ATTICI et quos alo vocant Sophistæ. Cum notis Meiskii, Schæferi et. Variorum. Opera et studio Gull. Steph. Dobson. Lond. J. F. Dove, 1828, 8vo. 16 vols. (pub. at 9l.) 5l. 3s., LARGE PAPER (pub. at 18l. 18s.) 6l. 6s., LARGEST PAPER, only 25 printed, (at 16l. 16s. each) 6l. 6s. Contains: Æschines, Andocides, Antiphon, Demades et Sophistarum, (Leobonactis, Herodis, Antisthenis, Alcidamantis, Gorgiæ), quæ extant; Demosthenes, Dinarchus, Isocrates, Isæus, Lycurgus, Lysias.

ORCHARD of Sion. — The Orcharde of Syon, in the whiche is conteyned the Reuelacyons of Scynt Katheryne of Sene, with ghostly Fruytes and precyous Plantes for the Helthe of Mannes Soule. Lond. 1519, folio.

An elegant specimen of W. de Worde's press, with cuts. By signatures it contains to B 4 in the second alphabet, in sixes, but the first alphabet has three characters after a. Prefixed are 9 leaves, containing prologues, &c. Sotheby's in 1823, wanting the prologue, 5l. 15s. 6d. A copy on VELLUM. Dent, pt. ii. 930, with the plates illuminated, bound in velvet, 63l. 2s.

ORDER and Disorder; or, the World made and undone. Being Meditations upon the Creation and the Fall; as it is recorded in the Beginning of Genesis. Lond. 1679, 4to.

Pp. 84. Bibl. Anglo-Poet. 944, 1l. 1s.

ORDER of the Hospitals. See HOSPITALS. NICHOLAS, Sir H.

ORDINAIRE, Abbé. The natural History of Volcanoes; including submarine Volcanoes, and other analogous Phenomena, translated by R. C. Dallas. Lond. 1801, 8vo. 5s.

ORDINALE. See DIRECTORIUM. PICA.

ORDINANCES and Orders. — All the several Ordinances and Orders made by the Lords and Commons assembled in Parliament, concerning sequestring the Estates of Delinquents, Papists, Spies, and Intelligencers, together with Instructions for such Persons as are employed in sequestring of such Delinquents' Estates. Published by order of the House of Commons. 1650, 4to.

This compilation contains some Acts not to be found in Scobell's Collection. *See* LITERAND.

ORDINARY OF CHRISTIANS. — The Ordynarye of Crystyanyte or Crysten Men, newely hystoryed and translated out of Frenshe into Englyshe. Lond. by W. de Worde, 1502, 4to.

This work was of high reputation; being very frequently printed in the original French. A copy of the second edition, printed on VELLUM by Verard (in 1492, French), is among the choice books in the Grenville Collection. The English translation extends to U 4, in sixes, with a table 4 leaves; is adorned with cuts. Towneley, pt. i. 720, 7l. — Lond. W. de Worde? 1506, 4to. 218 leaves, including the table, adorned with cuts. White Knights, 420s, russia, 15l. 15s. Inglis, 1125, 2l. 6s. Hibbert, 6025, russia, 115.17s. Kerr, 21l. Sotheby, April, 1857, 16l. 10s.

The Ordenarye for all faythfull Christians to lead a vertuous and godly Lyfe here in this Vale of Miserie. Translated out of Doutch into Inglysh by Anthony Scoloker. Lond. by Anthony Scoloker for William Seres, 8vo. With a number of woodcuts. — Lond. by Tho. Marshe, 1578, 16mo.

Ordynaries. Lond. by me Elysabeth Pykerynge, late Wyfe to Robert Redman, 1541, sm. 8vo. BLACK LETTER.

ORDNANCE SURVEYS AND MAPS. The Trigonometrical Surveys of Great Britain and Ireland, made by royal authority, were commenced as early as 1784, under the direction of General Roy; and the County of Kent was completed in 1790. The Surveys were continued by Capt. Colby and Capt. Mudge, and their Maps published in 1819, and seq. For many years past, the Ordnance Maps have been published under the direction of Lieut.-Col. Sir H. James, R.E., who is

ORDNANCE SURVEY—*continued.*
superintendent of the Ordnance Surveys. The official Catalogue of the numerous maps on sale may be had of the principal London agents, Messrs. Longman and Co. Paternoster Row, and Mr. Edward Stanford, Charing Cross.

It may be convenient to state here, that the principal Series is the ONE-INCH GENERAL MAPS OF ENGLAND AND WALES, which is in 110 divisions (also 40 in. by 27). Of these, 95 are completed, including all the counties excepting *Cumberland, Durham, Northumberland, Westmorland, and Yorkshire*, which are in progress, but are not unlikely to occupy the next five years. These 95 divisions are published at 2*s.* each plain, 4*s.* coloured, and 5*s.* extra if mounted on canvas for the pocket; or coloured and mounted in an oak case, 30*l.*

A sequence to the above, published at the same rate, is the ONE-INCH MAP OF SCOTLAND, arranged in counties; and the ONE-INCH MAP OF IRELAND, both as yet very imperfect, but proceeding regularly.

The following are indications of a few other of the Ordnance publications. Particulars must be sought in the official Catalogue.

SIX-INCH COUNTY MAPS OF ENGLAND, (size 40 inches by 27), of which only two are completed, viz. Lancashire, on 119 sheets, 24*l.*; Yorkshire, 311 sheets, 69*l.* 7*s.* 6*d.* Durham is to be 52 sheets, of which 10 are published at 4*l.*

SIX-INCH COUNTY MAPS OF SCOTLAND, (40 in. by 27), of which only seven counties are complete, viz.—
Edinburghshire, 35 sheets, 4*l.* 17*s.* 6*d.*
Fife and Kinross, 41 sheets, 8*l.*
Haddingtonshire, 21 sheets, 4*l.*
Kirkcudbrightshire, 58 sheets, 13*l.* 12*s.* 6*d.*
Linlithgowshire, 12 sheets, 1*l.* 17*s.* 6*d.*
Rossshire, &c., 49 sheets, 9*l.* 12*s.* 6*d.*
Wigtownshire, 35 sheets, 7*l.*

SIX-INCH COUNTY MAPS OF IRELAND, (40 in. by 27). Of this series the whole 32 counties are completed, viz.—
Antrim and Carrickfergus, 63 sheets, 13*l.* 9*s.* 6*d.*
Armagh, 29 sheets, 6*l.* 15*s.*
Carlow, 26 sheets, 4*l.* 17*s.* 6*d.*
Cavan, 44 sheets, 8*l.* 17*s.* 6*d.*
Clare, 76 sheets, 15*l.* 7*s.* 6*d.*
Cork, 153 sheets, 34*l.* 5*s.*
Donegal, 110 sheets, 21*l.* 7*s.* 6*d.*
Down, 57 sheets, 11*l.*
Dublin, 28 sheets, 5*l.* 10*s.*
Fermanagh, 43 sheets, 8*l.* 2*s.* 6*d.*
Galway, 137 sheets, 29*l.* 12*s.* 6*d.*
Kerry, 111 sheets, 23*l.* 5*s.*
Kildare, 40 sheets, 8*l.* 5*s.*
Kilkenny, 47 sheets, 9*l.* 17*s.* 6*d.*
King's County, 47 sheets, 9*l.* 5*s.*
Leitrim, 36 sheets, 7*l.* 7*s.* 6*d.*
Limerick, 60 sheets, 12*l.* 10*s.*
Londonderry, 49 sheets, 9*l.* 17*s.* 6*d.*
Longford, 27 sheets, 6*l.*
Louth, 25 sheets, 4*l.* 15*s.*
Mayo, 123 sheets, 29*l.*
Meath, 53 sheets, 10*l.* 17*s.* 6*d.*
Monaghan, 34 sheets, 6*l.* 7*s.* 6*d.*
Queen's County, 37 sheets, 8*l.* 2*s.* 6*d.*
Roscommon, 56 sheets, 11*l.* 17*s.* 6*d.*
Sligo, 47 sheets, 9*l.* 2*s.* 6*d.*
Tipperary, 91 sheets, 20*l.*
Tyrone, 69 sheets, 13*l.* 15*s.*
Waterford. 40 sheets, 8*l.* 15*s.*
Westmeath, 40 sheets, 8*l.* 10*s.*

It will be seen, that Ireland alone, on this six-inch scale, amounts to above 350*l.* without binding. By the time that Great Britain is completed, the entire set will cost upwards of a thousand pounds!

It must be sufficient here merely to intimate some of the other Ordnance publications.

TWENTY-FIVE-INCH PARISH MAPS, (nearly one square inch to an acre). Of *English Parishes*, only 10 in Northumberland, 14 in Westmorland, 8 in Surrey, 5 in Hampshire, 68 in Durham, and 1 in Lancashire, have been completed. Of *Scottish Parishes*, 46 in Ayrshire (complete), 53 in Berwickshire (complete), 1 in Buteshire, 43 in Dumfriesshire (including Gretna), 20 in Forfarshire, 13 in Linlithgowshire, 11 in Peebleshire, 17 in Lanarkshire, 17 in Roxburghshire, 8 in Selkirkshire, and 15 in Renfrewshire. And of *Ireland*, none. The cost of each Parish varies, according to the number of sheets, from 7*s.* to 2*l.* 2*s.*

SIXTY-INCH TOWN MAPS. Of these, about 60 *English* have been completed, of which the principal are: Blackburn, Bolton, Bradford, Halifax, Huddersfield, Hull, Lancaster, Leeds, Liverpool, London, Manchester, Preston, Rochdale, Sheffield, Wakefield, Warrington, and York; at an average, perhaps, of 2*l.* 2*s.* each. But London occupies 799 sheets, and therefore at 1*s.* each, costs 39*l.* 9*s.* Only 17 *Scottish* towns are complete, of which the principal are, Berwick, Edinburgh, Dumfries, and Peebles. Of the *Irish* towns, only Dublin is yet published, price 4*l.* 10*s.*

ORDNANCE SURVEY. BOOKS.
An Account of the Operations carried on for accomplishing a Trigonometrical Survey of England and Wales. By Capt. Mudge, R.A., Isaac Dalby, and Capt. Colby, F.E. Lond. 1799—1811, 4to. 3 vols. 29 plates, 2*l.* 2*s.*
Astronomical Observations made with Ramsden's Zenith Sector, &c. 1842, 7*s.* 6*d.*
An Account of the Measurement of the Lough Foyle Base, in Ireland, &c. By Capt. W. Yolland, F.R.A.S. 1847, 1*l.*

ORDNANCE BOOKS—*continued.*
Astronomical Observations made with Airy's Zenith Sector, from 1842 to 1850, &c. By Capt. W. Yolland. 1852, 1l. 1s.
— Abstracts from the Meteorological Observations taken at the Stations of the Royal Engineers in the year 1853-4. Edit. by Lieut. Col. F. James. 2s. 6d.
— Abstracts of Principal Lines of Spirit Levelling in Ireland, carried on during the years 1839 to 1843, under the direction of Major-General Colby. Lond. 1855, 4to. 5s.
— Meteorological Observations taken during the years 1829 to 1852, at the Ordnance Survey Office, Phœnix Park, Dublin. By Lieut.-Col. James, edited by Capt. Cameron. 1856, 4to. 5s.
— Account of the Observations and Calculations of the Principal Triangulation, and of the Figure and mean Density of the Earth, &c. Edited by Capt. Alexander Clarke. 1858, roy. 4to. with a volume of 28 plates, 1l. 15s.

O'REILLY, Bernard. Greenland, the adjacent Seas, and the northwest Passage to the Pacific Ocean, illustrated in a Voyage to Davis' Strait, during the Summer of 1817. Lond. 1818, 4to. 2l. 2s.
'One of the most bare-faced attempts at imposition which has occurred to us in the whole course of our literary labours.'—*Quart. Review.* Fonthill, 746, 16s.

— Edward. ? Sanas Gnoidhilge Sagsbhearla. An Irish-English Dictionary; to which is annexed, a compendious Irish Grammar. Dublin, 1817, 4to. 2l. 2s.
This work contains upwards of 50,000 words, collected from ancient and modern MSS. and from printed books. FINE PAPER. Published at 2l. 12s. 6d.

— An Essay on the nature and Influence of the Brehon Laws. Dublin, 1824, 4to.

— Catalogue of Irish works in verse and prose, with a chronological account of Irish writers, &c. Lond. 1820, 4to. 10s. 6d.
(Part 1 of the Transactions of the Iberno-Celtic Society, of which no more was published.) *See* IBERNO-CELTIC SOCIETY, and Transactions of Royal Irish Academy, in *Appendix.*

OREM, William. A Description of the Chanonry, Cathedral, and King's College of Old Aberdeen; together with many curious, entertaining, and pleasant remarks on the said Town, &c. for the years 1724-5. Edinb. 1791, 12mo. 3s.
A curious treatise. FINE PAPER, 5s. It was printed in J. Nichols' Bibl. Topog. Brit. no. iii. 1782.

ORFORD, Horatio Walpole, Earl of. *See* WALPOLE, Horace.
— George, Earl of. Hasty Productions (Poems). Norwich, 1791, 4to. 4l. 4s.
An obscene production, only twenty-five copies printed; and it is said that most of them were destroyed by order of the Hon. Mr. Damer. Hindley, pt. ii. 3087, 1l. 14s. Sotheby's, 1858, 9l. 10s.

ORICELLARIUS, B. *See* RUCCEL-LAI, Bernard.

ORIENTAL Tales, translated into English Verse by J. Hoppner, Esq. R.A. Lond. 1805, crown 8vo. 5s.
Pp. 123, with a frontispiece after Lancilas Hoppner.

The Oriental Navigator, or a new Direction for sailing to and from the East Indies, &c. Lond. 1794, 4to. with atlas in folio.

The Oriental Navigator, being a necessary Companion to the complete East India Pilot, in two large volumes of Charts and Plates. Lond. 1800, 4to. *See* PURDY, J.

Oriental Eclogues. *See* COLLINS, William.

Oriental Collections. *See* OUSELEY, Wm.

Oriental Field Sports. *See* WILLIAMSON, Thomas.

Oriental Translation Fund Publications. *See* APPENDIX.

Oriental Texts Society's Publications. *See* APPENDIX.

ORIGEN. Contra Celsum Libri VIII. ejusdem Philocalia, Gr. et Lat. cum Annotationibus Gul. Spenceri. Cantab. 1658, 4to. 5s.
A correct and well printed edition.— Cantab. 1677, 4to. 4s. Harwood styles this reprint 'as wretched an edition of a good book as ever was published.'

Origen against Celsus: translated from the Original into English by James Bellamy. Lond. 8vo. 7s. 6d. Book I. pp. 211, not including title. Book ii. pp. 1—203, including a half title. Hindley, pt. ii. 3028, morocco, 15s. Hibbert, 6899, morocco, 12s. 6d.
— De Oratione Liber, Gr. et Lat. Oxon. 1685, 18mo. 8s. Editio princeps. Drury, 2023, russia, 4s.

ORIGEN—*continued.*
Libellus De Oratione, Gr. et Lat. edente Guil. Reading. Lond. 1728, 4to. An excellent edition, with some notes by Bentley. Sir M. M. Sykes, pt. III. 500, 6s.

Omelia Origenis. Impressa in alma Civitate londoñ. ad rogatum Magistri Will'mi Menymē Socii Collegii Ricardi Whityngton. In Abchirche Lane. 16mo. Ten leaves, without numerals, signatures, or catchwords, printed by W. Faques. *See* Beloe's Anecdotes, v. 247–9.

Philosophomena, sive omnium Heresium Refutatio, e codd. Parīs, nunc primum edidit Em. Miller. Ox. 1851, 8vo. 10s.

An Homilie of Marye Magdalene, declaring her fervent Loue and Zele towards Christ: written by that famous Clerke Origine. An Homilie of Abraham, how he offered up his Soune Isaac, written by Origine, newly translated. Lond. by Reg. Wolfe, 1565, 16mo. At the close 'A prayer for married Persons,' and 'A Prayer generally for all Persons.'

A Letter of Resolution concerning Origen and the chief of his Opinions. Written to the learned and most ingenious C. L. Esq. and by him published. Lond. 1661. 4to. 4s. Reprinted in the first volume of the Phœnix, 1707, 8vo.

ORKNEY.—Rentals of the ancient Earldom and Bishoprick of Orkney; with some explanatory and relative Documents. Edited by Alexander Peterkin. Edinb. 1820, 8vo. 10s. 6d.
Not printed for sale. Some copies on LARGE PAPER.

On the Dissolution of Orkney from the Crown of Scotland. 1707, 4to.
Notes on Orkney and Zetland, illustrative of the History, Antiquities, Customs, &c. of those Islands, by Alexander Peterkin. Edinb. 1822, 8vo. 6s.

Poetical Description of Orkney, MDCLII. Edinb. 1835, 4to. Printed for private circulation only.
See BARRY, J. BRAND, J. HALL, James Low, G. MARTIN, M. STAFFORD, Marchioness of. WALLACE, J.

ORLANDO FURIOSO. *See* ARIOSTO, L. GREENE, Robert.

ORLEANS, Charles, Duke of. Poems. *See* ROXBURGHE CLUB, *Appendix.*

— Duchess of. Fragments of original Letters of Madame Charlotte Elizabeth of Bavaria, Duchess of Orleans: written from the year 1715–20, to his Serene Highness Antony Ulric Duke of B—W——; and to her Royal Highness Caroline Princess of Wales. Lond. 1760, 12mo. 2 vols.

ORLEANS, Jos. Père d'. Histoire des Révolutions d' Angleterre. Paris, 1693-4. 4to. 3 vols.
Roxburghe, 8365, 6s. Willett, 1774, 1l. 3s. 'Histoire ecrite avec jugement et eloquence, également estimée des Catholiques et des Protestants.'—*Du Fresnoy.* It is likewise recommended in the Earl of Chatham's Letters to his nephew, edited by Lord Grenville. The third volume of this work was translated by Captain John Stevens? and printed 1711 and 1722, 8vo. — Paris, 1695, 12mo. 3 vols.—Amst. 1714, 12mo. 3 vols. Roxburghe, 5366, 7s. 6d. Willett, 1858, 9s.—Paris, 1734, 12mo. 4 vols. Heath, 4463, 16s.—A la Haye, 1729, 4to. 3 vols. Paris, 1734, 4to. 3 vols. 10s. 6d.—1737, 12mo. 4 vols. with portraits. Dowdeswell, 531, 7s.—Paris, 1750, 12mo. 4 vols.—Suite, par M. Turpin. Paris, 1781, 12mo. 2 vols. 4s.

History of the Revolution in England under the family of the Stuarts, translated from the French of Father Orleans, by Capt. John Stevens. Lond. 1711, 8vo. 3s. 6d.

History of the Tartar Conquerors, who subdued China, 1680. Translated from the French, and edited by the Earl of Ellesmere, with an Introduction by R. H. Major, Esq. *See* HAKLUYT SOCIETY, *App.*

ORLEANS.—Histoire et Discours au Vray du Seige qui fut mis devant la Ville d'Orleans par les Anglois. Orleans, 1606, 12mo. 12s.
With a portrait of the Maid of Orleans, by L. Gaultier.—Orleans, 1576, 4to. Bright, 16s.—Orleans, 1621, 12mo.

ORME, Edward. An Essay on transparent Prints and on Transparencies in general. Lond. 1809, folio, plates, pub. at. 2l. 2s.
In English and French.

— Robert. A History of the military Transactions of the British Nation in Indostan, from the Year 1745 to 1761. Fourth edition, revised, with Indexes to the three volumes. Lond. 1803, 4to. 3 vols. maps, 3l. 3s.
This valuable historical work 'occupies so vast a field, that every future historian

ORME, Robert—*continued.*
of modern India must unavoidably trench in a greater or less degree upon his premises.—*Quart. Review.*— Lond. 1763-78. Willett, 3 vols. in 2, 2l. 7s.—Second edition, corrected; with index to the first volume, 1775-8, 4to. 6 vols. Nassau, 3l. 17s.—Third edition, corrected; with index to the first volume, 1780, 4to. 3 vols. Heath, 2591, 8l. 16s. Hibbert, 6037, with the historical Fragments, 4 vols. 4l. 16s.—1803, with the Fragments, 4 vols. Sotheby's, May, 1840. 4l. 4s.

Historical Fragments of the Mogul Empire. With Additions and a Memoir. Lond. 1805, 4to. A necessary accompaniment to this author's history of Indostan. Fonthill, 1746, 1l. 1s. Duke of York, 3659, 16s.—1782, 12mo. Gough, 2588, 8s. 6d. Roxburghe, 6666, 11s.

A general Idea of the Government and People of Indostan. Lond. 1811, 4to.

History of Sevaji (founder of the present nation of Morattoes). 8vo. Privately printed.

ORME, William. Bibliotheca Biblica; a select List of Books on Sacred Literature; with Notices, biographical, critical, and bibliographical. Edinb. 1824, 8vo. 12s.

Pp. xl and 491. A work to which the editor of these pages has been frequently indebted. 'The theological student cannot fail to derive much advantage from it; and the more learned divine will find it an excellent supplement to the Bibliotheca theologica selecta of the laborious Walchius, or to the erudite Bibliotheca Sacra of Le Long.'—*British Critic.*

Memoirs of the Life, Writings, and religious Connections of John Owen, D.D. Vice-Chancellor of Oxford during the Commonwealth. Lond. 1820, 8vo. with portrait, 12s.

Remarkable Passages in the Life of William Kiffin. Lond. 1823, 12mo.

Memoirs; including Letters and select Remains of John Urquhart, late of the University of St. Andrews. Lond. 1827, 12mo. 2 vols.

ORMEROD, George, D.C.L., F.R.S. The History of the County Palatine and City of Chester. Lond. 1819, folio, 3 vols. 30l.

A highly-valued county history, of which 350 were printed on small, and 65 on large paper. LARGE PAPER. Heath, pt. II. 932, with plates in three different states, viz. etchings, proofs, and proofs on India paper, morocco, 64l. 1s. Sotheby's in 1825, bds. 35l. 14s.; in russia, 42l. 10s. Gardner in 1834, morocco joints, 50l. *Collation.*—Vol. I. Containing the Introduction and Prolegomena, the County of the City of Chester, and Bucklow Hundred. Pp. liv and 556. Vol. II. Containing the Hundreds of Edisbury, Wirral, and Broxton. Pp. 472, not including the title and half-title. Vol. III. Containing the Hundreds of Northwich, Nantwich, and Macclesfield; Appendix and general index. Pp. 470, not including title and half-title. Pages 469-90 contain the list of embellishments and directions to the binder.

The Stanley Legend. (From Nichols' Collectanea, vol. vii.) Lond. 1839, 8vo. Privately printed.

Strigulensia; a Memoir on ancient Remains existing in the District adjacent to the Confluence of the Wye and the Severn. (From the Archæologia, vol. xxix.) Lond. 1841, 4to. Privately printed.

A Memoir of the Connexion of Arderne or Arden of Cheshire with the Ardens of Warwickshire. (From Nichols' Topographer.) Lond. 1843, 8vo. Privately printed.

Tracts relating to Military Proceedings in Lancashire during the great Civil War. (Printed by the Chetham Society.) 1844, 4to.

A Memoir on the Lancashire House of Le Norels or Norres, and its Speke Branch in particular. (From the Proceedings of the Historic Society of Lancashire and Cheshire.) Liverpool, 1850, 8vo. Privately printed.

Miscellanea Palatina, consisting of Genealogical Essays illustrative of Cheshire and Lancashire Families, and a Memoir on the lost Record called the Cheshire Domesday Roll. Lond. 1851, 8vo. Privately printed.

Parentalia: Genealogical Memoirs. Lond. 1851, 8vo. plates.

Calendars of Names of Families which entered Pedigrees in the successive Heraldic Visitations of Lancashire. (In the Chetham Society Miscellanies, vol. III.) Manchester, 1851, 4to.

A Memoir on British and Roman Remains, illustrative of the ancient Passages of the Bristol Channel, of former Communications with Venta Silurum, and of Antonine's Iter. xiv. (From Memoirs of the Bristol Congress of the Archæological Institute.) Lond. 1852, 4to. with many additional engravings. Privately printed.

Remarks on a Line of Earthworks in Tidenham, known as Offa's Dyke, existing in the Saxon Period, and terminating on Ledbury Cliffs. Lond. 1860, 4to. plates. Privately printed.

ORMEROD, Richard. A short Specimen for an Improvement in some Parts of the present Translation of the Old Testament. Lond. 1792.

ORMEROD, Oliver. The Picture of a Puritaine; or, a Relation of the Opinions, Qualities, and Practices of the Anabaptists in Germanie, and of the Puritanes in England. Lond. 1605, small 4to.
A work replete with classical allusions. Picture of a Papiste, and Discourse of Picture of Popish Paganisme. Lond. 1606. Bliss, both pieces, 15s. The two works together, Bright, 1608, 9s. 6d.

ORMOND, James Butler, Duke of. A Collection of original Letters and Papers, concerning the Affairs of England, 1641-1660, found among the Duke of Ormonde's Papers. Lond. 1739, 8vo. 2 vols.
Published by Thomas Carte. Bindley, pt. I. 1020, 18s. 6d. Hosburghe, 8481, 1l. 7s. & Carte, Thomas.
The Life of James Butler, late Duke of Ormonde. Lond. 1732, 8vo. 5s.—1739, 8vo. —1747, 8vo. with portrait, 6s.

— Mary Butler, Duchess of. A short Memorial and Character of the Duchess of Ormond. 8vo.

— Thomas Butler, Earl of. See MEARA, Dermitius.

ORMULUM, The, Anglo-Saxon and English. See APPENDIX.

ORNATUS and ARTESIA. — The most pleasant and delightful History of Ornatus and Artesia. (By Emanuel Foord or Ford, but issued by his friend, Robert Wood.) Lond. 1607, 4to.
In Dunn's Collection. With woodcuts. Sir M. M. Sykes, pt. II. 71, 3l. 3s.—1634, 4to. Steevens, in lot 1174. Bright, 9l. 15s. —1650, 4to. Utterson, 2l. 16s.—1669, 4to. North, pt. III. 740, 5s. 6d.—1683, 4to. White Knights, 3161, 1l. 1s. Bliss, 1l. 16s.

ORNITHOLOGIA BRITANNICA; seu Avium omnium Britannicarum tam terrestrium quam aquaticarum Catalogus, Sermone Latino, Anglico et Gallico redditus: cui subjicitur Appendix, Aves alienigenas, in Angliam raro advenientes, complectens. Lond. 1771, atlas folio.
Four leaves.
Ornithologie, or the Speech of Birds. See FULLER, Thomas, D.D.

ORNITHOPARCUS, Andreas. See DOULAND, John.

OROSIUS. Compendious History of the World; the Anglo-Saxon Version from the Historian Orosius, by Alfred the Great. Together with an English Translation from the Anglo-Saxon (by the Hon. Daines Barrington, with Remarks by Mr. John Reinhold Forster). Lond. 1773, 8vo.
A judicious and faithful translation of a work very valuable to the chronologist and antiquary. Horne Tooke, 503, 1l. 1s. Hollis, 150, 1l. 6s. Willett, 5, 1l. 8s.
The Life of Alfred the Great, translated from the German of Dr. R. Pauli. To which is appended, Alfred's Anglo-Saxon Version of OROSIUS, with a literal English Translation, and an Anglo-Saxon Alphabet and Glossary. By B. Thorpe, Esq. Lond. Bohn's Antiquarian Library, 1853, post 8vo. 5s.

OROURKE, John Count. A Treatise on the Art of War; or, Rules for conducting an Army in all the various Operations of regular Campaigns. Lond. 1778, 4to.

ORPHEUS. De Lapidibus Poema, Gr. et Lat. recensuit, Notasque adjecit T. Tyrwhitt. Simul prodit Auctarium Dissertationis de Babrio. Lond. 1781, 8vo. 5s.
An esteemed edition.
The mystical Hymns of Orpheus, translated from the original Greek; with a preliminary Dissertation on the Life and Theology of Orpheus, by Thomas Taylor. Lond. 1787 or 1792, 8vo. An esteemed translation. Drury, 2725, 3s.—1824, 8vo. 10s. 6d.
The Book of the Orphic Hymns. Lond. printed in uncial Letters by Julian Hibbert, 1827, 8vo. Bright, 2s. 6d.
See CALLIMACHUS, by W. Dodd.

ORPHEUS. — The Traitie of Orpheus Kyng and how he yeid to hewyn & to hel to seik his Quene and anether Ballad in the latter end. Edinb. by Walter Chepman and Andro Millar (1508), 4to.
By Robert Henryson. Twelve leaves, wanting the 3rd and 4th, which are supplied in the facsimile reprint of Chepman's tracts, 1827. It is preserved in the Advocates' Library at Edinburgh.

Orpheus his Journey to Hell, and his Musick to the Ghosts, by R. H. Lond. H. Johnes, 1595, 4to. Caldecott, M. 2s. 6d. A copy of this poetical tract is in the British Museum. It has no title-page, but commences on sig. B 1, and concludes on the reverse of sig. D 4.

Orpheus Junior's Golden Fleece. See VAUGHAN, (W.)

ORR, John, D.D. Sermons. Lond. 1739, 8vo. 2 vols.
Sermons (posthumous). 1778, 8vo. 3 vols.

ORRERY, Charles Boyle, Earl of. Dr. Bentley's Dissertation on the Epistles of Phalaris and the Fables of Æsop examin'd. Lond. 1698, 8vo.
Reprinted 1699, 8vo.—1745, 8vo. 5s. See BENTLEY, R. PHALARIS.

— John Boyle, Earl of. Remarks on the Life and Writings of Dr. Jonathan Swift. Lond. 1751, 8vo. 3s.
'Detestable letters.'—Bp. Warburton. It is said upwards of twelve thousand copies were sold.—1764, 8vo. 5s. LARGE PAPER. Williams, 1878, morocco, 19s.—Dublin, 1752, 8vo. Hibbert, 5s91, morocco, 12s.

Observations upon Lord Orrery's Remarks on the Life and Writings of Dr. Jonathan Swift. (By Dr. P. Delany.) Lond. 1754, 8vo.—Lond. 1772, with two original places by Dean Swift, never before published.

Dean Swift for ever; or, Mary the Cookmaid to the Earl of Orrery. Lond. 1752, folio.

First Ode of the first Book of Horace imitated (with the Latin text). Lond. 1741, folio.

Letters from Italy, in the Years 1754 and 1755, by the late Right Hon. John, Earl of Cork and Orrery, published from the Originals, with explanatory Notes, by John Duncombe, M.A. Lond. 1773, small 8vo. 3s. 6d.—1774. Drury, 1019, 5s.

— Earl of. An Answer to a scandalous Letter lately printed and subscribed by Peter Walsh. Dublin, by J. C. 1662, 4to.
For Reply, &c. see WALSH, Peter.

— Roger Boyle, Earl of. Dramatic Works. Lond. 1739, 8vo. 2 vols.
With portrait of the Earl. Garrick, 1716, a presentation copy, 1l. 11s. 6d. Roxburghe, 5919, 19s. Read, 8305, 7s. Heath, 1961, 5s. This collection does not contain the author's Mr. Anthony, a Comedy. Lond. 1690, 4to. but has his grandson's comedy of As you find it.

Parthenissa, a Romance, in four Parts. Lond. 1677, folio. Dedicated to my Lady Northumberland. Bindley, pt. II. 1927, 3s. 6d.

Parthenissa. The third Part, dedicated to the Ladie Sutherland. Lond. Herringman, 1655, sm. 4to. This volume contains Pt. 3 to 6 Books.

The Art of War. Lond. 1677, folio, with an equestrian portrait of Charles II. 'Commended by many expert captains for the best piece extant in English.'—Ant. à Wood. Bliss, 1s. 6d.

English Adventures, by a Person of Honour. 8vo.—Lond. in the Savoy, 1676, 8vo. Otway's Orphan is founded on the novel of Brandon, in p. 17 et seq. of this volume.

A Collection of State Letters of the Earl of Orrery, with his Life by Thomas Morrice. Lond. 1742, folio. Heber, pt. vii. 3s. 6d. LARGE PAPER. In the Grenville Collection. 'Well worthy the notice of the reader.'—Granger.—Dublin, 1743, 8vo. 2 vols. Garrick, Addenda, 14, a presentation copy, 2l.

Poems, on most of the Festivals of the Church. (Probably printed in Ireland), 1681, folio, unseen by Horace Walpole. Bliss, 19s.

ORTELIUS, Abr. The Theatre of the whole World (translated). Lond. 1606, folio.
Dedicated to K. James I. The maps are in Latin (from the Antwerp edition of 1595), but the descriptions are in English. Other editions, with abridged text, oblong 12mo.

ORTHUS, W. Oration touching the Lyfe and Death of A. Hyperius, by J. Ludham. Lond. T. East, 1577, 4to. See HYPERIUS.

ORTHODOX Churchman's Magazine and Review; or, a Treasure of divine and useful Knowledge. Lond. 1801-8, 8vo. 15 vols.
With portraits. Earl of Kerry, 371, 3l. 13s. 6d.

ORTHODOX COMMUNICANT, engraved on Copperplates by Sturt. Lond. 1721, small 8vo.
White Knights, 8014, 11s. Sir M. M. Sykes, pt. III. 752, 9s. Nassau, pt. I. 2472, morocco, 17s. Dent, pt. II. 54, morocco, 1l. 11s. 6d.

ORTHOGRAPHY.—English Orthographic. Oxford, II. Hall, 1668, 4to.
By Owen Price. FIRST EDITION. A-K 2, in fours, A 1 blank. Bliss, pt. II, 15s.—Oxford, L. Lichfield, 1670, 16mo. Bliss, 4s.

The Orthographicall Declaration: containing a briefe Advertisement of two new Inventions called Lineage and Fortage, whereby Writing-paper and Parchment are decently ruled and inlined, for to Ingrosse or write upon, after a more dexterous and beneficial Manner than is done or performed by the ordinary Way of hand-ruling with Plummet, Ruler, or Brasse-pen. Examples satisfactorie for Paper Books in quarto are annexed. 1616, 4to. *See* BRYDGES' Censura Literaria. BULLOKAR, Jo.

ORTIS, Ja. Ultimo Lettero di Jacopo Ortis: nuova Edisione. Lond. 1817, 12mo. 2 vols.
By Ugo Foscolo. The best edition, published under the inspection of the author, with 2 portraits. The edition of 1811 is mutilated.

Letters of Ortis to Lorenzo; taken from the original MSS. published at Milan in 1802. Translated from the Italian, 1814, 8s. 6d.

ORTIZ, Don Antonio. Relation of the Solemnitie wherewith Philip III. and Queen Margaret were received in the Inglish Colledge at Madrid, 1600. Translated by Francis Ryvers. Printed at N. with licence, 1601, 8vo.
Heber, pt. iv. 15s.

ORTON, Rev. Job. A short and plain Exposition of the Old Testament; with devotional and practical Reflections. Shrewsbury, 1788-91, 8vo. 6 vols.

This work, written by an English dissenting minister, inclined to Arianism, was designed for a companion to Doddridge's Exposition of the New Testament; but falls far short of its predecessor. Garrick, 1718, 1l. 10s.—1822, 8vo. 6 vols. 2l. 12s. 6d.

Letters from the Rev. Mr. Job Orton, and the Rev. Sir James Stonhouse, Bart. M.D. to the Rev. Thomas Stedman, M.A. Vicar of St. Chad's, Shrewsbury, 1800, small 8vo. 2 vols. 8s.

This eminent dissenting Divine published several volumes of sermons, &c., likewise a life of Dr. Doddridge, which has been frequently reprinted.

ORTUS Vocabulorum: alphabetico Ordine fere omnia quæ in Catholicon, breviloquo, Cornucopia, Gemma Vocabulorum, atque Medulla Grammaticæ, ponuntur cum perpulchris Additoribus Ascens. et vernacula Lingue Anglicane Expositionem continens. Westmynstre per Wynandum de Worde, 1500, folio.

FIRST EDITION of a work still of considerable importance to Grammatical Antiquaries. A copy is in the Grenville collection; it contains two hundred and sixty-six leaves. Sotheby, Jan. 1865, 17s. —Lond. per W. de Worde, 1508, 4to.—Lond. per Rich. Pynson, 1339, 4to.—Lond. per W. de Worde, 1511, 4to. Geo. Chalmers, pt. III, 3l. 12s. — Lond. per W. de Worde, 1514, 4to. Heber, pt. vi. 2l. 6s. —Lond. per W. de Worde, 1516, 4to. Bibl. Llwyd, 453, 4l. 14s. 6d. Heber, pt. vii. 1l. 10s. —Lond. per W. Worde, 1518, 4to. Gardner, mor. 7l. Sot Maittaire, Annal. Typog. p. 235, note a.

OSAIBA, Ibn, Abi. *See* ABDOLLATIPH.

OSBALDISTON, Wm. Aug. The British Sportsman; or, Dictionary of Recreation and Amusement. Lond. (1792), 4to. plates.

OSBECK, Peter. A Voyage to China and the East Indies, by Peter Osbeck; together with a Voyage to Suratte, by Olof Torren; and an Account of the Chinese Husbandry, by Captain Charles Gustavus Eckeberg. Translated from the German, by John Reinhold Forster; to which are added, a Faunula and Flora Sinensis. Lond. 1771, 8vo. 2 vols.
Drury, 2297, 11s. Roxburghe, 7312, 13d. Willett, 1656, 14s. Fonthill, 2928, 1l. 11s.

OSBORNE, Francis. The Works. Lond. 1673, 8vo. 8s.

These works, frequently reprinted, are now in little estimation. The author, Dr. Johnson styled 'A conceited fellow. Were a man to write so now, the boys would throw stones at him.'

Historical Memoires on the reign of Elizabeth and James. Lond. 1658, 12mo. With portraits of Elizabeth and James. White Knights, 1292, 7s. Nassau, pt. i. 1873, 7s. It was reprinted in the 'Secret History of the Court of King James I,' Edinb. 1811.

OSIANDER, Andrew. How and whither a Christian Man ought to flye the horrible Plage of the Pestilence. A Sermon. Translated out of hye Almayn into Englisshe by Myles Coverdale. Southwarke, by me James Nicolson for Jan. Gough, 1537, 16mo.

Annexed is 'A comforte concernynge yrn yt be dead. Howe wyfe, chyldren and other frendes shal be comforted ye husbondes beynge dead.'—Lond. by Leonarde Askell, 16mo. C, in eights. Another edit. printed by Nicolson, without date, 16mo. BLACK LETTER.

The Conlecpiures of the End of the Worlde, by Andrew Oslander, translated by George Joye, with many Things by him added. 1548, 16mo. Horner, 1l. 2s.

A very excellent and sweete exposition upon the xxiii Psalm of David, translated out of High Almayne, by Myles Coverdale, 12mo. BLACK LETTER. Nicolson, 1553. A to C v. in eights.

Sermon upon the xei Psalms, Lond. 1537, 16mo.

OSORIO, Jerome, Bishop of Sylves. The History of the Portuguese, during the Reign of Emmanuel, their Discoveries in Africk and the Brazils, with their Wars with the Moors, translated from the Latin by James Gibbs. Lond. 1752, 8vo. 2 vols.

Fonthill, 1656, 6s. Osorius is called by some the Cicero of Portugal.

Epistolæ ad Elizabetham Angliæ Reginam de Religione. Paris, 1563, 16mo. Roxburghe, 11s.—Lovanii, 1563, 16mo.

Epistle to the Princesse Elizabeth, Queene of England, &c. Translated into Englishe by Richard Shacklock. Antwerp. 1565, 16mo. Towneley, pt. i. 564, 12s. 6d. Heber, pt. v. 8s.

In Gnalterum Haddomum libellorum supplicum apud Helisabetham Angliæ Reginam, de Religione lib. tres. Dillingæ, ex off. Sebaldi Mayer. 1567.

A Treatise wherein be confuteth a certayne Auswere made by M. Walter Haddon against the Epistle vnto the Queenes Maiestie. Translated by Iohn Fen. Lovanii, 1568, 16mo. 10s.

Five Bookes contayninge a Discourse of civill and Christian Nobilitie. Translated into Englisshe by William Blandie. Lond. 1576, 4to. Dedicated to the 'Erle of Laycester.' Bindley, pt. iii. 978, 14s. 6d. Heber, pt. ix. 1l. 5s. Brand, 1l. 2s. Gardner, 18s.

De Gloria et de Nobilitate Libri. Lond. 1589, 16mo. See Retrosp. Review, L. 323-32.

The Library of Osorius was taken by Lord Essex at the siege or plunder of Cadiz, in 1596, and by him given to the Bodleian Library, then only recently founded. See Dixon's Memoirs of Q. Elisabeth, vol. 1, p. 64. HADDON, Walter.

OSSIAN.—The Poems of Ossian, in the original Gaelic, with a literal Translation into Latin by Robert Macfarlan; together with a Dissertation on the Authenticity of the Poems by Sir John Sinclair, Bart., and a Translation from Cesarotti's Dissertation on the Controversy respecting the Authenticity of Ossian, with Notes and supplemental Essay, by John M'Arthur, LL.D. Lond. 1807, roy. 8vo. 3 vols. 1l. 1s.

Published under the sanction of the Highland Society of London. LARGE PAPER, in imperial 8vo. Duke of York, 3l. 1s, morocco, 2l. 19s.

Other Editions.

Fragments of ancient Poetry, collected in the Highlands of Scotland, and translated from the Gaelic or Erse Language. Edinb. 1760. 8vo. pp. 70. The first Ossianic publication of James Macpherson, the 'discoverer' of this poet.

Fingal, an ancient epic Poem, in six Books; with several other Poems, (including the Songs of Selma), translated from the Gaelic Language by James Macpherson. Lond. 1762, and again, 1776, 4to.

Temora, an ancient epic Poem, in eight Books; with several other Poems, translated from the Gaelic Language by James Macpherson. Lond. 1763. 4to.

These two volumes are commonly found together in 1 vol. Willett, 1780, 7s. LARGE PAPER, 10s. 6d.

The Poems of Ossian, translated by James Macpherson. Third edition: to which is subjoined a critical Dissertation on the Poems of Ossian, by Dr. Hugh Blair. Lond. 1765, 8vo. 2 vols.—Lond. 1773, 8vo. 2 vols. Fonthill, 31, 1l. Garrick. 1790, a presentation copy, 1l. 19s.—Lond. 1794, 8vo. 3 vols. Willett, 1859, 6s.—Lond. 1796, 3 vols. Drury, 1929, russia, 17s.—Frankfort, 1785, 4 vols. in 2.—Edinb. 1792, 8vo.

The Poems of Ossian, containing the poetical Works of James Macpherson, in Prose and Rhyme, with Notes and Illustrations by Malcolm Laing. Edinb. 1805. 8vo. 2 vols. Dent, pt. i. 1573, 10s. Bright,

OSSIAN—*continued.*
9s.—Edinb. 1812, 8vo. 2 vols.—With an Appendix to Blair's Dissertation. Edinb. 1805, 12mo. 2 vols. 5s.

The Poems of Ossian, translated by James Macpherson. A new Edition, containing Macpherson's Dissertation on the Era and Poems of Ossian, and Dr. Blair's critical Dissertation; with Appendix containing a Review of the recent Controversy relative to the Authenticity of the Poems. Lond. Lackington, 1806, 12mo. 2 vols. with plates, 10s. 6 l. Strettell, 1061, 15s. 6d. FINE PAPER, CRN. 0 8vo. 11s. Republished, Edinb. Nelson, 1840, 18mo.

The Poems of Ossian, translated by Jas. Macpherson. To which are prefixed, three Dissertations on the Æra and Poems of Ossian. Lond. Cadell, &c. 1808, 12mo. 2 vols. LARGE PAPER.—Lond. Cadell, &c. 1807, 8vo. 2 vols. LARGE PAPER, roy. 8vo.

The Poems of Ossian. Lond. 1806, 12mo. 3 vols. With plates by Fittler.—Again, Lond. 1812. Brockett, 2l11, 1l. 5s.

The Poems of Ossian, translated by J. Macpherson. Authenticated and explained by Hugh Campbell. Lond. 1822, post 8vo. 2 vols. map and 3 plates. Duke of York, 3273, 1l. 5s. Bright, 5s. 6d.

Poems of Ossian, translated by James Macpherson, with the Dissertations on the Era and Poems of Ossian, and Dr. Blair's critical Dissertation. Lond. (Bohn's Miniature Classics) 1847, 24mo. front. 3s.

Versified Portions, &c.

The Battle of Lora, a Poem: with some Fragments written in the Erse or Irish Language, by Ossian the Son of Fingal, translated into English verse by Mr. Derrick. Lond. 1762, 4to. 1s. 6d.

Gisbal, an hyperborean Tale: translated from the Fragments of Ossian, the Son of Fingal. Lond. 1762, 8vo. Low and scurrilous abuse.

Carthon, in Verse, by Dr. J. Woodrow. Edinb. 1769, 12mo.

Fingal, in English Heroic Rhyme, by Dr. J. Woodrow. Edinb. 1771, 12mo. 2 vols.

The Fingal of Ossian, translated from the Galic, by J. Macpherson, and now rendered into heroic Verse by Ewen Cameron. Warrington, 1776, 4to.

Fingal, rendered into heroic Verse by Ewen Cameron. To which are prefixed, the Attestations and a Preface. Lond. 1777, 4to. with a frontispiece.

Sonnets and other Poems; with a Versification of the six Bards of Ossian (by Sir S. Egerton Brydges, Bart.) Lond. 1785, 8vo.

Some of Ossian's lesser Poems, rendered into English verse, with a preliminary Discourse in Answer to Mr. Laing's critical and historical Dissertation on the Antiquity of Ossian's Poems. By Arch. Macdonald. Lond. 1806, 8vo.

Fingal, an epic Poem, translated from the original Gaelic by the Rev. Tho. Ross. Edinb. 1807, 8vo. Only 50 copies printed.

Ossian's Fingal, rendered into Verse by Archibald Macdonald. Lond. 1808, 8vo.

Ossian's Fingal, rendered into English Verse by George Harvey. Lond. 1814, 8vo.

Temora, an epic Poem, in eight Cantos, versified from Macpherson's prose Translation of the Poems of Ossian, by T. Burke. Perth, 1818, 8vo.

Oina Morul, a Poem of Ossian, translated into English Verse by Wm. Day, Chelsea, 1817, 8vo.

Ossian's Poems attempted in English Verse, by the Rev. J. Shackleton. Birm 1817, 8vo. 2 vols. 7s.

Macpherson's Translation turned into Blank Verse, by the Rev. H. Davidson. Salisbury, n. d. 8vo.

Antient Erse Poems, collected among the Scottish Highlands, in order to illustrate the Ossian of Mr. Macpherson. (Lond. 1787), 8vo. pp. 34, 4s. The far greater part of this pamphlet (printed for private distribution) appeared in the Gentleman's Magazine for 1782 and 1783, under the signature of Tho. F. Hill.

Sean Duna: Le Oisian, Orran, Ulann, &c. Ancient Poems of Ossian, Orran, &c. collected in the Western Highlands and Isles: being the Originals of the Translations some time ago published in the Gaelic Antiquities, by John Smith, D.D. Edinb. 1787, 4to. 6s.

Dana Oiseanachta Fhinn, air an cnramach airson maith coitcheannta muinntir na Gaeltachd. Dun-Eidin (Edinb.) 1818, 8vo. A new edition of the Gaelic original, by J. Macgregor Murray.

Genuine Remains literally translated, with a preliminary Dissertation by Patrick Macgregor, M.A. Lond. 1841, post 8vo. Published by the Highland society.

TRANSLATIONS

into Greek, Latin, Italian, French, Spanish, German, Dutch, Swedish, Danish.

Ossiani Dathula, Græce reddita; accedunt Miscellanea, a Gul. Herbert. Lond. 1801, 8vo. Drury, 2030, 5s.

Temora Liber unus Versibus expressus, Auctore Roberto Macfarlan, A.M. Lond. 1769, 4to.

Phingalsis, sive Hibernia liberata, epicum Ossiani Poema e Celtico Sermone conversum, tribus premissis Disputationibus et subsequentibus Notis ab Alexandro Macdonald. Edinb. 1820, roy. 8vo.

Poesie, dell' Abate M. Cesarotti; con varie Annotazione de due Traduttori.

OSSIAN—*continued*.
Padova, 1763, 8vo. 2 vols. — Nizza, 1780-1, 12mo. 8 vols.—Firenze, 1807, 8vo. 4 vols.
Poesie. Pisa, 1801, 8vo. 4 vols.
Nuovi Canti di Ossian, publicati in Inglese da Giovanni Smith, e recati in Italiano da Michele Leoni. Ed. 8a riveduta. Venezia, 1818, sm. 8vo. 2 vols. Leoni translated also Shakespeare and Byron.
Poesies Galliques, par Le Tourneur. Paris, 1777, 8vo. 2 vols. 7s. LARGE PAPER, in 4to. — Paris, An vii. 8vo. 2 vols. 7s. VELLUM PAPER.—Précédé d'une Notice par Ginguené. Paris, 1810, 8vo. 2 vols. Best edition. YELLUM PAPER.
Poesies en Vers Francais, par M. Baour Lormian. Paris, 1801, 18mo.—2eme edition. Paris, 1827, 8vo. plates.
Ossian; Poemes Galliques. Paris, 1842, fcap. 8vo.
Obras, trad. del ingles a la prosa y verso castellano por Jos. Alonzo Ortiz. Valladol. 1788, 4to.
Fingal y Temora, trad. en verso castellano por Pt. Montengon. Madr. 1801, 8vo.
Ossian und Sined's Lieder, herausg. von Mch. Denis. Wien, Degen, 1799, 4to. VELLUM PAPER. An esteemed translation. Printed with Bodoni's types.
Die gedichte von Ossian aus dem Englischen Deutsche übers. Von F. Lp. Graf zu Stollberg. Hamb. 1806, 8vo. 3 vols.
Ossian's Gedichte rhythmisch übers. von J. G. Rhode. 2nd. ed. Berl. 1808, 8vo. 3 vols.
Ossian's Gedichte übers. von P. W. Jung. 1808, 8vo. 3 vols.
There are other German translations.
De Gedichten van Ossian in 't Nederduitsch door P. L. van de Kasteele. Amst. 1793, 8vo. pt. 1, all pub.
Gezangen van Ossian. Door den Baron de Harold naar het Engelsch in Nederduitsch Proza vertaald, Leyden, 1794, 8vo
Fingal, gevolgd by W. Bilderdyk. Amst. 1805-6, 8vo 2 vols.
Skaldentychen, oIversat. Upsala, 1794, 8vo. 2 pts.
Into Danish, by Alstrup. Kopenh. 1790.2, 8vo. 2 vols.

The Ossianic Controversy.

Three beautiful and important Passages omitted by the Translator of Fingal, restored by Donald Macdonald. Lond. 1761, 4to. A burlesque on the celebrated work entitled Fingal.
Remarks on the History of Fingal, and other Poems of Ossian, translated by Mr. Macpherson. By Ferdinand Warner, LL.D. Lond. 1762, 8vo.
Fingal reclaimed. Lond. 1763, 8vo.
A critical Dissertation on the Poems of Ossian, the Son of Fingal (by the Rev. Dr. Blair). Lond. 1763, 4to. 2s. 6d.
Memoirs sur les l'ossmen de Mr. Macpherson. Cologne, 1765, 12mo. This memoir originally appeared in the Journal des Savans.
Occasional Thoughts on the Study and Character of Classical Authors, with Comparisons between Homer and Ossian (by Dr. John Gordon). 1772, 8vo.
An Enquiry into the Authenticity of the Poems ascribed to Ossian. By W. Shaw, A.M. Lond. 1781, 8vo. 2s.
An Answer to Mr. Shaw's Enquiry into the Authenticity of the Poems ascribed to Ossian. By John Clark. Lond. 1781, 8vo.
Reply to Mr. Clark's Answer. By W. Shaw, A.M. Lond. 1782, 8vo.
Answer to Mr. Shaw's Reply. By John Clark. Lond. 1783, 8vo.
A Rejoinder to an Answer from Mr. Clark on the Subject of Ossian's Poems. By W. Shaw, M.A. Lond. 1784, 8vo. 1s. 6d.
The seven preceding works, bound in 1 vol. with some newspaper cuttings. Reed. 17s.
A Dissertation of the supposed Authenticity of Ossian's Poems. In Malcolm Laing's History of Scotland. 1800.
Report of the Committee of the Highland Society of Scotland, appointed to enquire into the Nature and Authenticity of the Poems of Ossian, drawn up by H. Mackenzie; with a copious Appendix, containing some of the principal Documents on which the Report is founded. Edinburgh, 1805, 8vo. 8s.
A Dissertation on the Authenticity of the Poems of Ossian. By Sir John Sinclair, Bart. Lond. 1806, 8vo.
An Essay on the Authenticity of the Poems of Ossian, in which the Objections of Malcolm Laing, Esq. are particularly considered and refuted, by Patrick Graham, D.D. Edinburgh, 1807, 8vo.
Observations relative to the Authenticity of the Poems of Ossian. 1813. See GRANT, James.
Essay on the Authenticity of Ossian's Poems, by Donald Campbell. Ayr, 1825.
The Claims of Ossian, examined and appreciated, by the Rev. Edw. Davies. Swansea, 1825, royal 8vo.
Macpherson's resentment of a criticism of Dr. Johnson's produced the very spirited letter which Boswell has preserved in his Memoirs.
See SMITH, John, D.D.

OSSOLINSKI, Lord George. A true Copy of the Latine Oration of Lord George Ossolinski, Count Palatine of Tenizyn and Sendomyris, as it was pronounced to his Majestie at

White-hall on Sunday the 11 of March, 1620, with the Translation of the same into English. London, for William Lee (1621), 4to.

In the Grenville Collection. Reprinted in the second volume of the Somers Collection of Tracts.

OSTEND.—Dialogue and Complaint made upon the Siege of Ostend by the King of Spaine, the Archduke, &c. Lond. 1602, 4to.
BLACK LETTER.

Relation of the defeating Card. Mazarine, and Oliver Cromwell's Design to have taken Ostend by Treachery in 1658. Lond. 1666, 12mo.

OSTERLEY LIBRARY and Menagery. *See* FAIRFAX, Bryan, HAYES, William.

OSTERVALD, John Frederick. Arguments of the Book and Chapters of the old and new Testaments, with practical Observations, translated by J. Chamberlayne. Lond. 1749, 8vo. 3 vols. 0s.

Published at the request and under the patronage of the Society for promoting Christian Knowledge, and still kept in print.—1716-18. 8vo. 8 vols. 7s. 6d. Williams, 1230, 1L.—1764, 8vo. 8 vols.—1779, 8vo. 2 vols.—1799, 8vo. 2 vols.—1819, 12mo. 3 vols.—1811, 8vo. 2 vols.—1833, 12mo. 8 vols.

A Treatise concerning the Causes of the present Corruption of Christians, and the Remedies thereof. Translated into English by C. Mutel. Second Edition, Lond. 1703, 8vo. 3s. Reprinted in Bp. Watson's Collection of Theological Tracts, who observes, 'This book was highly esteemed by Bp. Burnet; and indeed all the writings of Mr. Ostervald have been favourably received in the world in general.'

Grounds and Principles of the Christian Religion. Lond. 1704, 8vo. 3s. 'A work highly deserving of notice.'—*Bishop Watson.* It has been frequently reprinted.

The Nature of Uncleanness. Lond. 1708, 8vo.

Theologiæ Christianæ Compendium. Glasgow, 1757, 12mo. 3s.

Lectures on the Exercise of the sacred Ministry, translated from the French, with a Preface, and enlarged with occasional Notes by Tho. Stevens, M.A. Lond. 1781, 8vo. 5s. 'This work may be usefully read by serious-minded men.'—*Bishop Watson.* Williams, 1251, 14s.

Vie de J. F. Ostervald par David Durand. Lond. 1778, 8vo. 3s. 6d.

OSULLEVANUS, Philippus. Historiæ Catholicæ Hiberniæ Compendium, e D. Philippo Osulleuano Bearro Iberno. Vlyssipone, 1621, 4to. 4 parts in 1 vol.

A work 'full of groundless stories and ridiculous fooleries.'—*Nicholson.* A copy is in the British Museum. Gardner, in 1854, 6L. 10s. Bright, fine, 6L. 2s. 6d. Sotheby [Bp. Daly] June 29, 1858, 5L. 7s. 6d. Heber, pt. vii. 4L. 17s.; pL. iv. very fine, 1 1L. *Collation.*—A—Cc4, and Dd—Nn, in eights, the last leaf containing the errata. The introductory matter, viz. the title, 'licenc, A.S.' dedication 'Domino Philippo, Avitriaco IIII.' occupy four leaves.

Editio nova, edidit, notulisque ac Indicibus illustravit Matthæus Kelly. Dublin, 1850, royal 8vo. 7s. 6d. The work itself is divided into 4 vols. or books, the paging carried on to folio 234, including leaf of errata.

Patritiana Decas, sive Libri decem, quibus de Divi Patritij Vita, Purgatorio, Miraculis, Rebusq. gestis: de Religionis Ibernicæ casibus, Constantia, Martyribus Divis: de Anglorum iubrica fide; de An' globrevetion Ecclesiæ sectis, cacogramalibus, iubileis plenissimis, Liturgia, sacra pagina, ceremoniis & insitutis accuratè agitur. Anno 1629. Mairill, 4to. A copy is in the British Museum. Horner, 5L. Sotheby (Bp. Daly), June 26, 1858, 6L. 2s. 6d. Heber, pt. i. 15L. *Collation.*—A—Aaa 7, in fours, the last leaf containing the imprint. Prefixed to the volume are 16 leaves, containing the title, dedication to 'Michaeli Noronhæ, Lisbariam Comiti,' privilege, &c. complimentary Latin verses and contents. This work was replied to by Bp. H. Jones. *See* PATRICK, ST.

OSWALD, James. The Caledonian Pocket Companion. (1750, &c.) 12 books or parts in 2 vols. roy. 8vo.

Copies of a later issue; all without dates. The number of airs in these volumes is no less than between 5 and 600, and includes many very ancient, very excellent, and very curious pieces, nowhere else to be found, nor ever before printed. *See* Ritson's Scot. Songs, l. p. cviii.; and Laing's Introduction to Johnson's Scots' Musical Museum.

— James, D.D. An Appeal to common Sense in Behalf of Religion. Edinb. 1768-72, 8vo. 2 vols. 4s.

Horne Tooke, 505, with MS. notes by Tooke, 4L. 5s.

— Rt. Hon. James. Memorials of the public Life and Character of the Right Hon. James Oswald of Dunnikier, contained in a Correspondence with some of the most distinguished Men of the last Century. Edinb. 1825, 8vo.

Pp. xxiv. and 484, with port. by Lizars. Duke of York, 5525, morocco, 1l. 19s. Heber, l. 3s. 6d. Bright, 2s.

OSWESTRY.—The History of Oswestry from the earliest Period; its Antiquities and Customs; with a short Account of the Neighbourhood. Oswestry (1815), 8vo.

Collected from various authors, with much original information, by William Price. It consists of pages vii—xii, 1—168, with 7 woodcuts, a title page and dedication to the Hon. Thomas Kenyon.

OTES, Samuel. Explanation of the general Epistle of Saint Jude. Lond. 1633, folio, 9s.

OTHNIEL and ACHSAH. — The Loves of Othniel and Achsah, translated from the Chaldee. Lond. 1769, 8vo. 2 vols. 6s.

OTHO et OTHOBONE. Constitutiones Prouinciales et Othonis. Cum Interp. Joh. de Athon. Paris, 1504. folio.—Lond. Win. de Worde, 1529, 12mo.

The Constitutions of Othobone are annexed, though not mentioned in the title.

Constitutions Prouincialles, and of Otho and Octhobone. Translated into Englysshe. Cum priuilegio. Lond. Robert Redman, 1534, 12mo. 'After the address of "The Translatour to the readers," follow the copies of three oaths, which I know not where else are to be found: "The oths made by the bisshoppes to our soueraygne lorde the Kynge before theyr consecration; the olde othe of the prelates or bysshoppes of Englande made to the pope or bysshoppe of Rome; the new othe of the prelates or bysshoppes made to the pope or bysshoppe of Rome."'—Dibdin's Typ. Antiq.

Also attached to some editions of the Provinciale of Lindewood.

See CONSTITUTIONS. LINDEWOOD.

OTIA SACRA. See WESTMORELAND, Earl of.

OTTERBOURNE, Thomas. See HEARNE, Thomas.

OTTLEY, Wm. Young. An Inquiry into the Origin and early History of Engraving upon Copper and in Wood, with an Account of Engravers and their Works, from the Invention of Chalcography by Maso Finiguerra to the Time of Mark Antonio Raimondi. Lond. 1816, 4to. 2 vols. plates, 6l. 6s.

Strutsell, 1425, russia, 7l. LARGE PAPER, in imperial 4to. with proofs on India paper. Sixty copies printed. Dowdeswell, 623, 8l. 16s. 6d. Fonthill, 2578, 19l. 19s. Hibs, 9l. 15s.

A descriptive Catalogue of Pictures in the National Gallery, with critical Remarks on their Merits. 1826, fcap. 8vo. part I. The Angerstein collection.

The Italian School of Design, being a Series of Fac-similes of original Drawings by the most eminent Painters and Sculptors of Italy; with biographical Notices and Observations. Lond. 1823, super royal folio, with 84 plates, published at 12l. 12s. now 4l. 4s.—colombier folio, 18l. 18s. now 8l. 8s.; proofs, 25l. 4s.

Collection of 129 Facsimiles of scarce and curious Prints, by the early Masters of the Italian, German, and Flemish Schools, with 12 duplicate Plates of Niellos finished in silver. Lond. 1826, imp. 4to. published at 15l. 15s. Some copies contain only 100 plates, and were pub. at 12l. 12s.

Series of Engravings after the Paintings and Sculptures of the most eminent masters of the early Florentine School. Lond. (1826), imp. folio, 54 engravings after designs by Cimabue, Giotto di Lisondona, Giottino, Gaddi, Ucello, Ghiberti, Masaccio, Lippi, &c. pub. at 9l. 9s. now 2l. 12s. 6d.; PROOFS, colombier fol. 12l. 12s. now 4l. 4s. This work having been left unfinished, has no general title.

Notices of Engravers and their Works, being the Commencement of a new Dictionary, which it is not intended to continue. Lond. 1831, 8vo. pt. 1. (A to Bald, all published) 2s. 6d.; royal 8vo. 8s. 6d.

Observations on a MS. in the British Museum, believed to be of second or third century, containing Cicero's translation of the Astronomical Poem by Aratus. Lond. 1835, 4to.

See Galleries, p. 858.

OTUEL, Sir. A metrical Romance, from the Auchinleck MS. Edinb. 1836. See ABBOTSFORD CLUB, Appendix.

An abstract of this romance, from two MSS. will be found in the second volume of Ellis' Specimens.

OTWAY, Thomas. The Works, with Notes critical and explanatory, and a Life of the Author by Thos. Thornton. Lond. 1813, crown 8vo. 3 vols.

Best edition, with portrait of Otway and two plates. LARGE PAPER in demy 8vo. Bindley, pt. II. 2028, 1l. 9s. Sir M. M. Sykes, pt. II. 583, extra bound, 3l. 4s. Drury, 2433, russia, 5l. 4s.—1712, 12mo. 2 vols. with portrait. Heath, 1944, 7s. 6d. —1718, 12mo. 2 vols. Willett, 1861, 10s. 6d. —1728, 12mo. 2 vols.—1757, 18mo. 5 vols. 9s. Reed, 8306, 15s. Steevens, 1238, 1l. 12s.—1812, 8vo. 2 vols. 10s. Drury, 2932, 1l. 1s. Strettell, 1052, 16s.

OUFLE, M. A History of the ridiculous Extravagancies of Monsieur Oufle. Lond. 1711, 8vo.

This is a translation (from the French) of a work by the Abbé Laurent Bordelon, entitled L'Histoire des Imaginations extravagantes de M. Oufle, causées par la lecture des Livres qui traitent de la Magie, &c. of which there is a neat edition with plates and curious notes, Paris, 1754. Amsterdam, 1710, 2 vols. 12mo. The author's object was to do for magic, witchcraft, &c. what Cervantes did for knight-errantry. White Knights, 8019, 4s. Dent, pt. I. 1050, morocco, 12s.

OUGHTON, Tho. Ordo Judiciorum sive Methodus procedendi in Foro ecclesiastico-civili Britannico et Hibernico. Lond. 1728, 4to. 2 vols. 15s.

A useful work.—1738, 4to. 2 vols.

OUGHTRED, William. Key of the Mathematics. Lond. 1647, 8vo.

With portrait by Hollar. Towneley, pt. II. 569, 9s. 6d. Onghtred published many other mathematical works.

OULTON, Walley Chamberlain. The History of the Theatres of London, containing an Annual Register of all the Tragedies, Comedies, &c. performed from 1771 to 1795, with Notes and Anecdotes. Lond. 1796, 12mo. 2 vols.

Intended as a continuation to B. Victor's history of the Theatres. Duke of York, 2877, 6s.

A History of the Theatres of London, from 1795 to 1817, inclusive. Lond. 1818, 12mo. 3 vols. 10s. 6d. The 3 vols bound in 4, Southey, 1840, 1l. 1s.

Beauties of modern Dramatists. Lond. 1800, 19mo. 2 vols.

The Traveller's Guide, or English Itinerary. Lond. 1805, crown 8vo. 2 vols. Drury, 2934, 13s. Duke of York, 5878, 16s.
Picture of Margate and its Vicinity. Lond. 1820, 8vo. with a map and 20 views.

OUNDLE. — Strange and wonderful News from Oundle in Northamptonshire; giving an impartial Relation of the Drumming Well, commonly called Dobse's Well. Lond. 1692, 8vo.

Eight pages, including the title-page.

OUSELEY, Sir William, Knt. Travels in various Countries of the East, more particularly Persia. Lond. 1819, 21, 22, 4to. 3 vols.

In high estimation. Drury, 3211, 5l. 16s.
The author was secretary to his brother, Sir Gore Ouseley, Bart. ambassador extraordinary to the Court of Persia, 1810-12.

Persian Miscellanies; an Essay to facilitate the Reading of Persian Manuscripts; with engraved Specimens, philological Observations, and Notes critical and historical. Lond. 1795, 4to. pp. 240, with ten plates.

Oriental Collections illustrating the History, Antiquities, Literature, &c. of Asia. Lond. 1797--1800, 4to. 3 vols. An interesting publication.

Epitome of the ancient History of Persia, extracted and translated from the Jehan Ara, a Persian Manuscript; by William Ouseley, Esq. Lond. 1799, 12mo. 6s. pp. 92, with a map of Persia, a plate of the ruins of Persepolis, and two vignettes.

The Oriental Geography of Ebn Haukal, an Arabian Traveller of the tenth Century. Translated by Sir William Ouseley, Knt. Lond. 1800. 4to. pp. xxxvi and 317, also title and dedication to the king. Fonthill 353, 17s.

The Bakhtyar Nameh, or History of Prince Bakhtvar and the Viziers, a Series of Persian Tales (with a Translation). Lond. 1801, royal 8vo.

Observations on some Medals and Gems bearing Inscriptions in the Pahlavi, or ancient Persick Character. Lond. 1801, 4to. Brockett, 2312, 6s. Combe, 1444, 7s. Fonthill, 1638, 16s.

— Sir William Gore, Bart. Remarks on the Statistics and political Institutions of the United States. Lond. 1832, 8vo. 9s.

Notices of Persian Poets, with critical and explanatory Remarks; with a Memoir of the Author by James Reynolds. Lond. [Oriental Translation Fund] 1846, 8vo.

OUTRAM, William. De Sacrificiis Libri duo; quorum altero explicantur omnia Judæorum nonnulla Gentium profanarum Sacrificia; altero Sacrificium Christi. Lond. 1677, 4to. 8s.

This work, according to Horne, 'is of singular use to the divinity student, as affording, in a comparatively small compass, one of the most masterly vindications of the vicarious atonement of Christ that ever was published.'—Translated by J. Allen, 1817, 8vo.

OUVAROFF, M. An Essay on the Mysteries of Eleusis, translated from the French by J. D. Price, with Observations by J. Christie. Lond. 1817, 8vo.

Hibbert, 5902, 12s. Bright, 2s.

OUVILLE, Alonso de. An historical Relation of the Kingdom of Chile, 1646.

In the third volume of the Churchill Collection of Voyages and Travels, and in the fourteenth volume of Pinkerton's Collection.

OVERALL, John, successively Bishop of Lichfield and Norwich. Convocation Book, MDCVI, concerning the Government of God's catholick Church. Lond. 1690, 4to. 7s.

With portraits of Overall and Sancroft, by R. White.—Oxford, 1844, 8vo. port. of Overall only.

OVERBEKE, Bonav. Degli Avanzi dell' Antica Roma, da Paolo Rolli. Lond. 1739, 8vo. 3s. 6d.

With plates. LARGE PAPER. Willett, 1883, russia, 1l. 3s.

OVERBURY, Sir Thomas, Knight. Miscellaneous Works in Verse and Prose, with Memoirs of his Life. The tenth edition. Lond. 1756, 12mo. 3s.

Garrick, 1725, 4s. 6d. See Retrosp. Rev, ll. 92–105. It is stated in the Gent. Mag. for Feb. 1840, p. 125, that this tenth edition does not contain many articles which are to be found in the edition of 1638, as 'ad Comitissam Rutlandiæ,' 'Paradoxes,' 'Receipts,' 'The Mountebank's Song.'

Miscellaneous Works, verse and prose, with Notes, and a biographical Account of the Author, by E. F. Rimbault, LL.D. Lond. 1856, post 8vo. portrait, 5s.

A Wife now a Widowe. Lond. for Lawrence Lisle at the Tygre's head, in Paul's Churchyard, 1614, 12mo. This First Edition does not contain any characters. Copies in the Bodleian and Trinity Coll. Cambridge.

A Wife now the Widdow of Sir Thomas Overburye. Being a most exquisite and singular Poem of the Choice of a Wife. Whereunto are added many witty Characters, and conceited Newes, written by himselfe and other learned Gentlemen his Friends. Lond. for Lawrence Lisle, 1614, 4to. second edition, pp. 64, not numbered, with portrait by Simon Pass. This edition contains twenty-one characters. Lloyd, 1012, 2l. 2s. Bibl. Anglo-Poet. 502, 4l. 4s. Heber, pt. iv. 1l. 1s.—Fourth edit. Lond. 1614, 4to. Halliwell, 3l. 19s.—Sixth Impression, Lond. 1615, sm. 8vo. pp. 162, with port. by Simon Pass. Bibl. Anglo-Poet. 503, 1l. 11s. 6d. This edition contains a passage not in any other.—Seventh edition, Lond. 1616, small 8vo. pp. 292, with portrait by S. Pass. Lloyd, 905, 4s. Bindley, pt. II. 2042, 8s. 2043, 6s. Stanley, 680, 1l. 2s. Bibl. Anglo-Poet. 504, 1l. 15s.—Eighth edit. Lond. 1616, sm. 8vo. with port. by S. Pass. Bindley, pt. II. 2043, 6s. Skegg, 1l. 10s.—The ninth Impression augmented, with new Newes and characters. Lond. 1618, small 8vo. pp. 292, with portrait by S. Pass. Lloyd, 905, 4s. Bindley, pt. II. 2043, 8s. 2045, 6s. Stanley, 680, 1l. 2s. Bibl. Anglo-Poet. 504, 1l. 15s. Bright, 15s. North, 2l. 19s. Brand, 2l. 12s.—Tenth edit. Lond. 1618, sm. 8vo. White Knights, 3020, mor. 1l. 10s.—The eleventh edit. Lond. 1622, sm. 8vo. front. by Lisle, A–V, in eights.—Dubl. 1626, 12mo.—Twelfth edition, Lond. 1627, small 8vo. Lloyd, 904, 14s. Bindley, pt. II. 2045, Nassau, pt. I. 2474, with portrait of Overbery by Lisle, russia, 1l. Heber, pt. vii. 2s.—Thirteenth edition, Lond. 1628, small 8vo. Bright, 18s. Garrick, 1725, 7s. 6d.—Fourteenth edition, Lond. 1630, small 8vo. Bindley, pt. II. 2041. Stanley, 681, 18s.—Fifteenth Impression. Lond. 1632, small 8vo. pp. 320. Stanley, 682, 15s. Bibl. Anglo-Poet. 505, 1l. 1s. Bright, 18s.—The sixteenth edition, Lond. 1638, small 8vo. Nassau, pt. I. 2475, portrait inserted, 8s. Bindley, pt. II. 2044. Strettell, 1054, with portrait by Lisle, 12s. 6d. Caldecott, 6s.—Lond. 1664, small 8vo. Sotheby's in 1821, 6s. 6d. Sir Thomas Overbury's Wife will likewise be found in Capell's Prolusions, 1762.

The illustrious Wife, viz. that excellent Poem, Sir Thomas Overbvrie's Wife, illustrated by Giles Oldisworth, Nephew to the same Sir T. O. 1673. No copy known.

The first and second part of the Remedy of Love: Written by Sir Thomas Over-

OVERBURY, Sir T.—*continued.*
bury, Knight. Lond. N. Okes, 1620, 16mo.
A copy is in the British Museum. Sixteen
leaves, the first and last blank. Warton
quaries a former edition.

The just Downfall of Ambition, Adultery, Murder: at the end of which are added Weston's and Mrs. Turner's last Teares, shed for the Murder of Sir Thomas Overbury, poysoned in the Tower; who, for the Fact, suffered deserued Execution at Tiburne, the 14 of November last, 1615, 4to. Fifteen leaves, woodcut on title. Reed, 8781, 1l. 3s. Skegg, 5l.—1616, 4to. Hibbert, 6033, 2l. 6d. Strettell, 361, 1l. 13s. 6d. Saunders' in 1818, 2l. 12s. 6d. The title of this rare tract is given somewhat differently in Gent. Mag. Feb. 1840, p. 134, where we are told that it is in verse, with a portrait of Mrs. Turner, and bears no date.

Sir Thomas Overbury, his Observations in his Travailes, upon the State of the seventeen Provinces, as they stood in 1609; the Treatie of Peace being then on Foote, 1626. 4to. Fifteen leaves. Nassau, pt. ii. 577, 9s. Stevens, 1017, 10s. 6d. North. pt. iii. 591, 10s. 6d. Fonthill, 2755, 1l. 4s. Heber, pt. vi. 3s. There is probably an earlier edition, as it was licensed 24th Jan. 1615-16.—Lond. 1651, 12mo. pp. 60, with 'the lively portraiture of Sir Thomas Overbury,' by S. Pass. Nassau, pt. i. 2176, 5s. This tract is reprinted in the first volume of the Oxford Collection of Voyages and Travels, and in the 7th volume of the Harleian Miscellany. The original MS. is in the Lambeth Library.

A true and historical Relation of the Poysoning of Sir Thomas Overbury, with the several Arraignments and Speeches of those that were executed thereupon. Also, all the Passages concerning the Divorce between Robert late Earl of Essex, and the Lady Frances Howard; with King James's and other large Speeches. Collected out of the Papers of Sir Francis Bacon, the King's Attorney-General. Lond. 1651, 12mo. pp. 127, not including the title, with a portrait of Sir Thomas Overbury, Laur. L.isle sxcud. Bindley, pt. iii. 239, 13s. Nassau, pt. ii. 220, 13s. Skegg, 5s. *See* DAVIES, p. 608.

OVERBURY'S VISION. *See* NICCOLLS, Richard.

OVERS, John. The true History of the Life and sudden Death of old John Overs, the rich Ferry-Man of London, and of his Daughter Mary, who caused the Church of St. Mary Overs in Southwark to be built; and of the Building of London Bridge. Lond. 1744, 8vo. Pp. 30, exclusive of the title. First printed in 1637, 12mo. with woodcuts.

OVERTON, John. Jacobs troublesome Journey to Bethel, containing a briefe Exposition of the four first Verses of the 33rd Chapter of Genesis. Oxford, 1586, 16mo.
Dedicated to Maister Wm. Brent.

— John. The True Churchman ascertained. York, 1808, 8vo.
Williams, 1282, 13s.

The Chronology of the Apocalypse, investigated and defended. Lond. 1822, 8vo.

An Inquiry into the Truth and Use of the Book of Enoch, as to its Prophecies, Visions and Accounts of fallen Angels. Lond. 1822, 8vo.

— Richard. Articles of High Treason exhibited against Cheapside Crosse, with the last Will and Testament of the said Crosse, and certain Epitaphs upon her Tombe. Lond. 1642, 4to.
Four leaves. Lloyd, 1012, 11s. 6d. Skegg, 6s.

Man's Mortalitie; or a Treatise wherein 'tis proved, both theologically and philosophically, that the whole Man is a Compound wholly mortal, &c. Lond. 1644, 4to. With a frontispiece of Death, a clock, &c. with verses underneath, engraved by W. Bentley.
Overton published other tracts, most of which are in the British Museum.

— W. Exhortation to the Judges and Justices of Sussex, and the whole Countie assembled at the Assizes. Lond. by H. Newbery and H. Bynneman, 16mo.
Bright, 10s. 6d.

OVID. P. Ovidii Nasonis Opera, e Textu Burmanni; cum Notis Bentleii hactenus ineditis, necnon Harlesii, Gierigii, Burmanni, Lemairii, et aliorum selectissimis. Oxonii, 1825, 8vo. 5 vols. 2l. 2s.
A very neat and accurate edition. LARGE PAPER in royal 8vo. published at 5l. 5s. LARGE AND THICK PAPER. Twelve copies struck off.

Opera. Lond. 1582-3, 16mo. 3 vols. A neat edition, printed by Thomas Vautrollier.

OVID—*continued.*
Opera, curante M. Maittaire. Lond. 1715, 12mo. 3 vols. A neat and correct edition, with an index. Garrick, 1731, 10s. 6d. Roxburghe, 2004, 11s. LARGE PAPER. Hibbert, 5l. 5s. 2l. Dent, pt. i. 515, morocco by Roger Payne, 5l. 7s. 6d. Heath, 3l. 10s, ll. 19s.
Opera. Lond. 1745, 18mo. 5 vols. Brindley's edition. White Knights, 8l. 12s. 6s.
Opera, ex Editione Burmanni. Lond. 1815, 24mo. 8 vols. 10s. 6d. The Regent's edition.
Opera ex edit. Burmanniana, cum Notis in usum Delphini et Variorum curante Valpy. Lond. 1821, 8vo. 9 vols. published at 9l. 9s. now 2l. 2s. LARGE PAPER, royal 8vo. 3l. 3s.

METAMORPHOSES.
In Latin, or Latin and English.
Ovidiani Metamorphoseis moraliter a Tho. Walleys Anglico. Paris, in ædibus Ascensianis, 1511, 4to. — Par. Regnault, 1515, 8vo.
Metamorphoseon Libri XV. ab Andrea Naugerio castigati, at Vict. Giselini Scholiis illustrati. Lond. 1489, 18mo.—Lond. 1569, 16mo. Ea, in eights, printed in neat brevier italic.
Metamorphoseon Libri XV. Interpretations & Notis, ad Usum serenissimi Delphini. Lond. 1708, 8vo. Reprinted 1716, 1730, 1810, and since, 10s. 6d.
Cum Annotationibus Variorum. Dublin, 1729, 4to. A correct and splendid edition, printed by Grierson. LARGE PAPER. Mac Carthy, morocco, 80 francs.
Metamorphoses in Latin and English, translated by the most eminent Hands; with historical Explanations of the Fables, by the Abbé Banier. Adorned with Sculptures by Picart and other ancient Masters. Amsterdam, 1732, folio, 2 vols. Dent, pt. ii. 934, 3l. 6s. North, pt. ii. 1433, russia, 5l. LARGE PAPER. Hibbert, 6091, russia, 6l. 8s. 6d. Edwards, 791, russia, 10l. LARGEST PAPER. Stanley, 183, 2l. 5s.
Metamorphoses, cum variis Lectionibus. With Abbé Banier's Arguments and Explanations of the History and Mythology of each Fable in English. Lond. 1747, 8vo. Gough, 2000, 7s. 6d.
Metamorphoses, cum Versione Latina prosaica et Notis Anglicis, a Nathan. Halley. Lond. 1724, 8vo. Reprinted 1730, 1741, and since.
Metamorphoses, in Latin and English, by John Clarke. Lond. 1735, 8vo. A literal translation, reprinted in 1760, and since, 7s. 6d.
Metamorphoses, translated into English Prose, with the Latin Text and English Notes. Lond. 1748, 8vo. 7s. A correct and good prose translation with useful Notes, printed for Joseph Davidson. Reprinted, 1754, 1759, 1797, 1824, 6s.
Metamorphoses, translated by Thomas Orger, with the Latin Text printed in form of Notes. Lond. 1811, 8vo. 2 vols. 7s.
Metamorphoses, Selections from, Latin and English, on the Hamiltonian System. Lond. 1829, 12mo. 7s.

EPISTOLÆ, FASTI, TRISTIA, &c.
In Latin, or Latin and English.
P. Ovidii Nasonis Heroidum Epistolæ, Amorum Libri iii. De Arte Amandi Libri iii. De Remedio Amoris Libri ii. &c. Lond. 1583, 16mo.—Lond. 1594, 12mo.
Epistolarum Heroidum Liber, cum Interp. & Notis, ad Usum sereu. Delphini. Lond. 1702, 8vo. Reprinted 1714, 1729, &c.
Epistolæ, cum Versione Latina et Notis Anglicis a N. Bailey. Lond. 1744, 8vo. Reprinted 1752, &c.
Epistles, translated into English Prose, with Latin text and English Notes. Lond. published by Davidson, 1748, 8vo.—1752, &c.—1767, 6s. Other editions.
Heroides, ex editione P. Burmanni (edidit H. Homer). Lond. 1789, 8vo. 8s. LARGE PAPER in royal 8vo. Duke of Grafton, 546, 8s. 6d. Drury, 3215, russia. 6s.
P. Ouidii Nasonis Fastorum Libri vi. Tristium Libri v. De Ponto Libri iiii. In 1 bin. Ad Livium. Lond. 1583, 16mo.
Fasti, in Usum Delphini, recensuit et emendavit A. Tooke. Lond. 1720, 8vo. Other editions.
Fasti, with English Notes by T. Keightley. Dub. 1833, post 8vo. 6s. 6d.
Fasti, with Annotations by W. Toynne. Dub. 1833, 12mo.
Fasti, with English Notes by Stanford. Dub. 1838, 12mo.
P. Ovidii Nasonis de Tristibus Libri v. cum Interpretatione et Notis, in Usum Delphini. Cantab. 1709, 8vo. Reprinted 1705, 1719, &c.
Tristia, cum Versione Latina et Notis Anglicis a N. Bailey. Lond. 1726, 8vo. Reprinted in 1729.
De Tristibus Libri v. sive Analysis Ovidiana Ordine prosaico ad verbum, Paraphrasi et Notis Illustrata. Opera O. Dyke. Lond. 1797, 8vo.

TRANSLATIONS OF THE METAMORPHOSES.

Ouyde his Books of Metamorphose translated by William Caxton. Printed from a MS. in the Pepysian collection (No. 2124) at Cambridge containing the last five books of the Metamorphoses in prose. 1819, 4to. Presented to the Members of the Roxburghe Club by George Hibbert, Esq. Sir M. M. Sykes, 81. Bosweil, 3054, 4l. 6s. Dent, pt. ii. 1214, 6l. 10s. Crawford, mor. by Hayday, 12l.

OVID—*continued.*

The Fable of Ould treting of Narcissus, translated oute of Latin into Englysh Mytre, with a Moral thereunto, very plesaunte to rede. 1560. Lond. by Thomas Hackette, 4to. Eighteen leaves. At the end is 'Finis. Quod T. H.' These initials are by Ritson confidently attributed to Thomas Howell. *See* HOWELL, T. Rawd, £497, 3*l*. 19s. Bibl. Anglo-Poet. 325, 22*l*. resold Saunders' in 1818, 12*l*. 12s. Heber, pt. iv. 3*l*. 8s. Dolland, 7*l*. Utterson, 6*l*.

The pleasant Fable of Hermaphroditus and Salmacis. 1565. *See* PEEND, T.

Metamorphoses, The fyrst fower Bookes of the, translated oute of Latin into English Meter by Arthur Golding, Gent. Lond. by William Seres, 1565, 4to. A translation in lines of fourteen syllables. The first book contains fol. 12; the second 14; the third 12; and the fourth 12; exclusive of the dedication to 'Robert, Erle of Leycester,' and preface. Each book has a fresh set of signatures, with a colophon. Heber, pt. iv. 2*l*. 19s. Caldecott, 1*l*. 18s.

Metamorphosis, XV. Bookes of the, translated oute of Latin into English Meeter, by Arthur Golding, Gentleman. Lond. by Willyam Seres, 1567, 4to. FIRST EDITION of the complete translation. BLACK LETTER. Contains 200 leaves, besides a dedication to 'Robert, Erle of Leycester,' and a preface. Sir M. M. Sykes, pt. ii. 654, russia, 2*l*. 5s. — 1575, 4to. Contains, besides the prefixes, 190 leaves, numbered 191, no. 113 being omitted. Nassau, pt. ii. 579, 9s. Hand, 7l04, 1*l*. 18s. Heber, pt. iv. 1*l*. 15s.; pt. viii. 1*l*. 17s.; another, 1*l*. 11s.—Lond. 1584, 4to. —Lond. by Robert Waldegraue, 1587, 4to. folios 200, besides dedication and preface. Hibl. Anglo-Poet. 303, 6*l*. 6s. Steevens, 773, 11s. Bindley, pt. iii. 971, 12s.—Lond. by John Danter, 1593, 4to. A—Cc, in eights, including title. Sign. Z is omitted. Perry, pt. i. 2350, 10s. 6d. Sotheby's in 1823, 1*l*. 1s. — Lond. by W. W. 1603, 4to. 191 folios, with title, epistle dedicatory, and preface, 10 leaves. Bright, 9s.—1603, 4to. Boswell, 1642, 7s.—1612, 4to. Garrick, 1629. *See* Warton's Hist. of English Poetry, 8vo. vol. iv. 235-9.

Metamorphoses, the first five Books of, (by George Sandys). Second edition. Imprinted for W. D. 1621, 16mo. pp. 141, besides introduction. The title is engraved by F. Delaram, and a head of Ovid in an oval, with verses beneath, is prefixed.

Metamorphoses, englished by G(eorge) S(andys). Lond. 1626, folio. Sandys is pronounced by Dryden to be the best versifier of the last age: and Pope affirmed, in his notes to the Iliad, that English poetry owed much of its present beauty to his (Sandys') translations. The translation is accompanied with valuable notes collected from various authors. Dent, pt. ii. 1711, 6s. Bibl. Anglo-Poet. 650, 1*l*. 10s. Heber, pt. iv. 9s.—Lond. 1627.—Oxford, 1632, folio. Roxburghe, 2530, 7s. Bindley, pt. ii. 1712, 7s. LARGE PAPER. Bright, presentation copy, old mor. 2*l*. 17s. Heber, pt. iv. beautiful copy, gilt edges, 4*l*. 7s. resold Gardner in 1854, 9*l*. Nassau, pt. ii. 418, 19s. Heber, pt. iv. 14s.—Oxford, 1632.—Lond. 1638.—Lond. 1640, folio.—Lond. 1669, sm. 8vo.—Lond. 1673.—Lond. 1678.—Lond. 1682.—Eighth edition, 1690, 8vo.

Wisdom's Conquest, being an Explanation and grammatical Translation of the 13th Book of Ovid's Metamorphoses (by Tho. Hall). Lond. 1651, 8vo. A copy is in the Bodleian Library.

Phaeton's Folly, or the Downfall of Pride, transl. paraphrastically and grammatically, from the second Book of Ovid's Metamorphoses; also the first Elegy of Ovid's Book De Tristibus, by Tho. Hall. Lond. 1655. 8vo. 7s.

Metamorphosis translated grammatically, and also according to the Propriety of our English Tongue, by J. Bulloker. Lond. 1656, 12mo.

The Passion of Dyblis, made English, from Metam. lib. ix. by John Dennis. Lond. 1692, 4to.

Metamorphoses, in fifteen Books, translated by the most eminent Hands (viz. Dryden, Addison, Congreve, Nich. Rowe, Gay, Ambr. Phillips, Croxall, Sewell, and Garth), and adorned with Sculptures. Lond. 1717, folio. Prefixed to this translation is a portrait of the Princess of Wales, an elegant preface, giving a general idea of the work, the uses to which it may be applied, and how the poem may be read to most profit. Bindley, pt. ii. 1713, 13s. LARGE PAPER. Roxburghe, 2834, mor. 1*l*. 1s. Heber, pt. iv. old mor. 2*l*. 2s.

Lond. 1717, 12mo. 2 vols. 6s. — 1720, 12mo. 2 vols. Willett, 1568, 5s. 6d. Dent, pt. i. 715, with Ovid's Epistles, 1716, Art of Love and Amours, 1719, morocco by Roger Payne, 4*l*. 7s.—1724, 12mo. 2 vols. Roxburghe, 2632, 4s. Dent, pt. ii. 60, morocco, 12s. Garrick, 1732, 4s. 6d.—1727, 12mo. 3 vols.—1783, 12mo. 2 vols.—1746, 12mo. 2 vols. Fonthill, 3550, 18s.—1751, 12mo. 2 vols. 6s.—Dublin, 1769, 12mo. 2 vols. —Lond. 1778, 12mo. 2 vols. Nassau, pt. ii. 117, 11s. — Lond. 1807, 12mo. 2 vols. plates, 6s. This translation will also be found in the twentieth volume of Chalmers' Collection of the Poets, Walker's Classics, 1807, 3s. Valpy's Fam. Class. Lib. 12mo. 4s. 6d.

Metamorphosis epitomized in an English poetical Style. For the Use and

OVID—*continued*.
Entertainment of the Ladies of Great Britain. Lond. 1740, 12mo. An indifferent performance. Nassau, pt. i. 2479, 2s.
A new Translation of the second Book of the Metamorphoses by Wm. Green M.D. Liverpool, 1783, 12mo.
Metamorphoses, in English blank Verse, translated by J. J. Howard. Lond. 1807, 8vo. 2 vols. 5s.
The two first Books of the Metamorphoses, attempted in English Verse, by William Mills. 1808, 12mo. 5s.
Metamorphoses, literally translated into English Prose by H. T. Riley. Lond. 1852, [Vol. 2 of Ovid's Works, in Bohn's Classical Library], post 8vo. 5s.

TRANSLATIONS OF THE EPISTLES.

Heroycall Epistles, in English Verse, by George Tuberuile, Gent. with Aulus Sabinus' Answeres to certaines of the same. Lond. by Henry Denham, 1567, 8vo. FIRST EDITION. A copy in the Capell Collection. Heber, pt. iv. 1l. 19s.; made up of two editions, pt. viii. 16s. Contains 162 leaves, besides dedication to 'Lord Tho. Howarde, Viscount Byndon,' &c. 'The translator to his muse,' and his epistle 'To the reader.'—Lond. by H. Denham, 1569, 16mo. 2l. 3s. Perry, pt. ii. 693, title wanting, 10s. 6d. resold Bright, 5s. A to Y 4, in eights, A 1 blank, and Y 4 containing the colophon, dedicated to 'Lord Tho. Howarde, Viscount Byndon,' &c.—Lond. by Henry Denham, 16mo. Heber, pt. iv. apparently wanting two of the epistles and address, 16s. At the end of this edition are 11 six-lined stanzas from 'The translator to the captious sort of sycophants,' and correction of 'faultes escaped.'—Lond. by John Charlewood, n.d. (1567 ?) 16mo. X. in eights. Hibbert, 5927, 12s. 6d. Sir M. M. Sykes, pt. ii. 594, 14s. Nassau, pt. i. 2481, russia, 2l. 2s. Bibl. Anglo-Poet. 759, morocco, 12l. Bright, cut close, 1l. 12s.—Lond. by Simon Stafford, 1600, 16mo. X. in eights. Constable, 687, 13s. Sotheby's in 1821, morocco, 1l. 18s. Bibl. Anglo-Poet. 760, morocco, 8l. 8s.
Heroical Epistles, translated by Sir Ed. Sherburne. Lond. E. G. 1639, sm. 8vo. frost by Marshall, 5s.
Heroical Epistles, translated into English Verse by W(ye) S(altonstall), and illustrated with 24 Pictures. Lond. 1626.—1636, Nassau, pt. i. 2482, 4s.—Lond. 1663, 10s. 6d.—1671, 12mo.—Lond. 1673, sm. 8vo. pp. 702, with engravings pasted on the blank spaces at the commencement of the epistles. Bibl. Anglo-Poet. 719, 1l. 11s. 6d.—Lond. 1677, small 8vo. pp. 202, with frontispiece and plates by Glover. Hibbert, 5926, 6s. 6d. Bibl. Anglo-Poet. 718, 12s.—Lond. 1690, 12mo.

Heroical Epistles, translated into English by Francis Quarles. Lond. 1675, 8vo.
Epistles, transl. by several Hands, with the Addition of three Epistles of Aulus Sabinus, in Answer to as many of Ovid, made English by Salisbury. Lond. 1640, 8vo. with cuts. Skegg, 5s. Frequently reprinted.—Lond. 1683.—Lond. 1716, 12mo. An esteemed edition. Dent. pt. ii. 715, with Ovid's Metamorphoses, 1720, 2 vols. and his Art of Love and Amours, 1719, morocco by Roger Payne, 4l. 7s.—1725, 12mo. with his Amours, &c.—Lond. 1729, 12mo. 7s.—Lond. 1735, 12mo. 7s.
Epistles, translated into English Verse, with critical Essays and Notes, by S. Barrett, A.M. Lond. 1759, 8vo. 3s. A performance of no merit.
Heroids; or, Epistles from the Heroines of Antiquity, translated into English Verse by James Ewen. Lond. 1787, 8vo. 4s. A poor performance.
Four heroic Epistles, translated into English Verse. Atcester, 1803, crown 8vo. 2s. 6d.
Epistles, translated by E. D. Baynes. Lond. 1818, 8vo. vol. i.
Epistles, translated by Miss Garland. Lond. 1842, 8vo. 10s.
The Heroides, or Epistles of the Heroines, the Amours, Art of Love, Remedy of Love, and Minor Works of Ovid, literally translated, with Notes by H. T. Riley. Lond. 1852, [Vol. 3 of Ovid's Works in Bohn's Classical Library], post 8vo. 5s.

TRANSLATIONS OF THE FASTI.

Festivals; or, Romane Calendar, Englished by J. Gower. Camb. 1640, small 8vo. Hibbert, 5930, 8s. Coustable, 689, 8s. Steevens, 974, 8s. 6d. Nassau, pt. i. 2478, 10s. Garrick, 1735, 6s. 6d.
Fasti; or, the Romans sacred Calendar, translated into English Verse, with explanatory Notes by Wm. Massey, Master of a Boarding School at Wandsworth. Lond. 1757, 8vo. 4s. An unharmonious versification, with puerile and insignificant notes. Garrick, 1736, 5s.
Fasti, translated in English prose by Isaac Burt, LL.D. Dublin, 1833. Reprinted, 1844, 12mo. 3s. 6d.
Fasti, Tristia, Poetic Epistles, Ibis, and Halieuticon, literally translated, with notes, by H. T. Riley. Lond. [Vol I. of Ovid's Works in Bohn's Classical Library], 1851, post 8vo. 5s.

TRANSLATIONS OF THE ART OF LOVE.

The Flores of Ovide de Arte Amandi, with theyr Englysshe afore them, and Two alphabete Tables. Lond. in ædibus

OVID—*continued.*
Wynandl, de Worde, 1518, 4to. BLACK
LETTER. Unknown to Herbert or Dibdin,
and not noticed in Steevens' list prefixed
to Malone's Shakspeare. Geo. Chalmers,
pt. ii. 588, 21l. 10s.
Remedie of Loue. Translated (in Verse)
and intituled to the Youth of England, by
F. L. Printed by T(homas) C(reed) for
Iohn Browne, 1600, 4to.—A former edition, 1599, 4to.
Remedy of Love, by Sir T. Overbury.
Lond. 1620, 18mo. *See* OVERBURY.
Art of Love (in Verse). Middleburgh
(1598), 18mo.
Art of Love, by Francis Wolferston.
Lond. 1661. Dent, pt. ii. 61, morocco,
4s. 6d. Jadis, 126, morocco, 12s, Reed,
7904, 4s. 6d.
De Arte Amandi and the Remedy of
Love englished, in verse; as also the Loves
of Hero and Leander, a mock Poem; together with choice Poems and rare Pieces of
Drollery. Lond. 1662, 12mo. with head
by Marshall. Hibbert, 5915, morocco, 12s.
Heber, pt. iv. 5s. — Lond. 1677, 12mo. —
Skegg, 11s.—1696, 12mo. Bindley, pt. ii.
1l. 1s.—Lond. 1705, 12mo.
De Arte Amandi; or, the Art of Love.
16mo. Heber, pt. iv. 3s. A—F 6, in
eights, with an engraved title-page, at
the bottom of which is 'Gedruckt tot
Amsterdam by Nicolas Iansz. Visscher.'
The proheme commences 'If there be any
in this multitude,' and the first book,
'First thou that are a Freshman and are
bent,' &c.
De Arte Amandi, or the Art of Love:
the first Book. The latter, Hero and
Leander, from the Greek of Musæus, by
Tho. Hoy. Lond. 1682, 4to.
Art of Love, together with the Remedy
of Love, by several Hands. Lond. 1709,
8vo. Roxburghe, 2633, 8s. LARGE PAPER,
Dent, pt. ii. 62, morocco, 1l. 8s.—Lond.
1712, 8vo. cuts, 7s. 6d.—1719. Dent, pt. i.
715, with Ovid's Metamorphoses, 1720,
2 vols. and Epistles, 1716, morocco, by
Roger Payne, 4l. 7s.—1725. Willett, 1857,
8s. Bindley, pt. ii. 2052, morocco, 11s.—
Lond. 1785, 12mo., cuts, 6s.—Lond. 1791,
12mo. 4s.
The Art of Love, in Imitation of Ovid,
by Dr. William King. Lond. 1714, 8vo. 4s.
This work is divided into fourteen books,
most of them ending with some remarkable fable and interesting novel.
Art of Love, paraphrased and adapted
to the present State; with Notes, by Geo.
Fielding. Lond. 1747, 8vo.
Art of Love, Remedy of Love, and
Amours. Lond 1804, 12mo. with plates,
5s. 6d.; small 8vo. 10s. 6d.—Lond. 1813,
6s. 6d. Several editions printed with the
Metamorphoses.

For the only English prose translation
of 'The Art of Love,' see the previous column under 'Epistles.'

TRANSLATIONS OF THE TRISTIA, OR
ELEGIES, IBIS, &c.

De Tristibus, the first three Bookes,
translated into English by Tho. Churchyard. Lond. by Tho. Marsh, 1540, 4to.
Dedicated to Maister Christopher Hatton,
Esq. A copy is in the Bodleian Library.
Wood mentions an edition of the date of
1578. Farmer, 2l. 4s. Heber, pt. iv. 859,
wanting title and first leaf, 2l. 15s. The
only perfect copy known is in the library
of Earl Spencer, which was reprinted by
him, Lond. 1816, 4to. and presented to the
members of the Roxburghe Club. Sir
M. M. Sykes, 1817, 1l. 19s. Roswell, 3097,
4l. 1s. Dent, pt. ii. 1194, 2l. 10s. On
VELLUM. One copy struck off, now in Earl
Spencer's library.
Tristia, translated into English by
W(ye) S(altonstall). Lond. 1633, small
8vo. pp. 128. Bibl. Anglo-Poet. 717, 2l. 2s.
—1637—1673, with frontispiece. Bindley,
pt. ii. 2047, 8s.—Fourth edition, 1681, with
frontispiece by Cecil. Hibbert, 5929, 4s.
—Fifth edition, 1690, 5s.
De Tristibus: mournefull Elegies in
English Verse by Zach. Catlin. Lond.
1639, 8vo. Bindley, pt. ii. 2045, 9s. Towneley, pt. i. 588, 8s. Garrick. 871, 1l. 10s.
Tristia; containing five Books of mournful Elegies, newly translated by F. P.
Lond. 1713, 12mo.
All Ovid's Elegies: 3 Bookes, by C(ristopher) M(arlow). Epigrams (48) by J(ohn)
D(avis). At Middleboorgh, n. d. (1598),
16mo. A to F, in eights, including title,
forty-eight leaves. This volume was condemned and burnt at Stationers' Hall, by
an order of the Archb. of Canterbury
and the Bishop of London, dated June 1,
1599. There were at least three impressions, two titles commencing 'All,' the
other 'Certaine.' *Collation of copy with*
'All' *on the title.*—Title; Book 1. Elegia
8 is marked as 5; Book II. Elegia 7 is
marked as 5; Book III. Elegia 6 is numbered as 5, and so continued wrong to the
end. The same error occurs in the other
two copies from which Mr. Dyce prints;
but as the orthography differs, we give
the first few lines, to show the variation:—

'We which were *Ovid's* five bookes, now
are three,
For these before the rest preferreth he.
If reading five thou plainst of tediousness,
Two tane away, thy labour will be lesse.
With Muse prepar'd I meant to sing of
Armes,
Chusing a subject fit for fierce alarmes.

5 T

OVID—continued.

Both verses were alike, till love (men say) Began to smile and tooke one foot away.'

In Mr. Hanrott's copy the imprint was in capitals; and the Epigrammes by J. D. commenced on the reverse of E viii. and end on F viii. many words spelt in the other edition with the y final, are in this printed ie. In another impression differing only in title, 'Ovid,' &c. 'All 'Ovid's Elegies. Middleborough, n. d. The entire 48 Epigrammes (of which the second part consists) are given to J. D. 'I believe there were five if not six different impressions, in despite of ecclesiastical interdiction. The first of these had appeared in 1596, as Harington's Metamorphosis of Ajax sufficiently testifies. A duplicate version of Eleg. xv. lib. i. is ascribed to B. J. probably Ben. Jonson, and if so, must have been his earliest printed production.'—*Park*. Nassau, pt. i. 2479, 2l. 13s. White Knights, 8034, 4l. Hibbert, 5093, russia, 1l. Bindley, pt. iii. 2211, one leaf, A 4, wanting, 5l. 10s. Bindley, pt. i. 1778, 3l. 18s. 6d. — Another edition, pp. 59. White Knights, 3034, 4l. Nassau, pt. i. 2477, 2l. 15s. Strettell, 1055, mor. 6l. 12s. Crauford, in 1854, 2l. Sir M. M. Sykes, pt. ii. 583, morocco, 3l. Sotheby's in May 1823, 3l. 18s. 6d. Bibl. Anglo-Poet. 439, 7l. 7s. Heber, pt. iv. 2l. 1s. The 'Certaine' impression edited by Maitland, was reprinted, n. d. Twenty-five copies struck off. Constable, 688, 7s. 6d. It is likewise reprinted in Pickering's edition of Marlowe's Works, edited by the Rev. A. Dyce. See DAVIES, John, p. 592.

De Ponto, four Books of, translated into English by Wye Saltonstall. First edit. Lond. 1639, 12mo.—Lond. 1640, 12mo.

Invectiue against Ibis. Translated into English Meter (by Thos. Vnderdowne). Wherevnto is added by the Translator, a short Draught of all the Stories and Tales contained therein. Lond. T. East and H. Middleton, 1569, 8vo.—Lond. by Henry Bynneman, 1577, 16mo. M 4, in signs, with dedication to Lord Buckhurst and a preface. Bibl. Anglo-Poet. 757, 10l. 10s. Bright, corners of leaves slightly torn, 1l. 12s.

Invective, or Curse against Ibis, translated into English Verse by John Jones. Oxford, 1658, small 8vo. pp. 192. Bibl. Anglo-Poet. 599, 3l. 3s.—1657. Nassau, pt. i. 3426, 6s. Drury, 2950, 6s. Bright, 2l. 2s.

Banquet of Sence, &c. See CHAPMAN, George.

Walnut-Tree Transplanted, by Richard Hatton. (In Verse.) Lond. 1827, sm. 8vo. Bright, supposed unique, 7l. 7s. probably printed for private circulation, as the translator dedicated it to his mother.

OVIDIANA.

Clavis Ovidiana. A numerical Key to Ovid's Metamorphosis. Lond. 1715, 12mo.

Ovidius exulans, or Ovid travestie, a mock Poem on five Epistles of Ovid. Lond. 1673, 8vo. pp. 100, with head of Ovid. Towneley, pt. ii. 1544, 5s. Bibl. Anglo-Poet. 608, 1l. 11s. 6d. Nassau, pt. i. 2437, 6s. Bindley, pt. ii. 2055, 12s. Heber, pt. iv. 1s.

The Wits paraphras'd; or Paraphrase upon Paraphrase, in a Burlesque on the several late Translations of Ovid's Epistles. Lond. 1680, 8vo. pp. 180. Bindley, pt. iii. 1150, 10s.; 2185, 7s. 6d.; pt. iv. 456, 5s. 6d. Perry, pt. iv. 278, 2s. Bibl. Anglo-Poet. 839, 18s. Hibbert, 6545, 4s. Heber, pt. i. 5s. 6d.

Ovid travestie, a Burlesque upon Ovid's Epistles. By Capt. Alexander Ratcliffe, of Gray's Inn. Lond. — Second edition, enlarged, with ten Epistles never before printed. 1681.—Fourth edit. Lond. 1705, 8vo. pp. 142. Bibl. Anglo-Poet. 627, 1l. 4s.

The Speeches of Ajax and Ulysses on claiming the Armour of Achilles, translated by Hensley. Lond. 1815, 8vo. only 20 printed. Hibbs, 1l. 1s.

Ajax his Speech to the Grecian Knabbs, attempted in broad Buchans, by R(obert) F(orbes). Gent. &c. Glasg. 1755, 12mo.— Edinb. 1765, 12mo. 5s. To this edition the Pelemo-Middinia is subjoined.— Edinb. 1754, 8vo. Also in the 'Carmine Macaronica,' 1824, 8vo. It is also included in a Select Collection of Scots' Poems, chiefly in the Broad Buchan Dialect. Edinb. 1785, 12mo.

Ovid's WORKS, complete, literally translated into English prose, with copious notes, by H. T. Riley. Lond. [Bohn's Classical Library] 1852-59, 3 vols. post 8vo. 15s.

OVINGTON, John, M.A. Voyage to Suratt in 1689, with an Appendix containing, I. The History of a late Revolution in the Kingdom of Golconda. II. A Description of the Kingdoms of Aracan and Pegu. III. An Account of the Coins of India, Persia, Golconda, &c. IV. Observations concerning the Silk-worms. Lond. 1696, 8vo.

Willett, 1852, 5s. Hibbert, 5932, 5s. Fonthill, 2910, 7s. Heath, 2686, 7s.

On the Nature and Quality of Tea. Lond. 1697, 8vo. Bliss, 4s.

OWEN, Charles. Essay towards the Natural History of Serpents. Lond. 1742, 4to. 16s.

—— Chev. Voiage du Chev. Owen au Purgatoire de St. Patrix. folio, without place or date.

A popular legend of the middle ages, but the book, separately printed, is undescribed by bibliographers. Large black Gothic letter, a 1 to e v, on which is 'Deo Gratias,' without title, heading, or pagination. Bright, 8l. 8s.

—— Corbett. Carmen Pindaricum in Theatrum Sheldonianum, in solennibus magnifici Operis Encœniis. Oxon. 1669, 4to.

—— David. Herod and Pilate reconciled ; or, the Concord of Papist and Puritan (against Scripture, Fathers, Councels, and other Orthodoxall Writers) for the Coercion, Deposition, and Killing of Kings. Cambridge, 1610, 4to.

An interesting discourse on the same subject as Milton's Tenure of Kings and Magistrates.
Antiparæus: sive Determinatio de Jure Regio. Cant. 1622, 12mo.

—— Edward. Etchings. Lond. 1826, royal folio, portrait and 45 plates.
Privately printed. Lytton, 5l. 12s. 6d.

—— Henry, D.D. A brief Account, historical and critical, of the Septuagint Version of the Old Testament. To which is added, a Dissertation on the comparative Excellency of the Hebrew and Samaritan Pentateuch. Lond. 1787, 8vo.

This brief account 'should be read by every man who wishes to be acquainted with the history of that version.'—*Bishop Marsh*. The Rev. T. H. Horne observes, all Dr. Henry Owen's works are characterised by sound criticism and laborious research.

Observations on the four Gospels; tending, chiefly, to ascertain the Times of their Publication; and to illustrate the Form and Manner of their Composition. Lond. 1764, 8vo.

Short Directions to young Students in Divinity, and Candidates for holy Orders. Lond. 1703, 8vo.

An Enquiry into the present State of the Septuagint Version of the Old Testament. Lond. 1769, 8vo. 'A work very deserving of the reader's attention.'—*Bp. Watson.*
The Intent and Propriety of the Scripture Miracles considered and explained, in a Series of Sermons, preached in the Parish Church of St. Mary Le-Bow, in the Years 1769, 1770, and 1771; for the Lecture founded by the Hon. Robert Boyle, Esq. Lond. 1773, 8vo. 2 vols.—1755, 8vo. 1 vol.
Critica Sacra ; or a short Introduction to Hebrew Criticism. With a Supplement. Lond. 1774-5, 8vo.
Critica Sacra examined. By Raphael Daruh. Lond. 1775, 8vo. To this examination Dr. Owen replied in a 'Supplement to the Critica Sacra,' 1775. 8vo.
Collatio Codicis CottonianiGenesesos cum Editione Romana ab J. E. Grabe olim facta, nunc edita ab H. Owen. Lond. 1778, 8vo. 'A collation of the MSS. of the Septuagint, as recommended by Dr. Owen, would certainly be very acceptable to the learned world.'—*Bp. Watson.*
A brief Account of LXX. Version of the Old Testament. To which is added a Dissertation on the comparative Excellency of the Hebrew and Samaritan Pentateuch. Lond. 1787, 8vo.
The Modes of Quotation used by the Evangelical Writers explained and vindicated. Lond. 1789, 4to. A learned and elaborate work. Gosset, 2l. 6s., Bindley, pt. iii. 675, with a portrait inserted, 18s.
Critical Disquisitions ; containing some Remarks, I. On Masius's Edition of the Book of Joshua; and II. On Origen's celebrated Hexapla. Lond. 1784. 8vo.
Sixteen Sermons. Lond. 1797, 8vo.

OWEN, John. Joannis Audoeni Epigrammata. Lond. 1606, 18mo.
First edition of these esteemed Epigrams. Two impressions appeared in this year.—Lond. 1607, 16mo. Bright, 7s.—Lond. 1612, 12mo. Bright, mor. 6s. 6d.—Amst. 1624. — Lugd. Bat. 1628, 24mo. Roxburghe, 2252, morocco, 16s. — Lond. 1633, 12mo. with frontispiece. Amst. 1640, 32mo. — Amst. Elzevier, 1647, 24mo. Bright, morocco, 6s. 6d.—Hibbert, 5935, morocco, 6s. 6d.—Lond. 1650, 12mo. with portrait.—Lond. 1668, 12mo.—Lugd. 1688, 12mo.—Amst. 1669, 12mo. with portrait of Owen.—Basil. 1766, 12mo. — Paris, 1794, 18mo. 2 vols. 10s. Best edition, edited by Hanniard. LARGE PAPER in 12mo. LARGEST PAPER in 8vo. Four copies printed. On VELLUM. Four copies printed.
Certaine Epigrams ovt of the first fovre Bookes of Master Iohn Owen, translated into English by H(obart) H(ayman). Lond.

1628, 4to. A—F 3, in fours, dedicated 'To the Beauties of England.' Lloyd, 1l. 8s. This forms a portion of the Quodlibets by Robert Hayman.

John Owen's Latine Epigrams englished by Tho. Harvey, Gent. Lond. 1677, 12mo. pp. 220. Dowdeswell, 5s. 6d. Dent, pt. ii. 65, 6s. Lloyd, 907, 6s. 6d. Garrick, 1737, 5s. 6d. Inglis, 1080, 8s. 6d. Nassau, pt. i. 2190, 9s. Hibbert, 5037, 10s. Bindley, pt. ii. 2045, 10s. 6d. Roxburghe, 5409, 15s. 6d. Bibl. Anglo-Poet. 845, 1l. 5s. Heber, pt. iv. 4s.—1678. 12mo. Boswell, 2112, 5s. Sir M. M. Sykes, pt. ii. 508, 14s.

For other versions of these celebrated epigrams, see HARFLETE, Henry. PECKE, Thomas. VICARS, John.

OWEN, John, D.D. The whole Works of John Owen, D.D. carefully collated with the best Editions by Thomas Russell, M.A.; with Life by William Orme, and Index. Lond. 1826, 8vo. 21 vols. pub. 12l. 12s. reduced 6l. 5s.

As this does not contain the Exposition of the Epistle to the Hebrews, Wright's edition, 7 vols. 8vo. is usually added.

WORKS. A new edition, with his Latin Pieces and the Exposition of the Epistle to the Hebrews, edited by the Rev. Dr. W. H. Goold, with the co-operation of the Rev. J. Edmonstone. Edinb. Johnstone and Hunter, 1850-55, 24 vols. 8vo.; reissued by Clark, in 1859, at 5l. 15s. 6d.

The works of this learned non-conformist are much esteemed.

Of the divine Original, &c. of the Scriptures; also, a Vindication of the Purity and Integrity of the Hebrew and Greek Texts. Oxf. 1659, 18mo. 7s. Answered by Walton in 'The Considerator considered.'

An Exposition of the Epistle to the Hebrews, with preliminary Exercitations. By John Owen, D.D. Lond. 1668-84, folio, 4 vols. 2l. 13s. 6d. This work is particularly valuable for its illustration of the Epistle to the Hebrews by the aid of Rabbinical learning.—By James Wright. Edinb. 1812-14, 8vo. 7 vols. 2l. 12s. 6d. LARGE PAPER in royal 8vo. 4l. 14s. 6d.—Lond. Tegg, 1840, 8vo. 4 vols. 2l. 16s.

An Exposition of the Epistle to the Hebrews, revised and abridged by Edward Williams, D.D. Lond. 1790, 8vo. 4 vols. A well-executed abridgment.—Lond. 1815, 8vo. 4 vols.

A practical Exposition of the hundred and thirtieth Psalm. Lond. 1669, 4to. 5s.—Edinb. 1819, 12mo. 8s.

Discourses concerning the Holy Spirit, his Name, Nature, Operations and Effects. Lond. 1674. folio, 15s. LARGE PAPER, 1l. 1s.—Glasg. 1791, 8vo. 2 vols. 10s.—Glasg.

1817, 4to. It has been abridged by Geo Burder.

Works, containing several scarce and valuable Discourses. Lond. 1721, fol. with portrait by G. Vertue, 1l. 7s.

Collection of Sermons, Tracts, and Latin Orations. Lond. 1721, folio, with portrait by R. White, 1l. 1s. LARGE PAPER. Williams, 1423, mor. 7l. 12s. 6d. resold Bliss, 1l. 18s.

For extended notices of all the various works of this learned non-conformist, see Memoirs of him by Wm. Orme. Other memoirs of Dr. Owen appeared 1720. 1758, 8vo.

OWEN, H., and J. B. Blakeway. History of Shrewsbury. Lond. 1825, 2 vols. 4to. plates and woodcuts. 6l. 6s.

LARGE PAPER, royal 4to. 2 vols. 8l. 8s.

— John. A compleat and impartial History of the ancient Britons, from the earliest Accounts to the End of the Reign of Hen. VIII. vol. i. all printed. Lond. 1743, 8vo.

— John, A.M. Travels into different Parts of Europe, in the Years 1791 and 1792; with familiar Remarks on Places, Men, and Manners. Lond. 1796, 8vo. 2 vols. 9s.

Fonthill, 2012, 1l. 7s.

— Rev. John. The History of the British and Foreign Bible Society. Lond. 1816-20, 8vo. 3 vols. 16s. LARGE PAPER, 1l. 4s.

— Lewis. Specvlvm Jesviticvm, or the Jesuites Looking-glasse. Lond. 1626, 4to.

Thirty-nine leaves, A—K 3, dedicated to 'Sir Henrie Martin Knight.'—Lond. 1629, 4to. Gordonstoun, 1634, 18s.

The Running Register; recording a true Relation of the State of the English Colledges, Seminaries and Cloisters in all forraine Parts; &c. Lond. 1626, 4to. pp. 118. Steevens, 128, 10s. 6d. Gordonstoun, 1682, 1l. Bliss, 9s.

The Unmasking of all Popish Monks, Friers and Jesuites in generall, &c. Lond. 1628, 4to. Gordonstoun, 1683, 11s. Nassau, pt. ii. 580. 11s. Dright, 7s. 6d.

— Rev. N. British Remains; or, a Collection of Antiquities relating of the Britons. Lond. 1777 8vo.

'Comprehending, I. A concise History of the Lords Marchers; their Origin, Power, and Conquests in Wales. II. The Arms of the ancient Nobility and Gentry of North Wales. III. A Letter of Dr. Lloyd, Bishop of St. Asaph's, concerning Jeffrey of Monmouth's History. IV. An Account of the Discovery of America by the Welsh, three hundred Years before the Voyage of Columbus. V. A celebrated Poem of Taliesin, translated in Sapphic Verse. The whole selected from original MSS. and other authentic Records. To which are also added, Memoirs of Edward Llwyd, Antiquary, transcribed from a Manuscript in the Museum, Oxford.' Hibbert, 6932, 6s. Bent, pt. II. 67, 19s.

A History of the Island of Anglesey, with Memoirs of Owen Glendower. Lond. 1775, 4to.

OWEN, Richard. Memoir of the pearly Nautilus, with Illustrations of its external Form and internal Structure. Lond. 1832, 4to. 15s.

Catalogue of Physiological Series of Comparative Anatomy. Mus. Coll. of Surgeons. Lond. 1833-40, 4to. 5 vols. 7L 17s. 6d.

Catalogue of the Osteological Series of Comparative and Human Anatomy. Ib. Lond. 1853, 4to. 2 vols. 1L. 11s. 6d.

Catalogue of the Palæontological Series of Fossil Remains. Ib. London. 1854, 4to. 3 vols. 1l. 10s.

Catalogue of the Natural History, in the Mus. of the Coll. of Surgeons. 1830, 4to. 1 vol. 10s.

On the Structure of the Brain in Marsupial Animals. [Philosophical Transactions.] Lond. 1837, 4to.

A Description of the Fossil Mammalia collected during the Voyage of 'The Beagle,' with a Geological Introduction by Charles Darwin. Lond. 1838, 4to. 1L. 14s.

Odontography; or a Treatise of the Comparative Anatomy of the Teeth, their physiological Relations, mode of Development, and microscopic Structure, in the vertebrate Animals. Lond. 1840-5, 8vo. 2 vols. 6l. 6s.—Do. 4to, 10l. 10s.

Catalogue of Calculi and other animal Secretions. Lond. 1842, 4to. plain, 10s.; coloured, 1L. 11s. 6d.

Description of the Skeleton of an extinct gigantic Sloth; with Observations on the Osteology, natural Affinities, and probable Habits of the Megatherioid Quadrupeds in general. Lond. 1843, 4to. 1L. 12s. 6d.

Lectures on the Comparative Anatomy and Physiology of the Invertebrate and Vertebrate Animals. Lond. 1843-6, 8vo. 2 vols. 1l. 8s.

On the genus Dinornis. [Zoological Transactions, vol. iii. pts. 3, 4, 5; vol. iv. pt. 1.] Lond. 1844-50, 4to.

On the genus Dicynodon. [Geological Transactions.] Lond. 1845, 4to.

History of British Fossil Mammalia and Birds. Lond. 1846, 8vo. 1L. 11s. 6d.— Do. royal 8vo. 3l. 3s.

Parthenogenesis, or the successive Production of procreating Individuals from a single Ovum. Lond. 1849, 8vo. 5s.

On the Archetype and Homologies of the vertebrate Skeleton. Lond. 1849, 8vo. 10s.

On the Nature of Limbs. Lond. 1849, 8vo. 6s.

Monograph of the Fossil Reptilia of the London Clay. Pt. 1. Chelonia, by Owen and Bell. Pt. 2. Crocodilia and Ophidia, by Owen. Lond. 1849-51, 4to. 2 vols.

Monograph of the Fossil Reptilia of the Cretaceous Formations. [Palæontographical Transactions, pts. 1 to 5.] Lond. 1849-57, 4to. 5l.

On the Anatomy of the Indian Rhinoceros. [Zoological Transactions, vol. iv. pt. 2.] Lond. 1850, 4to.

On the Anatomy of the Nubian Giraffe. [Zoological Transactions, vol. ii. and vol. iii.] Lond. 1845, 4to.

On the Anatomy of the Great Anteater. [Zoological Transactions, vol. v.] Lond. 1853, 4to.

On the Anatomy of the Aurochs (Bison Europæus). Proceedings of the Zoological Society, 1848, 8vo.

Osteological Contributions to the Nat. Hist. of the Chimpanzees and Orangutans. [Zoological Transactions, vols. I. II. III. and iv.] Lond. 1835-53, 4to.

On a microscopic Worm in Human Muscles (Trichina spiralis). [Zoological Transactions, vol. 1.] Lond. 1835, 4to.

The Fossil Reptilia of the Wealden Period. [Palæontographical Transactions.] Lond. 1853, 4to.

British Fossil Reptiles of the Wealden Period. [Palæontographical Transactions.] Lond. 1858, 4to.

On the Classification and Geological Distribution of the Mammalia; on the Gorilla; and on the Extinction and Transmutation of Species. Lond. 1859, 8vo. 6s.

Palæontology, or a Systematic Summary of Extinct Animals and their Geological Relations. Edinb. 1860, 8vo. 12s.

Professor Owen is author of a considerable number of other treatises, as may be seen in the Bibliographia Zoologiæ, published by the Ray Society, vol. iv. pp. 55-67, where upwards of 230 titles are enumerated.

OWEN, Robt., of New Lanark. A New View of Society, or Essays on the Formation of the Human Character. Lond. 1816, 8vo. 5s.
The Revolution in the Mind and Practice of the Human Race. Lond. 1849, 8vo. 7s.
Mr. Owen has published other tracts.

— Tho. Reports in the Common Pleas. Lond. 1656, folio, 6s.
Pp. 77—80 are wanting in all copies.

— T. Agricultural Pursuits. Translated from the Greek. Lond. 1805, 8vo. 2 vols.
Hibbert, 5934, 6s. This clergyman also published translations of Terentius Varro, and Palladius.

— William. A Dictionary of the Welch Language, explained in English; with numerous Illustrations from the literary Remains, and from the living Speech of the Cymry. Lond. 1803, 8vo. 2 vols. 2l. 2s.
The first volume of this valuable work, containing 100,000 words, was published in 1793, the second in 1794, and both relssued with a new title in 1803. Prefixed is a Welsh Grammar. LARGE PAPER in 4to. 3l. 13s. 6d. See PUGHE.
Heroic Elegies and other Pieces of Llywarchen Hen, Prince of the Cambrian Britons; with a literal Translation. Lond. 1792, 8vo. Heber, pt. iv. 2s. There is much curious matter in the preface of this volume, and the translation is considered elegant and literal. See LLYWARCH HEN.
The Cambrian Biography; or, historical Notices of celebrated Men among the ancient Britons. Lond. 1803, 12mo. 6s. 'A very curious work.'—George Ellis.
See MYVYRIAN Archaiology, under Wales.

— W. Views on the River Thames. See COOKE, George.

OWLEGLASS. See HOWLEGLASS.

OWLS.—The Owles Almanacke, prognosticating many strange Accidents which shall happen to this Kingdome of Great Britaine this Yeare, 1618. Lond. 1618, 4to.
With a woodcut. Inglis, 1125, 1l. 15s. Gordonstoun, 1593, 3l. 10s. Jolley, 10s. 'A curious and humorous old pamphlet, in which every day of the month has its appropriate fortune annexed to it.'—Gifford.
Laus Ululæ, the Praise of Owls. 1727. Nassau, pt. L 1676, 2s.

The Owl, and the Nightingale, an early English Poem. Printed for the Percy Society.

OXBERRY, William. New English Drama. Lond., 1818, &c. sm. 8vo. 19 vols.
This series contains upwards of 100 plays, and is the only edition in which the business of the stage is marked.
Mr. Oxberry was at different periods of his life a comic actor, afterwards author and editor, and finally a printer.

OXENHAM, James. A true Relation of an Apparition in the Likeness of a Bird that appeared hovering over the Beds of some Children of J. Oxenham. Lond. 1641, 4to. 6s.
See also Roxburghe Club. APPENDIX.

OXFORD, Edward Harley, Earl of. A Catalogue of the Pictures, Coins, and Medals of Edward Harley, Earl of Oxford. Lond. 1741-2, 4to.
A copy is in the British Museum.
See Harleian Library, MSS. and Miscellany, also Voyages.

— Robert Harley, Earl of. An Essay upon publick Credit. Lond. 1710.
By some attributed to Daniel Defoe.—Lond. 1797, 8vo. It is reprinted in the thirteenth volume of the Somers Collection of Tracts.

OXFORD.—Publications relating to Oxford and its University.
Statuta Oxon. 1634, folio. On VELLUM, two copies printed; one with MS. additions, &c. is in the British Museum, the other in St. John's College Library, Oxford.

Statvta selecta è Corpore Staintorum Vniversitatis Oxon. Collectore T. Crossfield. Typis Ocil. Turner. 1638, 18mo. A, 4 leaves, B—O, in eights, P, 8 leaves, and Q, six leaves, the last containing the errata. At p. 20 should be a folded plate 'Encyclopædia seu Orbis Literarum,' by Bindley, pt. iii. 1065, 3l. 13s. 6d. Bright, &c. Several editions.

Parecbolæ sive axcarpta e corpore statvtorum Vniversitatis Oxon. Accedunt articuli religionis xxxix. in eccl̄esia Anglicana recepti, necnon juramenta fidelitatis et supremacia, Oxon. 1671, 1740, 1794, 1801, 1808, 1815, &c. Reprinted about every five or seven years.

OXFORD—continued.
Corpus Statutorum Universitatis Oxoniensis: sive Pandectae Constitutionum academicorum, e Libris publicis et Regestis Universitatis comparatarum. Oxonii, 1708, 12mo.—1768, 4to. 529 pages.

Statuta Aulae Regiae et Collegii de Brasen-Nose in Oxonio; subjicuntur Excerpta ex Compositionibus et Testamentis Benefactorum et alia quaedam Notatu digna ad idem Collegium pertinentia A.D. 1774, 8vo. Prefixed to each copy was the following request, printed on a separate strip and pasted within the cover. 'This book was printed solely for the private use of the Members of that particular society to which it relates, and cannot be interesting to any others. When, therefore, it shall have answered the owner's purpose, and can be no longer of service to him, it is hoped and expected that he or his heirs will cause it to be either destroyed or returned to the college; and not permit it to fall into the hands of a bookseller, and be sold to any accidental purchaser.' Collation.—The statutes, 108 pages, not including the title; varia lectiones, &c. 8 pages; the abstracts, 63 pages, not including the title; also contents, index and errata, 8 pages.

Foundation Documents of Merton College, edited by J. O. Halliwell, 1843, 8vo. 1s.

Foundation Statutes of Merton College, A.D. 1270, with subsequent Ordinances, edited by E. F. Percival. 1847, 8vo. 3s. 6d.

The Foundation Statutes of Bishop Fox for Corpus Christi College, A.D. 1517. Now first translated. With a Life of the Author, by G. R. M. Ward, M.A. Lond. 1843, 8vo. 5s.

The Statutes of All Souls College, now first translated by G. R. M. Ward, M.A. Lond. 1841, 8vo. 5s.

The Statutes of Magdalen College, now first translated by G. R. M. Ward, M.A. Oxf. 1840, 8vo. 5s.

University Statutes, translated by G. R. M. Ward and James Heywood. Lond. 1845-51, 8vo. 2 vols. Vol. I. (Caroline Code or Laudian Statutes promulgated.) Vol. II. containing the University Statutes from 1767 to 1850, 17s.

Marmora Arundeliana:—publicavit et Commentariolos adjecit Joannes Seldenus. I. C. Lond. 1629, 4to. Roxburghe, 8962, date 1628, 3s.

Marmorum Arundellianorum, Seldenianorum, aliorumque, Academiae Oxoniensi donatorum; cum variis Commentariis et Indice, secunda Editio (edidit Mich. Maittaire). Lond. 1732, folio. This edition contains several things omitted in that of 1763. Willets, 1514, 18s. 6d. Heath, 1468, 1l. 7s.

Marmora Oxoniensia (edidit Rich. Chandler). Oxonii, 1763, royal folio, 78 plates. Best edition. Drury, 2345, russia, 5l. 10s. Craufurd, russia, part of the Earl of Arundel inverted, 5l. 5s. A copy with the original Drawings, formerly valued at 100 guineas, was sold at Evans's in 1843 for 7l. 5s.

Marmorum Oxoniensium Inscriptiones Graecae, ad Chandleri Exemplar editae, coeante Gulielmo Roberts, A.M. Oxon. 1791, 12mo. 259 pages, 5s. LARGE PAPER, 4s. Combe, 1165, 10s.

A Catalogue of the Collection of Pictures in the Library of Christ Church (Oxford), which were bequeathed to that College by General Guise. To which is added a Catalogue of the Portraits in Christ Church Hall, 8vo. Oxf. 1833, 8vo.

Catalogvs Librorvm in Bibliotheca Aulae Magdalenae. Oxon. 1661, 12mo.

A Catalogue of the MSS. in the Ashmolean Collection has been made by W. H. Black, Esq. 1854, 4to, portrait.

Ashmolean Society Transactions. See APPENDIX.

Catalogue of the MSS. in the Library of All Souls College, by H. O. Coxe. 1842, 4to, not published.

Catalogue of all the Graduates in Divinity, Law, and Physick, and of all Masters of Arts, and Doctors of Musick, who have regularly proceeded or been created in the University of Oxford between Oct. 10th, 1659, and July, 1688. Oxford, 1689, 12mo.

Same, with the Chancellors, High Stewards, Vice-Chancellors, and Proctors, 1659—1727. Also the Parliament-men from 1603—1727. Oxford, 1727, 8vo.

Catalogve of all Graduates, &c. &c. 1659—1800. Oxford, 1801, 8vo.—New edit. continued to 1850 (edited by Dr. Bliss). Oxf. 1851.

The Oxford University Calendar is published annually at 6s. since 1810.

Oxoniensis Academiae Antiquitatis Assertio. 1568, 1574. See KAY, Thomas, TWYNE, Brian.

The Earliest Plan of Oxford known, is that taken by Ralph Aggas, and engraved in 1578, copied in 1728 by Geo. Varine, and other times, reduced copy; in Oxford Delineated, by Whissell and Bartlett, 1831.

Oxoniensis Academiae Funebre Officium in Memoriam Elizabethae nuper Angliae, Franciae, et Hiberniae Reginae. Oxoniae, Barnes, 1603, 4to.

The Answere of the Universitie of Oxford to the Petition of the Ministers of the Church of England desiring Reformation. Oxford, 1603, 4to. Bright, fine, 16s. —Oxford, 1604, 4to.

Iliam in Italiam. Oxonia ad Protectionem Regis sui omnium optimi filia, pediseqva. Oxon. 1608, 16mo.

OXFORD—continued.
This volume, edited by John Sansbyrry, Vicar of St. Giles, Oxford, contains woodcuts representing the arms of all the colleges at Oxford, with Latin verses beneath them. Bindley, pt. ii. 1087, 6l. 14s. 6d. Hibbert, 4086, morocco, 4l. Heber, pt. vii. 19s.

Justa Oxoniensum (Lachrymæ In Tumulum Principis Henrici). Lond. Bill, 1612, 4to.

The Oxford Act, a Poem. Lond. 1613, 4to. A copy is in the British Museum.

Academiæ Oxoniensis Funebria Sacra Memoriæ Annæ Jacobi L sponsæ dicata. Oxford, 1619.

Epithalamia in Nuptias Friderici Comitis Palatini et Elizabethæ Jacobi I. filiæ promigenitæ. Oxon. Barnes, 4to.

Epithalamia Oxoniensia in Caroli I. cum Henrietta Maria Connubium. Oxon. 1625, 4to.

The Character of an Oxford Incendiary. 1645, 4to. 8 pages. Reprinted in the fifth volume of the Harleian Miscellany. An edition of the date of 1645 is reprinted in Morgan's Phœnix Britannicus.

The Privileges of the University of Oxford in Point of Visitation; with the Universities Answer to the Summons of the Visitors. Anno 1647, 4to. Ascribed by Gough to Gerard Langbaine, D.D., but according to Bishop Humphreys, it is said to be written by Dr. Allestrey.

Judicium Universitatis de solenni Liga et Fœdere, Ordinationibus, &c. Lond. 1648, 8vo. Hibbert, 5839, 1s. 6d.—In English. Lond. 1659, 4to.

Pegasus; or the Flying Horse from Oxford, 4to. (1648). A severe Satire on the Earl of Pembroke and Montgomery, Chancellor of Oxford.

A third and fourth part of Pegasus; taught by Bankes's Ghost to dance in the Dorick mode. 1648, 4to. Bright, with pt. i. 11s.

Oxonii Lachrymæ. Rachell weeping for her children, or a pathetical Relation of the present grievances of the late famous University of Oxford. Lond. 1649 4to.

The Foundation of the Universitie of Oxford. 1651. See LANGBAINE, Gerard, D.D.

Conciones tres apud Academicos Oxonii nuper habitæ ab H.Wilkinson. Oxon. 1654, 8vo. 4s. 6d.

Sundry Things from several Hands concerning the University of Oxford, viz. I. A Petition from some well-affected therein. II. A Model for a College Reformation. III. Queries concerning the said University, and several Persons therein. Lond. 1659, 4to. 12 pages. Reprinted in the sixth volume of the Harleian Miscellany.

Notitia Oxoniensis Academia. Oxon. 1665. First edition, 4to. Oxford, 1675. See FULMAN, William.

Domiduca Oxoniensis sive Musæ Academicæ gratulatio ob Catherinæ Lusitanæ Regi suo desponsatæ in Anglia appulsum. Ox. 1662, 4to.

Oxford Almanacks, from their first publication in the year 1674 to 1856 inclusive. Oxford, folio. A complete set is scarce.

Theatri Oxoniensis Encænia Julii 6 celebrata. Oxon. 1677, folio.

Friendly Advice to the Correctour of the English Press at Oxford, concerning the English Orthographie. Lond. 1682, folio.

Habitus Academicorum Oxoniensium a Doctore ad Servientem. Sold by L. Oliver on Lugdate Hill, at the corner of the Old-Bailey, n. d. [about 1690] folio. A series of ten engraved plates, besides title. These full-length portraits in University costume are sometimes found attached to Loggan's Oxonia Antiqua; but they are very rare. A copy is in the Signet Library, Edinburgh.

Specimens of the several Sorts of Letter given to the Theatre by Bp. J. Fell. Oxf. 1695, 8vo.

Oxoniensis Universitatis Habitus academici. 1715. Bindley, pt. ii. 2064, 1l. 5s.

Academia; or the Humours of the University of Oxford in burlesque verse. Lond. 1716, 8vo. Heber, pt. iv. 6s.—1730. Shewg, 2s.

Merton Walks, or the Oxford Beauties. Oxf. Whistler, 1717, 8vo.

The present State of the new Buildings of Queen's College in Oxford. 1730. Eleven plates. A copy, apparently imperfect, but supposed unique, is in the Bodleian Library. Printed in 1718, with a plan only.

The Gentleman and the Lady's pocket Companion for Oxford. 1747. Frequently republished with large additions. In ridicule of the Oxford Guide there appeared a very humorous production entitled 'A Companion to the Guide and a Guide to the Companion.' See WARTON, Thomas.

An Epistle to Florio, at Oxford. 1749. See TRAWRITT, Tho.

Modus Salium. 1751. See JESTS.

Memoirs of an Oxford Scholar. 1756, 12mo. 6s.

Views (Twelve), of the Environs of Oxford, by John Malchair. 1763, 4to. Heber pt. iii. 11. 11s. 6d. Bliss, 870, pt. ii. See MALCHAIR.

The Oxford Sausage; or, select poetical Pieces written by the most celebrated Wits of the University of Oxford. Lond. 1764, 12mo. This first edition does not contain the likeness of Mrs. Dorothy Spreadbury, inventress of the Oxford sausage. Cuts by Bewick. Nassau, pt. i.

OXFORD—*continued.*
9493, 14s.—n. d. 12mo. 'Adorned with cuts engraved in a new taste, and designed by the best masters.' Bindley, pt. ii. 2054, 8s. 6d.—1777, 12mo. cuts. Nassau, pt. i. 2494, 10s.—1814, 8vo. with the original cuts. LARGE PAPER, royal 8vo. Strettell, 1053, 12s. 6d.—Lond. Longmans, 1815, post 8vo. cuts after Bewick. Bright, 8s.

Pietas Oxoniensis (by Sir Rd. Hill). 1768. In connexion with this pamphlet, which caused much attention, were printed Carmen Introductorum Piet. Oxon. Auctore G. Higginbrocolo (1768).—An Answer to Pietas, by T. Nowell, 1768.—The Contrast of Dr. Nowell, an Orator and Principal of St. Mary's Hall, 1768—The Admonisher admonished (by Hill), 1770. All in 8vo.

A Specimen of the several Sorts of Types belonging to the University of Oxford at the Clarendon Printing House. 1768, 8vo. —1788, 8vo.

Specimen pages of Bibles, with other types, were printed in 1829.

Registrum Privilegiorum Almae Universitatis Oxoniensis. Oxon. 1770, 4to.

The History of the University of Oxford to the Death of William the Conqueror. 1772, 8vo.—To the Demise of Q. Elizabeth. 1773, 4to. *See* PEHKALL, Sir John.

Oxonia explicata et ornata. 1773.— 1777. *See* TATHAM, Edward, D.D.

Specimen of a History of Oxfordshire. 1782.—1788, 4to. *See* WARTON, Thomas.

Inscriptiones Phoenicia Oxoniensis nova Interpretatio auctore J. D. Akerblad. Paris, 1802, 8vo. pp. 51.

Oxoniana, being selections from books and manuscripts deposited in the Bodleian Library. Lond. 12mo. 4 vols. (1807). Edited by the Rev. John Walker.

Copleston. Three Replies to the Edinburgh Review in its Attack on the Oxford System of Education. Oxf. 1810.

The Brasen-Nose Garland (by T. Duncan). 4to. Only 20 printed.

A History of the University of Oxford, its Colleges, Halls and Public Buildings. Lond. R. Ackermann, 1814, elephant 4to. 2 vols. One thousand copies with coloured plates printed. Nassau, pt. i. 141, russia, 5l. FOLIO. Twenty-five copies, with plates coloured. Dent, pt. i. 154, with a portrait of Lord Grenville upon India paper, 11l. FOLIO. Twenty-five copies on India paper, proofs. Some copies have Portraits of the Founders inserted.

A Series of Portraits (89 in number, coloured) of those distinguished Persons who were the Founders of Colleges and public Buildings in the University of Oxford; from Pictures in that University and from private Collections. Lond. elephant 4to. with arranged directions for the plates in the history of Oxford including the founders, one leaf. FOLIO. Twenty-five Copies on India paper, not coloured. The series issued to illustrate History published by Ackermann.

Musei Oxoniensis litterarii Conspectus et Specimina, edit. a T. Burgess. OXON. 1792-7, 8vo. fasc. 1 et 2.

Poemata Oxoniensia, Proemiis Cancellarii donata. OXON. 1810, 2 vols.

A correct Account of the Visit of His Royal Highness the Prince Regent and his Illustrious Guests to the University and City of Oxford, in June 1814. To which are added the English Poems recited on the Occasion, accompanied by some general Remarks. Oxford, 1814, 8vo. 53 pages.

An Account of the Visit of his Royal Highness the Prince Regent, and their Imperial and Royal Majesties the Emperor of Russia and King of Prussia, to the University of Oxford, in June, 1814. Oxford; printed at the Clarendon Press, 1815, 4to. LARGE PAPER, folio, pp. 96, with a ground plan of the Radcliffe Library, a view, in outline, of part of the interior of the theatre, and a sheet containing specimens of the various types used at the Clarendon Press. This volume was not printed for sale. Bindley, pt. i. 128, 2l. 12s. 6d. ON VELLUM. Twelve copies struck off for the Royal Personages who came to Oxford. Duke of York, 761, 4l. 14s. Now in the Grenville Collection.

The Oxford Spy, in four Dialogues, with an Introduction. Oxford, 1819, 12mo. Drury, 2562, 3s. 6d.

Account of the Lord Mayor's (Venables) Visit to Oxford in the Month of July, 1826; written, by the desire of the Party, by the Chaplain of the Mayoralty (R. C. Dillon, D.D.). Lond. 1826, sm. 8vo. Terribly quizzed by the reviewers, and afterwards suppressed. Sir F. Freeling, 5l. 5s.

Arms of the University of Oxford, and of all the Colleges therein; to which is added those of Winchester, Eton, and Westminster, also St. Paul's and Merchant Taylors' Schools, by W. Jackson, 12mo. Nassau, pt. i. 1722, 1l. 10s.

Oxford Architectural Society. *See* APPENDIX.

Oxford and Cambridge Miscellany Poems. Lond. 8vo. 17—

Oxford and Cambridge Nuts to Crack; or Quips, Quirks, Anecdotes, and Facetiae of Oxford and Cambridge Scholars. Lond. 18—, 12mo. cuts. Second edition. Lond. Bailey, 1835.

Oxford Prize Poems; being a Collection of all the English Poems that have obtained prizes in the University of Oxford, 12mo. Oxford, 1807. 12mo. LARGE

OXFORD—*continued.*
PAPER—completed to the year 1836. 12mo. Oxford, 1836, seventh edition, 7s.—Oxf. 1839, 12mo.
Oxford and Locke (by Lord Grenville). Lond. 1829, 8vo.
Oxford Delineated; or that celebrated University and City illustrated, by a series of Views drawn and engraved by J. Whitsell and T. Bartlett. Oxford, 1831, 4to. Proofs on India paper, 1l. 11s. 6d.
Oxford English Prize Essays, from 1771 to 1836. Oxford, Talboys, 1836, crown 8vo. 4 vols.—Oxford, Talboys, 1836, second edition, brought down to the present time, 5 vols. 2l. 5s.
Oxford Chronological Tables of Ancient, Medieval, and Modern History. Oxford, 1840, folio, 1l. 1s.
See BODLEIAN Library. CHRISTMAS PRINCE. FITZHERBERT, N. p. 804. HICKES, William. JAMES, T. p. 1188-9. KAY, T. LOGGAN, D. MALCHAIR. JOHN. NALUS, Tho. SHAW, Henry. SKELTON, Joseph. TORRE FILIUS. TWYNE, Brian.
In the second part of the Sale Catalogue of Dr. Bliss's Library, 1859, will be found the titles of numerous books published in or relating to the City and University, arranged in chronological order.

OXFORD Wendy; a Prospective for things and subjects, or a short discourse of some Treacheries acted against Charles I. & II. Leyden, 1652, 4to.
Bright, 8s. 6d.

OXINDEN, Henry. Religionis Funus et Hypocritæ Finis. Lond. 1647, 4to.
A Poem in Latin hexameters, consisting of 72 pages, with a portrait of the author. The portrait has been copied by Richardson.
Charles Triumphant (a Poem). Lond. 1660, 12mo. Bliss, 6s.
Eikon Basilike; or an Image Royal. Lond. 1660, 12mo. A Poem consisting of 15 leaves.
Jobus Triumphans. 1651, small 8vo. pp. 59. A Poem consisting of 766 hexameter verses. Prefixed are commendatory verses.
See Wood's Athen. Oxon. and Brydges' Censura Literaria.

OXLEY, John. Journals of two Expeditions behind the blue Mountains, and into the Interior of New South Wales, undertaken by Order of the British Government, in the Years 1817-18. Lond. 1820, 4to.
Pp. 408, with maps and views. A valuable work, particularly interesting from giving an authentic description of the interior of this singular country. Drury, 3724, 5l.

OZANAM, Ja. Recreations in Mathematics and natural Philosophy, recomposed and enlarged by M. Montucla, transl. and improved by C. Hutton, LL.D. Lond. 1803, 8vo. 4 vols.
A valuable work, illustrated with near 100 folding plates.—Second Edition. Lond. 1823, 8vo. 4 vols. New Edition, revised by C. Riddle. Lond. 1840, 8vo. in one volume, 12s.
Cursus Mathematicus; or a compleat Course of the Mathematics; done into English, with Additions and Corrections by several Hands. Lond. 1712, 8vo. 5 vols.

OZELL, John. Mons Testaceus, the Roman Laystall; or, the Augean Stable cleared of its heaps of Historical, Philological and Geographical trumpery, and other defects, in Mr. Bundy's translation of the Roman History, by Fathers Catrou and Rouille. Lond. 8vo. 1720, part 1, all printed. At the end is a translation (as a specimen) of the first canto of the Henriade of Voltaire.
Common Prayer not common Sense in several Places of the Portuguese, Spanish, Italian, French, Latin, and Greek Translations of the English Liturgy. Lond. 1722, 8vo. pp. 69.
Ozell translated FENELON's Telemachus, MOLIERE's Plays, RABELAIS' Works, and numerous other works, chiefly from the French.